D1583018

The World of
THEATRE
2003 Edition

iTi

The World of
THEATRE
2003 Edition

An account of the world's theatre seasons
1999–2000, 2000–2001 and 2001–2002

iTi

Edited for the
International Theatre Institute
by
Ian Herbert
assisted by
Nicole Leclercq

LONDON AND NEW YORK

First published 2003
by Routledge
11 New Fetter Lane, London EC4P 4EE

Simultaneously published in the USA and Canada
by Routledge
29 West 35th Street, New York, NY 10001

Routledge is an imprint of the Taylor & Francis Group

International Theatre Institute
UNESCO, 1 rue Miollis, 75732 Paris, Cedex 15, France
tel: (33) 1 45 68 26 50   fax: (33) 1 45 66 50 40
email: iti@unesco.org   http://www.iti-worldwide.org

Typeset by Xpress Design and Print
Strawberry Vale, England
Printed and bound in Great Britain by
TJ International Ltd, Padstow, Cornwall

British Library Cataloguing in Publication Data
A catalogue record for this book is available from the British Library

Library of Congress Cataloging in Publication Data
A catalog record for this book has been requested

ISBN 0–415–30621–3

World of Theatre ISSN 1564–2208

Publisher's Note
This book has been prepared from camera-ready
copy provided by the editors

Contents

Introduction

The last, Millennial edition of *The World of Theatre* represented a great leap forward for a publication that has been part of the International Theatre Institute's furniture for nearly twenty years now. Not only was it produced, to a higher standard than ever, by the Bangladesh ITI Centre for the use of the Institute's member Centres; it was also, for the first time, commercially published for the wider world by Routledge. Perhaps as a result of this, the book is beginning to emerge from shy obscurity into the limelight: *Theatre Notebook*, the leading journal of theatre scholarship in Britain, noted that it 'contains more information than any other single source, on activities from Argentina to Wales', calling it 'vastly informative and handsomely produced'. It is to be hoped that this edition will deserve a similar reaction.

What *The World of Theatre* sets out to do is to present a picture of the most recent theatre seasons in as many countries of the world as possible, in authoritative articles. The first source of these is the network of ITI Centres listed at the back of this book, nearly ninety of them, many of whom have commissioned leading authorities in their countries. Not all of those Centres are fully active, however, and there are some of them who have not been able to send reports out of sheer hardship, or worse.

Another valuable group of contributors has come from the parallel network of the International Association of Theatre Critics, of which I have the honour to be President – a position which has given me the possibility of gently twisting a few arms. Many of the ITI contributors are also IATC members: we are an organisation in cordial relationship with ITI, which represents our interests to UNESCO. Finally, I have been able to call on friends, and friends of friends, whom I have met over a long time of working in the field of international theatre, and who have once more come to my rescue with a generosity typical of true theatre people.

The result of this is that while not all ITI member countries appear in these pages (although you may find information about their activities in the long diary of ITI events at the end of the book), there are in compensation reports from major theatre nations, such as Brazil or South Africa, which do not have ITI Centres. The book is getting ever closer to achieving its aim, of recording the theatre of the whole world. Newcomers not in the last edition include Austria, Belarus, Cameroon, Costa Rica, Cuba, Ghana, Italy, Jamaica, Moldova, Nepal, the Netherlands and Singapore.

I have borne in mind that many of the readers of this book will not have English as their first language, and in places my attempts to simplify some complex aspects of critical theory may have rendered them less meaningful – possibly meaningless – for which the eminent contributors have my unreserved apologies.

The length and the emphasis of the articles vary as much as the theatre situations they describe. The articles on Germany and the USA, for instance, are relatively short, since their theatre scene is not unknown. England gets rather less coverage than her sister democracies Scotland and Wales, each boasting a completely separate theatre tradition. Hong Kong theatre has almost as long a section as its parent, China, because it has not been covered before. Accounts of new writing in the Western tradition show common trends, such as the rise of what the English call 'in-yer-face', the Germans 'blood and sperm' plays – the names of Sarah Kane, Marius von Mayenburg and Dejan Dukovski appear regularly. In other countries the priorities are different, often simple matters of survival and (in the best cases) recovery – from economic crisis in South America to religious upheaval in the Middle East, civil war and the ravages of AIDS in Africa, natural disasters in Asia.

Yet in all these pieces there is a recurrent theme: the power of theatre to transform even the ugliest of circumstances. It is a belief in this that unites the theatre community of every nation, and drives its representative body, the International Theatre Institute. ITI may not have great power or influence, and would not be so arrogant as to claim it; but if the Institute did not exist, it would be absolutely necessary to invent it.

Ian Herbert, *President, International Association of Theatre Critics*
Editor and Publisher, Theatre Record, *London.*

ACKNOWLEDGEMENTS

I should like to offer my warmest thanks to all those who have been involved in the production of this 2003 edition of *The World of Theatre*. First and foremost, to my dear friend Nicole Leclercq, of the francophone Belgian Centre of ITI, who has tirelessly given her time to soliciting articles, translating and editing them. Nicole has the parallel and even greater task of editing the ITI's other major reference, the *World Theatre Directory*. (This essential 'Yellow Pages' of world theatre can be consulted free on line at the address http://.iti.unesco.org.amt)

Next, to the contributors, so many of whom wrote their articles freely and generously out of respect for the ITI. Also to the many photographers who have supplied production pictures – we have tried to acknowledge them wherever possible. Then to all the ITI Centres who took the trouble to commission, prepare and often translate the articles. Further help with translations was given by many friends around the world, of whom we may mention Odette Beck, Etienne van der Belen, Penny Black, Paul Evans, Vladislava Felbabov, Cesar Herrera, Malgorzata Semil and above all Stephanie Regner. Allison Hancock and Ruth Keeley of *Theatre Record* provided essential office assistance, and Geoffrey Drew saved a lot of embarrassment with his keen proofreader's eye.

The technical preparation of the book would not have been possible without the generosity of Brendan Covile, of Xpress Design and Print, who prepared the camera copy; the Bangladesh Centre of ITI, led by Ramendu Majumdar and Mofidul Hoque, who oversaw the printing of the ITI edition; and Duncan Brothers (Bangladesh) Ltd, who supported that publication.

IH
October 2002

Foreword

The wealth of the International Theatre Institute (ITI) is first and foremost its network of National Centres. Since its formation, ITI has tried to bring together a maximum number of National Centres throughout the world. We have managed to do this, even if in the eyes of some we still have a way to go. But henceforth we favour quality as opposed to quantity. For a number of years now, we have not tried to have an exhaustive list. There was a time when UNESCO asked us to have the kind of representative spread expected of a great international intergovernmental organisation, including virtually all countries. Today we have reached an unquestionably respectable threshold with an exemplary geographical distribution. This is illustrated also in the membership of the governing bodies of our organisation.

As a consequence, what we want now is that requests for membership of ITI stem above all from a desire to know us and to be known by us, and express the will to enter into a free relationship of sharing – sharing with all the theatre communities throughout the world. ITI is not and never will be an organisation for defending individual interests, even less those of a professional group: there are other organisations to meet these needs. But do not conclude too rapidly that we have abandoned the idea of swift and immediate action – quite the contrary. We are well aware that we need to be in the forefront, with proposals for concrete and practical measures, designed to give tangible results. One needs only to look at the list of the events we have organised during the years covered by this volume.

What we wish above all is to concentrate our efforts on a number of essential priorities. Since the beginnings of ITI, we have especially wished to encourage international exchange in the practice of the live performing arts. This has been our first priority and remains one of the most important. The second is that of theatre education. Hence, a great number of our activities have been in this field. It is encouraging to note that our activities with regard to education have, over the years, become highlights in the world theatre panorama.

We have said before – but it certainly bears repeating – that we are confronted with what many call 'globalisation'. This is not a new discovery and whatever one may say it has always existed. Changes have not ceased to punctuate the march of our history. But today we are witnessing a stupefying acceleration of this process of change. In the past, time and space have constituted barriers. I am not so naïve as to believe the barriers have all disappeared, but they are very often being overcome.

It is through intercultural dialogue and the protection of our diversity that we will be able to arrest some of these fast-flowing currents. And it is by our presence at each others' sides that we will be able to mitigate the abruptness of these changes.

Some people in other places have given the impression that we could be moving towards a 'clash of civilisations'. This is not the danger that lies in wait for us, rather the 'clash of mutual ignorance'. We need to deepen our knowledge and understanding of others as much as we need to deepen knowledge and understanding of our own cultural identity. Any values we thus have can only be shared if we are aware of the values of others. Is not the theatre above all the art of dialogue? It is this dialogue that we must commit ourselves to protecting.

André-Louis Perinetti
Secretary General, International Theatre Institute

ARGENTINA

FRANCISCO JAVIER

In Argentina, and particularly in Buenos Aires, theatrical activity has for some years been divided between three important sectors: state theatre, commercial theatre and fringe, or 'off' theatre.

It goes without saying that the fringe is where the most innovative productions take place. It is the place where experiment can happen and where risks can be taken. Until now, it has been only in this fringe area that we could see the stirrings of change in our theatre. The two other sectors, on the other hand, entrench themselves in their success: the more they find it, commercially and artistically, the more fertile their rapport with the spectator looking for fashionable, frivolous entertainment.

We should nevertheless underline that, during these last years, there have been some remarkable exceptions to this rule, since a number of research and experimental productions have been seen on stages which were previously denied to such work. Today, it is possible to see a non-conventional production on a classical stage, that of the General San Martín Theatre. Not surprisingly, the theatre's audience feels disoriented; it cannot settle down in its usual comfortable ambience, and instead feels displaced, even to the extent of walking out of the theatre. This was more or less the case with Luis Cano's *Los murmullos (The Murmurs)*, staged by Emilio García Webhi. The audience of this traditional theatre cannot understand why the author should explain in the programme that the actors' spoken text is made up of dozens of quotations from well known authors, or from a list of source materials such as political speeches or periodical articles (a mechanism of heightened textuality) and how this plural speech can be related to the actors' performance, dry and stripped-down, interspersed with scenes of extreme violence: three times we watch a highly realistic simulation of the torture called 'the submarine' which consists in putting the head of the torture victim in a bowl of water and keeping it there until the last moment before suffocation). The setting is the deserted basement of a condemned building, which, for all its squalor, produces some strange and impressive images. Two years earlier, another breakaway production had already been seen in this establishment theatre in *Monterverdi. Método bélico (MMB) (Monteverdi: Battle Mode)*. This proves that San Martín Theatre is open to any kind of theatrical production.

Two other mould-breaking events of note took place in Buenos Aires. In one, popular music stormed the Colón Theatre, which is by tradition exclusively devoted to classical music, opera and ballet. A rock group gave a concert, backed by a symphony orchestra under the direction of a well known classical conductor. At the same time, the Luna Park, a place for sports events or big rock concerts, was chosen for an extraordinary production of an opera usually performed on big opera house stages, Giuseppe Verdi's *La Traviata*.

ARGENTINA

As for the Colón Theatre – our official theatre of lyric art – it succeeded in maintaining its seasons of opera and ballet. During the year 2001, for example, it presented Dmitri Shostakovitch's *Lady Macbeth of Mtsensk*. Mstislav Rostropovitch was the conductor and Sergio Renan the director.

It is interesting to see that the kind of crossover we have mentioned is also happening in other spheres of theatrical creation: playwrights are becoming actors or directors, just as actors are directing or writing, directors writing or acting. Designers. too, are emerging as directors. All this is probably following the mood of the time. It highlights the fragility of the boundary between literary genres and the fact that the different disciplines involved in theatrical performance will always be more or less important, in quality and quantity, so that a production may become a piece of visual theatre, or a performance, or even an installation.

Let us give another example. The owner of a consulting-room or office can use it as an apartment, to reduce expenses. He could even make a convertible desk, that will double as a bed, another kind of crossover. This is precisely the subject of Norman Briski's production *Rabattables (Convertibles)*, which he also wrote. It takes the audience by surprise, not only because of the kind of arguments the actors set up for the idea of exploiting a space for multiple use, but also because of the items of furniture which, in a clever and humorous way, demonstrate to the audience their use as 'convertibles'.

In all this varied theatrical activity, public and critical attention has been drawn to an unusual phenomenon: the cycle *Theatre for Identity* organised under the initiative of the Plaza de Mayo Grandmothers, a resistance movement which protests against the deaths and disappearances during the military dictatorship. During the year 2000, a production called *About Doubt* was presented. Bravely, it shows the dilemma of young people, who have to ask themselves if their parents are really their biological parents, or if they are born from parents killed or disappeared. The production was directed by Eudardo Fanego and performed by professional actors and theatre students. It was presented for free in commercial or fringe theatres, on days when they would normally be closed, and also in the halls of universities and other institutions. In the year 2001, the Plaza de Mayo Grandmothers group brought together 41 playwrights to write half-hour plays about identity. These plays were directed by 41 different directors, performed by hundreds of actors and presented over three months in 13 different theatres. Each performance was composed of three plays, again staged on the days when the theatre's own troupe was not playing.

To come back to the kind of theatre that wants to be different, we have to note that it is moving away from realism and the more obviously social subject matter. We could say that its proponents are looking for a philosophical way of expression. It does not trouble to tell a linear story but puts forward a mosaic of situations, a fragmentation, which invites the spectators to build their own a possible plot. The actor's spoken text seems to free itself from the situation and, to a large extent, determines the dramatic structure.

Daniel Veronese, the most representative playwright and director of this new wave, presented *Monteverdi, Método bélico (MMB)* and *Mujeres sueñan caballos (Some Women Dream of Horses)*. The first superimposes acts of cruelty and physical

From *Monteverdi. Método bélico (MMB) (Monteverdi: Battle Mode)* at the Teatro General San Martín, Buenos Aires
(*photo*: Carlos Firman)

violence, performed on the body of a defenceless dummy, over the clear beauty of Monteverdi's madrigals interpreted by a group of on stage musicians. The second one poses once more, in a very stripped-down manner, the problem of violence in the family environment, its gestation, flowering and final explosion.

Three playwright-director-actors worked together to create a production which explores the shadowy zones of the human condition, the mysterious and ambiguous links between crime and pleasure at the heart of a family. The performance is called *La escala humana (The Human Scale)* and its authors are Javier Daulte, Rafael Spregelburd and Alejandro Tantanián.

The group De la Guarda, whose productions rise above the theatrical currents predominating in Argentina, returned to Buenos Aires from an international tour to recreate their big success *Villa Villa*, a production applauded in London and New York. The major features of this spectacle are the performers' perilous jumps and movements in the air, with light, water, fire, and violent rock music coming together to compose strong and beautiful pictures.

Xibalba, by and with Guillermo Angelelli, is a production which experiments with the body of the actor, the expressive force of the voice and the incantatory power of ritual, following the creative precedents of Grotowski and Barba. With *Ganado en pie (Standing Cattle)* Paco Giménez, the founder of the Cordoba group La Cochera (The Garage), offers a production with a subtle and humorous performance style, which makes a parodic critique of aspects of Argentine idiosyncrasy and history. According to the director, the production's origin was a fundamental work of Argentine literature, Ezequiel Martinez Estrada's *Radiografía de la Pampa*. The subject and the style of Vivi Tella's *El precio de un brazo derecho (The Price of a Right Arm)* were original. In the hostile environment of a building site, the characters discuss the amount of compensation a workman would receive if he lost his right arm in an accident.

To the list of the playwrights who belong to the new theatre, we must add the names of Bernardo Cappa, Mario Cura, Marcelo Bertuccio and Omar Pacheco. Outstanding among the more established playwrights, who represent the traditional theatre and are regularly performed there, are Roberto Cossa, Griselda Gambaro, Ricardo Monti and Eduardo Pavlovsky. Pavlovsky renews himself constantly and aligns his work with that of younger playwrights and directors. This is, for example, the case with *La muerte de Marguerite Duras (The Death of Marguerite Duras)* where he is at the same time author and actor, under the direction of Daniel Veronese, who is, as mentioned, much engaged in a very personal breakaway aesthetic. As for Griselda Gambaro, she wrote *Lo que va dictando el sueño (What the Dream Dictates)*. Its character, an unhappy girl who is a maidservant in an old people's home, mixes dreams and reality. Her dreams do not modify reality but they do help to awaken paternal feelings in an old man. In *Finlandia (Finland)*, Ricardo Monti poses the problem of existential conflict that he had already developed in *Una passion sudamericana (A South American Passion)*: a political and military leader questions himself about his destiny, at the moment when he has to take action.

In the field of direction, there are also two different streams; the breakaway playwrights need, of course, to be directed by breakaway directors in order to produce coherent work. This explains why many playwrights (Daniel Veronese, Rafael Spregelburd, Alejandro Tantanian, Luis Cano...) direct their plays themselves.

Let us add that the nation's theatre also presents the theatre of the world: during this period the local audience has also had opportunities to see classical and modern plays from the world repertoire, presented by local and international groups. The ITI Centre of Argentina awarded the Saulo Benavente prize for the best foreign performance presented in Argentina in 2000 to the National Theatre of Greece for Sophocles' *Oedipus* and in 2001 to the group Zaranda from Spain for Gide's *La porte étroite*.

In these last years the dance theatre groups, all of them young, have also continued their chosen path of development. Modern dance, too, has seen some brilliant performances, as for example *The Four Seasons* to music by Vivaldi-Piazzola, by the General San Martín Theatre's ballet of Modern Dance, with choreography by Maurice Wainrot.

Before concluding this short summary of Argentine Theatre over these last years, one cannot avoid stressing a point which is perhaps not unusual but remains always surprising: the intensity of theatre activity seems to run counter to the serious social, political and economic situation which weighs on the country. The repertory has never been richer or more varied. There is a prevalence of productions put on by the companies themselves as co-operatives. A number of small spaces have appeared all over the city, both in and out of the downtown area. In some cases, there are no more than 20 spectators. Something else very surprising: some productions have been created by artists well known on the commercial circuit – as in the case of *Pequeños fantasmas* (*Little Ghosts*), directed by Manuel González Gil – where groups who have performed in the state or commercial theatre (as with Los Macocos) present their production and pass round the hat. The takings are considered as a minor commercial success. On the other hand, there are more and more actors available. The theatre schools and individual teachers still train young actors, but the Argentine Association of Actors tell us that only 10% of its 5000 actors are in work. The publishers complain about their disintegrating situation, too, but somehow there is always a new theatre book. It is the same for periodicals. And conferences, workshops, theatrical events are still being organised.

Another innovation of the new century was the rebirth of the national and international festival of the Cordoba province, the so-called Festival of Theatre of the Southern Cone, an emblematic event, because it sprang originally, with a significant reality, from the moment of the recovery of democracy in 1984. This Cordoba festival came to join the International Festivals of Buenos Aires, which took place in 1999 and 2001.

All this confirms, once again, that the theatre is deeply rooted in society, that it is closely linked with the vicissitudes which beset mankind and that, as always, it is these which furnish its best dramatic material.

Francisco Javier, *general secretary of the Argentine Centre of ITI, has a doctorate in Theatre Studies from the University of Paris VIII; a member of the Palmes Academiques de France, he is also an honorary professor in the philosophical faculty of the Unversity of Buenos Aires.*

AUSTRALIA

JEREMY ECCLES

Re-reading the thoughts I offered to *World of Theatre 2000*, I came to a depressing conclusion: either I was remarkably prescient in pointing to the things that were about to go wrong with the Australian theatre, or not much has changed. For issues like the funding imbalance between the big and smaller arts organizations, the international and domestic touring of product for political reasons rather than artistic ones, and the burden placed upon Aboriginal writing and performance to be both the conscience of the nation in increasingly conservative times and the exotic flag-bearer overseas of a mature and varied culture, were all discussed last time around.

If anything, with Australia now in the seventh year of a conservative central government, such tendencies have become more entrenched. And while the world may take note of our incarcerated refugees, our enthusiastic support for the Bush battle against Islamic terrorism, our rejection of the Kyoto Protocols on limiting greenhouse gases and our booming economy, our theatre prefers to entertain. Is this a slavish reflection of the prevailing *zeitgeist*, or the inevitable result of a funding system for the major performing arts companies that has forced the theatre to rely ever more on the box office, while the less ideas-based artforms – music, dance and opera – have been splendidly boosted?

Similarly, in the commercial world, exclamation-mark musicals like *Oliver!* and *Mamma Mia!* will get the money, along with tours by TV chefs or arena ballets, while commercial drama is dead – unless it's the Royal Shakespeare Company's 1964 confection, *The Hollow Crown,* gilded with aged Knights and Dames, preferably doubling as familiar faces from TV. God forbid we should see Sarah Kane.

It has to be admitted that the Sydney Theatre Company's house director, Benedict Andrews, has a penchant for Germany's 'in-yer-face' drama – Gieselmann's *Mr Kolpert* this year, von Mayenburg's *Fireface* in 2001. But it's kept firmly in the back of the subscription brochure, which is, one suspects, already pretty much fixed for 2004/5. This year (2002) in Sydney has felt like 'At last the 1999 show' with Michael Frayn's *Copenhagen,* Alan Bennett's *The Lady in the Van,* David Greig's *The Cosmonaut's Last Message,* David Hare's *My Zinc Bed* and Lee Hall's *Cooking with Elvis* all belatedly welcomed. Last year, we all laughed uproariously at Marie Jones' clever but utterly lightweight *Stones in His Pockets.* American plays are safer still – Richard Greenberg's *Three Days of Rain* or David Auburn's *Proof.* Nigh on perfect, especially if you can woo one of the New Aussie Hollywood actpack home to star…a Guy Pearce, a Geoffrey Rush or a Rachel Griffiths.

Even 'Dame' Ruth Cracknell in Donald Margulies' *Collected Stories* could sell a national tour in 2000. Sadly, it was Ruth's last tour – the great trouper died

From Marrageku's *Crying Baby*   (*photo*: Jon Greene)

this year after 46 years on the boards, with two shows still lined up. Director Richard Wherrett, the founder of both the Nimrod and Sydney Theatre Companies, also had at least one to go when he died in 2001. Significantly, it was a reprise of his world-wide 70s success, Steve J Spears' *The Elocution of Benjamin Franklin*. It's quite a feature of these times that we'd rather take another look at Jack Hibberd's *Stretch of the Imagination,* Ron Blair's *The Christian Brothers* or Patrick White's *A Cheery Soul* than write anything as imperishable today. We'd also rather adapt an international classic – Molière's *Don Juan,* Chekhov's *Three Sisters* or Webster's *Duchess of Malfi* – all serious revisions, mind you, which worked with widely varying degrees of success. To name the most successful, I've never felt I could enter Chekhov's hermetic world so completely before adapter Beatrix Christian got to work.

Is it the final victory of TV and film as the financially dominant media for writers in Australia? Certainly, Elizabeth Coleman's nationwide stage hit of 1999, *Secret Bridesmaids' Business,* has gone straight to telemovie – where it worked even better than on stage. Hannie Rayson and David Williamson, two of our senior playwrights, have, on the other hand, gone to London's West End. But what can one judge from their receptions there? Rayson's witty, moving and formally complex study of educational decline, *Life After George*, was pulled after a month – while in Australia its career seems to go on and on. Williamson's nakedly populist picture of greed in the art market was hand-picked and hand-reared (*i.e.* significantly altered) by pop-star Madonna to make her London stage debut – and seems destined for transatlantic glory. My interpretation is that the genuinely Australian experience is still only valued as exotic festival fodder; it doesn't yet have mainstream viability.

Which brings us to the government-sponsored wish for an international image that is 'cleverer' than kangaroos, beaches and Aussie Rules football. The biennial Performing Arts Markets have certainly encouraged the exotic in terms of physical and street theatre groups like Acrobat and Strange Fruit, Legs on the Wall and Erth. But there is also the Major Festivals Initiative, which funds work that is too big for any one producer, and seems to have had remarkable success in fostering work like the multi-national *The Theft of Sita,* Marrageku's *Crying Baby,* The Australian Art Orchestra's *Testimony* and Belvoir Street Theatre's *Cloudstreet*. One or all of them could have been found at international events like New York's BAM Festival, London's *HeadsUp* festival – both in 2001 – or this year's Australian promotion at the Hebbel Theater in Berlin. Several contemporary operas have emerged from the Initiative, too, such as Jonathan Mills' *The Ghost Wife,* which is featured as one of the London Barbican International Theatre Events in 2002.

The process begins with two or more festival directors in Australia agreeing to commission the work. That allows for big thinking, and big time to bed it down. *Sita*, for instance, wanted to add an Aussie flavour to a story from the *Ramayana*, together with Indonesian shadow puppets, Balinese gamelan and Western jazz. *Testimony* staged a tribute to the great American jazzman Charlie Parker with a Pulitzer Prize-winning poem and Australian music. *Cloudstreet*, which has been winning prizes ever since its 1998 start, is pure Oz, and 5 hours long. Only *Crying Baby* disappointed. More than a million dollars of public funds went into the multi-media development of an Aboriginal story from far north Arnhemland by a white street theatre director. But when two of the festival directors involved tried to question the confused dramaturgy, they were told they 'didn't know how Aboriginal stories came together' – so butt out!

This is a constant danger. There's a reluctance to criticise Aboriginal work – whether its under indigenous control or not – for fear of cultural insensitivity. Nowhere was this more apparent than in Peter Sellars' notorious 2002 Adelaide Festival. This dominated the period under review as the high-profile American opera and festival director charged on to the scene in 1999, wooed the crowd with his charismatic speech-making, and stole the hearts of the artists, offering commissions for local work that would be important enough to go to the world as a post-Colonial counter-thrust to the original Adelaide Festival philosophy, of simply importing the world's best practice. Unfortunately, Sellars then disappeared, as the whole project got bogged down in funding crises, administrative inadequacy and broken dreams.

It did happen, but only just. Attendance was the lowest in years, work commissioned by a panel of Associate Directors was largely unfinished, and little will go to the world. And the future of one of the oldest international festivals in the world is tainted by a creative and financial burden. Sellars may be right in saying that we don't need a supermarket trolley approach to festival curation any longer, and that the tyranny of distance between Australia and the rest of the world has been largely overcome. But it's something we're going to have to work out for ourselves: Australia didn't appreciate the brash Los Angeleno telling the *New York Times* that he was the first to discover and seek to overcome the local 'cringe' in self-confidence. Coincidentally, he said it just before 9/11.

Aspects of the Festival which need not go to the world, but matter deeply here, included the opening ceremony and the work of a company like Urban Theatre Projects. The opening was an all too rare piece of Aboriginal ceremonial in Southern, urban Australia. Local high-art snobs in Adelaide denied that it was 'art'. But to have pulled together concentric circles of indigenous peoples from South Australia, the traditional North, and the rest of the world (New Zealand, New Mexico, South Africa and Tibet) in such a respectful way required a vast amount of cultural negotiation. In Australia alone, the urban South and the tribal North find great difficulty in talking. In fact, Sydney, Adelaide and Melbourne see less of Aboriginal performance than the rest of the world's festivals. The resulting piece, *Kaurna Palti Meyunna*, spoke powerfully of survival against all the odds.

And while I wrote enthusiastically about the wave of urban Aboriginal theatre in *World of Theatre 2000*, it has barely advanced. Probably its greatest success was the belated production of the 1968 play, *The Cherry Pickers*, which indigenous playwright Kevin Gilbert stipulated could never be performed without an all-Aboriginal cast. Small groups have read it or performed it on the fringe since then. But it took Australia's Centenary of (white) Federation in 2001 to bring it provocatively into the mainstream.

The Adelaide Festival project, *Mamu*, on the other hand, about the tribes devastated by the British Maralinga atomic tests, arrived on stage so bloated by Western production values that its core was lost. Perhaps a group like

AUSTRALIA

Urban Theatre Projects has lessons for all such political theatre, theatre emerging from the communities of Australia. Embedding its theatre workers into the disadvantaged Western suburbs of Sydney or Adelaide, it regularly produces works that both reflect the lives of those people and are actually seen by them. The only drawback is that as the communities have no solution to their problems, so the resulting play can offer none. Sometimes a playwright's oversight comes in handy – Michael Futcher, for instance, wrote movingly for the 2000 production of *A Beautiful Life*, basing his material for Brisbane's Matrix Company on the first hand experiences of Iranian refugees. This rare piece tapping into the *zeitgeist* won four Green Room Awards in Melbourne.

Which is remarkably close to where I came in – generally underwhelmed by theatrical events of the past 3 years. An exception occurred in tiny, offshore Tasmania with the initiation of a festival reflecting island cultures. Created by the experienced Robyn Archer (formerly of the Australian Theatre Festival, two Adelaide Festivals and now the Melbourne International Festival), she sneaked Ten Days on the Island into Tassie lives in 2001, gently justifying her thesis that gathering artists in from Madagascar and Reunion, Singapore and Okinawa, the Shetlands and Iceland would provide evidence of a similarity based upon isolation and resilience. I look forward to further developments on the theme in 2003.

Jeremy Eccles *is a British-born critic, feature-writer and (since 1983) specialist commentator on Australia's cultural affairs. He writes for newspapers, magazines and electronic sites in Australia, Asia and Europe.*

AUSTRIA

Drama Theatre
HILDE HAIDER-PREGLER

The start of the new millennium saw not only Austria's political scene but also its theatre life in such turmoil as had not been experienced for a long time. Although it is true that in artistic and intellectual circles, the opposition to the ÖVP-FPÖ coalition was particularly sharply articulated, the structural changes and personal moves in the theatre sector cannot simply be attributed to the policies of the black-blue (ÖVP-FPÖ) 'Turning Point' government. Federal Chancellor Viktor Klima (SPÖ) had already transferred artistic affairs for the first time from a Federal Minister to a Secretary of State directly answerable to the Chancellor and with regard to subsidies had shown a preference for separations, (part) privatisation, sponsorship, efficient marketing etc. The 'black' (ÖVP) Secretary Franz Morak, a former Burgtheater actor who had moved into politics some years ago, carried on this line determinedly.

Naturally, there has been no lack of polemic. What some saw as a chance for a surge to previously inconceivable artistic heights produced in others fears of a regression into complacent mediocrity. That neither the one nor the other extreme resulted is hardly surprising. At any rate it is pleasing that in Austria the theatre is still a focus of public interest.

With the new organisational form of an intermediate Holding, Austrian Federal Theatres were forced into an economic corset, which though not really a restriction did demand careful budgeting of their still generous means. Nevertheless, in the second season for which he was responsible, Burgtheater Director Klaus Bachler could claim that the position in the German-speaking theatre achieved under Claus Peymann's spectacular direction had unquestionably been maintained. Committed Peymann fans had feared that Austria's State Theatre would sink into unimportance after the departure to the Berliner Ensemble of the much admired and much criticised man of theatre. In October 2000 the world première of Yasmina Reza's *Dreimal Leben* (*Life x 3*), translated by Eugen Helmlé and brilliantly directed by Luc Bondy with a quartet of high-quality actors, enticed prominent international critics to Vienna. In the form of an equally brilliant and amusingly multi-layered conversation piece, the French star dramatist presented a merciless soul striptease for two middle-aged couples on the academic career ladder. In this the same starting point was played with three different interactive possibilities, each of which turned into a nightmare. It's amazing what can happen when dinner guests mistake the date and stand at the door a day too soon ... Finally, Luc Bondy achieved the glittering high point of a Burgtheater season rich in highlights with a very nuanced production of Chekhov's *The Seagull*. Peter Zadek's psychologically finely honed and at the same time amusingly well-pointed production of Ibsen's *Rosmersholm*, with Angela Winkler and Gerd Voss, was enthusiastically received

AUSTRIA

Schiller: *Maria Stuart*, directed by Andrea Breth at the Burgtheater, Vienna

by critics and audiences alike. In spring, Zadek triumphed again with Neil LaBute's cycle of one-acters *Bash*, which uncovers 'the everyday evil', as a Festival guest production from Hamburg in the Akademietheater. Andrea Breth, engaged by Bachler as house producer at the Burgtheater, demonstrated once again her mastery of the precise plumbing of a dramatic text and her talent for designing impressive, symbolic pictures, with Ödön von Horváth's late work *Schuld und Sühne (Crime and Punishment)*. In her realisation of Pirandello's *Mit Leidenschaft ist nicht zu spassen!* in a mixture of German and Italian, the young Karin Beier unleashed a histrionic total theatre with a flood of pictures to delight the eye, which was only accepted by the critics with reservations. Like an erratic block came Martin Kusej's oppressive production, complete to the last detail, of Karl Schönherr's rustic tragedy *Glaube und Heimat (Belief and Home)*. Born in Austria and advanced in Germany to 'shooting star' status among the young directors, admired and disputed alike as a radical exponent of interpretative theatre, he set this work by the now seldom performed Tyrolean author, dealing with the religious wars of the Counter-Reformation, in a gloomy unlit set by Martin Zehetgruber on a muddy floor covered with clumps of earth and hardly any props. An artistically perfect and impressive evening, which nevertheless did not convince one of the need for a Schönherr renaissance. No less demanding than productions in the large house on the Ring and the Akademietheater were the offerings of the two subsidiary stages that function as theatre laboratories for the Burgtheater. A minimalist production of Sarah Kane's *Gier (Crave)* impressed in the Vestibule, while in the Kasino am Schwarzenbergplatz, with *Die Nervenwaage (The Nerve Scales)*, Joachim

Schlömer and an excellent, almost circus-like acrobatic young ensemble presented a lesson in applied Artaud exegesis (not only for theatre theoreticians) fully revealing the histrionic potential of the text without fighting shy of slapstick and thus bringing out its absurd, cryptic wit.

Thus it was hardly surprising that the Burg was nominated 'Theatre of the Year' by *Theater Heute* in its *Jahrbuch 2001* and represented at the 36th Berliner Theatertreffen with several of its productions. The Burgtheater was also successful at the 'Nestroy' awards, a theatre prize donated by the City of Vienna modelled on the Paris 'Molière' and awarded for the first time in October 2001. Luc Bondy was nominated Best Director and his production of *The Seagull* was declared the best German-language production of the season. (Peter Zadek and his *Rosmersholm* received the same acclaim a year later.) Among the actors, the jury were united over Gert Voss, while Martin Schwab received the 'Nestroy' for the best supporting role.

All the harsher was the reaction of international arts pages when the 2001/ 02 season fell below expectations, which were perhaps too high anyway. Whereas Peter Zadek's grand scheme of a confrontation with Christopher Marlowe's Elizabethan horror tragedy *The Jew of Malta* (newly translated by Elfriede Jelinek) found respectful and fairly enthusiastic recognition, opinions were considerably divided over Andrea Breth's production of Schiller's *Maria Stuart*; Luc Bondy's interpretation of *Anatol* with borrowings from the former 'regie' theatre displeased; and the attempt to open the Experiment, the rehearsal stage in the Arsenal near the South Railway Station, as a new performance area received little acceptance for the world première of Alfred Ostermeier's *Letzter Aufruf* (*Last Call*) as a high-powered technical stage show with authentic airport atmosphere from Andrea Breth. From a series of pleasant productions of contemporary dramatists – Botho Strauss, Jon Fosse, and the Martins McDonagh and Crimp – the long overdue Austrian first performance of Thomas Bernhard's *Elisabeth II* stood out, presented by Thomas Langhoff with the right feeling for ironic theatrics and in artistically frozen pictures as a feast for actors. That not only the Burgtheater but also a number of other stages – notably the Volkstheater and the Josefstadt – took advantage of the possibility presented by the waiver of the testamentary ban on Austrian performances of Bernhard's work to rediscover the once so disputed (and naturally all the more posthumously prized) author hardly needs emphasising. The year's top man among Austrian authors was unquestionably Johann Nestroy, the 200th anniversary of whose birth was celebrated by a veritable flood of more or less successful productions.

The numerous other Viennese stages, and especially the not exactly generously subsidised 'free scene', are in a difficult position beside the Burg, with its pluralistic programmes from the great classics to the experimental. The Theater in der Josefstadt, where Bernhard's *Der Schein trügt* (*Appearances Are Deceptive*) overstepped the tolerance of some of the audience, offered its predominantly middle-class conservative public, as always, elegant actors' theatre. It seemed almost a foregone conclusion that not much would change after Helmuth Lohners stepped down in Autumn 2003, since Lohner had taken pains to inaugurate as his successor the actor and producer Karlheinz Hackl, admittedly not an experienced theatre director but a genuine favourite of Viennese audiences (and one who has studied economics). However, events proved otherwise. The Vienna City elections in 2001 gave the Social Democrats an absolute majority. At city level this meant the end of the Red and Black (SPÖ-ÖVP) coalition. As a result, Andreas Mailath-Pokorny replaced Peter Marboe – esteemed on all sides – as Cultural Councillor. The decision to advertise the directorships of all publicly funded theatres openly in future naturally included the Josefstadt. Nevertheless, the appointment hearings took a quite wilful course, rich in surprises, which set the theatre world by the ears and provoked vigorous and exhaustive comment in the media. The majority of the Findings Commission, (a body which included Helmuth Lohner), decided against the candidate preferred by the departing director and chose Hermann Beil, long-time dramaturg and co-director with Claus Peymann, although he had not officially applied for the post. Beil resigned before signing his contract, having taken note of the desperate finances of the theatre and the rigid economy measures that this implied. That the choice finally fell on Hans Gratzer was no less of a surprise than his policy (ridiculed by a few), coming as it did from one linked for years with the dramatic avant-garde: from Autumn 2003 the Josefstadt would perform 'exclusively Austrian authors ... from Nestroy to Bernhard.'

One can trust that Hans Gratzer will again be successful in teaching the sceptics a lesson, just as he did at the end of his long period as director of the Vienna Schauspielhaus. Gratzer founded the 'off' stage in 1978 and led it at first until 1986, cleared the field for Georg Tabori's theatre laboratory 'Der Kreis' (The Circle) and then returned in 1991 with a rigid 'authors' theatre' policy, presenting exclusively world or German-language premières of plays eschewed by the established stages. Thus a productive unrest was created in the Viennese theatre world – and far beyond – with performances of Werner Schwab, Tony Kushner, Thomas Jonigk, Gustav Ernst, Sarah Kane and others, until the search for new artistic directions towards the end of the 90s seemed to lack orientation. As a result, in the last year of his direction Gratzer offered a contrasting programme which hit on a market gap. In season 2000/1, the Schauspielhaus became an exquisite music theatre studio where witty productions, at the same time full of poetry, of Baroque operas – G.F.Handel's *Acis and Galatea*, F.Gassmann's *La Contessina* and J.A.Hasse's *Piramo e Tisbe* – and rarely heard 20th century and contemporary experimental works followed one another in musically and scenically convincing performances. 'Authors' theatre' was placed (literally) in the shop window: every two weeks a world première, low-budget with small cast and lasting no longer than about one hour, in a roughly 60 square metre area, without technical finesse, with no dividing line between actors and audience and only separated from the street by a pane of glass. Without falling into trivial realism, almost all the texts dealt with the losers in the consumer society. Almost all caught the attention, although no new young genius was discovered. A pity that the shutters rattled down before the next workshop phase – for example, carefully aimed commissions – could begin.

The new artistic direction of the Schauspielhaus had other plans. From among the 77 applicants – Hans Gratzer did not offer himself – two young theatre men from the alternative scene, Airan Berg and Barrie Kosky, were the winners and announced that in the three years from Autumn 2001 they would make the house in the Porzellangasse into the 'interface between established and alternative, domestic and international theatre and other art forms' – without, however, a permanent ensemble. They opened with an exciting interpretation of Euripides' *Medea* which Barrie Kosky, often apostrophied as the *enfant terrible* of Australian theatre, directed as a timeless multicultural spectacle. None of the following productions (including a string of guest appearances) – from professional, witty Show Business to destructively stirring, scenic documentaries – could really match this, not even Kosky's puzzling, brilliantly realized 'Showbiz' piece *Dafke!*, the start of a Jewish trilogy presented as 'work in progress'.

A new wind has also been blowing in the 'Rabenhof' since Spring 2001, when Karl Welunschek took over as director of the former workshop stage of the Josefstadt Theatre and at once landed a sensational success with the world première of Wolfgang Bauer's *Tamagotchi* directed by Georg Staudacher; he has since greatly entertained his predominantly young audiences with 'fun and trash theatre', gleefully ignoring all criteria of good taste.

There have also been developments in the direction of the major festivals. The Vienna Festival, which was at last able to return in Spring 2001 to the halls of the renovated Museum Quarter, underwent a gradual transition: Luc Bondy, who was already responsible for theatre in the triumvirate with Hans-Peter Kehr (music theatre) and Hortensia Völckers (crossovers), has determined the artistic line as Intendant since 2002, supported by Hans Landesmann as music director and Marie Zimmermann as theatre director. With the 'forumfestwochen ff', the latter set a special accent: innovative, avant-garde and experimental productions, by young theatre people who have not yet arrived, would be presented in small venues and workshops, with groups from the Eastern European countries taking the foreground in 2002 and making almost as much of a sensation as the prominently cast major events. While in the previous year Peter Brook again enthralled – with *Le Costume* and a multiethnic *Hamlet* – this time Frank Castorf continued his fascinating, though severely taxing multimedia adaptations of Russian classic novels: after Dostoyevski's *Die Dämonen* (*The Devils*, 2000) and *Erniedrigte und Beleidigte* (*Humbled and Insulted*, 2001) came Bulgakov's *The Master and Margarita*. A genuine highlight was the guest appearance of the Hamburg Schauspielhaus with Michael Thalheimer's radically abridged and de-kitsched *Liliom*, while Robert Lepage's aesthetic and as always irreproachable Frida Kahlo homage *Apasionada* was received politely but not as enthusiastically as the millennium production *The Far Side of the Moon*, mirroring the centuries-old human dream of travelling to distant worlds, which the great theatre magician from Quebec had presented in 2000 at the 'Styrian Autumn', still Austria's most prestigious avant-garde festival.

In Salzburg Gérard Mortier's Festival era came to an end in Summer 2001 under the motto 'Questioning tradition' with much media hype and a real scandal around the ruthless deconstruction of *Die Fledermaus* by Hans Neuenfels. The 'Austrian slaughter of a suitable national holy cow' (*Die Zeit*, No.35/2001) enraged not a few in the audience – and some critics – so much that there was some debate as to whether there might not be a successful action for the return of the entrance fee on the grounds of false pretences. It must be separately emphasised that there were many highlights in the straight theatre sector. For example, Frank Castorf reanimated Tennessee Williams' aged psycho-thriller *A Streetcar Named Desire* in Summer 2000, Martin Kusej's wilful production and adaptation of *Hamlet* on the 'Perner Island' inflamed violent discussion and in the following year Austria's award-winning novelist Christoph Ransmayr made his debut as dramatist with a farewell to the theatre: condemned for her whole life to the prompter's box, the *Unsichtbare* (*The Invisible One*) – in the person of Kirsten Dene – made up for her hatred of all that had to do with the stage with a genuine passion for the cinema. Although awarded the authors' 'Nestroy' in 2001, the piece is not a great work. Claus Peymann directed, and also appeared in Summer 2002 under the incoming Intendant as director of Peter Turrini's new and heavily savaged *Don Giovanni in Santa Fé*.

After the political 'turning-point', Gérard Mortier had made no secret of the fact that he would under no circumstances prolong his contract under a black-blue (ÖVP-FPÖ) coalition. The modernisation slapped on the Festival by Mortier, who was not always as diplomatic as he might have been, with his director of plays Frank Baumbauer, was certainly not to everyone's taste. The engagement of Peter Ruzicka, cultural manager, composer and conductor in one, thus created, according to point of view, speculative hopes or fears that the 'old' elite Festival times would come back again. Ruzicka doubtless has a less shirt-sleeve image than his predecessor but a return to the (day before) yesterday does not seem to be on the cards. The eternal *Jedermann* on the Cathedral Square has already received a rejuvenation under Christian Stückl, whose Rocketing career began with the Oberammergau Passion plays.

Neither the Salzburg Festival nor the almost unsurveyable multitude of festivals and summer productions of every size between Lake Constance and Lake Neusiedl can complain of a lack of visitors. These are not concerned with scenic experiments but with solid, often demanding actors' theatre – between classic classics and modern classics. This recipe for success has won a faithful regular audience for Lower Austrian Reichenau, where Vienna's *fin-de-siècle* literary figures were wont to take their summer holidays. The 'genius loci' of the Spa Theatre was naturally Arthur Schnitzler but in Summer 2000 the artistic view was extended, with an interestingly designed production of *Die Letzten Tage der Menschheit* by Karl Kraus in the venerable Südbahn Hotel on the Semmering, which had been specially adapted for the purpose, and in the following year with a scenic arrangement of Thomas Mann's *Zauberberg*.

During the season the provincial theatres were well worth a closer look. As an example, mention may be made of the Carinthian Provincial Theatre in Klagenfurt, where Intendant Dietmar Pflegerl, a declared enemy of the FPÖ and Provincial Governor Jörg Haider, made committed theatre with endurance, earning respect well beyond the region, in opposition to a cultural policy that prefers to accuse critical artists of 'fouling the nest'.

In conclusion, only the question remains of which Austrian dramatists have come forward most recently. Elfriede Jelinek was declared Dramatist of the Year 2002 at the Mühlheim Theatre Days for her new text *Macht nichts* (*It Doesn't Matter*). The première, however, took place in Zurich, since Elfriede Jelinek has declined to be played on Austrian stages since the political 'turning-point'. On the other hand, Felix Mitterer, as always fighting against social abuses of every sort, still produces, with endless industry, on the thin line between committed literature and commercial plays, at least one play a year, whether for the Tyrolese Volksspielen or for an established professional stage. 'Schwab-mania' has abated in this country, although the plays of this dramatic genius who died early – despite or because of their at first sight untranslatable 'Swabian' – are beginning to be discovered outside the German-speaking area.

Whether Christoph Ransmayr's flirtation with the stage is more than an intermezzo remains to be seen. Among the younger generation the industrious Franz Obel indulges his tendency to overflowing whimsy – among others, the Volkstheater, still under Emmy Werner, presented his *Mayerling, österreichische Tragodie* in a production by Thirza Brucken – and there has been a series of premières which have made one curious. However, no great work was among them. It would appear that artistic interest has moved from writers' theatre to dance theatre, the latter having in recent years emphatically moved into the limelight and since the opening of the Dance Quarter (under the direction of Sigrid Gareis) in the Vienna Museum Quarter – and not only there – experienced a boom. But that is the start of another chapter.

Opera and Music Theatre
FRANZ EUGEN DOSTAL

In relation to the size of the country and the number of inhabitants (roughly 8 million) Austria has a dense network of music theatres. Vienna alone has seven music theatres, led by the State Opera and the Volksoper, both, like the major straight theatres (Burgtheater, Akademietheater, Theater in der Josefstadt, Kammerspiele and Volkstheater) repertory theatres with a daily change of programme and a ten-month season stretching from 1st September to 30th June. In addition, there are the Vienna Chamber Opera and the New Opera Vienna, both operating on the *stagione* principle. There are three further musical theatres, the Raimund Theatre, the Ronacher and the historic Theater an der Wien, the last also used by the State Opera and the Vienna Festival and where Beethoven's *Fidelio*, Johann Strauss' *Die Fledermaus* and Franz Lehár's *The Merry Widow* all received their first performances. All these three musical stages play the whole year round. Moreover, during his last season as Director of the Schauspielhaus (2001–2002) Hans Gratzer employed this theatre as an opera house and presented there a number of ambitious Baroque and modern music theatre works – a successful experiment that has not been taken up by the new direction of the Schauspielhaus. Nevertheless, Vienna, a city of 1.6 million inhabitants, still offers daily some 7,750 seats for music theatre, to which may be added some 6,500 seats in the Viennese concert halls which are used regularly several times a day. Attendance figures of between 85 and 100% result in concert and music theatre audiences of four million persons annually.

The 2001–2002 season can give an idea of the importance of the repertory of the State Opera: apart from ballets, the season offered 50 works, including 10 operas by Giuseppe Verdi (in 2000–2001, for the 100th anniversary of Verdi's death, it was 13: *Nabucco, Jérusalem, Ernani, Macbeth, Stiffelio, Rigoletto, Il Trovatore, La Traviata, I Vespri Siciliani, Un Ballo in maschera, Aida, Don Carlo* and *Otello,* together with a Verdi ballet and the *Requiem* under Riccardo Muti, which had been conducted at the Vienna Opera by Verdi himself in 1875), seven by Richard Wagner, five by Giacomo Puccini, four each by Wolfgang Amadeus Mozart and Richard Strauss, three by Gioacchino Rossini and 17 by other composers, one of which was a commission – *Der Riese vom Steinfeld* – from the dramatist Peter Turrini and the composer Friedrich Cerha; two works were produced especially for children. The most successful production of this season was, however, *Jenufa* by Leos Janácek, conducted by Seiji Ozawa, who has just been nominated Music Director of the State Opera, and produced by David Pountney, the Head designate of the Bregenz Festival. Among the most important productions of recent seasons, mention must be made at least of *La Juive* by Jacques Francois Fromental Halévy (conductor Simone Young, producer Günter Krämer) and *Billy Budd* by Benjamin Britten (Conductor Donald Runnicles, producer Willy Decker). The great success of the latter was the more remarkable as in the 1996–97 season the New Opera Vienna had set a very high standard with their own excellent production of *Billy Budd* by Leonard C. Prinsloo (conductor Walter Kobéra). Especially outstanding in both works was Neil Shicoff as Eleazar (*La Juive*) and Captain Vere (*Billy Budd*). Stefania Bonfadelli may be taken as representative of the feted female stars of the Vienna State Opera; she raised a furore both by taking over at short notice from Natalia Dessay as Amina in *La Sonnambula* by Vincenzo Bellini and as Juliette in *Romeo et Juliette* by Charles Gounod.

A change of director took place at the Volksoper, from Klaus Bachler, who took over the Burgtheater, to Dominique Mentha, who took up office with a truly missionary zeal and forfeited the sympathy of a large part of his audience by his first official act, preferring to pay off an exceptional artist like Edita Gruberová rather than allow her to sing Marie in *La fille du régiment* by Gaetano Donizetti for which she had been contracted by his predecessor. As a result, even such highlights of the programme as *Ritter Blaubart* by Jacques Offenbach (in a successful production by the director himself) and *The Pirates of Penzance* by Gilbert and Sullivan failed to attract many visitors and the responsible Secretary of State announced in the second year of his five-year contract that it would not be renewed.

Outside Vienna, all forms of music theatre are catered for all year round by the Graz Opera House and in Innsbruck, Klagenfurt, Linz and Salzburg, whereas the Stadttheaters of Baden and St. Pölten concentrate on operetta, to which the summer festivals of Bad Ischl and Mörbisch are also devoted. In two cases the administration changed from male to female hands: Karen Stone replaced Gerhard Brunner as Intendant in Graz, and Brigitte Fassbaender took over from Dominique Mentha in Innsbruck.

A speciality of Austrian music theatre, which also gives it its characteristic aspect and contributes not inconsiderably to the country's good reputation in music world, is that the orchestra pits of its opera houses are filled by a number of orchestras that have made a name for themselves on international concert plattforms and which range from just under to far above one hundred members: the Vienna Symphony Orchestra, the backbone of the Bregenz Festival, the Graz Philharmonic Orchestra, the Salzburg Mozarteum Orchestra, the Linz Bruckner Orchestra and above all the Vienna Philharmonic Orchestra, which is practically identical with the State Opera Orchestra.

Dance Theatre
IRA WERBOWSKY

The Austrian metropolis, Vienna, is also the centre of a very varied and lively dance scene ranging from classic to modern and from dance theatre to performance.

Incontestably, the venue with the highest quality is the Vienna State Opera. Under the direction of its Ballet Director Renato Zanella, a very broad repertory has crystallised, in which the classical ballet still has its regular place side by side with new paths in dance. The first highlight of the year 1999 was the highly acclaimed premiere of *La Bayadère* (music Ludwig Minkus), which came for the first time to Vienna 122 years after its world premiere in St Petersburg. Star dancer Vladimir Malakhov, who also danced Solor, made his debut as choreographer with this production. Although he kept closely to Marius Petipa's original, there were a few innovations: for example, Malakhov reduced the pantomime, choreographed a new waltz, gave the men an extra entry and added an additional variation for Solor. The story was told to its end in the union of the lovers in the realm of shades and the revealing of Hamsatti as murderess, with additional music from other ballets. The two female roles were danced by Brigitte Stadler (Nikia) and Simona Noja (Hamsatti).

With the revival of *Raymonda* in Rudolf Nureyev's choreography (with Simona Noja in the title role, Tamas Solymosi as Jean de Brienne and Christian Rovny as a splendid Abderachman) and *Manon* by Kenneth MacMillan (with Manuel Legris as Des Grieux and Simona Noja and Tamas Solymosi as Manon and Lescaut) two earlier productions returned to the repertory. The dance year closed with *Aschenbrödel (Cinderella),* which was Renato Zanella's contribution to the Johann Strauss year: an attempt at a symbiosis of the old fairy-tale and a contemporary modernity, whereby Johann Strauss, who had never seen a performance of his own ballet, also appeared and thus was enabled to do so quasi-posthumously. The French couturier Christian Lacroix created the colourful decorations and costumes, Eva Petters and Gregor Hatala danced the main roles.

As modern premieres in 2000, the three-part *Adagio Hammerklavier,* one of the most important choreographies by Hans van Manen, the dance joke *Black Cake* and *Beethoven Opus 73* appeared on the programme. The last, by Renato Zanella, was what he called his 'symphonic first born'. At the end of the year he choreographed a new version of *The Nutcracker* with Simona Noja as Clara-Maria and Jürgen Wagner as the Prince, replacing Yuri Grigorovitch's version after roughly twenty-five years.

The year 2001 brought *Verdi Ballett: Ein Maskenball* as Vladimir Malakhov's second work, this time wholly choreographed by him and based on the ballet music to Verdi's *Un Ballo in maschera*, which is almost always cut in performances of the opera. Malakhov himself appeared as Gustav III and the Amelia was Eva Petters. Finally, 2002 was marked by Renato Zanella's version of *Spartacus* (to the music of Aram Khachaturian), with Boris Nebyla in the title role.

The most successful production at the Volksoper was *Swan Lake Remixed* by the choreographer duo Liz King and Catherine Guerin, who took the well-known classic apart and put it together again in modern dance language, using computer graphics by Patrick Pulsinger and Erdem Tunakan. Rejected by traditionalists, it was always guaranteed a full house by mainly young audiences and was thus the greatest success of the Dominique Mentha era – extra performances had to be scheduled. This success was not repeated with *Caravaggio*, in which a team of four choreographers (Esther Balfe, Liz King, Mani Obeya and Daphne Strothmann) retold the life and works of the unconventional Baroque painter.

Apart from the two major stages, special mention should be made above all of the Tanztheater Homunculus, which recently celebrated the twentieth anniversary of its founding. Its two heads, Manfred Aichinger and Nikolaus Selimov, pioneers in the Freie Tanzszene in Vienna, managed with their fellow combatants to achieve the creation of a dance house in the newly reconstructed Museumsquartier. Unfortunately, however, performances and events have been presented there mainly for a very specialised audience, so that they have had to seek a new venue - which they found in the Halle 1030, where other representatives of contemporary dance like Elio Gervasi and Sebastian Prantl have also shown their creations.

Of the provincial theatres, Innsbruck remains the most important venue for dance theatre. Among their pieces, some of which received a very controversial reception, were *Strauss, Strauss, nur du allein* (choreography Marialuise Jaska), *Winter was hard* and *Sommerfrische und andere Ausflüchte* (choreography Manfred Aichinger) and *Diaghilew: Die Offenbarung* and *Casanova* (choreography Jochen Ulrich, who succeeded Jaska as head of the company).

The St. Pölten Festspielhaus has become established as the venue for very interesting guest performances. For example, the Rambert Dance Company, The Dallas Black Dance Theatre Company, the Zurich Ballet, the Leipzig Ballet, the Nederlands Dance Theatre, the Batsheva Dance Company and the Paris Opera Ballet School have all appeared here. The new Intendant is the former solo dancer of the Vienna State Opera Ballet, Michael Birkmeyer, who is working on the formation of the house's own ballet company under the leadership of Nicolas Musin.

Hilde Haider-Pregler is *Professor in the Institut für Theater-, Film- und Medienwissenschaften of the University of Vienna;* **Franz Eugen Dostal** *is a composer and producer, President of the Society for Music Theatre and committee member of the Austrian ITI Centre;* **Ira Werbowsky** *teaches ballet history at the Wolfsegg Ballet Centre and is ballet editor of the magazine Der Neue Merker.*

BANGLADESH

RAMENDU MAJUMDAR

For most theatre workers in Bangladesh, theatre is a part of life. They find meaning in theatre, which is their vehicle for artistic expression of the contemporary issues they confront in real life. Our mainstream theatre, termed 'group theatre', is a non-profit theatre comprising over 250 repertory companies run by dedicated men and women. For socio-economic reasons they cannot become theatre professionals in the strictest sense, but what they produce is of absolutely professional standard, done with a professional zeal. Theatre workers are engaged in different professions for their living and dedicate their leisure time to theatre. That is how theatre in Bangladesh is not only surviving, but blooming with a passion.

The new theatre movement of Bangladesh is as old as the country itself. Although relatively a young nation, born in 1971 out of a bloody but glorious war of independence which claimed the sacrifice of three million people, the history of its theatre dates back to the 6th century AD, when a Buddhist play was performed in Sanskrit. About four centuries later, Sanskrit gave way as court language to Bengali, the mother tongue of the people living in this part of the world.

Theatre researcher Dr Syed Jamil Ahmed has identified over seventy genres of indigenous theatre that still exist in Bangladesh today. Of these, nearly fifty are rooted in the various religious beliefs and faiths of the people; the rest are absolutely secular in nature. Of these, Jatra, featuring folk-plays of the operetta kind, is most popular. Over the years most of the forms of indigenous theatre have decayed and some are at the point of extinction. Modern Bengali proscenium-stage theatre was the direct result of the influence of European theatre, when the English expatriates set up a playhouse for English plays in Kolkata in 1753.

Bengali society then was in transition, moving from traditional feudalism to a modern society influenced by colonial domination. There was a fusion of ideas that drew both from the ethos of the land and from Europe. Over the years, especially since the early 1940s, theatre became a very popular form, celebrating the struggles and the passions of the Bengali middle class. This has brought theatre out from the recreation halls of the feudal lords to the consumption level of the man in the street. The audience is more mixed — 'groundlings' rather than 'Dress Circle'.

With the creation of Bangladesh, theatre became a much more vital art form. The country saw a creative upsurge in its entire cultural arena, embracing literature, painting and in particular theatre arts, which has become on the one hand a fashionable pastime for aspiring performers and good serious entertainment for the educated urban class on the other. While this is true for the mainstream productions of the major groups, there are interesting innovations that draw heavily on folk theatre traditions. There are also semi-theatrical innovations that have swept the streets of Dhaka and elsewhere during political upheavals and moments of national crisis.

What has happened can best be described as a growing linkage, penetrating deeper into a wider social milieu. It reflects the shifts in social trends, in political culture and above all in the reorientation of social bonds. The theatrical content has also come to incorporate these realities. Prominent among these initially were so-called leftist issues in the socialist sense – issues of class, exploitation, protest, alienation born of social inequality. Subsequently, the new left agenda – gender issues, environment, globalisation – has entered the scene. With time, resistance against fundamentalism has also become part of this inclusive trend. This has had a telling effect on the spectators. There is greater identification with the new theatre – the experience, the ethos, the action. At the same time, with the growing interest in ethnicity and heritage, theatre activists are trying to rediscover tradition in newer forms.

Bangladesh theatre, during the period under review (July 1999 to June 2002), experienced a severe crisis of performance space. With the increase in the number of new groups, the activities of the established groups had to be curtailed because of the non-availability of theatre houses. It might sound unbelievable that in a country where there are over 250 non-profit theatre groups, and theatre the most vibrant art form, there is not a single purpose-built theatre. In the capital, Dhaka, regular stagings of plays are held at two auditoria on the Bailey Road (which has been renamed Natok Sharoni, meaning Theatre Street). Our National Theatre is under construction: the experimental stage is ready, with all modern technical facilities, and has been waiting for the last nine months to be commissioned after crossing all the hurdles of government bureaucracy. The main stage is half completed and would not take more than six months to finish, should the work be resumed and funds made available. Once it becomes fully operational, the National Theatre should be a source of pride for Bangladesh.

The dilapidated condition of the theatre spaces in the capital, as well as the growing number of inferior quality plays produced by a large number of groups, were responsible for the rather alarming fall in audiences during this period. However, one of the auditoria (Mahila Samity) has been renovated and air-conditioned. There were a number of good productions, but these did not get many performances due to lack of space. The audience scene is changing: people have started coming back to theatre to enjoy good plays in a comfortable atmosphere.

Nagorik Natya Sampradaya, known for their excellence in production of both foreign plays in adaptation and original plays, especially those of Rabindranath Tagore and Syed Shamsul Haq, staged yet another Tagore play, *Raktakarobi* (*The Red Oleander*) directed by Ataur Rahman. The play brought a welcome change in the Dhaka theatre scene at a time when Bengali classics are not the favourite of the directors.

Dhaka Theatre, the group, has always sought a fusion of indigenous folk theatre traditions with contemporary theatre, The group's latest production, *Prachya* (*The Orient*), is no exception. The playwright Selim Al Deen goes deep into the theme of the relationship between the exploiter and the exploited.

ABOVE: *Raktakarabi*, produced by Nagorik Natya Sampradaya and directed by Ataur Rahman

BELOW: *Nityapuran*, produced by Desh Natok, written and directed by Masum Reza

BANGLADESH

The director, Nasiruddin Yousuff, has presented a brilliant vision of the play integrating folk rituals. The group's other production, *Na Nairamoni* (*Not a Bad Woman*), written by Selim Al Deen and directed by Saidur Rahman Lipon, looks at the life of a medieval poet, the status of women a thousand years ago and the society in general of the time.

Following their preference for social satires on contemporary issues, Theatre presented *Golapbagan*, written and directed by Abdullah Al-Mamun. The play deals with the issue of sex workers and shows how they are denied their legal rights on the excuse of morality. The group's other play *Choy Beharar Palki* (*Palanquin Carried by Six*) is based on the sensitive theme of cohabitation, which is not acceptable in our society. Written by Jaglul Alam, it was jointly directed by him and two young members of the group, Maruf Kabir and Tropa Majumdar.

Aranyak Natyadal's latest production *Shongkranti* (*Transition*), written and directed by Mamunur Rashid, is the story of a group of villagers practising a folk art form called 'Shong' which satirises known characters or incidents. The patrons tolerate it as long as they themselves are not portrayed. At times, the performers are even physically assaulted for their true portrayal of the characters.

The most talked about recent production is by a relatively new group, Desh Natok's *Nitya Puran* (*Myth Ever Present*), written by Masum Reza and directed by the playwright himself. In *Ekalabya*, he takes an insignificant character from the *Mahabharata* and gives it a new and logical interpretation. It is an excellent play of poetic language, emphasised by the brilliant performance of the young actor Dilip Chakraborty in the lead role. The group's other play, *Birsa Kabya* (*Ballad of Birsa*), also written by Masum Reza and directed by Shamsul Alam Bakul, portrays the heroic struggle of Birsa Munda, leader of a marginalised ethnic community.

The Bangladesh theatre community mourned the sudden death of playwright-director-actor-composer S.M. Solaiman at the age of 47. A trend-setter for musical comedy in our country, Solaiman directed his own play *Alal Dulaler Pala* (*The Story of Alal and Dulal*), based on a traditional ballad, for Dhaka Padatik and also directed his adaptation of Amjad Hossain's story *Kal Shakale* (*Tomorrow Morning*) for his own group Theatre Art Unit.

Natya Kendra presented an innovative, widely acclaimed production by Tariq Anam Khan, *Aroj Charitamrito* (*The Life of Aroj*) written by Masum Reza. The play is based on the life and struggle of a self-educated philosopher who led a humble life in a village in southern Bangladesh. His quest for the truth was threatened by religious fanatics but he never gave in to them. The urban elite discovered him at the end of his life.

Natyajon, another new group, mounted a one woman play, *Phulrani Ami Tia* (*Phulrani, I Am Tia*), written and directed by Kuntal Mukhapadhaya and performed by Munira Yousuf Memi. The productions of Dhaka Natya Niketan's *Dehadaho* (*Cremation of the Body*), written and directed by Aminur Rahman Mukul; Shomoy Sangskritic Gosthi's *Shada Ghora*, an adaptation of Ibsen's *Rosmersholm* by Gazi Rakayet (who also directed the play); Shubachon Natya Songsad's *Tirthankar* written by Samina Lutfa Nitra and directed by Faiz Zahir; Lokanatya Dal's *Madhumala* written by Kazi Nazrul Islam and directed by Liquat Ali Lucky and Prachyanat's *Koinya* (*The Girl*) written by Murad Khan and directed by Azad Abul Kalam, all deserve special mention.

The Center for Asian Theatre, which is lavishly funded by foreign donors, mounted productions of *Putuler Itikatha*, an adaptation of Ibsen's *Doll's House* by Kamaluddin Nilu; *Urubhanga*, adapted from the Sanskrit playwright Bhas by Niranjan Adhikary and directed by Kamaluddin Nilu; and *The Lesson*, a translation of Ionesco by Saidus Saklayen directed by Mejrema Reuter. CAT is in a position to maintain a repertory company which employs full time actors and actresses.

We have so far discussed the major productions of Dhaka. But theatre has an equally lively presence in many parts of the country. The groups do not get big audiences like those in Dhaka, but interesting productions are staged. To name a few, mention should be made of *Gunai Bibi*, based on a local folk legend and written by Biplob Bala, directed by Debaprasad Debnath, and *Shilari* (*Hail Stone Shaman*) written by Golam Shafi and directed by Aminur Rahman Mukul – both produced by Shabdabali Group Theatre, Barisal; *Madhumala* written by Kazi Nazrul Islam, directed by Ahmed Iqbal Haider and produced by Tirjok Natyadal, Chittagong; *Bahut Nama* (*Community Fishing*), written and directed by Aminur Rahman Mukul and produced by Tarun Sampradaya, Sirajgonj; *Shuru Kori Bhumir Namey* (*In the Name of Our Land*) written by Saymon Zakaria, directed by Sydur Rahman Lipon, produced by Bodhon Theatre, Kushtia.

A major development in our theatre scene is open-air theatre. There are many groups with very small resources – and also some established groups – involved in this movement. Performances are held in the dry season in parks, on street corners and at the base of some national monuments. People, most of whom cannot go to see a proscenium play, enjoy the performances, which usually have a political overtone. A National Open Air Theatre Festival is held every year in Dhaka in February, in which groups from all over the country participate. The Bangladesh Street Theatre Federation has been formed to co-ordinate the activities of these groups.

At least ten theatre festivals are held every year on the initiative of different groups, such as the National Academy of Fine and Performing Arts, the Bangladesh Group Theatre Federation, or the Bangladesh Centre of the International Theatre Institute. But these are not established festivals held at regular intervals. The Bangladesh Group Theatre Federation has entered into a long-term agreement with the Bengal Foundation – a private enterprise devoted mostly to the promotion of fine arts like painting and music – to fund, among other things, an annual National Theatre Festival. The first was held from 9–20 February, 2002, where twelve productions from Dhaka and nine from other parts of the country were staged. Most of the plays were original, though five were adaptations of foreign plays.

The biggest theatre festival so far was the one organised by Bangladesh ITI in February 2001, where plays were staged for seven days in seven different venues simultaneously. Performances of contemporary theatre groups, children's theatre, foreign companies, university theatre, traditional theatre and open air theatre made up the colourful spectrum of the Festival which was participated in by 83 groups with more than 3,000 artists. Recently, week-long festivals were organised by groups such as Dhaka Theatre, Desh Natok, Prachyant and the People's Theatre Association.

Children's theatre performances are not a regular experience for Bangladesh audiences but the People's Theatre Association has a country-wide network of children's groups and they try to hold a festival every year. Two recent interesting productions by Natya Chakra intended primarily for children were *Baritye Eka* (*Home Alone*) and *Bandhu Khujche Tantu* (*Tantu in Search of a Friend*), using the Grips method, where grown-ups act in the role of children to deal with problems familiar to them. Both plays were scripted by Zunayed Yousuf and directed by Debaprasad Debnath.

As far as theatre education is concerned, the universities of Dhaka, Chittagong, Jahangirnagar and Rajshahi all have drama departments where graduate and post-graduate courses are offered. Theatre School, established in 1990, offers a one-year certificate course in acting. Recently Prachyanat School of Acting and Design has also started to offer six-month courses.

The last three seasons have seen a positive change in the government's policy of theatre subsidy. On the recommendation of the Bangladesh Group Theatre Federation, the Ministry of Cultural Affairs gave grants to selected groups to cover part of the production cost for new plays. Unfortunately, their size was reduced in the last season. The main income of theatre still comes from its audience.

A big achievement of the long-time movement of the theatre workers was the repeal, on 30 January 2001, of the Dramatic Performance Control Act, introduced in this sub-continent by the British Raj in 1876 to curb the propagation of the nationalist freedom movement in British India. The law demanded pre-censorship of scripts by the police. Bengali theatre suffered 125 years of persecution in the name of this law, which was against the fundamental human right of freedom of expression.

During the period under review, there was a trend to rediscover tradition by way of writing plays, giving new interpretation of myths, using folk stories or going for a narrative style of storytelling. This is a welcome change from the over-dominance of social satire, and this intelligent mingling of tradition with innovation has opened up a new vista in our contemporary theatre.

Ramendu Majumdar, *actor and producer, is a leading figure in the cultural arena of Bangladesh. He is the President of the Bangladesh ITI and has edited the quarterly Theatre since 1972. He was the founder Chairman of the Bangladesh Group Theatre Federation.*

BELARUS

TATIANA ORLOVA

In spite of the rather difficult economic conditions of these last years in Belarus, our 28 theatres are still putting on plays. During the seasons 1999/2000, 2000/2001 and 2001/2002, there were more than 160 productions, varied in genre, theme and directing style. Theatres in Belarus are full: for some new productions, it is difficult to find a seat. Talking and writing about theatre is in fashion. For the first time, television and radio have started to publicise plays. Of course the capital of the Republic is the most active centre of artistic life. There are 14 theatres in Minsk, half of the country's total.

The old idealistic belief in the creation of a new civilization is no more and there is little impulse towards the creation of new artistic forms, apart perhaps from seeking it abroad. Unlike before, work is being performed for all tastes and preferences: well made 'boulevard' plays, absurdist works, postmodernist deconstructions and reinterpretations of the classics, and many Bielorussian pieces.

Season 2000/2001 was rich in plays by and about Chekhov, usually in radical and innovative interpretations. The Dze-Ja Little Theatre presented Chekhov's *Ivanov* in a production by Rid Talipov which treated it as a modern avant-garde play. No samovar, no birch trees, the usual indispensable accompaniments of this great author's plays. No nostalgia, no shouting, no scent of flowers from the garden. Our theatre has always seen Chekhov as something of a museum piece – his work was seldom played on the Bielorussian stage because he had become a symbol of boredom. Using a non-traditional theatre form with an arena stage and décor on the surrounding balconies, Talipov (who is also the production's designer) starts the play with one single chair for Ivanov. The audience watches as a table, a palm-tree and a clock are brought on. The actors descend to the stage from the balconies as if entering the hull of a ship or a cave, with no light or air for normal existence. It is his way of representing Chekhov as disembodied and out of time, with none of the usual connotations of comfort and entertainment. Ivanov scatters death around him without need of a pistol. His destructive influence is deadly in a manner familiar to young people today, because he cannot do anything, cannot change anything, cannot be of use to anyone.

According to the members of the Chekhov Committeee, the people sitting with their luggage at the junction, at the station, in Yuri Lezguinevitch's production of *The Cherry Orchard* at the Yakub Kolas National Academic Theatre, which subsequently toured to Moscow, 'opened a new dimension of Chekhov's text'. The same play, seen on the stage of the State Puppet Theatre under a new title, *No More Dreams of Paris*, was also impressive in its sharp contemporaneity. The cherry orchard in flower was symbolised by a little artificial tree in a glass belljar. The cherries were sunflower seeds,

BELARUS

scattered all over the stage, crushed under foot. The audience is blinded by the lights of the train arriving. Alexei Leliavsky, the director, stages the first act without puppets. When later they do arrive, they are full-sized. Only two characters do not have a puppet double : Lopakhin and Yasha – the opportunistic businessman and the insolent valet on the make. They alone respond to events; the other characters are mere marionettes, manipulated by anyone who wishes.

The young director Pavel Adamtchikov was awarded the Grand Prix at the national 'Hope 2001' festival for *More Than the Rain*, his musical and visual exploration of themes from *The Seagull*. This production was characterized by the minimalist style popular in Europe, making its point by the use of perfectly ordinary chairs to convey its scenographic language. Expressionism replaces the mannered realism characteristic of Bielorussian theatre in previous years. In this young director's production, the simple act of showing things just as they are becomes, unexpectedly, an emotional experience. Here we see two different schools of theatre coming together to suggest a possible new direction for the art of the new century.

One can see a rebirth of the art of movement and mime as it becomes more and more a part of performance. Several recent productions have made demands on actors that extend their traditional technique: the use of refined physical skills, barely perceptible subliminal movements, non-verbal communication at many levels and even a mixture of Western and Eastern styles, for example in the 'Gesture Theatre' of Viatcheslav Inozemtsev, in which we see a synthesis of the procedures and forms of the European and Japanese theatres, naturalism and avant-garde. Music is present at an instinctual level. All of this demands a considerable depth of theatrical training.

At the same time we have seen successful experimental productions of works by foreign authors on the stage of the Maxim Gorki National Academic Russian Drama Theatre in Minsk. The director Valentina Erenkova produced a very individual reading of Arthur Kopit's play *Oh Dad, Poor Dad*.... She staged it as a musical, which produced many varied critical reactions. Antonina Mikhaltsova presented a production which was unusual for the traditional Theatre of Ph. Lüscher, *A Night in Valparaiso*. It brought a new kind of poetry to the stage, musical and romantic. In the production the actors performed in front of a large video screen which enabled the director to give emphasis to the dominant theme of the play. There was much discussion of this production also among the critics, but like Erenkova's staging it was also successful with the public.

The state theatres traditionally choose to stage costume drama with plenty of scenery. The present interest in local themes and the arrival of a large number of historical plays linked to the work of the playwrights Alexei Dudarev and Sergei Kovaliov resulted in a lot of productions rich in choreography and special scenic effects. Plays such as *The Dark Lady of Nesvige, Tristan and Yseult* and *The Art of Love* appeared on the stages of Minsk, Vitebsk, Grodno and Moguiliov, striking the spectator with the splendour of their costumes and their strongly realistic recreation of past times.

A year earlier, the puppet theatre director Oleg Jugjda produced a lot of interesting stage work which would not have been possible in previous con-

Scene from *The Dark Lady of Nesvige*

BELARUS

ditions. For these efforts as a director he received several major prices at theatre festivals.

Bielorussian playwriting has made a great leap forward and gained new life with the appearance of talented new authors: we saw the debut of Svetlana Bartokhova at the Film Actors Theatre, and of Nikolai Rudkovsky at the Bielorussian Drama Theatre. By the age of 21, Andrei Koureitchik had produced no less than six original works.

Today's Bielorussian theatre has little interest in political or social themes. Playwrights prefer to look at the dilemmas of moral and spiritual conformism: they are concerned with anything that disturbs the sense of faith and tradition in the human spirit – some of them looking to God, others seeking solutions without Him. In their plays, our writers are seeking hope and reconciliation in a savage world. Several plays have been written as essays on loneliness, for example Nikolai Rudkovsky's *Bergman's Women*. Rudkovsky has set himself up as a kind or rival to the famous Swedish author-director, writing a unadorned play about people with broken lives. In Valery Anissenko's production, the seeker after spiritual truths is an actress with a Swedish name, Ingrid. Her destiny is beyond national boundaries, for all the world knows only too well the pain, incomprehension and bitterness of being alone. Throughout the play, this central character does not utter a single word.

One of the most successful Bielorussian theatres of the season 2001 was the Yakub Kolas National Theatre. The company made several overseas tours, winning a number of prizes at prestigious festivals. Its director Vitaly Barkovsky, a leading member of the country's theatre avant-garde, introduced an exceptional quality of emotion into a much anthologised work of the Soviet era, Yakub Kolas's poem 'New Land'. The movement of the actors varied from the ritualistic, in scenes of popular worship, to the dynamic, in scenes of angry turmoil. A powerful wave of humanity comes and goes, sweeping away the detritus on stage to reveal precious amber, which they clasp to themselves before covering it again with moss ; a sequence of mysterious human actions which conjures up the unknown yet seductive world of the seabed. Productions such as this confirm that Bielorussian theatre, like its neighbour theatre in Russia, is still above all a temple, whose acolytes are engaged in a search for harmony, though still prepared to tell pretty stories as distractions from the rigours of everyday life.

Tatiana Orlova, born in 1935, has a honorary doctorate from the State University of Belarus.

BELGIUM

Flemish Community - *Theatre*
PAUL VERDUYCKT

For once, let us not be modest: in recent years theatre in Flanders has become one of the most fascinating and versatile in Europe. During the season just past, the work of theatre-makers like Luk Perceval, Jan Fabre, Jan Lauwers, Arne Sierens and Alain Platel has been very well received abroad. Furthermore, these gentlemen – we lack ladies at the top of the Flemish theatre at the moment – were invited by several prestigious theatres and festivals to create new pieces of work *in situ*. Jan Lauwers, for instance, turned the Hamburg Schauspielhaus upside down with an innovative version of Shakespeare's *Tempest*; the Festival of Avignon provided Jan Fabre with no less a venue than the Cour d'Honneur of the prestigious Palais des Papes for his black fairy-tale *Je suis sang* (*I Am Blood*); and Luk Perceval directed a rather modest Chekhov (*The Cherry Orchard*) at Schauspiel Hannover. The trio's international order book for the years ahead is filling nicely. A younger team, the Antwerp theatre collective STAN, which occupied a place of honour at the Paris *Festival d'Automne* two years ago, also went South to make a production in French: *Les Antigones*. And we have not even mentioned our ambassadors of children's and youth theatre, with the Speeltheater, Victoria and Laika (formerly Blauw Vier) in the first division.

Besides this international recognition of Flemish theatre talent, two compatriots occupy key positions in the Dutch theatre. Four years ago, Guy Cassiers, a theatre-maker bitten by the visual media, assumed the artistic direction of the ro theatre, Rotterdam's municipal theatre. And early in 2001, Ivo Van Hove left Het Zuidelijk Toneel in Eindhoven to become Director of Toneelgroep Amsterdam, the largest company in the Low Countries in terms of financial resources, artistic prestige and acting talent. Combined with his identical position at the Holland Festival, this makes Van Hove an influential captain of culture in the Netherlands – until 2004 that is, when he relinquishes the direction of the festival. This double assignment took its toll over the previous season: Van Hove's tackling of the American rock musical *Rent* and his direction of the adaptation of Marlowe's *Massacre at Paris* bore little comparison with hits like *La dame aux camélias*. Dirk Tanghe, our third man in Holland, also had a lesser year at De Paardenkathedraal in Utrecht. His venomous burlesque parable *The Family Tòt* was no real match for the artistic success of *Reigen* (Schnitzler's *La Ronde*).

Our three large municipal theatres are also at the beginning of an interesting development, that should come to fruition in the seasons ahead. As of this season a fixed nucleus of actors and directors went to work at Het Toneelhuis in Antwerp, with the intention of giving the company a more coherent profile. The policy pursued during the past three years by Artistic Director Luk Perceval (see above), of giving opportunities to young talent and

BELGIUM

groups without a home, did not yield many ripe fruits – or it got lost on the vast playing area of his regular stage, the nineteenth-century Bourla theatre. Last season was no different in that respect: apart from the opening production of *Brandbakkes* (Marius von Mayenburg's *Feuergesicht*, directed by Tom Van Dyck), the high points, *Amlett* (written and directed by Jan Decorte) and Martin McDonagh's *Leenane Trilogy* (a co-production, by Johan Simons, with Het Zuidelijk Toneel-Hollandia), were the work of two interesting but veteran directors. And a charming programme of songs like *Jukebox 2000* could hardly be labelled as theatre. Even Artistic Director Luk Perceval seemed somewhat off form: his season opener *Aars!* and his young actors' project *Ridders* had only moderate appeal.

The Brussels KVS was already moving in a new direction last season. After Franz Marijnen's departure, a new directing team of experienced people in their twenties (led by Jan Goossens and Danny Op de Beeck) took the helm. They reopened the doors of the bottling factory – the temporary post-industrial home of KVS during the long-lasting renovation of its decrepit theatre – and linked up with dynamic theatre talent with a bent for music and violent body-language. The first signs of that change were seen during the second half of the season, with an uncommonly greedy and headstrong *Macbeth*, delivered by the Dutch-Syrian woman director Ola Mafalaani, as its pinnacle – although *Le nouveau KVS* tends to limit the role of music to yet another DJ in a production, as in Enda Walsh's *Disco Pigs, Macbeth* and, concluding the season, Koltés's *In the Solitude of Cotton Fields*.

Several *Macbeth*s wandered through the Low Countries last season. In addition to the KVS production, Gerardjan Rijnders directed – not without some irony – a very domestic reading at Toneelgroep Amsterdam (see above). The theatre presented its home port Rotterdam – Cultural Capital of Europe in 2001 – with a diptych that on separate nights confronted Shakespeare's play with *Bloedwollefduivel*, the icy adaptation made years ago by Jan Decorte.

But let us return to the Flemish municipal theatres. The NTG in Ghent has recently addressed itself to a broad public, with some success. On an artistic level, however, NTG's programme was uneven. Artistic Director Jean-Pierre De Decker realised this and, two years ago, engaged the talented young director Domien Van der Meiren. With his production of *Leonce and Lena* and especially with the repeat of *Celibaat* (an adaptation of a Flemish novel) he succeeded in raising the artistic level of the theatre a little. At the same time De Decker planned a merger with the artistically rudderless Arca, a smaller theatre in the same town. This operation culminated last summer in the Publiekstheater Gent, a new company with three stages (a traditional theatre, a medium-sized multifunctional house and a smaller single-level venue). The architect of the plan did not live to see the result: De Decker died of a heart attack. His task was taken over by a team of artistic directors who wish to continue his policy.

In contrast to the cautious renewal in the municipal theatres, a number of groups in Flanders, like De Tijd and Theater Zuidpool, continue to deliver work of a high standard season after season. During the 2000–2001 season De Tijd, the semi-permanent nucleus of actors around actor-director Lucas Vandervost, got their teeth into a kind of text theatre that is fairly unique in

Flanders – if we forget for a moment the solo performances by Bob De Moor, who often works with De Tijd. The narrative acting of De Tijd rose to great heights in the West-Flemish (anti) progress parable *Risquons-tout* and the intimate solo *De straat en het struikgewas*, both directed by Lucas Vandervost. At Theater Zuidpool actor-director Koen De Sutter increasingly sets his inventive and playful stamp on the Antwerp house, which has existed for ten years now. Both the season opener *De invreter* and the collective creation *Uitvreten!!!* testified to that. So did the production *Bremen is niet ver* that De Sutter directed at the Antwerp youth theatre Het Paleis. Last summer De Sutter deservedly rose to the position of Artistic Director of Theater Zuidpool.

You can also be sure that something exciting will happen with the Antwerp theatre collective STAN and the Brussels Dito'Dito. STAN were working abroad a lot last season, therefore we had to wait a long time for the very respectable close-of-season production *Lucia smelt*, the first theatrical text by the Dutch-Brussels author Oscar van den Boogaard. Dito'Dito did not spend so much time in other countries, and last autumn they showed us the results of their socio-artistic activities in a multicultural (capital) city. The interview project *U zegt/Vous dites* and the charming but rather short portrait of immigrants, *En daar ben ik gebleven/J'y suis resté depuis* certainly merited attention. And speaking of immigrants, *Niet alle Marokkanen zijn dieven*, Ghent theatre maker Arne Sierens's latest, received enormous attention from the media – and played to packed houses. Sierens's mix of the boxing context with the immigrant theme was not always smooth. Or was the production lacking the critical eye of Sierens's buddy Alain Platel, who was not involved in this one?

The Ghent theatre group Victoria, who have greatly supported the work of Sierens and Platel over the past years, are not averse to creating a little hype – hence the insubstantial portrait of young people *Discotheque* and the farcical exhibitions of artist-in-residence Wayn Traub. Even a talent scout of great integrity such as artistic director Dirk Pauwels can make a mistake from time to time. In Bruges, Josse De Pauw, his former compeer from Radeis, goes about things with more moderation but with no less acuity. He rechristened Theater De Korre as Het Net. But first, with the support of Victoria and the Brussels KunstenFESTIVALdesArts, he made the splendid *Übung*. In this production he blends film and theatre and holds up a mirror to children and adults alike.

De Roovers, the younger version of STAN, did not tread an easy path either last season. For the duration of one theatre year the Antwerp theatre collective immersed itself in music theatre. It was a genuine learning process for the collective. In *Histoire d'A*, a cross between the texts of Flemish writer of poetry and prose Peter Verhelst and composer Igor Stravinsky, the confrontation between De Roovers and the Prometheus Ensemble produced an uneven result. In the children's production *The Little Mermaid* a greater consistency was achieved and in *Leonce and Lena* De Roovers seemed to have finally found their bearings.

To other groups and theatre-makers the use of live music came more naturally. With *Vadria*, a typical Flemish family drama with a patina, Eric De Volder from Ghent continued the collaboration with composer Dick van der Harst that started two years ago with *Diep in het bos* (*Deep in the Woods*). The

BELGIUM

two very different productions of Büchner's *Woyzeck* that we saw on the domestic stages also made a keen use of music. In the literally wet Frankenstein nightmare that Johan Simons conjured up at Het Zuidelijk Toneel-Hollandia, the musicians looked down on guinea pig Woyzeck like cold hearted scientists. At the Turnhout Theater Stap, which works with mentally disabled actors, the music and sounds produced by the players became the voices in the head of the unstable protagonist.

The veterans Jan Decorte and Eric De Volder, who returned to the fore in the last two years, remained there during the last season. The Brussels composer Walter Hus used two existing Shakespeare adaptations by Decorte, the master of the childlike and the ridiculous, as libretti for two gripping mini-operas: *Meneer, de zot en tkind* (directed by Jan Ritsema at Limelight) and the already mentioned *Bloedwollefduivel* (directed by Guy Cassiers at the ro theatre). Decorte himself made the light-spirited *Sasja danse* with his younger fellows from De Onderneming (see also *Bêt Noir*). But with *Amlett* we were finally back to a Decorte with teeth. The young Dutch group 't Barre Land also ventured on an exciting approach to *Hamlet* under the direction of Jan Ritsema, premiered in the Brussels Kaaitheater. Starting from a new and snappy translation, they wanted to convey the 'flashing thinking' in Shakespeare as a verbal and mental relay race between actors, but did not entirely succeed in realising this fine project.

Wizard Jan Fabre reminded us of the physical power of his early theatre productions with the socio-political satire *As Long as the World Needs a Warrior's Soul*. This time he didn't use his own texts, but worked on the basis of improvisations with the actors, who also go all the way during the performances – *this is theatre like it was to be expected and foreseen* and *The Power of Theatrical Madness* revisited.

Flemish Community - *Dance*
Jetty Roels

The dance world is still a world of promise. PARTS (Performing Arts and Research Training Studio), established by the New York trained Anne Teresa De Keersmaeker, was five years old in 2001. The idea was to create a nursery for young talent in a country that lacks the basic foundation to feed and support such an explosion of dance. Unfortunately, in 2001 PARTS was still unable to award an official degree, although it continues to receive financial aid from both the Flemish and the European communities. The priorities are sometimes reversed: this international school auditions for students in 12 foreign countries and the percentage of Belgian students in the current class groups is between 0 and 20. In the same year, the period of study was extended from 3 to 4 years and in November the EC launched DEPART, a project connected to PARTS, in order to enable students to make a good start to their international careers while still involved in European projects. There is also Werkhuisproductie, supported by the company Rosas, a platform that can be used by anyone to create new dance pieces.

Ten times older, the ballet school at Antwerp celebrated its 50th anniversary in

2001. This may seem young from the European point of view, but for Flanders, until the second world war a dance desert, it constitutes an important achievement. For the occasion the school was awarded the title Royal, in the tradition of the first court ballet schools in Europe. This particular school was established in 1951 by Flanders' first lady of the ballet, Jeanne Brabants. In 1991 it came under the directorship of Marinella Paneda. Jeanne Brabants herself, turned 80, was offered a baronial title, but turned the honour down.

HID (Higher Institute for Dance), founded by the Belgian dancer and choreographer Aimé de Lignière, had a change of directors: the contemporary choreographer Maria De Corte took over in September 2001.

In 2000, a prestigious International Early Dance Conference was held in Ghent. It was organized by Lieven Baert, Belgian specialist in the field and director of The Institute of Historical Dance, and the university of Ghent. It included lots of lectures and demonstrations by international guests and was held under the auspices of the Dance Committee of ITI.

The Ballet of Flanders combined four dance pieces in its interesting and intense *Moving Views*, danced in the typically clean style of house choreographer Rosseel. The dances were set to modern scores by Arvo Pärt, Alfred Schnittke, Thomas Oboe Lee, George Crumb and Henryk Gorecki. For *Drifting Inwards* he used the striking music of the Finnish composer Kaija Saariaho and excellent lighting by Jaak Van De Velde.

There are two Flemish dance competitions: Kadans, for choreographers and young companies, and Terpsichore, an international competition for contemporary choreographers.

Les Ballets Contemporains De Belgique created a piece for eight dancers with the ironical title *Lac des Singes* (Monkey Lake), inspired by the chimpanzees at the Antwerp Zoo. Alain Platel, who refuses to be called a choreographer, never hides his admiration for Pina Bausch. Her controversial style was once again prominent in this piece. It was made by Hans Van den Broeck, who, together with Alain Platel, Koen Augustijnen and Christine Desmet, forms a trio in charge of the artistic aspect of this famous Belgian company.

Rain is a wonderful, repetitive, crisp piece, uniform in colour and texture. It bears the signature of De Keersmaeker's familiar clean and repetitive, minimalist ways. For the music she went back to her old love, Steve Reich. Belgium's favourite choreographer showed this new full-length work at La Monnaie, the Brussels opera house. Simple movements, variations of running, skipping, jumping and turning, were used as a perfect illustration of the De Keersmaeker style.

Wim Vandekeybus's *Scratching the Inner Fields*, inspired by and set to *Zwellend Fruit*, a fairy tale by Peter Verhelst, threw us back into his cruel world, with people itching and scratching themselves. The seven female dancers moved like animals and Iona Kewney, a double-jointed contortionist, definitely stole the show. This work could be seen as a mirror of *In Spite of Wishing and Wanting*, an all-male piece created in 1999.

Meg Stuart (1965), an American artist who lives in Belgium, studied dance at New York University. Between 1986 and 1992, she was a member of the Randy Warshaw Dance Company. In 1991, she created *Disfigure Study*, a production for the Klapstukfestival in Leuven. In 1994 she settled in Brussels and was given the opportunity to set up her company Damaged Goods. In 2000, Meg Stuart was awarded the Culture Prize of the Catholic University at Leuven. For 2000–2001 Stuart, in close cooperation with theatre director Stefan Pucher and Jorge Leon (video), created *Highway 101*, which was seen in Brussels, in Vienna (Wiener Festwochen), Paris (Centre Georges Pompidou), Rotterdam (Rotterdam Schouwburg) and Zürich (Schauspielhaus Zürich). The installation *The Sand Table* and the solos *Soft Wear, Private Room* and *I'm All Yours* were originally part of *Highway 101*. In the meantime, they have been given a new life and were performed in March 2001 in a program shared with Tim Etchells' Forced Entertainment. Damaged Goods then started its residence at the Schauspielhaus Zürich with the creation of *Alibi*. *Alibi*, first performed in November 2001.

The spaces of Kaaiteater were used during the KunstenFESTIVALdesArts, where the interesting work of Xavier Leroy could be seen in pieces with robot-like movements. In *Self Unfinished*, two bodies, an animal and a hermaphrodite, were transformed into one. For a week, Tom Plischke and his friends worked on a happening at the refurbished Beurs theater. Historical dance of the central European school was integrated with dance material of Dore Hoyer, who was the inspiration for the piece *Affects/Rework*. Fragments of film, text and music were used in *Re(sort)* a collage of images of the sixties. Alexander Baervoets's later work *Schauet doch* is of a meditative, repetitive nature. The Belgian Butoh artist Pé Vermeersch was an artist in residence in Tokyo and gave Butoh performances in Kyoto and Osaka.

At the beginning of 2000, the Flemish government reorganized its subsidy system for the country's 3,773 existing amateur groups. One should bear in mind that Belgium is the country of the so-called v.z.w., a particular kind of non-profit association. At present, this formula being very widespread, practically every single dancer has a small company or school registered under their own name. From now on, dancing will be one of the five options and financial support will be bundled into five year-envelopes. Dance groups of all kinds (folklore, modern, etc) that until now were independently subsidized, will be grouped together. As part of this greater whole, they will, for instance, have to share a single dance magazine, a common board, and give proof of a vision about their work. Any companies that do not join will automatically lose their financial support. The life of amateur groups is extremely important for the cultural growth of a country, because it has been statistically proven that this is the place where future artists are born. So Belgium's hope for future generations of dance genius is planted here.

French Community
NANCY DELHALLE

The most remarkable events for French-speaking theatre in Belgium in the last three seasons have been related to institutions, with much debate, discussion and reaction. The press, unaccustomed to such offstage animation, wrote a lot about it. The arrival of a new Minister of Culture, Richard Miller (born in Mons in the

Wallonia region), encouraged debate on new ways of distributing theatrical subsidy. He focussed the debate on geographical issues: not only are the majority of our theatres concentrated in Brussels, but in many regions, the range of cultural events on offer is poor. The Rogier Tower that housed the Théâtre National had to be demolished in May 2001. The first theatre of Belgium's French Community was to be relocated in another building. Such a crucial move needed serious organisation but the Ministry's decision on a new location was taken very late and this provoked the first agitation. Finally, while awaiting the construction of a new building, the Théâtre National was transferred to an old cinema, the Pathé Palace, bought by the Government. Because this location was much smaller it needed serious modifications. A critical audit of the theatre had to be done at the same time, because the contract for the Ministry's subsidy was ending. The Government wished to energize the Théâtre National and to implant it more efficiently in Wallonia, particularly in Mons. A lot of expertise was called in. Belgian theatre people were not used to such political interventionism and they mobilised to express their fears and claims.

The theatre in Belgium seems to be facing a kind of deadlock. The National Lottery has decided not to subsidise the arts any more, which represents a big loss. The existing structures cannot absorb all the graduates from the theatre schools (Conservatory of Brussels, Liège and Mons, Institut Superieur des Arts du Spectacle, Institut des Arts de Diffusion). While subsidies are not growing, applications for financial aid are getting more and more numerous. Also, the question of artistic status is more and more acute. Apart from those creators (often directors) based with a theatre, many others, usually the experimental ones, are forced to ask for support project by project, even if this kind of support is theoretically supposed to be devoted to newcomers.

Most of Lorent Wanson's productions are co-produced with the Théâtre National. That allows him to explore the repertoire with the socio-political emphasis that characterises his work (*Les Bonnes* from Genet, *En attendant Godot* from Beckett). But he is also working, in collaboration with ATD Quart Monde, on a more specialised project, *Les Ambassadeurs de l'Ombre*. It works with deprived families, who by expressing themselves on stage are able to explore a new way of life. The productions mix professional actors with welfare claimants, even addicts. Over several months, they can develop, write and rehearse a show that breaks the conventional no-hope view of poverty. Several disciplines (singing, chanting, music...) are employed to highlight individual or collective responsibilities, but also to change our views on the culture of the masses.

As for Charlie Degotte, he is giving new life to a Belgian tradition, in the *revue* that he presents, with others, at the Théâtre National. He left the Café Théâtre that he co-founded with Claude Semal in the same spirit of oppositional burlesque. Based on freedom of access, this venue continues to receive a variety of projects, sometimes very close to cabaret (*Cabaret politicomique* directed by Françoise Walot), sometimes more relevant to the *théâtre d'auteur*.

Christine Delmotte's company, housed at the Théâtre des Martyrs, gives priority to French-speaking Belgian playwrights such as Henry Bauchau, Paul Pourveur or Stanislas Cotton. She staged the latter's *Bureau national des allogènes*, a fable about immigration procedures that expresses in a poetic way the opposing points

BELGIUM

of view of the functionary and the refugee. The desire to reflect reality in crucial contemporary problems, like social and cultural exclusion, is also central to the work of many artists and appears today as a major theme in Belgian creations. This is reflected in the choice of the contemporary repertoire, with playwrights like Edward Bond (staged for example by Valerie Cordy), Lars Norèn (whose *Akt* was produced by Nathalie Mauger), Sarah Kane and even Dario Fo, many of whose plays were staged. But the same questions also provoked new plays, sometimes directed by their author. For example, *Zephira, les pieds dans la poussière* (*Zephira, Dusty Feet*) from Virginie Thirion transposes the Medea myth to the context of illegal immigration. Performed by three actresses, the production tells the story of Zephira who, after failing to live a decent life in Europe, is caught by her own dreams. The social and personal trap is closing in on her at the same time and, betrayed, she commits a last act of resistance. *Wanoulele que s'est-il passé?* (*Wanoulele, What Happened?*) from Layla Nabulsi tells the story of a Rwandan woman caught up in the genocide. Her words recount the paroxysm of physical and psychological violence, showing the monstrosity of the war. But she also talks about the survival instinct and how she was able to save her child. In between, moral values lose their sharpness and create real questions in the audience's mind.

A number of other productions have been built around reflections on Africa, with, as background, our colonial past and our ambiguous relationship with the dark continent. The wish to explain, but also to bear witness, is at the centre of *Rwanda 1994* from Groupov in Liège, a big production including Rwandan actors. The performance is still touring the world, costing so much money to the company that it is now in a difficult financial situation. *Bruxelles, Ville d'Afrique* (*Brussels, African City*), a production by Virginie Jortay with text by Antoine Pickels and Annick de Ville, is a critical and wide-ranging look at colonialism, physical brutality, enforced Christianization and the career of Patrice Lumumba. This play, which doesn't hesitate to criticise the influence of Belgian royalty, was first performed in Kinshasa with African actors.

There have been some changes among the institutions' leaders, while the opportunities for young creators remain precarious and there is still a lack of status for the actor. Jean-Louis Colinet, director of the Théâtre de la Place in Liège, took over the direction of the Festival Rencontres d'Octobre, renaming it the Festival de Liège and thus concentrating under his power almost all theatrical performance in the city. The first edition of the renewed Festival had great success with the public and saw the arrival in Liège of a new location for theatre, the former riding school of the Caserne Fonck. This place, a pleasant wooden structure, hosted performances from legendary international companies like Bread and Puppet and the Berliner Ensemble, and also less known productions from Eastern European countries, especially works by Biljana Srbljanovic, whose plays *Supermarket* and *The Supplication* were presented at the Théâtre de la Place the following season. As for the Compagnie Mezza Luna, which opened its own theatre, it prefers short plays, or has otherwise to count on the collaboration of the Théâtre de la Place.

On the other hand, while the Ensemble Théâtral Mobile of Marc Liebens, considered as one of the fathers of the 'Young Theatre' in French-speaking Belgium, has been deprived of its grant because of its deficit, the Théâtre

Varia, another of the institutions born from the 'Young Theatre' era, is looking for a new project. One of its directors, Philippe Sireuil, became head of
the Atelier Théâtral de Louvain-la-Neuve following Armand Delcampe. It is
probably by coincidence that these two directors, who do not share the same
aesthetic, agree about Jean Louvet's plays. Louvet defends Walloon culture and
identity while believing in a certain humanist utopia. He creates a theatre that
deconstructs the famous ideological mechanisms that alienate humanity. At the
Festival de Spa, Delcampe presented *Conversation en Wallonie, (Conversation in
Wallonia)* a play written in the 70's that examines the relationship between a
miner father and his intellectual son. Sireuil staged a monologue, *Devant le mur
élevé (In Front of the High Wall)*, where the author asks himself if our intimacy
still belongs to ourselves... At the same time poetic and politic, Louvet's work
has been regularly presented on Belgian stages. For example, *Jacob Seul (Jacob
Alone)*, which was presented twice, shows a man who is prisoner of a loneliness that can be seen as extreme individualism. Working in Mons, Frederic
Dussenne produced *L'Annonce faite à Benoît*, in which two men meet in a store
and build a relationship out of the stories they tell – true and false. In an
issue devoted to the author, *Alternatives Théâtrâles* magazine reported the experience of directors who had staged Louvet's plays.

Like those of Jean Louvet, Jean-Marie Piemme's plays are being staged more
and more in Belgium and abroad, for example in France, where he is often
presented at the Festival d'Avignon. Piemme presents human relationships in a
way that looks like boxers in a ring. But as they fight, the look of these relationships changes and the author shows not only what keeps us apart but
also what brings us together.

The contemporary French-speaking Belgian repertoire is made up of work
by Louvet and Piemme, Paul Emond, Jean-Pierre Dopagne and Philippe
Blasband. But the recognition – sometimes precarious – of these authors won't
erase fears about our dramatic writing. After a period of initiatives to promote these writers, we are now seeing a withdrawal. Writers often prefer to
stage their own plays instead of waiting for a hypothetical director or producer. Many theatres have no literary department and when the authors send
in plays, more often than not they don't even receive an acknowledgement.
While the Centre des Ecritures Dramatiques Wallonie-Bruxelles seems to have
difficulties working at full capacity, Temporalia, the association that organised
readings, has ceased its activities.

At the same time, we can note the return of a more classical repertoire.
Besides Molière (on whom members of Groupov like Jacques Delcuvellerie
or Matthias Simons are working), Marivaux and de Musset, who are staged a
lot, it is impossible to count all the different productions of Shakespeare or
Chekhov. On the other hand, contemporary French drama seems to be staged
less, except for Philippe Minyana's work. Directors prefer anglophone authors
like Michael Frayn, Daniel Keene, Martin Crimp, David Hare, Brian Friel and
Harold Pinter.

Projects devised by an author-director are getting more popular, which seems
to confirm a renewal of interest in collective work. For example, Laurence Vielle
is still doing her research on orality with *l'Abitasion brize le ven de notre jardin*, a
collage of texts written in a psychiatric institute. In a freak-out way that allies

absurdity and drollery, Isabelle Wéry wrote, directed and performed *Ms Ari Nue*, a surgical music hall. Writer and actor Philippe Grand'Henry played both mother and son in his autobiographical solo *Tout ça du vent*, directed by Françoise Bloch. Jean-Michel D'Hoop staged *Plat du jour*, a topical revue, in collaboration with the Théâtre des Martyrs. A collective with a very strong identity and increasing popularity is without doubt Transquinquennal. Its plays like *Chomage* or *Zugzwang*, or the ones made with the Flemish company Dito' Dito like *Enfin bref* (written by Rudi Bekaert) or *Vous dites?*, inspired by interviews from people in Brussels, are revived from season to season. These two companies are working together on language impurity, a topic that they never cease revisiting.

The number of venues that will house these young creators seems to be growing or at least remaining stable. For example, Les Tanneurs have welcomed projects from Xavier Lukomski (on Daniil Harms), and from Transquinquennal, and also from the choreographer Michèle Noiret. The theatre itself is also developing a project on and with the popular neighbourhood where it is located, the Marolles. L'L, still fighting to remain active, organised a festival of monologue with texts from Laurent Ancion, Stanislas Cotton, Veronika Mabarbi and others. Finally, the powerhouse of the younger creators, la Balsamine, opened in a totally renovated space with *Bruxelles nous appartient*, a project based on interviews taken in the city.

Attracting attention from other countries, while giving an international dimension to our stage and giving us visibility as part of an international dynamic, the Kunsten-Festivaldes Arts allows creations like those from Transquinquennal, Dito' Dito and Armel Roussel to gain a wider audience. The lack of touring possibilities remains a problem. But the ideas that drive the French-speaking Belgian theatre could, if well handled, lead to change. The sparkling – and cleverly promoted – return of Franco Dragone to La Louvière, where he intends to set up the workshop for his plays, confirms the new orientation towards the central region around Mons and Charleroi. It is also in this region that the 'Centre des Arts Scéniques' is located, with a mission to give opportunities to new actors. Creating good conditions for theatrical creations to tour is obviously the challenge for the years to come. Olivier Gourmet, in his speech after receiving the prize for interpretation in Cannes with the movie by Luc and Jean-Pierre Dardenne from Liège, told Belgian actors to keep faith and have courage, producing a wave of articles on the status of the actor. The government said that the question is being studied; it has already acquired the Theatre de l'Escalier, where the direction has been entrusted to Philippe Grombeer, ex-manager of the Halles de Schaerbeek. If these last seasons were spectacular for their backstage fighting, they were also fundamental proof that theatre is not artificial, but continues to awaken consciences on important issues.

Paul Verduyckt (b 1961) *studied German Philology and Theatre Sciences at K.U. Leuven. He was a theatre and dance critic of the newspaper* De Morgen *and later of the weekly* Knack *and for the last two years has been permanently associated with the Flemish radio KLARA (VRT) as a theatre reviewer. Since 1985 he has published regularly in specialised magazines in Flanders and the Netherlands and for two years he has been a member of the jury of the annual Theatre Festival, which presents the most interesting theatrical productions in the Low Countries.*

BENIN

OUSMANE ALEDJI

Let us say first, without any chauvinism, that Benin is one of the most fruitful countries for artistic expression in the whole of French-speaking Africa. In the field of plastic arts as well as those of music, dance or theatre, numerous lively talents have arisen as worthy representatives of Benin's artistic creation in the international forums. The Beninois Simplice Zannou was awarded in first prize in the plastic arts during the last 'jeux de la francophonie'. DAKART 2002, another event for the plastic arts, which takes place in Senegal, honoured another Beninois, Dominique Zinpke.

The three last MASA (Marché des Arts du Spectacle Africain) whose programming is the best in the whole of Africa, hosted Beninois groups in music and theatre. During the Theatre Festival FESTEF, which takes place every year in Lomé (Togo), Benin carried off four of the nine trophies awarded these three last years.

As for dance, besides the Ensemble Artistique National, which has been touring the whole world for two years with a remarkable production, other dance groups are growing in number and producing no less interesting work. Many of them are hacking their way through the dense jungle of contemporary dance.

It has to be admitted that this short but eloquent summary hides some severe threats which could alter what specialists have called 'The Beninois Miracle'. We will say a word on this later on.

Let us come back to theatre; this magic charm, this sacred fetish for which we have so long been pleasurably torturing ourselves. The theatre is going well in Benin, even very well. A lot of practitioners – actors, playwrights, directors and technicians – have come to maturity and their know-how provokes respect and admiration. They work regularly on the stages of Cotonou, Porto-Novo and Parakou, to name only those cities which have an important cultural activity.

The trend towards writer's theatre is beginning to supplant the so called popular or total theatre. The latter is no more than an assemblage of tom-toms, singing and dancing, with no content nor form. This occasionally interesting mixture of artifice and tasteful humour remains a theatre for holidays, which cheerfully sacrifices the text in place of sheer spectacle.

There is yet another theatre, which is a collection of domestic episodes (oh daddy, oh mammy, kiss kiss, I love you…) that was never clearly classified but was very successful until recently, winning full houses. But this theatre is beginning to disappear, because it has remained the exclusive speciality of feminine troupes, such as 'Qui dit mieux' and 'Les échos de la capitale'. The first one has not produced anything these last four years and the second no longer has its former energy and enthusiasm to perform.

Dramatised stories, too, once considered a major genre, are now losing ground in the face of an increasingly demanding public.

We could say that the wild beat of the tom-toms is no longer current; simple entertainment and unmotivated mockery has been replaced by the word, the text, the aesthetic and the beautiful. This is due to new authors and directors, young for the most part and still prolific, whose principal merit is to have reconciled Benin's audience – considered to be one of the most difficult in Africa – with its theatre.

Seasons 2000–2001 and 2001–2002 illustrate this thesis well: we have seen twelve authors' productions in Cotonou alone – and we have to remember that we are in a country where theatre is not subsidised.

The most successful creations were: *Atakoun* by Wassangari Theatre; Mohamed Benguettaf's *Arrêt fixe (Fixed Stop)* adapted and directed by Ousmane Aledji, a production which won the first prize in the Rencontres Théâtrales du Bénin (RETHEB), a festival initiated by the Beninois ITI Centre and the Beninois National Association of Theatre Artists (ANATTHEB); *Mains vides contre Kalachnikov (Empty Hands Against Kalachnikovs)* written and directed by Isidore Dokpa, original in more than one respect, with blind or partially-sighted actors and a text burning with raw truths and sadness; and *Imonlé*, written and directed by Ousmane Aledji.

These productions toured in Africa and Europe and some of them are still doing so. This is in particular the case of *Imonlê*, produced during the last Festival International de Théâtre du Bénin, FITHEB, the biggest theatre festival of French-Speaking Africa, which takes place every two years in six of Benin's cities. The last edition took place from 16–27 March 2002 and included fifteen countries and twenty-one performances. New companies are bringing new blood to the stage, and new trends are timidly putting their heads above the parapet as part of an advance guard which could wait no longer to show itself.

The KALETAS festival of schools' theatre pursues its merry way and continues to reveal young talents, still at school or at college, a fine crop to come.

Madmen can survive anything. I really do believe that. But as I was saying at the beginning, all this growth and ferment hides serious weaknesses. They could kill this creative and more particularly theatrical dynamism if the authorities in charge of management go on turning a blind eye, patting themselves on the back and saying that everything is going well. It is just not true. The political will is absent. The Government is not putting enough money into the theatre. The majority of politicians are culturally illiterate. The artist is still considered by them as some kind of beggar, who has to be given alms. The last Budget voted had not a single penny in it for culture. We still do not have a single theatre worthy of the name in Benin. Performances take place in sports halls or on plain concrete, more suited to political rallies than to an artistic production, even of poor quality.

Second complaint: unlike other countries where the theatre is considered as art for the elite or the middle-class, in Benin this part of the population never goes to the theatre, not even those who have the privilege of teaching theatre in our universities. The latter go on quietly teaching old-fashioned and archaic theories, from texts well defined by Koffi Kwaulé as 'the literature of the pedagogue'.

And what about ambition? You've got to have ambition, even to lift a grain of sand; there is no creation without ambition. We artists are suffering from lack of ambition.

Ousmane Aledji *is a playwright, director and head of the theatre company Agbo N'koko.*

BRAZIL

SILVANA GARCIA

Brazil is a huge country, a melting pot of great cultural diversity. There are many theatre productions in Brazil, but not as many nor of such a level as the country really deserves. Most of them are concentrated in the major capitals of the different States, especially in the south and south east, namely Rio de Janeiro and São Paulo. In the rest of the country, productions are still amateur and irregular – though there can be good performances in faraway regions. Unfortunately, one of the worst consequences of the country's huge size is that many productions are not widely seen, because they do not tour, since it would be so expensive. This is the main reason why this synopsis does not claim to cover the whole range of Brazilian theatre productions, and is instead focused principally on São Paulo.

The conditions for making theatre in Brazil are difficult: it is, of course, an expensive activity, but there is no single reason to explain the situation: we could point out the strong presence of Brazilian TV, the cost of tickets, even the lack of quality of the average production; but it is also true that audiences are relatively small for a population of about 170 million. In São Paulo, with some 37 million inhabitants, only 300 productions were staged in 2001, most of them for a short run (not longer than two months generally, and playing only from Friday to Sunday). Very few were sold out or came near that happy situation.

Many of the problems affecting theatre in Brazil are due to the lack, for many years, of an efficient cultural policy, that could stimulate both production and touring. Only very recently, and still very timidly, have municipalities and states – not yet on a federal scale, unfortunately – been able to subsidise productions and support groups for them to become more stable. By contrast, Tax Reduction Laws tend to delegate the investment in culture to private enterprises. In brief, theatre in Brazil comes far short of its true potential.

The best productions, at least the most stimulating, come from established theatre groups. Few can boast a regular programme: on the contrary, a huge number form and dissolve at a tremendous, dizzy speed. The few consistent ones are responsible for the ongoing renewal of Brazilian theatre.

Among them we can mention the Teatro da Vertigem (Vertigo Theatre). Directed by Antônio Araújo, a young director who graduated from the University of São Paulo, the group is committed to ensemble creation, with a long and dedicated period to prepare and stage performances of great impact in unconventional spaces. Its latest work, *Apocalipse 1, 11,* that toured recently in Portugal and Germany, opened at the end of 2000 and is part of a trilogy inspired by biblical episodes: the first, *Paraíso Perdido (Paradise Lost*, 1992) was performed in a catholic church; the second, *O livro de Jó (The Book of Job*, 1995) was performed in a disused hospital. Based mainly on St. John, *Apocalipse 1, 11* was performed in the large rooms and corridors of a former prison. Its tone is irreverent, blasphemous, iconoclastic, and beneath the threads of the biblical fable we can clearly perceive a critique of the political and social degradation in Brazil – beginning with the title, which refers to the 111 inmates who were murdered by the police in 1992 when they suppressed a rebellion in Carandiru, São Paulo's largest prison. *Apocalipse* received all the major awards of the season.

Another prominent group in this season was Galpão (The Barn), coming from Belo Horizonte (Minas Gerais). The group began by using circus and street theatre, but soon added some other contemporary influences. It has operated for over 20 years and has been responsible for memorable performances, like *Romeo and Juliet,* on stilts, which was performed for London audiences in 2000. Last season, 2001, they opened in São Paulo *Um trem chamado desejo* (*A Train Named Desire* – the title hints at Tennessee Williams's masterpiece – written by Luís Alberto de Abreu and directed by Chico Pelúcio, a simple story of a 'mambembe' theatre group (a kind of a modest touring company) from the beginning of last century, combining theatre and cinema, with a lovely sound track.

Also linked to the circus technique and inspired by research on folk tradition, the group Parlapatões, Patifes e Trapalhões (Braggarts, Rogues and Fumblers) dedicated its three latest seasons to preparing an adaptation of Rabelais. Hosted by the Teatro Brasileiro de Comédia (Brazilian Comedy Theatre) in one of its halls, it was able to develop a repertory programme staging six short plays: *Um chopps, dois pastel e uma porção de bobagem* (*One Bear, Two Tarts and a bit of Foolishness*) and *Mistérios Gulosos* (*Gluttonous Mysteries*), by Mário Viana; *Água fora da bacia* (*Water Spilt over the Basin),* by Avelino Alves, and *Os Manés (The Dumb)* and *Poemas Fesceninos* (*Obscene Poems*), by Hugo Possolo. These plays were meant to test their ability to stage *Pantagruel,* which opened in 2001, at the SESC Anchieta Theatre.

Another active theatre company was the Tapa, one of the few groups with institutional support and a venue. Based in São Paulo since 1986, the Tapa came from Rio de Janeiro, and espouses a repertory policy, which is unique in São Paulo theatre. Under its director, Eduardo Tolentino, the group staged *Navalha na carne* (*Knife in the Flesh,* 1999), a classic by Plínio Marcos, *A serpente (The Serpent,* 2000), by Nelson Rodrigues and *Órfãos de Jânio* (*Janio's Ophans* – a reference to President Jânio Quadros – 2001), by Millôr Fernandes. Together with these plays of the Brazilian mainstream, the group was also responsible for a remarkably successful staging of Shaw's *Major Barbara.*

Another venue-based group, which has recently come to São Paulo from the south, is Os sátyros (The Satyrs). In their small space near the centre of the city, the group has kept up a regular programme of their own work. Since they came to São Paulo, they have staged *Retábulo da Avareza, Luxúria e Morte* (*Triptych of Covetousness, Lechery and Death,* 2000), by Ramon Valle Inclan, *Sapho de Lesbos* (2001), by Ivam Cabral and Patricia Aguile, and are now presenting Oscar Wilde's *De Profundis,* adapted by Cabral from the poem Wilde wrote while he was in Reading Gaol. Rodolfo Garcia Vásquez directed all the productions.

One of the city's newest groups is the Companhia São Jorge de Variedades (Saint George Variety Company). Based since 2001 at the Teatro Eugênio Kusnet, the site of which was formerly the headquarters of the historic Teatro

ABOVE: *Teatro da Vertigem's apocalipse 1.1*, directed by Antônio Araújo

BELOW: Raul Barretto and Hugo Possolo of Parlapatões in *Pantagruel* (*photo:* Luiz Doro)

BRAZIL

de Arena in the 60s, the group is now running *Biedermann e os incendiários*, by Max Frisch, directed by Georgette Fadel, who in the same year directed *Bartolomeu, que será que nele deu? (What on Earth Is the Matter with Bartleby?)*, by Cláudia Schapira, inspired by Hermann Melville. A new generation is marking out its territory.

One of the oldest groups still operating in Brazil (since 1967), the Teatro União e Olho Vivo (Union Theatre and SharpEye) has remained totally devoted to folk theatre. At present it has been touring neighbourhoods and community centres with its performance of *João Cândido do Brasil – A revolta da chibata (João Cândido from Brazil – the Slender Whip Uprising*, 2001), focusing on an important episode of racist and social conflict in Brazilian history.

The Companhia do Latão (Tin Company) is still trying to establish an epic theatre in a national mode, in the footsteps of the committed Brazilian theatre of the 60s. It has performed, in 2000, *A comédia do trabalho (The Comedy of Work)*, an ensemble creation, and recently *Auto dos bons tratos (Play of Good Manners)*, by Márcio Marciano and Sérgio de Carvalho, the two directors of the company.

Among the best known theatre groups of Rio de Janeiro, the Companhia de Atores (Actors' Company), directed by Enrique Diaz, staged the comical *Melodrama* (1999), the result of research on this genre done by the group. In 2000, they again ventured boldly, with a new production of *O rei da vela (The Candle King)*, by Oswald de Andrade, which was acclaimed at the end of the 1960s in a historic staging by the group Oficina. We should also mention the work done, in 2000, by director Moacir Chaves with the Péssima Companhia (Lousy Company), who brought his own excellent *Bugiara* from Rio de Janeiro.

In any discussion of theatre for young audiences, the Grupo Pia Fraus should be mentioned. In 2000 they did *Farsa quixotesca (Quixotic Farce)*; their *Bichos do Brasil (Brazilian Animals)* is still running with tremendous success. Both performances were the result of a collaboration between Beto Andretta (from Pia) and Hugo Possolo (from Parlapatão).

As for directors, let us begin by mentioning some who have given Brazilian theatre its reputation. In the same historical venue where once was the former Oficina, now called Uzina Uzona, José Celso Martinez Corrêa continues as the most rebellious and creative director of our stage. In 1998 he won the main awards for *Cacilda!*, a play he wrote and directed, about one of the legends of our national theatre, the actress Cacilda Becker. In 1999, going against the trend towards long and complex performances, he staged a short version of *Boca de Ouro (Golden Mouth)*, remaining faithful to Nelson Rodrigues's original without discarding the mark of his own genius.

Another acclaimed director still operating is Antunes Filho. Sponsored by SESC – the Department of Social Service, which has since 1984 hosted the CPT (Centre for Theatrical Research), of which he is co-director, Antunes directed in 1999 the performance *Fragmentos Troianos (Trojan Fragments)* and in 2001 *Medéia (Medea)*, both adapted from Euripides, in a specially designed space at the SESC - Belenzinho.

We should also mention the high quality work of Felipe Hirsch, especially in partnership with Guilherme Weber and Erica Migon. He has directed his own play *Nostalgia* (Teatro Popular do SESI, 2001), and more recently Nicky

Silvers' *Os solitários (The Lonely Ones)*, at the Teatro Alfa, with two stars of the national theatre, Marieta Severo and Marco Nanini. Both featured effective sets by Daniela Thomas.

After having worked with director Zé Celso Martinez Corrêa, mainly as a lighting designer, Cibele Forjaz turned to directing and in 2000 presented *Toda a nudez será castigada (All Nakedness Will Be Punished)*, by Nelson Rodrigues, where the remarkable acting of Leona Cavalli won her an award. In 2001, with the same commitment and still with the same actress, she opened *Um bonde chamado desejo (A Streetcar Named Desire)*, by Tennessee Willliams, at the Teatro SESC Belenzinho.

The *enfant terrible* of the Brazilian theatre, Gerald Thomas, continued along his usual unconventional and polemic lines. We should note his inspired dramaturgy in casting a famous TV hostess, Marília Gabriela, in *Esperando Beckett (Waiting for Beckett*, 2001).

Gabriel Villela has lived up to his reputation as a creative director of exuberant profile by staging *Ópera do malandro (The Slicker's Opera*, 2000), a musical by Chico Buarque de Holanda, inspired by John Gay, *Gota d'água (Drop of Water*, 2001), by the same author with Paulo Pontes, and also a musical *Medéia (Medea)*, from Euripides.

Some other performances should be mentioned:

Silêncio (Silence, 2000), by Peter Handke, directed by Beth Lopes, with exceptional performances from a couple of young actors, Matteo Bonfitto and Yedda Chaves.

Copenhagen (2001), by Michael Frayn, directed by Marco António Rodrigues, with a special mention to the cast – Oswaldo Mendes, Selma Luchesi and Carlos Palma – who produced the show. Rodrigues also directed *Babilônia*, by Reinaldo Maia, in the venue which he runs together with his company, the Folias d'Arte (Art Follies).

On an unusually large scale by Brazilian standards, manager and actress Ruth Escobar produced *Os Lusíadas (The Lusiads* – the national epic of Portugal – 2002), in two consecutive versions, the first one directed by Iacov Hillel and the second by Márcio Aurélio.

Intimidade indecente (Indecent Intimacy, 2001), by Leilah Assumpção, with Marcos Caruso and Irene Ravache directed by Regina Galdino, was one of the major box office successes in the season. So also was *Honra (Honour*, 2000), by Joanna Murray-Smith, directed by Celso Nunes, with the same Caruso, paired with one of the *grandes dames* of Brazilian TV, Regina Duarte. We should also mention *Subúrbia (Outskirts*, 2000), by Eric Bogosian, directed by Francisco Medeiros, with an excelllent young cast: *Pobre Super-homem (Poor Superman)*, by Brad Fraser, directed by Sérgio Ferrara, and the Rio de Janeiro production of *A máquima (The Machine)*, by Adriana Falcão, directed by João Falcão, a director from the Northeast who is now celebrated as one of the brightest talents of the new generation. Theatres at the SESC hosted the three performances.

Among the several classics regularly revived here, a delicate *Tio Vânia (Uncle Vanya*, 2000), by Ágora, caught the attention. It was directed by Celso Frateschi, with set design by Sylvia Moreira and superb acting by a young actor, Fábio Herford, in the leading role.

BRAZIL

Touching on acting, we should mention the brilliant work of some veterans, who distinguished several productions by their presence, all in 2000: Berta Zemel, in *Anjo Duro (Tough Angel)*, written and directed by Luiz Valcazara, Paulo Autran in *Visitando o Sr. Green (Visiting Mr Green)*, by Jeff Baron, directed by Elias Andreato, and Raul Cortez in *Rei Lear (King Lear)*, directed by Ron Daniels.

One of the most interesting phenomena of the present Paulista theatrical landscape is the emergence of a new generation of authors who began writing during the 90s, breaking away from the rarefied theatre productions of the 80s that gave more attention to the work of directors than to playwrights. This new generation is generally associated with experiments in the more alternative circuits. They are all around the age of 30, mainly professionals with experience in other fields, have a strong personal style and are committed to the craft of writing, not only for theatre. Among them we should mention:

Fernando Bonassi, who besides being responsible for the text of the extraordinary *Apocalipse 1, 11*, also signed the text *Preso entre ferragens (Imprisoned in Shackles*, 2000), directed by Aliane Fonseca, at the Teatro Escobar. Márcio Aurélio, at the Teatro Popular of SESI, directed his most recent production *Souvenirs*.

Aimar Labaki, who as well as having his text *A Boa (The Good One*, 1999) directed by Ivan Feijó, was also responsible for two of the most awarded performances for young audiences: *Piratas na linha (Pirates in Line,* 1999) and *Motor Boy* (2001), both directed by Débora Dubois.

Samir Yazbek, the youngest of this generation, began his career by receiving a playwriting award for *O Fingidor (The Pretender)*, which he himself produced and directed. In 2001 his new play, *Terra Prometida (Promised Land)*, was directed by Luiz Arthur Nunes, at the Teatro SESC Anchieta.

Another award-winner, Bosco Brasil, is one of the most experienced authors of this generation. *O Acidente (The Accident,* 1999) opened under the direction of Ariela Goldman at the Centro Cultural São Paulo. In the present season, Bosco was responsible for the excellent *Novas Diretrizes em Tempos de Paz (New Rules in Times of Peace)*, also directed by Ariela Goldman with a moving performance by Dan Stulbach.

Mário Bortolotto received the drama award in 2000 for his play *Nossa vida não vale um Chevrolet (Our Life Is Not Worth a Chevrolet)*. Another immigrant from the south of Brazil, and undoubtedly one of the most productive of this generation, Bortolotto, who also directs and acts in his own plays, presented in the basement of the Centro Cultural de São Paulo, in the same year, a season assembling 14 of his plays. Now, to celebrate the 20th anniversary of his company, Cemitério de Automóveis (Automobile Graveyard), Bortolotto, together with producer and actress Fernanda Dumbra, has an even more daring encore: 26 of his plays, in a three month season, with two performances an evening, involving a total company of 80 actors.

The presence of this new generation of playwrights goes hand in hand with the movement to foster contemporary Brazilian drama, which has produced various interesting projects. In 2001, there was a Drama Showcase by Ágora, a small theatre co-directed by Celso Frateschi and Roberto Lage, which included the workshopping and eventual staging of a set of short plays, among which we may single out *Novas Diretrizes em Tenpos de Paz (New Rules in Times of Peace)* mentioned above.

Searching for a repertory to perform, actor Renato Borghi joined three other colleagues – the actresses Débora Duboc, Luaa Guimarães, and actor-director Elsio Nogueira – and commissioned plays, short ones like Ágora's, from fifteen playwrights. They organised a showcase of this repertory at the beginning of the present season, at the Teatro Popular do SESI, with invited directors. The authors were Aimar Labaki, Bosco Brasil, Dionísio Neto, Marici Salomão, Mário Bortolotto, Alberto Gusik, Hugo Possolo, Marcelo Rubens Paiva, Otávio Frias, Newton Moreno, Pedro Vicente, Samir Yazbek, Leonardo Alkmin, Sérgio Salvia, Fernando Bonassi (whose play was co-written with Victor Navas).

Among the playwrights of former generations who continue writing the best of Brazilian theatre, we should single out in 2001: Consuelo de Castro, with *Only You,* directed by José Renato, and Alcides Nogueira with *Pólvora e Poesia (Powder and Poetry).* The play by Nogueira, inspired by the meeting of Rimbaud and Verlaine, had an extraordinary, poetic staging by director Márcio Aurélio and won awards for best play, best director and best actor (Leopoldo Pacheco, who besides being an exceptional actor, has received awards as a costume designer).

As for adaptations, the best two of the latest seasons are*: Um porto para Elizabeth Bishop (A Port for Elizabeth Bishop,* 2000, at the Teatro SESC Anchieta), by Marta Góes, based on texts by Ms Bishop, and *O Evangelho segundo Jesus Cristo (The Gospel according to Jesus Christ,* 2001, at the Teatro SESC Vila Mariana), an excellent adaptation by Maria Adelaide Amaral of the novel by José Saramago with the same title. By coincidence, both plays were directed by José Possi Neto.

Finally, to complete this overview of Brazilian production, we should mention the role of the Universities in the training of young talents and the renewal of theatre artists. Among others, we may single out the delicate directing debut of Ana Roxo, *3x4 – 18x24* (Centro Cultural São Paulo, 2000), adapted from texts by Caio Fernando Abreu, and another by Luiz Fernando Marques, *Hysteria* (2002), shown in a big old house belonging to the University and delivered by an excellent young female cast.

On the level of political and cultural action in these last years, we should mention the group of artists and intellectuals, drawn mainly from the theatre workers of São Paulo, who organised the movement *Arte contra Barbárie (Art against Barbarism),* which now has a national dimension. This group, devoted to serious discussion of cultural policy, achieved, among other victories, the enactment of a law which allocates a considerable budget, on a municipal level, to productions by established companies.

Finally, to finish this synopsis, a special word for the book, published by SENAC, *Cem anos de teatro (A Hundred Years of Theatre),* written in tandem by the remarkable veteran critic Sábato Magaldi and the respected researcher Maria Theresa Vargas, acclaimed not only for its production quality, but also as a timely achievement in the desolate landscape of Brazilian theatre publishing.

Silvana Garcia *is a playwright and researcher, with a PhD in Performance Arts. She is Professor at the Dramatic Art School of São Paulo University and author of two books, Teatro da Militância (Editora Perspectiva, 1990) and As Trombetas de Jericó – Teatro das Vanguardas Históricas (Editora Hucitec, 1997), as well as Director of the Research Department of the Cultural Centre of São Paulo.*

CAMEROON

MBILE YAYA BITANG

During a colloquium organised some years ago by the Cameroon centre of the International Theatre Institute on the topic: 'Cameroon theatre: perspectives and achievements', Professor Polycarpe Oyie Ndzie described Cameroon theatre as a forest: we can sometimes see the fascinating movement of its canopy, but very scarcely does it show to its numerous researchers the secrets of its inner life.

Nowadays we see a relative standstill in the resolution of the problems at the roots of this deep reality. Efforts by the state, public and private institutions and the theatre community itself to create a new image of Cameroon theatre give reason to predict a healthier fate. But it won't allow us today to forget the wounds of the Cameroon theatre galaxy.

In the theatre training field, the absence of professional structures is very noticeable. Although there is a Performing Arts section at the Yaounde 1 University, created in 1993, unfortunately its direction is more theoretical than practical. Students graduating in the different branches of the theatre field have a mastery of the critical aspects of theatre but for practical training they are obliged to join University or other professional theatre groups and attend practical workshops, regularly organised in parallel with some cultural events such as CITFEST (Cameroon International Theatre Festival) and FITEJ (Festival International de Théâtre pour l'Enfance et la Jeunesse). In this way non professionals and professionals of drama have benefited from the skilled coming together of famous drama practitioners these last cultural seasons. Workshops have included:

  – a workshop on directing organised by the Swedish and Cameroon centres of the ITI, supervised by the Swedish directing teacher Martha Vestin

  – a workshop on stage design organised by Japanese and Cameroon centres of the ITI under the supervision of the Japanese Yoko Odagiri. At the end of that workshop, one young Cameroon student benefited from a scholarship to Japan.

  – a workshop on stage design supervised by the Swedish Marianne Carlberg

  – a workshop on lighting supervised by the Canadian lighting designer Claude Lemelin

  – a performing workshop conducted by the French mime Patrick Loriot under the title: 'language of body, language of silence'

  – a performing workshop on the use of the masks in theatre supervised by Michel Proc and Josiane Fritz during the 10th edition of CITFEST.

Apart from these workshops organised in the CITFEST and FATEJ, there were many other independent initiatives of theatre training from famous actors such as the Cameroonians Gerard Essomba and Were Were Liking who organised training sessions on acting, dance and vocal techniques, and Catherine Desazens (from Switzerland) who directed an initiation course on performance in March 2002.

In terms of playwriting, residencies are regularly organised for young authors by Compagnie Ngoti. The last one took place in April 2002, co-ordinated by Danielle Paume, of French origin.

All these actions put in place for theatre training demonstrate a real effort by public and private structures in that domain. And we hope that the new presidential decree concerning the creation of a national institute of arts will contribute to improving the level of theatre practice in Cameroon.

Concerning artistic production, these last seasons have witnessed a recovery of enthusiasm and vitality in the theatre field. After almost a decade of lethargy due to lack of funding, several theatre companies decided to make a vibrant come-back on stage, producing performances which went on to a beautiful international career. Among the most representative cases are the companies:

    – Bena Zingui, whose plays *Minkul mi nem* (*The Call of the Heart*) written by Felix Kama and directed by Louise Belinga, and *L'Epopée d'Angon Mana* written by Leon Marie Ayissi have been selected to participate in many international festivals, among them MASA (Marché des Arts du Spectacle Africain) in Abidjan (Ivory Coast) and FIA (Festival International de l'Acteur) in Kinshasa (D R Congo).

    – Ngoti, which represented Cameroon in famous international festivals such as MASA, FIA and FATEJ, with the play titled *Vivre mort* (*Living Dead*) by Mercedes Fouda, directed by Jean Mingele.

    – Les ateliers du COCRAD (Collectif des Créateurs d'Art Dramatique) selected for MASA 2001, Festival des Réalités in Bamako, Racines in Porto Novo and FITHEB (Festival International de Théâtre du Benin) with *Negrerrance*, a play by José Pliya directed by the Congolese Pascal Nzonzi.

During the seasons 1999–2000, 2000–2001 and 2001–2002, one may see a particular interest in co-productions with foreign theatre companies. The case of the project Eyala Peña is relevant. Formerly based on training sessions for authors, actors and theatre technicians, the project gave rise to several performances produced by Cité Peña of Douala (Cameroon) and In Excursus of Saint-Denis (France). Under the supervision of the French director Barbara Bouley, a tour in France was organised to make French people discover the results of the project, through performances of *Ekhaya le retour* directed by Barbara Bouley and *Saint Dallas*, a text of the Togolese Kossi Efoui (co-ordinator of the playwrights' forum in the same project) directed by the young and talented Stephane Tchonang. Eyala Peña also gave the opportunity to some young Cameroon stage designers to improve their knowledge through a one year scholarship for advanced courses. Returning to the country a few months ago, they are now practising their skill for the benefit of local and foreign theatre productions. In the same area of co-production we can mention the more recent case of the performance *Roméo et Juliette sous l'arbre*, an African adaptation of the Shakespeare play by the Cameroon company Sahre Théâtre,

CAMEROON

in partnership with Cartoun Sardine of Marseilles (France) under the direction of Philippe Car. Produced in June 2001 with the financial support of the French cultural centre, the play is now preparing for an international tour, after a national one in March 2002. In the same way was created the production of the play *Et Dieu l'avait créé* written by the Canadian Guy Dorval and directed by Thomas Amombo, artistic director of the company MUGRA (Mutants des Grands Arts). Apart from all these productions, financed mainly by francophone institutions, we have some cases of performances realised thanks to the goodwill of the German Goethe Institute. Such are the plays *Days in Black Satin* directed by Marc Deggeler, *Clara Schumann* written by Elfriede Jelinek and *Attitudes* (a collective work) both of them directed by Edwige Ntongon, and *Rue barrée* directed by Stephane Tchonang. Finally, a co-production between the festivals CITFEST and FIA had a great international success: the play *Les Dernières nouvelles ne sont pas bonnes* by Dave Wilson, directed by Nono Bakwa.

As far as theatre for children is concerned, the only professional company doing serious work in this field is the Théâtre du Chocolat, managed by Etoundi Zeyang, current president of the Cameroon section of ASSITEJ (Association Internationale de Théâtre pour l'Enfance et la Jeunesse). His legendary characters Bobo and Mangetout are the favourites of hundreds of children who always come in crowds to their performances regularly scheduled at the Yaounde Hilton hotel.

Cameroon theatre activists are certainly doing their best to stay in action in spite of the economic crisis. But productions over all the seasons are still rare, and real dramatic life in Cameroon is visible only during the various theatre festivals, particularly CITFEST.

The annual CITFEST (Cameroon International Theatre Festival), organised by the Cameroon centre of the ITI under the supervision of its president Ambroise Mbia, is a great occasion for training and exchange between the theatre public and artists coming from many African and other countries. The high quality of the plays scheduled in the festival always attracts many important buyers and personalities in the world of theatre. During recent editions a meeting has been organised for the experts of CITF (Commission Internationale du Théâtre Francophone), a seminar on the diffusion of central African plays, and several workshops for theatre technicians and artists, in addition to the numerous international plays in the programme of the festival. Many African companies have been selected to take part in some very important festivals thanks to their participation in CITFEST. Another interesting point in the programme of the festival is the distinctions given every year to honour some theatre figures. The Ebony Crown of theatre was given during the last edition to Bernard Dadié, the *doyen* of African playwrights.

Besides the CITFEST, the Cameroon centre of the ITI also organises every year the celebration of World Theatre Day through various events: carnivals, conferences, processions and performances.

Among other festivals with theatre content, we have:
- FATEJ (Festival International de Théâtre pour l'Enfance et la Jeunesse) organised by Etoundi Zeyang; many companies, including ones coming from Switzerland, Burkina Faso and Chad, participated in the last edition

in November 2000. The next edition of FATEJ takes place in October 2002.
– Net Plateau Vivant organised by André Bang and located in Douala, the economic capital of Cameroon.
– Other festivals like FENAC (Festival National des Arts et de Culture), UNIFAC (University Festival of Arts and Culture) and FATEA (Festival des Arts et Théâtre pour l'Enfant Africain) are not exclusively theatrical. Their programmes extend to other artistic disciplines such as music, dance and painting.

As for copyright, some adjustments are being made by the authorities in order to reorganise this sector, after the dissolution of the national copyright organisation SOCINADA (SOciété CIvile NAtionale des Droits d'Auteurs).

It goes without saying that if Cameroon theatre is still alive, it is mainly thanks to the financial and infrastructural support of foreign organisations, such as the SCAC (Service de Coopération et d'Action Culturelle) at the French embassy, which provides funding for training sessions, productions and touring; the French cultural centre and 'Alliances franco-camerounaises' whose infrastructures are very often put at the disposal of artists for rehearsals and performances; and Proculture, a European Union programme which finances projects from Central Africa.

In the final analysis of Cameroon theatre we can see a real improvement of theatre activity in the country these last seasons. But it is obvious that more efforts are still to be made to have better results, especially from the side of public institutions that should take more into consideration the problems related to theatre training, production and distribution of plays. We must hope that all the goodwill manifested these last years towards theatre development will continue growing each day, producing a bright image of Cameroon theatre.

CANADA

Alberta
MARTIN MORROW

The year 2001 marked the end of an era for Edmonton's Citadel Theatre –
one of the country's most ambitious regional companies – with the death
of its founder, the dynamic lawyer turned theatre builder, Joseph Shoctor. Few
major theatres in Canada owe their existence and character so much to one
individual, and Shoctor's vision had shaped the Citadel since its humble origins
in 1965 in a former Salvation Army headquarters.

The Citadel under Schoctor was next only to the Stratford Festival in
importing high profile artistic directors from the UK and one of the few
public theatres in Canada that made a continuous effort to build shows for
Broadway. However, the theatre's international profile waned somewhat since
the early 1990s, when it was run by Robin Phillips, whose biggest coup was
to salvage the Andrew Lloyd Webber flop, *Aspects of Love*, and give it a
respectable US tour. Shoctor's passing suggests an end to such ambitions, at
least for now. The Citadel's new artistic boss, Bob Baker – who took over
in 1999 – is the first Edmonton native actually to run the organisation and
his emphasis has been on strengthening the company's ties to its community.
More family shows, including an annual holiday production of *A Christmas
Carol*, and a greater use of the Citadel's multi-theatre facility, have been his
contributions to date.

In Calgary, meanwhile, the once-feisty Alberta Theatre Projects has also
begun to seek family audiences. The theatre that once courted controversy in this
conservative city (it actually produced the world premiere of Brad Fraser's
Unidentified Human Remains and the True Nature of Love and later staged a major
production of Tony Kushner's *Angels in America)* was forced to redefine itself
after a near-death financial crisis in 2000. Under new artistic leader Bob White,
the company sought to cultivate a broader audience while maintaining its nationalism by producing inoffensive and heartwarming Canadian fare such as Michael
Healey's national hit *The Drawer Boy*, Michel Tremblay's *For the Pleasure of Seeing
Her Again* and even a new adaptation of the trusty *Anne of Green Gables*. Predictably, ATP began to recover at the box office, at the price of losing much of its
adventurous edge. Even the plays premiered at playRites, its festival of new
work, were largely conventional and mainstream.

It was up to the smaller theatres to maintain Alberta's reputation for daring and new work. In 2001, One Yellow Rabbit, one of English Canada's
leading avant-garde troupes, premiered a verse fantasy, *Featherland,* a tender ode
to bestiality and individuality offered up by the incomparable dancer-chore-
ographer-playwright Denise Clarke. Meanwhile, Ghost River Theatre, another
Calgary company, mined the rich political and environmental issues in the

province that many Alberta playwrights seem reluctant to address. The troupe's musical satire, *An Eye For an Eye,* tackled the case of eco-terrorist Wiebo Ludwig and his holy war against the province's powerful oil and gas industry. Originally presented in Calgary in 2001, it was destined for a remount at the Edmonton Fringe – the largest and oldest fringe festival in North America – in 2002.

British Columbia
MALCOLM PAGE

The two major companies on Canada's west coast continue to be creations of the 60s – Vancouver's Arts Club, with two theatres, and the Playhouse, located in downtown Vancouver. Their successes during 2000 and 2001 have included some international and some new Canadian productions. The former include, at the Playhouse: *Wit,* with Seana McKenna magnificent in the lead, and *The Beauty Queen of Leenane;* and at the Arts Club: *Art* and the *Cripple of Inishmaan,* with a memorable performance by Bernard Cuffling. Successful revivals included *Amadeus* and *My Fair Lady* at the same locations and, more important, two recent Canadian dramas: *For the Pleasure of Seeing Her Again,* Michel Tremblay's tragi-comic youthful recollections of his mother (a role played with relish by Nicola Cavendish) and Timothy Findley's *Elizabeth Rex,* which depicts a night in 1601 when Elizabeth I (required to be more 'rex' than 'regina') is in a barn with Shakespeare and his actors. This last show won six of the annual Jessie awards, including best production, best actors (David Marr and Gabrielle Rose), best set (Ted Roberts) and best costumes (Mara Gottler).

Ms Gottler also designs lavish costumes for the company known as Bard on the Beach. Bard reached its 12th season in 2001, performing three Shakespeare plays each summer in two tents, with the rear of the stage left open for a view of sunset on the north shore mountains. Attendance, for 153 performances, rose to 65,000 (98 per cent of capacity). *The Tempest* was the highlight in 2000 and in 2001 Dean Paul Gibson directed *Two Gentlemen of Verona* with great success.

The major excitement of these last two years, however, has been the rise to prominence of three newer companies – Radix, Boca del Lupo and the Electric Company. Such terms as experimental and avant-garde are imprecise and over-worked. These three groups work in physical theatre, create collectively, are interdisciplinary, often use found spaces, blurring the lines and pushing stylistic boundaries. Members are young and able to stay together (many previously promising groups quickly dispersed for lack of money). One can say now that Vancouver at last has three groups on their way to equalling the best comparable troupes in Canada. There is a special thrill in going to a show by these companies, for it's sure to be fresh, different and surprising.

This said, it must be also acknowledged that Touchstone, led by Kattrina Dunn, with two productions annually, maintained its position as the leading alternative group, with Francois Archambault's play *15 Seconds*, Janet Munsil's

CANADA

Emphysema (seen in Britain as *Smoking with Lulu*) and a new play, *Unity, 1918*, by a local dramatist, Kevin Kerr. This last was an ambitious nine-character piece, set in Saskatchewan, and engaged with both the consequences of World War I and the great flu epidemic.

Another outstanding new play seen here was *Shape of a Girl*, by Joan MacLeod. Staged for Green Thumb, this 75-minute monologue by a teenage girl was amusing, truthful and touching as it took on such subjects as bullying and teenage violence.

Other companies such as Pink Ink, Headlines and Theatresports continued with good, worthwhile work, and Rumble and Shameless Hussies advanced to the higher ranks of the 30 or so alternative theatres in the city. Finally, the Vancouver Fringe Festival, held each September and now centred on Granville Island, presented, as usual, nearly 100 shows but during this period to a relatively low audience, of only about 30,000.

Ontario
RICHARD OUZOUNIAN

During the 2000 and 2001 seasons, theatres throughout Toronto and around Ontario – like theatre across most of the country – achieved peaks of excellence, but in between there were valleys of mediocrity, with a consistent level of excellence eluding almost everyone.

Canada's largest theatre, the Stratford Festival – located two hours to the west of Toronto – knew great financial success during this period, with multi-million dollar surpluses each year, mostly driven by their mainstage musical productions. It didn't seem to matter to their audiences if they were excellent (like *Fiddler On the Roof* in 2000) or substandard (as in 2001's *The Sound of Music*). Stratford continued to struggle with Shakespeare, but Antoni Cimolino's mediterranean *Twelfth Night* was a highlight and Timothy Findley's *Elizabeth Rex*, an imagined encounter between Shakespeare and Elizabeth I, provided a stimulating new script.

Stratford's major competition, the Shaw Festival – two hours to the east of Toronto – also had trouble with their namesake, with only Christopher Newton's striking take on *The Doctor's Dilemma* holding up the side. Newton also had a major triumph with his rediscovery of St John Rankin's forgotten *The Return Of The Prodigal*. Other successful productions at Shaw included lighter fare like Noel Coward's *Easy Virtue* and Thornton Wilder's *The Matchmaker*, as well as a fine production of William Inge's comedy-drama *Picnic* directed by Jackie Maxwell (who will take over the Festival when Christopher Newton retires after the 2002 season).

Toronto's largest not-for-profit theatre, CanStage, was less successful with its new work than it was in mounting versions of established hits. The latest works by established Canadian authors like Judith Thompson, Brad Fraser and George F. Walker provided less satisfying results than American successes such as *Wit* and Steve Martin's *Picasso at the Lapin Agile*.

Soulpepper Theatre Company continued its successful summer seasons of

ABOVE: (from left) Guy Bannerman, Blair Williams, Lorne Kennedy, Bernard Behrens, Jim Mezon and Neil Barclay in Shaw's *The Doctor's Dilemma* at the Shaw Festival, Niagara on the Lake (*photo:* David Cooper)

BELOW: *I, Claudia*, written and performed by Kristen Thomson, Tarragon Theatre, Toronto
(*photo:* Guntar Kravis)

classical repertory in Toronto, with ever growing audiences and solid support from the private sector. Their work provided a balance of the excellent and the uneven, with Pinter's *Betrayal* and Ionesco's *The Bald Soprano* proving real highlights.

Tarragon Theatre followed its long standing commitment to original work, but plays by established figures like David French and Jason Sherman as well as those by relative newcomers like Morwyn Brebner and Maja Ardal failed to make any real impression. Tarragon did have one surprise hit provided by actress Kristen Thomson – her writing debut in 2001 – *I, Claudia*. This deeply moving one-woman mask show about the inner life of a pre-adolescent girl scored with critics and audiences alike, and went on to a series of successful revivals, a national tour and performances in the spring of 2002 in Budapest and other Hungarian cities.

Theatre Passe Muraille continued to reap the benefits of Michael Healey's 1999 hit, *The Drawer Boy*, which was also being produced around the world, but the rest of their playbill wobbled uncertainly, with only Linda Griffiths' portrait of Canadian poet Gwendolyn McEwan, *Alien Creature*, and Daniel MacIvor's *You Are Here* providing real dramatic substance.

Factory Theatre also had its share of disappointing work, but scored two solid new hits with Florence Gibson's imagining of Reconstruction America, *Belle*, and Adam Pettle's smartly vernacular story of redemption, *Zadie's Shoes*, proving instant winners. Pettle may well prove to be one of Canada's major playwriting voices in the next few years.

In the commercial theatre, Ed and David Mirvish opened two smash musicals, *The Lion King* and *Mamma Mia!*, within a month of each other. Both were still selling out over two years later, which certainly pays the bills. Their heavily subscribed subscription seasons, on the other hand, have been featuring restaged versions of Canadian hits that began at smaller theatres (*The Drawer Boy* and *Zadie's Shoes* among them) as well as offering a home to an expanded version of a show that actually began at the Toronto Fringe Festival, *The Drowsy Chaperone*.

Of all the trends in recent years, this new willingness on the part of a strictly for-profit operation to commit to new Canadian plays may prove to be the healthiest development of all.

Quebec
SÉBASTIEN HARRISSON

Fashioned in the image of the society from which they emerged, Quebecois playwrights are rooted in a theatrical tradition and dramatic repertory still in its infancy. Despite its undeniable youth, French-language playwriting in North America can boast of having achieved an enviable place on both national and international stages. Most Montreal theatre companies now schedule at least one or two modern Quebec works among their seasonal offerings – testimony not only to the quality of the scripts but also to the concerted effort of the playwrights to band together to ensure that their unique vision of the world

Normand D'Amour, Dominique Quesnel, Marie-France Lambert and Isabelle Roy in *Le langue-à-langue des chiens de roche* by Daniel Danis at the Théâtre d'Aujourd'hui   (*photo:* Christian Desrochers)

CANADA

is carried from their desks to the major stages of the world. Founded by playwrights in the 1960s and administered and managed by them, the Centre des auteurs dramatiques (CEAD) is a leading voice for the development and recognition of playwriting in Quebec. The Centre, which focuses its activities on two main goals – promoting scripts to producers and providing literary support to writers – has enabled Quebec plays not only to find their legitimate place on stage but also literally to take flight artistically, by providing writers with a place for reflection and experimentation. As we will see below, the past three theatre seasons in Montreal have underscored the undeniable energy of the creative spirit of Quebec theatre with an impressive array of original productions that reflect the thoughts and aspirations of all of Quebec society. The family is at the heart of Quebecois imagery; so it is that the family inspired the first classics in Quebec's repertoire of works. Tremblay, Dubé, Laberge and Bouchard, to name just a few, made the family the cornerstone of their literary universe. This omnipresent theme of family, which some claim is symptomatic of a national tendency to withdraw within oneself, continues to be explored in current productions, although the image of the family created by today's playwrights has changed considerably with time.

There are powerful aesthetic differences, for example, between Serge Boucher's *24 poses (Portraits)* (Théâtre d'Aujourd'hui, 2001), in which the tragically banal life of a suburban family is examined under a microscope, and Dominick Parenteau-Lebeuf's fantasy *Poème pour une nuit d'anniversaire* (NTE, 2000), in which the family pet becomes the final repository of lost sanity. For her part, Lise Vaillancourt in *L'affaire Dumouchon* (La Licorne, 2001) casts an unforgiving eye on the traditional family through the character of a globetrotting vegetarian girl, while Geneviève Billette in *Crime contre l'humanité* (Théâtre Pàp, 1999) offers up the character of young Charotte, a literally rotting progeny of capitalists, who not only causes the explosive break-up of her parents but also throws into question the moral underpinnings of a performance-driven, get-rich-quick society. Wajdi Mouawad conjures up this same desire to revolt against society and question the idea of the clan in *Willy Protagoras enfermé dans les toilettes* (Théâtre Ô Parleur, 1999). Its teenage hero commandeers the WCs in the apartment to protest against the invasion of his family space by neighbouring clans.

Young playwrights, including François Archambault in *La nostalgie du paradis* (Théâtre d'Aujourd'hui, 2000) and Evelyne de La Chenelière in *Des fraises en janvier* (Théâtre d'Aujourd'hui, 2002), have also questioned such institutions as couples and marriage. In youth theatre, children portrayed on stage are often deprived of one or other of their parents, as in Dominick Parenteau-Lebeuf's *L'autoroute* (Le Caroussel, 1999) and Jasmine Dubé's *L'Arche de Noémie* (Théâtre Bouches décousues, 1999), thus reflecting the dismantling of the nuclear family in today's society.

Another socially isolated group has also taken centre stage: the elderly. René Richard Cyr, artistic director of Théâtre d'Aujourd'hui, has underscored in an interview how many scripts he receives that deal with ageing. Given the magnitude of the problem of Quebec's dwindling birth rate and the parallel growth of its ageing population, it is not surprising that the topic figures prominently in the minds of playwrights. The popular success of Jean-Pierre Boucher's *Les vieux ne courent pas les rues* (Théâtre d'Aujourd'hui, 2001), despite a lukewarm reception by critics, provides food for thought. Boucher's imagined collective suicide by residents of a seniors' home desperate to escape their endlessly boring lives, resonated with older patrons to such an extent that the play drew an unprecedented audience for Théâtre d'Aujourd'hui. Despite press coverage of the play's weaknesses, the show touched a nerve with the public and initiated a genuine dialogue with audiences.

Long isolated in North America because of language and independence leanings, Quebec and its theatrical imagery are experiencing, and have been for several years now, what can best be described as 'the call of the continent'. In presenting La Licorne's 2000–2001 theatre season, artistic director Jean-Denis Leduc defended the idea of a 'theatre that stands as a witness to our Americanism' by offering audiences a repeat of Jean-Marc Dalpé's success *Trick or treat* (Théâtre de la Manufacture, 1999), a resolutely North American play both in its writing style and genre that borrows from the thriller. This same sentiment has been echoed at Théâtre de Quat'sous, where the new artistic director, Wajdi Mouawad, chose to dedicate his first season to 'America as seen from the outside', including in the schedule *Le mouton et la baleine* by Moroccan-born Quebecker Ahmed Ghazali, a North-South tale of stowaways drawn by the riches of life in America who find themselves trapped on a cargo ship in the open seas. In his second season (2001–2002), Mouawad invited audiences to follow him on a journey through the myths of America in Sophie Faucher's *Apasionada* (Théâtre de Quat'sous, 2002), a co-production with Théâtre Ex-Machina, directed by Rober Lepage, that examined the life of South American artist Frida Kahlo, and then again led audiences through a stage adaptation of Peruvian novelist José Maria Arguedas's *Les fleuves profonds* (Théâtre de Quat'sous, 2002). A desire to explore the southernmost regions of the Americas moved the team of Persona Théâtre to schedule *Ushuaïa* (1999) by stage director Éric Jean, a fable set against the backdrop of Tierra del Fuego.

This interest in founding myths has also translated itself into a desire to explore First Nations on stage. Emmanuelle Roy's *Far West* (Théâtre Face Public, 2002), for example, presents the story of a young girl who travels to the north shore of the St Lawrence River to link up again with her aboriginal roots, while Daniel Danis's major work *Langue-à-langue des chiens de roche* (Théâtre d'Aujourd'hui, 2000) unravels the primitive customs of an insular society evocative of First Nations reserves.

The 'call of the continent' reverberates in a more formal way with the transformation of the road movie into road theatre in Christian Brisson-Dargis's *Ceci n'est pas un road-movie* (Théâtre du Grand jour, 2000), in which marginalized youth, devoid of ideals, take to the road in search of an imaginary Florida. This same theatrical form reappears in François Létourneau's *Stampede* (Théâtre Pàp, 2000), in which two truck drivers criss-cross Canada to the sounds of country music, and in Jean-Frédéric Messier's *Au moment de sa disparition* (Théâtre le Clou, 2000), a teen play that recounts one youth's search for his brother, lost somewhere on the highways of America.

With today's major shift away from separatist concerns – which monopolised the thinking of a large segment of the intellectual class for over 30 years – has come a willingness to redefine the artist's involvement in society, as reflected in the works of several contemporary Quebecois playwrights. The initiatives of Théâtre du Grand Jour, in particular, have lent support to this movement of ideas. The theatre company's production of Olivier Choinière's *Autodafé* (Le Grand Jour, 1999), an imposing fresco enveloping the whole of Quebec history, lays the partial groundwork for a much larger project. Since its founding, the young company has multiplied the number of events aimed at stimulating the political involvement of the theatre community. One of its most notable events was the October 2000 summit, where playwrights and the theatre community at large were invited to define what social involvement meant to them. In an interesting coincidence, at the same time (May 2002) as Théâtre d'Aujourd'hui was hosting the follow-up to the 2000 summit, Théâtre du Nouveau Monde was staging Michel Tremblay's play *L'État des lieux*, a balance sheet by which the prolific writer sounds the depth of political disillusionment among the generation of artists for which he served as inspiration.

This undercurrent of thought on the place of art in society has led other playwrights to seek inspiration through the visual arts and music. Geneviève Billette, in her play *Le goûteur* (Théâtre Pàp, 2002), describes an antiseptic business world where works of art deemed too subversive are banned, while Normand Chaurette, in his enigmatic and fascinating play *Petit Köchel* (Théâtre Ubu, 1999), focuses on a debate between four aficionados of Mozart about who is the mother of a cannibalistic and dictatorial son, thus weaving startling links between the creative process, patronage and fascism.

Aware that society is caught up in a media circus, several playwrights have also decided to question the responsibility of mounting a play in an atmosphere where everything is sensationalised. Stéphane Hogue's *Ceci n'est pas une pipe* (2001) denounces the exploitation of violence by the media, while Carole Fréchette's *Les sept jours de Simon Labrosse* (La Manufacture, 2000) focuses on the decision of a youth to turn his personal anguish into a show for his friends. In *Jacynthe de Laval* (Théâtre d'Aujourd' hui, 1999), René Gingras parodies the thirst for fame that motivates more than one character in his story of a social worker who takes over a TV studio by force in a vain attempt at glory. In *Rêves* (Théâtre Ô Parleur, 2000), Wajdi Mouawad delivers a dreamlike interrogation of a writer's motivations by his own characters, while in *Le ventriloque* (Théâtre Pàp, 2001) Larry Tremblay questions the mechanism behind the act of creation and gives a voice to ideas in his skilful and intricate weaving of a story within a story.

If this overview of the past three seasons of theatre helps isolate some of the guiding themes at the heart of Quebec plays, the most important lesson to be learned from reviewing this collection of works is the amazing variety of universes presented by the playwrights. The structure of the plays listed above is proof of a veritable explosion of styles, languages and themes that defies any suggestion of systematisation or of an 'umbrella' approach.

Whether poetic, realist, satirical, baroque, or surreal, these scripts and the universes that they conjure up are proof that local theatre production, as a mirror of our society, is becoming pluralistic, seeking inspiration from new sources within an ever-evolving social fabric and from different exchanges with the rest of the world. Many of the plays mentioned in this article have been performed in other countries, or translated into other languages.

In this same spirit of openness and discovery, a growing number of contemporary plays by foreign writers have shared the stage with Quebec plays over the past few years. Thanks to the translation efforts of writers such as Olivier Choinière, Carole Fréchette, René Gingras, Larry Tremblay, and Dominick Parenteau-Lebeuf, plays from English Canada, the United States, Ireland, Scotland and Mexico are now accessible to Quebec audiences. This exchange between Quebecois playwrights and their counterparts in other parts of the world will hopefully continue to stimulate the creation of works for the local stage, so that the words heard in Quebec theatres resonate with the world and what is happening today.

About the writers: **Sébastien Harrisson** *writes for stage, radio and television in Montreal. He is the author of the plays* Floes *and* Titanica, *presented in 2001 at the Théâtre d'Aujourd'hui.* **Martin Morrow** *is theatre critic for the* Calgary Straight. **Richard Ouzounian** *is the theatre critic for Canada's largest newspaper, the* Toronto Star. **Malcolm Page** *is Professor Emeritus of Theatre at Simon Fraser University and a regular theatre writer in Vancouver. The section of this article dealing with English-language theatres was edited for publication by* **Don Rubin**, *co-president of the Canadian Theatre Critics' Association and editor of Routledge's six-volume* World Encyclopedia of Contemporary Theatre.

CHINA

Mainland China
LIN LIN

1999

In this year, many large-scale events were held, including the Showcase Performance of National Excellent Plays (celebrating the 50th anniversary of the founding of the People's Republic of China), the 6th China National Theatre Festival, the 5th Chinese Yingshanhong Folk Drama Festival, the first Chinese Peking Opera Festival, the first International Yueju Opera Art Collection Performance, the first Chinese Chuanju Opera Festival, the first Chinese Folk Yueju Opera Festival and the Shantou International Chaoju Opera Festival. All of these demonstrated that at a turning point for China in the social, economic and political fields, Chinese drama – which has been deep in crisis for a long time – has gradually found ways of adapting to the immense economic pressure of the new social environment, in a situation of changing artistic appreciation.

There were revivals and adaptations of classical plays as well as new, innovative work. A representative example was the Beijing opera *Rickshaw Boy* (*Camel Xiangzi*, or *Luotuo Xiangzi*) performed by the Peking Opera Theatre of Jiangsu Province. An adaptation of the novel of the same name by the well-known playwright Lao She, it recounted the unfortunate life of a rickshaw boy, Xiangzi, who came from the bottom rung of the turbulent 20s society of battling warlords. Virtuous and hardworking, Xiangzi's highest ambition was to own a rickshaw, to make a living and to maintain a home. But no sooner had his dream been realized than it burst like a soap bubble. He bought a rickshaw, then lost it. He got married, then his home was destroyed and his wife died, leaving him completely dispirited. This was a modern Beijing opera rich in artistic merit, surpassing the Model Dramas of the 60s and 70s. In the past decades of modern Beijing opera, artists have worked hard to build heroic characters such as Li Yuhe in the Model Drama *The Red Lantern* and Yang Zirong in *Conquering Weihu Hill with Stratagem*, or to build positive characters such as Yang Bailao in the Model Drama *The White Haired Girl*. Characters such as Xiangzi, built up from many details, marked a new development in the production of modern Peking Opera, which was beginning to stagnate. This new style of creation was also embodied in the Discovery Opera, such as the Yue opera *Kong Yiji* and the Huangmei opera *Huizhou Woman*. Because of its spiritualized, poetic and uniquely expressive style, *Huizhou Woman* drew great interest from the circles of both dramatic criticism and dramatic theory, provoking a discussion which continues to the present day. *Huizhou Woman* took its inspiration from a tradition of the Huizhou region. Its script was based on the painter Ying Tianqi's print in the *Xidi County*

ABOVE: *Camel Xiangzi* (*Rickshaw Boy*) by Jiangsu Peking Opera Troupe

BELOW: *Mother*, by Wuhan Art Production Centre and Wuhan Modern Drama Theatre

series. The character of the title was an unsophisticated but elegant wife who was left behind (today's vogue saying). She sat in a flower-litter and got married at fifteen. Her only wish was to marry a good man and then help her husband by bringing up their children. The person who escorted her to the wedding was her husband's younger brother. Her husband left his long pigtail home (men had long pigtails in the Qing Dynasty) and ran away in order to avoid the arranged marriage. Ten years went by. Well-fed and well-clothed, the woman lived peacefully with her parents-in-law and her husband's younger brother. When she saw a frog jumping out of the well, she sighed with emotion. She carefully held the frog in her hands to take it home, and also shut the door in her soul to the outside world. Meanwhile her husband had gained a position as the head of a county and married another woman, by whom he had children. Another ten years went by. The woman lived on her own, without any thought of love. When she was 50 years old, her husband took his other 'wife' home. Having passed through a purgatorial life, she accepted all this calmly, without any complaint or regret. It is all to easy for us to accept the betrayer who has led a colourful public life, and pay less attention to the suffering wife. This play focused attention on the abandoned woman. The stage picture combined Chen Yifei's canvas (in the costumes and make-up) with Ying Tianqi's print (in the stage set) as its artistic style. Its artistic imagery and stage presentation were a great achievement.

The modern drama *Life and Death Scene* was an adaptation of the 1930s novel of the same name by Xiao Hong, performed by the Centre Experimental Drama Troupe. It depicted a suffering Chinese farmer who began to awake from the vicissitudes of life before and after '9.18', the seizure of Mukden in 1931, when the Japanese army launched its invasion of the three provinces of North East China. The director Tian Qinxin pursued a nationalized style of drama as well as using the representational techniques of the traditional Chinese opera. He applied the language of body movement and gesture to build his characters and express the theme, in an attempt to change the idea that modern drama is just actors speaking the lines.

A particularly interesting revival was *Malan Flower*, a fairy tale drama with a 50-year history, produced by the China Children's Art Theatre. This version adopted a brand new artistic vision. It retained the boisterous scene in which the actors and the children in the audience chase an old cat all over the theatre, but now there were four old cats; and the simple conflict between good and evil was also changed, for a sharp contrast between beauty and ugliness. The revision produced a modern music drama that was close to the taste of children today.

The famous play *Tea House*, which was revived by the Beijing People's Art Theatre, was originally written by Lao She in 1956. It portrayed the destiny of Tea House-keeper Wang Lifa and his household, as well as the ways of an array of his guests, during the dark and desperate period from the end of the Qing Dynasty right up to the eve of the liberation. the original production was one of the great achievements of Chinese drama, with a perfect pair of directors in Jiao Juyin and Xia Chun and performances by the older generation of the Beijing People's Art Theatre. The director of this revival, Lin Zhaohua, abandoned the pattern of the old *Tea House* and adapted the original script to re-illustrate the classic play. He chose young players such as Pu Cunxi, Liang Guanhua and others beloved by Chinese fans, to give a brand-new stage image. Since these players possessed tremendous box office appeal, the new *Tea House* was staged 50 times in its first run and gross earnings hit 5 million Yuan, a new record for the company. Lin's courage and innovative spirit were approved, although there were those who regretted that the revised play had lost much of the original's flavour.

The bold and insightful Chinese Youth Art Theatre showed its ability in performing foreign dramas. It rehearsed the French comedy *Les Palmes De M Schutz* by Jean-Noël Fenwick, translated and directed by Wei Xiaoping. This made use of French humour to express the conflict between the scientific spirit and secularity. Some parents brought their children to watch this piece in order to give them some understanding of the hard life of the scientist, but they found the result widely divergent from their original thoughts. This was a useful attempt at connecting today's Chinese artistic concepts with the popular artistic concepts of the West.

More and more theatres and troupes paid attention to marketing. As an example, the new Yue opera *Dream of the Red Chamber* (performed by Shanghai Yue Opera Theatre) made a great breakthrough in cross-industry collaboration between the theatre, the performers and the media and set up a production company, which applied commercial performance practice. The box-office's gross earnings hit 3.3 million Yuan, recovering its investment. The characteristics of this opera were a new content, new form and a new operating style. During the production and rehearsal period of *Jinzi*, produced by Chongqing Chuan Opera Theatre, the theatre also paid due attention to promotion, so that this opera, too, got its market share in spite of intense competition.

The level of performances of music drama was noticeably improved this year. The youth campus music drama *Future Combination* (from Sichuan) portrayed the life of 17-year-old high school students. It added modern rhythm to artistic performance, including pop music, bike dance, football dance and skating dance, all of which came from the students' daily life. The American musical *Beauty and the Beast* (performed in Beijing Guolun Xinxing Art Centre) cost more than 20 million Yuan; its absolutely splendid large-scale production drew applause. For the first time in the history of our domestic music drama, this was mounted as a normal commercial operation. The music drama *New Madam White Snake*, performed in a singing and dancing hall, was sponsored by an entrepreneur and performed in a nightclub setting. This kind of commercial enterprise became a new subject worthy of discussion. Another music drama *Xishi* (director: Mu Sen, composer: Zhang Guangtian) was performed in a Beijing singing and dancing hall. The actress Wang Ji played Fan Li and Hu Wenge (from Hong Kong) played Xishi, very different roles from their usual ones. Although this drama was not performed so many times and didn't produce a deep effect, this kind of performance can be considered a new trend.

In the 1990s, the emergence of an independent producers' network brought vitality to Chinese modern drama. Its experimental character drew great attention. But from 1999, the growth of independent production gradually diminished. Only Meng Jinghui from The Central Experimental Drama Theatre retained his special impetus. *The Amorous Rhinoceros*, produced by him, was staged 40 times during June and July of this year, and set up a new record for gross box-office earnings of 400 thousand Yuan, in the small theatre of the Chinese Youth Art Theatre, which has only 300 seats. *The Amorous Rhinoceros* is a love story with *fin de siècle* complexity. Malu loves Mingming desperately, but cannot win her love no matter what sweet words he expresses. Meanwhile, Mingming doggedly loves Chenfei (who never appears on stage), no matter what insults he gives her. Confusion all round. As in his previous dramas, Meng Jinghui used many special effects which were highly praised, as was his sensitivity to language. As an example, several people huddle together, with the audience only able to see one or two faces; they swing round and everybody lifts a handrail above their heads. Thus a crowded subway train appears in front of the audience. The passengers discuss how they would spend the money if they won prizes in a lottery. For the scene of the lottery draw, there should be a plaza which could hold tens of thousands of people. But what if there are only a few actors? The players raise a huge blue silk above their heads and charge jubilantly at the audience. With the blue silk swinging above their heads, the audience become the tens of thousands of people waiting for the lottery draw. Thus the atmosphere was built up – such handling of the relationship between audience and players is a speciality for Meng. At the end of this year, he rehearsed another small theatre drama, *The Pirate Faust*, an adaptation from Goethe's famous poetic drama. But the drama critics considered this more piracy than poetry, since what it expressed seemed not really to be what Goethe's *Faust* intended. Meng attempted to reveal Faust's spiritual pursuit as an intellectual for love, beauty, power and immortality in four scenes – First Love, Select Beauty, In the Country and Climb to The Moon. Although the drama didn't express these meanings clearly, it was still a work of high cultural intent. Also in this year, Huang Liguo set up his own waterside bar drama lab in Guangzhou. Many dramas were performed there, including *File Guangzhou*, *Shouting Abuses in the Long County's Street* (*Long Zhen Ma Jie*) and *You Have No Fire*.

2000

In this year, the national performing activities of opera and drama were based on past years' work, especially plays shown to celebrate the 50th anniversary of the founding of the People's Republic. These included the 6th China Art Festival, the first China Kun Drama Art Festival and Kun Drama Classic and Famous Play Show, South Drama International Learning Workshop and Wenzhou South Drama New Adapt Series Play Show, the first China Ping Drama Art Festival, the first China QinTune Art Festival, the 3rd International Guangzhou Yue Drama Festival, the National Children's Drama Excellent Play Show, Guangzhou Small Theatre Drama Show and other large-scale performance activities. All these were rich in themes, content and forms. There were also many new works welcoming the new century.

Boundless Love (*Feng Yue Wu Bian*), directed by Lin Zhaohua and Li Liuyi, produced by the Beijing People's Art Theatre, stirred up endless discussion with

Wuchang and Nudiao, performed by Beijing People's Art Theatre

its theme of love affairs. It told the story of the playwright Li Yu, who lived from the end of the Ming Dynasty to the beginning of the Qing Dynasty. Li Yu had excellent dramatic insight, which is honoured to this day. He was a skilful writer, but failed in the imperial examination. Since he couldn't get an official career, he devoted all his talents to acting and managing his family drama troupe, which had no social status in the feudal society of the day. Although there were many theatregoers at that time, the players were despised. This play made a careful analysis of the writer's feelings and intentions.

In commemoration of the 90th anniversary of Cao Yu's birth, this theatre also revived or revised classic dramas such as *The Thunderstorm*, *Sunrise* and *Wildness*. The revisions drew wide attention and led to heated theoretical discussion.

The Chinese Youth Art Theatre continued to show its strength in performing foreign drama, such as Gogol's comedy *The Inspector General* and Jean Genet's absurd drama *Les Bonnes*. The Central Experimental Drama Theatre put on a special experimental drama *Special Majiang* (directed by Li Liuyi) and a gory Canadian play, *Monument* (directed by Zha Mingzhe). Other art troupes released *Che Guevara*, *Love You Out of Question* and *The Butterfly Lovers* (*The Love Story of Liang Shanbo and Zhu Yingtai*). These works drew a large audience, exceeding that of previous years.

Special Majiang told a story of four brothers who agreed to say good-bye to Majiang and do something more constructive. The second brother never appears. The other three brothers enter into a hallucinatory waiting condition. Late at night, the lavatory upstairs makes noises, harshly drawing the brothers from beautiful dream or nightmare back to reality. After much discussion and allegation, we find that they killed the second brother together, because they didn't really want to give up Majiang. At the end of the drama, there is an unexpected knocking on the door. The eldest brother opens the door and introduces an invisible shadow. Then the three brothers sit with that shadow. The aim of the production was to combine Majiang with life. It made an excellent contrast to the fashion for more talk, less action.

The Canadian two-character drama *The Monument* (writer: Colleen Wagner, director: Zha Mingzhe) drew much attention. It pictured a mother who wanted to take a criminal, who had killed her daughter, into her home. The poetic and colourful experimental drama *Che Guevara* showed Che Guevara's political position as well as his love of galloping all over the world to change the destiny of the poor.

The military drama took action to widen its compass. 'Soldiers write about soldiers, soldiers perform as soldiers and for soldiers' had long been its writing tenet. But this changed when *Tiger Crouches in Zhong Mountain* (*Hu Ju Zhong Shan*) was produced in 1997. Now the military drama widened its vision from barrack room life to the whole of society. As an example, *El-Nino Report*, performed by Nanjing Military Front Modern Drama Troupe, mixed local settings with a military one, a cadre sanatorium. This drama expressed the effect on traditional military families during the marketing period. *Red Plastic Barrel in the Shade*, performed by Beijing Military Zhanyou Modern Drama Troupe, described a group of women college students joining in military training in the barracks. Encounters both comic and serious happened between the students, the squad leader and the soldiers. *Scenery of Life* (*Sui Yue Feng Jing*), performed by Guangzhou Military Soldiers' Modern Drama Troupe, showed the changes in the life of soldiers and their families from the military to the civilian. The Modern Drama Troupe of the General Political Department released an enjoyable large-scale modern music drama, *Taohua Ballad (Taohua Yao)*, a life-and-death love story between a girl, Taohua, and Zhang Husheng, a literature teacher of the New Fourth Army during the Wannan Incident.

In recent years, drama for small theatres has made great progress, with some traditional Chinese drama plays being rewritten for such groups. For example, Peking Opera Theatre of Beijing produced a small theatre Beijing opera, *Spill Water in Front of the Horse (Ma Qian Po Shui)*, rewritten from an old opera. We see three scenes in flashback: the first, when Zhu Maichen and Cuishi get married, he nearly 40 years old and very poor, she young and pretty; in the second, on a windy and snowy night after Zhu's ninth failed attempt at the imperial examination, Cuishi forces Zhu to go out and chop wood while she burns his books to do the cooking, then compels him to write a letter announcing their divorce; in the third, Zhu has become an official and returns home, while Cuishi, now a beggar, nags at Zhu and seeks reconciliation. But Zhu refuses her: 'Spilt water cannot be gathered up again'. The writer endowed the old opera with new meaning. Other examples included the small theatre drama *Farewell My Concubine (Ba Wang Bie Ji)*, rewritten by the Drama Troupe of the General Political Department. This production offered new insights on the play's story and characters.

2001

This year included national drama performances celebrating the 80th anniversary of the founding of Chinese Communism, commemorating the 120th anniversary of eminent Chinese writer Lu Xun's birth and the 65th anniversary of his death, the rare minority drama performance – the 2nd National Minority Literature Joint Performance, The 2nd International Small Theatre Drama Festival, The Best Drama Performance Season (in Beijing, Shanghai, Shenzhen and Hong Kong), the 2nd Ping Drama Art Festival and the 7th China Drama Festival, the largest of the year, and the China Peking Opera Art Festival.

The winning dramas in the 7th China Drama Festival were modified and further improved. The Chuan opera *Jinzi* was an adaptation of the drama *Wildness* by Cao Yu. The director and the players especially illuminated the character of Jinzi, who was untamed and had the courage to love and hate. The Ping opera *Wind of Hu and Moon of Han (Hu Feng Han Yue)* was also presented from a special point of view. Cai Wenji in that opera was different from the one in Guo Moruo's script. This Cai Wenji forgot her grief, and then met, knew, loved and parted from the Zuoxian King, all events revealing her love of life. The Pu opera *Women in the Adobe Kang* and the Yue opera *Tuoge's Flag* both gave pleasure. The modern drama *Mother* (performed by Wuhan Art Production Centre and Wuhan Modern Drama Theatre) described the legendary life of Ge Jianhao, the mother of Cai Heshen and Cai Chang, first-generation members of the Chinese Communist revolution. Posture techniques from traditional Chinese opera were used to show a revolutionary mother with bound feet, a strong visual expression which shook the audience.

CHINA

China Youth Art Drama Theatre performed Giles Cooper's absurd play *Everything In The Garden*. Its mode of expression was realistic and full of incident, very different from what we commonly understand by absurd drama. The plot developments threw the audience into astonishment now and then: Charlie, who was always worrying for lack of money, suddenly fishes out bundles of cash from under the floorboards; his 'dignified and virtuous' neighbours all turn out to be prostitutes – and so is his wife! This drama mixed moral fable, dramatic surprise and lively spirit in its internal form, offering a lot of suggestions to the writers of Chinese drama for small theatres.

As for modern work, dramas produced by private or independent companies were obviously much more frequent than those produced by national art theatres, and more plays were performed in small theatres than large, but with different qualities. The small theatre modern drama *www.com* (playwright: Yu Rongjun, company: Shanghai Modern Drama Art Centre) produced much reaction, using the Internet to express people's complex feelings and the spiritual distortion of modern society. The play's conclusion, especially, provided food for thought: after Cheng Zhuo and his wife Ai Yang divorce, they are eager to meet their new online lover – and find one other!

The background to *Death and the Maiden* by the Chilean playwright: Ariel Dorfman, presented by The Modern Drama Troupe of the Chinese Colliery Art Troupe, is the response to the atrocities of Chile's former fascist regime. The writer explores the complex motives of the drama's three characters, especially the doctor, Roberto, who had put his medical knowledge to the service of the regime, so that prisoners could survive in spite of being raped and tortured. When Roberto is finally forced to confess his crime and expose his ugly soul, the degree of realism left the audience 'astounded and disturbed', as one reviewer put it.

Fringe, or 'Coffee' drama has long been popular in western countries. Zhenhai Coffee Theatre was established in Shanghai several years ago. Many coffee dramas have been performed there and well received. This year Liu Shen's one-man drama *I Love Carrying the Coffin on Stout Poles* was performed. It told about the vicissitudes in the life of an old man whose job had been that of coffin-bearer. Script and performance alike were acclaimed by the public and the specialists.

This year saw the emergence of a force which can no longer be neglected on the modern stage, namely Campus drama. On the one hand there was the drama performed by the students of dramatic schools, such as *Lying Man* (from The Central Drama University) and *Cuihua Serves Bitter Vegetables* (*Cuihua, Shang Suan Cai*). The latter, a student adaptation of *Net-Worm Dairy*, was especially welcomed. On the other hand was drama performed by students of non-dramatic schools, such as *Zoology System – The Cat – Mr. Cazi* performed by the Oriental Campus Troupe organized by students from colleges and universities, *I Am Mentally Handicapped, I Am Innocent* performed by students of the People's University of China (Philosophy Department), *Spring Comes and Flowers Blossom* (Chun Nuan Hua Kai, the Chinese Language Department), *End Start* (the Economic School), *Woyzeck*, performed by the Sun Theatre of the University of Science and Engineering, Beijing, and *Dark Love: Peach Blossom Park* performed by the students' theatre of The Foreign Economic and

Commercial University. In *Woyzeck*, an adaptation from the German playwright Georg Buechner, the students applied a number of body movements to express the psychology of the characters. Chinese folk dances (*yangko*) were performed alternately, which gave the production life and vigour. Other original scripts revealed the students' own enthusiasms – their understanding of society, their sensitivity to current affairs and their thoughts on life and love. *End Start* discusses the burning issues of the young: Honghong chooses death to realize her dream of living with her beloved man. But her boyfriend and another lovelorn girl choose to face reality. The production conditions of the campus drama were not ideal – lack of funding and facilities resulted in imperfect performances. But the students persisted in making their own art creations, expressing their special point of view and mode of thinking as well as a spirit of courageous exploration. Campus Drama has become an effective and vigorous segment of the drama circle.

Hong Kong
JESSICA YEUNG
and MIKE INGHAM

The indigenous theatre of Hong Kong is Guangdong *Yueju*, the regional form of traditional Chinese theatre played in the *Yue* (Guangdong) dialect, known in English as Cantonese. *Huaju* (speech drama) joined *Yueju* at the turn of the 20th century, partly as a result of the amateur dramatics brought to the colony by British expatriates. Many English productions were performed by the English speaking local elite, but the segregated lifestyle of the two populations, Chinese and European, limited their influence. A greater influence was the practice of modern drama in the major Chinese cities. There was free entry between the colony and China at the time and travelling drama companies touring to Hong Kong performed *Huaju*. Subsequently, intellectuals and theatre personnel settling in Hong Kong early in the 20th century collaborated with local theatre workers. Some of these early productions were played in Mandarin, but more and more of them were played in the local dialect of Cantonese. In the latter half of the 20th century, *Huaju* became the main theatre form. Cantonese is used almost exclusively, alongside a relatively smaller number of English speaking productions among the various expatriate communities. A number of groups produce works in both languages. The earlier Seals Foundation and Chung Ying Theatre Company, the more recent Theatre Action, Eurasian performer Veronica Needa, the actress/director Carmen Lo and the playwright/director Dino Mahoney have all produced both English and Cantonese productions. Theatre du Pif tends to include both languages within a single production.

A big step forward was achieved in 1984 when the HK Academy for Performing Arts was established. It provides a variety of training courses for theatre practitioners. APA graduates have been the driving force in Hong Kong theatre since the 90s, alongside more established dramatists, many of whom produce work in the more familiar genre of stylistically realistic, text-based theatre. These younger generation artists generally follow the global trends of devised and movement-based theatre. They have practically taken over the current scene. The use of multi-media is abundant in their work; more traditional plot-oriented narrative is not favoured by this new generation.

The establishment of the Arts Development Council, which gives direct grants to arts companies, projects and productions, was another landmark. The majority of productions from the 90s onwards have been original devised works, often the result of workshops prior to a relatively short rehearsal stage. Besides these are adaptations of western classics. There are a small numbers of straight translations, and some English language productions by well-established groups from the expatriate communities. A handful of Chinese classics are also played in Cantonese every year, but the mainstream trend is toward original work.

Hong Kong always aspires to be international, for economic and cultural reasons, and cultural exchange is an integral part of its life. Theatre festivals are frequent. The Hong Kong International Arts Festival each February-March features top productions from all over the world. Running almost concurrently is the City or Fringe Festival, run by the Hong Kong Fringe Club. The other Independent Hong Kong Arts Centre also presents smaller scale theatre festivals, with productions from Hong Kong's Asian neighbours and some local theatre pieces. The Government presenter which manages almost all main venues, the Leisure and Cultural Services Department (responsible for the city sewage system as well as arts and sports), holds other larger-scale festivals on Chinese cultural themes, festivals for children and other events.

The number of venues and seats for theatre production has been stable in the second half of the 90s up to the present. There are 15 theatres, studios and halls run by the Government presenter, used for theatre and other performances. The total maximum capacity is 9647 seats. The two independent arts centres and the HKAPA run altogether 7 theatres and studios, comprising a further capacity of 2248. The occupancy of these theatres often reaches saturation. In other words, the territory has room for 11,895 people to attend theatre performances in one evening, out of the total population of just under 7 million. This does not take into account the larger multi-purpose stadia, such as the Hong Kong Coliseum, and the university theatres, which are also sometimes used in place of more commercial theatre venues.

Following the 1984 Sino-British Joint Declaration on the reversion of its sovereignty to China in 1997, Hong Kong experienced a long period of preparation and adjustment for the Handover. Social critics often described this period as 'a borrowed time and place', a way of life that one doesn't own, and one that could easily be taken away. Anticipatory sentiments were expressed as early as the 70s, when young university graduates were already staging anti-colonial plays on the threshold of the Red China of the Cultural Revolution, and supporting the campaign for the acceptance of Chinese as the second official language after English. Yet when decolonisation actually took place, such sentiments experienced drastic change. The problem lay with the perception among Hong Kong's artists of the post-1989 'motherland' as more threatening than nurturing.

Anticipation reached its peak in 1996, the year before the actual Handover.

The Hong Kong theatre scene, instead of reacting directly to the complex political actualities, turned to an almost collective reflection on national and cultural identity. The two large theatre companies, the Hong Kong Repertory Theatre and Chung Ying (literally meaning Chinese and English) Theatre Company, continued a stable production output, but the cutting edge was as ever represented by the small-scale companies, consisting of a couple of artistic and administrative personnel, working with other freelance artists for individual productions.

Chan Ping-chiu's Hong Kong Archeological Story, *Fly, Fly, Fly* (1996) was one of his series reflecting on the history of Hong Kong. Ho Ying-feng's *Ms Julie of Yuen Chow Street*, also exploring the theme of individual and collective identity and many critics' favourite theatre piece of the year, was lauded for its successful merging of text, movement and music, use of space on stage and technical arts. Zuni Icosahedron continued the cultural exchange series *Journey to the East* after a lapse of 10 years. The event comprised six 20-minute short works, on varied themes, by Chinese directors from local and overseas communities. The 1996 *Journey to the East* included shorts by Danny Yung, Zuni's Artistic Director, and stage works by the Hong Kong film director Stanley Kwan and Taiwan film director Edward Yang. Each made use of one table and two chairs (the basic stage set for traditional Chinese theatre) as its starting point. This event continued until 2000. Many of the works had a strong overtone of search for cultural identity. Tang Shu Wing and Jim Shui Man's collaboration, *No Man's Land*, is less political in its choice of themes but closer to the feelings of daily life. Spring-Time Productions, the only commercial theatre company in Hong Kong, was established in 1996, since when their productions have become increasingly populist and enjoyed commercial success. Musicals are also gaining popularity, with a number of local productions.

1997 was the golden year of the Arts Centre's theatre presentation. It facilitated some of the most thoughtful productions on the topic of Hong Kong identity. Chan Ping-chiu's highly acclaimed *Fly, Migrating Birds, Fly* started off by exploring individual in relation to collective history, developing into a more radical stance of questioning the stability and meaning of personal identity. Theatre games were an important component of the performance.

Such presentations show that independent presenters with vision can be very effective in facilitating and reinforcing certain cultural directions. Mok Chiu-yu's one-man show *The Story of Ng Chung-yin* reconstructed important episodes of the life of the late Trotskyist activist. Performances finished every evening with Ng's friends and comrades telling little stories of Ng's life, which were then acted out by a group of young actors in the form of Playback. The narrative presents another perspective of Hong Kong's history, relating social events to the life of an anti-establishment socialist. One long term consequence of this play has been the introduction of the Playback practice into Hong Kong. Since then this form has flourished.

Relating important past social events is also another popular theme. It can be understood as part of the reconstruction of a collective memory for the local community. Playwright Chan Kam-kuen's new play *1941* (the year of the Japanese occupation of Hong Kong) was produced after a revival of Chan's earlier play *1841* (the year of British colonization) which had first been staged in 1985. The veteran and highly regarded amateur Chi Kwan Drama Society continued their quest for a cultural relationship with China in *In Search of Spring Willow*, investigating the psychology of intellectual and patriotic theatre practice behind the pioneering Spring Willow Society, a group of returned students from Japan who first introduced speech drama into China. The indigenous traditional Chinese theatre of the region experienced a turning point in this year, namely the collaboration of critic/producer Lai Kin, film/Cantonese opera writer Yeung Chi-sum, theatre director/designer Ho Ying-feng, Beijing/Cantonese opera director Liu Xun and a number of Cantonese opera players in an ambitious attempt at merging traditional theatre convention with modern technical arts. The success of this production in attracting non-connoisseurs of the form was a big confidence boost for pursuing this direction in the years to come.

None of these productions could compare with the quintessentially theatrical performance of the Reunification ceremony. Never has a greater shock occurred in Hong Kong life than the handover of the territory to China on July 1, 1997. Never in the history of Hong Kong was a performance more performative than the flag-changing ritual and the tears of Chris Patten, the departing Governor, in the relentless rain. Nor had there been more heart-pounding music than the national anthem and those gestures of the players, so overcharged with significance, acted out to impress those without power to play but condemned to go on watching. The local audience of seven millions was overwhelmed by this performance of the century.

The explosion of creativity and social relevance in the theatre of 1997 could not be sustained in the year that followed. Indeed 1998 was not a very happy year. In the context of the macro-climate of the Asian economic slump, it was very difficult to determine the efficiency of the Special Administration Region's new government, headed by a Chief Executive and elected by an election committee consisting of 800 people rather than by general suffrage. Theatre, like other industries, suffered a decline in its vibrancy. In terms of trends, cultural identity continued as a popular theme. The most noted work in this direction was *Face*, a solo performance by Veronica Needa, a Eurasian who divides her time between Hong Kong and England. In separate English and Cantonese versions it tells the author's own history and confusion of identity. This production, revived very successfully in May 2002, is the only one that relates the identity issue from a perspective other than the Chinese one.

1999 was a more fruitful year for playwrights. Poon Wai-sum, artistic director of Prospect Theatre, was very successful with his *Ants Climbing Up the Tree*. The play is about the routine difficulties of life among the working public. The witty use of language, especially the humorous use of Hong Kong English, contributed greatly to the overall black humour of the piece. Chan Chi-wah, by profession a civil engineer, wrote the characteristically atmospheric two-hander *Getting Here and There, Climbing Up and Down*, set against a war background. He Qinpin, the Hong Kong Repertoire's resident playwright, employed from Beijing, wrote a grand royal court play entitled *Deling and Cixi*, an account of the friendship between the Manchurian Empress Dowager and the young court woman Deling. Its more traditional plot, narrative form and structure were atypical of most Hong Kong theatre.

Apart from the annual festivals, two important events of the year were the Chinese language theatre festival and The Wave. The former explored the idea of a Chinese language theatre rather than Chinese theatre, presenting works from other Chinese language communities. This is an ongoing project, with the collaboration of a number of major Chinese community cities including Hong Kong, Taipei, Shanghai, Macau, Singapore and others. The Wave was a small-scale festival presented by the Arts Centre, consisting of six hour-long works by six up and coming groups. The discussion it generated greatly assisted in promoting their work.

The year saw many changes in the artistic and cultural infrastructure of the city. The two Municipal Councils, the Urban Council and the Regional Council were dissolved, thus terminating the only councils in the ex-colony with both directly elected elements and executive powers. The executive arms of the councils taking care of cultural affairs were reorganized into the Leisure and Cultural Services Department, under the Home Affairs Bureau. A Cultural Commission was set up in this year, supposedly with the brief of making recommendations on the overall cultural administration of the Government, but it has yet to come up with any significant statement.

A well-equipped, medium-size theatre opened at Kwai Tsing, and this audience-friendly auditorium with excellent sight-lines and acoustics has been a valuable new venue for local as well as touring productions. The year also saw the publication of the bi-lingual, bi-weekly giveaway arts magazine *Xpressions*, a joint venture between the International Association of Theatre Critics (Hong Kong) and the *South China Morning Post*, with a grant from the Arts Development Council. It reached a circulation of 110,000 copies and was very successful, but its grant was discontinued after one year and it had to fold. In August the Arts Development Council commissioned four local associations, including On and On Theatre Workshop and the Hong Kong branch of the International Association of Theatre Critics, to organize the first Hong Kong Theatre and Education Conference at the Hong Kong Arts Centre.

The most active sector remained that of the theatre workers and theatre companies. Tang Shu-wing's direction of Chan Chi-wah's script, *My Murder Tale*, recounting the love and hate of an urban intellectual for the rural primitive, was many critics' favourite play of the year. The skilful fusion of puppetry, actors' movement and the atmospheric *mise-en-scène* affirmed the director's competence. Equally successful was Theatre Ensemble's radical adaptation of Ionesco's *The Chairs* which was injected with a strong local flavour. The most controversial production of the year had to be Edward Lam Dance Theatre's *Horrible Parents*, the result of workshops with secondary students, exploring their relationship with their families. The scenes are a succession of unconnected verbal and stage images, its lines typical of Cantonese nonsensical utterances, subverting the logic of established social and personal power relationships.

Major Cantonese productions in 2001-2 included the Actors Family musical *1941 Girl*, Chung Ying's *What a Blissful Encounter, Mr Ts'ai* and Theatre Ensemble's *The Green Bird*. Hong Kong Repertory Company offered a 7-hour epic, *A Dream like a Dream*, written by Lai Sheng Chuan (November 2001) and a newly translated version of Jean Genet's *Deathwatch* (June 2002). Zuni

CHINA

Icosahedron's multi-media encounter between Chinese culture and Western psychoanalysis, *Sigmund Freud in Search of Chinese Matter and Mind*, blended live traditional and avant-garde modes with electronic music and images. The Chinese Nobel-prize winning author Gao Xingjian had two of his works performed in different media: *Weekend Quartet* was adapted and directed by Dino Mahoney in English on Hong Kong's Radio 3 and the BBC World Service; and *Between Life and Death* was staged in Cantonese by No Man's Land, directed by Tang Shu Wing. The latter, with Theatre du Pif's experimental, bi-lingual adaptation of Lorca's *Bernarda Alba*, entitled simply *The House of...* were two locally commissioned productions in a richly varied Hong Kong Arts Festival for 2002, its 30th anniversary. Three major performing arts companies, Hong Kong Dance Company, Hong Kong Repertory Theatre (under its new Artistic Director, Frederic Mao) and Hong Kong Chinese Orchestra became an independent corporation and simultaneously registered as a charity, a significant move towards greater administrative autonomy.

In April, 2002 the Cultural and Heritage Commission released a consultation paper, encouraging the general public to voice their opinions and expectations regarding cultural development in Hong Kong. We eagerly await the results.

About the authors: **Lin Lin** *is a critic in Beijing, and acknowledges the help given in the preparation of this essay by writers of articles published in* China Drama, *including Liu Ping.* **Jessica Yeung** *was born in Hong Kong. She teaches at Hong Kong Baptist University and is also Chairman of the Hong Kong branch of the International Association of Theatre Critics and a committee member of the Hong Kong Arts Development Council. As producer, actor, interpreter and critic, she is an energetic promoter and* aficionado *of Chinese traditional theatre.* **Mike Ingham** *was born in the UK. He has lived in Hong Kong since 1989 and teaches at Lingnan, Hong Kong's Liberal Arts University. He is a founder member of Theatre Action, a bilingual intercultural theatre group.*

COLOMBIA

LUIS MIGUEL USUGA

For the last 30 years Colombia and its theatre have been playing out the same drama to the same script. The war which has affected us for more than 40 years now has had different protagonists: the State, the army, the drug traffickers, the guerrillas and the paramilitaries. However, they have all implacably pursued the same target, the ordinary citizen.

We can say the theatre has played its part in the struggle by denouncing injustice and offering various possible ways towards building a better future. Since the 70s, political violence has been kept down by the repression of a state wielding almost feudal powers against popular movements originating with peasants, workers and students, and giving rise to the guerrilla movements which still exist today. In that time, the theatre has established itself as one of the most important available platforms for political expression. Theatre companies, mostly starting as student groups, gave their support to political organisations in conflicts with the government. These groups took their work to the towns, villages and countryside. They were subjected to the repression, torture, abductions and beatings which were characteristic of the time. There was a huge public for this well developed touring theatre, which played not only indoors but also in the streets and squares, usually free of charge. This decade saw the birth or consolidation of important groups such as the Cali Experimental Theatre, La Candeleria from Bogota, the Little Theatre of Medellin and many other companies which developed a Colombian theatre aesthetic and still carry on their work in the community today.

The end of the 70s produced a slight reduction in State repression and with it came a change in the theatre which asked questions of practitioners about the content of their work. For the most part, this work had carried political messages, which led the theatre to establish itself exclusively as an instrument for the promotion of the ideas of left wing organisations.

The Festival of Manizales was a great agent for change. At it were produced works which had artistic expression as a fundamental component, without taking account of their origin in terms of the political orientation of the group or the play. The result was a new, fresher theatre, more modern and cosmopolitan, directed at a young public who were no longer so interested in politics but who wanted to be shown profound spiritual insights and reflections on life today.

This was a decade characterised by the arrival of the drug traffickers, bringing a bloody war which struck at the lives, the souls and the values of our society. Like the military powers of the 70s, the drug traffickers were not great followers of the theatre. Indeed theatre talked neither to them nor about them, though it often spoke of values that were not to their liking. It was a war which principally affected the theatres of Bogota, Cali and Medellin.

COLOMBIA

The repression of the time was directed against the whole population and one cannot talk of a systematic persecution of the theatre community. Night life in the cities disappeared completely, because people were afraid of the bombs and street battles going on. This fear spread out to the villages and the countryside.

In Medellin a *de facto* curfew was imposed by the organisation led by Pablo Escobar. Anyone caught in the street after 7 pm was assassinated. The theatres reacted by opening earlier, so that their audiences could get home safe and unharmed. Attendance dropped dramatically and there were times when productions played to no more than 15 spectators. In spite of this, the companies continued to play daily from Tuesday to Saturday throughout the period of crisis, which went on nevertheless for more than five years.

At the peak of the crisis, the Matacadelas theatre company put on a production of *O Marinheiro (The Sailor)* by Fernando Pessoa at midnight – and against all expectation got an audience. During this period we saw productions such as *Carro sin Frenos (Car Without Brakes)* directed by Luis Carlos Medina, *La Trasescena* from La Candeleria, *Que Jartera, que Pereza, aqui no Pasa Nada* de José Manuel Freidel, *Chicos Malos (Bad Boys)* from Guila Descalza, *Prometeme que no Griar (Promise Me Not to Cry)* by Victor Viviescas, and *Mi Barrio: Historia de un Amor* by Eli Fisgun. They reflected with a deep sensitivity the true essence of the problems which were affecting us at the time and particularly their effect on the collective imagination.

There were also events such as the Colombian Festival of Theatre for Young People, the National Theatre Festival, the Touring Theatre Circuit and the Theatre Fair, which besides being points of contact and exchange were evidence of the sector's working together in solidarity.

In Cali, Bogota and the other large towns, the crisis produced similar consequences - fear and declining audiences. Against all expectations, theatre activity itself increased, both in terms of the number of productions and the number of companies. During this time more than 15 professional theatre companies were established which are still in being today. In the whole of the country, more than a hundred theatre groups are still working, at the very heart of the conflict, in spite of minuscule support from the Ministry of Culture. The war which we experience every day has spread from the countryside to the towns. Armed groups fight over the villages with the usual results of death, threats and deportations. In spite of this, theatre is still there, still presenting shows in spaces that remain open. These are shows which seek to question, denounce and reflect on the causes and terrible consequences of the fear which engulfs us today.

Most of the protagonists in the zones of conflict see the theatres as neutral territory: Colombian theatre goes beyond the political beliefs of those who are suffering to cry out for peace and tolerance and the urgent need to unite to save the nation.

For all its universality, the Colombian theatre is the result of many personal initiatives. Both the theatres and the companies are independent. Unfortunately there is no State supported theatre or theatre group. Theatre is lively, varied, independent, pursuing its own path. It includes troupes that have more than 30 years' experience, others more recently established. There is street theatre as well as performances in larger or smaller spaces, in villages and in cities. This diversity has its effect on artistic initiatives, both their style and their content, which has resulted in a great variety in the theatre scene.

In Cali, there is a festival each year, Salas en Concierto, organised by Domos Teatro. In it, the city's theatre companies show their work alongside local, national and international groups. This is the cultural community's positive response to the deep economic crisis which affects the city.

As well as its traditional Festival of Latin-American Theatre, Manizales organizes the Latin-American Youth Days, an event which brings together more than 100.000 young people in a celebration of theatre, words and music.

In Medellin, there are more than 20 theatres showing their resistance to the conflict by presenting shows from Tuesday to Sunday throughout the year, without any Government support. Neiva, on the edge of the area of FARC activities, stages every year an event, Festigipa, which brings together specialist youth theatre groups with high national and international reputations. Pasto and Popayun, two towns surrounded by the escarpments of the Andes in the South of the country, have two international festivals as well as presenting indoor and outdoor shows from time to time. On the Atlantic coast, at Santa Marta, the Caribbean International Theatre Festival has now been going for seven years. In Urab, a banana-growing region in the North-West of the country, which has been heavily affected by the conflict, the local company have specialized in works which promote good community relations and at the same time speak out against some of the more cruel features of the conflict, such as driving people from their homes. Besides their year round work with the community, they also organise the annual National Festival of Community Theatre for Young People in Urab.

As well as the theatre groups named above, there are other companies, some more effective than others, but all of them well supported by the public and all aware of their importance in building a new society. It is obvious that present conditions are a tragedy for all the population of Colombia. The war has reached proportions previously unknown, and most of the population suffers from some form of discouragement, but the theatre is still there to bring its dreams. Day by day, in the middle of war, it continues to emphasize the possibility of a peaceful life together.

Dr Luis Miguel Usuga,, *born in 1966 in Medellin, is a leading cultural activist in Colombia where he has directed seminars, festivals and other cultural activities.*

CONGO - Brazzaville (Republic)

YVON LEWA-LET MANDHA

In June 1997 a civil war began in the Republic of Congo (Brazzaville) which resulted in the overthrow of President Lissouba by his adversary Général Sassou-Nguesso, on the 15th October. In December 1998, 'ninja' militiamen close to Bernard Kolekas, former Prime Minister of the fallen Government, restarted hostilities. Whole districts of Brazzaville were emptied as the population fled from exactions of all kinds. The South of the country fell prey to barbarism as the 'cocoyes' and the 'Zulus' still faithful to Pascal Lissouba brought the war to their zones of influence. In the face of this rebellion, the army was helped by Angolan troops and the 'cobras', militiamen close to Sassou, among others. Pointe-Noir, the country's economic capital, was spared these conflicts.

An agreement to suspend hostilities was signed in December 1999, under the mediation of Gabon's President Omar Bongo. Gradually, the country returned to peace. In March/April 2001, an 'all-embracing national conference' was called, but the leaders of the exiled opposition did not attend. From January to May 2002, the referendum, presidential, legislative, local and senate elections successively took place. But they were boycotted by a section of the internal opposition which complained of irregularities in the electoral process and rigging of the results. The new constitution established a presidency with a mandate extended to seven years. Denis Sassou Nguesso was elected with a high percentage (94%). But two weeks later (April 2002) a certain 'Pasteur Ntumi', from the far-off Pool area dug up the hatchet and launched the 'ninjas' again to attack Brazzaville. Once again, the rail link between Pointe-Noire and Brazzaville was cut. However, the other areas of the danger zone in the South – the Lékoumou, the Bouenze and the Niari – remained calm, as well as Pointe-Noire and the Northern part of the country. But the fights in the Pool and the incursions of the rebels into Brazzaville have kept up a climate of psychosis in the population.

It hardly needs to be said that this unhealthy climate is not likely to support an explosion of cultural activity, or the emergence of artistic talents and companies.

The Republic of Congo has not yet found a successor to its great and universally recognized playwright Sony Labou Tansi. In the same way, no company has yet made moves on the international chess-board like his Rocado Zulu Theatre. True, in Europe and in Africa, and in particular in France, some Congolese playwrights and actors today stand out for their work. Let us mention Kaya Makhele, Georges Mboussi and Gilbert Salladin, not forgetting Chrisostome Diangouaya among the leaders in dance. It should be explained that Sony himself was a link between the playwrights of his generation and the older one, among whom we may cite Antoine Letembet Ambily, Ferdinand Mouangassa, Patrice Lhoni and Guy Menga.

Today, because of the ravages of successive civil wars, the work of the present very deserving generation is being stifled in no uncertain manner. This is the case with Frédéric Pambou, who had been invited to take up a residency in Limoges a short time before war. All the same, the undisturbed and peaceful climate of Pointe-Noire harbours several young playwrights whose plays, some of them very fine, have been performed over the years by the city's companies.

In 2000, this brought about the creation of an 'Alliance Ponténégrine des Ecrivains d'Expression Française' (APEEF), under the patronage of the Centre Culturel Français (CCF). Their 'Anthology of the New Generation of Congolese Writers' is at present in search of a publisher. Among this new generation, we may mention Jean Jules Koukou, Yvon Lewa-Let Mandha, Ngoujel 1er, Stan Bakissi and Jean-Baptiste Tati Utaliane (not to be confused with J.B. Tati Loutard).

In these three last years Congolese theatre has moved noticeably towards a form of total performance, in which speech, song, bodily expression, dance and not least music exist equally together. And this in spite of the wars in the country and the lack of adequate training in the artistic field, or of appropriate structures. Nor let us forget that the Ministry of Culture is sadly famous for being the most impoverished of Congolese Ministries; it enjoys only a laughable percentage of the State budget, which does not allow it to subsidise projects. Theatre and dance suffer dreadfully from the lack of sponsorship in Congo-Brazzaville.

For all these reasons, those individuals or groups who do succeed in emerging in our country are hailed as either 'genius' or 'miraculous'. This is the case of Ballet Tiéri (Best Newcomer Award – RFI 2001) in Brazzaville. In Pointe-Noire, some theatre companies (Bivélas, Tshi Bili Tsi Si and Africa Graffitis) and dance companies (Yaninga, Bina-Ngoua and Lionceaux) have taken part in festivals in the Democratic Republic of Congo (FIA, CARE), in Cameroun (RETIC), in Burkina Faso (FITMO) and in Angola. Equally remarkable were the creation and development of the Pointe-Noire Festival JOUTHEC (Journées Théâtrales en Campagne), initiated by the Bivélas company and the Espace Culturel Yaro (founded in 1999, at the same time as the Festival). Its first edition was purely local, but in 2000 and 2001 it saw the participation of troupes from the Democratic Republic of Congo (Marabout, Ecurie Maloba, Tam Tam), Cameroon (Feugham) and Burkina Faso (Marionnettes).

As part of the 2000 edition the ITI Congo-Brazza Centre, with its office in Pointe-Noire, was created on the 28th of December in Diosso. Chaired by Frédéric Pambou (President) and Jean Léopold Ngoulou, known as Ngoujel 1er (General Secretary), the Centre has already set up the Tchicaya de Bouampire Prize, which is awarded to plays written in local languages. The first winner of this prize was Joseph Tchiamas (February 2002). Like the theatre and dance companies of the country, the ITI centre has difficulty finding the money to finance its activities; it lacks reliable structures and tools for its work.

It must be admitted that, with a few exceptions, nearly all our theatre and dance companies are still amateur. Even those exceptions are only semi-professional. Only Pointe-Noire, Brazzaville and, to some extent, Dolisie (before the war) have a theatrical activity worthy of the name. In the other cities of the country, contemporary dance has never really existed and theatre is confined to the efforts of schools or religious bodies.

In Pointe-Noire, the civil wars have had a surprisingly positive impact. Some playwrights and even whole companies (as for example Autopsie and Saka Saka) took refuge there and created a theatre dynamic in several venues. The Centre Culturel Français, the Direction Régionale de la Culture and the Centre de Formation SUECO have contributed strongly to artistic development. Numerous national and foreign productions have been presented there, as well as workshops in writing and directing, and the exchange of experience through conferences.

Brazzaville on the other hand has an air of theatrical renaissance after the dramatic events of 1997–99. As early as July 1999, the Association Nouvel'Art, whose President is the director and actor Matondo Kubu Ture, started a series of events every last Tuesday of the month, in partnership with the Centre Culturel Français, called 'Player of the Month'. This is a day rich in cultural events: discussions, talks, performances and an exhibition devoted to a playwright and his work. Works by Sylvain Memba, Jean Baptiste Tati Loutard, Sony Labou Tansi and Emmanuel Dongala have been staged.

Season 2000–2001 ended with a theatre celebration around the play *La Parenthèse de Sang* by Sony Labou Tansi. This performance was a lively theatrical event, with the participation of actors from different troupes of the region. Nicolas Bissi was the director. In February/March 2002, *La Cérémonie*, a new work by Emmanuel Dongala, staged (again) by Nicolas Bissi and performed by Guy Stan Matingou, was a big success with the public during a tour of the Centres Culturels Français in Central Africa.

Congolese theatre troupes follow the three 'classical' forms: tragedy (Saka Saka, Bivéla, among others), comedy (Théâtre des verts Unis, Tshi Bili Tsi Si) and tragicomedy (L'Arche de Ngoujel). But a 'theatre of social intervention' or theatre for development has also appeared, whose purpose is to respond to the material everyday needs of the population. An example is a series of performances presented in 2001 by Autopsie theatre in Pointe-Noire. This company's purpose is to draw attention, among other things, to the consequences of the war, such as rapes and robberies.

Because of the lack of theatre spaces (the rare existing private theatres, and also those of the CCF, are very expensive, and apply very selective criteria) some companies have simply opted for boulevard theatre, as, for example, the Théâtre de la Coulisse (Brazzaville) or the Théâtre de la Mer (Pointe-Noire). In the same tendency, Bivélas have in 2001 started a neighbourhood theatre in Pointe-Noire, playing popular group creations.

Story theatre is growing – exemplified by Africa Graffitis (Pointe-Noire) – as is the one man show or monologue theatre, featuring a single actor (Atelier Bobatu from Brazzaville). Last, there is the 'théâtre de chez nous' or 'sketch', a hybrid genre somewhere between theatre and cinema, which is played in the two national languages (munukutuba and lingala) and, very occasionally, in French. It is performed by companies from State radio and television, but one can also see private troupes emerging, such as Ata-Ndélé from Pointe-Noire.

Yvon Lewa-Let Mandha *is a playwright and writer on theatre.*

CONGO - Kinshasa (Democratic Republic)

JEAN MARIE NGAKI

Although the Democratic Republic of Congo has still not succeeded in bringing an end to the war that has been tearing it apart since the mid 90s, and is descending ever deeper into a crisis that has become endemic, contaminating all areas of national life, its theatre – paradoxically – is in splendid condition. Even on a shoestring budget, Kinshasa has managed to host several national and international meetings, the latest of which was the ITI African Regional Bureau Meeting, held in March 2002 during the celebrations commemorating the DRC ITI's 25th Anniversary, along with a well deserved tribute to Norbert Mobyem Mikanza, Congo's greatest man of the theatre, who passed away in 1995.

Although classical French language theatre is facing stiff competition from the so called 'popular', burlesque theatre, performed in the national language and very visible on private television channels, it manages nevertheless to remain on the scene. This is mainly due to enthusiastic and inventive theatre professionals, because the theatre (one might say the arts and cultural sector in general) neither receives nor expects any funding from the public authorities, who have never considered this an essential field of activity.

The State's indifference to the theatre is self-evident in the way it treated the Congolese National Theatre and the National Arts Institute, who were both made homeless when the Martyrs' Stadium was built in the late 80s: the best theatre in the country, the Cultrana Hall, was levelled, and the National Theatre Company was forced to squat in the former 'Ciné MPR' (re-named Mongita Hall by the company, in honour of a famous colonial era artist considered to be the pioneer of Congolese theatre), whilst the National Arts Institute was squeezed into an old building that was totally inappropriate for the type of courses being taught there.

Speaking of theatre spaces, none have been built for ages; the Palais du Peuple (Peoples' Palace) is off-limits and the new venues that are accessible to the public such as the Ciaj, the Place Léo Thuris/Saint Adrien, or the Jardin Na Moto were created on the initiative of the theatre troupes themselves. Almost all, unfortunately, are outdoor performing spaces, which presents drawbacks in a country which does not have the most pleasant of climates. A theatre also opened two years ago in the French Cultural Centre in Kinshasa (the Halle de la Gombe), but unfortunately it is merely a hastily constructed podium, totally exposed to prevailing weather conditions.

However, all these venues are in business, and witnessing a blossoming of theatrical activities. Over a hundred troupes are registered with the National

CONGO

Theatre Federation in the capital, Kinshasa, alone. Amongst them, at least a dozen work in a professional and coherent fashion.

Thus, the National Theatre has produced an abundance of fine creative work, even though it has been scourged by the country's difficult economic situation: its productions include *Barabbas*, by the playwright Michel de Ghelderode, directed by Norbert Viminde Segbia, and *Procès à Makala* (*Trial at Makala*) by the Congolese writer Norbert Mobyem Mikanza, directed by Jean Pierre Mukoko Kizubanata (2001); *Les enfants de l'exil* (*Children of Exile*, an adaptation of Aeschylus' *Suppliants*), directed by Viminde, as well as *Une Saison au Congo* (*A Season in Congo*) by Aimé Césaire directed by Mukoko (2000).

The troupe Théâtre des Intrigants has produced several very good works: *Pique-nique à sens unique* (*One Way Picnic*), a devised piece directed by Otto Huber from Switzerland; *La couronne de fer blanc* (*The Tin Crown*) by Michel de Ghelderode, directed by Valentin Miteldo Mwadi; *Le Président* (*The President*) by Maxime N'Debeka (Brazzaville), directed by Switzerland's Michel Faure; *Les souliers de la Princesse* (*The Princess's Shoes*) directed by Edo Kulumbi Nsin.

The Marabout theatre company produced a number of remarkable plays in a style all its own: *Pic-nic pour picpockets* and *Koffi papa tout* by Nzey Van Musala, both directed by the author; *Tanganyka, le viol du tablernacle* (*Tanganyka, or the Desecration of the Tabernacle*), also by Nzey, directed by Daniel Simon from Belgium; *Mwin* (or *Light in the Tunnel*), presented at the Hannover Universal Expo in 2000, a collective work directed by Nzey Van Musala and Ngaki Kosi.

The Ecurie Maloba company (born over 15 years ago from the fusion of three amateur theatre troupes, Malaïka, Lokole and Baobab), has preferred to co-produce works with actors from other African countries: *Les dernières nouvelles ne sont pas bonnes* (*The News Is Not Good*) by Dave Wilson, directed by Nono Bakwa, who also directed his own piece *Arrêt cardiaque* (*Heart Attack*). The problem with this sort of project is that it is hard to bring the artists together as often as they would wish to perform and the plays rarely survive their first tours.

One may also note the creations of the Tam-Tam theatre group, including *Les marionettes*, a collective work directed by Dilandwa and Mwambayi Kalengayi and *Y a trop de nègres dans le monde* (*There Are Too Many Negroes in the World*), by Mononembwe, directed by Dilandwa, as well as those of M Majuscule and interventionist theatre troupes such as Fcedar, Canacu de Bungu Omanga – who also recently won acclaim with their medium length film *Golgotha ou l'espoir d'une vie* (*Golgotha or the Hopes of a New Life*), a movie dedicated to womens' rights – Béjart, Tiza, Ata or Palmier Theatre.

A few groups have toured in Africa and Europe, such as the Théâtre des Intrigants, who are veterans at this exercise (they have been to several African countries and Switzerland with *Le Président*), the Marabout company (who have performed in West Africa and in Central Africa, more precisely in Congo-Brazzaville, with *Tanganyka*, *Koffi Papa tout* and *Pic nic pour pic-pockets*, and in Germany with *Mwin*), the Tam-Tam theatre company (who took *Les Marionettes* on a tour of Europe and Africa), and l'Ecurie Maloba (who performed *Arrêt cardiaque* in France and on the African continent as well as visiting Masa with *Les dernières nouvelles ne sont pas bonnes*).

One will have noticed that several of these works were by Belgian authors:

the policy of the Centre Wallonie-Bruxelles in Kinshasa – which is very active – is to support almost exclusively the production of such plays. Financially strapped Congolese theatre troupes have at least this means of recovering their financial footing.

In this overview of Congolese theatre, one should not forget to mention the theatre festivals that have been multiplying in Kinshasa, to the point where it has been said that 'Kinshasa is a land of festivals'.

The International Actor's Festival is held every two years, and in 2000 and in 2001 (special edition) the event gathered together troupes and artists from Congo-Brazzaville, Cameroon, the Ivory Coast, Burkina Faso and France. In the framework this festival there is also a regular workshop for stage managers.

The so-called Caré (Carrefour Artistique d'Echanges) or International Festival of Theatre in the City is an annual event that takes professional theatre to working class neighbourhoods of Central Africa (after eight editions it has become a travelling festival). During its 2000, 2001 and 2002 editions, groups from Congo (Pointe Noire and Brazzaville) Libreville (Gabon) and France participated in the Festival.

The Congolese Theatre Days for Childhood and Youth (Joucotej) which is an annual event, is open to professional troupes but is mostly for school groups. Its audiences are almost entirely composed of students.

The Congolese Theatre Meetings that have been hosted for the past two years by the National Theatre Federation have had the advantage of bringing to Kinshasa in that time groups from certain provinces of DR Congo (Bas-Congo, Bandundu, Equateur, Kasaï). Since the beginning of the 90s, provincial theatres had been living in relative isolation.

Apart from these, there is space to mention the Drame Scolaire Francophone (Dramscof), the Rural Theatre Festival (Fether) and the Meeting of Storytellers and Griots (RCG). This last festival has recently led to the development of a style in monodramas, a trend that is unquestionably led in Congo by Floribert Tawite Vusayiro, who was remarkable in his performance of *L'enfant-sorcier* (*The Witch-Child*). Like many of his colleagues, Tawite trained as an actor at the National Arts Institute in Kinshasa (INA), where he also teaches in the Arts and Humanities department.

Let us dwell for a moment on the INA. This teaching institution first opened in 1967 as a Music and Drama Conservatoire, and became the National Arts Institute in 1971, as a result of a general reform of the higher education system which integrated the INA into the National University. Currently the INA, which is directed by Professor Félix-Blaise Malutama Dima Ngo, who has a doctorate in Theatre Studies from the University of Louvain (Belgium), has 500 students divided into three different sections (Drama, Music, Cultural Animation). A great number of students have graduated from the Drama Department and most of the 'stars' of Congolese theatre today are graduates of this arts institute, which has acquired a regional reputation. All the main players of the Théâtre des Intrigants, the Marabout Théâtre company, the Tam-Tam or M Majuscule are INA alumni. Some former students have even appeared in popular theatre, which is a sure sign of the INA's influence. There exists a project supported by UNESCO to create regional centres of the INA, which should have been implemented years ago.

CONGO

In speaking of this tormented area of the African continent, one cannot avoid pinpointing the hardships the war has inflicted on our theatre: in the eastern part of DRC, members of the theatre community were hunted down because they were considered to represent the local conscience, or accused of helping NGOs, or were the standard-bearers of civil society in the struggle against the oppressor. Theatre halls were sullied by the blood of massacres, if they were not simply destroyed.

These past years have witnessed the passing of a few great figures of Congolese theatre: Mupey Katanga (actor and director of the Théâtre des Intrigants), who died in November 2001, Nono Bakwa (director of the Ecurie Maloba), who died in May 2002, and, before them, Kikanda Nzundu (a remarkable actor who had a memorable career with the DRC National Theatre), as well as Luzala Angèle Ntete (the first female Congolese theatre director), whose life ended suddenly in her forties.

To conclude, the theatre in DRC has managed to obtain some satisfying results, thanks to 'article 15' (getting by), as the saying goes here. It's time for the theatre community to lend a hand to bring it completely out of its isolation.

Jean Marie Ngaki Kosi Basak', actor and director; teacher of stage directing and theatre criticism at the INA; playwright; General Secretary of ITI for the Democratic Republic of Congo.

COSTA RICA

MARCO GUILLEN and FERNANDO VINOCOUR

The theatrical activity of Costa Rica is largely concentrated in the capital of San José, a city of about a million inhabitants, with about 20 theatrical spaces. Our theatre can be seen to reflect the different polarizing tendencies that arose from the transformation of the country's cultural and political institutions during the 80s. In the 70s, important developments had included the foundation of the National Theatre Company, two College Theatre Schools and the National Theatre Workshop (an introductory acting institute), along with the appearance of independent groups and the immigration of actors and directors from South America. For the Costa Rican theatre, it appeared to be the beginning of a long-awaited move towards professionalism. The second half of the 80s was a period in which a more individualistic and commercial model began to prevail, finally taking over in the 90s. Nevertheless, a few groups and individuals kept investigating new ideas with broader perspectives in the artistic, technical and ideological sense. They kept up the search for different stage languages with higher artistic demands.

Reviewing the theatre offerings of the last two years (2000–2001), we find a clear predominance of what we can refer to as the commercial theatre. Its shows are based on sexual innuendo and comic situations, and a type of urban folklore very acceptable to the taste and preferences of a mass audience. In this type of show, any artistic, technical or ideological concerns are neglected or very simplistic. The groups work as a producing entity, and their director-producer-managers generally create their own shows with a cast of amateurs. These actors are trained within the group, or at best by institutions with a very limited curriculum.

In this tendency – and with little difference between them – we find groups like Teatro Chaplin, Teatro del Angel, Teatro Arlequín, Teatro Moliere, Teatro La Máscara, and Teatro La Comedia. The titles of their shows are self-explanatory: *Viagra I and II, Give My Husband Some Viagra, Don't Give My Husband Any More Viagra, 90210 Colonia Kennedy, Eight People Trapped in an Elevator, Chingos o nada* (a version of the movie *The Full Monty,* which stayed on the stage for the longest run of the last two years). In recent years, Costa Rica has seen the arrival of TV productions that share many similar characteristics with the commercial theatre. The actors and crew of these shows move back and forth between the commercial (and sometimes official) theatre and TV. They reflect a very narrow profile of reality and of our identity.

On the other hand we have the work of the official institutions. Leading them is the Compañía Nacional de Teatro (CNT), which celebrated its 30th anniversary in 2001. The CNT has become a producing institution, staging three shows every year, having abandoned the promotional and educational activity performed in the past. In the last two years its shows have been high budget productions with a considerable number of actors. These productions did not show any significant innovation and were generally felt to be an artistic setback for the institution. Each production does an average of 30 performances in one of CNT's two playhouses in San José. They hire freelance actors and directors, since they do not have a permanent ensemble. The other theatre is rented out to individuals and groups, but with many economic and artistic restrictions which act as serious obstacles to rental.

Some of CNT's own plays in 2000–2001 were: *Richard III* by Shakespeare, *How I Learned to Drive* by Paula Vogel, *Les Femmes Savantes* by Molière (also presented at the Bogotá Theatre Festival in 2002), *Le Dindon* by Feydeau and *La Ronde (Reigen)* by Schnitzler. Despite the classical and contemporary importance of these titles, the shows lacked a coherent theatrical intention, resulting in very irregular work – artificial productions with very doubtful levels of professionalism. The CNT produced *Cuatro caballetes* by E Griffero as part of a programme to promote new directors. The production used clichés that made a very complex play even more obscure, although it had some successful performances in Uruguay in the year 2001.

As part of the Festival de Verano, sponsored by the Ministry of Culture, the CNT presented *Las fisgonas de Paso Ancho* by the Costa Rican playwright Samuel Rovinsky. They updated the play, which was based on an urban event of the 70s. Their stereotypical results only served to reveal the very basic problems and deficiencies of the text. The show was presented in the Festival Iberoamericano de Teatro in Cádiz, in Spain, the only Costa Rican presentation in a year dedicated to Central American Theatre. As could be expected, the show was received with disbelief and amazement. The critics had no hesitation in pointing out what we have mentioned. However, this work received the award for Best Director in 2001.

Another official initiative is the theatre supported by the state universities, although they work with very limited budgets. The Teatro Universitario of the Universidad de Costa Rica celebrated its 50 years in the year 2000. For this occasion they co-produced with CNT *Las bicicletas son para el verano* by the Spanish playwright Fernando Fernán Gómez, inviting the renowned Uruguayan director Júver Salcedo to direct it. In the same year, they presented *Entre Pancho Villa y una mujer desnuda* by the Mexican author Sabina Berman. This feminist play questions machismo in the context of the Mexican revolution. The production travelled to Belgium, Guatemala and Peru. The TU also presented a new stage production of *Punto de referencia,* written and directed by Daniel Gallegos, probably the most outstanding national playwright and one of his most intimate and complex plays. The show was also presented in Colombia and Venezuela. *Ecos de ceniza* was other of the TU's shows. Written by first timer Klaus Steinmetz, it deals with a contemporary criminal event and reflects on the justice system. Although the play's significant deficiencies meant that it gave only a limited perspective on the problem, it was judged Best Play of 2000.

The Fine Arts College of the UCR sponsored an interesting interdisciplinary show, *Detrás de la mascara*, created and co-directed by Leonardo Torres and Grettel Méndez. In the last few years the UCR's School of Theatre has

From the NET (Nucleo de Experimentación Teatral) production of *Pluma y la Tempestad* in San José

played an important role in the International Organization of University Theatre and of the Ibero-American Higher Education Theatre Schools (AIEST). They attended their international meetings and festivals in Belgium and Peru. During the second week of May 2002, the UCR hosted the latest meeting of the AIEST.

Teatro Estudio, recently created under the support of the School of Theatre at the Universidad Nacional (UNA), staged an adaptation of *Maria* by Jorge Isaacs, performed by students of the school. In 2001 they presented *Album de Familia*, adapted and directed by David Korish and Roxana Ávila from the play by Brazilian playwright Nelson Rodrigues.

The UCR has a number of student groups, like Teatro del Sol, completely sponsored by the students of the School of Theatre. They have a preference for light productions, sometimes close to those of the commercial theatre. Teatro Girasol of the Humanities Department is a group made up of students from different disciplines that works with a community and college bias. The Theatre project at the San Ramón branch of the UCR organised a regional theatre festival named *Por la vida*, honouring the fight against AIDS, with the participation of community and student groups from Central American countries. During it they offered workshops, performances and other presentations.

The Sala Vargas Calvo is a small playhouse sponsored by the Teatro Nacional, a symbol of the official culture of Costa Rica, which stages more intimate, small-cast plays for a limited audience. In 2000 they put on *El asilo* by the local author Guillermo Arriaga, performed by two veteran actresses, Gladys Catania and Eugenia Chaverri, who shared the year's Best Actress award. Another of their shows, *La estación del sueño*, consisting of three short plays by Melvin Méndez, received the awards for Best Play, Best Director and Best Supporting Actor for the same year.

The Teatro Popular Melico Salazar, another official institution, sponsored the Primer Festival de Monólogos, a contest dedicated to 20 minute monologues. The only prize was awarded to *El Nica*, a play dealing with Nicaraguan immigration, created and performed by César Meléndez.

The 7th Festival International de las Artes brings artistic expressions and creators from around the world to San José every two years. In 2000 we welcomed the Spanish group La Fura dels Baus, with their excellent show based on Federico García Lorca's life and works. Another notable show was *The Tempest*, a version of Shakespeare's play presented by the Argentine group Cuatro Vientos. In the same event, José Sanchís Sinisterra offered playwrights' workshops for local authors. The festival's many activities suffered overall from a lack of spaces and opportunities for discussion and critical reaction.

An alternative to the official and commercial theatre scene is the work of independent groups and creators. In the case of Costa Rica, it is difficult to refer to theatre groups in the sense of collectives in which the participants are engaged in a continuous search for a stage language. What we actually have are groups that spring up around one or two people who work with other individuals on specific projects. That does not mean an absence of theatrical rigour in their productions, whose standards are often very close to those of the collective works. The groups pursue different forms of research and generate projects of a high artistic level. They are self-supporting, hence constantly struggling to find resources, rent spaces, and promote their shows. It is important to mention the support given to the independent theatre by the non-governmental organizations (NGOs) and foreign embassies and cultural institutes, like Spain's Insitituto de Cooperación Iberoamericano. Among the independent groups we may mention Quetzal, Brecha, Giratablas, Abya Yala, Contraluz, NET (Núcleo de Experimentación Teatral), Teatro de La Rosa, Skené and Surco.

Quetzal develops one-man shows with resources of fragmentation and multiple characters in a minimalist approach. Their work is based on the performance of actor Rubén Pagura. During 2001, Quetzal presented an adaptation of *El cruce sobre el Niágara* by Alonso Alegría. The group has reached high artistic levels and often works abroad, in countries like Spain, Argentina and elsewhere. In 1999, Argentina recognized them with the award for Best Foreign Performance.

Abya Yala produce their own devised work or free adaptations of texts in a search for their own stage language and high artistic levels. Their most recent creation was *Sade*, based on several different sources. It was a very provocative show, not only in its artistic characteristics and level of professionalism but also in its confrontational statements. Abya Yala travelled through Central America in the summer of 2000, visiting different communities and sharing workshops and performances which recognised the local cultural traditions. In 2001, Abya Yala sponsored a conference led by Belgian director Tone Brulin, with whom they are preparing their next show.

The NET (Nucleo de Experimentación Teatral) is another provocative company doing important work. In recent years they have presented *Caleidoscopio*, a show based on texts by the Catalan Sergi Belbel, and *Pluma y la tempestad*. They present a significant number of shows outside the traditional theatrical spaces of San José. They are searching for new artistic languages to express a concern with our more immediate reality. The NET won the award for Best Group in 2000. As part of the opening of *Pluma* in San José, the company organized a debate with the participation of its author, the Argentine-Ecuadorian Arístides Vargas.

These three are the most interesting independent groups, not only because of their organizational system but also because of their artistic work. They maintain a permanent concern with the training, experimentation and development of artistic alternatives, looking for innovative stage language through contemporary authors and themes. They are also concerned with reaching new audiences and the projection of theatrical experience beyond performance.

The other independent groups are more or less limited to the sporadic production of shows. They are:

Contraluz, who recently presented *The Government Inspector* by Gogol. They also do some work in children's theatre.

Brecha have presented *Cuatro historias locas*, a collage of four short dramatic exercises.

Surco has its own theatre, where they presented *Luminaria, la última rumbera del caribe* by Emilio Carballido. They also staged the monologue *Baby boom en el paraíso* and *Hombres en escabeche*, both by the local poet, actress and playwright Ana Istarú. These plays are among the most important written in Costa Rica in recent years; both received awards in Spain during the 90s.

Teatro de La Rosa, which works from a feminist perspective, opened its own house and presented *La hora fuerte del sexo débil* by its director Claudia Barrionuevo. (At this point we should also mention the Costa Rican version of *The Vagina Monologues* by Eve Ensler, presented in our country by Producciones Gallito Pinto with the participation of three well known actresses.)

Ubú co-produced, with Teatro Universitario and the Fine Arts College at UCR, *Es una niña, ¿o no?*, a translation of *Baby with the Bathwater* by Christopher Durang.

Skené presented *Prometheus Bound* by Aeschylus and *Salomé* by Oscar Wilde.

Giratablas work under the sponsorship of an ONG (non governmental organization). They have their own building, dedicated mostly to workshops and classes for young people, with shows performed by the students.

Teatro Baco, although they describe themselves as a dance-theatre group, are more related to the promotion of literature, with very sporadic stage work.

Children's theatre in Costa Rica has been traditionally underestimated despite its broad potential public. There is an important but limited activity in this area, by groups like Contraluz, Giratablas, Ticotíteres, and Cucaramaca. Amateur theatre receives very little attention on the part of official institutions, but there is an important tradition of community theatre with several groups around the country, among them Grupo Vías in Puntarenas, Amubis y Santa Rosa de Lima in Cartago, and Antorcha in Alajuela. Some communities organize amateur festivals and performances at a national level.

Concerning playwriting, besides the plays mentioned above we should mention *PabloJosé*, by actress and playwright Roxana Campos, winner of the Premio Editorial Costa Rica 2001. The text is now in the process of being published and has not yet been staged, but no doubt marks a significant development in our national drama.

The state of criticism is another symptomatic aspect of our theatre; not only in the sense of the professional practice of the critics, but also in the lack of general opportunities for exchange, reflection and discussion. *Escena*, the only publication in the past completely dedicated to the theatre, nowadays comes out only twice a year, with very few theatre articles. Formal criticism is offered only in a single newspaper, by a couple of people who limit their comments to the level of basic information, or generalisations which go no further than the expression of simplistic likes and dislikes, often showing total disregard for basic aspects of the stage and theatre, with at the same time little sympathy for any non-conventional offering.

In this review of theatrical activity in Costa Rica during the years 2001–2002, we can see a steadily growing split into different interest groups, reinforcing their chosen positions in isolation. As this splitting process proceeds, different artistic options are significantly reduced, despite the growing number of possibilities for production and creation. Our pressing problems are the absence of opportunities for feedback and the exchange of ideas; the lack of initiatives to strengthen the educational venues; the significant absence of experimentation and research that might renew artistic levels and do away with traditional, tired stage concepts; and the strong resistance of most theatre sectors to developing professional standards. These are urgent problems, seen against the narrow range of possibilities for any qualitative development.

Any theatre with more artistic concerns and aspirations demands more ways for experimentation, confrontation, reflection and research. We need more and better spaces for educational and continuing training activities, and opportunities to promote national and international exchange. We urgently need to establish conditions for a real professionalization of our theatrical craft and practice. The theatre schools need to develop a strict system of higher levels of education, training and professional practice around the different modes of theatrical expression, not only in technical and artistic but also in ethical aspects. Other sectors, like those of the critics and the media, should also participate in such a process. On the other hand, we should be seeking a similar transformation and improvement of standards in the commercial theatre of entertainment. In every sector, there is an urgent need for the revision and restructuring of our national theatre practice.

Fernando Vinocour: *Actor, Director and University Professor. Since 1992 director of NET ((Núcleo de Experimentación Teatral), an experimental theatre group which he founded.* **Marco Guillen**: *Actor and University Professor. He has graduate studies in the USA specialising in Acting, General Theatre and Latin American Drama. Both are active members of ITI-Costa Rica.*

CROATIA

HRVOJE IVANKOVIC

The important political changes that occurred in Croatia after the elections in January 2000 were unfortunately not followed by more radical breakthroughs in the area of cultural politics. For Croatian theatre this primarily means that its organisational structure was left intact, although its foundations were established back in the socialist era. Moreover, the changes in the financing of theatrical activities did not significantly help or encourage the activity of independent theatres and companies. Croatian theatre thus remained an environment characterised by routine and lack of invention. During the last two years considerable chaos continued to rule in the repertoire of most institutional theatres and only a few productions managed to rise above the mediocre. Still, it is a consolation that attendances did not diminish. Two million people saw the performances in some thirty Croatian professional theatres (including children's and puppet theatres) in 2001 and 2002.

The most performed playwright in the last two years was Miroslav Krleza, the bard of Croatian literature. The twentieth anniversary of Krleza's death was commemorated at the end of the year 2001. On this occasion, the trunks containing his legacy were opened and that provoked an even greater interest in this writer. Krleza's drama, prose and essays have once again proved a unique theatrical challenge. Eight Croatian theatres and companies staged new productions of ten of his works, trying to interpret him from the point of view of contemporary theatrical expression, but also from the standpoint of the recent socio-political events. In doing this, they reaffirmed the openness of Krleza's dramaturgical and literary concepts and the repugnance they express towards any attempt at reducing theatrical expression to only one ethical or political dimension. By far the most spectacular and multi-layered of these performances proved to be *The Great Master of All Scoundrels (Veliki meštar sviju hulja)* based on a short story by Krleza and staged in the Zagreb Youth Theatre (Zagrebacko kazalište mladih – ZKM) by the eternal *enfant terrible* of the Croatian theatre, Branko Brezovec. Staging an early Krleza play, *Adam and Eve (Adam i Eva)*, for the Kufer company, the young director Franka Perkovic inaugurated a new theatrical space of intriguing ambience in the former Zagreb factory Jedinstvo.

With the exception of Krleza, the classics of Croatian drama of the past century were much less represented in Croatian theatres in the years 2000 and 2001 than those of their foreign contemporaries. Among others, works by Genet, Tennessee Williams, Beckett, Feydeau, Ibsen, Pirandello, Schnitzler, Strindberg and Anski were performed. Were it not, however, for the daring new production of the cult Pirandello play *Six Characters in Search of an Author* in the Croatian National Theatre in Split (HNK Split) by the French director François-Michel Pesenti, this segment of Croatian theatrical offerings in the last two years would be described as unoriginal, plain and average.

Productions of plays from the corpus of older European dramatic literature, which

ABOVE: Michel de Ghelderode's *Christopher Columbus*, directed by Georgij Paro, Dubrovnik Summer Festival 2001

BELOW: Filip Sovagovic, *Birds*, 2000, Croatian National Theatre in Split

traditionally make up at least a quarter of the repertoire of Croatian institutional theatres and summer festivals, received a pretty lukewarm reception. During the years 2000 and 2001 works by Shakespeare, Goethe, Gogol, Molière, Goldoni, Calderon, Sophocles, Rostand, Büchner, Euripides, Marivaux and Seneca were staged, often by foreign directors (such as Krzysztof Warlikowski and Janusz Kica from Poland, Tomi Janezic and Eduard Miler from Slovenia and Steven Kent from the USA) but on the whole none of these gave spectacular results. Our own drama heritage has practically vanished from the repertoire, with the exception of some performances in Dubrovnik and Varazdin. This phenomenon merits an analysis from the socio-political and theatrical points of view.

Stagings of contemporary Croatian writers were, on the other hand, rather frequent. Still, the unwritten rule still prevails that new works by domestic playwrights are generally staged as special previews. There is no chance for a different interpretation or – in the case of an unsuccessful premiere – an improvement, not even for the most valuable works. In the last two years, Filip Šovagovic established himself as an interesting dramatist. His plays *Little Birds (Pticice)* and *Festivals (Festivali)* were performed, with greater and lesser success respectively, at the Split Summer (Splitsko ljeto) in productions of the Croatian National Theatre in Split directed by Paolo Magelli. Yet another actor/writer, Elvis Bošnjak, must be mentioned as a true discovery of the theatre in Split. In 2001 he made a successful debut with his prison morality play *Father (Otac)* directed by Nenni Delmestre.

The fact that Ivan Vidic was the only one of the generation of writers who distinguished the late 80s and 90s to see his work produced, with the premiere of *The Great Tilda (Velika Tilda)* in the Ivan pl. Zajc Croatian National Theatre in Rijeka, testifies to the lack of communication between writers and managements in Croatian theatres. The new playwrights, the first of the generation whose plays will mark the Croatian theatre in the first decade of the 21st century, should also have their say regarding this situation. The most interesting among them so far are definitely Ivana Sajko (her play *An Orange in the Clouds (Naranca u oblacima)* had its first performance in the ZKM, and the collection of her plays entitled *Executed Characters (Smaknuta lica)* was published), Tomislav Zajec (The ITD Theatre (Teatar ITD) staged his play *The Assassins (Atentatori)* and the ZKM his grotesque *John Smith – Princess of Wales (John Smith – princeza od Walesa),* and Tena Štivicic (duodrama: *You Can't Run Away from Sunday (Nemreš pobjec od nedjelje)* in the ZKM and *Percival (Parsifal),* a play for the young in the Small Stage (Mala scena).

The fact that Croatian theatres, however unwillingly, follow world trends can be seen already from a cursory look at their repertoires. The years 2000 and 2001 saw the stagings of foreign mainstream writers like C P Taylor, James Goldman, Ronald Harwood, Paula Vogel, Juan Mayorge, Stephen Greenhorn, Neil Simon and David Hare (the dominance of Anglo-Saxon drama is conspicuous). On the other hand, Croatian theatres have not yet had the boldness to stage a drama by Sarah Kane, Marius von Mayenburg, Mark Ravenhill, Jon Fosse, Nikolaj Koljada or Enda Walsh, thus remaining conspicuously insensitive to the appearance of the so-called 'new European drama'. The greatest examples of boldness, stretched to the limit, in the years 2000 and 2001 were stagings of the works of David Ives, Dejan Dukovski, Gert Jonke, Mike Cullen, Marie Irene Fornes and Bernard-Marie Koltès. This undoubtedly points to the isolation of the Croatian institutional theatre.

The example of the Croatian National Theatre in Split, one of the four national theatres with drama, opera and ballet companies, demonstrated how difficult it could be to change the long-established ways of functioning in institutional theatres. Manager Mani Gotovac and drama director Ivica Buljan have been trying, over the past four years, to convert the theatre to an 'open system of cultural production'. Their endeavours have encountered numerous obstacles, and the theatre was often at the centre of public disputes and scandals (attentively followed by the local media) that partly prevented the envisaged 'transition'. Nevertheless, the Croatian National Theatre in Split merits a special place on the Croatian theatre map for its imaginative repertoire and the attention it devotes to domestic playwrights. The Ivan pl. Zajc Croatian National Theatre in Rijeka also showed an imaginative approach to the repertoire during the last two years. Its new drama director, Zlatko Sviben, 'opened' two interesting repertoire cycles: 'The European Millennium: Drama Epitome of the Epochs' ('Milenij Europe: dramski rezime epoha') and 'The Century of a City' ('Stoljece grada'). A shift towards new repertoire challenges finally started in the ZKM too. Slobodan Šnajder, a writer and until recently a dissident, became its manager at the beginning of 2001. This was the most significant personnel change in the Croatian theatre during the past two years. Although Šnajder's ambitious repertoire plans (directed towards the investigation of the pressure points of recent Croatian history) started to be realised only in the 2001/2002 season, the performance of *The Great Master of All Scoundrels* at the beginning of his term of office proved to be one of the most important Croatian plays of the last two years. In another successful production, inspired by the life and work of St Francis of Assisi, actor and director Rene Medvešek, with the great help of the ZKM ensemble, created the performance entitled *Brother Ass (Brat magarac)*, a witty, animated and above all, poetic stage fantasy about love, religion and the joy of life. Medvešek thus proved himself one of the most creative and original phenomena in the contemporary Croatian theatre.

The non-institutional theatres have vegetated over the last two years, managing to attract audiences only by an occasional performance. This is especially true of the Croatian Culture Hall Theatre in Rijeka (HKD teatar) that organises the International Festival of Small Stages (Meðunarodni festival malih scena). The exceptions are the only two non-institutional repertory theatres, both located in Zagreb: the Exit Theatre (Teatar Exit) that significantly marked Croatian theatre in the nineties, and the Small Stage, one of the best-organised and most vital of Croatian theatres. During the year 2001 the Small Stage moved towards the adult repertoire after seven years of exclusive devotion to children's and youth theatre, staging mostly contemporary international hits (*The Beauty Queen of Leenane* by Martin McDonagh and *Enigmatic Variations* by Erich Emmanuel Schmitt). Something completely opposite happened at the Exit Theatre, which after numerous financial problems started to stage children's and youth performances, and produced a very successful dramatisation of *Adrian Mole*; but its lead performances (during 2000 and 2001 *East* by Steven Berkoff and *Peaches* by Nick Grosso) slowly began to fall into routine patterns.

A number of different theatrical festivals should be mentioned as a special feature of the Croatian scene. The best known music and theatre festival, the Dubrovnik Summer Festival (Dubrovacke ljetne igre), faced in the past two years the most serious

CROATIA

management crisis of its fifty-year history. This, however, did not prevent a certain shift in its repertoire, up to now generally oriented towards atmospheric stagings of the classic works of Croatian and European drama. The summer of 2000 saw productions of *Uncle Maroje (Dundo Maroje)* by Marin Drzic and Pirandello's *Henry IV* on the medieval fortress of Lovrijenac, and the summer of 2001 was marked by de Ghelderode's *Christopher Columbus* directed by Georgij Paro (who staged it at the Porporela breakwater) and *The Fourth Sister* by Janusz Glowacki, directed by Ivica Boban, in one of the best performances of the season in Croatia, in the once elite Dubrovnik Belvedere hotel, now devastated by the war.

The Split Summer (Splitsko ljeto), the other big summer festival, was seen as a continuation of the season and repertoire ideas of its organiser – the Croatian National Theatre in Split. Two smaller Adriatic summer festivals brought some spark with their programmes: the Golden Lion Studio Theatre Festival (Festival komornog teatra Zlatni lav) in Umag (which mainly hosted performances of Slovene and Croatian theatres) and the dynamic International Youth Theatrical Festival (Međunarodni kazališni festival mladih) in Pula, characterised by a great number of interesting theatrical workshops. In the summer of 2001 the Istrian island of Mali Brijun hosted a performance surrounded by media attention unprecedented in Croatia in the last ten years – the old-fashioned and not entirely successful environmentally staged performance of Shakespeare's *King Lear* in the production of the Ulysses Theatre (Teatar Ulysses) and directed by Lenka Udovicki. It was marked by the return of Rade Šerbedzija, one of the greatest Croatian actors, after a long period of absence.

In addition to the summer festivals, during the years 2000 and 2001 several regular spring and autumn festivals were also held: The Marulic Days – Festival of Croatian Drama (Festival hrvatske drame Marulicevi dani) in Split, The Days of Satire (Dani satire) in Zagreb, Actor's Festival (Festival glumca) in Vinkovci, PIF – International Puppet Theatre Festival (PIF – međunarodni festival lutaka) in Zagreb, and many others. The International Festival of Small Stages in Rijeka as well as Eurokaz and Contemporary Dance Week (Tjedan suvremenog plesa) in Zagreb drew the greatest attention. These are traditionally the most important places for Croatian theatrical audiences to make contact with contemporary international theatrical events.

Regarding the presence of Croatian theatres in the world in the past two years, the best reception was for the performance of Bobo Jelcic's and Nataša Rajkovic's *An Uncertain Story (Nesigurna prica)* in a production of the ITD Theatre. After success at the Wiener Festwochen in 2000 it toured to several European cities. There were a number of other performances by Croatian theatres abroad, including the regular tours (Croatian National Theatre in Split, Gavella Drama Theatre (Dramsko kazalište Gavella) and ZKM) to major South American festivals. Finally, at the end of this panoramic survey it should be mentioned that during the years 2000 and 2001 several Croatian playwrights (Filip Šovagovic, Miro Gavran, Slobodan Šnajder, Darko Lukic) had premieres of their dramas in theatres abroad.

Hrvoje Ivankovic, *born in Dubrovnik in 1965, is a theatre critic for the Zagreb daily newspaper* Jutarnji list, *and an editor and dramaturg in the Drama Programme of the Croatian Radio.*

CUBA

VIVIAN MARTÍNEZ TABARES

For Cuban theatre, the 90s represented a period of fruitful ethical introspection, which could be seen in the general choice of themes and theoretical approaches. This was due in large part to the gradual emergence of an increasingly influential generation of graduates from the Instituto Superior de Arte (National Art Institute), who combined rigorous academic background with a demanding approach to the practice of their art, reflecting the times whilst respecting the traditions of their predecessors. In the triennial period under review (1999–2002), the Cuban stage has been showing signs of a paradigm shift, which has made it harder at times to identify its new purposes.

Today's theatre still highlights the missed opportunity for encounter between our playwrights and the celebrated directors who dominated the glorious period of the 'maestros' – Vicente Revuelta, Berta Martínez and Roberto Blanco – an era that forced remarkable playwrights such as Abelardo Estorino and Eugenio Hernández Espinosa to direct their own work. Literature and dramatic texts have followed parallel paths, to the former's detriment, because it cannot make its mark and is at this time in something of an impasse. What mostly predominate now are adaptations of classical texts, with the exception of Virgilio Piñera – neglected and forgotten during his lifetime – whose work is frequently staged by directors and choreographers.

The 1999–2002 period opened with a certain polarity, between an experimental form of theatre and one more involved with the portrayal of social reality, less preoccupied with artistic considerations. This dichotomy has been toned down, as new developments have appeared, and positions have shifted.

Today, the existence of almost 130 state funded groups (a high number, given the country's population of 11 million, its economic limitations and the lack of physical performance spaces) denotes the significant role society gives to culture, but also betrays – despite the far from negligible number of productions – an absence of discipline and an unimpressive level of quality in performances that do not fully develop existing potential, and confuse audiences and critics alike.

Although in other periods it showed greater stability and coherence as a movement or system, today's theatre is defined by a coexistence of groups, companies and potential projects. Higher cast turnover rates, reflecting the search for a better future elsewhere, or better pay in more recognised media such as film or television, have affected the inner structure of these collaborative enterprises, and converted them into disparate groups that are not always well organised amongst themselves and must learn – as some already have – to travel along new paths.

Thus, while on the one hand a few groups and people from different milieux try the options associated with commercial theatre (although this does

CUBA

not apply to the wages) – casting recognised television stars, intensively exploiting shows that cater to the public's tastes, or pursuing themes inspired by current events or laced with eroticism – a few small groups persist meanwhile in maintaining troupe ethics and dedicating themselves to the ideal of combining entertainment with experiment.

Amongst this latter group, three productions in 1999 proved to be effective examples of experimental approaches offering a lively exchange between text and context.

El alma buena de Se-Chuán (*The Good Person of Setzuan*), directed by Carlos Celdrán, takes the first of Brecht's plays to be performed in Cuba (in 1959) and re-interprets it in a contemporary context, in the light of the contradictions of a Cuban society that is immersed in material and economic difficulties which affect the individual conscience. This extremely creative performance, admirable in its scenography and spatial composition, attacks the reappearance of social distinctions within the socialist context, sounds a warning about the risks linked to the inevitable boom in the tourist industry, and is an ode to what is finest in the human spirit. (Celdrán's next production, *La vida es sueño* premiered in 2000 to commemorate Calderón de la Barca's 100th anniversary, also reflected something of prevailing Cuban conditions, through its set design and above all through the viewpoint represented by the main character, played by Alexis Díaz de Villegas. Strindberg's *La señorita Julia* followed, but this production focused more closely on the psychological aspect of the story and was much less referential to the surrounding context.)

Los Siervos (*The Slaves*), a complex work by Virigilio Piñera produced by the Teatro de la Luna under Raúl Martín's effective and subtle direction, avoids exploiting what would be today an easy propaganda opportunity (the play was published in 1953 to criticise Soviet socialist practices of the time, but never performed), to focus on portraying the essence of behaviour from a profoundly human and traditionally artistic viewpoint, integrating multiple expressive forms of language. *Los Siervos*, as well as *El Flaco y el Gordo* (*The Thin One and the Fat One*), *Electra Garrigó*, *La Boda* (*The Wedding*), and *El álbum* represent various stages of the group's work with the legacy of Piñera, who is considered the father of Cuban playwriting.

De Donde son los Cantantes (*Where the Singers are From*), presented by El Ciervo Encantado, directed by Nelda Castillo, is the result of coherent and systematic research on key aspects of Cuban culture in the collective memory, brought to the stage by the actors. The challenge of adapting for the stage a novel by Severo Sarduy, one of the most remarkable authors of the diaspora, is successfully met, with an expressive use of masks.

In a different vein, Carlos Pérez Peña, actor and director of the Teatro del Escambray, in his one man show *Como caña al viento* (*Like Sugar Cane in the Wind*), combines characters, poems, Cuban and Latin American songs to re-create his artistic history (to a certain extent the story of his group, somewhat isolated in the hills of the island's central region, well out of the mainstream), in a harmonious blend of talent, passion, technique and sincere emotion.

In 2000, the arrival of a new artistic director, the actress Antonia Fernández, gave a fresh impulse and fostered greater risk-taking within the theatre

ABOVE: *left,*. Zulema Clares and Ezequiel Verde in Carlos Celdrán's production of *the Good Person of Setzuan; right,* Ariel González and Roberto Gacio in *Los siervos (The Slaves)* by Virgilio Piñera
(*photo*: José Murrieta) (Yan Su)

BELOW: *Chorus perpetuus*, by Marianela Boán for DanzAbierta   (*photo*: Alejandro Aguilar)

CUBA

company Teatro Buendía (which had been directed from the mid 80s by Flora Lauten as a permanent workshop for actors), with her production *Historia de un caba-yo*. The title of Mark Rozovsky's Tolstoy adaptation is modified by replacing the noun 'caballo' (horse) by caba-yo, to emphasise, with the use of the personal pronoun yo (I/me), the involvement of all the participants in the performance. The Buendía performance recalls Vicente Revuelta's 1985 production, reflecting its groundbreaking nature, and using the youth of the cast members to reflect on our negative view of old age and differences. The actors move as if in a herd, using movements inspired by sports, rap or rock, with an energy that reaches out and resonates with their young and teenage audience. With its collective viewpoint, *Historia de un caba-yo* also revives the political sense of the play's discourse, while appealing to fundamental feelings which in turn spark an emotional response.

That same year, in Matanzas, the renowned marionette artist René Fernández and the Teatro Papalote performed an adapted version of Andersen's *Ugly Duckling*, entitled *Feo* (ugly), to defend, again with animal characters – and in this case, with puppets – the right to be different, to go beyond appearances in search of real values, to extol the value of freedom. Matanzas province, two hours away from the capital, is home to The Teatro Papalote and its offshoot, the Teatro de los Elementos, who have done remarkable work in marionette theatre. Every two years the former organises an international Puppet Theatre Workshop, which in 2002 will be entering its 5th edition.

Memory, exile, separation from one's family, are recurring themes. These, along with solitude, appear in *El Baile* (*The Dance*), written by master playwright Abelardo Estorino (who won the National Literary Award in 1992, and the National Theatre Award in 2002), and played by Adriana Santana, his closest collaborator. Nina, a 75 year old woman – as old as the author – recounts her life story, set off by the memory of a dance with a dashing young man during which she wore a pearl necklace for the first time, whilst she tries determinedly to contact her children in the United States. The woman's attachment to their letters, and her yearning to receive one containing an invitation that would enable her to see them again, mirrors her attachment to her home and her personal history, her land, which is a metaphor for the island itself. The realistic language switches between the pressures of daily life and the lonely woman's reveries. The play was first staged by the author with the Teatro de Repertorio Español of New York in 1999, and in Havana with the theatre company Hubert de Blanck, of which he is a member, in 2000.

The island mentality, viewed either as a source of continual curiosity towards the outside world and an open mindset (the celebrated essayist Graziella Poglotti says that the island's spirit lies in its ports), or as a fatalistic sense of imprisonment linking the word island to isolation and desolation, is another *leitmotiv* that left its mark on the literature of the early 90s, in works such as *Vagos Rumores* (*Vague Rumours*) or *Parece blanca* (*She Looks White*) by Estorino, *Manteca* (*Butter*) by Alberto Pedro, or *Santa Cecilia* by Abilio Estévez. Estévez returns to this theme in *El enano en la botella* (*The Dwarf in the Bottle*, 1994), which Raúl Martín premiered in 2001 with the Teatro de la Luna. A dwarf describes his confinement – and uses various metaphors to examine aspects of daily social life – only to discover that he is unable to move elsewhere.

Martín artfully stages the dense philosophical and literary content of the play, using a large blackboard on which the dwarf notes eloquent formulas, as well as gigantic rag dolls and, above all, versatile actors Grettel Trujillo and Mario Guerra, who stimulate the public's imagination. Grettel Trujillo won the Best Actress Award for her performance, shared with Adriana Santana in *El Baile*, in the First Monologue Festival held in Miami in May 2001.

Flora Lauten, a disciple of Revuelta, founder of Escambrey in the 1960s and mentor to young actors in Buendía, overcame an exodus of her actors by taking on new recruits for *Bacantes*, a version of Euripides' text adapted by herself and Raquel Carrió, constructing a metaphor of salvation through one's roots, embodied in both the group and the country. With remarkably rich imagery provided by the actors' bodies, and raw, elemental materials such as water, fire and sand, plus Greek songs sung with passion, Lauten highlights themes such as growth and upheaval, making a case for the Dionysiac forces that govern man's need for the enjoyment of life in spite of all its difficulties. Premiered in 2001 in the setting of an ancient Greek Orthodox Church that is home to the troupe, the play went on to dazzle audiences on the stage of the Teatro Nacional at the festival of Santo Domingo, as well as in other venues.

During this period it is essential to mention Carlos Díaz. His Teatro El Público, founded in the early 90s with a trilogy of American plays that broke taboos (social masks, rituals petrified by routine, homo-eroticism) and dazzled with the richness of their imagery in a time of material shortages, has been working since 1994 in the Trianón cinetheatre, located in the central district of Vedado, where he presents the most consistent theatre programme in the city, achieving long runs and full houses. From an artistic point of view, this director follows two different but always spectacular lines: on the one hand, a groundbreaking and satirical style, as demonstrated in the new production *Maria Antonieta o la maldita circunstancia del agua por todas partes*) (*Maria Antonieta, or the Cursed Situation of Water Everywhere*, 1999), profusely expressive through gestures and dance, which evokes Cuba's cultural history through the story of a Cuban family, based both on Piñera's poem 'La Isla en peso' (The Island in the Balance) — one of whose verses provides the title of the play — and on the Cuban songwriting tradition. The other trend, more respectful of the Gran Teatro tradition, informed the staging of Miller's *The Crucible* in 2002, which was nevertheless influenced by the first trend in that it incorporated transvestite characters and their corresponding ambiguity. His most recent production, Fernando Rojas' *la Celestina* (2002), which exploits nudity and eroticism in all its forms, aroused heated controversy, since many deemed the performance to be mere entertainment with no deep theme. It is still running after almost 100 performances, an extraordinary number in local practice.

In my opinion, however, the most impressive production of this period has been *Chorus Perpetuus*, by Marienela Boán and DanzAbierta, a group combining dance, theatre and any other means necessary to accomplish their goal of creating artistic forms in space that enable them to interact with their audience.

On stage, a small choir sings. Compositions by Mozart, Pergolesi, Moisés Simons, Gershwin, Curiel, or Ponjuán are both a uniting factor and a source of contradiction, as individuals struggle to express themselves personally and break away from the unison of the singing. Everyone tries to go their own way, changing tempo, introducing a new melody or simply staying silent. The choir goes through several crises and tensions erupt each time the group tries to quell a disturbance.

The setting is austere and minimalist: the only people present on stage are the six actor-dancer-singers, placed on a neutral floorcloth and surrounded by a black room with a lighting rig, bound by the 6 red ropes that hold them together at the wrists. There is no music or set design. The expressiveness of the ensemble is a creative construction that springs from intelligence, transforms a concept into bodily forms or vocal variations and inspires a variety of ideas, sensations and emotions. The tense bonds between individuals and groups, the dichotomy between human beings and the mosaic of objects which makes up contemporary society, and the need to reconcile their respective aspirations, lie behind each dramatic action, and are expressed through humming or translated into body movements. In the struggle between order and change, subtly sketched characters appear, portraying dramatic traits, each with their potential for contradiction and difference: the intransigent, the conciliator, the automaton, the apathetic soul, the eternal nonconformist, the enthusiast. Thus, controversy breaks the harmony of the initial artistic endeavour.

The piece embraces wider social issues, referring not only to the Cuban context in which the voluntary act of unity is essential to the nation's survival but which also demands space for diversity. In this it is similar to other contexts threatened by the homogenising effects of globalisation through the markets and the media. The dénouement results in an equilibrium that is neither ingenuous nor ironic: having defended their viewpoints and learnt to find a common ground beyond their differences, the group unite again, of their own will, without external bonds or attachments, because man alone is nothing. The production's closing spirituals, which are both cathartic and festive, offer another metaphor: that of a theatre which remains alive in spite of everything.

Vivian Martínez Tabares, *theatre critic and researcher, has written for national and international publications. She teaches theatre criticism at the Instituto Superior de Arte and is General Secretary of the Cuban Centre of the IATC, Director of the Teatro de la Casa de las Américas, for which she edits the review* Cojunto, *and in charge of organising the programming for the Latin American and Caribbean theatre season 'Mayo Teatral'.*

CYPRUS

CHRISTAKIS GEORGIOU

The Cyprus Centre of the ITI has for some time now been pressing for the adoption of a definite theatre policy, which would aim to attract new audiences to the island's five existing professional theatres. In its attempt to focus attention on the necessity of such a policy the Centre asked the Research Team of the Intercollege (an independent college) to carry out new research (the first was done by the Cyprus College – see the relevant article in *The World of Theatre 2000*) to examine why theatre attendance is far from satisfactory and make suggestions about how to improve the situation. In the same spirit, it staged the 6th Pancyprian Theatre Conference on the theme 'Practical Steps for Audience Development'. It also organized a Panhellenic Conference on Theatre in Education with the active involvement of the Ministry of Education and Culture of Cyprus and the Ministry of National Education of Greece. Audience development was also the subject of a seminar held in April 2001, organized by Morris Hargreaves McIntire. Gerald Lidstone and Jerry Morris gave lectures and held discussions covering a wide range of topics from both a theoretical and a practical point of view. The seminar was attended by professional and non-professional people of the theatre.

To look at the positive developments in our theatre scene, most theatres have continued to operate a second stage and even, in the case of the State Theatre and Theatre One, a third stage, which aim at producing more 'daring' plays – daring not only in terms of subject matter but also in presenting dramatic material involving the exploration of new ways of expression. In some cases, for the sake of attracting wider audiences, they even included in their repertoire plays written in the same spirit, technique and even the language of TV soap operas. A new term has to be coined to describe this kind of play – I have already made my suggestion in a letter to the press: 'fast-food' theatre. Typical examples of this kind of theatre are the plays produced in the 'second stages' of the State Theater (THOK) and Theatre One – respectively *Facing Evros* by Th. Papathanasiou and M. Reppas and *Senza Storia* by N. Ioannou.

Most of the professional theatres have been operating Children's Stages. Original plays, plays based on well-known fairy tales or novels belonging to the world literary heritage have been produced. If one casts a glance at the figures of the Main Stage audiences and those of the children's stages one will immediately see the big differences in numbers. However, one must take into account the fact that the numbers may sometimes be inflated due to organized visits of school children – a practice that has inherent in it an element of compulsion.

Another encouraging sign is that all the theatres, including the State Theatre, have been inviting, on a more systematic basis directors from other countries,

CYPRUS

including Greece, Germany, the USA and Bulgaria. These directors bring new ideas, sometimes interesting and sometimes less interesting, in the field of dramatic interpretation and presentation. Their philosophical approach stems from the prevailing tendencies in their respective countries and the way they direct reflects, in some cases, the intense experimentation that is taking place in a number of theatres in Europe and America. The tendency towards attracting big audiences with spectacular musicals has not taken root in Cyprus, due to the limited market and the high cost of such productions.

On the negative side, the absence of a dramaturg in almost all the professional theatres is a fact that has its effects on the choice of the repertory. It is true that in theatres without a dramaturg, the so-called artistic committees undertake to make relevant suggestions to their respective boards, which are ultimately responsible for the company's repertory. However, this is not done on a professional basis and most members do not have a global conception of the classical theatre repertory or current developments in the theatrical field.

In the last few years five national TV stations have been operating, plus 3-4 local stations, in an island whose population is not more than 700,000. The competition among these channels to attract the biggest possible number of viewers and thus rouse the interest of advertisers is great. In the last two or three years, commercial TV directors have discovered that Cypriot soap-operas are very popular; thus they have started producing and showing them on a big scale. Bearing in mind that the number of professional actors and actresses in Cyprus is limited, it is not surprising that many of them, in order to supplement their income, are compelled to appear nightly in more than one serial of very poor artistic quality. This is bound to erode their image as serious actors, and hamper efforts to attract bigger audiences to the theatres.

The State Theatre has been regularly visiting the world famous festival of Epidaurus, with either a classical Greek tragedy or a comedy. Not only do Greek theatres take part in this festival but also great directors from different European countries, such as Peter Stein, are invited to bring productions of classical Greek plays. In the summer of 2000 and 2001, the state theatre of Cyprus presented the *Acharnians* of Aristophanes and the *Seven against Thebes* of Aeschylus, while for the summer of 2002 it plans to stage *The Phoenician Women* of Euripides, a fine example of the humanistic approach of the great Greek tragedians to problems arising out of the defeat of an alien empire.

The plays of Cypriot dramatists did not receive the attention they merited. Directors still work under the illusion that a 'safe bet' creates by itself the preconditions for success. It has not yet been fully realized that a country's dramatic literature is an essential part of what we call 'theatre' and that without it theatrical groups cannot succeed in their mission. In the period we are examining, Satirikon and ETHAL staged *Spaghetti-Kleftikon* by A. Koukkides (a satirical attack on some current tendencies in Cypriot behaviour) and *Is Panther Alive?* based on a novel by Niki Marangou. Theatre One presented a farcical comedy, *Senza Storia* by N. Ioannou and a light revue, *Bir Gun Celecek* (*A Day Will Come*), by the same author. For the latter, the theatre functioned as a café or tavern theatre.

The Elizabethan theatre, especially Shakespeare, attracted the interest of directors co-operating with the State Theatre, (THOK) and some of the

ABOVE: the chorus in Aeschylus' *Seven Against Thebes*, presented by the State Theatre of Cyprus

BELOW: scene from *The Germans Invade Again*, by A Sklelarios and Chr. Yiannakopoulos, presented by Satirikon

CYPRUS

state-grant aided theatres. In 2000 THOK staged *Macbeth*, while Satirikon, in spite of its limited resources, attempted *King Lear*. Molière also proved popular with some directors. The Scala, one of our provincial theatres, staged his *Le bourgeois gentilhomme* while THOK chose *L'avare* for the opening play of the 2001–2002 season. Live music was used in the second case.

The modern Greek play proves to be among the most popular, especially farcical comedies. It seems that the majority of theatregoers are seeking innocuous entertainment that will let them forget the problems they are facing in real life. Again the numbers are revealing. Light comedies may attract 8–10,000 spectators; more serious plays, which touch social problems, anything between 3–5,000. All five theatres staged modern Greek plays: *Facing Evros* by Th. Athanasiou/M. Reppas (THOK), : *The Germans Invade Again* (Satirikon), *Stories by Grandfather Aristophanes* (rewritten by D. Potamitis – SCALA), *Thanasis the Politician* by Sakellarios/Yiannakopoulos (Theatre One), and *Stella Violanti* by G. Xenopoulos, *Mother Mammy Mam* by G. Dialegmenos, and *Stella in Red Gloves* by I. Kampanellis (ETHAL).

20th century European and American theatre offered a wide range of plays: Strindberg, *Crimes and Crimes*; Lorca, *Fascination, Passion and Death*, Dario Fo, *Accidental Death of an Anarchist*, Eugene O'Neill, *Desire Under the Elms*; Arthur Miller, *The Price*; Mark Medoff, *Children of a Lesser God*, Eugene Ionesco, *La Cantatrice Chauve* and others.

The children's stages seem to draw their repertory from plays written by Cypriot dramatists. Mainland Greeks and Russian authors are also popular. Children's plays are mostly staged on Sunday mornings or on particular week days by special arrangements with elementary schools. There are also children's stages independent from the professional theatres, run mainly by women directors who also run 'drama' workshops for children.

The Cyprus Centre of the ITI organizes four important activities connected with the ancient Greek drama. A biennial international symposium on ancient Greek drama where particular topics connected with interpretation and presentation are being discussed; an international summer school where academicians and theatre practitioners teach students from different countries the eternal values of classical Greek tragedies and comedies; an annual International Festival of Ancient Greek Drama held in the ancient theatre Odeion of Paphos – birthplace of Aphrodite and ancient capital of the island; and an International Higher Drama Schools Meeting and Festival – during which Drama Schools from America, Europe and Asia present scenes from ancient Greek tragedies and comedies.

Christakis Georgiou is President of the Cyprus Centre of ITI. An author and adapter of plays, he has also written novels and short stories.

CZECH REPUBLIC

MARIE RESLOVA

The ten years since the change of our social system have seen the transition of Czech theatres from a fully state-controlled (but also fully financed) network to a free (and unfortunately only partially successful) structure. Theatre people are still learning how to cope with this new situation and work within it. There have been attempts to make the system of subsidy more flexible and to transform theatres into self-sufficient and independent economic units. For the vast majority of Czech theatre ensembles, the actual running of the theatre, including its management and funding, is a decisive factor, which limits their possibilities. It tends to influence almost everything – the possibilities of the repertoire, the scenography, the choice and number of actors, the time allowed for rehearsals, and investment in technical equipment. Yet even today, as in the time of the totalitarian regime, genuine theatre talent can make its mark.

This situation came to its head two years ago, when the Board of the National Theatre began looking for a new head of its drama company in Prague. Suddenly there wasn't anybody whom the professionals (at least in private) would have willingly accepted in this rather prestigious position. The only person whom almost everybody would have accepted, despite the somewhat controversial reception given to his productions, and who with his repertoire and production standards endowed the small Theatre On the Balustrade (Divadlo Na zábradli) with the mantle of the leading Czech theatre, was Petr Lébl (*b* 1965), who staged, towards the end of 1999, the tragic end of his own life. Only after his death did people realize that his characteristic stage design and courageous production approach (seen for the last time in Chekhov's *Uncle Vanya*) had created the idiom and style of today's Czech theatre.

At the turn of the millennium, Czech theatre boasted, besides Lébl, several gifted theatre directors, who all succeeded, each in his own way, in disturbing the stagnant waters of our theatre production. Jan Antonín Pitínský (*b* 1956), playwright and director, had his roots, as did Lébl, in the theatre of the late 80s. Although he directed several plays at the National Theatre (Durych's *Wandering*, the Mrštíks' *Marysa*, Vanèura's *Marketa Lazarova*), it soon transpired that his lyrical-poetic staging of novels and the strongly cadenced, somewhat abstractly stylized gestures of the actors – actually the very basis of his fame – became, in the environment into which they had been implanted, little more than simple mannerisms. Jan Nebeský (*b* 1953), a director of esoteric spiritual depths, completed two years ago his series of productions of Strindberg and Ibsen with a remarkable production of *The Master Builder*. He convinced his casts of the need to establish a permanent dialogue between the actor and his character, between reality and stage fiction. His Beckett triptych – *Fin de partie (Endgame),Thérèse, Mal d'or* – and the production *JE SuiS*, with motifs from the novels of Bernanos, are a concise stage discussion about life's essentials, love and faith. Nebeský explores the extreme possibilities of the theatre and, in consequence, finds himself 'on the fringe' of the whole range of theatrical activity. Vladimír Morávek (*b* 1965) is, above all, a stage director of clear theatrical vision based on classical motifs – his 'naive', strikingly theatrical interpretations of Shakespeare (*Hamlet, Richard III*) or Chekhov (*The Three Sisters, The Seagull*) are simplified, frankly tragico-grotesque, provocatively open and unmistakable. At the regional Klicpera Theatre in Hradec Králové he has put together one of the most versatile ensembles in Bohemia. Michal Docekal (1965), formerly (together with Lébl) the youngest head of a theatre company in Bohemia (Comedy Theatre) is a director familiar with contemporary trends – he is inventive, with a clear tendency towards attractive, originally conceived form rather than intellectual depth (Shakespeare: *A Midsummer Night's Dream, The Taming of the Shrew*; Marlowe: *Doctor Faustus*). Starting in September 2002, he is the new head of the drama ensemble of the National Theatre. Jirí Pokorný (*b* 1967) is a playwright and producer who courageously and generously promotes contemporary world drama and incites his actors to go for unmistakable stylization and raw authenticity. He is responsible for the artistic side of the Brno HaTheatre (HaDivadlo).

These directors represent to a large extent the main trends in the contemporary Czech drama theatre. Most probably up to 90% of the repertoire of Czech theatres are box-office oriented plays and productions, most diverse in their professional qualities.

In some ensembles (Cinoherní klub/Drama Club, Spolek Kašpar/Association Punch, Dejvice Theatre, Divadlo u stolu/Theatre at the Table) we see a clear tendency towards the renaissance of the art of the actor, as a counterbalance to the too obvious concepts of the directors. More and more often, there are attempts to find adequate stage forms for contemporary drama – whether international: Bernhard, Schwab, Koltès, Ravenhill, Kane, Marber, McDonagh, or local: Balák, Jecelín, Pokorný, Bláhová, Tobiáš. The theatres that systematically look for and stage original Czech plays are Cinoherní studio (Drama Studio) Ústí nad Labem, HaTheatre, Divadlo Husa na provázku (Theatre Goose on a String).

The most highly praised recent new Czech play was the first play by Petr Zelenka, scriptwriter and film director, *Stories of Ordinary Madness*, produced at the Dejvice divadlo. We should note with sympathy the endeavours of some theatres, e.g. Dejvice, Klicpera Theatre in Hradec Králové, Divadlo v Dlouhé (Theatre in Dlouha Street), and the Comedy Theatre, to counteract the market and consumer-orientated environment with unwavering devotion to the fundamental human and professional ethics of systematic work in the theatre. These are long-term endeavours, seldom noticed by the media, but they bear fruit: productions whose strength is due not only to the power of theatre art, but also to human solidarity.

The existence of the drama theatre in the Czech Republic is somewhat precarious. Unfortunately, in many instances it lacks self-confidence. No new star emerged in the last three seasons. So far, the Czech drama theatre has yet to be seen at any of the major European theatre festivals, but it does have a great deal of vitality, and the support of regular theatregoers. It is not lack-

From the Czech-Japanese co-production of variations on Shakespeare's Romeo and Juliet under the title
A Plague on Both Your Houses! at the theatre Drak in Hradec Králové, with Josef Krofta as director

CZECH REPUBLIC

ing in its own special qualities, and is fully capable of competing with drama from other European cultures.

The situation of the opera is somewhat more optimistic – actually, we may speak of a quite unexpected renaissance, as confirmed by recent seasons. With the exception of Jan Nebeský, all the directors mentioned earlier have tried their hand at opera, thus strikingly upsetting the somewhat traditional ways of opera production. David Radok, producer at the Göteborg Opera, brought brio not only to Czech opera but also to drama productions. For two years running he was awarded the prestigious Alfred Radok Award for his opera productions at the Prague National Theatre (Shostakovitch: *Lady Macbeth of the Mtsensk District*, Berg: *Wozzeck*). This prize, named after his father, a famous Czech theatre producer and film director, is awarded every year by theatre critics for the best theatre production, regardless of genre. Because of the high quality of productions, theatre critics now regularly write about the opera.

The two Prague operatic houses – the opera of the National Theatre and the State Opera of Prague – are shaping their specific image. The National Theatre, wishing to give a modern form to opera productions, made it its policy to invite successful drama producers. J.A. Pitínský produced Wagner's *Tristan und Isolde* and Smetana's *Dalibor*, Vladimír Morávek Puccini's *Tosca* and Verdi's *Macbeth*. The National Theatre at long last succeeded in finding outstanding opera producers to stage Czech classics – David Pountney produced Smetana's *The Devil's Wall* and Robert Wilson Janácek's *Fate*. There were also several co-productions with European ensembles – Bohuslav Martinù's *Julietta* with Opera North from Leeds (UK) and Berg's *Wozzeck* with the opera from Göteborg.

The State Opera of Prague intends to keep alive the traditions of the former Neues Deutsches Theater, whose building it has taken over (hence Weiss's *The Polish Jew*); a significant component of its repertoire is productions of 20th-century operas – Benjamin Britten's *The Turn of the Screw*, Philip Glass's *The Fall of the House of Usher*, Bohuslav Martinù's *The Soldier and the Dancer* – and, above all, premières of contemporary operas: E.Viklický's *Phaedra*, entered for the competition Opera for Prague, the world première of *The Physicists* by the Swiss composer A. Pflüger. The idea of the French cycle of the State Opera was similar : Meyerbeer's *Robert le diable*, *Ariane et Barbe-Bleu* by Paul Dukas and the world première of the opera *Joseph Merrick, called the Elephant Man* by L. Petitgirard.

Petr Kofron, composer, conductor and head of the opera ensemble at the J.K. Tyl Theatre in Plzeò, has spent several years putting together an interesting regional ensemble. He arrived with a fascinating Czech repertoire – Fibich's *Šárka*, Foerster's *Simpleton*, Ostrcil's *Kunala's Eyes* – and the idea of modern stagings by young directors – Jirí Pokorný, Michal Docekal, Jirí Herman, whose production of Saint-Saens's *Samson et Dalila* promises well for his future. The Moravian-Silesian National Theatre, Ostrava continued its tradition of high standards in both repertoire and production – *Giovanna d'Arco* for the centenary of Verdi's death, Janácek's very first opera *Beginnings of a Love Story*, Borodin's *Prince Igor*. Productions of the ensembles in Liberec (Giordano's *Andréa Chénier*) and Brno (Janácek's *The Makropulos Case*) also attracted a good deal of attention.

The work of all Czech professional opera ensembles and musical academies was presented at the festivals Opera 99 and Opera 01, organized by the union of music theatre in Prague. The first festival focussed on Czech opera and presented the work of such composers as I.Hurník, M.Kanák and Z. Lukáš. The festival Smetana's Litomyšl was also entirely devoted to opera and in addition to major productions also had performances at the historic castle theatre (authentic interpretation of *Euridice* by J.Peri). It has its permanent place at Janácek's Hukvaldy and at the summer opera festivals in Kutná Hora and Loket. Two remarkble operas by young composers were produced in November 2001 at the Faculty of Music of the AMU (Academy of Performing Arts), M.Nejtek: *The Fool and the Nun*, M.Ivanovic: *Death and the Maiden*, directed by J. Herman.

Contemporary dance in Bohemia is also a rapidly developing theatre form. To define dance strictly geographically could be misleading – the true home of our dance is Central and possibly also Eastern Europe. In this sense Czech dance is still searching for its identity.

The last three years brought the revival and growth of contemporary dance styles. This was made possible by a number of organizations and, last but not least, by the somewhat forgotten traditions of pre-war expressive dance. The International Festival Dance Prague has now for a whole decade been supplying the art of dance with new ideas. Recently more intimate alternatives to this festival have cropped up: The festival of new dance, Confrontation, and Four Days in Movement, the focus being site-specific and crossover. This boom would be unthinkable without the existence of the theatre Archa (Ark), which systematically promotes the art of dance and puts its stage at the disposal of dance performances. Another new development is the recently opened Dance theatre Ponec, also the theatre Alfred in the Courtyard, which focuses on non-verbal theatre. In these and several other alternative theatres, dance is being transformed into an interdisciplinary genre combining movement, music, images and the human body as an existential issue. This new genre is a typical trait of European dance today.

The last influential element is the alternative dance conservatoire, the Duncan Centre, from which a whole range of young choreographers has graduated to supply the dance scene in Bohemia with new energy. They carry on the traditions of expressive dance, naturally adjusted to the present. Young Czech dancers are more at ease in this form of contemporary expression, and in contemporary dance techniques, than in the classical tradition, which never did suit the mentality and physical type of the Czechs. It has always been more compatible with the traditions of the pantomime and the grotesque elements of theatre.

This may be the reason why our dance theatre tends to come so near to clowning – one of its distinctive features. Eva Tálská in a non-verbal performance at the Theatre Husa na provázku (Goose on the String), *The Circus: or Death and Horse with Me* evokes the emotional myth of the circus – sentimental, naive, dream-like and grotesque, truly Fellini-like. The Czech-Italian group Déja Donné, led by the choreographic pair Simone Sandroni and Lenka Flory, has created their *Aria Spinta* (in great demand abroad) in the spirit of clowning, before probing the human soul in greater depth in the highly theatrical *In*

CZECH REPUBLIC

Bella Copia. The recently created group Krepsko (*A Pachyderm Trap, A Stone in Yoghurt*) could, hopefully, begin an original continuation of the traditions of absurd pantomime in Bohemia. Dance clowning of this kind was also evident in Mirka Eliášová's *Do You Feel Fine?* It is also the chosen path of quite a few young choreographers from the Duncan Centre.

Kristýna Lhotáková found herself in an international context with her *Venus with Rubik's Cube.* This dancer and choreographer recently attracted attention when she participated in a joint project with the Austrian–Swiss dancer and choreographer Anna Huber „*two,too*". Lhotáková works along the lines of dance minimalism, a great temptation for many young choreographers. It has certain features of laboratory work (each generation again and again investigates the body and its possibilities) and, moreover, it offers an atmosphere of ironic outrage. The well-established choreographer Petr Tyc (*The Little I Know about Sylphides*) has recently switched to minimalism and subtle dance allusions.

A well-travelled ensemble is the Theatre Novo G.O. Fronta, founded by the Czech–Russian performing couple Irina Andreieva and Aleš Janák. They are at their best in street performances – *The Vagabond Adam Kadmon.* They combine their market-place stand-up with the physical endurance and daring of buto-style performers, achieving spectacular effects with *De profundis clamavi.*

The work of Jan Kodet – *Jade; Gates* – and of Lenka Ottová – *Love, as they say; Bent Backward (Human Deviations)* features excellent dancers, a sudden dynamic explosion and a desire to go forward, towards a fully-fledged dance theatre.

A curious trend in Bohemia is a new mannerism of sorts, accompanied by a slight tendency towards mysticism. This is not surprising in Jan Komárek, a theatre director of the middle generation, who returned from the pursuit of mannerist and mysticising tendencies overseas with a nostalgic longing for magic Prague (*Shadows of Dreams, Martyrdom*), but we would hardly expect fairly introvert (if ironic) mannerism or mysticism in the younger generation of choreographers.

Jana Hudecková and Markéta Trpišovská have created in their *Ma dame blanche* a sophisticted, decadent dance idiom in pseudo-medieval scenes; Petra Hauerová's *Carmina Burana* in a way links medieval and modern political plagues; while in her *Charon's Brides* Kristýna Celbová covers herself with ashes as a true mourner. Enclosed by several mirrors, Kristýna Boková eats away her heart in her *Tetel.* At the extreme are the 'anonymous' group Envoi, saturated in esoteric science, and the solitary performer with an astonishingly beautiful body, Antonie Svobodová, who performs in churches, cellars and railway stations.

The greatest contemporary dance discovery in Bohemia is the Romanian dancer and choreographer Ioana Mona Popovici, who shone at this year's Czech dance platform with her *Buy a Soup and Get One Free; Breath, Shadow, Nothing...; Requiem for a Dog.* This extraordinary personality embodies the spirit of 'another' dancing Europe. The fairly new journal *Tanecní zóna (Dance Zone)*, which is itself part of the renaissance of dance in Bohemia described above, is trying to define it.

The Czech public is being courted by official puppet theatres (they have their own buildings and, far more important, subsidies from the municipality), independent professional groups and numerous highly inventive and increasingly aggressive amateur ensembles (Strípek in Plzen, Cmukari in Turnov, Cécko in Svitavy).

The Czech professional puppet theatre always had its strength in scenography. Its artists did not abandon experimenting, but in a matter-of-fact way put live actors into bold arrangements of the stage and its space. The technique of the shadow theatre had its comeback (lately in the successful *Sávitrí* of the independent group Divadlo Líšen). Work with light, projections and a multifunctional mobile stage steadily improved (the strongest performances were signed Petr Matásek – witness his scenography for the staging of *Kytice* (*A Bunch of Flowers*) at the Naivni divadlo (Naive theatre) in Liberec or the solution, based on the same principle, of the scenography for *The Three Golden Hairs of the Wise Old Man* by Marek Zákostelecký at the theatre Drak (Dragon). There was a search for new, non-traditional spaces – various street productions – or the utilization of 'non-theatrical' objects, such as the *Shed (La Baraque)* of the Voliere Dromesco company with the brothers Forman, who found yet another sanctuary for their project *The Purple Sails* in the Mystery Boat – a cargo vessel. Several puppet productions have taken place in circus tents, such as the circus musical *Pinocchio* with the participation of the theatre Drak, as well as the production by the independent group, Studio dell'arte, of the *Theatre Continuo Circus Vitae*. The Malé divadlo (Small Theatre) in Ceské Budejovice performs in manor and castle gardens. The puppet theatre has abandoned darkened halls to meet its audiences in the most bizarre spaces, attacking them with stage tricks and subterfuges, often inspired by the charm of old theatre productions.

In the repertoire, besides well-known authors (František Pavlícek, Milan Pavlík, Iva Perinová – her plays are by far the most frequently produced by Czech and foreign puppet theatres), we find some new names (Blanka Lunáková, Vlasta Špicnerová, the young and gifted Klára Perinová, René Levínský). Although not neglecting child audiences, the puppet theatres regularly include performances for adults in their repertoire – this is most obvious in the predominantly musical repertoire of the Brno theatre Radost (Joy). The most remarkable performance is the provocative play by Iva Perinová at the Divadlo Alfa (Alpha Theatre) in Plzen, *Gee Whizz, Dogheads!* with its allusions to the Czech national character. The well-known Divadlo Spejbla a Hurvínka (Theatre of Spejbl and Hurvinek) has regular performances for adults.

Stimulating puppet productions have made it for several seasons running to the so-called 'big' theatre festivals, such as the international festival Divadlo (Theatre) in Plzen or the Theatre of European Regions in Hradec Králové. On the other hand, 'traditional' Czech puppet festivals like Materinka in Iberec or Skupa's in Plzen, as well as such new festivals as Spectaculum Interesse (since 1995) in Ostrava or the World Festival of the Art of Puppets (for the first time in 1996) in Prague now welcome local and foreign independent groups and ensembles that make use of the resources of the puppet theatre for their productions. A good example is Jan Borna's successful production *How I Got Lost* at the Divadla v Dlouhé (Theatre in Dlouha Street), which in Ludvik Askenazy's story combines the possibilities of the drama and puppet theatre with 'hits' from the 'swinging sixties'.

CZECH REPUBLIC

When working on sophisticated projects for adolescent and adult audiences, professional puppet theatres often resort to international co-operation. One such example is the Czech-Japanese co-production of variations on Shakespeare's *Romeo and Juliet* under the title *A Plague on Both Your Houses!* at the theatre Drak in Hradec Králové with Josef Krofta as director.

Even after their ten-year existence, and the uneasy conditions notwithstanding, the ambitious independent groups Buchty a loutky (Cakes and Puppets) and Divadlo Continuo courageously defend their position. Their repertoire is primarily intended for adult audiences. Buchty a loutky, as confirmed by their latest production *Gilgamesh I and II*, seem to prefer more intimate performances, while Continuo frankly prefer street performances in the widest sense of the word. Several other productions of independent groups are an inspiration and challenge for professional puppet theatres: the previously mentioned work of the brothers Forman; Divadlo Kvelb (Theatre Closet), founded three years ago in Ceské Budejovice, which also focuses on street productions; and the appealing one-man show of the South-Bohemian puppeteer Vítezslav Marcík. A unique phenomenon is the art theatre of the sculptor and painter Petr Nikl, who brings to the Czech puppet theatre something totally unexpected – Dada-Surrealist productions. They may be found not only in his own performances of *Nests of Dreams* at the Gallery Rudolfinum in Prague, but also in joint projects with Jana Svobodová and the musicians Havel, husband and wife, for the Prague Divadla Archa (Ark Theatre): *In the Looking-Glass, Behind the Looking-Glass, Worn-Out Dreams*.

Since 1991, the professional Czech puppet theatre is every year confronted with the most striking productions of amateur ensembles at the festival 'One Flew Over the Puppets' Nest'. Since 1997 the ERIK prize has been awarded to the year's best production. Lately the award has gone to amateur ensembles – in the year 2001 to the young group DNO (Bottom) from Hradec Králové for their variations on the famous Cyrano motif.

Marie Reslová *trained at the Theatre Faculty of th Prague Academy of Arts, and is currently editor of* Divadelny Noviny (Theatre News). *She acknowledges the contributions of Radmila Hrdinová (opera), Nina Vangeli (dance) and Nina Malíková (puppetry).*

DENMARK

HEINO BYRGESEN

The drama of the 1999–2000 season seemed to lead a more interesting life behind the stage than on it. To be frank, the season appeared rather disjointed when viewed from the desk. Shows were cancelled, last minute rescues were attempted and first night performances were postponed again and again, as if the theatres hardly knew what they wanted.

No revolutionary new way of thinking found its way to the stage and we cannot expect to see the effect of the replacement of theatre managers for another season or two. There were no immediate exciting perspectives, however.

On stage, however, was more of a (melo)drama. The first premieres of the season were Eugene O'Neill's *Sælsomt Mellemspil (Strange Interlude)* at the Royal Theatre and the dangerously explosive work of wordart *København (Copenhagen)* by Michael Frayn at Betty Nansen Teatret. Together these two performances are fairly representative of the strength of the season: good and solid mainstream performances, verbal theatre with an appeal to brain and heart – the former definitely heart and the latter brain – carried by distinguished acting. Both became hits and were instrumental in reassuring the most anxious critics: when traditional drama could still prove its worth, there was no need to worry about the repertoire in general and the national stages in particular.

The Royal Theatre followed up its classics with Holberg, Strindberg, Shakespeare and Ibsen, of which *Gengangere (Ghosts)* by Ibsen can be described as the most consistent example of a gently modernised classic, in equal parts simple, touching and moving. Counting the two stagings of *Vildanden (The Wild Duck)* at Aalborg Teater and Rialto Teatret respectively, it is no exaggeration to say that Ibsen had a bit of a renaissance. Betty Nansen Teatret, regarded by some critics as our real national theatre, also followed the trend to take up classics, in this case in Per Olof Enquist's free adaptation. In spite of some rather feeble rewriting a new version of Chekhov's *Tre Søstre (The Three Sisters)* became yet another audience hit in the competent hands of the troika Bodil Udsen, Ghita Nørby and Susse Wold. Betty Nansen's faithful playwright Lars Norén, by now virtually playwright in residence, was of course in full combat mode this season. It was obvious that *Drengene i Skyggen (The Boys in the Shadows)* would attract great attention. The delicious list of sins attached to the principal characters of the play, on the heels of Norén's preceding play, the sensational convict drama *Sju Tre (Seven Three)* with its tragic consequences still fresh in the memory of the audience and the media. Can this be described as mainstream theatre? Betty Nansen Teatret certainly succeeded in making respectable theatregoers join the ranks of voyeurs, even if this time Noren's unpleasant details were well hidden outside the famous drawing room.

We experienced mainstream on a large as well as on a small scale. Aarhus Teater's ambition was to produce a well made and popular show, the result being a rather too glamorous stage version of the gigantic novel *100 års ensomhed (100 Years of Solitude)* by Gabriel Garcia Màrquez. Something similar can be said in the case of most of the repertoire at Folketeatret, in which *Anne Franks Dagbog (The Diary of Anne Frank)* certainly found a large audience of all ages.

The musical waves that kept rolling in at the regional theatres brought a load of oldish flotsam but also fresh attempts at renewing the genre. Niels Brunse and Lars Graugaard made an imposing heroic poem in an opera-like stage version of Dostoevski's *Idioten (The Idiot)* at Odense Teater. It may be described as a rather uneven and not completely successful performance, but the ambitious libretto did offer an interesting and very up-to-date drama about the murderer as identity and role. Aarhus Teater was also tossed back and forth on the waves of music theatre and emerged with a family show based on Astrid Lindgren's *Emil fra Lønneberg (Emil From Lonneberg)* as a sure winner. Not surprisingly, Aalborg Teater came up with the absolute hit within the traditional musical genre. Jonathan Larson's update of the *La Bohème* story, *Rent*, was tailored for the singing ensemble at Aalborg Teater and for Kasper Holten's youthful director's hand.

The boom in new Danish drama seen in the last seasons continued, but with diminished force. Nicoline Werdelin's *Den blinde maler (The Blind Painter)* and Line Knutzon's *Snart kommer tiden (Soon the Time Will Come)* both received a second look at Aarhus Teater and there was also room for Jens Christian Grøndahl's *Hvor var vi lykkelige (How Happy We Were)* and Per Hultberg's *Fædra*. Both of them were family dramas – the first a lengthy and unsuccessful attempt at infusing elements from tragedy and commedia dell'arte into a minor drama, the second restricting itself to a more straightforward style and a less daring genre. The term mainstream comes to mind. It is certainly the term for Stig Dalager's skilled family drama *Drømmen (The Dream)*, which offered, above all, solid character parts for three generations of women at Odense Teater.

From Juliane Preisler the season brought two premieres, on the theme of loneliness in various guises: *Forår (Spring)* at Folketeatret and *Meteor (Meteor)* at Café Teatret. Erling Jepsen made his mark on contemporary drama with a play about the solitude and absurdity of ordinary lives, *Snefnugget og øjeæblet (The Snowflake and the Eyeball)*, at Husets Teater and *Manden der bad om lov til at være her på jorden (The Man Who Asked Permission to Stay on the Earth)* at Rialto Teatret. Two valid presentations of modern mores on the periphery of more trendy city life.

Aalborg Teater launched an intimate stage for contemporary Danish drama. A small absurd exercise called *Familien Wondorcolor (The Family Wondorcolor)* created by Ege Arp-Hansen was coupled with Jan Sonnergaard's highly dramatic play *Sex* and made a neat prelude. The hothouse stage at Gladsaxe Teater opened with an equally fine adaptation of *Dinas Bog (Dina's Book)*, in a co-production with Jomfru Ane Teatret. Kim Fupz Aakeson's spaghetti western *Cowboy Cowboy* at Lille Scene worked nicely as a comic parody but did not come through with any particular message.

Instead we had to turn to the Radio Theatre in order to find Kim Fupz Aakeson's most successful piece of the season. *Parlør (Phrase Book)*, directed by

ABOVE: Lars Junggreen in Morti Vizki's monologue *Gray*   (*photo*: Bjarne Staehr)

BELOW: scene from Bob Wilson's production of Büchner's *Woyzeck* at the Betty Nansen Theatre
(*photo*: The Ocular One)

DENMARK

Emmet Feigenberg, turned out to be a chuckling mini-comedy about the inner tourist hell of a hotel guest. And while the theatre elsewhere steered a happy middle course, the Radio Theatre continued to creep off into the corners.

The world of reality was ambushed twice during the season. Daniel Wedel in *Polterabend* (*The Bachelor Party*), a play about a bachelor party gone way too far, toyed with authentic confessional journalism from an interesting angle. A second foot firmly planted in reality belonged to Morti Vizki. He managed to escape from the teacher-pupil scandal of his original premise and with the musical help of director Jacob F. Schokking his play succeeded in creeping into the dangerously fascinating grey zone of a teacher and her young lover. His *Australia*, probably the most whole-hearted pioneer work within broadcasting language in this season, was awarded the Danish Association of the Blind award for the best radio play.

The Danish Broadcasting Corporation gave free rein not only to the radio budget but also to the television screen. *Edderkoppen* (*The Spider*), in six popular episodes, bit off a chunk of the ever-amusing history of Denmark and chewed it with equal measures of poetry and drama. Among its actors were Jacob Cedergren, a representative of the young generation and Bent Mejding, an experienced theatre and television star; between them they served as a proof that the theatre over the recent years is able time and again to rear new actors and nurture seniors.

And how did the first season of the new century turn out? A new era began. And yet. It was as if the theatre – for good reasons probably – did not quite know what to do with itself in year nil. Time had moved imperceptibly but decisively from one century to another. But what about the theatre? The Danish season 2000–2001 in particular demonstrated how the theatre was still stuck in the 90s, unable to start over again. The view of the future was not clear. Or rather it was limited to theoretical performances.

Publications trying to wrestle with the theatre marked the season: an anthology on the drama of the future and another of theatre manifestos. The season was taking stock. The past was dealt with in writing and there were speculations about the future. In many ways it was a season of welcomes and farewells. Welcome to the new managing directors of the regional theatres – Aalborg Teater and Odense Teater – and in Copenhagen Dr Dantes Aveny, Folketeatret and Nørrebros Teater. A situation that marked off the season again as one of transition. A season of waiting for theatre managers to retire and to start, the past eyeing the future. And in relation to art: a poor season for an audience that was, with a few exceptions, left in the lurch. The time was spent mostly on goodbyes.

Preben Harris took his leave (at long last) from Folketeatret with almost nothing but revivals. Leon Feder left Nørrebros Teater after directing the musical *Show Boat* in a nostalgic cruise across the stage.

The Royal Theatre produced hardly more than one hit: Moliére's *Fruentimmerskolen* (*L'école des femmes*) directed by Alexa Ther. The play became a summit meeting between at one end the grand, regal actor from within the walls and at the other end the young, modern diva from outside: Jørgen Reenberg and Sidse Babett Knudsen, tradition versus present time, the master versus the pupil.

The season had its few but considerable peaks. At Betty Nansen Teatret the doors were thrown open to the American cult director Robert Wilson. His staging of *Woyzeck* with music by Tom Waits was indeed in an international class; but more important, it turned out to be a triumph for the Danish cast. Working with Robert Wilson marked out Betty Nansen Teatret yet again as the most influential theatre of today. In addition Hotel Pro Forma with Kirsten Delholm took a giant step within their genre with *Jesus*, performed in Malmø. Childish faith received a fatal blow, but faith, in particular faith in the theatre, was restored.

At Aalborg Teater Kasper Holten produced a *Hamlet* and at Østre Gasværk Lars Kaalund produced an *Othello*. However different they were, they both received much praise and became the focus of discussion. In short the discussion on classics begun in the nineties continued and involved two of the leading directors in the country.

New Danish drama was an entirely different matter: the *wunderkind* or the *enfant terrible* of the contemporary stage. The fact is that the new plays set off the season by being firmly anchored in the spirit of the 90s. Line Knutzon, Bo hr. Hansen, Erling Jepsen, Nicoline Werdelin, Jacob Weble, Stig Dalager, Gerz Feigenberg, Naja Marie Aidt, Peter Hugge, Morti Vizki and others all wrote themselves into the season, some to a better and more amusing extent than others, but without delivering a serious prelude to a new age. And if I may say so, resting on their laurels from the last one.

In this way criticism can be so unfair, if not unreasonable in its demand for constant renewal. Nevertheless the season 2000–2001 will be remembered as the time – the waiting time – during which everything and everyone on the Danish stage was retiring or resigning, clearing the decks and tidying up.

Having attended more than half the season 2001–2002 I would not be surprised if the audience were feeling slightly weary. It cannot be called an illness, just a feeling of weariness, a lack and weakening of initiative – not ill and not really well either. It is difficult to say precisely what is wrong. Something is wrong for sure. The strange thing is that if we look at what is being played right now in the middle of the season, there seem to be many reasons to be happy. Not everything has succeeded, but most of it has – and maybe especially those performances that have been dependent on one single actor: Nikolaj Lie Kaas as *Peer Gynt*, Sidse Babett Knudsen as Winnie in *Glade dage* (*Happy Days*). The new theatre managers have made a competent start. The contact with the audience was least effective on the smaller stages. Last but not least, *The Phantom of the Opera* is still running at Det Ny Teater. So there is no reason to panic. The best performances of the season have been in the regional theatres: Holberg's *Jean de France* in a radically new and up-to-date version at Aalborg Teater; Henri Nathansen's *Indenfor murene* (*Within the Walls*) reverently revived at Odense Teater; and Erling Jepsen's *Anna og tyngdeloven* (*Anna and the Law of Gravity*) at Aarhus Teater as a vigorous and satirical representative of the new Danish drama. Between them these three performances show what can become of the weary Danish stage when it overcomes its fatigue. It can blow new and contemporary life into an old classic. It can find its way into the life of a not so old classic. And it can take up a story of current interest and vary it in a new and provocative way. If these are

DENMARK

our only expectations and demands there is really no point in talking about weariness. So what is the problem? A certain type of performance is lacking on the Danish stage. Where is the drama that will seriously engage and confront us with our own world, that will denounce our reality and stir up our prejudices and habits? Where is the drama that will bring up problems for discussion? The focal point that will light up psychological, moral, social and political aspects of our lives here and now?

We do not find this in the slightly outdated news at the Royal Theatre, playing Sartre's *Urene hænder* (*Les mains sales*) and Joseph Kesselring's comedy thriller *Arsenik og gamle kniplinger* (*Arsenic and Old Lace*). Both of them are well intentioned but slightly impotent attempts at finding a new audience whereas it is left to the opera *Le Grand Macabre* to make out of yesterday's modernism something contemporary and relevant. Without wanting to be unfair to what is being played, I would argue that we need something different if we wish to move on. We need someone to take up the baton from Ibsen, Strindberg, Brecht and Dario Fo.

The weariness on stage comes not only from within. It is also a force from without. We have all the more reason to take up the fight – a fight that is shared by theatre managers, directors, playwrights and actors alike. Up to now we have seen very little of this. We may blame the weariness. That is the illness or the symptom of the illness. But there are signs of awakening, like the staging of Ibsen's *Når vi døde vågner* (*When We Dead Awaken*), Sarah Kane's performance *4:48 Psykose* and the last performance of the season, Morti Vizki's monologue *Gray*, based on Oscar Wilde's protagonist Dorian.

Heino Byrgesen, *Head of Radio Drama Production, Danmarks Radio and President of Danish ITI and Theatre Union.*

ECUADOR

EDUARDO ALMEIDA NAVEDA

The economic crisis which has ravaged Ecuador since 1995 worsened in 2000, after popular movements successfully lobbied for the resignation of President Janil Mahual, which led to a 500% devaluation and the replacement of the national currency, the sucre, by the US dollar in an attempt to slow down the ever-increasing rate of inflation. The social, economic and cultural crisis has deepened over the years and has sparked the emigration of large populations to various destinations in Europe and the United States, an exodus that has traumatised an increasing number of divided families. This form of forced emigration is progressing at an accelerated rate, and is following in the footsteps of neighbouring countries who have experienced similar crises as a result of the changes arising from the shake-up in the global economy and the inadequate response of national economies to these changes.

Within such a context of accentuated social contradictions, Ecuador's artists and intellectuals have had to adapt to these new social realities and find a more active approach to their search for answers within their personal spheres of creative activity.

Thus, women and men from the theatrical community have sought solutions to the new conditions in which they have had to develop their artistic occupations. These have not failed to appear: faced with a lack of funding and support from the State, artists have outdone themselves in finding ingenious means to support their activity.

One of the troupes which illustrates this approach is Malayerba. In *Nuestra Señora de Las Nubes* (*Our Lady of the Clouds*), written by Arístides Vargas, two characters, Bruna and Oscar, embody the solitude, frustrations, and dreams faced by migrants. Two suitcases set on an otherwise empty stage are the only elements that accompany them: battered suitcases which symbolise the couple's fruitless migration. Voted 'The Best of Latin American Theatre' by the *Diario de Managua* in 1999, in the city which played host to the 5th Nicaragua Monologue and Duologue Festival, the production has since toured venues in Latin America and in Spain.

The 2000–2001 season encapsulates the best of all three under review, since during this time the theatre defined itself more sharply and acquired greater strength, qualities which had been sketched out the preceding year and in 2000 reached maturity. After twenty years of activity, Malayerba received a tribute from the International Theatre School of Latin America and the Caribbean (Escuela internacional de America Latina y de Caribe/ EITALC) in August 2001. The theatre company held a workshop attended by 50 actors from different countries, who exchanged thoughts on acting and playwriting techniques with their hosts.

The theatre troupes Zero no Zero, Teatro del Cronopio and Contraelviento maintained their alternative acting schools which offered specific courses and scenic concepts. Tragaluz continued its policy of inviting a foreign director on an annual residency to lead their training seminars. In October 2001, The theatre group Mandrágora presented *Retrato Abierto (Open Portrait)*, in Quito, a fusion of dance and theatre, performed by Susana Nicolalde and directed by Wilson Pico. The theatre school and troupe Teatro del Cronopio staged *Farsa para Clown (Clown's Farce)* by Darío Fo, directed by Guido Navarro and based on a text by the same author entitled *Los Pintores no Tienen Recuerdos (Painters Have No Memories)*. In November 2000, the theatre company Espada de Madera presented *Al pie de la Campana (At the Foot of the Belltower)*, by Patricio Estrella, a tribute to those who are absent and who have left in their wake traces of both pain and hope. Several actresses stood out for the quality of their interpretation: Beatriz Vergara in *Medea, Call Back*, Toty Rodríguez in *Tres (Three)*; and in October 2001 *En el Umbral de Una Ciudad Invisible (On the Threshold of an Invisible City)*, based on texts of the Italian writer Italo Calvino, was premiered in Quito and performed by María Kulieva, Ximena Ferrín, Nidia Bermeo and Lorena Rodríguez.

2001 was an important year for national drama; the Premio Nacional de las Letras Eugenio Espejo (Eugenio Espejo National Literary Award) was awarded to playwright José Martínez Quierolo. Another playwright, Pecky Andion, premiered *Medea, Call Back* as well as Luis Miguel Campos who presented in Quito *La Tránsito Smith ha sido secuestrada (Transito Smith Has Been Taken)*, in April 2001. Patricio Guzmán premiered *La Cosa (The Thing)* in May 2001.

The International Festival of Manta hosted its 14th Edition, which included troupes from Europe and America, and was followed by a festival hosted by the Guyanaquil based troupe Sarao, as well as one sponsored by the theatre company Humanizarte in Quito. These festivals, held from August to October 2001, presented touring troupes from countries including Spain, Mexico, Peru, Colombia and Ecuador.

On the dance scene, the most remarkable event was the October 2001 staging of the No Más Luna en el Agua (No More Moon on the Water) Festival, held in the Casa de Cultura in Quito. Performing artists in the Festival included Paola Rettore from Brazil, Costaricans Carolina Vascones and Cecilia Andrade, as well as Mirelle Carone from Peru, all of whom offered works devoted to themes of solitude, migration and non-communication.

To summarise the events that occurred during this period, one can say that 'migration' was the predominant theme in productions. Most treatments of this subject used a large range of technical resources and reflected a high aesthetic standard, containing both artistic depth and a strong political message, as well as a heightened awareness of the impact this phenomenon has had on Ecuadorian society. Our national theatre proved its vitality and its willingness to find in its immediate surroundings the impetus for a most active level of creativity.

During the first months of 2002, theatre troupes continued to perform productions that had already joined the repertoire. The most interesting event of this period has been the organisation, for the second straight year, of an International Puppet festival, in Quito during the month of May. Troupes from

Susana Nicolalde in Mandragora's *Open Portrait*   (*photo:* Eduardo Quintana)

Spain, Italy, France, Argentina and Ecuador participated in the event, and the performance themes ranged from Ecuadorian immigration to Spain – performed by the Spanish group Karromato – to environmental protection, *via* the alienation induced by TV, which was presented by the French puppet troupe Marionettes en liberté. The puppetry gathering was organised by the company Tintintero, a group directed by Yolanda Navas.

Eduardo Almeida Naveda *directed the National Theatre company for two years; director from 1970 to the present of the Teatro Experimental Ecuatoriano; his writings include* The History of Theatre in Ecuador from 1900, *published by the Spanish Ministry of Culture, and articles for* El Publico *and* Latin American Theatre Review.

EGYPT

MOHSEN MOSILHI
and AHMED ZAKI

A strange phenomenon has crystallized in the Egyptian theatre during the last three seasons. We have seen a considerable increase in the volume of drama produced in the amateur environment, whereas the professional arena, both state theatre and private sector 'entertainment' theatre has become smaller.

A quick look at the amateur scene in Egypt indicates the existence of at least six authorities which present theatrical productions. Such shows are often presented in annual festivals or competitions. This activity is the shining face of the Egyptian theatre, a position reversed from earlier years. The most important of the authorities is the General Authority for Culture Palaces, which has a special department for theatrical production at various levels, including the national companies for governorates; companies of the culture palaces in greater cities; and culture houses in small towns and large villages. The production of this Department is varied and prolific, because it supervises the production of theatre all over Egypt. The present theatrical season 2001/2002, however, has suffered from a reassessment of the policy of quantity to be followed in the production of plays, which has led to delay in the start of the present theatrical season. Nevertheless, during the season 2000/2001 the Department presented 127 shows, presented by 132 companies at an average of ten evenings for each show. As for the present transitional year, the number of companies fell to ninety only. Future quantity and quality have not yet been decided.

The General Authority for Culture Palaces is an important cultural edifice for some additional reasons: it combines two other departments in charge of theatrical production for amateurs but within their cultural activity. The first Department is the Private Cultural Societies Dept. which produced 17 theatrical shows in 2000 alone. It held its festival in the following year, 2001, in Assiut Governorate in Upper Egypt. In recent months, it has started a new series of preliminary competitions, so that shows may be promoted to the Final Festival for 2002. The second Department is that of Child Culture, which produces plays for children every now and then.

The unsatisfactory matter in this phenomenon of amateur theatre is that, although the State produces or finances the greater part thereof, this huge and expensive activity is not positively reflected in the professional theatrical productions backed by the Government. Nobody knows where the amateur artists who participate in amateur productions sneak out. According to our personal opinion, the competition system on which such activities depend is sterile, because it does not lead to the accumulation of any kind of experience. Throughout the years, it has become 'a chance' for some professionals to be involved in such competitions.

Scene from *Jerusalem Shall Not Fall* (*Lan Taskot El Kods*) written by Sherif El Shobashy and directed by Fahmy El Kholy at the National Theatre

EGYPT

There are several other phenomena which should be noticed in our attempt to estimate the three theatrical seasons referred to, such as experimental theatre.

In September 2001, the Cairo International Festival for Experimental Theatre held its thirteenth session. Although it is an annual festival allocated for experimental shows only, its effects greatly exceeded the limits of small or experimental Egyptian shows. By accumulation, the Festival has been transformed into a major phenomenon in the Egyptian theatre.

For example, this year eighteen plays competed against each other to have the honour of representing Egypt officially in the Festival (Egypt, being the host state, is permitted two shows). At present, most of these shows are specially prepared for the Festival. Some of them 'die' because they are not selected to represent Egypt, but most of them are presented after the lapse of the ten days of the Festival. If we look at professional Government theatrical productions (decreasing year after year), we will discover that these experimental shows represent a high proportion of it. This means that the Egyptian audience will go on watching plays prepared according to the specifications of the Experimental Festival for most of the rest of the year.

On the other hand, the Experimental Festival has promoted a theatre which depends on the language of the visual picture and not the spoken word. We believe that while the visual element is necessary and indeed essential for international theatrical competition, *i.e.* in a different linguistic setting, the 'local' Egyptian theatre should not drift to this tendency, especially because the Egyptian literary heritage in general is linguistic in the first place. The percentage of illiteracy in Egypt is high, even according to Government figures. Hence, it is necessary to depend on spoken language to a large extent and not on the complex picture language which requires high 'artistic' culture in order to receive it and interpret its significance.

The activities referred to may form a bright picture of the reality of the Egyptian theatre during the last three years; nay, they may give promise of a flourishing future. Nobody can deny their importance. But hard reality shows the contrary of the results that might be expected from such activities. The Theatre Artistic House, which is the main Government theatrical producer, suffers from the small number of plays produced through its companies, as well as the small number of its audience, to the extent that it is sometimes obliged to restrict itself to presenting theatrical shows at weekends only.

The National Theatre, for example, presented only two large shows in the season 1999/2000: one was adapted from a work of the Syrian writer, Saadalla Wannous, titled *Adventure of the Mameluke Gaber* (*Moghamaret El Mamluke Gaber*), directed by Morad Monir in January 2000; the other was *Henry IV*, by Luigi Pirandello, directed by the Italian director Valts Manfrey which was presented by the theatre in October 2000. In the same season, the theatre presented three chamber plays (two of them translated) and received a Palestinian theatrical company for one week. In the season 2000–2001 the Theatre presented three shows only, two on the main stage. One was *Last Whisper* (*Akher Hamsa*), written and directed by Hany Motawe, the present Head of the Theatre Artistic House, in August 2000; the other was *People in the Third* (*El Nas Elly Fil Thaleth*), written by Osama Anwar Okasha. Among the reasons for its success were the distinguished TV reputation of the writer and its star cast.

The current 2001–2002 season has witnessed some improvement in theatrical performances. January 2002 has presented us with the play *Jerusalem Shall Not Fall* (*Lan Taskot El Kods*) written by Sherif El Shobashy and directed by Fahmy El Kholy, followed by Shakespeare's masterpiece *King Lear*, directed by Ahmed Abdel Hamil, which drew the attention of the public through its leading actor, the TV star Yahia El Fakharany.

The picture is no different in the rest of the companies affiliated to the Theatre Artistic House. Each of the eight presented a number of plays no greater than the fingers of one hand (apart from the company of the Youth Theatre, which presents poor and small shows in haphazard presentation places). For example, among the most important works presented by the Modern Theatre company is *The Dancer and the Dervish* (*El Ghazia Wal Darwish*). It also presented a comprehensive reconsideration of an old work by the Egyptian dramatist Mikhail Roman, who died in 1973, titled *Isis My Love* (*Isis Habibty*). The new version was presented in August 2000 by the director, Samir El Asfoury, who transformed it into a strange, hybrid and directionless show, titled *My Love...* (*Habibty Ya...*). The title itself was a sarcastic imitation of one of the most successful shows of the commercial sector by the same director, titled *My Belt ...* (*Hazemny Ya*) in which the famous eastern dancer, Fifi Abdu, played the heroine.

The same pattern was repeated with the shows of the Modern Theatre in 2001. It presented a small number of plays, the most important of which were *Sons of Anger and Love* (*Awlad El Ghadab Wal Hob*), written by Karam El Naggar and directed by Nasser Abdel Moneim, and *Hello Land* (*Alo Ya Ard*) written by Nabil Badran and directed by Hesham Gomaa. The company began the year 2002 by presenting the *Barber of Baghdad* (*Hallak Baghdad*) written by Alfred Farag and directed by Hanaa Abdel Fattah.

The other companies of the Theatre Artistic House presented in the last months of 2001 a small number of 'great' plays. El Taliaa company, for example, presented *War of Basous* (*Harb El Basous*) written by Shawky Abdel Hakim and directed by Mohammed El Kholy, with its plot, depending on inheritance, projected on to contemporary Arab world disputes. The Tomorrow Theatre company presented *Harem of Salt and Sugar* (*Harim El Malh Wal Sukar*), written by Mohammed El Gheity and directed by Mahmoud Hassan, dealing with the strangeness of some traditions of revenge in Upper Egypt.

Our view of the recession in Government theatrical production can be confirmed by the book published by the Theatre Artistic House itself about its activities during the period from 1990 till 2000. The book clearly indicates the remarkable decrease in audience numbers from the middle of the 90s. Figures we have obtained from other sources prove the continuance of this decrease in numbers after 2000, when the official book stops. In our opinion, this decrease is not necessarily connected with the shrinkage in the theatrical production of the State only: it has other social, economic and political reasons. The foregoing represent mere samples of Government theatrical production. The total image also includes the production of El Hanager Theatre, the Educational Cultural National Centre (Opera) and the Artistic House for Popular and Musical Arts. But what we have said about the production of the Theatre Artistic House applies to some extent to these production authorities also.

EGYPT

The companies of the private sector are also suffering from a severe drop in the number of visitors although such companies are interested in comedy, farce, singing and musicals aimed mainly at entertainment. Most of these companies were obliged to close down for long periods. When they resumed their shows, they presented them for two or three days per week as a maximum, although these companies make use of great cinema stars and are extensively promoted. In the present season, 2001–02, some companies have presented old works again. There have been few new works, the most important of which are *Pamper Yourself Dossa* (*Edalacy Ya Dossa*), written by Ezzat Adam and directed by Hassan Abdel Salam, in which the eastern dancing star, Fifi Abdu, is again heroine. The most expressive sign of general depression in the production atmosphere is the entire absence of the disciplined and brilliant actor-manager Mohamed Sobhy from the theatrical arena during 2001.

To be sure, we cannot ignore non-artistic factors which affect theatre attendance, such as the economic one (annual individual income has shrunk in the beginnings of 2002, due to the rise in the Dollar rate) and the artists' demand for space and private TV channels. But in our opinion the real reason is the continuous deterioration in the development of the theatre art, to the extent that real creativity has become rare and risky. This is surely the outcome of previous years, too full of work on the trial and error principle.

Ignoring fundamental planning in the Government theatre, for example, has led to the fact that the State spent much money on the amateur theatre through different ministries without finding a practical means through which the professional Governmental theatre might benefit from this activity. There is no longer any energy poured into the professional theatrical production machine, so it has become weaker and weaker. For this reason, the creativity level has lowered year after year. The whole matter has been transformed into a task to be performed, a festival to be held or a competition to be accomplished, all against a background of low prices, which has disgusted the real innovators. They have lost interest in the theatre. The number of new writers introduced by the amateur theatre during the last three years can hardly be counted on the fingers of one hand. None of them promises much for the future.

The general image of the Egyptian theatre during the last three years may seem to be bright and flourishing in one aspect, but it is dark in the other. The State is still intensively producing shows for amateurs (some for political reasons) through several production authorities, but it is miserly – or obliged to be so – in producing serious professional theatre.

*Mohsin Mosilhi is a leading Egyptian theatrologist; Dr **Ahmed Zaki** is Professor at the Arts Academy, Head of the Egyptian ITI Centre; formerly Under-Secretary of State and Head of the Theatre and Folkloric Arts Sector.*

ESTONIA

KADI HERKÜL

'There's no business, like show business…' For the Estonian theatre, the last few seasons have been a real illustration of this half-century old quotation from Irving Berlin. A little more than ten years of independence have brought show-business-as-usual on to Estonian stages, as well as less conventional performing spaces.

In November 2001 we saw the first Cameron Mackintosh production in Estonia, and in Estonian – Alain Boublil and Claude Michel Schönberg's *Les Miserables*, directed by Georg Malvius from Sweden, was staged in Tallinn to packed audiences and critical approval. In June 2002 Andrew Lloyd Webber's *Evita* followed – this time in Tartu, staged as an open-air performance in the Town Hall Square and directed by the young and promising Tiit Ojasoo. In November 2002 *Miss Saigon* is due to open.

Although Estonian state subsidized theatres along with private companies have produced quite a number of (mostly) old musicals from the 50s and 60s during previous seasons, *Les Miz* was the first real full-scale musical on Estonian stages.

Along with musicals, all kinds of showbiz-type theatre events have taken place and are becoming more and more popular. In 1995 Estonian theatre saw the revival of an open-air summer theatre tradition (of the same kind as is very popular in Finland – probably influenced by our short but bright season of summer nights); during the last seasons summer theatre has become more and more popular with dozens of open-air productions by both professional state theatres, private companies and amateur groups taking place all over Estonia through June-July-August.

It should be stated here that the scope of summer theatre is rather large – it includes small intimate productions in manor houses or city museums for 60 to 100 spectators as well as full-scale panoramic open-air events for up to 1000 viewers.

In 2001 summer productions received more than 100,000 visitors – an amazing number compared to the overall number of Estonians living in Estonia, which is less than a million.

During the summer of 2002 approximately 20 professional summer productions could be seen all over Estonia (including the first swamp-theatre production, *Elk-woman*, staged on a bog island near the town of Rakvere) and the total number of visitors will probably increase.

In some ways the success of show-business events and summer theatre indicates that traditional theatre has lost part of its importance and the theatre landscape has become far more diverse. Or the other way round, the word 'theatre' has come to mean much more than productions in dusty playhouses.

At the same time, traditional Estonian theatre has survived rather well. Despite huge changes in society and the overwhelming market-orientated liberalism of the Estonian economy, state subsidies have remained the most important source of funding for theatres. In 2002 18 Estonian theatres received some funding from the state budget out of the total amount of a little more than 10 million US$. It should be specified, though, that the eleven state or municipal theatres gathered most of the money, with seven small private companies receiving only about 2.5% of the sum.

This funding system has been criticized from different sides, mostly because it makes practically no allowance for projects and new ideas. The current system of subsidy has proven to be quite suitable only for preserving Estonian theatre as it is. At the same time it needs extreme persistence to change the funding. In October 2001 there was an initiative from the Ministry of Culture to merge two Tallinn-based theatres – Vanalinnastuudio, staging mostly comedies, and the Estonian Drama Theatre (a kind of national theatre in all but name) – and thus create some extra money for new and emerging theatres or projects. Unfortunately enough, the initiative was abandoned (or postponed) after some weeks of warm dispute.

Even though great ideas do not depend straightforwardly on money, the lack of the latter could be considered one of the reasons why the Estonian theatre landscape has been rather flat during the last years. Estonian theatre is dominated by quite well made but rather old-fashioned productions, focusing on human psychology. It doesn't mean that this type of theatre can't be contemporary and eloquent. For example the productions of Brian Friel's *Aristocrats* (2000, directed by Priit Pedajas), Michael Frayn's *Copenhagen* (2002, directed by Mikk Mikiver), or Per Olov Enquist's *Image-makers* (*Bildmakarna*, 2000, directed by Kaarin Raid) have granted the audiences highly adorable evenings. Yet along with these successes there are dozens and dozens of productions that lack individuality.

Somewhat aside from this central stream of Estonian theatre lies the work of novelist and director Mati Unt. His recent productions, including *The Wedding* by Witold Gombrowicz, *The Master and Margarita* by Mikhail Bulgakov and *The Cherry Orchard* by Anton Chekov all use a fragmented style, mixing elements of 'high' and 'low' in a quite grotesque manner. And although this kind of theatre was popular in the world some decades ago and is now considered pretty old-fashioned, it can be seen as something more or less new, even experimental, in the context of Estonian theatre.

At the same time it would be precipitate to consider Estonian theatre dead. The last few seasons have brought a handful of new young directors with distinguishable styles to Estonian theatres. These young men (Tiit Ojasoo, Hendrik Toompere, Tõnu Lensment) are stepping away from traditional psychology, trying to explore the unconscious and unspoken sides of human nature. This emerging group has been called 'cold', due to the absence of compassion or mercy in their work.

Dealing with the last three seasons in our theatre there seems to be at least one production one could not omit – *Connecting People*, written by the *enfant terrible* of Finnish theatre, Jouko Turkka and directed by his compatriot Erik Söderblom.

Connecting People, probably the most scandalous theatre event of the decade, took place in the tiny Von Krahl Theatre in Tallinn. The play grotesquely and awkwardly portrays the most famous business personality in neighbouring Finland, the CEO of the cell-phone company Nokia. Although in places disgusting, the play received rather positive repercussions in the Estonian media. Probably they were partly due to the fact that this kind of rough theatre is extremely rare on our stages. At the same time, the fact that *Connecting People* was banned in Finland made it an especially attractive event for Estonians (and even for Finns).

In the field of new dramatic writing, Estonia is far beyond its Nordic neighbours. Our contemporary theatre is mostly dominated by Anglo-American and

ABOVE: Ain Lutsepp and Guido Kangur in Michael Frayn's *Copenhagen*, directed by Mikk Mikiver
(*photo*: Harri Rospu)

BELOW: Andrew Lloyd Webber's *Evita* at the Town Hall Square in Tartu, directed by Tiit Ojasoo
(*photo*: Ove Maidla)

The World of Theatre

– during recent seasons – Irish writing. Brian Friel has been on Estonian stages for a decade; the last seasons have added the names of Martin McDonagh and Conor McPherson to the list.

Among new Estonian plays *The Bridge* (*Sild*), by actor-songwriter Jaan Tätte, is worth mentioning. the central character of the play – a beautiful young woman – is going to die very soon and is looking for someone to love and be loved by. The play's best part is a heartbreakingly sincere monologue from the girl, depicting the outworn everyday issues like beauty and love.

The first summer productions of 2002 seem to suggest quite a new tendency in Estonian dramatic writing – an incredible amount of self-irony is emerging on Estonian stages. The Estonian Drama Theatre celebrated summer with a production by a promising young playwright, Andrus Kivirähk, called *Estonian Funeral*. The work openly laughs at the issues that have been considered most valuable and basic in Estonian national identity: workaholism, endurance under occupation(s), etc.

A week later, *The Dawn Concert*, by satiric writer Toomas Kall, opened in the courtyard of a decaying Northern Estonian manor house. Inspired probably by the Eurovision song contest held in Tallinn in May 2002, the play offered a totally laughable portrayal of Estonian 'hospitality', or in other words willingness to do everything (and more) to please every single foreigner and construct a picture of Estonia as a really first-class Eastern European democracy.

As for music and dance, the last decade has been quite a hard experience for Estonian stages. As the borders more or less opened up, a huge number of our high quality professionals left the country. The problem has been most burning for dancers – the Estonian school of classical ballet is considered pretty good in the west (due to our Soviet heritage), so our best artists dance anywhere but in Estonia. The best-known success story is that of Agnes Oakes and Thomas Edur, now enjoying the status of senior guest principals at the English National Ballet. For nearly a decade this has created quite an empty space at the Estonian national opera. Fortunately enough the situation seems to be changing. In 2001 Tiit Härm, a former principal of the national opera who has been working for La Scala ballet for 10 years, took over the role of artistic director of the ballet. He has brought a new and demanding repertoire (*Cassandra* by Luciano Cannito, *Coppelia* by Mauro Bigonzetti) to the national opera.

In addition a handful of small dance companies (Fine 5, ZUGA, SPA) has emerged during the last decade. Their efforts in the field of post-modern dance have been considered quite promising, but the lack of modern dance experience and techniques – due to the fact that modern dance was virtually banned by the former Soviet regime – seems to be a stumbling block for them. No new dance company in Estonia has (yet) achieved the artistic importance and meaningfulness of Pina Bausch, Sasha Walz, or Alain Platel.

In conclusion it could be stated that Estonian theatre is at the crossroads. It has survived rather well through ten years of drastic economic change. In the future, its well being depends more and more on the clarity of its artistic aims. To stay competitive in the fast growing entertainment market, theatre needs to be flexible and diverse in themes, styles, and finding funds.

Kadi Herkül *is a theatre critic and deputy editor-in-chief of the Estonian daily* Postimees.

FINLAND

RIITTA WIKSTRÖM

'Small is beautiful'. These were the words used by Vivica Bandler when in 1989 she became artistic director of the Tampere International Theatre Festival, an organisation rapidly running out of money. At the beginning of the 90s the festival had to be content with showing small-scale visiting productions involving only a few actors and it was from this that the audience had to experience the wonder and greatness of the theatre. This was not a conscious policy, rather it was an attempt to turn the inevitable to the festival's advantage. Nonetheless, this was something to be repeated several times in the years to come. The effectiveness of these words is something which has stayed in the minds of those groups of actors who, at the beginning of the 90s, were forced to be extremely frugal with production costs and to concentrate far more on ideas and concepts than on the scale of performances.

There have been no drastic changes in Finnish theatre in the last few years and in consequence many people have accused it of being unimaginative and dull. Despite this the Finnish theatre-going public has remained faithful to theatres throughout the country. The huge popularity of many fine, well-known older actors is testament to this. It is because of these actors that theatres have been able to count on the success of individual plays and, indeed, of entire seasons. An example is Ronald Harwood's *Quartet* at Helsinki City Theatre in spring 2002 starring Kyllikki Forsell, Ritva Valkama, Pentti Siimes and Lasse Pöysti. The actor Esko Salminen, too, has been a crowd-puller in the Brecht play *Herr Puntila und sein Knecht Matti* (autumn 2001) and in KOM theatre's production of *Festen* (spring 2002).

It is essential to consider the factors which affect the appeal of programming and individual productions in larger theatres. In addition to musicals and hilarious farces, which have traditionally always attracted large audiences, a form of expression based on the power of visual images has grown in popularity. The work of a skilled scenographer is primarily called for in showy musicals and historical costume dramas. During the years of financial difficulty at the beginning of the 90s the work of set designer Kari Junnikkala and Kaija Salaspuro, who often collaborated on productions, attracted large audiences to the main stage of Lahti City Theatre. Starlit skies (as in the Lahti production of *Juha*, directed by Ensio Suominen and Eija-Elina Bergholm) and even ice rinks seem to present no problem for those with a passion for new theatrical techniques, and after all, it is not their fault if the narrative is upstaged by the design.

Set design and costume have been given ample opportunity to grow and develop in the larger theatres. Musicals and large-scale spectacular productions, which regularly sell out, have made particular use of these areas of expertise. Such productions require big casts and enormous budgets and have all but sidelined the passion for more experimental theatre. Programming with depth, which challenges the traditional approach to form, is more likely to be found in smaller theatres or on smaller stages.

Yet there are many recent examples of exceptional productions on a similar scale to these routinely performed and now somewhat hackneyed musicals. An example is the opera *Paavo Nurmi*, directed by Kalle Holmberg at the Olympic Stadium in Helsinki during summer 2001. Paavo Haavikko wrote the story of the legendary long distance runner in the libretto and also set it in a wider historical context. The performance, produced by Helsinki City Theatre, worked extremely well in the enormous arena, regardless of the rain which took the actors by surprise on several occasions.

In recent years there has been a clear shift of focus in the programming of 'the classics'. William Shakespeare's great examinations of power have become surprisingly rare sights on the Finnish stage. A decade or so ago there were several productions of *Macbeth* and *King Lear* across the country, reflecting the cold war era and the use of weaponry. On the other hand there are several examples of more light-hearted, comedic Shakespeare plays in recent programmes and *Romeo and Juliet* is no longer conspicuous by its absence. The great plays of Anton Chekhov, which were once the mainstay of many theatres' repertoire, have also become rarities. Only one of the theatres in the Helsinki area (Teatteri Takomo) has taken on the challenge of *Uncle Vanya* and in doing so found links between the play's characters and contemporary society in a sensitive and powerful way.

Conversely, the stern troll of Nordic drama, the Norwegian playwright Henrik Ibsen, has assumed an important role in a time when we are once again forced to question the problematic identity of the individual and to find solutions for it. Nora's solution to this problem in *A Doll's House* has appealed to audiences in a production in Lahti City Theatre (dir. Cilla Back, 2001) and in a version in the Finnish National Theatre (dir. Katariina Lahti, 2002), which considers the problems of men's and women's duty from a modern-day egalitarian perspective. The small Takomo Theatre got to grips with *Hedda Gabler*, nowadays somewhat rarely performed, in a production which sidelined the conventional interpretation of Hedda as the portrait of a diva and instead brought her cruelty acutely to the fore.

Old Hollywood musicals received many an outing in Finland during the end of the 90s, their sunny optimism bringing a little light to the needs of an audience living in hardship or otherwise in low spirits. In line with this, a new image of the relationship between family and environment has arisen. In Finland half of all marriages end in divorce, which indicates that 'the family' is in a bad way. The problems faced by families and children have begun to appear on stage as side issues or central themes.

This issue was dealt with very powerfully when KOM Theatre performed the play *Aina joku eksyy* (*Someone Always Goes Astray*), written and directed by Reko Lundán, and a year later its continuation *Teillä ei ollut nimiä* (*Can You Hear the Howling?*); both productions toured widely throughout Finland. Each play deals with various stages of a family's life, focussing on a household troubled by the parents' problems and the difficulties experienced by the children as they grow up. Both plays employ a flashback technique and the story is told in short,

Part of Lahti City Theatre's policy is that it invests time and effort in musical theatre. A musical adaptation of Tolstoy's *Anna Karenina* was produced as part of an EU project. This Finnish-Russian production was directed by Jotaarkka Pennanen

skilfully written fragments of dialogue. The humour on the surface initially hides the stark reality which both plays hold within them. The generation of people raising children during the 60s is given critical examination with all its self-absorbed ideas, its freedom, everything. Reko Lundán is one of the great surprises of recent years. In addition to being a gifted playwright he is also a skilled, intelligent and analytical director (*Death of a Salesman* at Helsinki City Theatre and *Cat on a Hot Tin Roof* at the Finnish National Theatre) and is now one of the three directors of the Tampere International Theatre Festival.

The last few years have also seen Finnish historical dramas trying to attract an audience, which has perhaps not fully relinquished its rather simple Finnish identity in favour of a rather more colourful EU nationality – other than the change to the single currency. Various periods of history have been put on the stage in lavish spectacles (for example Laila Hietamies' plays at the Finnish National Theatre, set amidst the romanticism of Tsarist Russia) or following the story of Finnish cultural figures – *Vanhempieni romaani* (*My Family's Novel*) at Lahti City Theatre in 2001. In both of these the audience is taken back in history on something of a sight-seeing tour, to a time of wealth, flamboyance and exuberance. Once again, set and costume designers (Ralf Forsström, Kari Junnikkala, Kaija Salaspuro) came into their own.

A production which also belongs to the group of historical spectacles is TTT-Theatre of Tampere's centenary celebration production of Maija Lassila's *Tulitikkuja lainaamassa* (*Borrowing Matches*). This play had previously been considered merely a genial folk comedy. In this production it opened up into an expansive portrait of the Finnish temperament and being, Kalle Holmberg's direction depicting the various stages in the country's history in the shadow of death, yet within the context of the comedic picaresque journey. The presence of death was made concrete in the red, earthy set depicting the yard, on to which were painted imitations of Hugo Simberg's highly original and captivatingly primitive paintings.

A production both interesting and radically different in its mentality to others in this historical series was performed at Helsinki City Theatre in spring 2001. The Swedish director Frej Lindqvist directed his own play *Armfelt*, a drama about the relations between Finland, Sweden and Russia. The performance was both charming and intelligent, gently playing with historical themes. It was at once a thoroughly enjoyable farce, where people fought battles in caricatured ballet steps, and a perceptive interpretation of the various turns of history.

Artistically speaking, Finnish theatre has not tried to cross the minefield that is 'biographical theatre' and the unavoidable sense of parody which comes with that. In a country in which every single public monument sparks a passionate debate for or against modern art, successful young artists are tolerated alongside such people as old Field Marshall Mannerheim, General Airo and other political figures in recent history. Indeed, the springboard for many romanticised historical plays is often a genuinely fascinating personal history (for example Elisabeth Järnefelt in *My Parents' Novel*) or the life and times of a well-known political figure and an explanation of their list of misdemeanours (the play *Isä* (*Father*), which dealt with the life of Ahti Karjalainen, at Helsinki City Theatre in autumn 2001).

In recent years extensive works of literature have provided new challenges for dramaturgs. One example of this was the performance at Hämeenlinna City Theatre of Olli Jalonen's enormous novel *Yksityiset tähtitaivaat* (*Personal Heavens*) in a dramatisation by Marja Louhija. It charts the story of a small, ordinary person in the ideological struggles of early 20th century St Petersburg, in the grip of hunger and freezing cold, and depicts the development of a family over three generations in different parts of the world.

Turku City Theatre managed to produce a stage version of Marquez' *One Hundred Years of Solitude*. The dramatisation by Ilpo Tuomarila, directed by Maarit Ruikka, succeeded in bringing the colourful and mystical world of Marquez' text to the stage.

The musical version of Leo Tolstoy's novel *Anna Karenina* at Lahti City Theatre was an enormous event, with its numerous costumes and huge international cast. This production, created and directed by Jotaarkka Pennanen, represents a first in many ways. An enormous EU grant, the size of which has never been seen in Finland before, was awarded for the realisation of this project. Many artists from the St Petersburg area collaborated on the project: the music was composed by Vladislav Uspenski and the libretto was written by Tatjana Kalinina. The dance group and the choreography were Russian, the actors Finnish. The production was performed during a short and intense autumn – spring period 2001–2002. The commercial spirit of the production was accordingly built upon: the audience could purchase a range of Anna Karenina jewellery, local restaurants served up an Anna menu and in the interval Anna pastries were served.

One of the most surprising phenomena of the past three years has been the growing popularity of Finnish plays. During 2000 there were several dozen premières of new Finnish plays in theatres around the country, both in small theatres and on the smaller stages of large theatres. The desire to examine the nature of Finnishness can be seen in the search for images of national identity, largely through dramatisations based on Finnish literature. Also unprecedented was the fact that the most popular new plays moved on to other theatres after their premières. In previous years, even the most popular plays had always remained in a single theatre.

The image of Finnish dramatists has also changed during the past few years. Young playwrights are generally professional dramaturgs in their own right and welcome the opportunity to direct their own work. The Direction and Dramaturgy department of the Finnish Theatre Academy seems to have developed into a school for playwrights as well. Some of the very best young dramatists have graduated from the academy, including Juha Siltanen, Laura Ruohonen, Juha Lehtola, Michael Baran, Reko Lundán, Anne Koski and Kristian Smeds.

Of course many playwrights come from places other than the Finnish Theatre Academy. However, they often experience difficulty in forging contacts with theatres. To help young writers, KOM Theatre has developed a completely new way of working. KOM-Text looks through scripts and even synopses of work in progress. Various dramaturgs and directors read through the material and give feedback to the writers. Promising ideas are developed first as rehearsed readings and then into finished productions. There are many other theatres involved in this process of text development besides KOM.

FINLAND

Confidence in the ability of Finnish plays to attract a substantial audience is not a new phenomenon amongst our smaller theatres. The first theatre to make a decision to perform only new Finnish texts was Ryhmäteatteri (The Group Theatre) towards the end of the 80s. At the end of the 90s, many other theatres began to follow suit, realising that without serious dedication to new Finnish drama there would soon not be any at all. In different parts of the country, for example in Oulu, there were attempts to make contact with young writers, whilst in Lahti the theatre Vanha Juko was founded, a theatre which looks exclusively for new Finnish drama. These theatres encountered the same problems as those so-called 'groups', who had already established their position and who had long since supported and in many respects paved the way for new Finnish drama.

The furore over Jouko Turkka's play *Osta pientä ihmistä* (*Connecting People*) even before its première, which led to rehearsals at KOM Theatre being discontinued, was in a league of its own. People feared that the play had gone beyond the limits of decency by portraying a living person, the managing director of Nokia, in a potentially detrimental fashion. Those who bothered to read the play or who managed to see its production by the Estonian Von Krahl Theatre will have noticed that the way in which it deals with the multi-millionaire, a leading figure in the mobile communications industry, revered by young financiers, in fact reflects in an exaggerated and even surreal way the financial situation in Finland today; it has nothing to do with the real life or persona of the person in question. The play has yet to be performed in Finland.

In recent years, Finnish theatre and plays have made their way beyond the language barrier and on to international stages. Laura Ruohonen's play *Olga* has been translated into several languages and was performed to great critical acclaim at the Traverse Theatre in Edinburgh, Scotland.

In a class of their own are the plays written and directed by Kristian Smeds, both in Takomo Theatre and more recently in Kajaani City Theatre. Chekhov's *Uncle Vanya*, the play *Jumala on kauneus* (*God is Beauty*) depicting the destiny of a Finnish artist and his most recent play *Huutavan ääni korvessa* (*One Crying in the Wilderness*), which looks deep into the Finnish soul, have been given characteristically austere physical performances, almost frightening in their primitive energy. The deeply human 'message' of these plays hits home despite language barriers – which explains the growing demand for them at international theatre festivals.

Everyone has had money troubles, both the affluent and the poor. All arts organisations, including theatres, have felt the strain of financial demands more than ever before. This has been a time when the pressure to reduce public funding has grown considerably. A general trust in continued support is still very strong – after all, Finland is a country which prides itself on its support for artistic life. The law in Finland guarantees the existence of theatres as well as orchestras, museums and libraries. Recent years have seen an increase in the pressure to implement strategies to save money and thus theatres have been presented with unrealistic targets.

A law regarding theatres and orchestras, passed in 1993, supported the Finnish theatre network during the financial crisis of the mid-90s in a special way.

State funding alone is not enough to support the running of theatres. The provinces, of which there are so many and which already suffer from the difficulties involved in moving about within the country, have been forced to choose between the demands of arts organisations, education, teaching institutions and health care. In the light of this, many small provinces were forced to cut funding to theatres on the premise that theatres had the ability to fund themselves through box office takings. There followed a heated debate, in which it was argued that art can serve as an attraction to these very provinces and thus recover the money spent on it – with interest – straight back into the local council coffers. It was because of this that people began to examine and count up all the influence art had on work, tax levels and other aspects of public funding.

At the same time many of those who were not covered by the theatre law condemned it strongly and demanded that it be revised, since it supported only large theatre organisations, based on the number of staff, and thus made size a virtue in its own right. New smaller theatres, which the younger generation has been founding in rapid succession, had no chance of meeting the criteria outlined for state support and were forced to settle for a meagre grant at the discretion of the funding body. These groups have become concentrated in a few large towns, usually ones with a university, where there is a wide audience and where television and cinema can also offer actors essential work opportunities.

It often feels as though each successive generation needs a group of theatres of its own as a guarantee of their existence and as a channel for their feelings. It will not be long before many of them will have established themselves and will begin to demand state funding. Even in Finland, which considers itself a 'theatre country', people have begun to wonder how the state can fund all of these theatres without having to make cuts at one end of the scale or the other. And which end should that be? Should we shut down a bad theatre in the far north? Who is to say what is quality theatre and what is not?

Riitta Wikström *is a theatre critic with one of the major Finnish newspapers,* Etelä-Suomen Sanomat.

FRANCE

IRÈNE SADOWSKA GUILLON

In March 2000, with the arrival of Catherine Tasca as Minister of Culture, the reformist policy of her predecessor in the first Government of the leftist coalition, Catherine Trautmann, was replaced by a policy of consensus, smoothing over conflicts by increasing the budget of important theatre institutions and revitalising a number of more marginal bodies. Under Tasca, the cultural budget exceeded one percent of the total national budget for the first time. Between 1998 and 2002, the money allocated to the performing arts increased by 30%. This increase strengthened State support around four areas of priority:

1   to support new disciplines, new spaces for artistic expression and independent production
2   to redirect attention to the needs of less mainstream media and the performing arts outside the capital
3   to put artistic training and practice at the centre of State support
4   to give impulse to research and validation of the past as well as training in theatre disciplines with an emphasis on new technology.

These priorities were an expression of a desire to re-establish the balance between Paris and the regions by reinforcing the partnership between central and regional government. As a response to the new artistic realities which came up against a static and overburdened institutional system, a large part of the new funding, more than half, was earmarked for the support of new disciplines: dance, circus, street theatre, contemporary music and experimental work carried out in new venues described as 'intermediate' or 'alternative'. Added to this were new resources (6 million euros) for the Centres Dramatiques Nationaux, the National Theatres, regional Opera Houses, Parisian theatres and Festivals with an international dimension, all intended to reinforce their capacity to create and promote work.

During this time, the building policy for the performing arts, with a budget of 52 million euros for 2002, was particularly chaotic: a number of urgent projects such as the refurbishment of the Théâtre National de Chaillot and the construction of a new performance space for the Odéon were abandoned in favour of new undertakings.

Catherine Tasca's policy was an opportunist one, which sought to avoid conflict and follow fashionable new tendencies without serious examination. Circus, dance and street arts were the undoubted beneficiaries of a policy built on publicity stunts and themed events like the Year of the Circus in 2001–2002 and the Bicentenary of Victor Hugo, 2002, or on cultural events bolstering French foreign policy: The Year of Morocco, The Year of Hungary, of Algeria and so on.

The Public Services Charter, which was supposed to come into force in

2002 and redefine the relationships between the State, local authorities and the directors of subsidised organisations, setting out their cultural practice and their artistic obligations, was already a dead letter. Equally, the directive of Catherine Trautmann that there should be a single reduced price once a week, in order to democratise access, was abandoned. The theatres simply set up their own systems of reduced prices appropriate to their own audiences.

The many changes of directors in subsidised theatres pursued the existing policy of promoting young talent (Emmanuel Demarcy Motta, Sylvain Maurice…) but looked for them to be more careful in their planning, doubt-less in the hope of avoiding financial disasters like that of Stanislas Nordey's 'People's Theatre' in Saint-Denis, where Alain Ollivier took over in 2002.

Notable appointments included the arrival of Marcel Bozonnet to run the Comédie-Française; Ariel Goldenberg taking on Chaillot from Jérôme Savary, who went to the Opéra Comique; Christian Schiaretti inheriting the TNP at Villeurbanne, the long-time fiefdom of Roger Planchon; Jean-Louis Martinelli, ousted from Strasbourg by Stefan Braunschweig, in turn taking over Nanterre from Jean-Pierre Vincent; further afield, Daniel Benoin arrived in Nice, Jean-Louis Benoit at La Criée in Marseilles and Pierre Pradinas followed Sylviu Purcarete in Limoges. Women directors made some inroads, with appointments including Catherine Anne at the Théâtre de l'Est Parisien, Gilberte Tsaï in Montreuil and Claudia Stavisky at the Célestins in Lyon.

The struggle of writers to gain responsibility for the running of theatres began to bear fruit, with Jean-Michel Ribes (founder of a playwrights' pres-sure group) taking on the Rond-Point in Paris. Whether this trend will con-tinue remains to be seen. What is certain is the increasingly urgent need for reform and regional redistribution, in the light of changes in socio-economic patterns and the status of the artist. This will probably be a job for Jean-Jacques Aillagon, Minister of Culture in the new right-wing government appointed after the re-election of Jacques Chirac to the Presidency of the Republic in May 2002.

Generous state subsidy in the 80s led to an explosion of professional and semi-professional companies, so that at the end of the 90s it became neces-sary for the Ministry of Culture to take radical measures to reform the sub-sidy system. They cut the system of annual grants to independent companies and replaced it with two levels of aid, the one over two or three years to selected groups, the other in the form of grants for single projects which had already secured at least a third of their funding. Necessary and urgent as this reform was, by limiting the number of those benefiting from State subsidy it contributed to the growth of an artistic fringe; as did the new legislation which turned theatre companies into commercial cultural undertakings. There were other important factors which helped create this fringe: while its members were reacting against the establishment's mainstream aesthetics and mass-produced productions, the establishment itself was resistant to work which went off the beaten artistic track.

This deep division between the two camps made the hierarchical structure of the subsidised system more and more apparent. Vast amounts of money were poured into the top companies, who operated a closed shop on the in-ternational level, where smaller regional theatres and festivals had to work alone

FRANCE

in financially precarious conditions. At the bottom of the ladder were the small independent companies, some of whom benefited from much sought after residencies in the regional theatres, while others had to seek out their own new places of performance. From this arose a trend towards squatting and occupation of disused buildings which produced considerable creativity both in their usage and the work which emerged from them. Often working in a social context and taking account of their immediate environment, the success of this movement and its 'alternative' spaces forced the state to accept its existence. As a rather paradoxical result, the state went some way towards institutionalising the fringe by setting up support for 'New Artistic Territories'.

Economic difficulties and the need for publicity forced the private theatre sector, an almost completely Parisian phenomenon, to turn to successful joint action. Since 2000 the managers of the 42 large and small private theatres have got together twice a year to announce their future programmes at star-studded press conferences. They also now publish a monthly guide, *Rappel*. Another strong factor affecting the growth of audiences in this sector has without doubt been adventurous new programming. As well as the usual *divertissements* there is now a higher quality of repertoire, including much new and often previously unknown work from contemporary French and foreign writers. As the star system declines, to be replaced by a more homogenous system of casting, the barrier between state and private theatre is coming down, with numbers of subsidised productions transferring to the private sector – and occasionally the reverse.

Among the big hits of the private sector may be mentioned Marguerite Duras' *L'Amante anglaise*, which played throughout the 1999–2000 season in Patrice Kerbrat's production; Marion Bierry's production of Sergi Belbel's *Après la pluie*, which played for two seasons; Gildas Bourdet's revival of *L'Atelier* by Jean-Claude Grumberg which played from September 1998 through to the end of 2000; and Marcel Bluwal's production of *Le Grand retour de Boris S.* by the Belgian Serge Kribus, which won the Critics' Prize for 2000–2001. Many private theatre productions were recognised with 'Molière' awards, including Richard Kalinovski's *Beast on the Moon* (2001), which confirmed the directing talents of Irina Brook, while a 2002 award for comedy went to *Ladies' Night*, by Anthony McCarten, Stephen Sinclair and Jacques Collard, a play which was despised by the London critics when it appeared there.

The subsidised theatres in these three seasons began to tire of some of the fashionable labels of the 90s – 'people's theatre', 'art theatre', 'theatre of social concern' – though there were plenty of directors working with new and old plays examining contemporary problems: violence, immigration, war and the rise of various forms of extremism.

This in part explains the enormous number of productions in France of the work of Edward Bond, and with it an increasing interest in the violent young playwrights who have come to the fore in Britain, Germany and Austria. Recent French exponents of a similar theatre have been Xavier Durringer, Mohamed Rouabhi and, most recently, the veteran Michel Vinaver with *11 septembre 2001*.

Nevertheless, new writing remains the poor relation in the subsidised sector. In spite of pressure from both the ministry and the Society of Dramatic

ABOVE: from Marcial Di Fonzo Bo's production of Copi's *Eva Peron* for the Théâtre National de Bretagne, Rennes   (*photo*: Alain Dugas)

BELOW: *left*, Peter Brook's *Le Costume* at the Bouffes du Nord *right*, Euripides' *Bakkhantes*, directed by Omar Porras at the Théâtre de la Ville, Abbesses Paris (*photos*: Pascal Victor,Birgit)

FRANCE

Authors and Composers, it accounts for just 8% of the total production, with much of the rest consisting of adaptations from other genres and revivals of domestic and foreign classics. In this respect Shakespeare, Molière and Chekhov lead the field – in 2001–2002 there were eight revivals of *L'Ecole des femmes* and any number of *Uncle Vanya*s.

The most frequently performed modern authors seem to be dead ones – Beckett, Koltès, Copi. Among the living, some (Michel Azama, Philippe Minyana, Valère Novarina, Noëlle Renaude, Serge Valletti) have remained in the limelight thanks to a continuing relationship with a known director, while others (Xavier Durringer, Joël Jouanneau, Jean-Paul Wenzel) have staged their own work.

There have been no notable developments in staging, only imitations of earlier 'masters' (Brook, Kantor…) and variations on the post-modern aesthetic, some using minimalism or new technology (Bob Wilson), others revelling in an aesthetic of ugliness. Among the works of today's French 'masters' may be mentioned Ariane Mnouchkine's *Tambours sur la digue* (1999), Benno Besson's *Caucasian Chalk Circle* (2001), Bernard Sobel's *Ubu Roi* (Avignon, 2001).

Within the younger generation one can observe a number of similarities, such as a retreat from realism and character in favour of minimalism and deconstruction. In playwriting this will often appear as an absence of dramatic structure, a stripping down of language, sometimes leading to the dialogue conventions of sitcom or strip cartoon. At the opposite end of the scale is the baroque extravagance of Olivier Py. Between these two extremes are a number of authors who have achieved a wide audience without falling into repeating old styles: Daniel Besnehard, Jean-Marie Besset, Enzo Cormann, Véronique Olmi, Jean-Yves Picq and Christian Siméon.

Promising directors include Eric Lacascade from Caen who won the Critics' Prize 2000–2001 for his Chekhov trilogy; Thierry de Peretti whose production of Koltès' *Retour au desert* in 1999 was a revelation; and Laurent Laffargue, a fine company leader whose work stretches from Shakespeare to Bond, Brecht to Daniel Keene.

The state has given considerable support to dance, an area which has enjoyed great creativity in recent years. This support has been as much for the development of an infrastructure as for choreographic creation itself. Major events in contemporary dance over the last three seasons include the world premiere of *Rire de la lyre* by Jose Montalvo (Opéra Garnier, 1999); Roland Petit's *Notre Dame de Paris*, with original music by Maurice Jarre (Opéra Garnier, 2001); Meg Stuart's *Highway 101* (Centre Pompidou, 2000); Saburo Teshigawara's *Absolute Zero* (Créteil, 2000); and finally Merce Cunningham's *Way Station* (Théâtre de la Ville, 2001).

Also worthy of note are Daniel Larrieu, whose + *qu'hier, pleins feux et Petit Bateau* (Théâtre de la Ville, 2001) is a look back at his career; Régine Chopinot, whose latest work *Chair obscur* (Théâtre de la Ville, 2002) examines touching and distance, bodies and the space between them, in both visual and physical terms. Odile Duboc who has developed a whole universe of texture, colour and light tinged with poetry in *J'ai mis du sable exprès, vite fait, comme ça, dans mes chaussures* (Brest, 2002); while Jean-Claude Gallotta, Mathilde Monnier and Angelin Prejlocaj continue to present work of quality. If the major choreographers have continued in their known ways (opening up to other disciplines such as theatre, circus, plastic arts; the introduction of spoken text; use of technology; oriental influences), the young have pursued more varied paths.

The increasing number of new spaces devoted to dance, as well as national and international dance events (including the new Paris International Dance Festival and the Rendez-vous Chorégraphique de Sceaux) have encouraged a meeting of different forms and the emergence of new talents.

The extraordinary richness of lyric theatre and opera which was noted at the end of the 90s continues to grow. The opera audience has increased in spectacular fashion over the last three seasons, both in Paris and outside – a different, younger audience. The great popularity of lyric theatre is due both to a public hunger for works which combine speech and song, music and image, and to the innovation and originality of their high quality productions, more and more of them by experienced theatre directors such as Mathias Langhoff, Jorge Lavelli, Robert Lepage and Andrei Serban. What is now on offer is a varied repertory of new work and inventive revivals, available at prices no greater than those of the cinema, which makes them accessible as never before to an audience of young people which has been greatly encouraged in the school environment.

The artistic policy developed by Jean-Pierre Brossmann since he took over the refurbished Châtelet in 1999, with its emphasis on new and commissioned work, has done much to develop the contemporary repertoire. Particularly notable were Ushio Amagatsu's staging of *Three Sisters* by Peter Eötvös and Peter Sellars' production of Kaija Saariaho's *L'amour de loin*. Brossmann has also developed relationships with big international festivals such as Salzburg and has created the Festival des Régions which welcomes productions from companies outside Paris each year to Châtelet (Lyon in 2002) in celebration of the growth of music theatre throughout the country. Another great success with the public has been Jérôme Savary's development of the Opéra Comique into a major popular music theatre, helped by the new repertoire of musical comedy.

International exchange has always been part of French cultural life, promoted by institutions such as the Odéon and the festivals in Avignon, Grenoble and elsewhere. Now overseas influence has increased considerably in other fields; it has expanded from opera and dance into every part of the theatre, with a growing interest in other countries' playwrights as well as their practitioners – Jon Fosse from Norway, Daniel Keene from Australia, Biljana Srbljanovic from Serbia have all had their work performed in a number of French theatres. There has also been a growth in co-productions with theatres in Spain and Germany.

The international and national festivals which grow in number year by year have become real rivals to the permanent theatres in seeking out new work and new techniques. Where the established festivals have usually been multidisciplinary, the new ones tend to concentrate on a single sector such as mime, dance, street theatre or new writing.

Irène Sadowska Guillon *writes for a number of specialised theatre journals in France and overseas. A specialist in contemporary theatre, especially that of Spain, she is the founder of a programme of dramatic exchange between France and Spain, 'Hispanité Eplorations'.*

GERMANY

KNUT LENNARTZ

The last two theatre seasons in Germany were marked by many personnel changes. But although directors and managers came and went in many of the big theatres, it would nonetheless be premature to call this a changing of the generational guard.

Take the Berliner Ensemble, for example. Founded by Bertolt Brecht and Helene Weigel in what was once East Berlin, this renowned theatre had been adrift following the death of Heiner Müller in 1995 until Claus Peymann, after nearly 12 years as director of Vienna's Burgtheater, returned to Germany. In the 70s and 80s Peymann was one of the leading directors in Germany – and one with unambiguous political intentions. He came to Berlin with grand plans at a time in which the city was returning to the centre of the political stage with the government's relocation from Bonn. In this new context, Peymann saw the opportunity to assume the role of a critical observer of political events, seeing himself as an 'incisor' in the flesh of the powerful and raising hopes for a new era of political theatre. His success in this regard remained modest. In February 2000 he directed *Das Ende der Paarung* (*The End of the Pairing*) by Franz Xaver Kroetz, a play based on the tragic suicides of Green Party politicians Petra Kelly and Gerd Bastian, who had withdrawn from political life in the 1990s. But the production only served as proof that dramatising the life of political personalities does not necessarily translate into political theatre. Despite several notable productions, the Berliner Ensemble has yet to live up to the expectations that it has raised in this area. Like the numerous other productions of that were mounted after the terrorist attacks of 11 September, even Peymann's rendition of Lessing's *Nathan der Weise*, which was added to the programme of the Berliner Ensemble in early 2002, can hardly be regarded as a satisfactory reaction to the new face of terrorism, religious fundamentalism, globalisation and other pressing questions.

These issues have attracted the attention of representatives of the generation in their thirties during the past two years. In Berlin, a young team associated with director Thomas Ostermeier took over the Schaubühne am Lehniner Platz, a theatre that has sustained itself on the legendary productions of Peter Stein and Luc Bondy during the 70s and 80s. After the fall of the Berlin Wall in 1989, the Schaubühne survived as the only prominent traditional theatre in the city's western half, but it could no longer boast of the artistic quality of its founding years. This was an opportunity for Thomas, who had made a name for himself at the so-called 'Barracks' at the Deutsches Theater with socially critical productions – the majority of them British transplants. Choreographer Sasha Waltz joined him at the Schaubühne in 2000. Hopes were high for a mutually productive relationship and there were even visions of joint projects between the dance theatre and its dramatic counterpart. The results after two years are rather sobering. With its productions *Körper* (*Bodies*) and *nobody*, Sasha Waltz's dance troupe has recently prompted international recognition. But the dramatic and dance theatres seem to be following their own paths; a major collaboration has yet to materialise. Ostermeier began his directorship with the German premiere of *Personenkreis 3.1* by the Swedish author Lars Norén, and continued to stage works by authors with whom he had successfully worked before at the Barracks. These included plays by Sarah Kane and younger German playwrights whom he brought to the Schaubühne as in-house authors. He directed *Parasiten* by Marius von Mayenburg as well as Roland Schimmelpfennig's *Push Up 3.1*, which has been a success this season. It's a play that focuses on representatives of the so-called 'Neue Mitte' or new middle class, dynamic young managers competing with one another to get to the top.

An era has come to a close in Berlin at the Deutsches Theater. Since 1991 Thomas Langhoff had been in charge of the theatre, where his father, Wolfgang Langhoff, had left his mark following World War II and into the 70s. Thomas Langhoff played to the strengths of the Deutsches Theater, which, ever since the legendary productions of the classics by Max Reinhardt in the 20s, had been regarded as the premier theatre for great acting. In recent years, however, Langhoff had been unable to recreate his past successes and his contract at the Deutsches Theater expired at the end of the 2000/01 season. Many critics found it symptomatic that he chose to end his tenure with a production of Shakespeare's *King Lear*, with Christian Grashof, a house regular, in the principal role: Langhoff being driven out of his theatre as Lear is expelled from his kingdom. His successor was Bernd Wilms, who had headed Berlin's Maxim Gorki Theater in the 90s and found favour with the public by featuring stars from television and film, such as Harald Juhnke (*Der Hauptmann von Köpenick*) and Ben Becker (*Berlin Alexanderplatz*). At the Deutsches Theater he also signed on young directors like Michael Thalheimer, whose deconstructive approach continues to polarise the public, as was the case with his Hamburg Thalia Theater production of Ferenc Molnár's *Liliom*, which caused the former city mayor to remark that despite Thalheimer, *Liliom* was in fact a respectable play that could have been staged in a respectable manner. This being as it may, Thalheimer's production was selected for inclusion in the annual Berlin Theatre Meeting, which features the year's most outstanding performances from Germany, Austria and Switzerland. Thalheimer presented a second work there as well – his Dresden production of *Das Fest* (*Festen*) based on the eponymous Danish film by Lars von Trier. Lessing's *Emilia Galotti* was another production that provoked dissonant critical echoes, but it was nonetheless an important sign of a new beginning at the Deutsches Theater.

The Maxim Gorki Theater enjoyed a less auspicious new start last season. New theatre manager Volker Hesse, who left Zurich's Neumarkt Theater to come to Berlin, inaugurated his tenure with a new play by Theresia Walser, *Die Heldin von Potsdam* (*The Heroine of Potsdam*). The theme sounded contemporary and exciting: a staged skinhead attack faked by the supposed victim. Hesse has not been able to duplicate his Zurich accomplishments, where, collaborating with dramatist Urs Widmer, he had succeeded in translating current issues into the theatrical realm. Among such productions was *Top Dogs*, a play about unemployed high-level managers.

GERMANY

Only an optimist would have believed ten years ago what has in fact come to pass at the Volksbühne am Rosa-Luxemburg-Platz. Frank Castorf, once the *enfant terrible* of German directors, is now the longest-serving theatre manager in Berlin. Better than anyone else, he has been able to stabilise his theatre during a time in which everything in and around Berlin was in a state of upheaval. His productions are expressions of a specific sense of the times that is typical for the young, post-unification generation in East Berlin. His most recent works, *Endstation Amerika* (*A Streetcar Named America*), adapted from Tennessee Williams, and his interpretations of Dostoevsky's *Erniedrigte und Beleidigte* and *Demons* are evidence of Castorf's indefatigable creativity.

There were also considerable changes on the German theatre scene beyond Berlin. The two major Hamburg theatres changed managers. The Hamburger Schauspielhaus under Frank Baumberger has been one of the best addresses for theatre in Germany. This is where Christoph Marthaler, who has in the meantime taken charge of the Zurich Schauspielhaus, directed on a regular basis and it is was the site of intense collaborations with Frank Castorf's Volksbühne. Baumbauer, now at Munich's Kammerspiele, was replaced by Tom Stromberg, who has long experience in the alternative scene, in theatres such as Frankfurt's TAT (Theater am Turm). In Hamburg Stromberg gave young directors a chance to prove themselves, but he has yet to enjoy the same success as his predecessor. Ulrich Khuon left Hanover to assume the direction of Hamburg's Thalia Theater, taking over the reins from Jürgen Flimm. In Hanover Khuon had featured new dramas and he is adhering to this concept in Hamburg as well, with productions by Moritz Rinke (*Republik Vineta*) and two plays by Dea Loher, *Klaras Verhältnisse* (*Klara's Conditions*) and *Der Dritte Sektor* (*The Third Sector*).

For many years, Dieter Dorn had assured continuity in the work of the Kammerspiele in Munich. This year Dorn left to join the Staatsschauspiel, taking many outstanding actors with him, among them Rolf Boysen and Thomas Holtzmann, who had contributed to the brilliance of the Kammerspiele. That Dorn assigned them the roles of Shylock and Antonio in his opening production of Shakespeare's *The Merchant of Venice* is an indication of his estimation of their talents. With this production Dorn made a definitive statement about his approach to theatre: large-scale productions of the classics with great actors. This makes him something of an exception among theatre heads and directors in Germany. In the generation of 40-year-olds, the only comparable figure would perhaps be Matthias Hartmann, a director who also worked at the Staatsschauspiel in Munich during the 90s and is now head of the city theatre in Bochum. Remarkable is his ongoing collaboration with dramatist Botho Strauß; Hartmann mounted a premier of Strauß's new work *Der Narr und seine Frau heute Abend in Pancomedia* (*The Fool and His Wife This Evening in Pancomedia*) last season. This year he scored a publicity coup by casting Harald Schmidt, who is well-known in Germany for his late-night talk-show, in the role of Lucky in Beckett's *Waiting for Godot*.

The German theatre landscape continues to be characterised by the so-called multi-stage theatres (mehrspartentheater) housing opera, dance and theatre ensembles. Approximately forty such theatres exist, and they still determine theatre life outside the major theatre centres of Berlin, Munich, Hamburg, Frankfurt

From Frank Castorf's production of Dostoevsky's *Erniedrigte und Beleidigte (The Insulted and the Injured)* at the Volksbühne, Berlin   (*photo*: Iko Freese / DRAMA)

and Stuttgart. That small theatres are also more than capable of extraordinary artistic accomplishments was proven once again last year by the Meininger Theater in Thuringia. The music theatre here focused its energies in peerless fashion to stage a production of Richard Wagner's 'Ring' under the direction of Christine Mielitz, who heads the theatre. The Meininger Theater succeeded in presenting all four parts of the cycle, a feat that one would usually expect from the traditional Wagnerian stronghold of Bayreuth, which has far greater means at its disposal in terms of actors and finance. But in Meiningen the whole theatre – indeed the whole city and region – supported this event. Meiningen is well-known in Germany for its theatre tradition. This is where in the nineteenth century 'Theatre Duke' Georg II founded the 'Meininger style' – a theatre of illusion – with his Shakespeare productions. Critics showered Meiningen with praise for the 'Ring' cycle. Projects like this are responsible for the fact that this city of only 26,000 inhabitants was able to attract 180,000 people to the theatre. This would be a remarkable achievement for any theatre today.

The struggle surrounding the stage was often as dramatic and exhausting as the actions taking place on it during the past few years. Many theatres have been forced to make considerable cuts in the face of the spending strictures imposed by cultural officials; some theatres must even fear for their very existence. Even major theatres are feeling the strain. Will Berlin be able to afford three operas in the future? Will there continue to be money for the Berliner Ensemble *and* the Schaubühne am Lehniner Platz? Scenarios are already being played out according to which one of these two theatres will be closed. The situation is not much better in other German cities. Bonn's municipal theatres are facing a 30% reduction in funding, since the federal government has drastically reduced its sponsorship of the arts in the former capital. The federal state of Brandenburg also experienced radical cuts. In Frankfurt/ Oder, to cite just one example, the multi-stage theatre – consisting of opera, drama and ballet – was first reduced to a purely dramatic venue and then closed altogether. In other places, attempts to create savings included mergers between neighbouring theatres. This has saved many theatres in the past. But when earlier this year in Thuringia plans were aired to amalgamate the Theater der Landeshauptstadt Thüringen and the Deutsches Nationaltheater in Weimar, the public cried out in protest. It is not yet clear whether this citizen's initiative to preserve an autonomous theatre in Weimar will be successful. In any case, it is a sign that the diversity of Germany's theatre landscape is being threatened in many ways.

Knut Lennartz *(b 1944) studied theatre and philosophy in East Berlin (Humboldt University) in the 60s and served as a dramaturg thereafter in Karl-Marx-Stadt (now Chemnitz) and Frankfurt (Oder). Since 1988 he has worked for the German Theatre Association and as an editor of the theatre journal* Die Deutsche Bühne.

GHANA

EVANS OMA HUNTER

In Ghana the National Commission On Culture (NCC), which is equivalent to a Ministry of Culture, is in charge administratively of all activities for the Arts in the country. It is headed by Professor George Hagan, who also happens to be the honorary President of the Ghana National Centre of ITI. Under the NCC, there are several bodies or Associations representing artistic disciplines. Though independent, they work somewhat under the auspices of the NCC. These are:

The Musicians Union of Ghana
Ghana Actors Guild
Ghana Association of Writers
The Visual Arts Association
The Ghana Union of Theatre Societies
The Concert Parties Union of Ghana
The Ghana Dance Associations
The Audience Awareness Artistic Organisation

All these associations are governed by elected Presidents or chairpersons and can be contacted through the National Commission on Culture, 1 Abdal Gamel Nasser Avenue, Private Mail Bag, Ministry Post Office, Accra, Ghana. *Tel* 021 233 663440.

The Ghana National Theatre was established about a decade ago and is headed by an Executive Director in the person of Professor Komlah Amoako. Within the National Theatre set-up there are several artistic resident groups, such as the Abibigromma drama company, the National Dance Company and the National Symphony Orchestra; the complex also houses an Art Gallery.

Under its administrative wing, the NCC has a number of Centres of National Culture. Each centre is managed by a director; these, though they are expected to operate independently and finance their own cultural programme activities, receive a Government subvention budget for staff salaries through the NCC.

The Artistic Associations, however, do not receive any financial assistance. They will have to find their own financial support, which usually proves to be very difficult. A few have been able to survive through their own ingenuity over the years. Some start their groups enthusiastically but in no time succumb to this non-support disease and become dormant.

The management of the National Theatre host a weekly live drama and music programme on their premises, with financial support in the form of sponsorship from the Unilever company, manufacturers of soaps and detergents. The same performances are televised on Ghana Broadcasting Television (GBCTV).

Abibigromma, the resident theatre group of the National Theatre, is under the artistic directorship of Ms Dzifa Glikpoe. The group is seriously involved in drama performance in the regions and in schools.

The National Dance company, also resident at the National Theatre building, is also subsidised by the Government and has in the past two years turned out a number of dance drama productions such as *Solma, Sayl-Da, Musu, Nkulunkuulu, The Lost Warrior, The King's Dilemma, Images of Conflict* and others. The dance troupe is under the artistic Directorship of Professor Francis Nii Yartey, ably assisted by Ms Grace Dzagbatey.

The Awareness Theatre International Group, which is a wing of the Audience Awareness Artistic Organisation, is headed by Emmanuel Tetteh, assisted by James Tetteh and Silas Hibbert, Ms Vera Larbi and Grace Awositey. The group's Artistic Director is Evans Oma Hunter. In the last two years the group, in collaboration with Alliance Francaise D'Accra, have produced and performed these plays: *You Can't Believe All You See* by Nana Banyin Wartemberg, *Oh, When the Raining Seasons Come* by Oma Hunter, *Little Princess Korkor*, also by Oma Hunter, *Sumanguru Kante*, by Chris Atta Pappoe and *The King Must Dance Naked*, by Fred Agbeyegbe.

The Awareness Theatre International Group have also collaborated with the Ghana Centre for Culture in The Neighbourhood, a community Theatre For Development (TFD) project in Ursher Town, James Town and The Osu Children's Home – all in Accra – at the beginning of the year 2002. The Awareness Theatre International Group rehearses at the premises of the National Museums of Ghana. Very soon it has plans to mount a weekly theatre programme of performances for schools and the general public. The greater Accra Regional Centre For National Culture (CNC) Arts Centre has a performance space where a number of drama groups rehearse and perform. The groups that use the facilities there include: the Kozi Kozi Theatre, Mirrors, Talent Theatre Group, Nyankontum Theatre Group, Adabraka Drama Group and the Efiritete Drama Group.

The Efua Sutherland Drama Studio at Legon is also active most of the time, with performances by the resident University theatre company and drama students' productions from the School of Performing Arts, University of Ghana under the directorship of Professor Martin Owusu. Professor Asiedu Yirenkyi is the Head of the Drama Department. Video film production in the country has greatly affected the frequency of live drama performances, because all the actors find it an easy way out, for which they are much better remunerated compared to live theatre productions.

The National Organizer of the ITI Ghana Centre, Mr Torgbi Ehlahhas, mounted a programme throughout the country to encourage students in the various secondary schools to form Arts Clubs as branches of ITI. This exercise, if successful, will enable ITI Ghana to disseminate information about world theatre programmes and also introduce theatrical activities among students in the country and help to sustain their interest in the arts.

The Labone Secondary school embraced the initiative and launched their branch of the Arts Club in June 2002, where three theatre personalities were invited to deliver lectures. Evans Oma Hunter delivered a paper on 'Possible Careers for Artists in Future'. David Dontoh, Actor/Director of Kozi Kozi Theatre Group, delivered a lecture on 'Theatre and the Way Forward', while Mr Sefa, Director of the Greater Accra Centre for National Culture, gave a lecture on 'Arts and Nation Building'.

Evans Oma Hunter *is Artistic director of the Awareness Theatre International Group, for whom he has written a number of plays.*

GREECE

DINA ZIROPOULOU

Before reviewing the theatrical events of the past three years, it may be useful to present a picture of the way theatre operates in Greece.

There are two state theatres – the National Theatre and the National Theatre of Northern Greece – based in Athens and Thessaloniki respectively. Additionally, since 1985 Municipal and Regional Theatres have been operating officially in 16 Greek cities, subsidised to a great extent by the state.

A further twelve companies (Notos Theatre, Karolos Koun Art Theatre, Amphi-Theatre, Nea Skini, Praxis Company, Embros Theatre, Phasma Company, Nea Skini Technis, Open Theatre, Stoa Theatre – mostly staging modern Greek plays, Mikri Porta Company – staging plays for children – and Piramatiki Skini – based in the city of Thessaloniki) are also partly subsidised by the state, within the framework of a two year contract.

Some of these groups have a long tradition in mainstream Greek theatre, whereas others started with a more experimental and often 'marginal' character, but in the course of time their work has been gradually systematised and more widely acknowledged. Fifty more companies are subsidised on an annual basis. A large number of companies, often presenting a particularly notable output, are privately run or supported by sponsors. One may also mention the so-called commercial theatres, whose productions are undertaken and supported by theatre owners.

Approximately 80% of Greek theatrical production is concentrated in Athens. The theatre season normally runs from October to April, although in recent years another season has been created, from the beginning of April to the end of May. In summer, theatrical activity takes place mainly in the provinces. There is a varied repertory, including a considerable number of ancient drama productions which are usually presented within the framework of various Festivals. In Athens, some commercial theatres operate during the summer, usually staging comedies, musicals and revues. Other Athenian companies often go on summer tour around the country with the plays they have staged in the capital during the winter.

The drama repertory adopted by the companies from autumn 1999 to spring 2002 included classical, contemporary, Greek and foreign works. The classical repertory was represented by Aeschylus, Sophocles, Euripides, Aristophanes, Menander, Shakespeare, Marlowe, Aphra Behn, Molière, Marivaux, Lesage, Lope de Vega, Goldoni, von Kleist, Goethe, Büchner, Ibsen, Strindberg, Chekhov and others.

With regard to the contemporary foreign theatre, there is a clear preference for works by English playwrights, among them Harold Pinter, Sarah Kane, Kevin Elyot, Patrick Marber, Mark Ravenhill, Caryl Churchill, David Hare, Shelagh Stephenson, Lee Hall, Martin Crimp and Edward Bond.

GREECE

Works by a number of American playwrights also appeared on the Greek stage, such as Tennessee Williams, Arthur Miller, Eve Ensler, Martin Sherman, David Mamet, Tony Kushner, Terrence McNally, Neil Simon, Christopher Durang, Neil Labute and Lee Breuer.

The French repertory was represented by Labiche, Feydeau, Camus, Anouilh, Genet, Sartre, Beckett, Koltes, Veber and Yasmina Reza. From other countries came work by German playwrights such as Brecht, Bernhard, Wolf, Rilke and Marius von Mayenburg, Italy's Dario Fo, Spain's José Sanchis Sinisterra, M. Rammer from Australia, Brian Friel from Ireland, the Bulgarians Hristo Boytchev and Topalov, the Serb Kovasevic, and the Brazilians Nelson Rodrigues and Roberto Athaide.

Dramatisations of Greek and foreign prose continued. Amongst the foreign novelists adapted for the theatre, Dostoievsky is the most popular example. In particular, the staging of his play *Crime and Punishment* directed by N. Milivojevic (Notos Theatre, 1999–2000) generated an extremely favourable response, whereas the adaptation of the Japanese novel, Y. Kavabata's *The House of the Sleeping Girls* directed by G. Chouvardas (Notos Theatre, 2001–2002) divided critics and audiences alike.

During the same period, comedy performances were in blossom and enjoyed remarkable box office success. The detective comedy set in a hairdressing salon, *Sheer Madness* by B. Jordan and M. Adams, directed by K. Arvanitakis (Apothiki Theatre, 2001–2002) which ran for three years to a steady audience, is a characteristic example.

The public preference for musicals – which has been taken up by our National stages – ought also to be noted. Only a few are worth serious attention, such as G. Xenopoulos' play *The Students,* which was turned into a musical and performed at the National Theatre (2000–2001), and Marguerite Monnot's *Irma la douce,* staged by the National Theatre of Northern Greece (2002).

Shakespeare's plays were presented in many notable performances during the three seasons in question. Among them were the Notos Theatre Company production of *Much Ado About Nothing* directed by Th. Moschopoulos (2001), which was also presented in London, and the rarely performed *Love's Labour's Lost*, directed by S. Livathinos (National Theatre, 2002), which was met with high praise from both critics and public.

In parallel to the classical repertory, the Greek stage also showed a strong preference for contemporary foreign playwrights. A heated debate was established after the performance of plays by Sarah Kane and other contemporary, mostly English, playwrights, whose work reflects the desperate cry of the extreme human experience and discusses the psychosis of the contemporary individual and society. The varied and controversial reactions of the audience and the drama critics to these shows raised numerous questions regarding the very nature of dramatic art and preoccupied theorists and dramatists alike. A great sensation was caused by the performances of *Cleansed*, directed by L. Vogiatzis (Nea Skini, 2001) and *4.48 Psychosis*, directed by Roula Pateraki (Dramatiko Theatro, 2002) both by Sarah Kane.

Amongst the other English playwrights staged in Greece one could note a distinct preference for the work of Pinter. His plays enjoyed great success during the 1999–2000 season, whereas during the next one the 'Pinter trend' continued but with less successful performances.

Amalia Moutoussi and Lefteris Vogiatzis in the latter's Nea Skini production of Sarah Kane's *Cleansed* (*photo*: Athina Kasolea)

GREECE

A series of important performances were based on works of American playwrights, such as Tony Kushner's version of *L'Illusion comique,* and David Mamet's *Glengarry Glen Ross*, both directed by S. Livathinos (Dolichos Company, 2000–2001 and 2001–2002 respectively), and *Every Thursday Mr Green* by J. Baron, directed and performed by G. Michalacopoulos (1999–2001). What is more, Martin Sherman's stirring monologue *Rose*, directed by K. Damatis (Ilisia Theatre 2000–2001), with Antigoni Valakou in one of her best interpretations, was a great artistic success, together with the performance *The Whales of August* by D. Berry, (National Theatre, 2001–2002), featuring remarkable performances by the leading actresses Nelly Angelidou, Antigoni Valakou and Vera Zavitsianou. A play by an American author of Armenian origin, Richard Kalinoski's *Beast on the Moon,* (Apo Mihanis Theatre, 1999–2000) constituted one of the most stirring performances of the last three years.

High quality interpretations were also given by Reni Pittaki and Betty Arvaniti in the play *The Siege of Leningrad,* by the Spanish playwright José Sanchis Sinisterra, directed by M. Kougioumtzis (Art Theatre and Praxis Company). Amongst the highlights of the season, one should also mention Büchner's *Woyzeck,* directed by G. Lazanis (Art Theatre, 2001–2002) and of course Thomas Bernhard's two well known plays *Vor dem Ruhestand,* directed by S. Livathinos (Praxis Company, 1999–2000) and *Am Ziel,* directed by M. Limberopoulou, (Art Theatre, 2001–2002). Of particular interest also was the performance of the play *Feuergesicht,* (Praxis Company, 1999–2000), by the young playwright Marius von Mayenburg, directed by E. Sapountzi whose untimely death was a notable loss.

During this same period, the Balkan and Russian repertory provided the Greek stage with significant contributions. As for the contemporary Russian theatre, it was successfully represented by two outstanding performances of plays by women, *Dekaimero ton ginekon* (*Ten Days for Women,* Ivi Theatre, 2000–2001) and *Dear Helena* (Epi Kolono Theatre, 2000–2002), by T. Vosnesenskaia and L. Rosmoskaia respectively.

As far as plays from the modern Greek repertory are concerned, although they were relatively absent from the Greek stage during the 1999–2000 period, the companies took a turn during the 2000–2001 and 2001–2002 seasons and incorporated a large number of them in their seasons. Many productions drew on old comedy plays and several film scripts – mainly from 60s blockbusters – were adapted for the stage. We saw plays by older and younger writers, such as A. Matessis, G. Xenopoulos, P. Horn, P. Vizantios, I. Kapetanakis, I. Kambanellis, P. Matessis, Loula Anagnostaki, G. Skourtis, D. Kehaidis, F. Politis, D. Haritopoulos, M. Pontikas, G. Veltsos, D. Kordatos, P. Mentis, A. Dimou, D. Dimitriadis, Maria Efstathiadi, Elena Pegka, L. Christidis, M. Reppas and D. Papathanassiou.

In the same period, a new series of notable works emerged, some of which were written by Greek actors. This is the case of Chrisa Spilioti, G. Iliopoulos and Ìaria Skaftoura – who was awarded 1st prize in the young writers competition, organised by the Notos Theatre with the aim of promoting new Greek plays. Great sensations were caused by the performances of *Angela Papazoglou* (Metaxourgio Theatre, 2000–2002), which ran for two years, *O ehthros tou piiti* (*The Poet's Enemy*) by G. Himonas, directed by Maya Limberopoulou,

Art Theatre – Municipal and Regional Theatre of Patras, 2000–2001), *Eleni*, by G. Ritsos, directed by V. Papavasiliou (Art Theatre, 2000–2002) and *Ethnikos Imnos* (*National Anthem*), directed by M. Marmarinos, Diplous Eros 2001–2002 – a performance based on improvisation and praised for its subject matter, originality and genuineness.

During the three seasons in question, the trend towards dramatisation of non-theatrical texts continued: the high quality performances *Fonissa* (*Murderess*) by A. Papadiamantis with Lydia Koniordou, and *Morfes apo to ergo tou Biziinou* (*Figures from the Work of Viziinos*) starring Anna Kokkinou, reappeared on stage, the works of V. Solomou-Xanthaki, E. Roidis, G. Skabardonis, P. Delta and M. Karapanou were dramatised, and *Evdomo rouho* by E. Fakinou (*The Seventh Garment*), directed by D. Mavrikios, Nea Skini 2000–2002, was also appreciated. One should also mention the performance of the play *Ligo apo ola* (*A Little Bit of Everything*, Sfendoni Theatre, 2001–2002*)*, which stood out through its innovative use of shadow theatre techniques and the actors' interpretation that produced interesting aesthetic results.

During the 1999–2000 and 2000–2001 seasons, a large number of ancient dramas were staged by important directors, using a variety of approaches. None of them, however, managed to stand out by bringing to the stage something beyond the limits of a conventional ancient drama performance. In this short article there is only space to mention a few of the works from the ancient Greek repertory staged in the past three years, as productions of the National Theatre, the National Theatre of Northern Greece, the Municipal and Regional Theatres, and many other privately run companies, subsidised or not, within the framework of the Athens and the Epidaurus Festivals.

Aeschylus was present in such works as *Oresteia, Persians, Seven Against Thebes* and *Prometheus Bound;* Sophocles with *Ajax, Philoctetes, Electra, Oedipus Rex* and *Antigone;* Euripides with *Alcestis, Iphigenia, Medea, Hecuba, Bacchae, Hercules Furens, Cyclops, Trojan Women* and *Orestes*. It is worth noting that the 2000 production of *Oedipus Rex* was first staged at the Coliseum in Rome. During the winter season 1999–2000, Aeschylus's *Agamemnon* was performed, and in winter 2001–2002 *Oedipus Rex* and *Oedipus Coloneus* were staged together. Additionally, seven out of the eleven surviving comedies of Aristophanes were staged – namely *Acharnians, Frogs, Peace, Women in Parliament, Knights, Clouds* and *Plutus*; the National Theatre of Northern Greece presented Menander's *Woman of Samos*.

A certain qualitative improvement in ancient Greek drama production is expected for the 2002 summer season, as many performances will come alive on stage – some of them under the aegis of the 'Cultural Olympiad' – with the participation of important Greek and foreign directors.

Some important companies from abroad have visited us in the context of various festivals, and individual foreign artists have collaborated with Greek companies (N. Milivojevic, Alla Demidova, Maya Morgenstern). In the same context, we should mention the considerable contribution of the Piramatiki Skini in Thessaloniki, which organises the annual 'Spring Festival', to which foreign companies are invited. Moreover, the National Theatre of Northern Greece, a member of the European Theatre Union, co-organises productions with other member states. Similar initiatives towards international drama collaboration are taken by the Notos Theatre in Athens.

GREECE

In another interesting tendency, many companies are working in 'unconventional' theatrical venues; there has been a gradual increase in the number of 'bar theatres'. A play based on Hitchcock's film of Ethel Lina Wait's *The Lady Vanishes* (Treno sto Rouf Theatre, 1999–2002) was successfully staged, for three years in a row, in a real train which was specially converted for the purpose. During the period under discussion, even greater emphasis was laid on stage design, which is nowadays much influenced by the use of various electronic means. The example of *The Skriker,* by Caryl Churchill (Porta Theatre, 1999–2000), a performance which made extended use of technical effects, best illustrates the trend.

The expanding theatrical map of Greece, where theatre productions are framed by congresses, events and meetings – to a certain extent encouraged by the activity of the various University Theatre Studies departments – undoubtedly shows an increasing interest in the mechanics of theatre, which carries along artists and theorists, but not yet the wide public, which, in fact, should be the primary objective.

The fact that the abundant variety of theatrical productions is not matched by a corresponding increase in theatre audiences has caused great arguments regarding the theatre's need to reconsider its objectives. It has also initiated much debate about the 'theatre crisis'. The plethora of theatrical events seems to have created the impression that the industry is repeating itself, and has resulted in a certain mistrust, not only of the theatre's ability to converse with reality, but of its potential to deepen our understanding of that reality.

For the time being, however, the constant search that characterises Greek theatrical reality both confirms its great potential and allows us to be optimistic in an era during which change of all kinds occurs at high speed and the 'media theatre' is violently imposed on our life; the latter is, of course, an issue that affects not only Greek theatrical reality, but the whole world that expresses itself through the theatrical *praxis*.

An examination of the theatrical events of this period in Greece leads us to the following safe conclusion: there is, clearly, a need to renew the code of communication between the artist and the public; and also a need for dramatic art to go beyond the limits set by the theatrical *status quo*, so as to seek the appropriate means of bringing to the theatre an innovative and pioneer spirit.

Dina Ziropoulou: *MA in Drama (Essex University, UK), MA in Theatre Studies (Athens University), PhD student in Drama (Aristotelian University of Thessaloniki); teacher at the Drama School of the Athens Conservatory and other schools of drama.*

HUNGARY

ANDRÁS FORGÁCH

Nothing is new in the Hungarian theatre scene nowadays, although everything is constantly changing, without our being able to perceive these fundamental changes in their depth. This is a rather typical situation for Hungary, always a country in transition. Theatre had a real renaissance in the 60s, and then, after a short period of calm in the late 70s and early 80s, an eruption of a new, more realistic, harsh, important, complex theatrical style: the theatre in general became a focus, a prism of cultural (and political) life. In the 90s, this role has diminished (with the new freedom of the press, and the 'real-life' parliament): but still it has a very strong infrastructure imbedded in the life of the cities, especially in Budapest, where the state and the town secure the financial survival of these structures (although we hear a lot of complaints from the theatres, and the money is never enough). This is more or less the German model, but with much less money. The middle-generation of directors today is very wary because of this continuous thinning of the money-shield; they speak of the danger to their own existence, not simply the survival of the theatre itself. The spectre of commercialisation is also very present in the anxieties of this middle-generation.

The best development of the last few years: the new generations are not killing their fathers, trying to take over their positions – they simply create their own studios, workshops, institutions (Árpád Schilling, Bárka Theatre, Béla Pintér, Csaba Horváth and others). Some of the younger ones blend beautifully into the existing system, being very mobile, moving easily from theatre to theatre, and still not losing their own very peculiar dialect (Sándor Zsótér, Róbert Alföldy, János Szász, László Keszég, Péter Forgács and others). A lot of talented actors are now directors too; sometimes they even play in the plays they direct, and define the new style of old institutions (Enikö Eszenyi for example, who has become in the meantime a director-star in Prague too, or Andor Lukáts, or Géza Tordy, or Gábor Máté). And a new generation of actors, who were children in the days of the so called 'system-change', can show their talents without any restraint: they can play anything, speak any way they want, they can undress, sing, dance, build up new mythologies. They play in films and work in several companies at the same time. They learn, they make their own 'image'. I've never seen so many 'new' faces at the same time.

What we see is an eclectic and gaudy style: anything can happen. As the selector for the 2001 Theatre Festival in Pécs (from now on Pécs will be a stable site for these yearly festivals, which is also a very positive development) I saw more than a hundred performances, and in the following pages I'll try to give a few impressions, concrete details of what I saw. I must admit, it is not an easy task.

Let's start with the strongest and most successful company in Hungary, the

HUNGARY

Katona József Theatre. 2000–2001 was a very strong year for them, with very convincing productions of *Tartuffe, Der Theatermacher* (Thomas Bernhard), *Kalldewey Farce* (Botho Strauss), *Der Talisman* (Nestroy) and the *Threepenny Opera* (Brecht/Weill), as well as Yvette Bozsik's *János Vitéz,* a very modern and ironical rethinking and reconstruction of a very well known popular epic of the 19th century, written by the greatest Hungarian poet, Sándor Petöfi. All the same, the company is now at a turning point: some of its best actors are being lured away by the new National Theatre. This monumental building is not yet finished, but it already functions as a new magnet, with its higher salaries and prestige, and paradoxically it is also a destabilising factor, shedding some light on the biggest problem here (as in all of Europe): how can theatre as an expensive (highly subsidised) collective art of big towns and big communities be accommodated in a market-economy? In the long run, I suspect this disorienting and disintegrating component will have a positive effect, because it will challenge all kinds of routines.

The Katona József Theatre has a very creative duplicity: in the Kamra (which is a kind of chamber theatre in a longish cellar two blocks away from the main building) they experiment, and invite all kinds of – mostly young – directors, who can develop their very different language with the excellent actors of the group, while in the main hall, one sees more classic productions. *Talisman* (directed by Gábor Máté, an actor-director, with a 'Kaposvár-background', and a renowned professor of the Academy of Theatrical Arts, who is now also the new 'chief director', because Gábor Zsámbéki is rather occupied throughout the year with managing the Théâtre de L'Europe) served as a very refreshing musical play, about the problem of 'minorities', the 'redheads': it is a real *Volksstück*, with a mixture of gimmicks and simplicity, emphasising the inventiveness of the actors, and a big success with the audience. *Tartuffe* (staged by Zsámbéki) gave a very pointed (rather acid) analysis of the current political-moral situation in Hungary. The weakest point was surprisingly the *Threepenny Opera*, directed by one of the best directors here, Tamás Ascher, and with all the company's stars. It all looked so right – the misery, the beggars, all these by-products of the painful system-change in Eastern Europe. The only thing missing was the true indignation, the real hatred, the emotional ground for all the fuss: the production is a bit too elegant, and maybe too ironical. The *Theatre Maker* by Thomas Bernhard in the Kamra was a big occasion for a great actor, Péter Haumann, to show what he knows about desperate situations and his art. The director Péter Gothár, who is also one of the leading film-directors today in Hungary, has an impeccable sense for ambiance, and a very special kind of vicious humour, and film-like details. With János Szikora's production of *Kalldewey Farce* by Botho Strauss, who is not an easy author for the Hungarian stage, with all his linguistic riddles (and this rather early play is one of his more enigmatic ones), the German playwright is established as someone who is also our contemporary, or rather, a representative of the new reality (the linguistic relativism, the intellectual shallowness, the new media, the insecurity of any job, any position) is much closer to what we experience now in Budapest, than Bertolt Brecht's vision of Berlin in the late twenties, be it as rude and direct as it may.

From Krétakör Theatre's production of *Woyzek* (*photo*: Mátyás Erdélyi)

HUNGARY

Árpád Schilling, who now has his own company, the Krétakör Theatre, has created – in respect of their aesthetics – two almost diametrically opposed spectacles: one is *NEXXT (The Plastic Chicken Show)*, a new play, or rather text, or let's say script, written by István Tasnádi, who is the regular collaborator of Schilling's totally interesting experiments; and the other is Ferenc Molnár's classic *Liliom* (a remake of a production he made while he was still in the Academy of Theatrical Arts). *NEXXT* is a very ambitious project, which was also shown in Avignon this year, and was created in cooperation with the Bárka Theatre. It is a combination of two famous books, *A Clockwork Orange* and *American Psycho* – a courageous, but in my estimation half-baked show, heroic and a little bit futile at the same time. The big problem: you can't make a parody of two books and the media at the same time, and you can't expect that everybody will take it seriously. The dramaturgy has serious flaws, the scenic solutions are sometimes brilliant, but the old paradox works here again: the more brilliant the scenic solutions, the less essential the plot. They change places so to speak, and the balance is never there. It is a success with a certain generation, who take it as it is: a rather superficial parody of the brutal chatshows of today; but it is in the end rather shallow. Still, the qualities of the group around Schilling, the actors, and the background financial organization is excellent. *Liliom* is another matter: full of funny little *chansons*, and still going deep, under the surface of the light-heavy play in a very simple white set. It has won two or three prizes this year, and they can't play it enough in their studio at the Thalia Theatre. Schilling has very good connections in the European theatre world: his new *Woyzeck* was sponsored by the Berliner Festspiele and it had its premiere there in September of this year. He is regularly travelling throughout Europe with a wonderful adaptation of Heinrich von Kleist's *Michael Kolhaas*, renamed *Enemy of the People* and originally produced in the Kamra of the Katona József Theatre.

Another young director of consequence is Béla Pintér, who every year produces one or two important performances with his group, the Picaro, founded in 1992, from the Arvisura Dance Theatre. He offered this year the *Sehova kapuja* (*Gates of Nowhere* – with the Hungarian word 'sehova' alluding, with a wordplay to 'Jehova', that is, the religious sects): a very fresh and insolent sequence of scenes leading us from the headquarters of a tiny sect somewhere in Budapest, to a remote little village in Transylvania, where the ambitious sect-leader (played by Béla Pintér, who is usually the protagonist of his plays, closing the gaps of the classic theatrical vicious circle, and thereby showing that it is possible to direct, act, and play, and still be interesting or even more). The two communities are played, at times brilliantly and convincingly, by the same young actors (most of them coming, so to speak, from the 'street', with no formal actor-training, so that, with all their inevitable technical weaknesses very much present on the stage, they are still daring, adventurous, less inhibited than the so-called professionals). Hilarious and also sombre, funny and tragic at the same time, it is a real achievement.

Pintér has grown up to be one of the most important trend-setters in the Hungarian theatre scene. When he started, he was a dancer, a so-called 'folk-dancer', later working together with Csaba Horváth, who also has his own group, the Közép-Európa Táncszínház, that is, the 'Middle-Europe Dance

Theatre', producing two or three excellent and refreshing dance-shows (more than shows: events, essential, almost metaphysical dance-evenings, with only a few dancers, sometimes only him and his regular partner Andrea Ladányi). Thus folk-dance, which was sometimes rejected rather snobbishly by the cultural elite, has produced some very strong individuals, with a strong sense for movement and music, and a rather raw way of throwing emotions and expressive moments in the face of a public that has been accustomed to more sophisticated, subdued or sublime ways of self-expression. In the last season Csaba Horváth has produced three important evenings in a series: the first is *Alkonyodó* (dusking would be the proper word for it – the Hungarian title doesn't sound very regular either): six ageing dancers in 50 minutes show their bodies in a very poetic and simple sequence of scenes, which all centre around wood and water, cutting wood and bringing, pouring water; the second is *Nero, My Love*, in which a wonderful (and rather stout) actor György Gazsó dances (for the first time in his life – and he is forty-something now) with Andrea Ladányi, following the invisible script of a famous Hungarian novel written by Dezsö Kosztolányi, about the deviant and desperate Nero of Rome: a strange collage of two cultures, as the actor makes a physically and mentally very straining effort to express himself without words, and be equal to one of the best dancers of the Hungarian dance-scene of today. The third production caused a kind of a scandal: its title is *Mandarin*, and it is based on Bartók's music *The Miraculous Mandarin*. Because of certain details (among others, little naked children in 'cages') the family of the composer withdrew the rights, and then a real miracle happened: the choreography, danced by Csaba Horváth and Andrea Ladányi, worked like a time-bomb without a note of accompaniment. This Bartók-piece without music is one of the most interesting theatrical experiments we had here. We can only be grateful to the stern guardians of the rights of the composer: they showed us that nobody can silence the music we hear in ourselves.

One of the most original Hungarian directors of today is the young János Mohácsi, who lives and works in Kaposvár: the Kaposvár theatre has been for the last three decades one of the leading companies in this country. It is a legend, but also a very strong and impressive reality: while other companies have struggled, faded and had their setbacks, or gone back to the secure ways of routine, in Kaposvár, with the leadership of first Gábor Zsámbéki, then László Babarczy (and also Tamás Ascher), something always 'happened', and the nucleus of the company of actors, designers and directors is still strong enough to be one of the 'beacons' (to put it romantically) of today's theatre-life in Hungary, against all odds. Mohácsi was discovered by this theatre, today he produces one or two plays, sometimes he uses classical stuff, but with the text completely reworked, by himself, his brother and the actors, until it becomes their own. This year they produced the award-winning *We Bombed in Kaposvár*, based Joseph Heller's *We Bombed in New Haven*: it is a wild and funny, and extra-long Odyssey of the actors and the whole theatre around the theme of militarism and war, but also theatre as a way of living. Mohácsi's plays almost explode with the energy of the actors. They are absolute partners, they are themselves, they are individuals, they have a very great and special sense of humour, when they work with him – he is one of those directors who work in the so-called 'stone-theatres', but never give up their peculiar way of seeing. He is not very comfortable in other theatres, except the one in Nyíregyháza, where he has produced some wonderful things in the last few years, such as Brecht's *Caucasian Chalk Circle*, and this year Erdmann's *Mandate*. He has a keen interest in technical things, he invents special machines for his productions. In the end of the Heller play, the planes (three of them) that we see before us on the stage, bomb the theatre itself, where we sit (with the help of a video-film). He also has a very special talent to create credible mass-scenes on the stage: in a given moment some thirty actors can swarm on stage without being simply chaotic or formless: everybody finds his place spontaneously in the big picture, and it is never boring. *The Mandate* is a very biting parody of so-called communism and the petit-bourgeois existence – two seemingly opposite but in reality intertwined ways and forms of living. In certain moments Mohácsi can create the most absurd situations on stage one can imagine. And in Kaposvár there were other interesting productions, among them the *Operetta* of Gombrowicz, or the *Chioggia (Brawl)* of Goldoni, or *Platonov* by Chekhov, all by very young directors, who are regularly given their chance in this small and (apart from the theatre) rather boring southern town. Maybe that is the secret of the constant rejuvenation of this workshop.

Sándor Zsótér is a very special case: he is a kind of travelling ambassador for himself, with no fixed abode, he moves from theatre to theatre (with his congenial set-designer Mária Ambrus), or like a preacher in the desert: he provokes, he explores: sometimes with great originality, as happened in the case of Benjamin Britten's *Midsummer Night's Dream* at the Szeged Opera, some-times repeating his mannerisms (as in the case of *Timon of Athens* in the Radnóti Theatre, in Budapest, which is rather cold). Britten's opera was one of the highlights of this season: a truly original performance, showing the mechanism of alienation, to use a once fashionable word, to demonstrate the bleak truth of a great theatrical myth: the gap between the imagined and the real. Here Puck, the young and insolent servant of Oberon, is an old and clumsy fellow, dressed more like an asylum seeker than a fairy. The fairies in general are like working women, riding their bicycles home from the factory, and singing as they go (a wonderful feat, not simply in the idea, but its realisation.) The magical ointment that changes the young lovers' emotional drives is more or less a joint, that Oberon or Puck smokes near them, and so on.

To get back to the Radnóti Theatre: this great group wasn't very lucky in this season with other productions: although it has one of the best companies in the country, with very high quality actors in every age-group, and has produced some of the best 'conservative' theatre in the last ten years under the leadership of András Bálint, the very intelligent and experienced, nay, inspired actor-manager of this small company. This year they tried to swap their tiny stage for a bigger one. They wanted to test themselves on a 'real' stage, in a bigger house, the Thalia Theatre, that houses many guest productions (this is one of its main functions; it has opera and dance performances, and hosts several festivals a year). The Thalia is in the same street, the 'Broadway of Budapest', Nagymezo street, about a hundred metres away from Radnóti. The choice seemed to be perfect, Ben Jonson's *Volpone*, with the best actors in the roles of their lives, but something went awry: there was not enough time, or the mixture of styles didn't work. The director, Péter Valló, who is one of the most diligent and professional directors in Hungary (and also a very good set-designer) simply opened up too many styles, too many directions: and in the end, it produced a lukewarm effort, albeit with some interesting details. *The Birthday Party* by Harold Pinter, directed by Péter Gothár, was also an unbalanced evening, with convincing elements side by side with empty and untidy details.

One of the legends of the Hungarian theatre-scene, is Péter Halász, who after being expelled from Hungary with his group in the mid-seventies was a co-founder of the Squat Theatre in New York, and had world wide success with some of their productions, such as *Pig, Child, Fire* or *Andy Warhol's Last Love*. He is able to provoke year after year with new productions: this year he showed *Gyerekünk* (*Our Child*), a play based on his own text, at the Új Színház (New Theatre), a well-established new theatre in the heart of the city. The play is a kind of collage of texts, a fusion of very different theatrical means: and conventional actors, if they are able to tune themselves to Halász, can discover their hidden abilities. In Halász's theatre there is no way of 'imitating'. Presence is the most important factor, the ability to connect the different levels of theatre (film, sound, movement, ideas, words) with their physical presence, so to speak. The texts don't really have a psychological background, although there is always a hidden story. Halász also worked for years before in the Kamra. He is in a way a pedagogue, and for certain actors, he is a blessing. Last year, with András Jeles, who as film-director and also playwright, theatre-director, and writer is one of the most important persons in today's Hungarian artistic life, he founded the Városi Theatre (Town Theatre) in a rather poor and socially desolate district of Budapest. The two are in their mid-fifties, they can't be called young anymore, but it is clear that they are absolutely unconventional in all that they do. Halász played in some of Jeles's films, and although they have a rather different approach to acting or theatre as a form, their collaboration, if they can get the money to reconstruct the building they received for a symbolic sum, could be one of the most interesting events in the next decade. One of the scandals of the last year is that they haven't received enough from the state, or the foundations, to survive. It seems that in Hungary productivity is always deeply connected to problems; yet theatre flourishes in this country, even though the complaints grow. I hope that this rather sketchy essay has proved my point.

Andras Forgach *(b 1952) after finishing university in 1976 dramaturg (literary consultant) in several theatres. Freelance since 1984. Translator, playwright, essayist, novelist. His first play* The Player *(after Dostoievski) was produced in the Katona József theatre in 1982. Published four books:* Two Plays *(1991),* A Figure Like Figaro *(1993),* Who Isn't *(1999),* Vicious Success *(2000). His translations include plays by Beaumarchais, Kleist, Wedekind, Marlowe, Shakespeare, Pinter, Genet, Tennessee Williams.*

ICELAND

MAGNUS THOR THORBERGSSON

The last three years in Icelandic theatre have been an interesting period of upheaval and change, in spite of an ongoing financial and artistic crisis. Its distinctive themes were loud and often uninformed debate on popularity, commercialism and numbers of tickets sold, in step with the main story of the period: The Rise and Fall of Leikfelag Islands (The Icelandic Theatre Company). This debate culminated in accusations put forward by the Association of Independent Theatres against the two major theatres in Reykjavik, Leikfelag Rekjavikur (The Reykjavik Theatre Company) and Thjodleikhusid (The National Theatre), regarding alleged misuse of their official funding and abuse of their dominant competitive position. Other controversial happenings were the change of artistic directors at The Reykjavik Theatre Company and the change in the laws on The National Theatre, allowing the artistic director to be rehired beyond the former maximum of eight years at the helm.

In many ways the most important theatre in Iceland in the years between 1999 and 2002 was The Icelandic Theatre Company. Founded a few years earlier, around a performance of Jim Cartwright's *Stone Free*, the ITC soon rose to some fame and in 1998 the City of Reykjavik put it in charge of the oldest theatre house in Reykjavik, Idno, where the Reykjavik Theatre Company had been founded some 100 years before. Idno had been closed and under reconstruction for some years, more or less since the Reykjavik Theatre Company moved to the newly built City Theatre in 1989.

To some extent the ITC blew fresh winds across the somewhat stagnant theatre landscape, in spite of its rather conservative artistic direction and its emphasis on commercial theatre. Among the ITC's most interesting novelties was the Lunch Theatre, short performances accompanied by soup at lunchtime. More importantly, the ITC shook up the Icelandic theatre landscape with effective PR work and noisy claims of success, forcing the two large theatres to revaluate their position and strategies. In the 1999–2000 season, the ITC received attention for some quite well made (although very traditional) productions of popular plays, such as Terrence McNally's *Frankie and Johnny in the Clair de Lune* and Galin's *Stjörnur á morgunhimni (Stars in the Morning Sky)*. In these productions, as in most of its work, the ITC made no attempt to distance itself artistically from the National Theatre or the Reykjavik Theatre Company. Its main aim was to create a popular theatre.

By the beginning of the 1999–2000 season the ITC was claiming that it was able to make theatre just as good as, or even better than that in the two large institutional theatres, boasting of extreme popularity, which had allegedly been achieved without any official support. This triggered a lively discussion on the justification and distribution of official funds for theatre activities, which then led to the charges made against the Reykjavik Theatre Company and the National Theatre, of alleged undercutting of ticket prices, and misuse of their ruling competitive position. The Competition Authority later commented on these

And Björk of Course... by Thorvaldur Thorsteinsson, directed by Benedikt Erlingsson for The Reykjavik Theatre Company (*photo*: Sigfus Mar Petursson)

charges, although very vaguely, but by that time the heat of the matter had more or less dissipated.

In May 2000 the ITC united with Loftkastalinn (The Air Castle) and Hljodsetning (Sound Dubbing), a leading company in dubbing for television. The Air Castle had been successful with its first production, the musical *Hair*, and by the time of the merger it was occupying a theatre space in the western part of Reykjavik, where it had established some popularity. The new theatre, which still went under the name of The Icelandic Theatre Company, under the artistic direction of young director Magnus Geir Thordarson, now had two stages, a larger one in The Air Castle's space and a smaller one in Idno. In the press, especially in the daily newspaper *DV*, the ITC soon established an image as a 'theatre giant', a third large theatre to set beside the Reykjavik Theatre Company and The National Theatre.

The next season started with a series of loud declarations and statements in the press. The daily *DV* stated that the *crème de la crème* of Icelandic theatre artists had decided to join the 'new giant' on the theatre market, a statement that turned out to be highly exaggerated. In the press these issues developed into a kind of 'battle of the stars', where some of the leading figures of Icelandic theatre denied rumours of being under contract at the ITC, and the ITC in turn declared such rumours to be a 'misunderstanding'.

The ITC promised up to 12 premières in the 2000–2001 season, including co-productions with other theatre groups and smaller cabaret shows. But although the number of ITC's full-scale private productions was much smaller, it soon became evident that the ITC had set their sights too high. In addition, private businesses, whose support the ITC relied heavily upon, suffered

ICELAND

crisis in 2000 and 2001, forcing them to cut back on cultural support. The ITC had to cancel about half of their announced premières and by the summer of 2001 it had more or less ceased to operate. It closed in the fall and earlier this year the Icelandic Theatre Company was declared bankrupt, proving a professional theatre performing on a regular basis without official support to be more or less impossible in the small Icelandic society.

The first professional stage in Iceland, The National Theatre, celebrated its 50th anniversary in April 2000. On the occasion of the celebration the National Theatre launched a playwriting competition, which hauled in 40 new plays. The winning play was *Landkrabbinn (The Landlubber)* by Ragnar Arnalds, former Member of Parliament, who had written a number of plays for the National Theatre. The premiere of *The Landlubber* in March 2000 brought heavy disappointment; and the negative reception of the runner-up play *Vatn Lifsins (The Water of Life)* by Benony Ægisson, premiered in October 2001, launched a vivid discussion on the value and form of playwriting competitions, which in the last decade had failed to provide innovative, high quality plays. The results of the National Theatre's competition also provided grounds for speculation on the state of Icelandic playwriting, causing theatre critics and artists alike to be concerned about the future of Icelandic plays.

The National Theatre's artistic director, Stefan Baldursson, was harshly criticised for failing to nourish and encourage new Icelandic writing for the stage. Although one of the main aims of the National Theatre according to law, the development of new Icelandic plays has been regarded as a secondary issue, culminating in the fact that in the last three years only four new Icelandic plays were staged at the National Theatre, excluding plays for children.

Stefan Baldursson has also suffered the criticism of being in many ways too commercial. The emphasis has often been on plays or productions that have been popular elsewhere, like *Stones in His Pockets* or *Singin' in the Rain*. But the truth is that the National Theatre has also focused a lot on the staging of classic drama, often resulting in very good productions, such as Brecht's *Caucasian Chalk Circle* and Shakespeare's *A Midsummer Night's Dream*. In fact, the National Theatre is the only theatre in Iceland which has the financial capability to produce such productions, and in this respect it has been doing good work.

The Reykjavik Theatre Company, located in the City Theatre, decided in December 1999 to call for applications for the post of artistic director, a controversial decision, as the artistic director, Thorhildur Thorleifsdottir, was only just finishing her four year period and would normally have had the option to apply for a renewal of her contract. The matter received some attention in the press, especially when the chairman of the RTC's board, responsible for the hiring of the artistic director, decided to apply for the post. In the end, Thorhildur Thorleifsdottir decided to withdraw her application for the post, and finally Gudjon Pedersen, one of Iceland's leading directors, was hired.

Thorhildur Thorleifsdottir's artistic policy could be characterized as a mixture of extremes. Under her management the RTC had rejoiced in some of its biggest commercial successes, including musicals such as *Grease* and *Little Shop of Horrors*, and its biggest success ever, Marc Camoletti's *Sex í sveit (Pyjamas pour six)*, with a total audience of over 50,000. On the other hand the RTC, under her direction, had also focused on highly artistic performances, aiming at a very selective audience, as in the cases of the poetic plays of Sigurdur Palsson or the productions of Russian director Alexei Borodin.

Gudjon Pedersen launched his first season in October 2000 with his own sombre production of *King Lear*. It became soon clear, however, in the light of RTC's poor financial situation, that the theatre could not afford an artistic direction with its emphasis on such large-scale, expensive productions of classic drama, which did not achieve any general popularity. The RTC had suffered a continuing financial crisis ever since the company moved into the City Theatre in 1989, a situation with no end in sight in the near future.

In contrast to the somewhat extremist policy of Thorhildur Thorleifsdottir, Gudjon Pedersen decided last season to focus on popularity on the theatre's Big Stage, without giving in to hardcore commercialism such as producing only musicals and farce, which would be most likely to gain the biggest success at the box office. Thus the emphasis was laid on dramatisations like Laura Esquivel's *Like Water for Chocolate* and Halldor Laxness' *Kristnihald undir Jökli (Under the Glacier)*, plus a new play by the most popular contemporary Icelandic playwright, Olafur Haukur Simonarson.

The Small Stage of the City Theatre was handed over by the RTC to smaller theatre groups; and a new stage was opened in the City Theatre in October 2001, which has become the space for some of the most innovative and creative theatre activities seen in Iceland for years. The New Stage opened with a modern production of *Waiting for Godot*, and has since then been the home of a group of artists within the RTC, led by 34-year-old director Benedikt Erlingsson, who have been given the opportunity to work together as an ensemble for some length of time.

Independent theatre groups have suffered something of a crisis in the last few years. To some extent, the rise and fall of the Icelandic Theatre Company may have contributed to this, but judging from the performances chosen for realisation on the City Theatre's Small Stage, the independent groups were not doing much innovative or new theatre. There are some exceptions to be found, for example The Icelandic Take-Away Theatre or Dansleikhus med Ekka (The Sobbing Dance Theatre), but their (and others') experiments went almost unnoticed.

Among the independent theatres, Hafnarfjardarleikhusid (The Hafnarfjördur Theatre), situated in a suburban town near Reykjavik, has received the greatest attention, focusing entirely on new Icelandic playwriting. Its specialization was rewarded in 2000, when the theatre signed a contract with the ministry of culture and the town council of Hafnarfjördur, which secured the theatre financial support for the next three years, enough for two productions per year.

This period of financial and artistic crisis with its focus on commercial and competitive issues has resulted in a growing impatience among many Icelandic theatre artists; an impatience, which has been breaking loose during the last season. Their craving for increased emphasis on artistic matters and more experiment in the theatre has resulted in the founding of the special group within the Reykjavik Theatre Company mentioned earlier and Vesturport (West Port), a small theatre created by a group of young artists. Although there seems to be no end in sight to the financial crisis, in artistic terms Icelandic theatre is, hopefully, seeing some light at the end of the tunnel.

Magnus Thor Thorbergsson *studied literature at the University of Iceland and theatre studies at the Free University of Berlin. He works as a dramaturg at the Icelandic Academy of the Arts and as a theatre critic for the Public Broadcasting Service.*

INDIA

REOTI SARAN SHARMA
and J N KAUSHAL

In the sub-continental situation of India, where plays are being written and performed in over 22 major languages and in vastly distanced regions, it has always been difficult to evaluate and assess the Indian theatre in its totality. However, geographical distances have been overcome and linguistic barriers partially scaled down with the holding since 1999 in New Delhi of a festival of the best Indian plays, under the aegis of the National School of Drama, the premier institute of theatre training which over the past 45 years has significantly imparted a professional quality to the largely amateur theatre, through a cadre of approximately 800 actors, directors and designers trained by it.

In the four festivals held so far, an average of 80–90 outstanding plays have been performed. These served as the shop window of Indian theatre in its linguistic and artistic diversity, reflecting its strengths – and weaknesses – as never before.

A number of our playwrights have survived the evaporating forces of time. Though writing in their own regional languages they have become national playwrights, as their plays have been translated into other Indian languages and still retain their potential for revival. Notable among this group are Badal Sircar, Utpal Dutt, Habib Tanvir, P.L. Deshpande, Vijay Tendulkar, Girish Karnad, Mohan Rakesh, Dharmvir Bharati, Adya Rangacharya, Chandrasekhar Kambar and recently Mahesh Dattani. In their own languages and regions, the following also enjoy recognition and popularity: Romesh Mehta, P.K. Atre, K.N. Pannikar, J.P. Das, Manoj Mitra, Balwant Gargi, Gursharan Singh, Dr. Atamjit, Satish Alekar, Mahesh Elkunchwar and Motilal Kemu.

Similarly, due to their striking theatrical acumen, unique talent for visualisation and rich theatrical aesthetics, drawing upon both the classical and folk traditions of Indian and Western traditions, the following directors have come to occupy the commanding heights of modern Indian theatre: Sombhu Mitra, Utpal Dutt, Habib Tanvir, Ebrahim Alkazi, Alyque Padamasi, Shyamanand Jalan, B.V. Karanth, Ratan Thiyam, H. Kanhai Lal, Jabbar Patel, Arun Mukherjee, Rudraprasad Sengupta, Usha Ganguly, Romesh Mehta, K.N. Pannikar.

However, the festival simultaneously exposed the Achilles heel of the 'art' theatre. While the commercial theatre, touring theatre companies and some forms of folk theatre (like Jatra and Tamasha theatre in the states of Bengal and Maharashtra) enjoy strong financial, community and audience support, the professional artistic theatre perches upon a very fragile base. It lacks in infrastructure, financial and audience support. By and large it is a sporadic, individual activity, invariably triggered by the availability of production grants from the government and corporate sponsorships. Generally experimental in nature,

ABOVE: *Andha Yug (Blind Age)*

BELOW: *Agni Matter Male (Fire & Rain)*

INDIA

this theatre lacks mass appeal. In it the audience miss what sets, lighting, costumes and music can contribute to create a spectacular presentation on stage. Its magic is restricted to that of the words and the actors. Even in the matter of actors, plays with a very small cast are preferred, because professionally trained directors have failed to form viable teams of actors, theatre technicians and playwrights, capable of varied and sustained theatre practice. This has particularly affected the emergence of new stage writers. Those who venture into the field of writing for the stage soon become disillusioned, as they do not find regular opportunities to see their work presented on the stage, or to work with worthwhile directors who could fine tune their dramatic skills and impregnate their literary sensibilities with the complex needs and visual aesthetics of the theatre.

As a result, old plays are more often repeated, foreign plays adapted, or directors write their own scripts in the context of their material constraints or their unrealised artistic ambitions. This trend has popularised the writing of one-actor plays and increased the dramatic rendering of short stories on stage – a genre perfected by director Devendra Raj Ankur and spread by theatre actors working in movies.

Strangely, in the sector of street theatre there is no dearth of playwrights. Street theatre (agitprop in the West) is proliferating at a very fast pace in small towns and industrial townships. Street plays are written by amateur playwrights almost as soon as any event of social concern takes place. Nor in the sector of popular amateur theatre is there any shortage of playwrights. It is indeed tragic that serious professional theatre is stuck with a few authors, who often resort to historical, mythological and folk tales as content for their new plays, ignoring the contemporary themes that would make their writings original, contemporary and in consonance with the role theatre is expected to play in transforming societies and liberating the human psyche to take the future by the horns. In desperate moments, one is tempted to conclude that our playwrights have unwittingly strayed into the wilderness of their ethnic past, in search of the pretty pictures and folk motifs that the young breed of trained directors prefer, for conveniently creating spectacles and illusions of ethnic splendour. The death of idealism and ideology in our age has further accelerated this process.

The National School of Drama Festival, called Bharat Rang Mahotasava (Indian Theatre Festival) is primarily a national festival, but its windows open upon world theatre. In the 2002 festival five foreign troupes came to participate. *Bhelua Sundari*, (*The Damsel Bhelua*) a play from Bangladesh directed by Sydur Rahman Lipon, *Dancing With Dad*, a solo performance written, directed and acted by Yitzhak Weingarten from Israel, and *Moby Dick*, the novel by Herman Melville, presented in a theatre version by Erik Schaeffer and staged by Theatre Triebwerk of Hamburg, were specially noted for their theatrical excellence.

There were also significant productions based on world classics by Sophocles, Euripides, Shakespeare, Brecht, Molière, Bernard Shaw, Nikolai Gogol, Stephan Zweig, Lu Xun, Karel Capek, Dario Fo, Doris Lessing, Ariel Dorfman, Arthur Miller, Jean Anouilh, Luigi Pirandello and John Steinbeck. But a marked difference was noted: most of the directors did not follow the Western format of presentation, but created their own theatre language using indigenous styles of presentation. Often they took the liberty of interpreting and visualising the play in their own innovative way, thus creating new sub-texts and different aesthetic experience.

Most of the Indian plays were set in a rural environment. The characters depicted belonged to the lower middle classes, presenting their trials, tribulations and existential dilemmas in a way that facilitated instant rapport with the audience. There was no elitist approach to theatre or life. In quite a few plays, women were the protagonists because in India, like other developing societies, they suffer the ultimate tyranny perpetrated on them by males – as individuals as well as social and religious groups. To illustrate: amongst the 13 solo performances six dealt with women. Though a few concentrated on the 'other woman' syndrome, there were others which concentrated on the denial of space to women in society.

The depiction of women and their destiny was not limited to solo performances. Gunakar Dev's play *Veerangana* (*The Brave Lady*) was a story of valour taken from the pages of history in which a great lady, at the cost of her life, united people of different castes, creeds and religions to weld them into what has come to be known as the Assamese race in the North Eastern state of India.

Similarly *Didi Thakuran* (*Sister Thakuran*), based on a novel by Renu and directed by Satish Anand, depicted the turmoil in the psyche of the refugees from East Bengal and the original inhabitants of the Indian state of Bihar. The female protagonist Pavitra, a refugee from Bengal, faces the antagonism, discrimination, exploitation and character assassination which refugees face all over the world. But an incidental intervention of Mother Nature, in the form of rain and floods, turns the tables and the original inhabitants, too, become refugees in their own land, giving them a realisation of what it is to be homeless and landless. Pavitra open-heartedly joins the original inhabitants in their calamity and succeeds in creating a sense of common human destiny and togetherness.

Jatra (*Journey*) written by Imran Hussain and directed by Baharul Islam, impressed as a saga of a Muslim woman, Rubaiya, who faces the gender bias that women face in Muslim society due to the non-Islamic practices that have crept into their religion, promulgated by semi-literate clerics. Rubaiya is divorced by her husband and suffers discriminations that are not sanctioned by religion but perpetrated through unchallenged false religious practices. She stands up gallantly to challenge the humiliating conditions imposed for re-marriage to her former husband and thus defend her self-respect and her rights over her body.

Suman Mukherjee accomplished the very difficult task of creating theatre out of a novel with remarkable ease. His production of Debesh Roy's *Teesta Parer Britanto* (*Tale from the Other Side of the Teesta River*) was an excellent example of creating spectacle without much ado about anything. Apart from creating the right ambience with a skeletal set and selective lighting, his actors never showed a chink in their performances. The production had a languid pace, like the river in the title.

Using a new language of theatre better understood by today's fast-track MTV generation, Nirmal Pande committed an act of sacrilege by presenting

INDIA

Dharamvir Bharatis Andha Yug (*The Blind Age*) a Hindi classic based on the Indian epic of *Mahabharata*, introduced to the world by Peter Brook through his landmark production with a multinational cast of actors. Nirmal used a jazzy and fizzy style, like *West Side Story*, for his production, which brought a different kind of youthful synergy to a play that had always been performed at a reverentially placid pace.

Playwright Mahesh Elkunchwar writes with great restraint and sensitivity and in his new English play *Sonata* surveys a group of women who had aligned themselves with the Women's movement but thirty years later abandoned it and retreated into their private world of reality and fantasy, opting for the conventional life style of marriage and children. The play is constructed as a mosaic of their experiences, with fragmented memories of childhood and youth constantly invading and interrupting the present. It came out as a poignant tale of self-discovery, self-denial and self-betrayal. Nissar Allana's design and Amal Allana's direction created a perfect example of theatre of realism.

The internationally renowned director Ratan Thiyam came with a very different production, based on *Ritu Samhar* (*Ode to Seasons*) a descriptive poem by Kalidasa, the Sanskrit poet and dramatist. *Ritu Samhar* is not a play in the conventional sense. It has no tangible story. It is a description of the Indian cycle of seasons, portraying the close interaction of life and nature, showing the impact of the seasons not only on living beings but also on inanimate nature. Using movement, gaits, acrobatic skills and symbolic gestures from the rich theatrical vocabulary of light, sound, movement and music he possesses, Ratan creates stunning stage pictures that dissolve into each other to create a flow of visual poetry on stage.

During the last decade in India, too, there has been an unprecedented proliferation of TV channels and satellite telecasts. Television has, undeniably, wooed away significant chunks of the theatre audience, as well as theatre artists, and has become the prime medium for entertainment. But theatre has always been more than entertainment: a ritual, a social celebration, a cultural exercise and finally, the never dying urge in man to witness performers enacting *Leelas* (marvellous acts), taking the risks normally associated with those who walk on tightropes. Live experience being irreplaceable, theatre will always be a necessary part of man's spiritual journey.

J N **Kaushal** *is Vice-President, and* **Reoti Saran Sharma** *General Secretary, of the Indian Centre of the International Theatre Institute.*

IRAN

FARAH YEGANEH

Iranian theatre has become more varied in its styles of expression in recent years. Some plays are socially minded, some maintain a traditional style, while the younger generation produce interesting experimental plays on small stages, and their ambitious artistic endeavours aim at creating an ensemble spirit.

An extensive guild union was established in 1999. Called Khane-ye-theatre (The House for Theatre), it embraces all theatre professionals in its various societies with the purpose of supporting theatre activity. The Iranian ITI Centre was also established in the same year, and has attempted to promote the art of theatre in our country in addition to expanding international relations. A new phase of its activity was initiated in March 2002.

The Iranian professional theatre movement is especially active in our main city, Tehran, with about 150 shows each year. This professional activity is reinforced by work done in the country's other major cities. There are a lot of permanent theatre groups, whose repertoires combine Iranian plays with contemporary and classical world theatre. Every year, the Iranian theatre enjoys a 15,000,000 audience, and the number of daily stage performances in public and private theatre spaces adds up to 4000 all over the country, with a further 8000 street theatre performances.

Contacts with the outside world have grown considerably in the last three years. We have attempted to attend international festivals such as the Edinburgh Festival and Theater der Welt, and have been able to communicate with national and international theatrical institutions all over the world such as the ITI, the puppet union UNIMA (since seven years ago; one member of its board is Iranian) and the International Association of Theatre Critics (since around ten years ago). We hope and wish for more extensive mutual relationships in future.

Universities are fundamental to the growth of our national theatre. In the last ten years, the number of students in theatre schools and colleges has steadily increased, with the universities alone now accounting for one thousand graduates each year. Apart from the universities offering majors and courses on different fields in theatre, there is a growing number of private academies and institutes teaching theatre at basic, intermediate and advanced levels. Never before in its history has Iran had more young people studying drama and other types of performance. This applies to writing as well: courses and workshops have spread throughout the country, with many more of them sparked by the demands of multi-channel television. A new generation of actors and directors is arriving, with fresh visions of their own. Thus, theatre studies have achieved a high level of development. The Theatre Research Centre of The Art University, established in 2001, is a fresh centre in this field, the results of whose researches will nourish our theatre very soon.

The government and the parliament approve the budget for theatre, since

IRAN

both the legislative and the executive powers have to confirm it. Dramatic Arts Centre (DAC), which has represented the Iranian ITI Centre since 1999, was established after the Revolution, under an act of parliament, as the theatrical branch of the Ministry of Culture for specific purposes such as promoting Iranian theatrical activities and providing financial assistance to performing artists. The Theatre Society is a collaborating body that assists DAC in some of its duties.

The current president of DAC, Majid Sharifkhodaei, (who has a doctorate in the political history and sociology of Iran) knows the needs and requirements of theatre in Iran very well, and with his understanding of the phenomenon has been able to solve a lot of problems, promote the Iranian stage, and communicate at an international level. There are, in total, around 290 regional theatre societies in towns, cities and districts, all associated with DAC and funded by it, supporting regional theatre troupes and producing plays all through the year.

DAC has established the most active centre for theatrical books in its Publication Department, and published twenty-nine books in the 2001–2002 season alone. It also publishes *Namayesh* (*Theatre*), a monthly journal and one of the most respected professional theatre magazines in our country. Other noteworthy theatre journals are *Honarha-ye-Namayeshi* (*Dramatic Arts* – monthly), *Theatre Quarterly*, *Honar* (*Arts* – quarterly), and *Sahneh* (*The Stage* – monthly). All have helped to spread knowledge of the work of researchers studying the theatre as a cultural and artistic phenomenon.

Four main theatre halls and complexes are owned, maintained and managed by the DAC in Tehran: The City Theatre Complex, with its seven stages, built in 1972, has been hosting big audiences, and is a true cultural centre with national impact; the Sangeladj Hall is one of our oldest theatre buildings, constructed in 1962; the Honar Hall (The Art Hall) is mostly used for puppetry; Vahdat Hall is the biggest and most magnificent, used for large, sometimes more commercial productions.

DAC has an important mission to make the theatre more accessible to all, and is found at the centre of every development in Iranian theatre. It has attempted to stimulate theatrical life in smaller towns, and in offering opportunities to young artists, university graduates and other talented newcomers has produced their performances to offer a new lease of life to them.

As far as the reform of the state theatres and network of stages across the country is concerned, all theatre makers agree that the civic subsidy guarantees not only creative freedom but also access to the arts for all citizens. However, it is a matter of considerable concern to the President of DAC that the cultural identity of subsidized theatre in the different states should be maintained. He uses his considerable influence to ensure the continued existence of the smaller theatre groups. The country's public theatres receive public funds within the framework of a subsidy system. Most performances cannot cover more than a fraction of their production and operating costs.

In addition, the municipal authorities of various districts of Tehran and other towns and cities have established small halls called Farhang-sara (meaning 'a little home for culture') in which theatrical activities take place, usually amateur or semi-professional.

ABOVE: Mahtab Nasirpoor and Ahmad Aghaloo in *Khoroos* (The Rooster) by Mohammad Rahmanian; Sayeh Hall, Teheran, 2002

BELOW: *Shabha-ye-Avignon* (Avignon Nights), written and directed by Koorosh Narimani, Teheran 1999

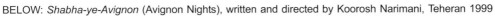

IRAN

Every geographical state in Iran holds a festival each year, the total number all over the country being 29. Their budgets are funded by the Bureau of Culture – the state branch of the Ministry of Culture – in each state. From every state festival, two theatrical works are chosen to participate in a Regional Festival – the country is divided to six regions. From each Regional Festival, three performances go forward, (making a total of 18) to The International Fajr (Freedom) Theatre Festival – the most significant theatrical event in our country, which takes place toward the end of the Iranian year and the beginning of the Christian one.

An International Puppet Festival is held every two years in August in Tehran with the participation of various Iranian groups and famous foreign companies. The festival is one of the most interesting ones because of the presence of beautiful puppetry works with their rich variety from all over the world. It is a ten-day period of fantasy and dream taking the audience to the land of marionettes and puppets. The last festival took place in August 2002.

Another biennial Iranian festival is The National Traditional-Ritualistic Festival, featuring various traditional and ritualistic theatrical performances in stage and street theatre forms. Groups from all parts of the country take part, in order to reveal and reinterpret the traditional way of performance.

A national Children and Young Adults Theatre Festival titled 'Omid' (Hope) takes place every autumn in a different city or town. In addition, there are a few other small festivals such as The Nomad Theatre Festival (annual, Aligoodarz, August) and The Defence Theatre Festival (annual, Tehran, June). All Iranian festivals are funded and produced by the government, to encourage graduates and practitioners to produce quality work. These festivals have become one of the most important channels for enhancing theatre life in our country.

The International Fajr Theatre Festival is annually held in Tehran at the end of January, with the participation of Iranian and foreign theatre companies, in four different sections: the domestic competition (for the young or less established professionals; the fringe (for the Iranian theatre masters); the foreign companies section; and the street theatre section – of which the first and the fourth sections are competitive. The festival, in a nutshell, reflects the characteristics of Iranian theatre, and has contributed both to international exchange and to the development of our national theatre movement. Its total budget is an estimated 700,000 Euros, all paid by the government through the Ministry of Culture.

In the 1999–2000 theatrical season, the 18th Festival took place with the participation of 57 Iranian groups, five foreign companies from Germany, Armenia, Sweden, Norway and Italy, and 46 Iranian street theatre troupes. In its twelve-day run, the festival enjoyed the attendance of 160,000 audience members. Two performances, *Shabha-ye-Avignon* (*Avignon Nights*) and *Vaghti Ma Bargardim* (*When We Come Back*), directed respectively by Koorosh Narimani and Ebrahim Poshtekoohi, jointly won the prize for the best director. *Avignon Nights* was also awarded the first prize for its dramatic text. Pantea Bahram was selected as the best actress in *Pas, Ta Farda* (*So, Till Tomorrow*), and Siamak Safari who had played in *Avignon Nights* took the prize for best actor. Following its goals of communication between the West and Asia, the German Theater an der Ruhr started its theatrical activity in Iran for the first time with this festival, with productions such as *Kaspar* and *Before the Millennium Makes Us Apart*. Its presence has continued up to the present in the form of a contract.

All Iranian plays accepted for Fajr will have further public performance over the next year. Works by great and famous directors are placed on the Fringe so that the young have enough opportunity in the competition.

In 2000–2001, the 19th Fajr was held in January 2001 with the participation of 37 Iranian groups, 13 foreign companies from Greece, Germany, Italy, Bulgaria and China, 21 productions on the Fringe and 43 Iranian street theatre troupes. In this season, a student section was added to the Festival, with 25 university student groups taking part. *Saadat-e Larzan-e Mardoman-e Tirehrooz* (*Unfortunate People's Shaky Happiness*), written by Alireza Naderi, won the first prize for its text. The best actor selected was Amir Jafari for his acting in *Yek Daghigheh Sokoot* (*One Minute's Silence*) and *Regisseurha Nemimirand* (*Directors Don't Die*), and Setareh Eskandari was awarded the prize for best actress for her acting in *Unfortunate People's Shaky Happiness*.

Awards were offered to the late Hooshang Hessami for his directing of *Poof*, and to Ali Rafiyi for his adaptation and stage-direction of a famous stream-of-consciousness novel, *Shazdeh Ehtejab* (*Prince Ehtejab*). Hamid Samandarian and Akbar Radi were honoured as masters, and in the Fringe section, Ahmad Aghaloo was awarded a commemorative plaque for his acting in *Khoroos* (*The Rooster*). The undoubted hits of the 2000–2001 season were *Gong-e Khabdideh* (*The Mute Who Was Dreamed*) directed by our theatre wizard Atila Pessiani, and a fresh production of *Antigone* directed by Pari Saberi which mixed Iranian Tazieh elements into a Greek tragedy. The most significant event of the festival was the attendance of the Peking Opera with their fantastic performance of *Lady Yang*, which amazed and charmed its Iranian audience. A workshop on sound and movement techniques was held for theatre students during the festival, with English tutors. The Festival attracted an attendance of 200,000.

The 20th International Fajr Theatre Festival, held in January 2002, included the participation of 33 Iranian groups for the competition section, 20 Iranian groups in the fringe section (the masters), 10 foreign companies from Russia, Germany, Italy, Greece, Syria, Egypt and Canada, 31 street theatre groups, and 27 student troupes. Neda Hengami won the prize for her direction of *Azhedahak*, Mohammad-Bagher Banayi was awarded the writing prize for the script of *Sabz, Sohrab, Sorkh* (*Green, Sohrab, Crimson*). Sima Tirandaz won the best actress prize for *Mahale Fekr Konin Iynjouri Ham Momkeneh Besheh* (*You May Not Guess It Possible*), and Davar Farmani got the prize for the best actor for *Green, Sohrab, Crimson*. Amir Koohestani, the competent young director of *Raghs Rooye Livanha* (*Dance on Glasses*) attracted the attention of the German authorities and was invited to present his play in Germany.

A trend which goes against the tendency to big international productions at the beginning of the new millennium is that of the monologue. The standard-bearer of the Persian monologue is Ghotbeddin Sadeghi who has certainly influenced other young directors. A central theme of his work is the interior struggle of the individual, ill at ease in a world that revolves around materialism and hypocrisy. He received an award in the fringe section for his play *Sahoori* (*Reveille*), for his focus on old Iranian fables, and their revival in new theatrical forms. Its solo actor, Mikael Shahrestani, has long been making an impression on Iranian stages. Ali Rafyi, with his production of Genet's *Les Bonnes*, Davood Fat-halibeigi with his adaptation of Shakespeare's *Taming of The Shrew* to Iranian traditional theatre, Mohammad Rahmanian with his *Shahadat-khani-e Ghadamshad-e Motreb dar Tehran (Minstrel Ghadamshad's Passion Play at Tehran)*, and Atila Pessiani's *Bass-e Dige Khafeh Shou (That's Enough, Shut Up!)* were among the performances to be enjoyed – the last was invited to tour in Britain. The Theater an der Ruhr, in collaboration with DAC, worked on *The House of Bernarda Alba* by Federico Garcia Lorca, directed by Roberto Ciulli and performed by Iranian actresses – the production had its premiere in the Main Hall of the City Theatre in June 2002. The Festival also held a workshop on lighting and scenography, with German tutors. With so many attractions, it is not surprising that 250,000 people attended the Festival.

In these three seasons, classics have been the staple fare of both traditional and avant-garde companies. Dramatic texts have been mounted either with meticulous respect or with a sense of complete reinterpretation. The great works of Shakespeare have been performed, while Chekhov, Sartre and Genet have also been solidly present.

Besides festivals, national seminars and conferences on different aspects of theatre are held all through the year. The annual National Seminar on Tazieh – the famous Islamic-Iranian passion play – was held in May 2001 for three days with 12 lectures on the subject in the mornings and 12 Tazieh performances in various traditional places in Kashan, a town famous for its mosques and Takiehs (a special performance stage for Tazieh). Iran has traditionally been and still is world-famous for its Tazieh, and the Seminar is held every year in one of the states, preferably in those with the tradition.

The spectrum of Iranian theatre ranges from the commercial ones, presenting popular entertainment, to the fringe groups and so-called alternative theatres. Due to their enormous range of artistic expression, these independent ensembles are reaching a highly diversified audience, and exercising an increasing influence on high culture. Although, in recent years, the government has made a determined effort to promote alternative theatre more effectively, many of these groups are working under permanently precarious financial conditions. Most private theatres, dependent on the box office, offer commercial and/or traditional plays, though they do receive support from DAC in other aspects.

The different trends and approaches in Iranian theatre reflect the debate going on among artists and critics. On one side are the nationalists, who think that the future of our theatre lies in rediscovering the truest national form, which has been lost due to long negligence and ideological indifference. On the other hand are the proponents of modernity, who think that our theatre in the new millennium can develop only in close conjunction with the theatres of the world, and claim that the futile search for purity will deny theatre its vigour and originality. Today, Iran is overcoming economic depression and entering a promising new phase. Henceforth, we can hope to construct a sound theatre infrastructure.

Farah Yeganeh *is a university lecturer, theatre critic and translator. She is the Secretary of the Iranian ITI Centre, and the editor of* International Department of Dramatic Arts Journal.

IRELAND

STEVE WILMER

The Irish theatre has continued to benefit from a rapidly expanding economy and a sizeable increase in government subsidy. John O'Donoghue, the new arts minister who was appointed in June 2002 and whose portfolio was redefined to include sports and tourism, reported that the government had increased its spending on the arts from 1997 to 2002 by 80%, from 26.4 million to 47.8 million Euros. Before leaving office, his predecessor, Sile de Valera, announced an ambitious five-year plan that the funding would increase to 79.8 million Euros by 2006. (However, with a recent downturn in the economy and announced cutbacks in governmental budgeting, it remains to be seen whether the government will sustain this level of growth.) In tandem with the increased expenditure on the arts, many new theatres have been built or upgraded both in the Dublin area (such as the new Pavilion Theatre in Dun Laoghaire) and around the country. Furthermore, rather than providing only annual funding to arts organisations, the arts council has provided increased security for thirteen subsidized theatres and theatre-oriented organisations (such as Rough Magic, Fishamble and Meridian theatre companies), providing them with three-year funding.

The National Theatre (known as the Abbey Theatre), under the leadership of its artistic director Ben Barnes, has continued to maintain its national and international success in the wake of Patrick Mason's impressive leadership. Deborah Warner staged a version of *Medea* (2000) with Fiona Shaw in the title role that used an Irish-speaking chorus and featured a bloodthirsty Shaw brandishing a butcher's knife as she chased her children off the stage. Clearly a star vehicle for Shaw, the production moved to London in 2001 minus the local Irish cast, and is due for a New York production. A tribute to the playwright Tom Murphy (whose *The House* was premiered in 2000) was staged during the 2001 Dublin theatre festival, with six of his plays receiving an airing, including *A Whistle in the Dark*, *Bailegangaire*, *The Sanctuary Lamp*, *The Morning after Optimism* and *The Gigli Concert*. Important new work continued to be produced, such as two plays about small town life: Eugene O'Brien's *Eden* (2001) about a husband and wife who live in separate fantasy worlds and *On Such as We* (2001), about an affable barber, amiably played by Brendan Gleeson and written by Billy Roche (whose *Wexford Trilogy* was revived in London in 2000), as well as Mark O'Rowe's *Made in China* (2001), about Dublin's underworld.

Sebastian Barry's *Hinterland* (2002), directed by Max Stafford-Clark (and co-produced by Out of Joint Theatre Company) about a character reminiscent of the former Prime Minister Charles Haughey, caused a storm of criticism because of its treatment of a living (and disgraced) politician who continues to be investigated for alleged financial misdealing. Part of the concern expressed was that the life of the politician had been travestied, with the son of the character in the play attempting suicide, his mistress showing up in his house and confronting his wife, and his former colleague, now dead, appearing from a cupboard to haunt him.

IRELAND

Irish classics were also revived at the Abbey, including an impressive production of *Big Maggie* by John B Keane (who died in 2002) directed by Garry Hynes and with Marie Mullen in the title role; and J M Synge's *Playboy of the Western World* in a sparse production directed by Niall Henry with Olwen Fouéré as Pegeen. The Abbey and Ben Barnes also became embroiled in a political dispute as to where to house the theatre in the future. With more government funds available, grand plans were projected about moving the Abbey to a different location and expanding its facilities or building an entirely new edifice. After much discussion the matter has not been settled, but for the moment the Abbey will continue to remain where its is.

The Gate theatre, under the ongoing leadership of Michael Colgan, continued to mount elegant productions, mostly of the classics, with the occasional new play by established writers such as a triple bill of short plays by Brian Friel (*The Yalta Game* – adapted from a Chekhov short story), Conor McPherson (*Come on Over*) and Neil Jordan (*Wild Horses*) in 2001. Frank McGuinness, in *Gates of Gold* (2002), focused on the two gay impresarios who had run the Gate Theatre earlier in the century. Conor McPherson (whose *The Weir* ran for two years in London) continued to supply plays via London, with his *Port Authority* reaching the Gate in April 2001. Michael Colgan, who staged all nineteen of Samuel Beckett's stage plays in a Beckett Festival in 1991 and has continued to tour them abroad, furthered his Beckett industry by filming all of these plays in separate productions, using illustrious directors such as David Mamet and Neil Jordan. This collection of films is being marketed on DVD. Colgan also continued his series of Pinter revivals with a splendid production, directed by Robin Lefevre, of *The Homecoming* (2001) with Ian Holm, later restaging it at Lincoln Center in New York.

The Druid Theatre and the Gate Theatre mounted Marina Carr's depressing but emotionally gripping *On Raftery's Hill* (2000), which dealt with the topical subject of sexual abuse in Irish families. Carr's *By the Bog of Cats*, which premiered at the Abbey in 1998, was revived in the USA in 2001 with performances in Chicago and in a major production in San Jose with Holly Hunter in the leading role. The smaller touring companies continued to do interesting new work. Rough Magic produced *Midden* (2001) by Morna Regan and a revival of *Dead Funny* (2001) by Terry Johnson. The Passion Machine presented an updated version of *Diarmuid and Grainne*(2001) by Paul Mercier as well as a revival of his football play *Studs* to coincide with World Cup fever. The inventive Corn Exchange continued to develop new scripts for its small audience (on the back seat) *Car Show*. The Ann Bogart-inspired Blue Raincoat Theatre Company of Sligo continued its investigation of Lewis Carroll's work with *Alice in Wonderland* and *Alice Through the Looking Glass*, adapted by Jocelyn Clarke and directed by Niall Henry. Calypso Theatre Company, which has focused on racial and immigrant issues and seems increasingly important in an atmosphere of hostility to increased immigration, refugees and asylum seekers, produced Roddy Doyle's new play with the familiar-sounding title, *Guess Who's Coming to the Dinner*. Enda Walsh (whose earlier *Disco Pigs* has toured successfully for years) directed his new play *Bedbound* in the Dublin Theatre Festival in 2000.

Commercial successes that started small and ended up touring abroad included John Breen's *Alone it Stands* (originally staged by Yew Tree Theatre Company in County Mayo) and Marie Jones' delightful two-hander *Stones in His Pockets* (with Conleth Hill and Sean Campion), which followed the lead of Martin McDonagh's *The Cripple of Inishmaan* in commenting on the influence of the American film industry in Ireland.

The fledgling Irish modern dance movement received a significant boost with the first International Dance Theatre Festival Ireland taking place in Dublin in May 2002.

Jane Brenan in the Abbey, Dublin production of *The Secret Fall of Constance Wilde* by Frank McGuinness (*photo*: Amelia Stein)

It included a visit from the Merce Cunningham Dance Company. Other important festivals included the biennial international theatre symposium organized by Pan Pan Theatre Company (2001) and a festival of new work by Barabbas (2002)

Several useful new books appeared about the burgeoning Irish theatre: Dermot Bolger's *Druids, Dudes and Beauty Queens* (published by New Island Books, 2001); Eamonn Jordan's *Theatre Stuff: Critical Essays on Contemporary Irish Theatre* (Carysfort Press, 2000), Lillian Chambers, Ger FitzGibbon and Eamonn Jordan, *Theatre Talk: Voices of Irish Theatre Practitioners*, Chistopher Morash's *History of Irish Theatre 1601-2000* (Cambridge University Press, 2002), Lionel Pilkington and Nicholas Grene's *The Politics of Irish Drama* (Cambridge University Press, 1999). The *Irish Theatre Magazine*, edited by Karen Fricker, continues to provide excellent quarterly commentary on theatre events and trends.

Steve Wilmer *is a Senior Lecturer in the School of Drama at Trinity College Dublin. Recent work includes* Theatre Worlds in Motion: Structures, Politics and Developments in the Countries of Western Europe, *edited with Hans van Maanen and published by Rodopi in 1998. His* Theatre, Society and the Nation: Staging American Identities *will be published in 2002 by Cambridge University Press.*

ITALY

FABIO MANGOLINI and
MARINO PEDRONI

Italian theatre is going through a process of serious change. On the one hand, audiences continue to grow: there are more and more new theatres, refurbished theatres and alternative spaces where one can attend a performance. On the other hand, artistic creativity is well represented, with new creators arriving to take their place alongside those of older generations, all of them producing interesting work. At first sight, this is the general shape of Italian theatre in these last seasons. A series of elements, however, show it to be at a real turning point, between a 'before' and an 'after' which can be given temporal form. Two different episodes have led to a real take-over, in the artistic landscape, by the younger generation.

The first is unfortunately linked to two painful events: the deaths of Giorgio Strehler and Carmelo Bene. Strehler's decease not only provoked a change in the artistic direction of Milan's Piccolo Teatro, with the appointment of Luca Ronconi (to tell the truth, Strehler had left his position a few years ago, but he still retained a central place within the organisation); it also produced a flurry of activity among innumerable creators, who tried to take over his teaching and translate it into new forms with new content. As for Carmelo Bene, his art had for years been an influence on a whole generation of creators. The second fundamental event was the award of the 1997 Nobel Prize for Literature to Dario Fo, representing institutional and international recognition for a distinctive local vision of theatre and its practice.

The arrival of young people at the helm of important centres of production is a sign of a movement towards the acceptance of new forms of theatrical creation: Giorgio Barerio-Corsetti took over the direction of the Venice Theatre Biennale, while the appointment of a number of other leading lights of the experimental theatre of the 80s, Gabriele Vacis, Marco Martinelli, Federico Tiezzi, Romeo Castellucci, Mario Martone, confirmed their final recognition by both institutions and public alike.

In Italy, there are some theatrically very well developed geographical areas – for example Emilia-Romagna (a region boasting three permanent (*stabile*) theatres); and their panorama is extremely varied, from the Societas Raffaello Sanzio to the Teatro de la Valdoca, from Albe in Ravenna to Parma's Teatro delle Briciole, to name just a few. But there are also underdeveloped areas such as Basilicate, where the very few troupes in existence are in charge not only of theatrical creation but also of the creation of an audience (a concrete example of this is Matera's Teatro dei Sassi under the direction of Massimo Lanzetta).

However, even in the economically disadvantaged areas, performances are plentiful and there is a dynamic artistic set-up. Even if we exclude Naples, the traditional fount of Italian theatre and the crossroads of tradition and innovation (one example is the work of Toni Servillo's Teatri Uniti), a disadvantaged area such as Apulia or Sardinia can still produce quality projects (such as Taranto's CREST or Bari's Teatro Kismet).

In the current Italian theatrical landscape, we are present at an osmosis between language and genre. It is the litmus paper for the state of current theatre: so many different theatrical languages, structures, objectives, all of them impossible to reconcile, none of them strong enough to become dominant. We are, in fact, unable to impose a unifying framework from the critical and linguistic point of view: neither a hierarchy of shared values, nor a universally applicable vocabulary.

It is impossible today to speak of a single specific form of theatre, a definable art. This situation is confirmed by the state of Italian production and programming. It has resulted in a new receptivity, which has made possible a profitable exchange between traditional and experimental theatre. So, though it is difficult to produce a clear outline of the Italian situation, it is still possible to give some significant indications of the nature of this theatrical period. Theatrical spaces are more and more becoming places for the exchange of experience, where the dramatic impulse is represented by 'thinking the other's thinking'.

Several groups have been inspired by the example of Judaism, its history, its culture. Moni Ovadia rediscovered a world almost totally unknown in our country with productions like *Oylem Golem* or *Ballata di fine millennio (Song for the End of the Millennium)*. His pupil Enrico Fink carries on with *Lokshen: patrileneare, un racconto*.

In the tradition of 'public theatre' Marco Baliani, Marco Paolini, Lara Curino, Eugenio Allegri and Enrico Messina, to name a few, have arrived as actor-narrators. From Paolini, we remember especially *Vajont*, a performance which meticulously reconstructs the tragedy of 1963 which struck a whole valley in the Veneto, or some narratives ('public speeches') like *Ustica*, based on documents about the 80's tragedy in which a civilian aeroplane was destroyed by military aircraft, responsibility for which was never admitted by the authorities.

Further, Marco Baliane has for several years been leading a project for ETI (Ente Teatrale Italiano): 'The Ports of the Mediterranean'. Productions like *Migranti (Migrants)* and *Giufà* are the fruit of this research. They mix together narrative models (and actors) peculiar to the Mediterranean world, from the occidental tradition as much as the North African or Balkan. An equally original initiative is that of Ravenna Teatro, who have been able to link the oral tradition of the Senegalese *griot* and the storytellers of the Romagna, giving birth to a true theatrical crossover.

But the 'other's thinking' came especially to the fore with a number of productions which have had a great impact on the stage in these last years: *Barboni (Tramps)* and *Esodo (Exodus)* from the Pippo Delbono Company; Compagnia della Fortezza's productions under Armando Punzo's direction (*Marat-Sade, Les Négres*) and other creators like Anonio Vigano with the Teatro della Ribalta. Their productions have brought to the stage prisoners, the homeless, the mentally ill: bodies and languages, which have until now served only as objects for observation and had never before acquired a theatrical subjectivity of their own.

ITALY

On the other hand playwriting discovered its most original features the moment it succeeded in bridging the gap between language and dialect: Enzo Moscato, Mario Martone or Toni Servillo's Neapolitan, Marco Paoloni's Venetian, Ravenna Teatro and Teatro della Valdoca's Romagnole, Kripton company's Calabrese, Franco Scaldati or Spiro Scimone's Sicilian. This exploration has led to an encounter between the 'paternal' national language and dialect, the maternal language of the subconscious.

Recent generations of theatre people have been characterised, above all, by their refusal to follow the theatre's 'grand masters'. Instead, they have focused their interest more towards the visual arts or to the philosophers of psychoanalysis (Lacan, Foucault, Derrida). In this field, even if we cannot speak of a common poetics, there still exists a link between such different groups as Fanny and Alexander, Marco Sgrosso and Elena Bucci's Le Belle Bandiere, Anna Amadori and Fulvio Ianneo's Teatro Reon, Motus, Teatrino Clandestino or Terzadecade, Danilo Conti and Antonella Piroli's Tanticosiprogetti, all working and performing in Emilia-Romagna, probably the most prolific of the Italian regions. Let's add Antonio Marfella's Rosso Tiziano, in Naples, which unites actor's theatre with deep research on the text.

From the institutional point of view, one year ago we could have started this article with the words, 'The long awaited law of the Italian theatre, which should bring some order to the chaotic landscape of production, is about see the light of day'. This law should have redefined existing theatrical reality in simple terms, by confirming the important institutional production structures (*teatri stabili*) and giving a guarantee of support to the touring companies (*compagnie de giro*). It should have also finally reaffirmed the value of the sectors linked to experiment and to the young public. The new development enshrined in the law was to be the setting up of regional networks with a new overall management, linked to the local communities, to supervise the creation of 'resident' companies which would serve local needs.

For Italy, 'land of a hundred cities', the creation under the law of a new National Theatre Centre, which would replace the Ente Teatrale Italiano (ETI), and be more attentive to localised needs, would have developed both the production and the 'consumption' of theatrical performances. On the other hand, the concept of 'resident' companies, somewhat along the lines of the French model, would have guaranteed the future of a large number of producing institutions, which would otherwise be dissipated, by allowing them to produce with their continuity assured.

The new law should have been the historical turning point for a decaying institutional framework. But this law, so long promised and promoted by the previous Government (1996–2001) was never to be born; and the present Government intends to go in a completely different direction, although it has not yet made any concrete proposal apart from the threat, still hypothetical, to strike at the Italian theatre by suppressing public subsidy of any kind. Caught between the violent political infighting and vendettas being waged between opposing political parties, it is the Italian theatre that bears the brunt: more enterprising than ever in its artistic spirit, yet more than ever the victim of confused and confusing institutional *diktat*.

A stated in this article's introduction, the Italian theatre still survives in lively

Giulio Cesare after Shakespeare by Romeo Castellucci

health, in spite of the present chronic lack of efficient institutional structures that might prove capable of building a secure future for the artistic potential of old and new generations. Perhaps is it 'thanks to' those difficulties that the interesting experiences described here continue to be born and grow.

In this sense, Italian theatre is very much alive. It is nevertheless permissible to ask ourselves what the situation would be, if an institutional structure could be established that was as lively as the artistic one. In its absence, the Italian theatre continues to bear up, at least until now.

JAMAICA

MICHAEL RECKORD

Jamaica has for hundreds of years been a nation with a passion for performing, and there have been theatres and performing groups in the island for most of the last three hundred of them. With the coming of Independence in 1962, dramatic productions began to boom. Popular music grew faster, and reggae quickly became the island's best known Performing Arts export. Dance grew too, but less quickly than the other performing art forms.

For more than a decade, the island, with a population of two and a half million people, and more specifically the capital Kingston and its environs with a million, was responsible for more than three dozen dramatic productions a year. The island has no government-subsidised theatre, and as the cost of mounting theatre productions escalates, producers have been finding it more difficult to finance productions. Many have given up, which is one reason why, over the past decade, the number of productions mounted in the island has fallen by about 40 per cent.

In 1999, revues and 'roots plays' dominated the Jamaican theatre scene, making up the bulk of the new productions mounted, out of a total of some 33 shows for the year. Both types of drama comment directly on the country's distressing socio-economic situation. The 'roots' play is a sex farce mounted with a minimal set and featuring working class characters. The setting is always domestic and usually depicts a living room and a bedroom. Veteran 'roots' producers who staged shows in 1999 were Paul Beale, Balfour Anderson and the granddaddy of them all, Ralph Holness, the man who coined the term. 'Roots' plays tend to mock the foibles of the segment of the population featured; revues tend to hold the government and big business up to ridicule.

A fine production came from a group which usually does award-winning work, the Jamaica Junior Theatre, an amateur children's and young people's theatre company. Their version of the Broadway hit, *The Lion King*, was spectacular and featured fine acting all round. An outstanding show and one with special significance was The Company Limited's *Once On This Island*. Featuring a number of trained singers from the Eastern Caribbean, as well as top Jamaican talent, it was ironically one of TCL's best productions and, regrettably, its last. After serving Jamaica well for more than a decade, the Company bowed to economic pressure.

If TCL had been able to get a franchise from David Heron to produce his plays, it wouldn't have folded. That relative newcomer opened his fourth straight crowd-pleaser, *Love and Marriage and New York City*, in September, started touring the island in December and subsequently took the show to Britain and the USA.

Amina Blackwood Meeks' one woman show (a rarity in Jamaica) *Invocation*, was a tour de force. The actress/playwright literally and figuratively had the audience eating out of her hands – she served pudding towards the end of the show.

Two big musical productions, *Bugsie*, the Little Theatre Movement's annual 'pantomime',

andrew
brodber

pat
gooden

terri
salmon

karl
williams

Private
Lives

By **Noel Coward**
Directed by Norman Rae

For
Tickets
Call 926-6163

Little Little Theatre
Playing Weekends Fri. & Sat. 8pm • Sun. 5pm & 8pm

JAMAICA

(so called because of the genre's vague similarities to British pantomimes), and Jambiz International's *Breadfruit Kingdom* closed the 1999 season on a high note.

The sharp decline in the number of productions continued in 2000; happily quality decreased only marginally. In the recent past Jamaica produced some 20 new dramatic works in a year. In 2000, there were 15. Admittedly, 15 new shows (plays, revues and musicals) is good for an island of Jamaica's size, but the general quality of the productions followed the numbers downward.

Most producers opted for comedy rather than drama. Only two commercial producers faced the challenge of looking at serious issues seriously. Two educational institutions did mount dramas. From the University of the West Indies, the University Dramatic Arts Society staged Errol John's *Moon on a Rainbow Shawl* in March and, with the Edna Manley College behind it, the School of Drama gave the tiny public which attends the School's productions Lorraine Hansberry's *A Raisin in the Sun* in April and Samuel Beckett's *Endgame* in November. The other producers relied on comedy to pull in audiences but not all comic productions did well. Failure at the box office does not necessarily mean artistic failure and a group of International Theatre Institute members, including ITI Jamaica President David Heron, suggested that poor marketing could be blamed for at least one financial failure.

Fr. Richard Ho Lung and Friends, the group which has been staging the Roman Catholic priest's musicals and revues for some 20 years, put on their biggest production ever with *Jesus 2000*. It featured a huge cast in 31 scenes performing 26 musical numbers, with the Prima! Chamber String Orchestra of Florida providing beautiful accompaniment.

Jamaica played host to the 4th Biennial Caribbean Secondary Schools' Drama Festival which saw school drama groups coming from St Kitts-Nevis, Guyana, Trinidad and Tobago and Antigua to compete with local schools. The excellent performances given by some students augured well for the future of regional drama.

Dance concerts provided the best theatre fare for 2001. Though it's not the first time it has happened, last year the 'contest' between dance and dramatic/musical theatre was particularly uneven. There were fewer dramatic productions than usual, only about 22 commercial works. Of the 22, only eight of those staged up to the end of the year were new Jamaican plays; and generally, the shows were lightweight. The serious decline in numbers started in recent years, but even up to 2000 there were some 15 new productions. On the other hand, there was a veritable explosion of dance concerts in 2001. Most were at least interesting; some were excellent.

In December, a visiting British theatre company, Travelling Light, played at the Edna Manley College, and the 60th annual Pantomime of the Little Theatre Movement (LTM) opened as usual on Boxing Day in the 100 year-old Ward Theatre. The LTM got much congratulation for staging a one-day, first-of-its-kind colloquium on the Pantomime, in October 2001.

In December, the fine Dance Theatre Xaymaca opened its sixth season of dance at the Little Theatre. Its Artistic Director, Barbara McDaniel, who received a national honour on Heroes' Day for her contribution to dance, was the main choreographer. Other professional dance companies which provided pleasurable seasons of dance in 2001 were the National Dance Theatre Company (NDTC), Movements Dance Company, the Stella Maris Dance Ensemble and, to a lesser degree, the Dance Theatre

Company of Jamaica. The oldest of the companies, the NDTC, is 40 in 2002; the youngest, the Stella Maris Ensemble, is nine.

School based troupes also delighted. They were the Tivoli Gardens High School Dance Troupe (who showed off 14 Gold awards) Wolmers' Dance Troupe and the St Jago Dance Society (who showed off their four Gold award dances).

Happily, in the last four months of 2001, the pace of drama productions increased. We got the JamBiz International production *Dirty Diana* by Patrick Brown, the Area Youth Foundation's *Link-Up* by Sheila Graham and Owen Ellis (script) and Winston Bell and the Area Crew (music), the School of Drama's *Malcauchon* by Derek Walcott, Father Ho Lung and Friends' *Spirit* and the Drama School's production of *Lysistrata* by Aristophanes. Though it was not the most professionally produced or written, *Link-Up* was for many the most inspiring. The core membership of the Area Youth Foundation comes from inner-city communities.

Non-commercial theatre generally fared better than commercial theatre. The usual three major drama competitions/festivals – that of the Jamaica Cultural Development Commission (JCDC), the Secondary Schools' Drama Festival and the University's Tallawah – were staged. The JCDC drama competition drew good response from across the island and 11 plays got the required 95% and over to be eligible for the National Finals in Kingston. Tallawah's organisers were happy with their 54 entries last year, especially the fact that they included a large number of original pieces. Unfortunately, the Secondary Schools' Drama Festival had, in one respect, its worst year. Only seven schools entered the festival, where there used to be 20 to 30 entries.

Jamaican Theatre has started looking to the future. In August 2001, a first-of-its kind meeting was held which augured well for Jamaica's cultural landscape. A Cabinet-appointed Entertainment Advisory Board, based in the Ministry of Tourism and Sports, was formed and mandated with the task of advising the Ministry on issues regarding the formulation of an Entertainment policy covering the development of human, intellectual and capital resources within the ministry.

In mid-April, the Chairperson of the Entertainment Advisory Board's Arts and Affiliates Subcommittee and the Entertainment Director jointly presided over an Arts in Education meeting at the Ministry of Tourism, which was attended by high-level representatives of the University of the West Indies, the Government's Department of Culture and the Edna Manley College for the Visual and Performing Arts, among others.

These developments should impact strongly, if not directly, on theatre. What will affect theatre directly, though, is the product of another meeting at the Jamaica Tourist Board in November last. It was a meeting of scores of theatre practitioners, who set up a Steering Committee which led to the formation of the Jamaica Association of Dramatic Artists (JADA) in February 2002. JADA, too, has been having frequent subcommittee meetings. As a result of these initiatives, one may confidently expect the decline in theatre productions which started a few years ago to be halted.

Michael Reckord *is a writer and educator who has been working in and writing about Jamaica theatre and dance for the past 40 years. He reviews theatre and dance for Jamaica's major daily newspaper.*

JAPAN

GORO MINAMOTO

By and large, the situation of Japanese contemporary theatre reflects the history of theatre in Japan. Noh, Kabuki, classic and contemporary theatre, all of these are separate genres with their own history. For example, in Japan it is almost unthinkable for an actor who has played Hamlet to play Jimmy Porter in John Osborne's *Look Back in Anger*. Different genres are separated by a very deep gulf. For a time, Osanai Kaoru, the man considered to be the father of Japanese modern theatre, even argued vigorously that it was necessary to break off completely from the traditional performing arts. Today, very occasionally, actors from the classical genres appear in modern dramas. This is a important form of experimentation, but from the standpoint of the theatre world as a whole, such examples are rare exceptions to the rule. In this report, I will concentrate on contemporary theatre where movement has been relatively vigorous. With other genres, I will comment simply on outstanding developments.

It has been three years since the opening of the New National Theatre. There have been many outstanding productions that have received various awards and, for the most part, the critical reception of the theatre has been positive. The 1999–2000 season featured such plays from before and during World War II as Kato Michio's *Nayotake* and Morimoto Kaoru's *Doto* (*The Angry Waves*) and *Hanabanashiki Ichizoku* (*The Colourful Family*). *Nayotake* is a play with a powerful presence in in postwar theatre. It is based on an idea from the ancient classic, *Taketori Monogatari* (*The Tale of the Bamboo Cutter*). It questions the nature of Japanese culture and how an artist should live. In a bit of very ambitious casting, the main role was played by kabuki actor Nakamura Hashinosuke. *Doto* is based on the story of the world famous blood researcher Kitazato Shibasaburo, and shows the struggle to establish the foundations of modern science in a Japan just awakening from a feudal system. Makino Nozomi as director and Takahachi Kouji as Kitazato were particularly well received. *Hanabanashiki Ichizoku* is a satirical play in the manner of Noel Coward and together with *Doto* shows the range of the playwright Morimoto, who was considered an *enfant terrible* and died very young. Among translated plays, Kuriyama Tamiya as director and Mita Kazuyo as Mary in Eugene O'Neill's *Long Day's Journey into Night* were highly praised. Beginning with the 2000–2001 season, Kuriyama became artistic director for drama of the New National Theatre and gave the concept of 'Historical Age and Memory' as the theme of his directorship. In this regard, two plays by Inoue Hisashi were particular striking, the revival of *Kamiyacho Sakura Hoteru* (*Kamiyacho Sakura Hotel*) and the new play *Yume no Sakeme* (*The Seam of the Dream*). These plays questioned responsibility for World War II, the first play focusing on the emperor, the second on the common people. These plays drew attention by showing the

Ichikawa Shinnosuke and Nakamura Jakuemon in *Sukeroku*

playwright's unique world and examining what lies beneath contemporary Japanese society, treating the theme with great complexity combined with a light comic touch. *Haha-tachi no Kuni e* (*To the Land of the Mothers*) by Matsuda Masataka showed the experience of the atomic blast at Nagasaki, an event that still casts a shadow on the youth of today, with a powerful depiction of the complexity of the human emotions surrounding the event. *Pikadon Kijimunaa* by Sakate Yoji was set in the period around the time of the return of Okinawa to Japan, bringing out the contradictions of post-war society by connecting the atomic blast at Hiroshima with Okinawa under a military government. *Konnichiwa Okaasan* (*Hello Mother*) written and directed by Nagai Ai showed the very serious economic problems of old age in a portrait of contemporary life with a light touch, and both play and production were very highly praised. Noda Hideki staged a new production of his play, *Gansaku Sakura no Mori no Mankai no Shita* (*Fake – Underneath the Trees of the Cherry Forest in Full Bloom*). This play treated the development of the ancient imperial court in Japan with a fantastic approach full of surprises, directly taking on the myth of the eternal unbroken line of the imperial family. Horio Yukio, the designer for the play, created a cherry forest that extended into the audience, making for an unprecedentedly deep perspective and emphasizing the animist atmosphere of the play. *Bijo de Yaju* (*The Beauty is a Beast*) by Rabelais expert Ogino Anna did not live up to its expectations.

Among translated plays, Michael Frayn's *Copenhagen*, directed by Uyama Hitoshi, attracted the most attention and there was less criticism than before for such productions as *Macbeth*, *Pacific Overtures* and *A Streetcar Named Desire*. For the series of activities of the producing department of the New National Theatre under the direction of Kuriyama Tamiya and his theme of 'Historical Age and Memory,' the department was awarded the group award of the Kinokuniya Theatre Prize, one of the most distinguished awards in modern theatre in Japan. One of the intentions of awarding the prize to the New National Theatre was to attract public attention to the crisis of theatre, since Prime Minister Koizumi has suggested cutting off public aid to theatre as part of his plan to restructure the government.

In order to produce the plays of modern playwrights, in contrast with the private sector the New National Theatre has many economic advantages. It can assemble excellent casts and stage staff, so perhaps it is only natural that there are many superior productions. However, since it doesn't have its own company of actors or a training programme, there is also the risk that an excellent production will not have a lasting influence. The New National Theatre still has many problems to deal with.

Notable new works that were produced include Inoue Hisashi's *Rensagai no Hitobito* (*The People on the Block*), Saito Ren's *Koi Uta* (*Love Song*), Obata Kinji's *Kanoko Kannon*, Makino Nozomi's *Takaki Kanomono*, and *Aka Shatsu* (*Red Shirt*), Nagai Ai's *Hagike no Sanshimai* (*The Three Hagi Sisters*), Sakate Yoji's *Nanyo Kujira Butai* (*Whales in the South Seas*), Kaneshita Tatsuo's *Sasori* (*Scorpion*), Shinagawa Yoshimasa's *Hibakari* (a Japanese-Korean joint production), Betsuyaku Minoru's *Saigo no Bansan* (*The Last Supper*) and *Chiri mo Tsumoreba* (*If Dust Accumulates*), Yagi Syuchiro's *Ashura no Tsuma* (*The Warrior's Wife*), and Hirata Oriza's *Ueno Dobutsu-en Sai-sai-sai Shugeki* (*The Fourth Attack on the Ueno Zoo*).

There were many productions of translated plays already widely known in this country and so many plays in general that I will just list some of the notable productions with foreign directors. Alexander Marin directed *The Grapes of Wrath*, Ion Caramitru directed *The Merchant of Venice*, Prosper Diaz directed Michel Azama's *Jujigun (Parade sauvage)* and David Lebow directed David Hare's *The Blue Room*.

Two Japanese directors who are known internationally are Ninagawa (Yukio) and Asari (Keita). Ninagawa directed a highly acclaimed production of John Burton and Kenneth Cavander's *The Greeks* with a cast drawn from a wide range including talented modern theatre actors such as Hira Mikijiro, Watanabe Misako, Asami Rei and Shiraishi Kayoko, and performers from other genres, including young kabuki actor Onoe Kikunosuke. Asari Keita staged a new musical, *Ikoku no Oka (The Hill of a Foreign Land)*, producing, directing and designing the play as well as participating in writing the script. It is a work on a grand scale with a story that spans America, Japan, China and Russia and concentrates on the theme of the inequalities of the negotiations at the end of World War II and the situation of Japanese prisoners of war incarcerated in the Soviet Union. A play on an important theme like this should have received more detailed critical attention, whether positive or negative.

New talented directors include Miyata Keiko, who has directed a wide range of plays with a firm sense of control; Suzuki Hiromi, the director of *OUT*; Shirai Akira, the director and dramatist of *Moon Palace*, and Carolino Sandorovich, the director and playwright of *Shitsuon (Room Temperature)*.

To conclude this section on contemporary theatre, I would like to mention two theatre troupes outside of Tokyo. One is the Hirosaki Gekijo, in the northenmost part of the main island of Honshu, directed by Hasegawa Koji. In such plays as *Mikkagetsudo Shoten (The Mikkagetsudo Bookstore)*, which he wrote and directed, he uses the striking technique of looking at the current age by depicting life in the region with great detail, paying special attention to the flavour of the distinctive dialect of the region. The other group is the Hyogo Butai Geijutsu in Hyogo Prefecture, with playwright and critic Yamazaki Masakazu as artistic director. Most of the productions are translations of plays from Broadway or the West End like *Proof* or *Peggy for You*, but they also produced a new play by Yamazaki, *Niju Seiki (Twentieth Century)* about the world-famous woman photographer Margaret Bourke-White. As befits the title, the play was on a grand scale and the smooth interaction of Asami Rei in the leading role and the direction of Kuriyama Tamiya, was highly praised. Of course the scale of these two groups is totally different, the one an independent semi-pro theatre troupe and the other an institution supported by a prefectural government, but both deserve attention for very high quality work.

Takizawa Osamu, one of the most noted actors in Japanese modern theatre, died in June 2000. For nearly seventy years, he maintained a leading position in contemporary theatre. His attention to detail and intelligence in his acting was legendary: there is a story that in order to play Lenin, he read through all his collected works in preparation. In later life, he turned his talents to directing as well, with remarkable results.

In the world of kabuki, at the beginning of 2000, Ichikawa Shinnosuke performed the difficult role of *Sukeroku* for the first time. His striking good looks and handsome figure gave a breath of today to an Edo period youth. Shinnosuke is now one of the most celebrated young stars in kabuki. In the new kabuki play *Genji Monogatari* (*The Tale of Genji*), dramatized by Oyabu Ikuko, he played the handsome ideal lover of classical Japan. There were several attempts at new plays featuring kabuki actors, such as Nakamura Kankuro in *Guzu Roku* by Mizutani Ryuji and Matsumoto Koshiro in *Yume no Nakazo* but the results fell somewhat short of expectations. But Kankuro also built a temporary structure reproducing an Edo period kabuki theatre on the shores of the Sumida River in the Asakusa district, the heart of the traditional *shitamachi* area. It is called the Heisei Nakamura-za and here he produced the kabuki play *Hokaibo*. It was enormously popular and felt like being taken back to the Edo period.

At the beginning of 2001, the kabuki actor Bando Yasosuke took the distinguished name of Mitsugoro and this was commemorated by two months of performances at Kabuki-za. This was an appropriate honour for an actor of great ability. On the other hand, the kabuki world also suffered great losses with the death of *onnagata* female role specialist Sawamura Sojuro, an actor with a very distinctive style, and Ichimura Uzaemon, the most senior of actors playing male leading roles. But the loss with the greatest symbolic significance was the death of *onnagata* Nakamura Utaemon. He ruled as post-war kabuki's highest-ranking *onnagata*, with the cool surface of a clear acting style, painstaking with every stroke, and the energy of magma underneath. It was always impossible to tear one's eyes away from the characters he created on stage. Kankuro's activities were particularly striking, taking a central position in the production of *Sannin Kichisa* (*Three Thieves Named Kichisa*) at the Theatre Cocoon in Shibuya, a full-length performance combining the staging techniques of kabuki and modern theatre. At Kabuki-za, Kankuro had contemporary director Noda Hideki rework the script and direct *Togitatsu no Utare* (*The Revenge on Togitatsu*), by the mid-20th century playwright Kimura Kinka. At his temporary theatre Heisei Nakamura-za, Kankuro played the main roles of Tomomori, Gonta and Tadanobu. There were mixed reactions to the results, but the energy and ideas that Kankuro has used to bring life to kabuki have attracted attention far beyond the limited world of existing kabuki fans. At the same time, Onoe Kikugoro has performed a variety of roles, both classical roles in his acting tradition and fresh new roles, including Enya Hangan and Kampei in *Chushingura* (*The Treasury of Forty-Seven Loyal Retainers*), the title role in *Ten Ichibo*, a rarely performed play about a villain who pretended to be the son of the shogun, and Tamate Gozen in *Sesshu Gappo ga Tsuji*. To each of these roles he brought a convincing feeling of inner reality.

The National Theatre has the weakness of not having its own troupe of actors. However, it overcomes this handicap by doing things that are difficult in the commercial kabuki theatre. The National Theatre's main reason for existence is producing plays as a whole, including sections that are never played and reviving plays that have not been performed in a long time, combining a spirit of research and experimentation. In these two years, there were ten major productions of kabuki, nine of them full-length plays full of variety. Kabuki produced by the Shochiku production company usually has programmes of the most famous acts of classical plays featuring star actors. These two ways of producing kabuki have increased the range of choice for audiences and increased the variety within kabuki as well.

In the world of commercial theatre, senior actresses showed their vigour. Yamada Isuzu received the medal of Culture and Mori Mitsuko's signature play *Horoki* (*Diary of a Wandering Life*) received the Yomiuri Theatre prize. However, as a whole in commercial theatre, there were no striking new plays and there were mostly revivals or rewrites of old plays. Among plays produced by Shochiku was a collaboration of the popular Kansai theatre troupe Gekidan Shinkansen with young kabuki actor Ichikawa Somegoro in the play *Ashurajo no Hitomi* and popular kabuki actors Bando Tamasaburo and Ichikawa Shinnosuke in Izumi Kyoka's fantasy, *Kaijin Besso* (*The Palace of the Sea God*). This could be described as being somewhat experimental. There were ambitious productions among musicals. *Elisabeth*, produced by Toho is a musical originating in Vienna which was produced once by the all-female Takarazuka troupe, but the Toho production attracted attention by staging the original version. It was also popular because of the casting, with Ichiji Maki in the title role, but also popular young actor Uchino Masaaki as Tot in his first appearance in a musical and veteran actor Yamaguchi Yuichiro as Dabul. The direction by Koike Shuichiro and choreography by Oshima Sakiko was also highly praised. The Takarazuka troupe showed its continuing vitality by opening the new Takarazuka Gekijo Theatre in Tokyo in January 2001 and over two years, performing one of the favorites in the repertory, *The Rose of Versailles*, in three different versions.

Unfortunately there is not enough space to discuss Noh and Bunraku puppet theatre in detail. In 2000, Noh was designated a world cultural treasure by UNESCO. After ten years of activity, the Nohgaku no Za disbanded. This group was formed by talented *shite* main actors Umewaka Rokuro and Otsuki Bunzo together with Noh researcher and theatre critic Domoto Masaki as director. The activities of this group had great significance. They aimed to bring new life to Noh by opposing its petrifaction and mystification, trying to restore the acting style of Noh in its earliest days, improving plays in the existing repertory, reviving forgotten plays and creating new plays.

Most of the performers in the Bunraku theatre troupe come from the training programme run by the National Theatre. The National Theatre runs several training programmes for the traditional performing arts including Kabuki and Bunraku and their graduates form a significant part of all the genres it trains, playing a crucial role in the development and preservation of the traditional performing arts. This has been one of the most significant achievements of the National Theatre and has been a strong argument for the necessity of public funding for the arts, just as the government is discussing cutting all aid to theatre.

JORDAN

SAWSAN DARWAZA
and LINA AL-TALL

Jordan is a small but ambitious country known for its unique mix of tradition and modernity. The theatre arena in our country is a reflection of the political and social aspirations of our community of artists. From 1999 until the beginning of 2001 was a flourishing period of theatrical and artistic projects and productions, not only in the capital, Amman, but also in the rural areas and small cities, through small festivals and touring young companies.

1999 was a year of preparation for the new millennium. In the theatre community the atmosphere was one of hope and positive vibrations, especially in the light of the sponsorship of the Amman municipality, the European Union and the private sector, all of which enhance the theatrical movement in Amman and outside.

It was also the year when the Performing Arts Center (PAC) became effective and functional, having been founded in new premises in the year 1995, under the umbrella of the Nour al Hussein Foundation and the direction of Lina Al-Tall. Its aims are to establish training in theatre arts, dance and production management skills.

Among the most important performances of season 1999 was the play *The Memory of Three Boxes*, written in spoken Arabic by Sawsan Darwaza, Haya Husseini, and Nasser Omar and directed by Sawsan Darwaza. It concerns three friends discussing and re-evaluating their lives in an attempt to find a new formula to enter the new Millennium. The play has toured in Jordan, Egypt and Tunisia.

The Moment (Al-Lahza) was a joint writing work supervised by the late Jeff Gillaham, directed by Lina Al-Tall and produced by the Performing Arts Center. The play is designed to fit the drama in education format. It traces the voyage of two youngsters through time as they evaluate their past and head towards a supposedly better future. The young director Hakeem Harb adapted and directed *Medea*, which toured in Jordan under the umbrella of the Ministry of Culture.

Of the productions in the Jordanian Theatre Festival, it is worth mentioning the play *Halima*, written by Mohamad Btouch and conceptualized and directed by Mohamad Dmour. The play discussed the problem of honour crimes in Jordan and had much impact on the jury, which awarded it most of the festival prizes including best directing, best actor and actress, playwriting and scenography.

The Amman International Festival, an independent festival organized by the Al-Fawanees Troupe, hosted many plays of which the most important was their own production, written and directed by Nader Omran, director of the troupe, *Jissr Al Awdah (The Return Bridge)*. The play is about the Palestinian Diaspora and tells the painful story from the expulsion of the Palestinian people in 1948 to the present day.

The season of 2000 was an especially interesting one, with much potential: joint theatre projects and co-productions between Jordanian companies or artists and foreign troupes and artists from other countries of the region and further afield.

The Performing Arts Center (PAC) of The Nour Al Hussein Foundation (NHF) was requested by the International Centre for Theatre in Education (ICTIE), to host their biennial International Conference on Theatre for Social Development, entitled *People in Movement*, which was held for the first time outside the UK from the 24–29 August 2000. The ICTIE conference was held under the Patronage of HM Queen Nour al Hussein, in cooperation with the British Council, Jordan. At least 200 people from all over the world attended the conference, from about 16 countries. The conference for theatre artists explored the use of theatre as a tool for change and social development, with the participation of eight key speakers of different nationalities. Six theatre performances from different parts of the world were performed during the conference and were attended by a large number of spectators from Jordan.

A joint production of Mira't media of Jordan, Ashtar theatre of Palestine and Elteatro of Tunisia, entitled *Of Soil and Crimson*, was produced by the European Community and the UNDP during the Bethlehem 2000 festivities. It took the format of a touring workshop between its Pan Arab cast and crew in preparation for the final performance. *Of Soil and Crimson* attempts to recapture and shed light on the grand and sophisticated Canaanite mythology, of a people whose history and culture were falsified, stolen and deliberately buried away despite the immense contribution that the Canaanites provided to civilizations in the entire region. The script stems from the spirit of the Canaanite verses that were found on the Ugaritic tablets, which archeologists uncovered at the beginning of the twentieth century at Ras Shamra in northern Syria. The writing is so vivid that the events in the play seem as if they are happening now, even though over 3400 years have passed since they occurred. These tablets demonstrate the three main pillars of Canaanite life: the various Gods, the King (who was the son of the Gods on this earth), and a tolerant people with a love for life and innovation. These three principles have been preserved to this very day, despite the consistent threat and ugliness of wars and political turbulence in the Palestinian land. The play opened in Nativity Square in Bethlehem and toured to Jerusalem, Nazareth and Ramallah; it visited Jordan in the Jerash Festival and was a prizewinner in the Carthage Theatre Days. It was written by Naser Omar and Tawfeq Al-Jebaly, directed by Sawsan Darwaza, with choreography by Raja'a Ben Ammar.

Another interesting project was *Humanity. Go*, a black comedy that portrays the decline of humanity within a world of fast changing values. The play takes you on a thought-provoking journey through the minds of metaphorical characters with conflicting views and ambitions, all aspiring to live in dignity. *Humanity. Go* was directed by Lina Al-Tall, from a script by Najeh Abu Al Zein, with choreography by Rania Kamhawi. It was produced as part of the Peace, Democracy and Human Rights programme with the support of the European Union, and performed both locally and internationally – in Thessaloniki, Greece, as part of the Second Festival of Women Creators of the Two Seas: The Mediterranean and The Black Sea in 2000; and in Bosnia-Herzegovina as part of the Sarajevo International Festival, Winter 2002.

2000 was also an interesting year for the Artists' Union, a non-profit body, which has introduced a new theatre festival, entitled Petra, in which the union produced and sponsored a number of Jordanian plays by professionals and young troupes.

As for the Ministry of Culture, it was still organizing and sponsoring its yearly festival for theatre as a local competitive festival – it was not until the year 2000 and in its 8th session that the festival became Pan-Arab. The production *Al-Khayte (The String)* by Mohammad Dmour was its prizewinning play and the actress Nadera Omran was awarded the best actor prize. The Ministry had also established a new Forum Festival for Amateurs to give a chance for theatre to be introduced in rural areas.

In late September a reversal in the state of events took place: a second Palestinian uprising, which was a shock to all positive dreams in our small region. Artists became very sensitive to this *coup de théâtre*. Not only artistic projects were affected but also the whole of the political and economic arena. The complex relationship between Jordan and Palestine and the region made all subjects shift to one priority, the re-evaluation of the Arab-Israeli conflict and the serious search for a real just peace and not a paper-thin facade. With this grave tone we have entered the season of 2001.

The Jerash Festival dedicated its 20th session to the Palestinian uprising and hosted performances of an engaged nature. It opened with a musical installation by the musician Bashar Zarkan around the poem prologue of the renowned Palestinian poet Mahmood Darwish. The Sabreen music band from Jerusalem also gave a special performance from their repertoire, known for its originality and nationalistic engagement. The show took place in the northern Roman amphitheatre. The festival also hosted Arab and International performances, as a boost to theatre in the ancient Roman city of Jerash.

The Ministry of Culture opened its ninth Jordanian Theatre Festival on time in November and hosted Arab and Jordanian troupes. Best examples: *Hadikat Al Mawta (The Garden of Death)*, a play that says death has become as normal as a public park in which the Arab strolls naturally every day. It asks, did we really live that much to die all these deaths? The play was written by Ibraheem Jaber and directed by Khalil Nasserite. *Sedra*, a mythological play adapted by Khazal al Majidi and directed by Abdul Kareem Jarah, revolves around the idea of Cain and Abel and the evil force that drives humankind. The play *Hayat Hayat (Life Life)* written and directed by Ghannam Ghannam, was a work that moves towards the abstraction of the idea of life versus life relived, in a dialogue between an actress and her inner self in their search for truth.

International joint projects were also predominant in this season. *A Snake in the Grass* is a surreal mosaic of haunting episodes, the ensemble of actors and dancers exploring vanished childhood. They struggle to confront the precarious present. This joint performance written, directed and choreographed by the internationally acclaimed artists Adam Darius and Kazimir Kolesnik, was performed by 14 Jordanian actors and dancers from the Jordanian Independent Youth Actors and PAC team. It is a fusion of text in Arabic and English, chorus chants, expressive mime, dance and music.

As for 2001's musical productions we can mention *Youth Holds the Future*, a musical play depicting the theme of the 21st Arab Children's Congress. Directed by Lina Al-Tall, with script by Najeh Abu Al Zein, choreographed by Rania Kamhawi, musical composition and songs by Wael Sharkawi. This production was performed by students from the dance and theatre departments and professional artists from Jordan at the Roman Amphitheatre in downtown Amman to an audience of 5000 spectators.

We notice here to our surprise that theatre projects increased in number and became diversified, as if the incidence of turbulence is a catalyst to the artistic arena, as the need for artists to represent their ideas and visions becomes stronger and more vital at this point in time.

The season of 2002 was a season of putting forward our objection as artists to what is happening to the world and to our region. The incidents of September 11 made it clear to us that we are not well represented in the eyes of the globe: we fear being over-simplified in a great misunderstanding of cultures and politics. Once again, the platonic vision of the city as a global village has proven that it is far fetched and unrealistic. The role of artists as visionaries and avant-gardists has became ever more necessary but, alas, much more strenuous and painful. The theme of resistance against racism and the definition of terror, and the killing of innocent people from all over the globe – and in Palestine in particular – came through many theatre and filmed productions like the two mentioned below.

100 Arab Artists Speak Out is a message in the bottle sent by the artists to the globe, each through his/her artistic expression, whether it is a dance, a poem, a dramatic scene, an installation or a music piece and more. The project is the work and the joint product of a collective body of artists through independent networks in the Middle East, envisioned by Sawsan Darwaza and Zeinab Farhat, executed and filmed by Pioneers Production Company in Jordan and diffused in the region by volunteers and Pan-Arab production companies of an engaged nature.

Nour is a music and multimedia show by the Rum Troupe's composer and director Tarek Al Nasser with the 20 members of his young band. They have presented an original piece, using film material, slides and music, which focuses on the painful and inhuman conditions the Palestinian people are enduring.

In this year, we found ourselves all of sudden in a Catch 22 situation: the community of artists felt stifled as a category and on the defensive. The theatre arena in Jordan turned to themes inspired by the serious conflict of West and East in the new world. The urge of artists to produce works related to Arab culture was more predominant. For subject matter, they turned back to mythology and history in productions that emphasised Arab identity and the tolerant religions that stemmed from the very soul and heart of our holy lands.

The play *Jerusalem* is a project worth mentioning. Medmedia has been engaged in a multimedia theatrical production, in collaboration with PAC, the Nour Al Hussein Foundation, the European Union and Jordanian Television, opening in the Jerash Festival in June 2002. The production uses an innovative mix of theatre, choreography, music and audio-visual techniques. It involves a professional team of over 40 artists from the region. As a cradle of peace and a focal point in the universe, Jerusalem is the setting for a love story, in a situation that seems impossible, one that appears to have lost any sense of meaning, time or place and is no longer like the vision, nor like the scent of our childhood memory. *Jerusalem* communicates positive messages of peace, and humanity. It looks back and forward, beyond harsh reality, spanning more than ten thousand years into the past and as far as the imagination can take you into the future. The production portrays Arab culture and its people's profound history, aesthetic affinities and spiritual heritage, while maintaining an eternal bond with the universe. It is a serious attempt at bridging civilizations through culture, art, music and dance. The play is written and directed by Sade Batayneh and choreographed by Rania Kamhawi.

JORDAN

We have also noticed the amazing continuity of the 9th session of the Amman Theatre Days, under a joint management from Al Fawanees Theatre (Jordan) and Al Warsha Troupe (Egypt). It is an international festival and an opportunity for Arab and international troupes and artists to meet in a friendly and professional atmosphere that includes plays, workshops, films and round tables, and offers possibilities for founding an 'Arab Network' for theatre and the performing arts.

The festival, in co-operation with the greater Amman municipality, hosted many performances including *Kahrab* from Syria, a provocative play of love and hope, written and directed by Basim Kahar; and *Dancing on the Dead*, a bilingual performance from Collectif 12 (France) directed by Katherine Boskovitch and performed by Sawsan Bu Khalid from Lebanon. It is the story of a clown who stands in defiance of war and the horrible violence: 'What's happening right now gives us the right to laugh at our pain while listening joyfully to the poetry of those who died in the Shatila massacre.'

Shrapnel is a music, theatre and video art piece improvised by musician and singer Najeeb Sharadi from Morocco, and Kamelia Jubran from Jerusalem, directed by Sawsan Darwaza, with scenography by Nader Omran. The performance was dedicated and simultaneously given with a show in Jerusalem for Palestinian Artists and Intellectuals during a strike in objection to Israeli atrocities in the Jenin Camp. *Le Fou* was the jewel of the festival, prepared and directed by Tawfiq Jebali from El Teatro theatre, Tunisia, using texts of the Lebanese poet Jibran Khalil Jibran. The play came in a multimedia format to elevate the excellence of poetry in the mind of the Fou (the madman) of Jibran, who found in his madness freedom and liberation. *Layla, in the Red Bermudas* from Al-Fawanees Theatre came as a positive and friendly comedy performance for children, to incite laughter and love of life. The play was directed and prepared by Ashraf Awadi and Bashar Sharaf.

More events are worth mentioning in the theatre arena in Jordan. We can mention here the yearly Festival of Children's Theatre which is organized by the Ministry of Culture; the Youth Festival, which has also maintained its tradition yearly and is organized by the Directorate of Theatres under Hatem Al-Sayed; and the Festival of Arab Song, which has succeeded in continuing on a yearly basis under the supervision of Wafa' Al-Qusoos. Through these festivals the Ministry of Culture tries to back up the theatre movement in the country and spread the theatre traditions within its community. Theatre, in spite of all the problems, the dramas, and the *coups de théâtre*, remains a powerful tool that can effectively promote, educate and empower people to better understand the complexities of human behaviour. As a creative expressive medium, it can cross both tangible and intangible borders.

Sawsan Darwaza *is President of The Jordanian Centre of ITI. Theatre and TV Director at Mira't Media Production House, she is known for her engagement in theatre and arts and for her experimental and collective work in the field.* **Lina Al-Tall**, *director & founder of the Performing Art Center and a theatre actor and director, is known for her theatre in education projects. She succeeded in establishing the School of Theatre and Arts in Jordan University in 2002, and has been awarded The King Hussein Medal for Distinction of the 1st order for her achievements in the field of theatre.*

KENYA

ERIC GICHIRA

Is Kenyan theatre dead? I'd like to take a hard and unsentimental look at this question. In a sense, there's little or nothing in our theatres that can be termed 'Kenyan theatre'. Thus, where this phrase is used, I have to mean theatre with a Kenyan cast, or written by a Kenyan. For purposes of identity, we Kenyans rush to identify anything put on our stage as 'Kenyan theatre'. God forbid. It is easier to talk of 'theatre in Kenya', than of 'Kenyan theatre'.

The irony as I see it is that Kenya imports more theatre annually than any other 'product', be it from the US, Britain, Israel, the Caribbean or elsewhere. And since we hardly export any theatre to these and other countries, the imbalance of this 'theatre-trade' certainly works to our disadvantage.

In the 60s, 70s and 80s, Kenya's theatre scene was vibrant, in spite of the then Government's continuous harassment of actors and playwrights. Their orgy of play censorship was, to say the least, lustful. Between the 70s and now, we have seen some major figures spearheading our theatre scene, including among others Ngugi wa Thiong'o, Micere Mugo, Henry Kuria, Ken Watene, Francis Imbuga, John Ruganda, Nigel Slade, Allan Konya, David Mulwa, Tirus Gathwe and Wahome Mutahi.

The insecurity resulting from the ethnic clashes that characterised the 90s had a significant effect on Kenya's theatre, not to mention the political tensions that are part of every Election Year (1992, 1997 and of course 2002) in Kenya's recent past. Other minor influences on our theatre in the last decade or so include both student unrest and teachers' strikes, or threats to strike.

As our theatre now struggles to redefine itself, these gales seem to have blown out the flame of creativity. Re-inventing its proper place in our social set-up has not been an easy task. Today, harsh economic realities, worse than in the last four decades, bedevil the prospects for growth. The theatre community is now grappling with means and ways of becoming self-sustaining. Theatre groups and companies that thrived in the past have folded or disappeared into oblivion. The old theatre generation, that could have fed inspiration and skills to our present actors, is either dormant, forgotten or long dead. Able and visionary leaders are hard to come by. Our theatre today lacks role-models. Hence the uphill task of trying to rekindle the bygone era's fires. Unlike Uganda and even more Tanzania, Kenya's theatre lacks a 'culture of patriotism' – not that there's a lot for us citizens to be patriotic about, with all the daily problems we face. But in all sincerity, there's a time when a 'culture of patriotism' can help develop a country's theatre into what could then be referred to as 'our theatre'. That is lacking in Kenya.

Probably the greatest barrier to our theatrical development is the lack of a clearly defined cultural policy – a government failure. This has made theatre and similar cultural initiatives in Kenya lag, while our neighbours Uganda and Tanzania continue to make great strides in arts and culture.

KENYA

While the government of Kenya has shown some little political will to have a cultural policy put in place, it still lacks the commitment to implement it. Sadly, our government seems unapproachable on matters concerning theatre. Efforts by writers and scholars to offer advice to the Government have fallen on deaf ears. I'd speculate that it is afraid to have a culturally-sensitised citizenry, but the reasons for this are beyond my comprehension. This lack of support or show of concern for matters cultural and theatrical has produced a young generation of 'cultural infidels'.

Compared to Uganda and Tanzania, Kenya's theatre standards are, supposedly, slightly higher – but not as high or as good as they ought to be. The embarrassing odour of mediocrity still hangs about our theatres, conventional or otherwise.

A constraining sense of competition has lately made most theatre groups in the country strive to outdo each other in all aspects other than in staging quality productions. The price that Kenya's theatre has had to pay in touting mediocrity on stage has been reflected in playing to near-empty houses. There's little benefit that will emerge from our theatre as long as it continues to be seen as an occupation for clowns or school dropouts. This is the fatalistic 'Kenyan' attitude that needs to change. In my view, actors in Kenya still suffer from social ostracism by the public for not being serious people in life. Most parents discourage their children from pursuing any theatrical ambition. Our society needs to be educated and informed about the value of theatre, with its practical benefits being stressed. Changing Kenya's theatre into something positive might seem to need nothing less than the miraculous, yet, if experience is anything to go by, theatrical miracles can happen – even in Kenya.

For a start, hiring rates for our theatres are above what many average theatre groups and companies can afford. The consequent pedestrian approach to theatre as a means of making a quick buck, coupled with little or no rehearsal, poor publicity and crass marketing concepts, only serves to compound the problem further. Occasionally, where good funding is available, corrupt practices and misappropriation of donated funds give Kenya's theatre a bad name. This drains any goodwill and support that might exist.

The mass production of mediocrity on stage has inevitably produced a disinterested audience with little regard (or respect) for Kenya's theatre or her theatre workers. And it's easy to see where the blame squarely lies. Nowhere in the world has theatre been known to grow without the support of a home grown, paying audience.

Nevertheless, we do still have some things to shout about. Celebrated events in our theatre calendar include the Mavuno Christian Drama Festival; the Mbalamwezi Theatre Awards; the Nairobi Theatre Extravaganza; and the Kenya Schools and Colleges Drama Festival. At the University level, the FTT theatre concept in our public (state) universities has produced some of Kenya's finest dramatists.

Our most consistent foreign donor agencies include the British Government – especially for their commitment to build a theatre in Kisumu City – the British Council and The Ford Foundation. All three have been quite supportive of East Africa's theatre.

'Man cannot live by bread alone', says the Good Book. Over the last three years, most of what can be referred to as Community or Civic Theatre in Kenya has been donor-driven. This is not to mean that there's anything wrong in that. The problem is, most Kenyan actors' minds are so 'donor-infested' that they won't go near a theatrical production that's not funded. Unless, of course, they are school set texts, most of which guarantee a ready audience and good returns. My worry and question is: what will happen when the funding stops? What happened to bygone days, when innovative, 'unfunded' productions enjoyed a good run, and were quite capable of sustaining themselves and their cast?

Kenya is urgently in need of a theatre that addresses our societal affairs. By this I mean one that touches on our hopes, pains, aspirations and failures. I also envisage it highlighting our historical background as a nation: our political milestones and setbacks, our constitutional issues, as well as social and religious matters. Until it does, the so called 'Kenyan theatre' is pretentious and undeserving of the name. It needs radical re-organisation to make it a 'people's theatre'. A theatre whose traditions, style and touch we can identify with – not one that's borrowed, or jerry-built, from Western cultures or ideologies.

Kenya's historical and cultural pot still has a lot of wealth to draw from. Our myths and traditions, too often seen under the banner of folklore, still offer a rich source which scriptwriters, actors and directors can tap. Unfortunately, a genre like children's theatre seems to have died in the 90s, after having been popularised by the now defunct children's theatre group, The StoryTellers (TST). Stand-up comedy (with all its theatrics) seems to be the only area that has grown to attract a good audience and corporate support. Stand-up comedians or groups like Redykylass, Fanya and Family, Kachumbari, Doom and Jerry, and Publik Noisemakers have lately been enjoying an enviable audience in Nairobi and elsewhere in the country.

Encouragingly, Phoenix Players (the Capital's elitist expatriate theatre) has recently opened its doors to numerous new stage plays by Kenyan playwrights. The latest beneficiaries include J P R Ochieng Odero, Oby Obyerodhyambo and Cajetan Boy.

Prevailing economic hardships notwithstanding, a few other theatre groups still manage to get a full house every so often, Heartstrings Ensemble in Nairobi currently being a good example. And dramatised narratives and folklore, popularised in Nairobi by Bantu Mwaura, Oby Obyerodhyambo, Aghan Odero, Amadi Atsiaya and the late Erastus Owuor, have managed to pull good houses to our theatres and open spaces. The opening last year of Citrus Whispers Theatre – the latest of Nairobi's playhouses – was a welcome relief. Indigenous and vernacular plays enjoy a good staging there.

Theatre in Education, Theatre for Development and other forms of Community Theatre have recently been rekindled by Black Odanyiro Wamukoya and the late Lenin Ogolla, who have greatly influenced and sensitised Kenya's rural communities, using theatre to bring about change: be it on the gender front, domestic violence, legal issues, behavioural change or otherwise.

However, our theatre still suffers more from 'individualistic exhibitionism' than collective team ventures on stage. This ingrained attitude has inevitably put 'brother against brother' and one theatre company against another. This lack of collaborative effort has marginalised the theatre's impact on society.

KENYA

I'm longing for the day when our actors will outgrow petty theatre politics and theatrical indiscipline, to live 'sober' lives. When all is said and done, Kenyans urgently need a thriving and attractive theatre with which they can associate, and be proud of it. Interestingly, most young actors now want their theatre 'artistic' and 'iconic'. Devoting time to develop new talents, and giving credibility to outbursts of 'experimental theatre' needs attention. Kenyan actors are notoriously shy of experimenting on new or diverse forms of theatre. This maybe another reason why Kenya's theatre is in stagnation.

Unfortunately, our theatre lacks good leaders who can steer it to new heights. In the last three years, we have seen the demise, among others, of Erastus Owuor, Lenin Ogolla, Joni Nderito, Opiyo Mumma and Samson 'E T' Ochieng. And in their deaths, Kenya's theatre has suffered a huge blow: the leadership vacuum they have left still cries out to be filled. The existing poor management of theatre groups, companies, associations and clubs illustrates the effect of incompetent leadership in our theatre. Lack of training in the field is equally to blame – poorly trained managers produce a poorly trained workforce. Yet this inefficiency and the resulting poor morale among our theatre community is only the aftershock of a huge 'theatrequake'.

The financial constraints which are a national problem have not spared our theatre workers. Most of them are forced to live from hand to mouth, with circumstances forcing them to care only about their basic needs. This lack of adequate material resources has also taken its toll on our theatre structures. Our very own Kenya National Theatre, for instance, is presently in bad shape – and in dire need of a functioning lighting system.

There's a need to lay emphasis on professionalism. The way forward for Kenya's theatre is to move from a hobby approach to a serious business approach. Government support, especially in formulating a working Cultural Policy, would be a good start. We might then hope to see moves towards a conducive funding environment, whether from the state itself, or from the corporate world and donor agencies. This funding kitty could be directed towards setting up more theatres and theatre training centres, organising more theatre workshops and theatre festivals, facilitating theatre research projects and, last but by no means least, organising training programmes, especially in theatre management.

In spite of all I have said, there's a favourable climate for progressive theatre in Kenya. And, no, Kenya's (and indeed East Africa's) theatre is not, as many people would have you believe, on its deathbed. Hopefully, our national culture will one day be reflected in and around our theatres. There's no better place to preach a nation's culture than on her own stages.

Eric Gichira *is a Kenyan journalist, covering theatre for* The People Daily; *he is also an aspiring poet and playwright.*

KOREA

HAN SANG-CHUL

The end and the beginning of a century gave special meaning to the Korean theatre. Under the military government, the Korean theatre, as a movement for democratisation, had struggled for years for democracy and the restitution of human rights against the repressive dictatorial regime. The military regime had finally collapsed in the mid 90s, but in 1997 the new democratic government, named 'Mun-min', was confronted with a national economic crisis. An IMF loan to Korea was necessary to ward off economic collapse. As a result of this difficult situation, many company managers had to declare bankruptcy and many businessmen who had been excluded from reconstructing had to be driven out from their companies. The audience was also disappearing like an ebb tide. The present government, inaugurated in 1998, has begun to support Korean culture and art as well as trying to restore the Korean economy. It could mark a welcome change in the Korean dramatic world, which has always suffered from financial difficulties.

Since 2000, the Korean theatre has been engrossed in escaping from the past. Throwing out the gloomy and depressive legacies of the military regime and the theatre of political struggle, it has concentrated its energies on producing light and sensuous work, looking for amusement and an escape from real life rather than the intellectualism and thoughtfulness of the past.

Most of the works produced were by young playwrights in their twenties and thirties; the actors, too, were also young and unskilled. The impact of the IMF on Korea made it difficult for dramatic companies to employ older, more experienced actors, due to the shortage of money. However, the Korean dramatic world was full of energy and desire, as a result of the large endorsement of the government, whose support made it possible to establish many new theatre companies, albeit composed of inexperienced young actors, directors and staff, who presented a large number of plays.

Until recently, one of the more important phenomena in the Korean dramatic world was its interest in neglected traditional plays such as *Gut* and *Sadangpae Nori*. Increasingly, would-be actors wanted to learn about those things too. This was confirmed by the fact that the number of university theatre and film departments has increased by approximately 80 in recent years, and theatre has been admitted to the middle and high school curriculum for the first time. The impact of theatre in education and society in Korea has increased greatly, with a corresponding increase in the theatre community and its activities. Young people's activities, especially, were characterised by the setting up of a number of festivals with youth as a common theme, as well as playing their part in the existing dramatic set-up. Examples were the 'One-Act Play Festival', 'The Festival of New Directors', the 'Fringe Festival', the 'Independence-Art Festival' and the 'Two-Character Play Festival'.

KOREA

The Rural Gentleman, Cho Nam-Myung, was written by Lee Yun-taek to celebrate the 500th anniversary of the birth of Cho, an historical figure

On the whole, the Korean theatre over the past two years has neglected the most important part of its homework: developing creative work. The lack of new creative work and companies with a shared commitment to it still causes worries to the present-day Korean theatre. On the other hand, Cha Bum-suk and Lee Gun-sam, the masters in the world of Korean playwriting, both wrote new works in 2000–2001. Noh Kyung-sik, Yun Dae-sung and Yun Cho-byung also announced new works in 2001 after a long absence, but their work showed little freshness; moreover their directors could not express their talents well.

Between 2000 and 2001, the new writers Park Gun-hyung, Kim Tae-woong, Kim Yun-mi and Kim Myung-hwa attracted attention in the world of Korean theatre. Whenever Park Gun-hyung published a play, he showed his superiority to other writers in both theme and approach. In his work *Adoring the Youth*, which was about looking back over the actor's young days when he had been severely affected by the meaninglessness of life, he raised the questions, 'Does not the young person who is living with hopelessness and autism have a meaning in life?' and 'Does the meaningless life have a place in the world?'. Kim Tae-woong wrote and directed the work *Yi*, which was an imaginary reconstruction of the relationship between the King and a Royal actor in the period of Youn-San, during the Choson Dynasty. The real change and loss of motivation in the student movement was treated in her work *Dol-Nal* by Kim Myung-hwa. *The Rural Gentleman, Cho Nam-Myung*, which was produced by Lee Yun-taek to celebrate the 500th anniversary of his birth, was evaluated the best work among them in recent years. Its story was based on the real person Cho Nam-Myung, who had been living in a rural area without yielding up his critical spirit as a gentleman (Sonbi) to the real world.

With regard to translated works, free adaptations of Shakespeare plays were preferred to performing them in the original form. Another notable event was the performance, by a group of students who had been studying in Moscow, of the four great works of Chekhov, which brought out the real intention of the plays. The opening of the 'Heiner Müller Festival' gave another opportunity to increase our understanding of foreign writers.

Visiting performances from abroad were infrequent, but a few major works left a strong impression on Korean audiences. For the first time in Korea, the French Théâtre du Soleil of Ariane Mnouchkine performed *Tambours sur la digue*. The Russian Maly Theatre of St Petersburg performed *Gaudeamus* by Lev Dodin and the Bulgarian Credo Theatre brought *The Overcoat* by Gogol. The Royal Shakespeare Company visited Korea for the first time and presented *The Taming of the Shrew*.

Musical comedy became more active. The number of musical performances increased and the audience showed high interest. *The Phantom of the Opera* was the best example of these tendencies. The producers invested 10 million US dollars to present this great musical to standards equivalent to the work of America and England. It attracted enough of an audience to be able to recover its investment within three months and was due to perform for a run of seven months.

Han Sang-Chul *is a former president of the Korean Section of the International Association of Theatre Critics and a Professor at Hallym University. His book,* Korean Theatre: Its Conflicts & Reflections *was published by Hyundaimihaksa, Seoul 1992.*

KUWAIT

SALEH AL-GHAREEB
and SHAHER OBEID

For more than 20 years now, the Kuwaiti theatre movement has been suffering from what might be called growing pains, a not unusual situation in drama in any country in the world. This situation in the State of Kuwait, as recent theatre seasons have shown, is generally characterized by low production output.

A few remarkable presentations are produced by the four national theatre groups which form the Kuwait Federation for Domestic Theatres (KFDT), which is encouraging, but they cannot really be considered a good yield, sufficient to meet the theatre community's aspiration toward excellence. Most productions are weak.

In the almost complete absence of much needed analytical studies and serious research, which might help pinpoint the crucial factors required by the theatre movement in Kuwait to return to its glorious era of the 60s and 70s of the last century, it is widely believed that the low annual budgets allotted to the four groups under the KFDT largely accounts for the present failure.

Theatre in Kuwait is Government subsidised, previously by the Ministry of Social Affairs and Labour and now by the National Council for Culture, Arts and Letters (NCCAL). Paradoxically enough, the support given to theatre groups has lately been increased and is nowadays considerably higher than it was during the 80s and early 90s; but this financial support is still not enough to make the situation better or help in motivating theatre activity. On the contrary, the amounts paid to the theatre groups, supposedly for improving their work, are hardly enough to meet the salaries of the personnel, the ever rising costs of production and general expenditure.

On the other hand, the Kuwait theatre movement is part and parcel of the larger Arab theatre and cultural situation. Therefore, it is taken for granted that it is suffering from all the same social and cultural problems which have so far prevented development of Arab theatre as a serious creative art. Again, theatre in Kuwait – the subsidised theatre in particular – has a critical situation similar to that of the monetary problem: good serious productions require much work, more money and a better environment.

Such difficulties and problems have imposed themselves on the scene; as a result theatre activity in the last three seasons was very limited, apart from those produced and presented in the Kuwait Theatre Festival, which became monumental.

The Festival is an annual competitive cultural event, and offers a good opportunity to host leading Arab theatre personalities, who are invited to participate, as jury members or experts, in the festivities which usually include, in addition to visiting Arab productions and cultural symposia, debates on

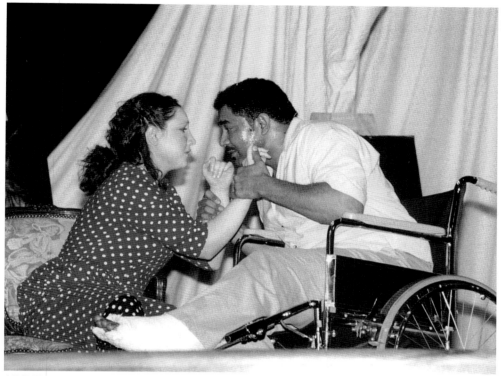

ABOVE: *At the Heart of the Lantern* (*Fi Qulb Al-Qundeel*), Al-Shabi Theatre

BELOW: *A Grain of Sand* (*Habbat Ruml*), Al-Khaleej Al-Arabi Theatre

theatre experiences in general and discussions about the presentations themselves. They come to Kuwait and exchange views on the development of Arab theatre movements.

On the other hand, Kuwait gives much attention to youth; the Kuwait Theatre Festival itself plays a great role in encouraging the participation of the younger generation in its productions – especially in the two latest editions of the Festival.

The Festival is organised by the National Council for Culture, Arts and Letters in close cooperation with the Kuwait Federation of Domestic Theatres, and is the largest State subsidized dramatic event in the country. The first and second editions of the Festival were organized in the late 80s. After that it had to stop, due to the Iraqi invasion of Kuwait in 1990, only to be restarted in 1999, with many controversial presentations, in its third edition.

The fourth edition of the Kuwait Theatre Festival was held from 27 March – 5 April 2000, giving an opportunity to celebrate World Theatre Day. Many productions competed in that event, including: *The Owl* (*Al-Buma*) by Fatima Al-Ali, directed by Nasser Karmani; *It Is Red, But* (*Hamra Wa Lakin*), adapted and directed by Ahmad Al-Shatti; *We Are All in the Same Boat* (*Kullona fil Marjoha*) by Mohammad M. Belal, directed by Ahmad Mussaed; *An Evening with Dogs* (*Sahra Ma Al Kelab*) by Fawzi Ghareeb, directed by Ahmad Salman; *Ship Builder* (*Sane As-sufon*) by Ahmad Shahabi, directed by Ahlam Hassan. In his above-mentioned play *We Are All in the Same Boat*, Dr Mohammad Mubarak Belal was recognised as a playwright to note, even though this was not his first contribution to the local theatre.

The 2000 edition of the Festival can be described as mostly youthful, as many young actors and directors had the chance to participate side by side with the pioneers of the Kuwait theatre. It seems that the decision taken by the theatre leaders to encourage young artists was deliberate, with an eye to finding new blood in Kuwait theatre. Some of these young people were students and undergraduates of the Higher Institute of Dramatic Arts, who made a successful start to their career.

This new orientation was also very fruitful in the fifth edition of the Theatre Festival, in 2001, in which actors, directors and particularly playwrights showed far more skill overall. New names imposed themselves: Ahmad Al-Shatti, Khaled Al- Mofidi and Jaber Mohammadi (directors); Mahmoud Esmael and Sharifeh Al-Kandari (both directors and writers); and Anaam Saud, Fatami Al-Attar and Fadel Muel in the field of playwriting.

In the framework of the fifth edition of the Festival, productions presented in the main competition included *L'Ecole des femmes* (*Morabbi Az-Zawjat*), adapted and directed by Ahmad Al Shatti; *Escaped with His Lot* (*Tar Brezquh*) by Fatami Al-Attar, directed by Jehad Al Attar; and *Question Mark* (*Alamat Estifham*) written and directed by Mahmoud Esmael. On the fringe of the competition a production of *Hamlet* was presented by Solaiman Al-Bassam, a Kuwaiti dramatist working in Britain, who directed the play for his company.

Aware of the importance of criticism in motivating creativity, the Kuwait Federation of Domestic Theatres, the main dramatic authority in Kuwait, in co-operation with the National Council for Culture, Arts and Letters, created an annual prize the for the best article about theatre productions; Fadi

Abdullah, a journalist, won the prize for the year 2000, while in 2001 Dr. Nader Al-Qunnah won the prize for his commentary on the fifth edition of the Festival.

The Annual Dramatic Competition, announced at the official opening of the fifth National Theatre Festival, was also intended to encourage dramatic work. The competition set out regulations covering dramatic production, its work, aims, participation, management and period. Various special and general provisions govern the nine prizes awarded in the framework of every edition. The Competition is organized in cooperation between the National Council for Culture, Arts and Letters and the Kuwait Federation of Domestic Theatres.

Both the Competition and the Festival have proved good means for creation, as the fifth and sixth editions of the Festival have shown. Ten theatre productions were presented by the four main theatre groups (Al-Arabi, Al-Shabi, Al-Khaleej Al-Arabi and Al-Kuwaiti) and other groups, including the University theatre group, the theatre group of the Public Authority for Youth and Sports, the Schools Theatre and the Higher Institute of Dramatic Arts.

There were essentially four competing productions: *The Column (Al-Amood)* by Ossama Fuad Al-Shatti, directed by Mohammad Solaiman, presented by Al-Arabi Theatre; *At the Heart of the Lantern (Fi Qulb Al-Qundeel)* from the Shabi Theatre; *My Love Zakaraya (Zakaraya Habeebi)* from the Kuwaiti Theatre; and *A Grain of Sand (Habbat Ruml)* from the Khaleej Al-Arabi Theatre.

In spite of the financial difficulties and its relative failure over the last two decades, the theatre movement in Kuwait still holds a pioneer position in the Gulf Arab Countries, not only through the activities of the festival, the symposia, and the local workshops which are organized in the country during the theatrical seasons, but also for its regional exchanges and participation initiatives. For example, Kuwait is always represented in Sharja Theatre Days (United Arab Emirates), the Cairo Experimental Theatre Festival and the regular Gulf Theatre Festival.

During 2001 theatre made its presence felt while Kuwait celebrated much cultural and artistic activity as Capital of Arab Culture. Many Arab and world intellectuals were invited by Kuwait to participate in cultural and artistic activities, which included theatre productions from Syria, Egypt, Lebanon, Saudi Arabia, Tunisia, UAE, France and Switzerland.

Locally, apart from the Theatre Festival many other theatre events were organized in Kuwait over the last three theatre seasons; one of these was the workshop by Al Khallej Al Arabi Theatre which resulted in the production *Amazement (Heirah)*, a philosophical play that embodies the emotional conflict of the human psyche. The play was written and directed by a young writer, Emad Mansour. The same theatre group also contributed in 2001 an adaptation of Tolstoy's *The First Man Who Made Wine*, directed by Monqed Al Suraye; the play speaks about the relation between man and the Devil, as a mirror to man's good nature.

It is well known that the private theatre sector (or what can be called the commercial theatre) gives priority to monetary gain in its work; nevertheless, it plays a good role in bridging the gap in dramatic production which is a result of the failure of the Government subsidized groups in this field. Productions in the private sector are usually farces, seeking mainly to satisfy

KUWAIT

ordinary audience members who need laughter to help them find shelter from the increasing concerns of life. During the last three seasons, the private theatres staged a good number of productions (bartering entertainment for money, it might be said) and it is true that among the gales of laughter exists a variety of social and political problems which are examined, if lightly, by some of these presentations. Productions like: *Santroon Bantloons* by Saad Al Faraj, *Khairan to and Fro* (*Khairan Raeh Jai*) and *You Should Judge Well* (*Kullak Nadar*), or *Girls Fondling* (*Dala Al-Banat*), *Only At the Door, Young Men* (*Albab Ya Shabab*) and *Bo Mtaih*, which were presented in the three seasons under review, and many others which are generally described as commercial, often pose societal problems. They are mainly related to family, society, bringing up children, and divorce, commenting sometimes on their consequences for succeeding generations, the victims of such problems.

Theatre for children is plentiful in Kuwait, although not in every season, due to more than one reason, but mainly the intense competition for the limited number of theatre spaces in the country, and consequently their failure to cope even with the large number of presentations for older people.

However, the theatre for children in Kuwait is mainly concerned with the educational and pedagogical side of society. Most of its plays are concerned with the everlasting conflict between Good and Evil, a theme which is always loved by children. The most notable recent examples are: *Gasper 2000*, *Planet of Happiness* (*Kawkab As-sadah*) and *TeleTubbies* during 2000; in 2001 there were many other presentations, for example *Zahra and City Dreams* (*Zahra wa Ahlam Al-Madinah*).

Productions for children are highly varied but are mostly dominated by children's songs, which tends to make them rather showy, with a poor story line. That is particularly evident in such presentations in 2000 as: *The Wonderful Fiddle* (*An-nay Al-Ajeeb*), *Murjanah and the Pact* (*Murjanah Wa lAssabah*), which takes its theme from the legends of *One Thousand Nights and One Night*, *The Investigator* (*Al-Mohaqeq*), *Peccacho*, which tells the story of a young girl who dreams of meeting beloved figures, and *Konan in the Land of the Pokemon* (*Konan Fi Ard Al- Bokemon*) which focuses attention on the importance of protecting the environment, and the numerous presentations of 2001, the most significant of which is *The School in Plot 13* (*Madrasat Qetah 13*).

During the first quarter of 2002 a large number of presentations for children flooded the national theatre houses; they got a lot of publicity, and offered a serious opportunity to demand new stages in the country as well as the rehabilitation of the old ones.

Among the most publicised productions in that period were *Sindibad*, a play which moves in an inventive way between adventures and conflicts, *Ant Kingdom* (*Mumlakat Al-Naml*), *The One With Three Heads* (*Abo Al-rous Al-thalathah*) and *Reemi and the Enchanted Palace*, (*Reemi WalQasr Al-mashour*), which is an invitation to children to learn wisdom.

The limited number of stages in the country is especially noticeable during certain holidays (Al-adha and Al-fatr Eids), when producers compete to present children's shows. The short period allocated to each producer for presenting his work (except for comic works, which are allotted more time) results in slim profits, which adds to their problems.

Besides the private commercial theatres and the domestic theatre groups, there are a handful of institutions which take an interest in producing dramatic presentations which relate to their own interests and orientation. For example, Bashaer Al-Kher, an Islamic Kuwaiti Institution, offered in 1999 a presentation entitled *An Ignorant Young Man* (*Shab Tafi*), a light comedy that deals with the problems of addiction and social responsibility. Other similar presentations included *Beloved and Lover* (Asheq Wa Mashouq), about the steadfastness of the Kuwaiti people during the Iraqi occupation of their country.

In 2000 the Islamic Theatre for Dramatic Production Group, another Islamic institution, produced a historical play about the assassination of Hussain near the city of Karbalaa, *Winds of Karbalaa* (*Riah Karbalaa*), followed by *Christ and Hussain* in 2002; both plays were written and directed by Mohammad Al-Gazzaf. More contributions to the dramatic activity came from the School Theatre which presented a play titled *Birds Without Nests* (Toyour Bela AShash); the National Theatre Group also resumed its work, producing in 2001 *The Souq*, an adaptation from the well known Arab play *Letters of the Seville Judge* (Rasael Khadi Eshpelia).

Other state institutions offered dramatic presentations during the 1999–2002 seasons; they include The Higher Institute of Dramatic Arts, with many important presentations such as: *Death of a Clerk* (*Wafat Muadhaf*), *Tube Men* (*Rejal Al-Anabib*), and *My Love is Yours* (*Laka Hobby*). The Youth Theatre of the Authority for Youth and Sports presented two plays: *The Nile* and *A Fork, a Spoon and a Knife*. The Kuwait Martyrs' Bureau also presented the play *Law of the Earth* (*Qanoun Al-Ardh*) which focuses attention on the Kuwaiti Missing and Prisoners of War and problems of the occupation period; the play can be described as a call to promoting national awareness in the younger generations.

Saleh Al-Ghareeb *is a writer, journalist and editor of many profiles of Kuwaiti intellectuals, especially theatre people;* **Shaher Obeid**, *translator and writer, is author of five translations and many articles and short stories.*

LATVIA

GUNA ZELTINA

After twelve years in a 'market-place' situation after the country regained its independence in 1990, Latvian theatre has more or less adapted to its severe economic conditions. In a situation where state subsidies for our nine professional repertory theatres cover just about 20% of their running costs, this adaptation mainly resulted in a complicated balance between art and entertainment in the repertoire of our theatres. Another balance has also recently been achieved, that between the wish of Latvian theatre professionals (especially the younger generation) to accumulate international theatre experience and their desire for self-realisation through national material.

This phenomenon has become more evident in the last three seasons, when the direction of the theatre repertoire has changed towards Latvian contemporary drama. During the 90s, when all the theatres were forced to rely more on their own earnings than state subsidies and they turned desperate looks to the models of foreign commercial theatres, the number of 'less commercial' Latvian original plays in the repertoire sank to a dangerous minimum. The natural ties between the national theatre and drama were destroyed and Latvian contemporary drama experienced a sort of stagnation. New, original drama in our theatre landscape became as rare as the species of so called 'blue' or 'Moon' cows that still exists – precariously – in Latvia.

A positive and stimulating shift in the attitude of theatres towards the national contemporary drama was evidenced by the festival 'Latvian Contemporary Drama 2001' initiated by the Latvian Drama Agency and the Latvian Playwrights' Guild and financed by the Latvian Culture Capital Foundation (Latvijas Kulturkapitala fonds), the Riga City Council and the Ministry of Culture of Latvia. It comprised 88 productions of national contemporary plays submitted and 66 presented, in both professional and amateur theatres, for the selection of the final programme. In the final programme of this festival, 21 productions of plays by 14 authors were presented in Riga (12–18 November 2001). Afterwards it became clear that the final programme was too dense and motley, reflecting more the overall panorama of Latvian contemporary drama than its highest achievements. But it was the first time that such a large festival of national drama was organised in the history of Latvian contemporary theatre and its main objective was achieved: now theatres turned to original plays with a renewed interest and foreign guests and experts could experience Latvian drama and its translations. The next festival is planned to be held in 2003. Last but not least, a financial mechanism has been created for the regular support of original drama, performances for children, regional guest tours for professional theatres and other activities, adding support to insufficient state subsidies and grants from the Cultural Endowment: in 2002, the Ministry of Culture and this foundation have launched particular competition-based target programmes for other essential spheres of national culture.

ABOVE: Akvelina Livmane, Peteris Liepins and Valdis Liepins in *Laba tiribas sajuta (That Fine Feeling of Being Clean)* by Pauls Putninš, directed by J.J. Jillinger at The Arts Theatre (*photo*: Janis Deinats)

BELOW: FROM Alvis Hermanis's production of *Panny z Wilka* by Jaroslaw Waszkiewisz for The New Riga Theatre (*photo*: Andris Draznieks)

LATVIA

The most active national playwrights include the poet and dramatist Mara Zalite (*b* 1952) and the playwright and director Lauris Gundars (*b* 1958) who is developing his own version of the absurd theatre in such plays as *Livingstons* (*Livingstone*, 1999) and others. Lauris Gundars started the first BA programme for playwrights at the Latvian Academy of Culture in 1997, and one of its graduates, the gifted young writer Inga Abele (*b* 1972), has made the most promising debut of the decade with her play *Tumsie briezi* (*The Dark Deer*). It has already been staged in three theatres and was performed at the Bonner Biennale 2002. The director Viesturs Kairiss from the New Riga Theatre presented this play in the programme of European Cultural Month in Riga (2001); it is a magical interplay of theatrical images, feelings, associations and impulses of the subconscious. Mara Kimele's production of the same play in the Valmiera Drama Theatre (2001) is based on a very tense psychological realism, creating a harsh story of injured human lives and destinies. A different staging of the play by the director Charlotte Koppenhöfer at the Theater im Depo in Stuttgart (2002) discovers the theatrical potential of new Latvian drama.

The poetic gift of Mara Zalite, who has written five librettos for musicals, rock operas and an opera staged in Latvian theatres during the last three seasons, has contributed to a unique situation not only in our theatre but also in the whole panorama of Baltic theatre: productions of national musicals and rock operas have become the most popular performances for the widest audiences. Her librettos are more poetic dramas with remarkable literary quality than 'simple' librettos and they usually deal with key historical and spiritual problems touching on the nation's destiny. Especially popular was the rock opera *Kaupens, mans milais!* (*Kaupens, My Love!*) with music by Janis Lusens in the Liepaja Theatre (1999), a poetically tense drama of ideas about a society turning an anti-hero (the criminal Kaupens) into a hero.

Two productions of rock operas by Mara Zalite and Janis Lusens, *Indrika hronika* (*The Chronicles of Henry of Livonia*, 2000) and *Sfinksa* (*The Sphinx*, 2001), staged in the Latvian National Theatre by its artistic director Edmunds Freibergs, have become national hits. The musical *Tobago!* by Mara Zalite and the composer Uldis Marhilevics in the Latvian Dailes (Arts) Theatre has also been one of our recent public and box office successes.

Our youngest professional theatre, the New Riga Theatre (founded in 1992), can be considered the artistic leader on the Latvian theatre scene. Due to its strong artistic strategy and support from different cultural foundations it has managed to avoid the commercialisation of its repertoire. Productions of its artistic director Alvis Hermanis (*b* 1965) and director Viesturs Kairiss (*b* 1971) are regularly presented in international theatre festivals. Hermanis' recent stage works include the visually impressive *Panny z Wilka* (based on a work by Jaroslaw Iwaszkiewicz, 2000) which was awarded the First Prize in the Latvian annual theatre awards for the 2000/2001 season, as well as a dynamic production of the play *Ristumine peateega* (*Highway Crossing*, 2000) by Estonian author Jaan Tatte and an innovative interpretation of Gogol's *The Government Inspector* (2002), set in the surroundings and atmosphere of the so-called 'Brezhnev stagnation'.

Along with his productions of *Tumsie briezi* and Mara Zalite's *Margareta*, a contemporary paraphrase of Goethe's Faust and Margareta theme (2000),

Kairiss has staged *The Serpent* (2000), based on the novel by Mircea Eliade and also presented in the Hebbel Teater in Berlin. Together with his stage designer Ieva Jurjane, Viesturs Kairiss participated in the international project *Hotel Europa* (2000). He is also a film and opera director, receiving The Grand Music Prize of 1999 for his production of Tchaikovsky's *Yevgeny Onegin* in the Latvian National Opera, where he also made a controversial production of Mozart's *The Magic Flute* (2000).

The New Riga Theatre has successfully developed a co-operation with foreign colleagues, and performances have been staged here by Yevgeny Grishkovets from Russia, the now Latvian-based Banuta Rubess from Canada and others. The production of Grishkovets' play *The City* (2001) by Alvis Hermanis in the intimate atmosphere of a private apartment in Riga was among the best performances of the year. Banuta Rubess has found a colourful scenic image for her interpretation of Caryl Churchill's *Top Girls* (2001).

The director Mikhail Gruzdov from St. Petersburg has become one of the leading personalities in the Latvian theatre, regularly staging performances in our theatres. His co-operation with the Arts Theatre brought about the exciting production of Gogol's *The Marriage* (2000) that received the First Prize for the 1999/2000 season in the Latvian annual theatre awards. Gruzdov has also staged Alexander Ostrovsky's *Late Love* (2001), as well as realising such a serious and complex work as *Fiesta* (an adaptation of Ernest Hemingway's *The Sun Also Rises*) in the Liepaja Theatre, 2001.

The best productions of such directors as Mara Kimele, Olgerts Kroders and Felikss Deics who are praised as masters of psychological analysis in the Latvian theatre are marked by brilliant acting achievements. Mara Kimele has found a fascinating way for her interpretations of Chekhov's *The Seagull* (2001) and *Pazudusais dels* (*The Prodigal Son*, 2002) by the Latvian classic playwright Rudolfs Blaumanis in the Valmiera Drama Theatre while Felikss Deics has explored the complex ethical issues and human relationships in his productions of Ibsen's *Ghosts* (1999) and Blaumanis' *Baltais* (*The White One*, 2001). Olgerts Kroders presented a nuanced study of individual dramas of alienated society in his production of Patrick Marber's *Closer* (the Arts Theatre, 2001).

The National Theatre continues to maintain the national directing and acting traditions in its productions of contemporary Latvian drama (Harijs Gulbis' *Veverisi*, 2000; Pauls Putnins' *Kveli ilgota/The Passionately Desired*, 2001) as well as in interpretations of foreign plays such as Agneta Pleijel's *Standard Selection* (2000) or Alexey Vampilov's *The Eldest Son* (1999) and *Last Summer in Chulimsk* (2000). The two latest ones manifest a new shift from eccentric avant-garde theatre forms to more traditional theatre language, a transition that typifies not only the director of both Vampilov's performances, Regnars Vaivars, but almost all the Latvian stage directors of the younger generation.

A sort of directing crisis has recently become more evident in the largest professional theatre of Latvia, the Arts Theatre. In the spring of 2002, its previous artistic director Karlis Auskaps, after mounting large-scale popular productions, such as the Latvian classic Martins Ziverts' *Aksts* (*The Court Jester*, 2000), gave up his post, though staying in the theatre as one of its stage directors. His decision was the result of an inner 'revolution' of the troupe against the excessive number of 'mass-market' performances in the repertoire.

LATVIA

Now the theatre is to be led by a collective artistic council of experts in different artistic areas. Perhaps the new council will find a more satisfactory balance between the actors' urge to development through their art and their enforced prostitution for the audience's pleasure.

An example of an intelligent popular performance, along with the afore-mentioned *Tobago!* and *Aksts*, is a musical production of Dumas' *Monte-Cristo* (2000) by Arnis Ozols, with music by the prominent composer Raimonds Pauls. The director most open to the new stylistics, technologies and experiments in this theatre is J.J. Jillinger (*b* 1968) who has made witty and dynamic productions of several contemporary Latvian plays – *Rit atbrauks Florinda* (*Florinda Arrives Tomorrow*, 2001) by Dace Ruksane and *Laba tiribas sajuta* (*That Fine Feeling of Being Clean*, 2002) by Pauls Putnins.

In the Riga Russian Drama Theatre, the director Genady Trostyanetski has made successful productions of Raimonds Pauls' musical adaptation of Theodore Dreiser's *Sister Carrie* (2000) and Molière's *Les Fourberies de Scapin* (2000), staging as well such a complex material as Solomon Anski's *Dybbuk* (2002) known from the famous Yevgeny Vakhtangov interpretation in the Habimah Theatre in the 20s. The regional Daugavpils Theatre, with two troupes, Latvian and Russian, is just about surviving; but recent lively productions of Latvian classical plays and works of contemporary national authors prove the creative potential of this theatre.

Among Latvian independent theatres working without state subsidy, the most active are Kabata (The Pocket), Skatuve (The Stage), the Liepaja Travelling Puppet Theatre and the independent private theatre Muris (The Wall). The second national festival devoted to the interpretations of the classic Latvian writer Rudolfs Blaumanis' plays, with guest performances from neighbouring countries, was held by the Valmiera Drama Theatre in 2002. The international theatre festivals Homo Novus (since 1995, biannual) and Homo Alibi (since 2000, annual), organised by the non-governmental New Theatre Institute of Latvia, have become larger and increasingly influential. Both of them present guest performances from abroad, simultaneously being a showcase of Latvian new productions for foreign visitors and making contacts for the Latvian 'blue cows' with their professional neighbours in the European theatre.

Dr. art. **Guna Zeltina** *is a theatre critic, author of several books on Latvian theatre and head of the Department of Theatre, Music and Cinema at the Institute of Literature, Folklore and Art in Riga, Latvia.*

LEBANON

ABIDO BACHA

The last century, a hundred years of enormous change, has come to a close with a formidable revolution in computer science. Yet its effects have not meant the death of theatre at the end of the century, any more than did the threat of cinema at its beginning. Theatre is just as strong, and it persists in proving its own power before being influenced by any other form of expression.

What has been accomplished in Lebanon in recent years is not completely satisfactory, because of the tendency of some to miss good opportunities, such as Beirut being declared Arab Cultural Capital in 1999, or the preparations for the Year of Francophony.

A lot has been said about the decline of theatre in Lebanon and in the Arab World. The debate has spread from Lebanon to other Arab countries, because Lebanon is a pioneer of theatre in the region. Some have gone so far as to contest the celebration of World Theatre Day, a tradition since 1961. But Lebanon has been present, and has been celebrating that occasion, ever since it joined the ITI as a regular member.

How can one refuse to celebrate that day? The world has sacrificed enough for the unity of colour and spirit, in the absence of ideology, 'because theatre is based on ideology.' Theatre could be lost without these criteria. Such a point of view, though, has not prevented many from participating in World Theatre Day, especially the ITI members of the Lebanese Centre. The Centre organised a celebration in 2001 at the Gulbenkian Theatre of the Lebanese-American University (LAU), during which theatre people (writers, critics, actors, directors, scholars and organisers) were given awards, and the LAU shared in the production of scenes and sketches. The ITI Centre again organised a celebration at the Beryte Theatre of St. Joseph University in 2002.

Many have prophesied the disappearance of theatre, but there have never been more performances in Lebanon than in the past three years. Theatre remains theatre, without which there would be no actors. The only way to defend it is to continue working. There were so many more plays than in preceding years, that the Lebanese State acquired the appearance of a Theatre State. This was strongly felt during the year 1999, when Beirut was chosen by UNESCO to be Arab Cultural Capital, and one cannot describe this phase as commonplace. Theatre people predicted its death even before a new page of theatre began, and without looking for a new social significance or new styles. Finally, they went beyond the proposals of the old trend in 1999, with simple plays bearing easy concepts.

2001, too, had a rich calendar: *Mounamnamaat Tarikhiyat* (*Historic Miniatures*), by Nidal al Achkar, based on a text by Saadallah Wannous, *Lucy, al Marat al Aamoudiyat,* (*Lucy, the Vertical Woman*), by Roger Assaf, based on a short story by francophone writer Andrée Chedid. The 'Ayloul' (September) Festival presented six events, a combination of theatre, dance and conferences. Thomas Linen from Germany produced *Masafat* (*Distances*), and Xavier Leroy presented

LEBANON

Nitaj el Zourouf (*The Result of Circumstances*), an autobiographical work. Thomas Argai presented *Al Janna* (*Paradise*).

There were five foreign plays in the Festival of International University Theatre: *Al Mouchkila* (*The Problem*), performed by LAU students, *Serele,* directed by Rima al Koudaissi of the Saint Esprit University of Kaslik, *Al Farachaat Hourra* (*Butterflies are Free*), directed by Malaak Fattal, and *The Double Bass*, by Patrick Susskind directed by Pauline Haddad.

The 'Chams' Festival distinguished itself by encouraging short films, with a further 26 theatre productions, and five dance performances. In many of the performances between 2000 and 2001, scenography returned to a classic style. All types of theatre were thus represented: comedy, dance, group works, monodramas, and even a variety show. They included productions by both local and visiting companies.

In Lebanon, foreigners have often been invited to direct performances: the Italian Kabaliani, whose workshop ended with the presentation of *Sourat Orss* (*Photo of a Wedding*) in 2000; James Sloviak, a student of Grotowski, who directed in 2001 a performance in one of the annexes of the UNESCO compound in Beirut. The show ended with *Aoujea Faust* (*The Ills of Faust*). Sloviak came to Beirut to teach the Lebanese what they had already assimilated and digested during the past 50 years. They had seen Grotowski himself present his work in Lebanon, an example of devotion and absolute sacrifice.

Marco Baliani came for a second time in 2001 to direct a new workshop, which culminated in a play entitled *Tadhiyat* (*Sacrifice*). It was presented in Lebanon, in Italy, in Albania and in Egypt.

Accomplishment is not an end in itself, but a means to an end. The benefit of foreign experimenting in Lebanon, after some 50 years, is ready to be questioned.

Vaudeville is a popular but superficial type of theatre. It has neither analysis, nor romantic scenes, nor poetic characters, nor even clearly outlined characters. It is a theatre which is more and more self-centred, without any introductory touches. And the more it becomes self-centred, the more it moves away from sensations and feelings, because its spirit has become its cosmos. The two latest vaudevilles in Lebanon are *Kabset Zirr* (*Pushing a Button*), in 2000 at the Piccadilly Theatre, directed by Michel Jabre, and a revival of *Aarissain Midri Min Wain* (*Two Bridegrooms, Who Knows from Where*), at the Georges V Theatre, directed by Rana Najjar. Both plays are by Marwan Najjar, a prolific writer for theatre and television.

Group theatre, varieties, educative theatre, political drama, futurist writing, the modern, the post-modern, vaudeville, satirical theatre (called here, as in France, chansonniers), all seem to have become an open market. The new production policy of the Ministry of Culture has led theatre people to re-evaluate and re-launch it in what looks like a minor bourgeois revolution. Thus, suddenly, theatre has acquired a large number of plays, though initially attempts were reserved to the few who had always struggled, and still do, to continue their work. The result is that no terminology can describe with precision what is happening in Lebanon. Dozens of plays, untouched by change or a sense of polemic, have emerged in the country, and just transform old debates into new ones. Innovation is largely absent, as are the ideoligical concepts which could illustrate theatrical creativity within cultural circles.

A great period of historic progress, and valuable accomplishments based on sound technique have, however, marked the golden age of Lebanese Theatre. Such names as Chakib Khoury, Antoine and Latifé Moultaka, Raymond Gebara, Yacoub el Chedrawi, Roger Assaf, Jalal Khoury, Nidale el Achkar, Mounir Abou Debs, and the Rahbani brothers stand out, and have left their indelible mark on the Lebanese scene.

Festivals like the University Theatre Festival and the Ayloul Festival help in renewing the spirit of theatre. The University Theatre Festival, alone, has triggered at its outcome in 2001, sixteen new works. Patrick Susskind's well-known monodrama, *The Double Bass*, directed by the young Pauline Haddad, was one of them, and at its presentation in Amman, Jordan, the actor performing it, Jihad el Andari, received an important award. Also worthy of note are the shows given by the Faculty of Education of the Lebanese University, under the guidance of Karim Dakroub, professor of drama. There was also the play *Moukaabat (Cubes)*, presented by the technical institute of the Kafaat society. In it, scenes unfold without chronology or a sense of drama, linked to each other only by the notion of death. Yet another play, *Antigone*, based on the Sophocles text, is reinterpreted with scenes taken from other works, the whole directed by Rabih Mroué.

In 2000, Beirut celebrated the 22nd anniversary of the death of Egyptian writer and director Nagib Srour. But before that, there was an outpouring of other productions representing many facets of theatre.

Has theatre died? At this point it is only suffering from exhaustion, and is merely the reflection of the present spirit of the cultural Lebanese mosaic. We have to add to this the dire economic crisis which has obliged those theatre students who graduate from Lebanese universities to direct their energies towards local television. A great negative influence, too, has been the disappearance of the middle class, which was principally responsible for the production of cultural theatre, and for Lebanese culture as a whole. A source of anxiety for theatre people in the last ten years has been, first of all, the absence of public spaces. Their presence is an essential condition for the development of a democracy, without which theatre cannot prosper. The absence of these spaces has erected a thick wall separating actual life and the practice of theatre, and the soul of the city has been crushed because of their disappearance.

On another level, one portion of our society has experienced the spirit of Arab progressivism, another that of nationalism, while remaining attached to tradition; a third has lived ensconced in group problems, and a last portion of society has felt deep individual suffering in the quest for a window on the world community.

Theatre people in Lebanon are also worried by the ever growing development of technique throughout the world. All signs, all discourses indicate promises which will transform the whole world into a village, and this is driven not by chance, but by the desire to dominate. Likewise, development in Lebanese theatre has slowed down, and television has become the sole resource for many actors. It has the power to paralyse their theatrical talent. In fact, dozens of students register in theatre schools in the sole hope of being saved from their economic crisis by television. Theatre is private no more, and not even technique can save it. We hear far-off sounds that obsess us, and yet hope to be able to put our house in order.

Abido Bacha *(b 1957), is a theatre critic with the Beirut daily newspaper* As-Safir, *also an actor, author and teacher. His publications include a study of Arab theatre at the turn of the twentieth century.*

LITHUANIA

RASA VASINAUSKAITE

During the last decade, classical tragedy has been very rare on the Lithuanian stage. Directors, considering that the different genres have been so levelled and mixed, and that reality itself is so tragic that theatre is not strong enough to stand comparison with it, have turned back to the dramas and comedies of the 60s to 80s, or contemporary plays, changing them on stage to tragic farces or tragi-comedies, grotesqueries or even romantic melodrama. It is twenty years since Sophocles was performed and ten for Shakespeare's tragedies: a time when theatre was very sensitive to its surroundings and still trying to resolve the conflict between the individual character and an anonymous, monochrome society.

The changes in society and its differentiation, the arrival of a new generation of theatregoing public, began to transform the objectives of theatre art. The border between serious art and entertainment or mass culture became very thin and delicate and only a few artists have succeeded in keeping their bearings on this frontier. Jonas Vaitkus, a director, declared in an interview, 'Lithuanian theatre needs to be reformed. The profession – directing, the art of the actor – is becoming impoverished. The theatres are engulfed by stagnation and routine and they are presenting few performances, most of them being Boulevard and mass entertainment. There is no exchange of creative ideas between companies. Moreover, young artists have no decent conditions or work opportunities.' This is perhaps the reason why this director, in 2002, is staging *Love, Jazz and the Devil* (1965) a play from our playwright from the 60s, Juozas Grusas, to show that the actors have not changed over the years and that the rebellion of his youth was a myth that has to be demystified to-day.

Eimuntas Nekrosius's ideas are very close to those I have mentioned: 'The theatre, in an attempt to get the audience's attention, consciously started to simplify and caricature the situations on stage. Today the theatre is copying movies, television and the other arts: it is efficient, it is beautiful, but most of the time its effects hide an emptiness. The more we think only about modern means of expression, the more we move away from the essence of theatre. But everything depends on the creator's personality and on the view he has of the world. Usually, good theatre is eternal. The passage of time corrects it but does not change it'.

After his *Hamlet* (1997), Nekrosius is almost the only one still presenting classical tragedy: in *Macbeth* (1998–1999) and *Othello* (2000), he tries to speak about a situation which is not of the moment. Gintaras Varnas, a younger director who, after long researches into tragic theatre, staged Ibsen's *Hedda Gabler* and O'Neill's *Mourning Becomes Electra* in 1997–1998, turned in 2000 to Calderon's *Life is a Dream* and, in 2001, to contemporary tragedy with *Le pays lointain* by Jean-Luc Lagarce. This play is written in a very poetic and moving way; the performance was also very moving and very faithful to Varnas in spite of the fact that the new drama, with its colloquial language and style of writing, has never previously been attractive to him.

ABOVE: Egle Spokaite with Vladas Bagdonas in Eimuntas Nekrosius' production of Shakespeare's *Othello*   (*photo*: Dmitrij Matvejev)

BELOW: Gintaras Varnas turned in 2001 to contemporary tragedy with *Le pays lointain* by Jean-Luc Lagarce at the Kaunas Drama Theatre   (*photo*: Dmitrij Matvejev)

LITHUANIA

Nekrosius, Rimas Tuminas (both born in 1952) and Jonas Vaitkus (born in 1943) are the most productive and interesting among the established generation of directors. Although their stagings are quite different, they all have a great influence on the present state of Lithuanian theatre. The experiments of Vaitkus, at present the best directing and acting teacher, with their powerful suggestion and richness of expression, often enter into competition with the work of younger directors (as for example, Oskaras Korsunovas, at 33 the best known example, worldwide, of the younger generation of Lithuanian directors).

Tuminas, after his staging of Lermontov's *Masquerade* (1995), Sophocles's *Oedipus Rex* and Shakespeare's *Richard III* (1997–1998), turned to classic comedy by directing Gogol's *The Government Inspector* (2001) and showed the old time situation as being no different from our own. For Tuminas, theatre is a celebration, merry and sad at the same time, and this can be seen in his most recent creations where it seems that he is trying to bring together the theatre's possibilities and the needs of the public. This is the reason why *Oedipus Rex* and *The Government Inspector* have been transformed into romantic dramas with all the elements of the romantic aesthetic.

On the other hand Nekrosius, with his Shakespeare trilogy, created a universal meditation on the way man has to reconcile himself to his cruel fate. There is thus no need to read *Othello*, for example, before going to the performance. It is more important so stay quite objective in front of Othello's suffering, which leads him from love to murder, after which death is the only choice. Nekrosius stays faithful to his poetic-metaphorical theatre in which he links, in a subtle way, a psychological, or rather naturalistic way of acting with traditional means of expression. But in his latest productions, *Othello* for example, the staging has become more simple and concrete, the atmosphere more clear and warm. The director characterises his productions as follows: 'Confessional theatre, which goes simultaneously to the limits of naiveté, excess and fragility.'

During the last decade, Lithuanian theatre has gone through a catastrophic decline not only of the spoken word on stage, but also of the drama in general. Playwrights and theatre people have several times analysed the sad situation of Lithuanian dramaturgy: a national theatre cannot be imagined without a tradition of national playwriting and the evolution of this one stopped in the 80s. This is the reason why the independent Centre for Training and Information on Theatre and Cinema, which is very active and has been working for six years, publishes a yearly 'Bulletin of New Playwriting' where extracts from recent plays by Lithuanian and foreign writers are published. In this way the centre gives impetus to new works looking for directors, presenting some in staged readings during a festival called 'Action for New Playwriting'. This festival takes place every year in June. Each time, one can get a glimpse of the productions to be presented the next season. Most of the new performances, directed by Varnas, Vaitkus, Korsunovas, and also Ignas Jonynas, V-Cezaris Grauzinis, Gintaras Liutkevicius, Ramune Kudzmanaite, Povilas Laurinkus, the young and younger directors, have been originally presented during this 'Action' which unites creators in the common search for a new scenic language. Let us note that the 'Action' does not only present the works of Lithuanian directors. Other artists from neighbouring countries – Latvia, Estonia, the United Kingdom, Poland, France, Germany – come to

Vilnius to present the latest theatre news and show the direction of their work. Under the influence of foreign artists, Lithuanian theatre has finally developed a tendency towards social analysis of our time, which has led our playwrights and directors to reassess their own possibilities.

The emergence of a new dramaturgy (mostly foreign) was necessary because the more the Lithuanian theatre refines its ways of artistic expression by using metaphor, stylisation and an ever-increasing symbolism, the more theatre has become introverted towards the theatrical (the apogee was reached in the 90s). Hence the more the gap between theatre and society, between theatre and real life has become noticeable. In recent years, it became evident that theatre is incomprehensible or even remote, not only for the young generation but also for the spectator who wants a recognisable hero, identifiable with his daily problems. The theatre lost its object of provocation, its target audience. It obeyed the tendencies of pure aesthetic and artistic elitism and became, according to Korsunovas 'a feast for the greedy' and it is now forced to change or, inevitably, to die. This is why, in these last years, the theatre has turned to the richness of the new playwriting which looks at the real situation of man in the face of a fickle reality, describing it and proposing an objective diagnosis of the contemporary state of mind and the new reality. This tendency was evident in the productions of the 1999–2002 season, where a critical-ironic, sarcastic and provocative, non-conformist view of ourselves and our environment dominated.

Korsunovas was the first to organise such a tête-à-tête between theatre and life: after his production of Ravenhill's *Shopping and Fucking*, he staged *Feuergesicht* (*Fireface*) by Marius von Mayenburg and, later on, *Parasiten* by the same author and, with a young director, Laurinkus, *Crave* by Sarah Kane (1999–2002). Besides his productions of Shakespeare's *A Midsummer Night's Dream* (1999) and Bulgakov's *Master and Margarita* (2000, staged for the Festival d'Avignon) where the staging was very expressively theatrical and imaginative and had nothing to do with the reality of life, the first ones were rather shocking because they were so full of the mundanities of daily life. It can be said that in these productions, staged in his new Oskaras Korsunovas Theatre, he poses questions and provokes answers, first of all about life itself but also about the Lithuanian theatre tradition. The Lithuanian theatre had never been directed towards social matters, only moral ones. It is still rather traditional, in continuing to use the theatrical methods of imagination and metaphor. Most of our directors despise the realistic form as something left over from the Soviet era and its artistic rules. Korsunovas was the first who not only revived a modern theatre form but also tried to give another dimension to this form by linking the tradition of theatricality, of theatre as play and visionary game, to today's techniques, which we could call postmodern. The new production that we are expecting in autumn 2002 from this director who, in every performance, is looking for a new approach, is *Oedipus Rex*, where the classic text will be confronted with a contemporary setting, by unexpected means. Among the other new performances will be a Nekrosius production, based on ancient Lithuanian texts. So that the next theatre season will confront a tragedy and a myth, setting them down in the life of to-day. The result of this remains to be enjoyed.

Rasa Vasinauskaite *is a theatre critic and professor at the Theatre Academy. She works for several magazines and periodicals about theatre in Lithuania and abroad and is Theatre editor of the cultural magazine* 7 *meno dienos.*

MACEDONIA

LJUBISHA NIKODINOVSKI-BISH

'In Macedonia even the air smells of theatre. At the very beginning of the third millennium AD, on the international stage, Macedonia is again on the front pages of the world's media, not because of the word theatre, but because of the black name for armed action – terror. Maybe terror wants to eliminate the word theatre from Macedonian soil...' so said Jordan Plevnes, in March 2001, in the Macedonian message for World Theatre Day.

In these turbulent times of the metaphorical 'powder keg', Macedonian theatre in the last three seasons faced the most dramatic challenges in its existence – to remain young and full of energy in the face of the collective Macedonian depression, and to be open in times when terrorism (local and global) has driven the life of the spirit underground.

At a ceremony in the Macedonian Academy of Sciences and Arts in Skopje on the 20th November, 2000, commemorating the first performance of the drama *Macedonian Blood Wedding* by Vojdan Cernodrinski (1887–1951), which took place in Sofia in dramatic circumstances on the 20th November 1900, academician Mateja Matevski called it 'a defining moment of the Macedonian theatre, that opened the way for a new approach in a new time, the new century.' Cernodrinski, as writer, director and actor in his own theatre *Skrb i uteha (The Sorrow and Consolation)*, was a man who understood theatre as a weapon, and has acquired the status of the Father of Macedonian theatre. This occasion was marked by the publication of a monograph, *Makedonska krvava svadba sto godini podocna (Macedonian Blood Wedding – a hundred years later*, 2000, by Jelena Luzina, Ph.D), and a specially recorded TV documentary.

Later, the Institute of Theatrology at the Faculty of Dramatic Arts issued a CD entitled *Teatarot na makedonska pocva – enciklopedija (Theatre on Macedonian Soil – Encyclopaedia, 2002)*, describing the history and development of theatre in Macedonia over twenty-five centuries, produced under the supervision of Professor Luzina.

The celebration of this legendary play was confirmed by the prize for best performance at the 35th anniversary of the Macedonian Theatre Festival *Vojdan Cernodrinski* in 2000, which was given to a revival of *Macedonian Blood Wedding*, performed by the Bitola National Theatre, and through the award for best director, which went to Ljupco Gorgievski (*b* 1956) for his inventive direction of this pseudo-historical melodrama, in which he created a new vision of the traumas arising from five centuries under Turkish occupation (until 1912/1913). In the same year another classic writer, Anton Panov (1905–1968), was revived with great success in a production of *Pecalbari (Migrant Workers*, February 2000) by Branko Brezovac (*b* 1955), a Zagreb director who works frequently in Macedonia. With its transformation of folk culture and tradition, it took the award for stage dramatisation in the performance of the Bitola

National Theatre, which used the style of a contemporary musical to high-light the eternal anxiety of the migrant worker's life. Two years later, the performance *Parite se otepuvacka* (*Money Kills*, March 2002) from a third classic writer, Risto Krle (1900–1975), won the award for best performance, again at the Bitola National Theatre. Ljupco Gorgievski once more received the prize for best directing, melting the modern and folklore traditions in this strong ethno-theatrical tragedy, where parents blinded by the greed for his money kill their own son, not recognising their own child after he returns from emigra-tion.

In the relatively small Macedonian theatre scene, about thirty new plays and adaptations have been staged between 1999–2002.

One of the best young Macedonian playwrights, Jugoslav Petrovski (*b* 1969), who in 1995 won the Shakespeare Award at an international drama competi-tion in Exeter, Great Britain for his play *Porcelanska vazna* (*Porcelain Vase*), was awarded in 2000 as the best text at the Macedonian Theatre Festival, for his latest text *Eleshnik* (National Theatre, April 2000), directed by Dimitar Stankoski. The wind 'Eleshnik' which according to legend, blows over Lake Ohrid and foretells misfortunes, was the inspiration for Petrovski to wrote a forceful tragedy on the migrant workers' life, which here goes beyond the borders of humanity into crime.

In the same Festival the already well known, prizewinning Macedonian writer and playwright Venko Andonovski (*b* 1964) received the award for best text in 2001 for his play *Kandid vo zemjata na cudata* (*Candide in Wonderland*, Dramski Theatre, October 2000), directed by Saso Milenkovski. Obviously modelled on Voltaire's hero, and burdened with the same naive optimism, Andonovski's Candide moves in the land of miracles – more precisely in the prison of the land of miracles – pitting his naivety against the madness of the authorities or, better, the technology of power.

Inspired by the millennial celebration of two thousand years of Christian-ity, Ljubisha Georgievski (*b* 1937), an eminent director and the President of the Macedonian ITI Centre, directed his own new text *Armagedon* (January, 2000) in the Bitola National Theatre; his adaptation/text for the Macedonian Na-tional Theatre, *Play Shakespeare* (May, 2000) was a step away from the 'main-stream' in which he has worked lately: a creative adventure of the Shakespeare heroes who capture the spirit of our time, creating a picture of the world as a global circus. Starting from the screenplay for the film *The Passion of Joan of Arc* by Carl Dreyer, Georgievski wrote and directed the play *Jovana Orleanska* (*Joan from Orleans*, Dramski Theatre, July, 2000) with a post-script suggesting that our nihilist age should be reminded of the impossibility of existing and surviving without faith, even a fanatical one.

A quality young director, Dritro Kasapi (*b* 1975), staged a play by Teki Dervisi, *Utre odime vo rajot* (*Tommorow We Go to Heaven*, April 2000), at the Albanian drama of the Theatre of Nationalities in Skopje as a co-production with the National Theatres from Tirana and Pristina. Performed in Albanian, it dramatised the happenings in April 1999, during the war in Kosovo; at its centre is a family locked in a basement, waiting for the end of the war.

In two performances in two decades, the play *Divo meso* (*Proud Flesh*) by the well-known playwright Goran Stefanovski, marks two peaks of the

MACEDONIA

Macedonian theatre. The first performance (Dramski theatre, 1979) directed by Slobodan Unkovski was voted the best performance in Macedonia and in ex-Yugoslavia in 1980 – and was later pronounced to be the best Macedonian performance of the 20th century. In the revival directed by Aleksandar Popovski (*b* 1969) again in the Dramski theatre (December 2000), it represents the peak of the Macedonian theatre's 'new generation' and received the prizes for best performance and best directing in 2001 at the Macedonian Theatre Festival (with subsequent successful guest performances in several countries of Europe). *Proud Flesh* shows, through the fall of a family, the sin we have done to ourselves, and also the great errors which take us away from what we might be. Stefanovski says that when he wrote it, he thought that he had written a play for the past; now he realizes that he has written a play for the future.

Aleksandar Popovski has returned regularly over the last ten years to *Balkanot ne e mrtov* (*Balkan is not Dead*), by Dejan Dukovski, most recently in the Macedonian National Theatre (October 2001). (Its premiere was successfully directed by Saso Milenkovski in the Bitola National Theatre, 1991). Just as *Proud Flesh* found its time again, so *Balkan is not Dead* found its place to be performed today. The story is rooted in Macedonian drama tradition, reflecting Cernodrinski in its examination of the decay endemic in the system, the country, the regulations, the morale – something that fits all too well with the time we live in. The playing of young and brave actors led by Nikola Ristanovski, in these two performances and others, transformed the text and the director's idea of the crises in the modern world, expressed in the theatre as a 'Love drama in a world in which love is impossible'.

Global change, especially after the fall of the Berlin wall, opened a gateway for the cultures of countries with a limited language diffusion to step out into the European and world stages, with opportunity to confirm their own (and their country's) identity through language. The appearance of Macedonian drama on the international stage resulted in the translation, publication and staging of plays by Stefanovski, Plevnes, Dukovski and others. We should mention the book *Ten Modern Macedonian Plays* (co-published by Matica Makedonska and Macedonian ITI, Skopje, 2000), edited by Jelena Luzina, Ph.D, a selection of ten contemporary/modern Macedonian plays, translated into English, with theoretical and critical commentary.

The big international production, *Hotel Europa* (Vienna, June 2000), with concept and text by Goran Stefanovski, was directed by seven of Eastern Europe's most talented directors and choreographers, in a co-production by Chris Torch of Intercult from Sweden and several European festivals. Hotel Europa is a seedy and tragicomic old hotel (1900). Each invited artist has created a 'room', encompassing the themes of loneliness, love, mobility, migration and homelessness in the transition; two of the directors were Macedonian – Dritro Kasapi (*Room Service*) and Ivan Popovski, who lives and works in Moscow (*Maiden Voyage*).

Within the Festival of the Dramski Theatre from Macedonia, from 3–11 May 2001, on the stage of the Theatre D'Oprime in Paris were presented the performances *Phyloctetes*, *Proud Flesh*, *Closer*, *Candide in Wonderland* and the première of *The Last Man, the Last Woman*, by Jordan Plevnes, directed by

Nina Kosenkova from Russia in two versions created simultaneously – Macedonian and French. An unknown man who calls himself the Balkan Chopin wants in one night to resolve all 68 of the crisis spots of the world. The Last Woman follows him on his unique way.

In the Satirical Theatre Kerempuh (Zagreb, Croatia, 2000) Aleksandar Popovski revived the hit play *Bure barut (Powder keg)* by Dejan Dukovski, who now works as a scenarist and playwright in the Schauspielhaus in Hamburg; Popovski also staged the world premiere of Dukovski's latest play *Dracula* (January 2002), in the Slovenian National Theatre in Maribor. In what became a cult performance in Slovenia, Dracula is a hospital patient, and while good and evil remain the focus, the border between them has been made relative.

The Albanian drama of the Theatre of Nationalities in Skopje took part in the Bonner Biennale for the first time in 2000 with a performance of *Koskite sto docna doagaat (Late Coming Bones,* 1998) based on the text by Teki Dervisi and performed in Albanian, directed by Vladimir Milcin.

The Turkish Drama of the Theatre of Nationalities, in a co-production with the City Theatre from Istanbul and the National Theatre in Marseilles (October 1999), made a successful production of the dream-play with a Shooting, *R* by Jordan Plevnes, directed by Mehmet Ulusoj from Turkey and performed in four languages – Macedonian, Turkish, Albanian and French.

Contemporary dance is gaining favour in Macedonia, partly due to the support of the MOT festival which has put on a great number of performances, workshops and seminars. At the First Balkan Dance Platform held in Sofia (December 2001), where the achievements of contemporary dance in the Balkans were presented, the appearance of promising choreographer and dancer Iskra Sukarova, with her *QB2*, and the video presentation of works by Jagoda Slaneva, Gordana Dean-Pop Hristova and Rismima Risimkin, confirmed that Macedonian contemporary dance holds it own. For the celebration of International Dance Day, 29th of April, Sukarova (*b* 1973), a graduate student at the Laban Centre in London, showed the results of her dance research in the performance *Play Me* in the MOT/Youth Cultural Centre.

In January 2002, the Macedonian Theatre Platform, initiated and organised by the MOT festival, the Dramski Theatre, the Bitola National Theatre and the Macedonian National Theatre in co-operation with the French Cultural Centres in Skopje and Bitola, was an effort of the organisers to showcase Macedonian theatre to twenty representatives of European theatre festivals, among them members of the 'Theorem' association, as well as other promoters and organisers. Twelve plays were performed by the host companies and the Albanian drama of the Theatre of Nationalities. The mission was also important as a chance to get acquainted with theatre life and theatre workers in Macedonia in order to co-operate in the future.

In the period under review, not only Shakespeare but also other masters of world drama have been seen regularly on the stage, from ancient Greek authors to Molière and Brecht; Chekhov's *Platonov,* Ibsen's *Peer Gynt* and Klaus Mann's *Mephisto* were successfully directed by Dimitar Stankovski, Zlatko Slavenski and Kole Angelovski, with a world première of the contemporary Russian playwright Nikolaj Koljada, *Surveyor* (March 2000), directed by Vladimir Milcin. Patrick Marber emerged as a major playwright with *Closer* (December

MACEDONIA

1999), directed by Slobodan Unkovski, one of the best of Macedonian directors, who was welcomed back after seven years directing in USA, Yugoslavia and Slovenia.

On the 12th of July, for the opening ceremony of 41st Ohrid Summer festival and the première of the spectacle *mACEDOINE: Odiseja (Odyssey)* 2001, the prominent actress Nada Gesovska read a message from one of the great names of world theatre, Peter Brook: 'The universe is yours: that's why you should not kill each other but love each other!' He recommended people from the whole planet to come and to enjoy the excavated and reconstructed antique theatre from the 3rd century BC, one of the most beautiful in Europe – Lychnidos, in Ohrid.

The story of *Odyssey 2001* begins in antiquity and ends today, or maybe tomorrow, as an paean to love, mutual understanding and tolerance, which sets aside the differences between human beings (racial, religious, national and linguistic). Dramatically arranged by Zoja Buzalkovska and the director Ivan Popovski, it used segments from ancient dramatic authors and contemporary Macedonian playwrights, writers and poets, in the Macedonian, Turkish and Albanian languages, with folk songs and stories. This impressive product of the director's vision, with the engagement of a great number of first class collaborators, actors and musicians, using effective visual and audio effects, opened a new page in Macedonian theatre life, and beyond.

The Bitola National Theatre and the Dramski Theatre took part in this grandiose (*sic*) project with as co-producers the Ohrid Summer Festival and MOT. The performance was repeated at the antique theatre on the Heraclea site near Bitola, and afterwards it opened the 26th International Theatre Festival MOT, when it was adapted for the main stage of the Macedonian National Theatre in Skopje (September, 2001).

Choosing Lennon's eternal refrain 'Give Peace a Chance' as its motto, MOT's *The Theatre of Power* faced up to a Macedonia at war and gave peace a chance – at least in the evenings of our 'booming' everyday life. With 16 different performances from 8 countries, MOT broke our isolation and brought back a piece of artistic (as well as essential) sense to our living. The great number of 10,000 visitors showed that this is the only acceptable response which the audience can give to the current authors of our ongoing real-life drama.

Since 1997, the Macedonian ITI Centre, together with the international message on the occasion of World Theatre Day, 27 March, has distributed a Macedonian national message, whose authors are top names of Macedonian theatre: the last three messages have come from Dejan Dukovski (2000), the leader of contemporary Macedonian drama and a professor at the Faculty of Dramatic Arts in Skopje; Jordan Plevnes (2001), one of the most important Macedonian playwrights of the middle generation who has served as Ambassador of the Republic of Macedonia in France, Portugal and UNESCO; and Sasko Nasev, Ph.D (2002), theatrologist and popular playwright.

Ljubisha Nikodinovski-Bish is Secretary General of the Macedonian Centre of the ITI and Artistic Director of the MOT International Theatre Festival; he is also a theatre writer and editor of the book Oresteia in Action.

MEXICO

ISABEL QUINTANAR

The field of theatre in Mexico is a very wide one. The large daily listing of theatre in the newspapers compiled by the Mexican theatre producers' association contains both art theatres and commercial theatres. In it we can find all types of production, from the very popular to the most serious, with musical comedy in between.

State and university theatre has its own channels of information. In Mexico City there is a weekly listings newspaper called *Tiempo Libre* (*Free Time*) which is read and used by the theatre community as well as the public at large.

Theatre in the provinces is largely amateur, which is not say that the work is poor or elementary, but simply to explain that theatre people do not make a living from their art, since taking part in the theatre may mean having to do up to ten other jobs.

The leading productions of the year take part in the National Theatre Festival, which the National Institute of Fine Arts has organised for 25 years now in various cities of the Mexican Republic. Participating companies are chosen by a selection committee composed of five personalities from the theatre community.

As well as the National Institute of Fine Arts, the National Theatre Co-ordinating Committee, headed by the theatre director Otto Minera, develops theatre at pre-school, primary and secondary level through a programme which gives theatre its place in the national programme of education. For its part, the National Dance Co-ordinating Committee, under Héctor Garay, promotes dance at a professional level with the National Dance Company and gives opportunities for the independent groups to appear in its Dance Theatre.

The Mexican Centre of the International Theatre Institute is an authentic voice of the theatre which has done much to gain the support of the authorities, the national press and the public for the work of the theatre community. The Centre is made up of the Mexican sections of international non-governmental organisations (NGOs) such as IATA, ASSITEJ, IATC, FIRT, OISTAT, UNIMA and the Seki Sano Foundation. Each of these bodies is active within its own domain, with its own statutes.

Every year, the Mexican Centre organises activities such as the 'Theatre-Lovers Conference' which has its own committee elected to pursue its work in different festivals, both national and international. Every two years, in Ciudad Victoria, Tamaulipas, it stages the Intercontinental Festival of World Cultures. It publishes the journal *Teatro* in English, French and Spanish, and will be showing its 13th issue this year at the XXIX Congress of ITI in Athens.

The 'World of Theatre in Mexico' took place in March 2001 over twelve days in three provinces of the republic, including the first Intercontinental Festival of World Cultures, in which ten countries took part, the Symposium

MEXICO

on Cultural Identity and Development, with delegates from fifteen Universities, and a board meeting of CIDC. This took place in Victoria, Tamaulipas. It was followed, in Mexico City, by a tribute to the playwright Alberto Sastre, with the staging of *Esquadra hacia la Muerte* which he wrote fifty years before. The production was directed by the director Manuel Montoro, a board member of ITI. On the same day an exhibition opened, organised by OISTAT Mexico under its president, the leading designer and teacher Félida Medina, and entitled *Fifty Years, Nineteen Designers*. Representatives of national centres of ITI were present at these events, travelling the following day to Jalapa, in Vera Cruz, where they celebrated World Theatre Day with the inauguration of the 'My Life in Theatre' medal, which is to be awarded to important national and international personalities. The medal is accompanied by a citation on parchment signed by representatives of all the cultural institutions of the country.

This event was followed by the opening of the meeting of national centres of the ITI for the Americas and the Caribbean.

We should finish by noting the production of *Oedipus Rex* by José Solé, director, teacher and President of Mexican ITI, which was so successful that it was invited to take part in the festival of Greek tragedy in Athens. Unfortunately, our country's economic recession meant that it was not possible to send a Mexican company of forty to Greece.

Isabel Quintanar *is a leading actress and Director General of the Mexican Centre of the International Theatre Institute.*

MOLDOVA

ANGELINA ROSCA

During the last season the theatrical art (and the culture in general) of the Republic of Moldova has become not only the most economically vulnerable realm of public life, but also a zone of attacks. After the communists came to power in February 2001 they tried to resume control of the theatre, a control that had been renounced by the state in 1991, simultaneously with the *Declaration of Independence of the Republic of Moldova*. To achieve that gain Parliament published a bill regarding the activity of *Theatres, circus and concert organisations*, a part of a whole policy seeking the return of a time long past.

The first organised reaction of the opposition (and of the public at large) can be considered the mass meetings which have taken place regularly, from January 9th, 2002, in The Square of the Great National Gathering, under the guidance of the PPCD (People's Christian Democratic Party). The main impetus for these protests was the decision regarding the compulsory study of Russian in schools. Subsequently, the decisions of the communist Government have been increasingly retrograde. In February, a bill was approved stipulating the substitution of the curriculum course on the *History of Romanians* with the *History of Moldova*. A study of our history that omitted the history of Romanians would be inconceivable, for the greater part of historical Moldova lies in the territory of Romania. Tailored to communist specifications by some nostalgists of the former USSR, the *History of Moldova* was doomed to become a pro-Soviet falsification that would be thrust upon our young. But the scope of the popular protest (a general strike, with the participation of the cultural institutions, students and school pupils) forced the communists to abrogate the above-named law a week later. For all that, the opposition continued the organisation of mass meetings demanding the removal of censorship in the mass media, a referendum, and the collective resignation of the communist Government. The democratic response continually gained in scope (the TV went on hunger strike, and about a hundred tents belonging to demonstrators appeared in front of the Parliament building, thus making the movement in defence of democratic values a non-stop activity).

The unceasing degradation of the political climate in Moldova was cause for concern in the European Community. In the long run, by the efforts of the Council of Europe a temporary compromise was finally achieved in April 2002. But before it happened the League of Theatre Critics and several theatres had pitched their tents in the street. That of the Eugène Ionesco Theatre was decorated with playbills of *The History of Communism Told for the Mentally Ill*, by Matei Visniec, staged by Charles Lee from France (premiered in February 2000 and seen later that year on the Edinburgh Festival Fringe in Scotland). And the Satiricus Theatre was there almost daily, performing scenes of political satire for the demonstrators. That experience found its reflection in the production of *A Lost Letter*, by I. L. Caragiale (April 2002).

MOLDOVA

In its turn, the National Theatre is keeping up with the times with a number of performances which stand out both by their social impact and artistic value. In his creations Mihai Fusu managed to sound faint notes of the betrayal in the electoral turmoil (*A Lost Letter* by I. L. Caragiale, July 1999), and the necessity of the struggle for national liberation (*Mowgli* by Rudyard Kipling, May 2000). The staging of *One Flew Over The Cuckoo's Nest* by Ken Kesey proved to be extremely timely. It became possible as a result of the collaboration with three artists from Romania: director Mihai Lungeanu, composer George Marcu and the actor Anca Paslaru.

Naturally, the present situation of the theatre is also an echo of some previous actions. Inspired by experience with advanced cultural spaces, the Government in 1995 suspended the subsidy of three out of the thirteen theatres then existent, condemning them to raise their own income in a country where there was no law regarding sponsorship and where the living standard of the population was in the penultimate place among the former socialist states. The theatres put out an SOS call to be, at least, delivered from the taxes imposed on theatre tickets and a reduction in the exaggerated tariffs charged them for public utilities, telephone, and so on. But the powers that be looked on coolly at the theatres' death-agony.

The situation of other theatres, which from 1998–1999 functioned on the basis of partial self-financing, is not much more better. Only 30–40% of their needs are covered by the state. Several years ago public opinion, which considered the Mihai Eminescu National Theatre a temple of the arts, was shocked when the only way it could find to survive was to lease some of its space to a casino. Time proved it to be not the most radical solution applied by a theatre out of necessity. Fundraising became the theatre's main function, while the artistic function was left far behind. The phenomenon was debated at the International Theatre Symposium *Artistic And Commercial Value of the Performance* (October 10–13th, 1999, organised by the Luceafarul Theatre).

The theatrical situation is falling into decay. For the Bogdan-Petriceicu Hasdeu Republican Musical-Dramatic Theatre (with a troupe of 17 actors headed by Alexandru Turcanu) and the Eugène Ionesco Theatre, which have no stage at present, tours are the only way to maintain standards.

The average earnings of an actor are now about 150–250 lei (US$11–18.50, a fifth of the living wage). The initiative of the directors to go over to contract-based hiring is hampered by the Code of Work approved in 1995 and by the Payment Law approved in 1994. The law provides that the remuneration of an actor's labour should be calculated not in conformity with his real contribution, but with his length of service. A considerable number of actors have left the theatre. In these extremely favourable conditions (for him at least) the Italian impresario Batistini recruits the best performers for his projects. As a consequence the M. Eminescu and the E. Ionesco theatres had to resort during the 2001–2002 season to unplanned changes of cast or even to omit some performances from the repertory.

The municipal theatres are slightly more protected: Satiricus, Guguta, Theatre of a Single Actor. But their employees are also haunted by the feeling that it could be the last season for them. To remedy the situation, the National Debate on the Cultural Policy of Moldova took place in October 2001 under the aegis of the General Secretariat of the Council of Europe and the Ministry of Culture. A group of experts from the Council of Europe,

ABOVE: Matei Visniec's *The History of Communism Told for the Mentally Ill* (*photo*: Ken Reynolds)

BELOW: left, *The Seventh Coffeehouse*, directed by Mihai Fusu; right, *The Wolves And The Sheep*, directed by Petru Vutcarau (*photos*: Eugen Verebceanu, Serghei Cartashoff)

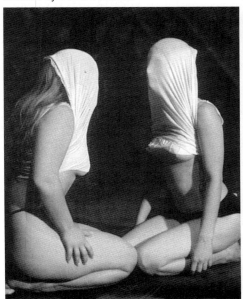

together with the Ministry of Culture, worked out an analytic program regarding the perspective of the further development of arts, literature and culture in the Republic of Moldova. The lack of cultural policies has prompted many events, such as the International Theatre Symposium *The Actor in the Context of New Cultural Policies*, which took place in Chisinau, also in October 2001, within the framework of *One Man Show*, an important theatre festival which was in its second edition, organised by the Theatre of a Single Actor led by Dumitru Fusu.

Looking into the last three seasons, one must take into account the last decade of the millennium, a period when the most sound successes of the Moldavian stage were closely associated with the names of Sandu Vasilache, Petru Vutcarau and Mihai Fusu. Especially turbulent were 1993–1997, when the above named directors held leading posts in the most important stages of the country. After 1997 grave disturbances, bound up with those names, began. Sandu Vasilache, accompanied by eight actors, left the National Theatre for Bucharest. Mihai Fusu forsook the Luceafarul Theatre in favour of the Coliseum Arts Centre, becoming its president in 2000. Petru Vutcarau is frustrated by the lack of a stage (an extremely significant fact is that the former premises of the E. Ionesco Theatre now belong to the State Chancellery), by the long struggle with the Ministry of Culture and by the retirement of his economic manager Veaceslav Reabcinski.

Those theatres practically achieved the impossible in holding out against the ordeals. The academic conference *Creators and Critics: face to face* (organised by the M. Eminescu National Theatre and the Romanian section of the International Theatre Critics Association in April 2001, with the participation of a group of eighteen people, most of them theatre critics and journalists from the most important publications of Romania) established that the collective guided by Vitalie Caraus could manage to fill the gap in the repertory produced by Vasilache's resignation with seven new, high quality titles. An unanimous opinion was reached: the M. Eminescu National Theatre has a valuable troupe of actors, capable of satisfying the requirements of any director – both from inside the country and those invited.

The troupe keeps up its relationship with Petre Bokor from Canada, who several years ago staged here *The Godmothers* by Tremblay and *Our Country's Good* by Wertenbaker. This time he has been invited to stage for the opening of the 2001–2002 season *Don Quixote* by Miguel de Cervantes, in the musical adaptation belonging to Dale Wasserman, *Man of la Mancha*. At the end of the season a grand event happened – *The Gamblers* by N. V. Gogol. In the second half of the 2001–2002 season the M. Eminescu National Theatre is to launch a programme to encourage national playwriting, introducing to the audience seven rehearsed readings of works by Nicolae Negru, Val Butnaru, Nicolae Rusu, Angelina Rosca, Irina Nechit, Constantin Cheianu and Larisa Turea.

The E. Ionesco Theatre lays emphasis on classical texts, performed in a modern language. *Hamlet* by W. Shakespeare, directed by Ion Sapdaru (premiere January 2002) can be held up as a pattern of shocking theatricality, with a hefty dose of stunning sensuality. The production is founded on signs, codes and complex images.

In *The Wolves And The Sheep* (July 2002) E. Ionesco Theatre tries to present its own image. Undoubtedly, Vutcarau exploits the themes that are central to his creation: that of death (death of content, sense, emotion, word, inner life, of a reaction and attitude) and the temptation to destroy the rigid schemes that bind the author's text. He keeps on declaring for a continual exchange of energy, states, emotions, information and pauses. He also presents on the stage a minimal decor and some costumes of a defiant conventionality. But if before the group effort was stressed, now the individual act is of the greatest value. That's why the performances stand out against the general background of the aggressive *mise en scène*, where the rhythm and structure of the direction hides the inventiveness of the actors.

From that point of view should also be noted *Ciuleandra* by L.Rebreanu (directed by Boris Focsa, dramatisation by Angelina Rosca) – a psychological performance, placed in the framework of an easily understood conventionality. It's notable because it puts the actor's creation in the foreground, being concentrated on the inner resonances. The first night of *Ciuleandra* opened the fourteenth season of the Luceafarul Theatre, in October 1999.

The Republic of Moldova has for many years practised a theatricality based on the interaction of various arts within the theatrical act, and on the interaction of theatre with other arts, intensifying the forms of image-theatre, dance-theatre, music-theatre. From this point of view two director-producers' performances are interesting: Sandu Grecu at Satiricus Theatre (*The Metamorphoses-II* by Ovid, April 2000; *The Master and Margarita,* based on his own adaptation, December 2000) and Boris Focsa at Luceafarul Theatre (*Smiles of a Summer Night* by Ingmar Bergman, stage adaptation by Angelina Rosca, September 2000; *Masquerade* by M. I. Lermontov, March 2002). Also very noteworthy is the combination of the dramatic theatre with the puppet-show in *Ivan Turbinca* by Ion Creanga, a performance produced by Leonid Cibotaru at the Vasile Alecsandri Theatre from Balti (July 2001).

Unfortunately, in this cultural arena new techniques of composition and conception are late in making their appearance. An exception in this sense is *The Seventh Coffeehouse,* a performance directed by Mihai Fusu – a result of collaboration between the Coliseum Arts Centre (a group of independent artists) and the Swiss Agency For Development and Co-operation (SDC). The subject of the play, that is made up of incoherent events, is the distressing problem of the traffic in prostitution. It is based, not on dramatic fictions, but on real events recorded by Mihai Fusu, Dumitru Crudu and Nicoleta Esinenco. This social situation, very characteristic of today's Moldova, is hardly accepted by the civilised world, a fact also proved by the press reaction to its recent presentation at the Bonner Biennale.

The theatres try, and often succeed, to prove their competitiveness within the framework of theatrical festivals, including Bucharest, Edinburgh, Grenoble and Avignon (France), Bonn (Germany), Cairo (Egypt), Klaypeda (Lithuania), Trabzon (Turkey), Gdansk (Poland), Kiev and Kerch (Ukraine) and Razgrad (Bulgaria). As to festival life inside the country, it is poorly developed. There are no more than two festivals that have progressed beyond a single edition (Eugène Ionesco Theatre's Biennale and One Man Show). Both of them are international and take place in the capital. In celebration of the 180 years from the birth of Vasile Alecsandri at the theatre that bears his name, in Balti, the *Republican Festival of Classical Universal Drama* took place in October 2001.

In the circle of producers of established reputation are the young producers: Mihai Tarna with *Run for Your Wife* by Ray Cooney (E. Ionesco Theatre, May 2001); Anatol Durbala with *The Death Of Tarelkin* by Suhovo-Kobylin (December 1999); Nelly Cozaru with *Medea* after her own scenario and *Frankie and Johnny in the Clair de Lune* by Terrence McNally (Coliseum Arts Centre, March 2002); Calin Ursu with *A Blind Man And A Blind Woman On The Caucasian Mountains* by Dumitru Crudu (May 2002); Corneliu Pavaloi with *That's The Carnival* by I. L. Caragiale (Luceafarul Theatre, May 2001); Valeriu Andriuta with *The Murderers' Night* by Jose Triana (Luceafarul Theatre, October 2001); Petru Hadirca with *A Wild Night* by I. L. Caragiale (the Ginta Latina Centre, December 2001) and so on. But their creation is, largely, an imitation of successful productions of their already recognised colleagues. The fascination of the *mise en scène* coexists with the desire for metaphysics and paradox. A lot is staked on the outward appearance: white faces, coloured wigs and so on. Some of them even take artificiality for art. Theatricality is compromised with a commercial view, counting on a vulgarised illusionism. There are cases when the dramatic material is hyper-simplified and astonishment is the only aesthetic value.

It should be noted that even the established producers are in relative crisis. The situation is provoked by artistic factors as well as purely economic ones.

With the 10 years of glory of the E. Ionesco Theatre came to an end an entire existential period, both in art and in society, making some people feel diffidence or even panic. Everyone notes that now, at a crossroads of thousands of years, those who themselves once changed and developed the image of the entire theatrical movement are themsleves in need of a change under the badge of theatricality.

The idea that one should shun the principles of the Shchukin School from Moscow and the Vakhtangovian aesthetic promoted by it has lately become popular. But an analysis of the development of the followers of Vakhtangov in our theatrical space suggests that the redefinition of our theatricality needs not a giving up of Vakhtangov, but his rediscovery. The prescriptions of the Shchukin School have been adopted by four generations of artists from this cultural space, for that institution is very close to the temperament and tradition of the Romanian theatre.

In fact, the problem is that in Moldavian theatrical space the Vakhtangovian aesthetic takes a one-dimensional projection. The Comic Grotesque becomes the only point of attraction, disregarding the Tragic Grotesque, the Zone of Fantastic Realism and the Philosophic Stratum from Vakhtangov's creation. The performance creators are supposed to meet their audience half way, sometimes overcoming not the Vakhtangovian aesthetic, but some rigid patterns. Since the Vahtangovian aesthetic is an open value system, the Bessarabian theatres have the freedom to resort to a synthesis of forms. That way we might keep abreast with that free-style, based on the conjunction of aesthetic formulae from the most varied artistic systems, that characterises the World Theatre at this cross roads of thousands of years.

Angelica Rosca, *Doctor in Theatre Sciences, is Head of the Department of History and Theory of Theatre at the State Art University of Chisinau. Editor-in-chief and director of the magazine* Coliseum-Teatru (Coliseum-Theatre).

NEPAL

ABHI SUBEDI

Nepali theatre in the last three years has undergone important changes in terms of both textual and theatrical innovation. In a country whose dramatic traditions have strong bases in both culture and performance, change in theatrical practice should not be seen as something of recent origin. Nepali theatre at the turn of the century has revived some traditions, produced some new plays and accepted certain intercultural innovations in both text and performance. Traditional Nepali society, which has always nurtured and continued the theatrical tradition, has suddenly awakened to a new mode of reality and new forms of challenge. In a short period of time, it became divided between old values and aspirations for change.

The democratic change of 1990 in the political structure of the country opened up many avenues of culture that had lain dormant during thirty years of one-party rule. It also exposed some existing problems to the limelight. The conditions of performance were the same; theatre houses were the same; the minimal government patronage of the development of theatre was more or less the same; grants and subsidies did not change significantly in the days after the restoration of democracy in 1990. Something did nevertheless change. People in recent years have realised that they are freer to speak and that they have responsibilities to protect and preserve indigenous traditions. The performance culture that has been continuing for thousands of years assumed a new significance in the recent ones. Indigenous cultural forms were now presented with confidence to an audience of natives as well as visitors.

Nepali theatre became more broad-based than before, more problem-oriented and innovative. At the same time, many fledgling theatre groups realised that they had greater challenges than they had anticipated when they started, such as finding suitable halls or theatres in the city where they lived. Kathmandu has a few theatre houses, mostly run by the government or under semi-governmental management. Outside the Kathmandu valley, except in a few places like Pokhara in the west and Dharan in the east, no significant theatre works were carried out.

One important challenge to theatre artists in recent years has come from political performances. The newly created political parties made it almost a daily practice to stage their political programmes, creating personas and performers, using tableaux and other forms to project their political ideologies. Street theatre, started by a group of young theatre workers in 1980 to provide a symbolic opposition to the non-party rule of the country, felt a challenge, ironically, from these political performances. Audiences became interested in these real life dramas. They accepted them. The existing forms of street theatre almost gave way to performances of a political nature.

The other serious turn in Nepali history was the emergence of the insurgency. Many young people went underground to fight for what they considered a system of government that would be different from the present, parliamentary form. Nepali dramatists and theatre persons accepted the significance of the new mode of performance, expressing the moods and challenges of these developments.

Nepali performance art of recent years can be examined under the following headings: continuity of performance art and ritual performances; dance and dance drama; experiments and innovations in proscenium theatre; play writing; organisational structures; and regional contacts.

A survey of the the scenario shows that performance culture in Nepal over the years has continued to appear in both traditional and modern forms. Indic performance culture continues as the leading influence in the traditional performance culture of Nepal even today. Ralph Yarrow's categorisation of the Indic theatre (*Indian Theatre: Theatre of Origin, Theatre of Freedom* p. 67: Surrey, Curzon, 2001) as 'epic; historical; didactic; documentary; dialectic; socially cohesive; controversial; entertainment/diversion; sentimental; demanding/empowering; elevating' is equally applicable to the Nepali traditional theatre. Its main attributes in the last few years continue to be the same as they have been for centuries.

Marching remains one of the important features of Nepali performance, especially in the Kathmandu valley which has a long tradition of performance arts. 'The spatio-cultural and human settlement patterns have continued to form the heritage of ritual travels within the Nepal mandala for millennia. These ritual movements have the physical, intercultural and message oriented dimensions. These performances can be seen in the traditional ritual and contemporary movements of the performers along the contours within the urban space in the mandala. These different modes of travels have also undergone various processes of assimilation.' (*see* Abhi Subedi, 'Travel as Theatre in Nepal Mandala', *Mandala*, bulletin of Nepal Centre of ITI)

The heritage of traditional ritual dance and dance-drama, especially in the Kathmandu valley, has maintained the vibrant tradition that follows the old choreography, and they are carried out each year in traditionally mandated order. In short, the three categories of performance that Schechner defines as *efficacy* for ritual, *transportation* for devotional and *entertainment* for modern exist in the Nepali performance of today. On the face of it, it is difficult to see the nuances of the changes, but if we look closely, we can see that the people perform the rituals, dances and dance-dramas under new conditions of individual inspiration.

The *Gaijatra* festival, the pulling of Indra's chariot, the King's worship of the virgin goddess who lives behind exquisitely carved wooden windows and doors, the dance-drama of Harishiddhi, the Janakpur festival of Ram and Sita's wedding, the Bisket festival of Bhaktapur and its vibrant form, the *Lakhe* dance and the chariot procession of the Machendranath, the Buddhist dance dramas of the monasteries and the musical performances of singers and musicians like the maestro of serious modern music, Ambar Gurung, and the classical singer and musician, Nararaj Dhakal – all these continue to be performed. Classical dance forms, too, have been presented over the years by the famous maestro Mrigendraman Singh Pradhan.

In the traditional performances the King and the common people become a unity. Though the structure remains the same, the people who perform it express the anguish of the times. Nepali traditional performance art has been performed in the last three years with greater earnestness than before, because of the difficult times that the Nepalis have been experiencing, but yet as an expression of power and confidence. Even the huge stone Buddhas at the foot of the hill of Swoyambhu monastery in Kathmandu have become participants in this silent but meaningful drama, because many young people turn to them and use them as icons representing performances of the Buddhist drama; as in the 60s and 70s when the youth of the West, the 'hippies', came over and sat with these statues, making postures of the cosmic drama, which also had its influence on Nepali youth. In other words, traditional performance art and iconicity has generated a great sense of performance in Nepal.

Diverse groups of theatre workers felt a need to get membership of the International Theatre Institute, which they obtained in March 2000, becoming also a member of the Asia Pacific Bureau of ITI. Since then the contacts established by the ITI, calls for performances, and discussions have helped establish a system for the organisation and performance of dramas and dances on the stage.

The main theatrical performances during these years have been in proscenium theatres, mainly of two kinds. Directors of the younger generation, many of them trained in Indian schools, have been guided by a mélange of expressionistic and realistic theatre. Experimentation has been the dominant impulse of these theatre directors. Sunil Pokhrel and Anup Baral, both trained in the Delhi School of Drama, have certain commonalities in their techniques. Sunil Pokhrel uses the cultural semiotics of the Nepali tradition in his proscenium theatre. In a play written by Ashesh Malla titled *Kumari* (the name of the living virgin goddess of the Kathmandu valley), and *Dreams of Peach Blossoms*, a poetic play by Abhi Subedi, which Pokhrel has performed in Nepal, India and Bangladesh several times over the years, he has created a unique mix of tradition and modernity. The constant tension between different times and conditions of different spaces is resolved through the interpolation of traditional performance forms, like dances, singing, festival and mythological enactment of scenes. Similarly Anup Baral, in a play by Sarubhakta Shrestha titled *Thangla*, has combined cultural dynamism and anthropological formations. In a play based on the story of a polyandric society, Baral combines realism with the expressive interpretation of unique anthropological forms.

Street theatre tradition has been fostered by the Sarwanam group, led by the dramatist and director Ashesh Malla. In *Ko Gardaicha Yuddhako Ghosana*, a play based on the dilemma faced by the people of this land in the wake of the insurgency and the government's resistance to it, Ashesh Malla has sought to project the pain by employing the expressive techniques of street theatre.

New theatre groups like Sangya Theatre, a group of young academics formed in 2000, and other groups of younger theatre workers like Akhyan theatre group, Yuba Chetana Abhiyan, Anam Natya Jamat in the eastern region, have performed over these years, mostly in proscenium theatres. We may also mention Arohan theatre group, Dabali theatre group (led by the well-known theatre artist Puskar Gurung), Studio 7 (of Sabine Lehmann, a Kathmandu-based German theatre creator), Royal Nepal Academy (which has probably the best theatre and also organises theatre festival each year), and the Pratibimba group from Pokhara in the western region. Rastriya Nachghar has started a tradition of organising a theatre festival each year from 2001. This, plus the institution of various awards for the theatre people, are the major theatrical landmarks in Nepal over the last three years.

Theatre groups in Nepal have also worked in association with social service groups and international non-governmental organisations, but the dramatic quality of this work is not the main focus of attention here. The symbiosis of the Nepali theatre with the socio-political experience of the country in the last three years has played an important role, but a strong desire for change among the smaller and established theatre groups can be seen from a study of their performances, choice of the text for performance, musical soirées, classical singing and dancing. Over the last three years, dancing has suffered most, with very few performances of ballads and dance-dramas.

In spite of state indifference to matters of theatrical art, we can applaud the tenacity of stage performers, playwrights and musicians in presenting their own works and their resolve to press ahead, however difficult conditions may be. Directors, theatre artists and playwrights have been exploring new avenues of multi-cultural contacts with institutions and groups. They have over the years presented plays, taken part in seminars and workshops and invited theatre creators from India and the West to exchange experiences. Many well-known Indian theatres, dance groups and musicians have given performances as part of that exchange.

The Nepali audience in the past 4 or so years has changed significantly in terms of their broadened horizons of expectation: some power must come out, some confidence be built, some gaps in audience expectations filled.

A great body of theatre criticism, plays and research works about theatre seems to have developed over the years. The canons of drama pedagogy have been working quite successfully in the universities and criticism. Including dramatic texts in the university curriculum, however, does not fill the gap between theatre and text. In other words, those who may have read a play but never seen it staged, have started coming to the theatre to see it. But over the years, no central agency has appeared to galvanise the dispersed energy of drama and theatre and give it an institutional shape. The problem, as said earlier, is that a weak civil society is failing to claim its cultural rights and perform its own responsibilities at a time when the Nepali state is caught in the maelstrom of insurgency, slow economic growth and unstable institutions.

The future of Nepali theatre is full of challenges, but there is ample energy for experimentation, opening theatrical institutions and working, even with scant resources, for the performance arts. Themes for drama are being wrought out of our difficult and bloody history itself, through a unique and unusual mix of democratic innovations and very strong politico-institutional challenges to this system. Difficult days can be, ironically, productive times for the Nepali theatre. But the experience of past millennia shows that the basic thrust of Nepali theatre has always been towards both continuity of theatrical tradition and new experimentation.

Professor **Abhi Subedi** is a poet, playwright and writer. He is the president of the Nepal Centre of the ITI.

NETHERLANDS

CECILE BROMMER

The majority of Dutch theatre-makers and choreographers have long seen the credible portrayal of a better or more beautiful world as something 'improper'. One can see in this the inheritance of Calvinism, which had a particularly formative effect on the north–western region of the Netherlands. Or perhaps it is the emphasis on the individual, which characterizes the whole of Europe. In the last few years, though, a need for fantasy and storytelling has begun to become apparent in the theatre and dance world, a need that has long been exploited by commercial television, film and musical producers. Contemporary theatre and dance performances have increasingly acquired a narrative character; they display a wonder at existence, they search for meaning and they offer the audience consolation or even a flicker of hope.

In these times, the popularity of Postmodernism, and the non-hierarchic juxtaposition of diverse forms of life, is declining. It is tempting to draw a parallel with our society's current shift to the right, as a result of which there is less tolerance for the various cultures living in the Netherlands. In the theatre and dance world, however, the national and international exchange of knowledge and culture progresses without diminution. Dutch companies provide space for the work of foreign immigrants, the young and amateurs; they conduct research on other cultures, perform abroad regularly, and maintain numerous international co-operative links.

Since the 70s, individuality and sincerity have been flown high on the flagpole of Dutch theatre-makers and choreographers. The latter of those, in particular, is remarkable in an art form that stems, fundamentally, from the well-presented lie. 'Show that you are lying', is a striking description of text treatment, dance and scenography within this tendency. Through 'honest dance' or 'honest acting' directors and choreographers aim to increase the involvement of the audience, because they 'take the audience seriously' and they address it personally. Choreographers show the vulnerable, mortal quality of the dancer's body, which has the capacity to grow emotional, sad, cheerful or angry. Theatre-makers show the actor behind the character and present design and text as the possible personal vision of the designer and writer upon a particular theme.

The paradox of honest theatre was suggested by Maatschappij Discordia, where the performers even occasionally addressed the audience with the text in their hands, with an incidental item of clothing draped over their shoulder as a reference to the character. A company that followed their lead is 't Barre land; in this case, the performers gave a demonstration of detached, 'quote acting' in *Hamle't* (January 2001). The text of the play was divided among the actors without taking any account of the characters. The concentrated energy of the performers emphasised their sincere wish to relate those particular texts at that particular moment.

NETHERLANDS

In the Netherlands, there is not much by way of political theatre, which is no surprise in such a comparatively well-balanced and economically stable society as the Dutch. Nevertheless, there are increasing numbers of theatre-makers who have their eyes focused on what is happening in the world around them. To freelance director Ola Mafaalani, for example, the classics are an opportunity to draw attention to the wrongs of the world. In her recent productions, she has expressly made use of audience participation to seek answers to the fundamental question of shared norms and values. In *Ajax* (Fact, September 2000), she had members of the audience take up places in a jury, as if in the American justice system, to decide the fate of the hero. A year later, in *Macbeth* (De Bottelarij/Koninklijke Vlaamse Schouwburg, September 2001), they handed out tomatoes for the audience, to pelt the guilty.

To enhance the involvement of the audience, Mafaalani uses the physicality of her actors to add an element of tension and the personal to the performance. In her early, small-auditorium performances, the acting area was surrounded by bedsprings or vertical bars, through which the exertions of the actors and their human presence remained visible and tangible throughout. In *The Merchant of Venice* (Toneelgroep Amsterdam, March 2002), the unhappy Portia hauled three wheeled chests around with her, meant to contain gold, silver and lead. Thus Mafaalani symbolised Portia's attachment to the chests from which, in accordance with her father's will, her future husband would have to make the correct choice. The actress was seen sighing and sweating from the effort of dragging the chests around. It was she, with a stuck-on moustache, dressed up as a lawyer, who finally settled the dispute between the merchants with a great deal of rhetoric and satire.

The above mentioned performances are devoted to text interpretation, often making use of slender theatrical resources. The exuberant and bestially sensual productions of Dirk Tanghe, with the Paardenkathedraal, are an exception to this trend. His production of Schnitzler's *Reigen* (November 1999) was bathed in red light. In the centre of the stage was the front of an enormous racing car, upon which the wheels spun and roared as the tension between the characters mounted. The two actors stood on a belt, which ran across the width of the stage, and had to keep moving continually if they wished to stay out of each other's reach. All five couples made up a different pair of animals, their voices transformed into animal sounds; their relationships were characterized by instinctive, animal lust. His successful *Midsummer Night's Dream* (November 2001) was a feast of frolicking elves, exuberant design, light and sound effects, hilarious vocal effects and exaggerated diction from the actors.

Tanghe does in the playhouse what theatre companies such as Dogtroep and Vis à Vis do out of doors or at other non-theatrical sites, such as hospitals and prisons. The latter create extremely expressive and humorous scenes – with sound installations, video projections, fire and water, bicycles and cars, everyday objects and grotesque, illustrative movements and gestures – usually to relate a simple story.

Video projections of previously recorded and live images create new spaces, within which stories can unfold. De Châtel created a choreography based on the computer game Tomb Raider (*Lara*, October 1998). A large projection screen at

ABOVE: from Dirk Tanghe's production of Shakespeare's *Midsummer Night's Dream* for De Paardenkathedraal (*photo*: Sjouke Dijkstra)

BELOW: from Toneelgroep Amsterdam's *Snaren (Strings)*, directed by Gerardjan Rijnders (*photo*: Chris Van der Burght)

the back of the stage showed the actions of Lara Croft, those of the dancers and the overflowing images in between them. Thus, an extra stage came into existence upon which the dancers could interact with the computer heroine.

The new media have been an inextricable component of the productions of the artistic director of the Ro theatre, Guy Cassiers, for a considerable time. He opened Rotterdam's year as Cultural Capital 2001 with *La Grande Suite*, based on the travel stories that Marco Polo wrote in prison. On an enormous projection screen, one could see associative colours, forms and images, which helped to build up dramatic tension through their alternation. Marc Warning designed a choreography for flying bars, whereby they moved up and down automatically, first as the bars behind which Marco Polo was imprisoned, and secondly as an undulating sea.

Carina Molier built a house for Toneelgroep Amsterdam, with walls made of cambric (*Ruigoord, een virtuele dood*, December 2000). On them were shown projections of what people were doing inside the house, whilst at the same time the spectators were able to see through them: a living Big Brother house, so to speak – this sensational television programme was originally produced by the Dutch.

Con Amore (February 2002) by Toneelgroep Amsterdam, created by their new artistic director Ivo van Hove, also portrayed a group of people in their daily life: he depicted the present generation of young people with a hopeful vision, yet with a knowledge of the less pleasant aspects of life: a generation that possesses an abstract, new-age belief in the goodness of humanity and life in general. The performance covered a day in the life of a group of young people – the actors showered on stage, cooked and ate, kissed and made love, went to the toilet, quarrelled, laughed.

The emphasis upon sensual experience in performances by Van Hove is characteristic. With *India Song* (June 1999) he made his aspiration for sensory theatre explicit by making use of scents, which were blown over the heads of the spectators via a propeller. The audience, seated around the stage, thus smelled the sultry atmosphere of India, the scent of sweet perfume, of bitter lemon and of an acrid crematorium. In *De dame met de camelias* (June 1999), he was successful in creating, partly by means of a significantly slowed tempo, an atmosphere of silence and stillness, something which has all but disappeared from Western Culture.

A recent production for Toneelgroep Amsterdam by their former artistic director Gerardjan Rijnders illustrated the current transformation from mistrust, lovelessness and rhetoric towards wonder and tentative optimism. The independent role of the scenography, again by Marc Warning, was striking. *Snaren* (April 2002) began with an explanation of the smallest possible units from which the world is composed, called 'strings' (snaren), which led to a philosophical discussion about the beginning of the beginning of the world – which was directly and rhetorically spoken, very much in the Calvinist tradition, in a black space by an actor dressed in black, lit only by a single spotlight. Occasionally, a light flashed on in the space behind the speakers where a number of actors clothed in rags clattered around. In one of the flashes, a man stepped out of a portable WC cabin, naked. Disillusion gave way to hope when the back of the stage slowly lit up and a gigantic baby descended from the rafters. The baby was followed by cuddly toys and then bottles, not of milk but of cola and mineral water. In the closing image, vertical rows of coloured discs hung on long ropes as a sort of backdrop, and slowly moved towards each other. Meanwhile, the people on stage, who had been portrayed in all their banality and were by now dressed in brightly coloured clothes, sought consolation from one another.

These signs of hope were a welcome change after the trend in England called 'Cool Britannia', which also shocked spectators in the Netherlands around the turn of the millennium. Sex, violence and drugs are emphatically present in the work of such writers as Enda Walsh, Sarah Kane and Mark Ravenhill. Their controversial, topical portrayal of degenerate, broken families appealed to many Dutch theatre-makers. The melancholic, violent *Leenane Trilogy* from Hollandia (September 2001), based on texts by the Anglo-Irishman Martin McDonagh, was a highpoint of the season. The plays portrayed people for whom violence is a means of communication – people who made no connection between beating each other's heads in and their own mortality.

The logic of dance is the presentation of the physical presence of the body. (Post)modern dance starts with the body itself as the aesthetic and designing object and subject of the performance. The repetitive movements of Krisztina de Châtel, the ironic witticisms of Hans van Manen, the emotive dancers of Truus Bronkhorst and the theatrical jokes of Paul Lightfoot are all in deliberate opposition to the illusion of the fluently moving, perfectly formed and unfailing body of the classical ballet (and of American films and television series). But, just as in the theatre, recent choreography is not as abstract as before. In contemporary works that combine dance with theatre, new media and the visual arts, recognizable forms and story lines are being sketched.

The work of Jiri Kylian is still authoritative within the Dutch dance world. The internationally admired dance master, who has created so many dance works for the Nederlands Dans Theater, draws from both the classical ballet tradition and newer dance techniques. His creativity has produced a wealth of new forms, which are an inspiration to the younger generation. The striking and idiosyncratic work of Emio Greco, developed in close collaboration with the dramaturge Pieter C. Scholten, evokes associations with performance art and the visual arts. Such dance companies as that of Conny Janssen Danst and the Hans Hof Ensemble create works that are narrative, idealistic, personal and theatrical, and within which the dancers make contact with one another as human individuals. In *Álbum familiar* (February 2001), Conny Janssen expressed the spirit of the age, in which globalisation stimulates a contrary longing for family, tradition and folklore, by depicting people's need for intimacy and security.

The performances described above show once again the great diversity of Dutch theatre and dance. Disciplines such as youth theatre, mime and puppetry (including Stuffed Puppet Theatre and Speeltheater Holland) haven't even been mentioned. The popularity of crossover projects makes the diversity endless. What they all have in common is the increasing visibility of the personality of the maker and the actors or dancers, who are aware that they are playing a character and show it – which promotes identification and engagement, making possible new forms of narration.

Cecile Brommer *is a dramaturg; her article was translated by Paul Evans.*

PERÚ

FERNANDO TORRES
and VIOLETA CACERES

1999 was a particularly difficult year for Peruvians because of the political situation created by the government in seeking re-election for a third time. 2000 was an election year, which ended with the unwanted re-election of the president. These results caused a lot of social turmoil, culminating in meetings and riots to protest against a very ill-defined and manipulated process. La Marcha de los Cuatro Suyos was a most effective protest march, that brought together thousands of Peruvians claiming their right to democracy. The airing on television of a series of videos that were clear testimony of corruption forced the president to flee the country. An emergency government was elected by the National Congress, to be responsible for creating the right climate for democratic elections.

After eight months, Alejandro Toledo was elected President of Perú. Democracy was re-established, but the dream was too short and it only took a few months before new riots began. These difficulties were reflected in all sectors, the arts being probably among those most affected. The complete lack of cultural direction forced the private institutions to take on projects that should otherwise have been the responsibility of the Instituto Nacional de Cultura (our equivalent of the ministry of culture). As a result of the indifference of the state, the arts and cultural expression are now mostly funded by private institutions, some of which have become important cultural forces after organising events that have already become landmarks in the cultural panorama of the country.

In an attempt to solve the problem, the new government created the Comisión Nacional de Cultura, headed by a well known sculptor, Víctor Delfín, who called in professionals from the visual and performing arts as well as other intellectuals from a vast number of cultural fields. This committee was in charge of defining cultural policies in the country. After one year, we have not yet seen anything that might make us hope for the best. Poverty and unemployment seem to remain as the worst enemies of democracy, to the point that entities like the Teatro National have been affected; its Director was forced to quit a year ago and since then it has remained closed. This institution had developed an unparalleled body of work for the benefit of Peruvian playwrights, including both outstanding theatre productions and the printing of theatre scripts.

Private institutions like the Pontificia Universidad Católica or the so-called bi-national institutions, among others the Alianza Francesa, the Asociación Peruano Británica, the Instituto Cultural Peruano Norteamericano, the Instituto Peruano Japonés, the Instituto Italiano de Cultura, the Centro Cultural de España, are cultural centres with a permanent programme in the performing arts as well as the visual arts.

Les Mains Sales directed by Jorge Chiarella at the Universidad Católica.

The Instituto Cultural Peruano Norteamericano (ICPNA) supports a number of international festivals in Contemporary dance, theatre, *lieder* and diverse forms of musical expression. Some of these festivals have been running for more that 15 years, which has generated important platforms for different disciplines of the performing arts. These events have also served as a very positive way to establish contacts between Peruvian and foreign artists.

The Centro de Artes Escénicas de la Municipalidad de Lima has also created a Festival Internacional de Danza y Teatro that started four years ago and seems to be quite well established. This event includes national and international companies as well as workshops and performances by Peruvian and visiting artists.

The representative theatre groups have been reduced to a few, probably because of the economic limitations. Yuyachkany still remains as the most professional theatre association, followed by Cuatro Tablas, La Tarumba, Maguey, Raíces and Grupo de Teatro de Villa El Salvador. The latter is located in one of the marginal areas of Lima where a theatre group has an exceptional connotation. Yawar is another group that has similar position; it has already toured Europe.

The Movimiento de Teatro Independiente – MOTIN-PERU – brings together most of the independent theatre groups in the country. This institution organizes the national theatre convention and the Muestra Nacional de Teatro that takes place every two years in different cities of the country. The Asociación Prolírica is devoted to organizing the opera season that takes place once a year in Lima. They invite national and international singers to perform

PERU

in big productions sponsored by private funders. This year, *Aida* was performed with La Huaca Pucllana, an historical and archaeological site, as a natural setting. Several thousand people filled the space every night.

In spite of a context dominated by political and economy instability the theatre groups have managed to keep the show going on, not only in the regular theatres but in the open air, where productions take place in some of the most disadvantaged areas, like Comas, Villa El Salvador and Independencia. These places have their own theatre groups that keep up a regular schedule of performances throughout the year. The same is true of other Peruvian cities like Cajamarca, Arequipa, Huancayo, Trujillo and Cuzco.

1999–2000 was particularly active in the theatre field, especially for the emphasis given to the classics: Shakespeare, Brecht, Tennessee Williams, García Lorca as well as new creations by Peruvian groups and playwrights. Among the most outstanding pieces we recognise: Brecht's *Galileo Galilei*, directed by Luis Peirano at the Universidad Católica; José Watanave's *Antígona*, directed by Miguel Rubio for Yuyashkani; *King Lear* (director, Edgar Saba) and *The Taming of the Shrew* (director, Donald van der Maaten), both at the Universidad Católica; *Los Ruperto* by Juan Rivera Saavedra, directed by Ruth Escudero at the Teatro Nacional; *Kathy and the Hippopotamus* by Mario Vargas Llosa, directed by Maria Pacheco in the ICPNA Festival; Tennessee Williams' *A Streetcar Named Desire*, directed by Chela de Ferrari at the Universidad Católica.

In 2000–2001, once again the lack of stability during the transition from one kind of government to another generated natural fears for the future of our economy, as was demonstrated by the limitations in funding for theatre projects. To overcome this situation, groups of young actors, playwrights and directors presented a series of plays that described the gloomy atmosphere the country was facing at that particular moment. The following are some of the pieces that received more attention from audiences and media: *Los charcos de la ciudad (City Puddles)*, written and directed by Mariana de Althaus; *El viaje (The Journey)* and *El sueño de las palomas (The Doves' Dream)*, both written and directed by Jorge Villanueva; *Carmen*, written and directed by Kathy Serrano; *Dulces sueños (Sweet Dreams)*, written and directed by Ruth Vásquez.

The two most ambitious productions of the season were R. Angeles' *Macbeth* for ICPNA and Goethe's *Faust,* directed by J. Guerra for the Universidad Católica.

The first semester of 2001–2002 has not been very prosperous in terms of new productions, with a few exceptions. We consider it indispensable to name: Frank Wedekind's *Spring Awakening*, directed by R. Angeles for ICPNA, Sartre's *Les Mains sales*, directed by Jorge Chiarella, and Vaclav Havel's *Largo Desolato*, directed by Mateo Chiarella, both at the Universidad Católica.

In this rather limited panorama the Centro Peruano of ITI has been promoting a series of activities in order to increase audience appreciation as well as produce a healthy exchange of ideas among professionals in the theatre field, among them playwrights, actors, directors and also students. A series of round tables and lectures has been scheduled every year, with the participation of the best representatives from the national scene. At the same time we are always attentive to international events like the Sinaia Congress in Romania, where the Escuela Nacional de Arte Dramático of Peru participated with great success.

PHILIPPINES

MALOU JACOB

Stage Directors Anton Juan and Nonon Padilla have dominated Philippine theatre with their extraordinary creative work for decades, season after season up to the present. Juan, who is with the 26 year old Dulaang University Players, went to the Centre Universitaire International de Formation et des Recherches Dramatiques in Nancy for higher studies in theatre under Michelle Kokossowski, Augusto Boal, Radu Penciulescu (Grotowsky School), Dario Fo, and Donatello Sartori. He also studied Butoh with Kazuo Ohno, and Noh Theatre at the Kita School under Takabayashi Sensei. His memorable productions include: *Medea*, *Bacchae*, *The Maids*, *Miss Julie*, *Marat/Sade*, *Waiting for Godot*, *Yerma* and *Death in the Form of a Rose*.

Nonon Padilla, artistic director of Tanghalang Pilipino, the resident company of the Cultural Centre of the Philippines (CCP) since 1987, started his career at the Ateneo, trained with Cecile Guidote at the Philippine Educational Theatre Association (PETA), the Czech director-playwright Ladislav Smocek and the American director Brooks Jones. Among Padilla's stunning works are: *Hoy*, *Boyet*, *Cabesang Tales*, and the musicals *Noli Me Tangere* and *El Filibusterismo*, which toured Japan.

For 2001, Anton Juan directed Sara Kane's *Crave*, a dramatic poem telling the story of a distraught young woman on the verge of self destruction. The complex web of stories told in scraps and fragments by the characters reveals the sexual abuse and rejection inflicted by members of her own family during a very stormy childhood. Usually given a chamber quartet rendering, Juan's directorial approach to the piece was described by dramaturg Jon Lazam as 'a seascape of restless voices and corporeal images relentlessly surfacing the sea of unsound consciousness', emphasising Kane's defiance of all the rules of linear narrative.

Nonon Padilla directed *Carmen* as a chamber opera in Filipino. In his production, Padilla juxtaposed *Carmen* in an experimental collage with the lives of Filipinos living abroad, experiencing a gypsy life and state of mind of total freedom, against the perspective of patriotism that asked the hard questions about being Filipino.

Among emerging theatre groups we should mention the New Voice Company (NVC), established in 1994 by Monique Wilson who played the lead in the West End production of *Miss Saigon*. She was a student of Zenaida Amador of Repertory Philippines, home of Broadway plays. As artistic director of NVC, Wilson has steered her company into making its mark as the feminist theatre group that has made Philippine theatre honest, provocative, challenging and bold. Its repertoire includes plays that deal with women's rights, sexuality, incest and globalisation.

For 2001, its major production was Eve Ensler's *The Vagina Monologues*. It premiered in Manila, toured the provinces and Asian venues including Hong

PHILIPPINES

Kong and Singapore. It was translated into Filipino by Glecy Atienza, Joi Barrios and Luna Sicat.

With this production, the Philippines joined more than a dozen other countries that have produced Eve Ensler's play, described by the *New York Times* as 'a bona fide phenomenon' and by *Variety* as 'a work of art and a piece of cultural history.' Proceeds of the NVC production went to various local groups that provide relief and support to women and children who suffer abuse and poverty.

Under the helm of Paul Morales, Dulaang Talyer (founded in 1993) has evolved into, perhaps, the most experimental and original theatre company in the Philippines. Morales, a University of the Philippines Theatre graduate, has directed for PETA, Performing Artists International and Ballet Philippines. He took up further studies at the London Laban Centre of Movement under a British Council and CCP grant. For 2001, he directed Andrew Bovell's *Speaking in Tongues* and Nic Pitchay's *Bilog*, the company's most critically acclaimed production to date. Dulaang Talyer (DT) is a pioneering company, committed to the pursuit of innovative and professional theatre. The company believes in the value of a working ensemble: a Talyer or workshop is a place where people work together to create and experiment. DT is composed of young, dynamic artists like Nicolas Pichay, an award-winning poet and playwright, versatile actor Herbert Go, and organizer Roli Inocencio.

With the emergence of talented young directors Paul Morales of Dulaang Talyer, Tami Monsod (director of *My Sister in This House*) of New Voice Company, and Josefina Estrella (director of *Divinas Palabras*) of Dulaang UP to join the veteran directors, Philippine theatre will be in very good hands in the years to come. They just have to see to it that they follow the tradition of the Philippine Educational Theatre Association (PETA), of producing numerous Filipino original works, which has made it an institution in Philippine theatre since it was founded by Cecile Guidote in 1967. Cecile is a leading figure in the Philippines Centre of the International Theatre Institute, which since its inception has been consistent in its support for theatre for the poor, the marginalised, children with special needs and the Indigenous peoples. With one third of the population living below the poverty line, it is continuing its priority programs in providing theatre training for special needs children and out of school youth through links with community, civic, religious and school groups and with the government, demonstrating the power of theatre for human resource development, rehabilitation, and education.

The Centre has the distinction of producing and sustaining a national Broadcast Theatre Programme that reaches out to the masses for their entertainment and enlightenment. *Balintataw* was recently featured by CNN and introduced by Jane Fonda as a model soap opera for change. With Folk Arts for Communication and Education (FACE), it runs the Earthsavers Dreams Academy/Ensemble (EDE), a co-operative of artists, educators, and civic leaders who aspire to democratise culture and apply arts as a catalyst for social change by providing arts education services for persons with disabilities and the marginalised, including street children and tribal youth. In August 2001 FACE/Earthsavers joined the Culture Olympiad 2001 hosted by FACE (Denmark) and Naestved Kommune in Naestved, Daenmark.

Scene from Dulaang UP's presentation of *Oedipus Rex* directed by Anton Juan in a Filipino translation by Rolando Tinio

The Philippine ITI Centre also supports efforts in the development of playwrights, the key to a dynamic and provocative theatre. It has helped the national chapter of Women Playwrights International (WPI Philippines) in its search for gifted, budding writers among the Muslim and Indigenous communities of Mindanao for its Playwriting Workshops.

Further, the Centre plays a leading role in promoting a Culture of Peace, Social Justice and Sustainable Development by giving mobile workshops in the provinces for marginalized communities. It has co-operated with the local government of Bohol and the Bohol Foreign Friendship Foundation to give an environmental theme for the International Arts Festival held in July 2002. For the World Environment Month in Boracay, a world famous beach, the Centre has organised a gallery of the sea – featuring paintings on 50 sailboats – and a water festival of plays, music, and dance.

Malou Jacob, *co-chair of the Playwrights Committee of ITI Philippines, is an award-winning playwright whose works include* Juan Tamban, Pepe, Macli-Ing *and* Anatomiya ng Korupsyon.

POLAND

WOJCIECH MAJCHEREK

There is nothing the Poles like more than to complain. To a routine question like 'How's it going?', a Pole will respond with a martyred air, 'Badly', even if he has just returned from a holiday in Majorca. Maybe social psychologists could explain in some way the phenomenon of our national discontent. Anyway, it is not the reasons for but the consequences of such an approach that are significant. My compatriots would find a source of dissatisfaction in any domain of their lives. Naturally, in the theatre, too.

Obviously, theatre life in Poland is beset by a number of problems. First of all, the theatre has not yet overcome the institutional and financial crisis which is a troublesome legacy of the past regime. Theatres in the so-called People's Poland did quite well financially, as they were harnessed to implementing the cultural policy of the state. Artists from the West truly envied their Polish colleagues' permanent employment, with salaries and social benefits provided by the employing entity – the theatre. As of 1989, Poland has taken the path of liberalisation, as a result of which theatres found themselves in a situation similar to the state factories whose fate, for lack of a private investor, was uncertain. The government withdrew from its former role of patron (the Ministry of Culture provides funds for only two theatres: Stary in Cracow and Narodowy, the National, in Warsaw). Following the state administration reform of 1998, local authorities have taken control of several dozen theatres. Since money is sparse and expenses considerable, no wonder theatres are financially unstable. Subsidies are modest. As managers would say: 'too little to live on, too much to die from'.

However, everyday problems should not be allowed to distort the overall image of the Polish theatre of the last two seasons. There are a few signs suggesting that our drab reality might be viewed in a more optimistic manner.

Throughout the 90s, the best achievements of the Polish theatre were associated with the work of three directors: Jerzy Jarocki, Jerzy Grzegorzewski and Krystian Lupa. Jarocki, who made his debut in the 50s, is probably the only artist of that generation who has managed to maintain an extremely high level in his productions, although recently he has been less active. Grzegorzewski, who has persistently pursued his original, personal vision of the theatre from the beginning of his career in the 60s, became the focus of public attention after his appointment in 1997 as the director of the reopened National Theatre in Warsaw (which had been closed down for reconstruction for many years, following a fire). Murmurs were heard that Grzegorzewski would tend to dominate the national stage, which, in spite of its ups and downs in the past, was always held in high esteem. Indeed, though he keeps on inviting directors from both the older and the younger generation, his personality prevails. What is interesting is that, without giving up his distinctive style of

Maja Komorowska, Piotr Skriba and Waldemar Barwinski in Thomas Bernhard's *Auslöschung*, adapted and directed by Krystian Lupa at the Teatr Dramatyczny, Warsaw   (*photo*: Stefan Okolowicz)

staging (fine blending of words, images, sounds and acting), Grzegorzewski tried to enter into a serious dialogue with the Polish cultural and literary tradition. Stanislaw Wyspianski, a distinguished dramatist of the turn of the 20th century, has been adopted as the house dramatist. In his poetic drama, Wyspianski proceeded to challenge the ever present Romantic tradition in Polish art. At the same time, as the author of *Wesele (The Wedding)*, he carried out a penetrating social and psychological analysis of a nation which had been enslaved for long decades. By successively staging such plays as *Noc listopadowa (November Night)*, *Sedziowie (Judges)*, or *Wesele (The Wedding)*, Grzegorzewski seemed to be testing the validity of Wyspianski's diagnosis today. And yet, none of these performances manifested documentary immediacy. As a matter of fact, several critics charged Grzegorzewski with failing to address real life in his theatre. Nevertheless, Grzegorzewski has succeeded in turning the National Theatre into a major artistic institution in Poland. The theatre's prestige has been confirmed by staging *Slub (The Marriage)* and *Operetka (Operetta)* by Witold Gombrowicz (June, 2000). The paramount role of Grzegorzewski at the National may be evidenced by the fact that, during his leave of absence in the 2000/2001, the season was generally considered unsuccessful.

Undoubtedly, Krystian Lupa has led the field throughout the past decade and the last two seasons prove his supremacy. Lupa, the outstanding Polish stage director of the present day, once again tried his hand with the work of Thomas Bernhard. Following an excellent adaptation of his *Kalkwerk* and the staging of two plays: *Ritter, Dene, Voss* and *Immanuel Kant*, Lupa produced another long performance at Teatr Dramatyczny in Warsaw, based on the Austrian writer's last novel – *Auslöschung (Redemption,* March 2001). Lupa seems to be fascinated by Bernhard's hero's inextinguishable desire to come to terms with his work, life, family and surrounding. Such a self-vivisection has a personal/psychological as well as a social/historical dimension. The latter may be found in Bernhard's obsessive inquiry into Austria's links with fascism. At the same time, the performance means for Lupa the summing up of his theatrical experience – the act of 'auslöschung' of the title is his attempt to discover the true sense of art. In the opinion of many, the performance was a major event of the season 2000/2001.

Lupa's theatre is more and more being recognised abroad. His adaptations of Broch's *The Sleepwalkers* and Dostoievsky's *The Brothers Karamazov*, premiered 10 years ago at Stary Teatr in Cracow, have recently been revived and presented at various theatre festivals abroad.

It is not only artists of the older generation who are making their presence felt in the lively current of the Polish theatre. In the late 80s and early 90s, a group of directors, sometimes called 'the younger and more talented' made their debuts. They have not formed a generation group with a specific aesthetic or ideological manifesto. On the contrary, they have tried hard to preserve their individual identities which were manifested in their successive productions. After ten years, their dominant position in the Polish theatre (at some point they were joined by a few more new figures) has been confirmed. These are disciples of Krystian Lupa, who are trying to break away from his influence. Grzegorz Jarzyna and Krzysztof Warlikowski exhibit the strongest personalities and have already managed to win international acclaim. Their productions were shown at recent festivals in Avignon, Amsterdam, Düsseldorf, Nitra and Vilnius. During the last two seasons, they staged their performances at Teatr Rozmaitosci in Warsaw, where Jarzyna holds the position of artistic director. As a result of their efforts, the theatre is highly valued and also very popular, especially with the younger audience. Jarzyna and Warlikowski, in spite of their different styles, have succeeded in winning over the fans of contemporary film, music and fashion. They reap the benefits of the inspiration coming from other forms of art. They adapt classics to meet present day aesthetic expectations. Warlikowski favours Shakespeare and ancient drama. His most recent productions are: *Hamlet* (October 1999) and Euripides' *Bacchae* (February 2001). Both productions proved highly controversial due to his radical manner of interpretation and staging – few directors are so able to irritate both the public and the critics. Hence, he often has to face very trivial charges. Excessive exposure of homosexual motifs was imputed to his *Hamlet*. *Bacchae*, in spite of a somewhat mannered contemporary form, seemed to represent an interesting attempt to address the problem of a religious crisis.

Jarzyna, a star among young Polish directors after his first productions were hailed with enthusiasm, suffered a serious defeat with his adaptation of Thomas Mann's *Doctor Faustus* staged at Teatr Polski in Wroclaw (October 1999). His next production, *Ksiaze Myszkin* (*Prince Myshkin*) (May 2000), after Dostoievsky's *The Idiot*, was also criticised. Jarzyna once again proved his superior directing skill, his ability to create images, moods and emotions on the stage; unfortunately, the attractiveness of his staging hardly supported the basic meaning of the novel. In Jarzyna's production, the novel was reduced to a story of unhappy love between Myshkin and Nastasia Filipovna. On the other hand, his most recent production, *Festen* by Thomas Vinterberg and Mogens Rukov (June 2001), which was earlier filmed by the Danish group Dogma, was generally appreciated. The performance addressed the problem of sexual abuse in a family, an issue eliciting wide response everywhere including Poland. Jarzyna's handling of the subject transcended a mere documentary approach.

Piotr Cieplak occupies a separate position among younger directors (though 'young' in a man means around forty, by Polish standards). Like his colleagues, he does not turn his back on the cultural background of his audience (an important role is given in his theatre to music, played by the underground group Kormorany). His stage images are possibly less striking than Jarzyna's and his productions display less destructive power than Warlikowski's. His adaptation of *Winnie the Pooh* at Teatr Studio in Warsaw (October 1999), addressed to the grown-up audience, won great popularity. In the last season, Cieplak mounted two interesting productions: *Historia Jakuba (The Story of Jacob)*, after Stanislaw Wyspianski's drama *Akropolis*, at Teatr Wspolczesny in Wroclaw (January 2001) and *King Lear* at Teatr Powszechny in Warsaw (May 2001). In his own characteristic style, he presented these almost archetypal stories in terms of a distinct and immediate human experience. His interpretation of Shakespeare's tragedy was highly symptomatic in this case, with an emphasis on a family drama devoid of the historical context.

The general weakness of the middle-aged directors induces a constant quest for young talent. First productions of young directors often evoke greater response than new productions from those who have been active for the last 20 or 30 years. Though the efforts of the young often betray immaturity in form or intellectual content, yet they produce ferment in the theatre. As a result, the theatre landscape in Poland has been recently reshaped. The unrivalled position of the Stary Teatr in Cracow, dominating throughout the 60s, 70s, 80s and even the 90s, was finally shaken. Internal crisis eroded the crucial component of its former prominence: the acting ensemble. A number of eminent actors from Stary Teatr started to perform elsewhere, for instance at Teatr Narodowy in Warsaw. Likewise, many directors held in high repute have ended their co-operation with this theatre (Krystian Lupa, apart from the revival of his *Brothers Karamazov*, returns after a long break to the Stary with an adaptation of *The Master and Margarita*). Thus, it is difficult to name the best theatre in Poland, while it is quite possible to mention several centres of some interest. Undoubtedly, the already mentioned Teatr Rozmaitosci in Warsaw forms such a centre. Krystyna Meissner – a well known organiser of the 'Kontakt' festival in Torun – following her failure as manager of the Stary Teatr, did not surrender but went on to successfully resurrect the formerly second-rate Teatr Wspolczesny in Wroclaw. Her success owed much to the support of young directors, such as Piotr Cieplak, Pawel Miskiewicz, Pawel Szkotak and Grzegorz Wisniewski. Meissner's energy seems inexhaustible. On her initiative, a new festival in Wroclaw, 'Dialog', was started; it has been conceived as a confrontation of the Polish and foreign theatres (in October 2001, the Polish theatre was represented by productions of Grzegorzewski, Lupa, Cieplak, Jarzyna, Warlikowski and Szkotak; among foreign artists, one should mention Robert Wilson, Christoph Marthaler, Oskaras Korsunovas and Stefan Pucher).

Teatr Nowy in Lodz, whose days of greatness were over about 20 years ago, has also revived. It was taken over by Mikolaj Grabowski, an established director who has also relied on younger talents. Yet, during the first two successful seasons, Grabowski's own productions have also met with a very favourable reception: *Prorok Ilja* (*The Prophet Elias*) by Slobodzianek, one of the most interesting contemporary dramatists in Poland (November 1999) and *King Lear*, pronounced the best Shakespeare production of the 2000/2001 season (October 2000).

Finally, the third theatre which received wide acclaim after years of stagnation was Teatr Polski in Poznan. And again, it owed its revival to young directors, Pawel Wodzinski and Pawel Lysak, who have taken over the management of the theatre. Both keep trying to transplant to the Polish theatre the current fashion in the Western drama, the so-called 'new brutalists'. Earlier, they staged plays by Mark Ravenhill and Sarah Kane, then they introduced plays by Theresia Walser (*King Kongs Töchter*) (November 2000) and Lars Norén (*Personkrets 3:1*) (March 2001). Their radical view of the theatre gave rise to fierce discussions in Poznan and brought attacks from the conservative circles of local authorities. So far, the directors have not backed down. In collaboration with Teatr Rozmaitosci and Teatr Wspolczesny from Wroclaw, they mounted (January 2002) the première of *Cleansed* by Sarah Kane, directed by Krzysztof Warlikowski.

The Helena Modrzejewska Theatre in Legnica has stood out in a remote region, far from the major theatre centres. Its manager and director Jacek Glomb and his team belong, again, to the younger generation. They have managed to infuse life into an area almost doomed to provincialism (after the war, a Soviet garrison was stationed in the town). Glomb adopted a programme, according to which the theatre should come out and welcome people instead of waiting for a handful of spectators. Therefore, many performances are staged outside the theatre building: in old factory plants, in the open air or closed down cinemas, like, for example *Ballada o Zakaczawiu* (*The Ballad of Zakaczawie*, October 2000) which was a hit of the last season. It presents a story of a Legnica district stricken with poverty. In Polish theatre, it is a rare example of a theatre project in a real, down-to-earth setting, which has not lost, however, its universal implications. The theatre's presence at the Edinburgh Fringe festival (with an energetic, pageant production of *Coriolanus*) may be treated as a sign of recognition.

The last two seasons brought a new life to the Polish drama. To a great extent, this was due to efforts of an author hiding behind the pseudonym Ingmar Villqist. He is a 41 year old art historian who made his debut at the end of the 90s as the founder of his own theatre Kriket with its base at Krolewska Huta (Chorzow). For a long time, no native dramatist could boast of such a success in the Polish theatre. The number of productions of his plays in the 2000/2001 season equals the productions of plays by the modern master, Slawomir Mrozek. What is the reason for the unprecedented success of his plays? Perhaps it's because they seem so ... foreign. The author himself does not deny the inspiration of great Scandinavian artists, on the one hand (Ibsen, Strindberg, Bergman) and German expressionism, on the other. He has given our stage directors and actors something they dreamed of after years of fulfilling national duties: characters with personal problems. At the same time, the dramatist has not subjected his heroes to any kind of grotesque or absurd distortions, nor has he used them to create any intellectual constructions. Nothing in his work would suggest that Villqist might come from the country of Witkacy, Gombrowicz, Rozewicz and Mrozek. His dramatic method may be observed in the cycle *Beztlenowce* which includes small scale sketches of psychological character. Its heroes hide secrets from their past – all kind of traumas. Yet these experiences (such as sexual abuse in childhood) have been perfectly universalised. The author is also fond of analysing complex psychological relationships (two homosexuals raising a child in the titular one-act play *Beztlenowce*, a married couple suffering an imaginary parenthood in *Fantom*). *Noc Helvera* (*Helver's Night*), Villqist's most popular play, tells the story of a relationship between a woman and her mentally handicapped adopted son. History, in the shape of nascent fascism, brutally intrudes into their lives. Yet the real historical experience is only a symbol of our oppression of vulnerable poor people. Villqist's success came from the fact that he gave the actors what they like best and what they rarely get from other dramatists: material for acting. The dramatist skilfully builds dialogues and the language does not jar on our ears. Villqist follows the method that usually ensures success: he conceals crucial problems of the *dramatis personae* behind trivial, seemingly unrelated utterances, understatements, meaningful pauses. He sketches situations with ease; a few strokes are enough to create a character and his/her issue. Details are filled in by the actors. Villqist's plays are usually taken up by younger directors and sometimes by the author himself. Critics keep arguing about particular performances and mainly about the real value of his art. Maybe his success will break through the theatre's traditional mistrust of new authors. After all, today the Polish theatre does not lack interesting personalities among directors and actors (if only actors devoted more attention to perfecting their acting instead of chasing after money in film, TV and advertising). Neither does it lack the audience. What it lacks are contemporary plays that try to answer the question who we are, at the turn of the century.

Wojciech Majcherek *is a theatre critic and essayist for the Warsaw-based monthly journal* Teatr.

PORTUGAL

MARIA HELENA SERÔDIO

By the beginning of 2000 there were major signs in Portugal of an imminent crisis in both the political and the cultural spheres. It was the beginning of a second term for the Socialist Party's programme, intended to implement a kind of a modest Welfare State, but the many contradictions arising out of different strategies – even within the party itself – made it difficult to form a clear policy. An ambiguous policy could hardly survive some hard facts it had to face: tough rules prescribed by the European Community, a decline in economic growth (factories closing and fields left untilled, with claims in both cases that the cost of production would be too high), low productivity, an inefficient managerial class, a tax policy favouring fiscal evasion for the big enterprises and penalising workers. The difficult financial situation brought the inevitable social disquiet, and the cultural realm was bound to be affected.

The Minister for Culture was the first to react, by resigning in May 2000, hinting at a shortage of financial support. This jeopardised some expectations, left theatre practitioners at a loss, and brought about the immediate resignation of the Director of the National Theatre in Porto (Teatro Nacional de S. João), Ricardo Pais. The incoming Minister faced a delicate situation: Porto as European Capital of Culture 2001 was a difficult case, its subsidies having been decided by a jury that the present Minister apparently did not ratify. All the theatre groups who felt mistreated by the former Minister rapidly sought new criteria for their subsidies, paralysing the whole process. It brought chaos to the beginning of the season of 2000–2001. It also showed how fragile the system is, at the same time revealing the discontent and rivalry between different companies: regions against big cities, alternative theatre against more established groups, personal grudges before seriously based cultural choices.

About half way through its term, the Government resigned. New elections hoisted a right wing coalition into power, with a new programme: cuts everywhere (especially in health, education and culture); the idea that the State was in a calamitous financial condition that would not allow the new Government to take any step towards a proper solution (including new taxes); a low profile for the Ministry of Culture, which made culture look somewhat irrelevant. The situation for culture in general, and for theatre in particular, is not comfortable. Those who are trying to keep theatre alive in Portugal are certainly going to experience difficulties not only now, but in the future.

The case of the National Theatre in Lisbon (Teatro Nacional D. Maria II) is a good example. In September 2000 its retiring director, Carlos Avilez, directed *The Royal Hunt of the Sun*, (with a rich design concept, but overall lacking in energy), as a farewell to the theatre he had presided over for several years. It was then closed for many months, while the Ministry tried to cancel the contracts of most of its permanent staff. Nothing was staged during that period. Several personalities were invited to be the new director (none accepted), and no specific policy was defined. Its present director, João Grosso, a relatively young actor, is trying hard to recover some normality, but a large institution is difficult to reanimate: audiences tend to lose the habit of going. Not surprisingly, it lacks a firm idea of what a National Theatre should be, especially in regard to Portuguese drama, classical and contemporary.

The unstable situation of the National Theatre in Lisbon may have been one of the reasons why no play by Gil Vicente was running there in June 2002, when we celebrated the 500th anniversary of the very beginning of the Portuguese theatre. Indeed, the celebrated author of the *Boat Plays* (*Glory, Purgatory, Hell*), wrote and played in his first court play – the first play ever written in Portugal – *Auto da visitação* (*Visit*) in June 1502, to celebrate the birth of the future King John III.

However the Centre for Theatre Research, at the University of Lisbon, did commemorate the event: it staged a major congress, which gathered scholars and researchers from all over the world, and issued his *Complete Works* (*Vicente: Todas as obras*) on CD-ROM and in print. Several theatre companies did stage his work: A Barraca, under the direction of Maria do Céu Guerra, produced *Comédia de Rubena* (*Comedy of Rubena*), and in Évora, CENDREV chose *Romagem dos Agravados* (*Pilgrimage of the Aggrieved*), directed by Mário Barradas, who staged it in a palace, with the audience on both sides of a long platform where the actors exposed their grievances. Other Vicente productions, sometimes collages, were done by groups in the regions, among them Teatro de Portalegre, Trigo Limpo, Teatro das Beiras, Filandorra.

Anticipating the event, Cornucópia in 2000 staged a most stimulating amalgam of two of Vicente's plays: *Frágoa de amores* (*Forge of Love*) and *Floresta de enganos* (*Forest of Errors*) in the performance *Amores Enganos* (*Love's Errors*). With a magnificent set by Cristina Reis (following her ideas of space, construction from fragments, and strong colour) and imaginative direction by Luís Miguel Cintra, the performance featured splendid acting. It also showed how Vicente can trigger the contemporary imagination.

Going against the grain of the idea that the Portuguese are more prone to writing poetry than drama, we have seen interesting initiatives to attract young people to playwriting, including DRAMAT (formerly directed by Fernando Mora Ramos and now by Maria João Vicente), a structure linked to the National Theatre in Porto.

Not a new writer but still young, Abel Neves deserves attention for his recent work, *Além as estrelas são a nossa casa* (*Up There the Stars Are Our Home*), which has been staged in these three latest seasons by a number of groups. Its attraction lies in the fact that it is written as a sequence of short scenes, each with no more than three characters, which can be reconstructed by any director choosing from them and making it differently meaningful. A performance can turn out to be funny, dreamlike, frightful or nostalgic, but it will definitely be a very efficient and contemporary fictional world.

Among other new plays in performance, four interesting examples confirm that a contemporary Portuguese repertoire exists and can provoke stimulating productions. Novelist and playwright Mário de Carvalho wrote an amusing collection of short plays, *A vida tem destas coisas* (*Life's Like That*), which José Peixoto directed for the Teatro dos Aloés in 2001. Another example of good comedy based on close observation of human frailties is Teresa Rita Lopes's recent *Esse tal alguém* (*That So *and So)*, a sequence of hilarious monologues by a Woman and a Man (intersected by a chorus), which Rogério de Carvalho directed for Teatro de Almada in 2001. The play deservedly won a major award (from the Portuguese Writers' Association) in 2001, while in 2000 that award went to another play by a woman – Maria Velho da Costa – author of intelligent, aesthetically tantalizing novels. Responding to an invitation addressed by director Ricardo Pais who wanted a vehicle for two well known actresses, da Costa imagined a possible meeting of the heroines of two late nineteenth century novels: *Os Maias*, by Eça de Queirós, and *Dom Casmurro*, by Machado de Assis. *Madame* (2000), is intelligent and well-written for a début play, not only capturing the breadth and size of the two characters, but also adding engaging life and dialogue to their meeting in Paris as older 'women with a past'. Pais' production for the National Theatre in Porto pushed this play slightly towards a kind of rich *divertissement*, with what could have been two drag queens.

A fourth case is Jaime Rocha, a former journalist, who has recently turned to playwriting. His *Casa de pássaros* (*House of Birds*) combined a Tennessee Williams view of character with Hitchcockian suspense. Directed by Carlos Avilez for the Teatro Experimental de Cascais, the play depicted an intriguing relationship between an elderly lady and her maid (who had become mute), living in and through a symbolic relationship with birds. The lady is visited by her daughter and her boyfriend; what triggers the main action is the irresistible attraction the lady feels towards this man, in whom she sees a lover she had refused in her youth.

Other more established Portuguese authors have also been staged, and Jaime Salazar Sampaio, Augusto Sobral and Luiz Francisco Rebello saw their *Complete Works* published. The latter saw an arresting staging of his play *Páginas arrancadas* (*Torn Pages*) by Comuna, under the direction of João Mota, who also played the leading role of a present day politician, disturbed not only by the memory of his betrayal of left wing fellow students, but also by the revelation of his long concealed homosexuality.

But in evoking our near past – the Salazar regime – it was *O magnífico reitor* (*His Excellency the Dean*), by Freitas do Amaral, which caught the attention of the media. Though not *ad hominem*, it certainly alluded to Marcello Caetano, who was Dean of the University of Lisbon at the time of a student demonstration in 1962. He handled the situation with some skill (not specially cherished by the political police or the regime itself), but when he stepped into Cabinet as Minister for Education (and potential successor to Salazar) he was much less tolerant. The play has its faults, as might be expected in a first play, but received a very polemical production at the Teatro da Trindade (in 2001), directed by Fraga, which attracted a large audience. It included music by important composers and singers of the time, as well as videos – showing daily life, the student riots, the beginnings of the colonial war in Africa – which caught some nostalgia. The author is a well known politician, in a way a disciple of Marcelo Caetano. Criticised by his fellow right wing politicians for revising history, and by the left for simplifying and distorting the facts, Freitas do Amaral brought theatre to the front pages for some days.

Another political statement was *O navio dos negros* (*The Negroes' Boat*), by Jorge Silva Melo, based on Herman Melville's *Benito Cereno*. It demonstrated three major features of Melo's playwriting: the importance accorded to words and narrative (he retained Melville's long descriptions, as a kind of litany), the idea of choral intervention (two groups of black sailors), as well as a more direct reference to present politics in the form of an added insert on the new 'slavery' in Portugal, involving not only Africans, but also people from Eastern Europe. Perhaps the staging at Culturgest (in 2000) did not meet the expectations aroused by the text, but it showed that its author-actor-director is highly talented, with firm ideas about directing his company, Artistas Unidos.

One of Melo's new ideas, since Artistas Unidos has taken over a derelict former newspaper building in Bairro Alto, is to build a repertoire theatre, staging short contemporary plays in small scale productions, with a couple of premieres every month in the different studios of the building, running for overlapping periods. He likes to present mini-seasons: several plays by Sarah Kane, a few incursions into Dutch theatre, some contemporary Scots playwrights (including David Harrower's *Knives in Hens,* a work done by Paulo Claro, Joana Bárcia and Américo Silva, assisted by Jorge Silva Melo, in 2000), and a very interesting Irish play by Mark O' Rowe, *Howie the Rookie,* imaginatively translated by Fracisco Luís Parreira into *Agá o Piolho,* also in 2000. Further, he has encouraged young writers to translate plays (which are then published in Artistas Unidos' journal), and actors to direct; he has invited choreographers to stage canonical plays (João Fiadeiro directed *Waiting for Godot* in 2000, and Madalena Victorino *Happy Days* in 2001). In 2002 the company staged a major Harold Pinter season, on their own and in co-production, including *The Dumb Waiter, Betrayal, Old Times, Ashes to Ashes* (with a company from Porto, Assédio) and *One for the Road* (with a superb performance by Melo himself).

Another group that tries to keep its productions in repertory is O Bando, but in a very different way. Indeed, since they moved to the outskirts of Lisbon they have tried to maintain their own kind of visual, handcrafted performances, but are more keen on presenting them in the open air. Directed by João Brites, both *Merlin,* by Tankred Dorst, in 2000, and *Alma Grande (Great Soul)* by Miguel Torga, in 2002, were visually arresting open air performances, delighting their faithful audience. At the same time, they tour brief scenes built around characters from previous shows, since it is Brites's speciality to turn them into vivid symbols.

In a very different approach to repertory, Cornucópia, under the direction of Luís Miguel Cintra, visited the classics in a consistent, deep and imaginative way: in 2000, they did a splendid creation out of Shakespeare's *Cymbeline,* directed by Cintra with set design by Cristina Reis, and later dedicated a season to German romanticism: *A morte de Empédocles (Empedocles's Death),* by Hölderlin, *O novo Menoza ou História do Príncipe Tandi de Cumba (New Menoza, or the Story of Prince Tandi of Cumba),* by Jakob Lenz, and *Dom João e Fausto (Don Juan and Faustus),* by Christian Dietrich Grabbe, all in 2001. Both Hölderlin's play (directed by Cintra) and Grabbe's text (directed by Christine Laurent) included music, the former having a musician (Nuno Vieira de Almeida) playing sonatas by Schubert, the latter interspersed with brief moments of song.

Luís Miguel Cintra has staged some operas and shows a delicate sensitivity to rhythm and music in many of his productions. Recently, in 2000, he directed *The English Cat,* by Hans Werner Henze (libretto by Edward Bond) in a co-production by Cornucópia with our own San Carlos opera house and other institutions. In 2002 he staged a beautiful *História do soldado (Soldier's Tale)* by Ramuz and Stravinsky, with a chamber orchestra directed by João Paulo Santos. His production kept the piece's fairy tale atmosphere, in a funny but well choreographed and acted performance.

A new Lisbon venue also opened with theatre and music: the Teatro Aberto (Open Theatre). Directed by João Lourenço, the company behind this new construction, Novo Grupo (New Group), decided to put on *Peer Gynt*, with new music by Eurico Carrapatoso, played by an orchestra of 27 musicians, again conducted by João Paulo Santos. With excellent acting by young João Pedro Vaz and Irene Cruz, among others, it paid excellent homage to Ibsen's masterpiece. It is interesting to remember that in 1976, this same director was responsible for the opening of another venue, also called Teatro Aberto, and now due to be pulled down. For that occasion he directed Brecht's *The Caucasian Chalk Circle*. *Peer Gynt* is perhaps as appropriate now, in catching the spirit of a historical moment, as Brecht was then.

It is mainly on these and similar independent subsidized groups that theatre life in Portugal is based. They are the real backbone of our theatre system. In 2001, around 50 different groups were allocated a long-term subsidy, decided by a mixed jury of independent members and a representative of the Institute for the Performance Arts, a branch of the Ministry of Culture. Other more occasional productions also receive a subsidy but on an annual basis (there were about 30 in 2001).

Municipalities also support some of these companies, especially those in the regions. Such is the case with the Teatro de Almada (directed by Joaquim Benite), which besides staging its own productions holds a very important festival in June. It has been growing in importance, spreading across the Tagus into Lisbon in joint ventures with large halls like the Cultural Centre in Belém, Culturgest and Teatro da Trindade.

Many other groups in the regions stage festivals, as a good pretext to enlarge audiences and involve the city where they are based. Seiva Trupe in Porto holds the oldest and most important one, FITEI, featuring productions from the Iberian countries (including Spain and the former Portuguese provinces in Africa, Central and South America). In the framework of Porto as Capital of Culture in 2001, the Festival PoNTI (International Festival of Porto at Christmas), staged every two years by the National Theatre of S. João, went one step further in hosting major international companies, as well as co-producing with many of the city's own theatre groups.

Among the other companies set in the northern capital, Assédio did an interesting *Faith Healer* (*O fantástico Francis Hardy, curandeiro*), by Brian Friel, in 2000, directed by Nuno Carinhas; Teatro de Marionetas do Porto invented a fabulous *Macbeth* for puppets (designed and directed by João Paulo Seara Cardoso), and As Boas Raparigas... (The Good Girls Go to Heaven, The Bad Ones Where They Please) produced two most engaging performances: *Vanya*, by Howard Barker, in 2000, and *Uriel Acosta*, in 2001. These two works by director Rogério de Carvalho, continuing a long and successful career, were the main reason for him to be awarded the most important prize of the Ministry of Culture (the Prémio Almada) in 2001.

The year before, the award was given to Luís Miguel Cintra (for his excellent work as actor, director and co-translator of *Cymbeline*), whereas the newcomer's prize was awarded jointly to João Pedro Vaz, for his direction of Martin Crimp's play *Attempts on Her Life ((A)tentados)* for Assédio, in 2000, and Armando Nascimento Rosa, for his play *Lianor no país sem pilhas* (*Lianor in the Land Without Batteries*) which João Mota directed most charmingly for his company Comuna in 2000.

Other small productions proved that there is plenty of talent and imagination not yet recognized by the authorities: *Agamemnon or the Crime* (a work based on Marguerite Yourcenar's *Clytemenestra or the Crime*), was well directed by Antonino Solmer and beautifully acted by Fernanda Lapa and António Rana, in production by Lapa's company Escola de Mulheres (School for Women) in a derelict house in downtown Lisbon (the former kitchen of the Palace Marim Olhão). Under the direction of Pedro Penim, the theatre Praga staged a very creative *Madame de Sade* by Yukio Mishima, with costumes and music from the 70s; and Teatro Meridional continued its delicate and expert work on both the poetical world of Mia Couto (*Mar me quer*) in 2001 (directed by Miguel Seabra and Natália Luiza) and *Delírios dell'arte*, in *commedia dell'arte* style, also directed by Miguel Seabra, based on a text by Mário Botequilha.

Two actresses on the fringe have been mapping out very personal territory, both in choice of venue and in acting and directing style: Mónica Calle staged Fassbinder's *As lágrimas amargas de Petra von Kant* (*The Bitter Tears of Petra von Kant*) in her tiny Casa Conveniente in Cais do Sodré (renowned for its bars, clubs and prostitution), and Lúcia Sigalho took her company Sensurround to Armazém do Ferro (Iron Warehouse) to do a provocative *Birra da viva* (*Living Woman's Tiff*) by Adília Lopes.

I would single out two other performances as pointing to very different ways of doing theatre. One is the only musical of reasonable quality that was a real box office success: *Amália,* staged and produced by Filipe La Féria. Intended as a biography of our great *fado* singer Amália Rodrigues (who died recently), it is based on a very simple dramaturgy – its main weakness – but succeeds in staging her voice with three different singers, representing the three ages of Amália: little girl, young woman and mature woman. The choice of songs is perfect, the atmosphere beautifully created by voices, sometimes showing the different styles, sometimes displaying rivalries between the singers. This was a final triumph for a director from the subsidised theatre who has been trying for ten years to stage a commercial success.

CENDREV in Évora did the other performance I would like to mention. Based on Brecht's play *A venda do pão* (*Brotladen*), it was directed by Pierre-Etienne Heymann in a translation by Marc-Vincent Howlett. It involved the whole company, including its acting school. It was an excellent performance, not only because of its imaginative dramaturgy and lively direction, but also because it created an incredible energy from the presence of so many actors – and musicians – on stage.

The first of these shows aimed at creating an audience, the second was more concerned with preparing actors in the great canvas of human activity. Both are important, but it is the second which paves the way to a more meaningful future.

Maria Helena Serôdio *is a Professor at the University of Lisbon (English Literature and Theatre Studies), a theatre critic contributing to various periodicals; she is also Director of the Centre for Theatre Studies (University of Lisbon) and author of three books:* Leituras do texto dramático *(Horizonte, 1989),* William Shakespeare: A seduão dos sentidos *(Cosmos, 1996), and* Questionar apaixonadamente: o teatro na vida de Luís Miguel Cintra *(Cotovia, 2001).*

ROMANIA

ALICE GEORGESCU

In the past three years, Romanian theatre has faithfully reflected the dynamics of present day Romanian society. It is a society which is still unstable, floating aimlessly on the waters of an insecure present, between the temptations (and also the tentacles) of a past from which it cannot be separated, and the rigours of a future to which it is being forced to adapt.

Successive attempts to introduce institutional reform were hindered by an unexpectedly powerful inertia, which led to delays in the necessary transformations or – even worse – to distortions capable of inspiring a fear of change. For example, a welcome initiative, aimed at the decentralisation of finance for the cultural institutions, turned out to be a dangerous trap in which many theatre managers were caught, as well as, unfortunately, the theatres themselves. We are talking about a Government decision which envisaged switching control of the performing arts institutions – except, originally, the national theatres and opera houses – from the Ministry of Culture (which became, after the 2000 elections and the subsequent changes, the Ministry of Culture, Religion and Heritage) to the local power structures (county or municipal councils). In theory, this decision was meant to encourage a more direct involvement of these local structures in the upkeep of institutions of spiritual value to the population of a defined geographical and cultural area – and also to free the above mentioned ministry from a pretty heavy budgetary burden at a time when Romania remained, sadly, one of the few European countries which allocated a trifling amount of its GDP (less than one per cent) to culture.

In practice, this measure turned out to be an opportunity to stir up various local quarrels, some theatre managers having to pay with their job for the thirst for revenge of narrow-minded bureaucrats or envious colleagues. The most recent victims include the manager of the Youth Theatre in Piatra Neamtz (the scene of a very interesting international festival, which ceased to exist as a result) and also the manager of the Lucia Sturza Bulandra Theatre in Bucharest (a theatre which, after a period of probing and re-evaluation, finally regained its best shape, as proven by an excellent show, Chekhov's *Uncle Vanya*, directed by the guest Russian director Yuri Kordonsky (May 2001).

On the other hand, it is true that the above mentioned administrative measure proved useful to those communities which wanted to establish professional theatres inside their territory, either completely new ones or those created by the institutionalisation of amateur troupes; that is what happened to the theatres in Focsani, Tulcea and Targoviste in the period under review.

During the last season (2001–2002), three of the six National theatres, namely those from Craiova, Timisoara and Targu-Mures, underwent the same decentralisation. They were chosen for this experiment on the strange criterion of

ABOVE: B. Angi Gabriella and Palffy Tibor in *Kasimir und Karoline* by Ödön von Horváth, at the 'Tamasi Aron' Theatre, Sfantu Gheorghe   (*photo*: Barabas Zsolt)

BELOW: *Die Kanibalen* by George Tabori, 'Radu Stanca' Theatre, Sibiu

historical importance; the National theatres which remained attached to the Ministry of Culture and to its budget, namely those in Bucharest, Cluj and Iasi, being considered to represent provinces of greater 'historical significance' than the ones where the first three are located.

These decisions – perceived by the theatrical community as random and arbitrary, considering the administrative consequences they produced – were the reason for a pretty strong movement in favour of a law of theatres (similar to the one in force in inter-war Romania), seen as an unique chance to regulate relations between theatres and authorities on the one side, and between theatre professionals, in case of potential work conflicts, on another.

The explosive situation which took place at the Nottara Theatre in Bucharest, during the 1999–2000 season, when the company refused to work under a manager considered corrupt and abusive, a situation which was both legally insoluble and morally damaging – to the prestige of the profession as much as to the public interest – seems to confirm the necessity of such particular regulations.

At the same time, such a law would prove unworkable at a time when broader legal measures are still in force in Romania, such as the labour act (Codul Muncii), which contains provisions from the communist era. A number of projects to initiate this much-needed law of theatre are still in circulation in the profession; but, for the time being, they mainly refer to salary levels for theatre staff (attempting especially to reduce the huge gap between the incomes of directors and designers, who generally work on a contract, and those of actors, of whom the overwhelming majority are still paid by loss-making subsidised companies, the state and municipal theatres) and to means of changing the repertory theatres (which means almost all Romanian theatres) into project-based theatres or receiving houses.

So how does the present theatrical scene appear, under these circumstances of legal and to some extent social chaos?

The first obvious assertion would be that, during the three years considered here, the 'average' show has come to represent the norm, where five or six years ago the analysts were bewailing the absence of these particular shows, productions which could give the theatrical season a buffer of respectability between the stand-out hit shows and the absolute flops. The overwhelming majority of the fare in Romanian theatres now consists of decent shows, of an acceptable level in terms of directing, design and acting. Normally, there are no huge failures; but nor are there the exceptional or revolutionary masterpieces likely to beget tendencies or counter-tendencies, imitations or derivatives, capable of inspiring blind admiration or strong controversy; in short, productions which are able to promote the theatre both as an art and as a social and cultural phenomenon.

I think the motives for this state of affairs may be identified in the fact that, for various reasons, many of the really important, inspired directors of the mature generation have stopped working or are wasting their time with minor works of no significance for their artistic career. Also, we should consider the fact that the young directors (products of a school which is in need of serious reform in its methods and objectives) have developed inside a value system that is inherently insecure and lacking in professional role-models.

Vlad Mugur was, in past years, such a role model. Despite his old age, he was the creator of an important number of remarkable shows, characterised by imagination and fantasy and most of all by refinement and elegance. Though seriously ill, he still managed to stage no less than five shows during the years in question, including *Right You Are (If You Think You Are)(Cosi e (se vi pare))* by Luigi Pirandello (the National Theatre in Craiova, October 1999 and the State Hungarian Theatre in Cluj, September 2000), *The Venetian Twins* (*I due gemelli*) and *The Gossips' Carnival* (*I petegolezzi delle donne*) (Nottara Theatre, Bucharest, February 2000 and the National Theatre in Craiova, October 2000); and also a strange, rough, testamentary *Hamlet* (the National Theatre in Cluj, June 2001). Liviu Ciulei, an almost legendary figure in the Romanian theatre and also author of a manifesto regarding the 'retheatralisation of theatre' during the 50s (therefore right at the peak of the socialist realist period) came back to work in Bucharest for a short time; his *Hamlet* (Bulandra, June 2000), however, disappointed the young audience because of its unexpectedly classical vision.

No imposing names, able to create new tendencies or trends, have sprung, unfortunately, from among the new generation; one might at least mention László Bocsárdi for his original and strong conception, as well as for the attempt to create a new style of acting with his troupe in the Tamási Áron theatre in Sfantu-Gheorghe (*Blood Wedding*, by F. Garcia Lorca, June 2000; *Kasimir and Karoline*, by Ödön von Horváth, June 2001) and also the very young Radu Apostol, author of a socio-theatrical experiment in which he used homeless children as actors (*At Home*, by the Russian playwright Ludmila Razumovskaia, at the Ion Creanga theatre, Bucharest, June 2001).

The Romanian theatre, once accustomed to genuine creative interplay between directors of various ages and artistic orientations, seems to have taken a revitalising break lately; against this 'restful' background, controversial, modern and provocative shows are a rare phenomenon. In this context, considering the three theatrical seasons, we should first mention the Ukrainian director, Andrej Zholdak, who staged versions of *The Idiot* by Dostoievski (January 2001) and *Othello?!* by Shakespeare (March 2002) at the Radu Stanca Theatre in Sibiu (a town which hosts a very important international festival, modelling itself on the Avignon Festival). These shows expose a violently counter-traditionalist and innovative vision regarding not only the written text but also the stage performance in general, a delirious fantasy (yet rigorously supervised) and also an intensive exploitation of the actor and all the aspects of his creativity (these are only a few characteristics of this 'theatre of risk', described by the critic Georges Banu). Second would be the director Alexander Hausvater, advocate of a sensual but equally intellectual theatre, whose shows – among which I quote *The Cherry Orchard*, by Chekhov (National Theatre, Iasi, October 2000) and *The Cannibals*, by George Tabori (Radu Stanca Theatre, Sibiu, January 2002) – proved shocking because of the unexpected harshness of their stage performance. Finally we should talk about the demystifying (and in some ways highly debatable) approach proposed by Alexandru Tocilescu to a classical, fundamental text in the Romanian drama: *A Lost Letter* (*O scrisoare pierduta*), by Ion Luca Caragiale (National Theatre, Bucharest, September 1999). We should also take into consideration young Radu Afrim, who after a few questionable attempts at experiment for its own sake showed the fruits of a rich and purposeful creativity in *Ocean Café* (based on texts by young Romanian writers), at the Youth Theatre in Piatra Neamtz, December 2000, and *Seaweed: Bernarda's House Remix* (after Lorca) at the Andrei Muresanu Theatre, Sfantu-Gheorghe, February 2002. We could also mention the show *Pilafs and Donkey Scent*, based on a story from *1001 Nights*, part of a vast international project which director Silviu Purcarete inaugurated at the Radu Stanca theatre in Sibiu in May 2001.

This brief resume of the Romanian theatre in the last three seasons should be rounded off by noting the more noticeable (yet still far from satisfactory) presence of national plays in the repertory, a more substantial and informed audience for modern world drama, as well as the growing importance of dance theatre and modern dance. Our picture would not be complete without mentioning the important number of stagings (alas, rarely successful) of plays by Ion Luca Caragiale (1852–1912), the greatest Romanian playwright, produced or in course of production in 2002, decreed by the Romanian government as 'The Caragiale Year' (an anniversary supported by UNESCO). There could also be enumerated the large number of projects and programmes initiated and carried out by the Theatre Union in Romania (UNITER), as well as an important number of national and international festivals (most important of which is the one that takes place every fall in Bucharest, entitled simply The National Theatre Festival), events which create an image of a theatrical life that is vital and effervescent. Which is why it may seem bizarre, with this background, that the main wish of Romanian artistes should be for a theatrical life that is nothing more than normal ...

Alice Georgescu is a drama critic, editor of the theatre page in Ziarul de Duminica, *the weekly cultural supplement of the daily* Ziarul Financiar. *In 2001, she won the critics' prize of UNITER, for the second time.*

RUSSIA

VALERY KHASANOV

2001 was marked by two events, different in character but equal in importance. First, the Theatre Workers' Union of the Russian Federation held its national congress. This association, which brings together interested parties from all over Russia, plays a major part in the country's theatre life. Their congress took place on 22nd and 23rd October. The delegates discussed the running of their organisation in the perturbed social circumstances which have arisen from the radical changes presented by the market economy. The last decade has been an extremely difficult one. Theatres have had to contend with the ever-increasing necessity to adapt to an existence in which competition and commercial success have become determining factors. Alexander Kaliagin was re-elected as Chairman of the Union.

In the second, Moscow hosted the third Theatre Olympics, following Greece and Japan. This was an exceptional worldwide event. This great world theatre festival, organized by the International Confederation of Theatre Associations and the International Chekhov Theatre Festival opened in April and continued until the end of June. The great metropolitan city experienced vivid emotions.

The celebration overflowed from the theatres to the streets and quays of Moscow. The opening ceremony in front of the Bolshoi Theatre carried on next door, at the Maly Theatre, with a production of *Arlecchino* as directed by Giorgio Strehler, in commemoration of one of the great masters of the past century. One show followed another: every night the theatres of Moscow were packed and their audiences deeply moved. The Olympics produced a unique musical spectacle, *Polyphony of the World*, with a hundred people taking part, including maestro Gidon Kremer and his string ensemble 'Kremerata Baltica' and musicians, actors, dancers and folk artists from several countries across the world. The production was staged by the director Kama Ginkas and stage-designer Serguei Barkhin with original music by Alexander Bakchi, and production by Valery Khasanov. For a whole month long, audiences were able to see the *Zingaro* equestrian show from Paris, a discovery for the Russian public. In order to host this show, the organizers built a new stage with the necessary infrastructure to welcome audiences, in the Kolomenskoie park.

The programme of the Olympics included several sections – Great World Theatre (with Peter Stein, Luca Ronconi, Tadashi Suzuki, Yuri Liubimov and other great masters of contemporary theatre), Experimental Theatre and Theatre Workshops, an International Festival of Drama Schools, and a Street Theatre programme, directed by Viatcheslav Polunin.

The Olympics have of course influenced Moscow's theatrical life. The 5th International Monodrama Festival was postponed to 2002 (when it will take place from 4-11 October). The International Dance Theatre Festival, traditionally

RUSSIA

organized by the National Lyric Theatre of Stanislavski and Nemirovitch-Danchenko, with the help of the British Council and the Centre Culturel Français, took place in autumn. Its programme did not provoke the same enthusiasm as previously. The productions proposed by the participating countries were not exceptional discoveries for Moscow's audience, for two reasons: Moscow is more and more 'spoilt' by the quality of touring performances; and higher quality costs too much for the organizers of this particular project. All the available budget had been swallowed up by the Olympics.

The traditional festival of Russian theatre in small towns was organised in 2001 in Moscow by the Theatre of Nations, the very first festival of the new century. Theatres from the little cities presented mostly classical plays, among them *Vassa Yeleznova* by Gorki (Omnibus theatre, city of Zlatoust, staged by B. Gorbatchevski), the *Cherry Orchard* by Chekhov (Pushkin drama theatre from Magnetogorsk, staged by V. Akhadov), *Blood Wedding* by Lorca (Cossack drama theatre from Novocherkassk, staged by L. Chatokhin). The presence of a theatre in small Russian towns is very important, because cultural life is concentrated around it.

The Baltic House Festival in St Petersburg was an important event outside Moscow. There were plenty of different styles to please everyone. Selection often depend on what entries are offered. In a difficult economic situation like Russia's in the matter of theatre finance, the organisers' attitude, that they will accept anything that enables the Festival to take place, is understandable. St Petersburg must have an International Festival, and this is the Baltic city's very own.

During the 2001–2002 season, Russia and Turkey collaborated on a contemporary dramatic art festival organised by the Theatre of Nations in Moscow and the National Theatres of Turkey. Several Turkish plays were translated and staged in a number of Russian cities including Moscow, Samara, Yaroslavl, Oufa, and Ryazan.

What is positive about Russian theatre is that it has regained its former cultural and social role. Performances are sold out, and theatre companies are staging all manner of different genres.

A new style of theatre, growing in popularity in Moscow, is copies of Broadway musicals. After the hit *Metro* comes *North-West*, inspired by Alexander Kaverin's novel *Two Captains* (music, book and direction by A. Ivachtchenko and G. Vassiliev) which has played every day for months.

The established theatres are adapting to the new conditions. Small-scale productions with two, three and more actors are attracting the public instead of big productions like before. One of them is *Laughter School* written by the Japanese author Koki Mitani and staged by Roman Kozak (promoted to artistic director of the Pushkin drama theatre). Two actors play a comedy on a small stage. Their acting represents a remarkable synthesis of psychological theatre and Brechtian alienation, with a precision of movement that adds an extraordinary dimension of absurdity to the play's realism.

Following *Cyrano de Bergerac*, staged by Vladimir Mirzoev at the Vakhtangov Theatre, Pavel Khomsky presented his own *Bergerac* at the Mossoviet. Andrei Jitinkin, now leader of the Malaya Bronnaya Theatre, presented the first staging of Frank Wedekind's *Lulu*. The acclaimed show *No. 13* by R. Kouni

Maxim Sukhanov in *Cyrano de Bergerac*, staged by Vladimir Mirzoev at the Vakhtangov Theatre

was staged by V. Machkov at the Art Theatre. This theatre has also presented two new dramas, *The Sacred Flame* by S. Moham, directed by S. Vragova, and *Molière* (*Kabala Sviatosh*), from Bulgakov, staged by Adolf Shapiro with Oleg Tabakov playing the title role. The Taganka Theatre, which can count on a faithful public, staged for the first time *Zhivago*, inspired by Boris Pasternak's novel and directed by Yuri Liubimov, presented in memory of A. Schnitke. Liubimov also staged *Socrates/Oracle* for the first time, in July 2001, in Athens.

Yugo-Zapad Theatre (South-West), which this year celebrates its thirtieth anniversary, toured the United States. It presented *Samoubijtsa* (*The Suicide*) by Nikolai Erdman. This company has previously staged Shakespeare (*Midsummer Night's Dream, The Taming of the Shrew, Romeo and Juliet*), and also Goldoni's *La Locandiera*, Brecht/Weill's *Dreigroschenoper*, *The Master and Margarita* and *Molière* from Bulgakov and several works by Chekhov. Yugo-Zapad's artistic director, Valery Beliakovitch, has succeeded in building an interesting repertoire for his theatre.

The Sovremennik Theatre, directed by Galina Voltchek, remodelled *Balalaikin and Co* from the Russian classic by M. Saltykhov-Shchedrin, which was once staged by the Russian master of theatre Georgi Tovstogonov. *Playing Schiller*, based on *Maria Stuart*, staged by the Lithuanian director Rimas Tuminas and acted by Marina Neelova and Elena Yakovleva, two extraordinary actresses, was also acclaimed by the Russian public. This performance was presented in Mannheim (Germany) during the Schiller-Tage. Some other productions from this theatre may be mentioned, such as Erich Maria Remarque's *Three Comrades* and E. Ginzburg's *Krutoi Marcheroute (Tales from the Time of Personality Cult)* both staged by Galina Voltchek. This last performance has been part of the repertoire for several years and still attracts a large audience.

An important number of small theatre companies are at work in Moscow. The Historical and Ethnographical Theatre has as its mission the restoration of traditional Russian theatre from past centuries. Their repertoire includes the music theatre performance *Kazachye Deistvo* (*The Cossack Game*) directed by M. Miziukov. The action, accompanied by Cossack and Orthodox songs, takes place in a Cossack village. A young Cossack couple live out the happy and tragic moments of their life – like Christmas, a wedding, and the departure of young men for the war. In another production, the ritual mystery *The Russian Calendar*, the audience discovers the world of ancient Slavonic ceremonies and celebrations.

The Theatre 'School of Contemporary Drama' directed by Iossif Reikhelgauz, who has already staged Chekhov's *The Seagull*, put on performances by Yevgeni Grishkovets, the acclaimed actor and playwright who debuted recently with his first monodrama. Grishkovets produces an intellectual theatre, apparently very simple but very deep in its content. He created three performances that are now in the repertoire of the theatre, *At the Same Time* (monodrama written, acted and staged by himself), *Notes of a Russian Traveller* (written by Grishkovets and staged by Reikhelgauz with two actors, V. Steklov and V. Botchkarev) and the premiere of *Planet* (written and directed by Grishkovets, performed by himself and A. Doubrovskaya).

Mark Rozovski has recently staged Chekhov's *Cherry Orchard* in his Nikitski Vorot Theatre. Another little theatre, Na Pokrovke, which has Sergei Artsibachev as its artistic director, created *Five Evenings* by Alexander Volodin, a melodrama about the life, dreams and lost illusions of a modern woman, and *In Silence*, from the contemporary author V. Malyagin, both staged by Artsibachev.

In Russia there is always a great number of premières featuring appearances by popular actors. Their quality is not always consistent but they occupy a large part of the market. The Independent Theatre Project produced Carlo Goldoni's *La Locandiera*, staged by Viktor Chamirov, with Russian theatre and movie stars Tatiana Vassilieva and Valery Garkalin. The theatre agency Art-Partner XXI put on Aldo Nicolai's play *The Temptation* with two other stars, Liubov Polichtchuk and Boris Cherbakov. The Vadim Dubovitski production centre presented the Neil Simon comedy *Rumours*, with Olga Volkova, Yefim Chifrin, Yelena Safonova and others.

It is impossible to mention all the theatres and theatre companies which work permanently in Moscow. *The Moscow Playbill* (a magazine which announces theatre programmes) advertises the productions of a hundred theatres but is not exhaustive: there are hundreds more, of many different styles. This article has simply mentioned a number of productions which have been appreciated by the press and the critics.

In St Petersburg, the Tovstogonov Dramatic Theatre always draws attention. The company still works according to the precepts and teaching of their genius master. The theatre has evolved since Tovstogonov but it is still his personality that makes it different from the others. The company still numbers many stars trained by the master. It has a great artistic responsibility, to maintain the same quality it had before. This theatre can be considered like an Academy, because it is the point of reference for performances of the highest quality. It came to Moscow with eight different productions (Racine's *Phèdre,* Anouilh's *Antigone,* Hauptmann's *Before Sunset, Macbeth, Boris Godunov,* but also *California Suite* by Neil Simon, *Long-Legged Lie* by Eduardo de Filippo and *Arcadia* by Tom Stoppard). Three performances were directed by Temour Tchkheidze who is in a sense Tovstonogov's heir. His *Antigone* is rich in poetic metaphors, its conceptualism carefully subordinated to Anouilh's own reading of this classical story. At the same time the director allows his actors their freedom to create complex characters, driven by the same predominant passion. Racine's *Phèdre* staged by G. Ditiatkovski, is an extraordinary performance stripped of any extraneous symbolism. The aesthetic is purely classical – even the translation is one made in the nineteenth century. The total respect for the period, mentality and style of Racine brings to the performance a moving modern characteristic. For classical theatre is eternal, and every age can relate to it. This performance is not about passion. It is the tragedy of a pure feeling, condemned without trial by traditional society because of its conflict with normal standards of relationships – there, no one can ever be free. The company's performances in Moscow are still being discussed. The only certainty is that Theatre, as ever, is an essential part of art and life that deserves its capital letter.

The Vakghtangov Academic Drama Theatre from the Republic of Ossetia-Alania (Vladikavkaz) is one of the oldest in North Caucasia. It celebrated its 130th anniversary in 2001. After the restoration of its stage, the company is now working on it again. Chekhov's *Cherry Orchard*, staged by artistic director

RUSSIA

Yu. Tamerian, was premiered for the reopening of the building. This theatre selects young people who are sent to study at the Chepkin Drama School, attached to Moscow's Maly Theatre.

The Republican Theatre contest 'Tchontorlo Tcharchav' took place on the occasion of International Theatre Day, in the republic of Tchouvachia. Among several nominations, the jury proclaimed *Retro*, by Alexander Galin, best production of the year 2001 (direction: Achot Voskanian).

Theatre Meetings devoted to Anton Chekhov's heritage were organized in May 2001 in Lipetsk. Sergei Artsibachev, artistic director of Moscow's Na Pokrovke theatre, presented *Three Sisters*. This production, although premiered ten years ago, still arouses great interest among its audiences. The reason for this is that the director has succeeded in linking the eras to say 'They're just like us'. The performance starts in the audience. The actors talk to the public and invite them to 'dinner *chez* Prozorov' to make them feel the atmosphere of a provincial town and introduce them to a refined world which is exceptionally well delineated.

For the occasion Lipstek Dramatic Theatre created *Love the One That Mocks* from Yu. Bytchkov, based on Anton Chekhov's correspondence with Lika Mizinova and Lydia Avilova's memoirs. In two years, this Festival has become a firm fixture in the theatre calendar.

The Siberian Transit festival took place in May 2001 in Novosibirsk, with the participation of the most important theatres of the region: Altai drama theatre (in Bertolt Brecht's *Dreigroschenoper*), Irkutsk's Okhlopkov drama theatre (with Grigori Gorin's *A Mass for the Dead)*, Novokuznetsk drama theatre (*Our Benefactor*, from the short story *The Village of Stepantchikovo* by Dostoievski), Tiumen drama and comedy theatre (Chekhov's *Cherry Orchard)*, Tomsk drama theatre (*Dulcinea of Tobos* by Alexander Volodin), Kemerovo drama theatre (*An Ingenious Mistress* by Lope de Vega), Pushkin drama theatre, Krasnoiarsk (*Macbeth*), Omsk drama theatre (Nabokov's *Invitation to a Beheading*), Krasny Fakel drama theatre, Novosibirsk (Chekhov's *Three Sisters*). The principle of this Festival is to select the best performance of the season from each theatre.

In the Mordovian Republic, Saransk drama theatre opened its 2001–2002 season with the premiere of a play called *Thou Shalt Not Kill, Thou Shalt Not Steal!*, the work of a contemporary Mordovian woman playwright, V. Michanina. It was directed by Yu. Khvostikov, artistic director of the theatre. 'To overcome', what does it mean? This is the question posed by this production. Lack of spiritual values and cupidity bring about a murder. A man dies. The action takes place in a village church. The play's characters are the decorators restoring the church, the church officials and the parishioners. Among other premieres, let us quote Garcia Lorca's *House of Bernarda Alba* (directed by Yu. Khvostikov) and a production for young people, *The Golden Feather*, from a play by I. Tokmakova.

A highlight of the 2002 season was the Golden Mask festival in Moscow. Under its dynamic young director, Edward Boyakov, the event has grown rapidly since its inception in 1994. Originally a Moscow-only festival, since 1995 it has made its selection from the whole of the Russian Federation, and it now covers not only drama but opera, operetta, dance (modern and classical) and puppetry. As well as the competitive section of the festival, its final week has for the last three years included a showcase section, intended for overseas visitors such as directors of festivals.

This year's third Russian Case was curated by a Russian critic, Elena Kovalskaya, and an American critic working in Moscow, John Freedman of the *Moscow Times*. They presented their wares in three sections: dance, new writing and 'Directors' Theatre', reflecting what is still the dominant influence in Russian theatre. Opera was represented by the Maryinsky with a version of *Tsar Demyan*, originally conducted by Valery Gergiev, while a category-defying production, *Olonkho (The Woman Warrior)* came from Siberia, having already been seen on the 2001 Edinburgh Fringe.

The six short modern works in the dance section included two from companies in Ekaterinburg and one from Chelyabinsk, with the other three from Moscow. The new writing section included Yevgeny Grishkovets, with *Planet*, and Vasily Sigarev's *Plasticine*. The other two 'new' plays were by Mikhail Ugarov (*An Urban Romance*, also known as *Deadbeat*, since it concerns the seduction of a respectable wife by a low-life) directed by Alexander Galibin for the Liteiny theatre of St Petersburg, and *You*, Olga Mukhina's newest play, presented in the studio of the Moscow Arts Theatre. Mukhina has had considerable success with the dreamy *Tanya Tanya* (1996), and her blend of fantasy and feyness, while compared by some to Chekhov, may strike observers of modern Russian theatre as closer to *Cerceau*, by Victor Slavkin. As with *Cerceau*, Mukhina coops up a group of people in a confined space and observes their attempts to escape it, both physical and emotional.

In the Golden Mask itself, a production of *The Seagull* by Lev Dodin for the Maly Theatre of St Petersburg won the award for best large-scale play. Maxim Sukhanov was Best Actor in Vladimir Mirzoev's staging of *Cyrano de Bergerac* at the Vakhtangov Theatre. Pyotr Fomenko's four-hour staging of *War and Peace: the beginning of a novel*, a reminder, if one were needed, that good Russian actors are the best in the world, picked up Golden Mask awards for best small-scale production, best actress (Galina Tumina) and best director.

Valery Khazanov, *critic, theatre producer and researcher, is secretary of the Russian Centre of the International Theatre Institute. He is responsible for the international network of monodrama festivals and runs his own annual festival in Moscow. His article includes additional material by Ian Herbert.*

SINGAPORE

FELIX and JEFFREY TAN

Singapore is only a little dot on the map of the world. Located east near the equator, made up of 3.2 million people – Chinese, Malay, Indian and Eurasian – Singapore has always taken pride in its survival success story in the area of business and cultural cohesion. Primarily made up of migrants in the early generations, the current generation of Singaporeans has grown up in the period since independence from British rule was won in 1965. Today in 2002, the current concern of Singaporeans about being a soulless society, made up of 'stayers and quitters' has led the People's Action Party (the long time ruling political party) to embark on wide-ranging discussion and reflection at a national level with a view to 'Remaking Singapore'.

Singapore's performing arts scene, from its very early stages, saw itself as something of an oddball in Singapore society. While Singapore prided itself on becoming an important economic hub, a booming society that needed to hang on to its traditional 'Asian values', the arts scene took a back seat. But as the years went by, the small and relatively 'unnoticed' arts community grew, as Singapore began to realise that something was missing from its make-up – vibrancy. That is when the government made a concerted effort to consolidate and push for a more lively arts scene, which culminated in the creation in the early 90s of the National Arts Council. And since then, there has been no turning back.

Indeed, the opening in 2002 of the biggest and most extravagant performing arts venue in Singapore, Esplanade – Theatres on the Bay, which started construction slightly more than three years ago has been touted as the arrival of the best performing venue in Southeast Asia. Given the massive structure of the Esplanade, which hopes to rival not only the Sydney Opera House but also other such performing arts venues around the world, one problem still stands – how sustainable is such a venue in the long run? That aside, the Esplanade also reflects the aspirations of Singapore society to make the arts an important part of its cultural identity.

The National Arts Council (NAC) has over the last three years shaken itself free of the dust of scepticism and cynicism. While many initially thought the NAC was a mere mouthpiece, a pseudo-censorship board to 'govern' the arts in Singapore, it is now looked to as the number one supporter of the arts. From providing scholarships to Singaporeans who want to pursue studies in the arts, it has gone on to provide housing to budding arts groups. In addition, the NAC has made sure that a majority of arts groups – be it in the visual or performing arts, traditional or contemporary – now has access to a pool of funds that will ensure their growth. Last but not least, the NAC organises the annual Singapore International Arts Festival, which has been compared to the Edinburgh Festival. The role of the National Arts Council is thus not merely that of a governmental board to regulate the arts in Singapore. It also plays a very substantial role in cultivating its arts scene.

From its humble beginnings, the Singapore International Arts Festival has, over the last three years, taken arts participation in Singapore society to a level never seen before. The number of performances, both local and foreign, has increased, with dance performances this year outweighing theatre performances. The Singapore International Arts Festival is just one small piece of the jigsaw of a vibrant arts scene.

A major problem today is that one can no longer see a clear demarcation between what is theatre and what exactly is dance. While the creative endeavours of up and coming dance groups have constantly crossed the boundaries, they have split Singapore society into two distinct segments, with one group demanding that such performances of dance-theatre should be seen as explorations into the realm of dance, while the other has criticised them for failing to find a definitive direction within their own performance style.

There is also the Arts Education Programme in Singapore, whereby arts practitioners, for example, teach theatre and dance in primary and secondary schools. These practitioners are both local and from around the region. This sort of activity has been actively sought not only by the Singapore government, but also by the population, who have clamoured for more involvement of the arts with our younger generation. Furthermore, educational institutions, such as Nanyang Academy of Fine Arts and LaSalle-SIA College of the Arts in Singapore have seen an increase in student intake in the performing arts. Such institutions not only teach traditional Asian theatre forms, but also cover other related fields, such as music and dance. Other tertiary institutions also have their own theatre studies department, including the National University of Singapore and the Nanyang Technological University. The creation of such courses and departments by recognised local institutions indicates a new awareness of the importance of cultivating the arts and sustaining their growth. It also reflects the public openness to the arts as now not merely peripheral, but an integral part of a mature and established society.

Another very important part of Singapore's thriving arts scene is the Arts Housing Scheme, which finds suitable spaces to house theatre and dance groups. Over the last three years, a stretch of houses along Waterloo Street has been turned into an arts hub. Local theatre groups, such as Action Theatre and Dance Ensemble Singapore, can be found there. Further along the street one can also find the Stamford Arts Centre, where many other theatre and dance companies are housed. Even community centres around Singapore have given space to supporting the arts. This scheme has helped theatre and dance companies, who are more often than not desperately in need of administrative space in order to function as a company. Furthermore, the 'housing' can mean not only a performance space but also a venue for rehearsals, something that is sorely lacking in land-scarce Singapore.

All this increased interplay between the performing arts scene and ordinary Singaporeans reflects the fact that Singapore is more than ready to embrace this once 'ostracised' segment of society. Nevertheless, Singapore has merely reached the starting point of its process of development towards a cultured society that many cosmopolitan cities around the world might boast of.

On the Singapore theatre stage, there has not been a more exciting, dynamic and encouraging time in the short 37 years since independence. The announcement of an increase in arts funding by 97.4 % to $7.5 million in 2000 with an additional $4 million to follow was due to the recommendation of the 'Renaissance City Report' by the National Arts Council, envisioning Singapore to become an International Arts City.

SINGAPORE

With four major co-existing cultures, Chinese, Malay, Indian and Eurasian, Singapore has yet found enough of one national culture to have its own National theatre company. The focus of the Singapore theatre has also developed from finding the Singapore voice on stage, in the early 80s, to interdisciplinary, intra-cultural, inter-cultural and post-modern works today.

Over the last three seasons from 1999 till July 2002, there have been many rapid changes on the Singapore stage in all four languages. However, it is the Singapore English theatre that has seen the most vibrant changes, both locally and internationally. New players have emerged and the older companies have revamped their existing structures and production methods, making the cultural landscape one of constant metamorphosis, in true Singaporean survival style. This article will highlight some of the major changes of three of the four flagship arts companies (companies receiving the two year major grant given by the National Arts Council in 2000) and some of the newer emerging theatre companies in Singapore.

Established in 1985, Theatreworks (S) Ltd is Singapore's premier English theatre company. Led by Artistic Director Ong Keng Sen since 1988, the company has grown from premiering Singapore comedies and musicals, running mini festivals (Theatre Carnival on the Hill 1992, Got-to-Go 1998), site specific works (*Yang Family*, 1996) to presenting post-modern, intercultural works such as *Lear* in 1999; premiering in Hong Kong, Singapore then touring to Jakarta and Perth in Feb 2000, *Desdemona*, which opened the Singapore Arts Festival in 2000; and *Search Hamlet*, Aug 2002.

Ong, who has become known for the reinvention of traditional performances through a juxtaposition of cultures, was invited to curate for the Berlin Laboratory 'In Transit' Festival in June 2002–03. In 2000, Theatreworks was named one of the four flagship companies and in 2002, the group re-organized into three sections: Theatreworks (International Wing), headed by Ong Keng Sen, Theatreworks (Singapore Wing), headed by Associate Artistic Director Tan Tarn How and Theatreworks (Education and Outreach), headed by Associate Artistic Director Jeffrey Tan.

The Theatre Practice (TTP) is Singapore's oldest bilingual theatre company, spearheaded by its Artistic Director, Kuo Pao Kun, who is also sometimes known as the father of Singapore theatre. Most practising theatre directors and actors have in one way or another studied with him in the late 70s, 80s and 90s. Known for landmark works such as *Silly Little Girl and the Funny Old Tree* (Mandarin version in 1997 using Grotowski's presentation method, English version in 1999); and the multilingual *Mama Looking For Her Cat* (1988) features seven different languages spoken on stage. The focus of the company has grown from producing locally devised stories to revisiting classics such as Cao Yu's *Family* in 1998, *The Island* (Mandarin version) in May 2002, *Oleanna* (Mandarin version) in Aug 2002 and *Animal Farm* Nov 2002. TTP has also revamped its core artistic team in 2002 with younger members, Nelson Chia (director), Wu Xi (director from China), Judy Ngo (Actor) and Alvin Chiam (Actor), assisted by Assistant Artistic Director Wong May Lan. To date, this is the only Singapore theatre company with full time actors.

Besides the TTP, Kuo is also responsible for setting up the non-certificate awarding Theatre Training Research Programme (TTRP), the only three year consolidated professional actor training programme to draw from Asian classical theatre systems (Beijing Opera, Noh theatre, Bharata Natyam, Kudiyattam or Kathakali and Wayangwong) while training for contemporary theatre.

The Necessary Stage (TNS), established in 1988 by Alvin Tan and Haresh Sharma, is known for collaborative, group-devised, socially relevant work. Since moving into Marine Parade Community Building in 2000, the company have expanded their repertoire to include more community-focused work through the 'Marine Parade Theatre Festival 2000, 2001', and the publications *Programme* and *Focus*, while still developing artistically challenging works through the experimental platform 'Names Changed To Protect The Innocent'. Every March, TNS continues with their yearly MI Youth Connection, the Young People's Theatre Festival. 2002 marks the sixth year of this collaboration with Mobil One, the cellphone company. TNS refocused in 2002 to have a longer rehearsal period of up to six months per show, dropping the Community Theatre Festival and two publications.

The other non-flagship companies, who continue actively to produce good work, include Toy Factory Ensemble, headed by Artistic Director Goh Boon Teck and Associate Artistic Director Beatice Chia. They won the Straits Times' 'LIFE' Award for best director with '*Shopping and Fucking*' in Feb 2001. Controversy is the norm for most theatres in culturally sensitive Singapore. For Toy's latest play *Fireface* (Sep 2002), they were asked to retract their brochures because some members of the public found them too offensive. The Tamil theatre company, Agni Kootthu (Theatre of Fire) also had one of their plays, *Talaq* (*Divorce*), banned in 2000 because some members of the Muslim Indian community found the play race sensitive and caused a public furore.

In Aug 2002, the Singapore Repertory Theatre (SRT) was added to the list of two-year major grant companies for 2002–2004. SRT continues to produce musicals (*Rent*, 2001, *Honk!*, 2002) and well known plays (*Barefoot in the Park*, 2001). In 2002, SRT will be producing *Forbidden Place* for the opening of the Esplanade, and it is also slated to travel round the region. Despite the controversies, Singapore theatre continues to grow and travel beyond its shores of origin. Theatre Ox (1998) headed by Ang Gey Pin, has been travelling since 2001 with the Jerzy Grotowski and Thomas Richards Laboratory in Pontedera, Italy with *One Breath Left*.

In November 2001, the Association for Singapore Actors (ASA) was launched, giving a voice to the actors in Singapore. In the area of arts education, the Singapore Drama Educators Association will be launched in September 2002, marking yet another collaboration between the several theatre companies, educators and teachers. Later in October 2002, the Singapore Critics Association will also be formed.

The rapid change in Singapore theatre reflect the changing landscape of the minds of the current society. Let's hope that in the mist of all this vibrant change, some of the new found gems will survive for the next generation, who may capture some of the imagination, memories and stories of our time.

Felix Tan *is currently a journalist with Radio Singapore International. His programmes include Arts Arena, where he takes a look at the performing arts scene around the world. He is part of the organising committee looking into setting up an Association of Theatre Critics in Singapore.*
Jeffrey Tan *is an Australian-trained theatre director who also lectures part time at the National Institute of Education, designs stage lighting, and writes. He also sits on the Singapore Arts Festival Programming Committee 2003–04 and is President of the Singapore Drama Educators Association.*

SLOVAKIA

ZUZANA ULICIANSKA

During the past three seasons, it is possible to trace different tendencies in Slovak Theatre that can, within limits, be called progress. Jaroslav Hasek, father of the famous Good Soldier Svejk and activist for the Party for Small Progress Within the Legal Limits, would love these minor, but still noticeable, developments.

Statistically speaking, the number of premieres grew steadily from 114 in 1999 to 155 in 2001. Also in 2001, the total number of productions presented by theatres (theatres in Slovakia still work mostly under the repertory system) reached its peak with 578 productions. The total number of performances that took place in Slovakia was 5,781. This represents the second best result in the last ten years, leaving the year 1999 as the best. The number of theatre visitors in 2001 reached 1.32 million (out of 5 million inhabitants of Slovakia), a slightly smaller attendance than in some previous years.

The year 2002 has been marked by governmental reform in Slovakia. Naturally, this also has an impact in the sphere of the arts. Since April 2002, 19 former state theatres are run by the newly established, self-governing regions. At the end of the 2001/2002 season, only the four biggest theatres (including the Slovak National Theatre) remained under the direct control of the centralised Ministry of Culture. One of the four, the New Scene Theatre in Bratislava, is currently undergoing the transition from an organisation financed and strictly controlled by the state to a non-profit organisation led by an independent board. This is a radical change that was only made possible by the 'transformation law' passed in the Slovak parliament in December 2001. The consequences of this law in the cultural sphere are only now beginning to be seen. It may prove to be stimulating, giving much more freedom and flexibility to theatre life, but may also be harmful if misused for commercial or political purposes. The involvement of city councils in theatre is still minimal; cities directly run only two small theatres. The number of independent theatres varies. In 2001, only 20 filed official forms. The ongoing problem of any independent theatre activity (including festivals or journals) is finance. The grant system is administratively slow and discriminatory in many areas. As far as building is concerned, the renovation of a historical theatre building in Presov and the building of two smaller venues for puppet theatres in Kosice and Banska Bystrica was completed in this period.

However, figures do not tell the whole story. It is extremely important that the past few seasons saw the staging for the first time in Slovakia of several plays that are considered to be an integral part of the world repertory. This applies not only to recently written texts, but also to plays from different periods that have not been staged before in Slovakia.

A good example of this 'pioneering' tendency in dramaturgy is *The Cocktail Party* by T. S. Eliot. It was translated into Slovak for the first time and staged in the Bratislava Astorka Korzo '90 Theatre in March 2001. The same theatre put on Harold Pinter's *Birthday Party* a year later. This theatre also staged Heiner Müller's *Quartett* in June 2001

ABOVE: *The Dreamplay* by August Strindberg, presented at the Andrej Bagar Theatre in Nitra
(*photo*: Ctibor Bachraty)

BELOW: *The Dance Hall – Tanciaren*, directed by Martin Huba at The Slovak National Theatre – Drama
(*photo*: Jana Nemokova)

and it is now rehearsing a text by Jon Fosse. While the experienced directors Juraj Nvota and Vladimir Strnisko took on the first two plays, it is almost natural that a young woman director – Sonia Ferancova – did the controversial *Quartett* with very distinct, strong visual imagery.

The Andrej Bagar Theatre in Nitra has been continuing its policy of co-operation with foreign directors. The theatre hired the young Lithuanian director Gintaras Varnas to work on a demanding project for the first Slovak staging of *The Dreamplay* (*Ett Drömspel*) by August Strindberg (December 2000). With the support of Slovak designers (Alexandra Gruskova and Ales Votava), he succeeded in making an impressive production, which was awarded the critics' choice Dosky (Boards) award for Best Scenography of the Season 2000/2001.

The Drama Ensemble of the Slovak National Theatre, Bratislava, has also tried to be innovative in its dramaturgy. One of the most popular productions was Jean Claude Grumberg's *L'Atelier*, which opened in April 2002. A new play, *Portugal*, written by the young Hungarian playwright Zoltan Egressy, was already popular all over Eastern Europe when it was staged in Bratislava in September 2001. One of the most distinguished productions was certainly a stylised production of David Harrower's rural drama, *Knives in Hens*, directed by the young Silvester Lavrik, which had its premiere in March 2001.

'In-yer face' drama is not extremely popular in Slovakia, although we can find a few traces of it. Svetozar Sprusansky directed a decent production of Marius von Mayenburg's *Fireface (Feuergesicht)* produced by the Zdvih Association in the Andrej Bagar Theatre (June 2000). Students of the Academy of Music and Dramatic Arts performed Mayenburg's *Parasites* in February 2002. *Phaedra's Love* by Sarah Kane had its Slovak premiere (March 2002) in Studio 12, the new venue established in the premises of the Theatre Institute in Bratislava. This space, the former Radio Studio, was made available for students, alternative groups and regional theatre companies. In the Bratislava Studio L+S premises, a few other independent productions, such as the play *Disco Pigs* by Enda Walsh, were presented.

Another big achievement was director Roman Polak daring to touch the taboo playwright Bernard-Marie Koltès. Having successfully directed *The Return to the Desert* in the Drama Club in Prague with a Slovak protagonist, Emilia Vasaryova, Polak staged two other plays by Koltès in the Studio of the State Theatre in the eastern Slovak city of Kosice. The same theatre also staged for the first time Stanislaw Ignacy Witkiewicz's *In the Small Court* (*W malym dworku*) (June 2001), and Sam Shepard's *Buried Child* (April 2002).

It must be said that some of these artistically varied projects were not very successful with the general public, which prefers lighter musical or dance comedies. Nevertheless, they represented a very important development in Slovak dramaturgy. They opened new social and political issues and presented different theatrical poetics. These positive trends in staging contemporary world drama eventually led to some successes with the public. The first Slovak production of *Closer* by Patrick Marber, directed by the Dutch director Jan-Willem van den Bosch, was in May 2002. This work is becoming popular both with critics and the general public. The production, supported by the British Council, was a good example of international co-operation that brought to Slovakia a slightly different, less theatrical school of acting. A similar attempt at staging Molière's *Don Juan* by the French director Patrice Kerbrat in the Slovak National Theatre proved to be too academic.

Positive tendencies can be traced also in the publication by the Theatre Institute Bratislava or small independent publishing houses, such as Drewo a srd or L.A.C. Levice, of foreign plays that have been translated into Slovak.

And what about new Slovak plays? New writing is the salt of national theatre life. In this respect, Slovaks have been on a restricted diet for a couple of years. The prescribed cure was the competition for new texts, Drama 2000 and 2001, or the participation of Slovak authors in the Alfréd Radok competition for the best Czech and Slovak plays. However, only a few new texts get staged. The only original Slovak play staged by the Slovak National Theatre in the last three years was *The Woodsman's Wife* (*Horor v horarni*). The experienced author, Lubomir Feldek, wrote this as a post-modern joke on a nineteenth-century drama written by national poet P. O. Hviezdoslav. An interesting attempt to approach some feminist issues appeared in the Puppet Theatre at the Crossroads in Banska Bystrica under the title *Don't Cry, Anna* (*Neplac, Anna*).

The former leader among theatres working with original texts, STOKA, has recently undergone a change. A smaller group remained under the leadership of the director, Blaho Uhlar. A second group that split from STOKA, called the Association for Contemporary Opera, produced several projects, including provocative and challenging contemporary operas. The GUnaGU theatre, led by author Viliam Klimacek, continued as another prolific centre for new writing. Another author, Stanislav Stepka, works exclusively with his Radosina Naïve Theatre with its down-to-earth humour and loyal audience.

The most successful original text in the last few seasons was in fact not a text, but a script for a dance performance inspired by the project of Théatre du Campagnol *Le Bal* and adopted to the Slovak context by Martin Huba and Martin Porubjak. A year after its premiere, this Best Production of the 2000/2001 season, *The Dance Hall* (*Tanciareni*), is still one of the hottest tickets in Bratislava. Using no words, this production of the Slovak National Theatre provides the audience with both amusement and insight into Slovak history. The production was also given the second prize at the Kontakt Festival in Torun, Poland.

Contemporary texts, or better, scripts, can be found in contemporary dance projects. The Dance Studio in Banska Bystrica presented several inspiring projects (*Twins*, with choreographers Zuzana Hajkova and Milan Kozanek, and *Rooms* (*Izby*), choreographed by Marta Polakova). The work produced by the Association of Contemporary Dance or by Bratislava Dance Theatre is of interest as well. The mime artist Milan Sladek declared the end of his involvement in the Arena theatre in Bratislava.

The most ambitious performances of the 1999/2000 season are certainly those in the Slovak National Theatre production of Ionesco's *The Chairs*. Director Lubomir Vajdicka gave the audience an opportunity to watch two star performances from Emilia Vasaryova and Emil Horvath. Emilia Vasaryova was awarded the Dosky prize for Best Actress in the 1999/2000 season for her role.

The 1999/2000 season in the Slovak National Theatre was also marked by one of the most eminent Slovak actors Martin Huba. He played Prospero in Shakespeare's *The Tempest*, directed by Peter Mikulik. (The amazing set design of this production was made by one of the most talented young Slovak scenographers, Ales Votava. To the theatre community's sorrow, he died in 2001.)

The acting of Zita Furkova and Vladimir Hajdu in *Quartett* in the Astorka Korzo '90 Theatre, Bratislava, was highly appreciated as well. Vladimir Hajdu was awarded the critics' choice Dosky Prize for Best Acting for the 2001/2001 season. His colleague from the same theatre, Anna Siskova, received, in the same year, the same award for her role as Celia in Eliot's *The Cocktail Party*.

Probably the biggest role of the last season belongs to Emilia Vasaryova, who lent her distinctive talent and character to the lurid story of Maria Callas in Terrence McNally's *Master Class*, directed by Jozef Bednarik in the Opera of the Slovak National Theatre.

We can stay with this director for a little while. Jozef Bednarik is known for his inspiring work with actors. For several years, he worked mostly on musical and opera productions in Prague. In recent year he has returned to Nitra and Bratislava, where he has staged several musical comedies with touching messages that have reached the widest possible audiences. This applies to the New Scene Bratislava production of Jerry Herman and Harvey Fierstein's *La Cage aux folles*, with the deeply moving transvestite Zaza performed by Csongor Kassai and Miro Noga. In addition, he staged *Zorba the Greek* (starring Leopold Haverl and Marian Slovak, together with a splendid Bozidara Turzonovova) in the Andrej Bagar Theatre in Nitra. Nor should we omit Bednarik's successful direction of *Don Giovanni* in the Opera of the Slovak National Theatre in June 2001, which was among the most accomplished opera pieces in the last period. Speaking of important roles in recent years, I should mention quickly Diana Morova as Cleopatra in Shakespeare's *Antony and Cleopatra*, directed by Hungarian directress Eniko Ezsényi in the Slovak National Theatre, and the female version of *Don Juan* performed by Jana Olihova in the theatre in Martin.

Slovakia has a range of regular international theatre events. One of the biggest one-off international events was the hosting of the Eurothalia festival, organised by the Slovak National theatre for the European Theatre Convention, that took place in Bratislava in June 2002. However, Slovak companies do not frequently make international tours.

Possibly the biggest international success of the last period was *Macbeth,* premiered in March 1999 and directed by the Czech director Vladimir Moravek in the Andrej Bagar Theatre in Nitra. The production was presented in the Thalia Theatre in Budapest, in Prague, Brno, at the Shakespeare festival in Gdansk, the Bath Shakespeare Festival in Great Britain, and at several other events. The ambitious production of *Hamlet* from the same theatre, directed by Hungarian actor and director Robert Alföldi, also had a few foreign showings. However, to see any Slovak production, the best choice is still to travel to Slovakia. A good opportunity is, for instance, the International Festival Divadelna Nitra, the Puppet Festival in Banska Bystrica, the contemporary dance festival, Bratislava in Movement, or the Istropolitana Project in Bratislava for student groups.

Zuzana Ulicianska *is a theatre critic. She works for the Theatre Institute in Bratislava while teaching theatre management at the Academy of Music and Dramatic Arts in Bratislava.*

SLOVENIA

HENRIK NEUBAUER

'Theatre is a space that we enter as individuals, to become participants in a collective happening; and the theatre performance binds us into a temporary community. But we are taught through the experience that such a thing doesn't occur in every performance. The power to bind individuals into a community, therefore, isn't *a priori* given to the theatre art. A common bond is only formed if an aesthetic level of common experience is established. And it can be established through the contents of the performance and through the manner in which these contents are presented'. Those were the words of the selector of the last drama festival in Maribor, who also stressed that over the last years performances of contemporary plays with serious content, and classical plays from the world literary treasury, prevailed.

The growth in both attendance and productions, which we have spoken about in past editions of *World of Theatre*, continued in the last three seasons in all branches of Slovenian theatre life, including opera and ballet. We can speak of a growth of 8% in the last three theatrical seasons from 1997/98 to 2000/01 with regard to the attendance and 22% for the number of staged works. Statistically, if in 1992 one in three Slovenians visited a theatre performance, in 2000 the figure was one in two. This can partly be attributed to the growth of commercial theatres with popular and boulevard comedies. In 2000 two commercial theatres around Ljubljana registered more visitors than the National Drama Theatre in Ljubljana. Especially during the summer time there is a growing number of festivals, which enable the same performances to be seen in other surroundings than those for which they were originally conceived.

An important factor in the existence and development of Slovenian theatre is the subsidy from the Ministry of Culture of Slovenia, which is slowly rising. The Slovenian cultural budget rose from 26.25 billion tolars (about 118 million euro) in 2001 (altogether 0.57% of GDP) to 28.5 billion tolars in 2002; in 2003 it should go up to 30.3 billion tolars. 35% of the cultural budget is devoted to theatre.

This increase is, of course, partly also due to the inflation rate. The state interest in theatres is also seen through investments in theatrical institutions: among other projects in 2002 and 2003, priority will be given to the completion of the reconstruction of the old stage and hall of Maribor theatre and the preparation of the documentation for the much needed reconstruction of both metropolitan theatres, the Drama and the Opera and Ballet of the Slovenian National Theatre in Ljubljana. Because of a change of government, the formerly announced Slovenian National Cultural Programme has still not been adopted. Now a Law on the Implementation of Public Interest in the Field of Culture is being debated in Parliament.

On the positive side in the Dramatic Theatres, we can speak of quite a few

SLOVENIA

highlights in direction, scenography and acting as a consequence of a successful realisation of directors' concepts and a coming together of all those factors that could have an influence on the performance. These range from the selection of suitable and provocative texts, which enabled powerful and authoritative approaches from the directors, to the quality of the actors' creations, as well as the vision of the theatres' artistic leadership. In the seasons we are writing about we can again see the opening up of horizons for the younger generation of directors. Besides the older generation of Slovene directors, drama theatres also opened their doors to guest directors from other countries including Poland, Macedonia, Croatia, Bosnia and Italy.

On the other side, there was a slight decrease in premieres of Slovene playwrights in the seasons under review. That is also evident in the programme of the most important theatre festival in Slovenia, Borštnikovo srecanje (Borštnik Meeting), which shows each autumn in Maribor the best dramatic productions of Slovenian theatres. Out of 16 performances in 1999 there were only three chosen by Slovene playwrights, the same in 2000 and 2001, and for 2002 only one out of 10 performances is by a Slovene author.

Nevertheless we can see that most Slovenian theatres are in touch with what is happening on drama stages abroad: they are presenting many of the newest contemporary plays by European and American authors, of course translated into the Slovenian language. Besides the classic repertoire (Molière, Shakespeare, Corneille, Chekhov, Goldoni, Racine, Ibsen, Lorca) and the modern classic authors of the 20th century (Beckett, Brecht, Ionesco, Stoppard, Toller, von Horváth, Tennessee Williams) there were a lot of current plays on the programmes for 1999-2002. The list is quite comprehensive and includes authors like Hare, Koltès, Koljada, Glowacki, Belbel, McDonagh, Srbljenovic, Hübner, Harrower, Kane.

Apart from the non-institutional groups that are growing 'like mushrooms in the rain', a new drama theatre was opened in 2001 in Koper, a city on the Slovenian sea-coast near Trieste, which had already existed for some years after World War II, but was closed in 1957 due to governmental restrictions; it joined theatres in Ptuj and Kranj, which were re-opened earlier (Kranj in 1987, Ptuj in 1997).

Of the past three seasons, that of 1999/2000 was considered the best. Among non-institutional performances, there are two which should be especially mentioned: *Gravitacija 0* (*Gravitation 0*) produced by Dragan Zivadinov – eleven theatrical scenes with a duration of 20 seconds each, which were repeated twice in a non-gravitational space in a plane which took off from the Star-city near Moscow with actors and spectators; and *Drive in Camillo*, produced by Emil Hrvatin, who stretched a net between two high buildings and put a moving person there. The latter was part of the Festival Manifesta 3.

The Drama of the Slovene National Theatre in Ljubljana, which had the greatest acting potential in 1999/2000, stood out with performances of Dostoievsky's *Idiot*, *Waiting for Godot* by Beckett and Molière's *Misanthrope*. The next two seasons didn't reach that level but still showed a very fresh *Kasandra* (*Cassandra*) by Slovenian playwright B. A. Novak and *Škofjeloški pasijon* (*The Passion of Škofja Loka*) after a medieval mystery and *Knives in Hens* by David Harrower, highly awarded at the Borštnik Meeting in 2001. Last season's *Razmadezna* (*Cleansed*)

Lorca's *The House of Bernarda Alba*, directed by Matjaz Pograjc at the Mladinsko Theatre, Ljubljana, March 2000
(*photo*: Barbara Sršen)

SLOVENIA

by Sarah Kane and *Praznovanje (Festen)* by Danish playwrights Vinterberg, Rukov and Hansen were both up to now unknown to Slovenian audiences and both were directed by young directors at a very high level – mature, direct and exact.

In the Drama of the Slovene National Theatre in Maribor the best productions were by Slovenian playwrights: *Filio ni doma (Filio is not at home)* by Berta Bojetu with its uneasy and aggressive atmosphere; and the tragicomedy *Zalezujoc Godota (Stalking Godot)* by one of the best contemporary Slovenian playwrights Drago Jancar, based on Beckett's *Waiting for Godot.* The latter, set in the post-totalitarian time, is a cruel struggle for domination between two former spies. But the highest point was without doubt *Amadeus* by Peter Shaffer, in 2001, which made use of the full potential of the actors, singers, musicians and dancers of the theatre. In the last reported season *Jobova knjiga (The Book of Job)* in an adaptation by a Czech theatrical team (director, designer, music) was much praised as spiritual theatre and describers as a 'concert for the Word of God'.

The Municipal Theatre of Ljubljana was praised first for its revival of Goldoni's *Sluga dveh gospodov (Il servitore di due patroni)* in the original Commedia dell'arte style, then for the very theatrically conceived *Cyrano de Bergerac* by Rostand and finally for the Irish play by Martin McDonagh *Kripl iz Inishmaana (The Cripple of Inishmaan)*, which created a recognisable situation, full of temperament and authentic comic accents.

From the Slovensko Mladinsko gledališče we should note the performance in 1999/00 of *Hinkemann* by Ernst Toller. The invalid and impotent main character was pretty much shock-free as the production was based on a cabaret atmosphere and expressive acting. In 2000/01, critics stressed the lack of internal consistency in the productions of the theatre, which has a historic reputation and a very mobile group of actors. However in 2001/02 *Tri sestre (Three Sisters)* by Chekhov and a double-bill by Sarah Kane *Fedrina ljubezen (Phaedra's Love)* and *4.48 Psihoza (4.48 Psychosis)* again showed the strength of that theatre.

From the three theatres in Celje, Nova Gorica and Kranj in 1999/2000 the highlights were plays by Molière and Shakespeare: *Don Giovanni* in Celje, *Hamlet* in Nova Gorica and *L'Avare* in Kranj. In the next seasons they were *King Lear* and *Lev pozimi (The Lion in Winter)* by James Goldman in Celje, *Tistega lepega dne (That Lovely Day)*, an adaptation of a novel by Slovenian writer Ciril Kosmac, in Nova Gorica and a play on paedophilia *Kako sem se naucila voziti (How I Learned to Drive)* by Paula Vogel in Kranj. In 2001/02 Nova Gorica theatre showed Goldoni's *Zdrahe (Le baruffe chiozzotte)*; in Celje they introduced a musical for the first time, *Chicago* by Kander and Ebb, and in Kranj von Horváth's *Ljubezen, vera, upanje (Faith, Hope and Charity)* subtitled as a 'little Dance of Death'.

Of the newcomers the Ptuj Theatre has in 1999/00 shown Lutz Hübner's *Marjetka, str. 89 (Gretchen 89ff)*, Gretchen's monologue from Goethe's *Faust* that shows the theatre life behind the curtain, not usually seen by the audience. The play won the first Prize of the public at Dnevi komedije (Comedy Days) in Celje. Next season the theme of its mini-repertoire of three plays was love and relations between the sexes. The Koper Theatre has finished its first complete season but up to now without making much of a stir. They still need time to grow.

The improvement of the situation in both the Slovenian Opera and Ballet houses, in Ljubljana and Maribor, tentatively announced in the last issue of *World of Theatre*, showed its fruits in the quality of their artistic achievements and, in Ljubljana, efforts to increase both the number of productions and the attendance. Comparing 2000/01 with 1997/98, the number of productions stayed on the same level in both theatres, but the attendance has already risen in Ljubljana by 108%, even if it still has not reached the level of past decades. In Maribor, the figures stayed as they were or even slightly diminished. In both theatres, foreign directors and conductors prevailed; in Ljubljana those from Germany and in Maribor those from Italy.

In 1999/2000 all four premieres in Ljubljana (*Madam Butterfly, Le Nozze di Figaro, Medea* and *Ivan Susanin*) showed a clear theatrical concept and some extraordinary achievements from their lead singers – Ana Pusar Jeric as Cio-Cio-San, Marko Fink as Figaro, Irena Baar as Medea and Janez Lotric as Sobinin. The Ljubljana ballet ensemble gave their first performance of John Cranko's famous *Taming of the Shrew* in the original choreography, staged by Georgette Tsinguirides, as well as the no less known *Green Table* by Kurt Joos, staged by Anne Markand. The latter, however, was not on the same level. The Romanian dancer E. Clug showed his short ballet *One – Bachelorette* on Bach's music and – briefly – *Giselle* (there were only two performances because of some choreographically unsuitable changes).

In 2000/01 the critical response was mixed. Mirjam Kalin was much praised as the Witch in Dvorak's *Rusalka, Don Pasquale* was a 'solid, fluent performance with little sparkle', *Don Giovanni* was 'presented as collecting experiences' as the title role was staged by Austrian director Hochstraate 'not profound enough, as if he wasn't interested in the fascinating figure of the seducer'. Verdi's *Nabucco*, on the other hand, was staged with great professionalism but too much emphasis on the stage decor. Ballet showed first a classic *Swan Lake* with promising young dancers and beautiful decor from English National Ballet. For the second evening two ballets by Slovenian composers were chosen, first the revival of *Trobenta in vrag* (*The Trumpet and the Devil*) by Alojz Srebotnjak and as a novelty *Nori malar* (*The Mad Painter*) by Janez Gregorc both choreographed by Vlasto Dedovic, a former dancer of the company. The last one especially, showing the miserable life of a Slovenian painter, gained much praise. In the season 2001/02 the Ljubljana Opera presented two old Slovenian operas by Viktor Parma in a semi-concert version. Verdi's *Il Trovatore* was staged with a static chorus above stage level and soloists acting below, which deprived the performance of its dramaturgical development. The end of the season showed a solid *Lustige Witwe* by Lehár and the same can be said of Tchaikovsky's *Evgen Onegin* though 'without a great impetus'. Ballet presented first the traditional *La fille mal gardée* in Spoerli's version and an 'acrobatic' ballet named *Ta ljubezen ...* (*That love...*) with just a few dancers.

Maribor Opera and Ballet marked its 1999/2000 season with the first International Singers' Competition in September 1999 where the Armenian bass Tigran Martirosian was awarded first prize. One of the best productions on the Maribor stage was Puccini's *Turandot*, again with the much praised Janez Lotric, followed by Verdi's *Don Carlos*, which was not on the same level, and a quite acceptable *Elisir d'amore* by Donizetti. At the end there were some guest performances of Bernstein's *West Side Story* in a production for La Scala from Milan with the Maribor orchestra. Ballet only showed a revival of the short ballet

SLOVENIA

Graduation Ball after D. Lichine. In 2000/01 two Verdi operas, *Macbeth* and *Ernani*, were presented as well as *Hymnus*, the first opera composition by Maribor-based Italian conductor Stefano Pellegrino Amato. The realisation wasn't very successful. The ballet *Spartacus* by A. Khatchaturian had a changed libretto with a shift to the personal drama of the heroes but with good dancers. The second production, the ballet *Pohujšanje*, after the drama *Scandal in the St. Florian Valley* by the leading Slovenian playwright Ivan Cankar, did not come up to expectations. The season 2001/02 showed a lifeless *La Bohème* and Verdi's *I due Foscari*, with very good singers and charming costumes but poor stage direction. The ballet ensemble presented Delibes' *Coppélia* 'without real dynamism' and *Transylvania*, a charming folkdance ballet based on dances and legends from Romania staged by Maribor-based Romanian Marin Turcu.

Puppet theatres as always gave joy to their young public but there were also some performances deliberately staged for the older audience, for example Büchner's *Woyzeck*. Puppets are always part of the magic; life has to be given to a dead object and there are different ways of doing it. Slovene puppeteers are very vital and address the above question with all possible methods. That was especially evident in the First Biennial of Puppet Creators in November 2001 in Maribor, the first result of the recently established Institution of Puppet Creators which links 17 institutional and non-institutional groups.

The impression of the last seasons was really fresh. There was new leadership for both main theatres in Ljubljana and Maribor. The first fruit of the Studio for Puppets in Ljubljana was the performance *Od ena do nic (From One to Zero)*; the Puppet Centre, a miniature theatre in Ljubljana Castle, also began functioning. In the puppet world, roles are being taken over by a generation of young, impulsive and highly skilled puppeteers who have chosen the puppet as their artistic mean of expression. Among the highlights were *Rumeno cudo (The Yellow Wonder)* by the playwright Renate Schupp, a 'strip cartoon' performance with actors as puppets, *Noge in krila (Legs and Wings)*, a typical female performance in Ljubljana, *Škrat Kuzma (Dwarf Kuzma)*, a playful romp in Maribor and *Zgodbe iz gozdicka (Tales from the Wood)* by Theatre Joze Pengov in Ljubljana. Numerous different non-institutional theatres were also active, like the Puppet Group 'Konj' of Silvan Omerzu with his author's project *Zbogom, princ (Goodbye, Prince)*. The breakthrough of puppetry into the national TV programmes is also very encouraging.

We can conclude that in the last three years the Slovenian theatre is very vital and active in all its branches, always searching new ways and presenting to its audiences the classic as well as the contemporary repertoire.

Dr **Henrik Neubauer** *is a director, choreographer, publicist, historian and Associate Professor at the University of Ljubljana. The entry is based on the yearly overall reviews published in the* Slovene Theatre Annual *and newspaper articles.*

SOUTH AFRICA

PETRUS DU PREEZ

The South African stage is probably one of the best barometers to show the diversity of a rapidly changing society. In less than a decade, our theatre has undergone quick and sometimes painful changes. With the changes in the South African state, the system for financing the country's arts also changed drastically. The previous structure of financial support had been biased towards the benefit of 'elitist arts' introduced to the country by the colonial powers for the consumption of generally white audiences, as reflected by the Performing Arts Councils (PACs) in the different provinces. The change of government not only meant a new political dispensation: the amount of money provided for the arts by the government, to support the drama, music, opera and ballet companies housed in the PACs' theatres, was drastically diminished. All art forms were now to receive equal support from the government. State patronage of the arts is now based on the principle that access to, participation in, and enjoyment of the arts, cultural expression, and the preservation of one's heritage are basic human rights; they are not luxuries, nor are they privileges, as the population under the Apartheid years had generally been led to believe. Government's role is to facilitate the optimum conditions in which these rights may be enjoyed and practised and the distribution of funds allocated for the arts must mirror this policy. This policy is of course not as simple, but it was the changes in the allocation of funds that changed the image of South African theatre and the performing arts and it is only now that the industry is finding its feet again.

The loss of grants to the PACs resulted in the disintegration of the various orchestras and theatre companies. Workers in the theatre had to find new jobs or to start their own companies. This is one of the reasons why South African arts festivals grew in number and in size. Festivals include the National Arts festival in Grahamstown, in Oudtshoorn the Klein Karoo Nasionale Kunstefees (Small Karoo National Arts Festival), Whale festival (in Hermanus), 'Kalfie'-festival, Macufe-festival (in Bloemfontein), Aardklop festival (in Potchefstroom), Spier Summer Arts Festival in Stellenbosch, the Cape Town festival and a number of others that come and go in smaller towns or venues during the year, for example the Melkbos Arts Festival.

It is in these festivals that new works are mostly presented and companies tour from one festival to another with these productions. Corporate sponsorships help to maintain festivals, with the granting of funds to specific performing companies or to the festival as a whole. The governments of the different provinces where these festivals are held (as well as the Ministry of Arts, Culture, Science and Technology) also support them, not only to promote diversity in the arts, but also to help stimulate the local economy where the different festivals are held.

SOUTH AFRICA

Vumile Nomanyama in *Yiimimangaliso – The Mysteries*, directed for Broomhill Opera by Mark Dornford-May   (*photo*: John Haynes)

In 1999 the festival in Oudtshoorn, the Klein Karoo National Arts Festival, yielded a crop of incredible performance and visual work, setting the stage for both national and international artists. The State Theatre Dance company (subsequently dissolved) performed a piece by Anton van Niekerk with music by Richard Carter, *Raka*, based on the Afrikaans prophetic epic poem with the same name by N.P. van Wyk Louw. With the focus on movement and music, the text of the poem, in conjunction with the performers of different races, changed into an ironic representation, not only of a Post-Apartheid South African society, but also of the arts in this society. Another example of an old work put into a new context was the modern Afrikaans classic, *Ek, Anna van Wyk*, (*I, Anna van Wyk*) by Pieter Fourie, directed by Marthinus Basson, in which recent South African history was re-examined. The patriarchal system with its dominant white, Christian-nationalist male figure (read the Apartheid regime) was juxtaposed with strong female characters pushed to the limits of sanity. In Basson's production, the male body was transformed to help portray the character of Anna and some of the other female characters, showing the distance we have travelled since the first performance of this play in the middle 80s. Like many of the productions at the festivals, this production toured the country to rave reviews, not only for its brilliant direction and acting, but also for the design that contributed to a striking presentation.

At the 1999 Standard Bank National Arts Festival in Grahamstown, the re-examination of South Africa's past on stage was well represented. The activities of the Truth and Reconciliation Commission under the leadership of Bishop Desmond Tutu were still in full swing. The country's artists and performers joined in a spirit of reconciliation by telling their stories – true or fictional. This can be seen as a natural process, mirroring the change in political circumstances, as well as the next step in the development of protest theatre in South Africa. In *The Story I Am About to Tell* (*Indaba Engizoyixoxa*) the cast consisted of professional actors and 'ordinary people' telling their stories and capturing a period of the country's history that the people still need to deal with. The text, written by the cast with Lesego Rampolokeng and directed by Robert Coman, was originally workshopped at the Market Theatre Laboratory in Johannesburg. Apart from the performances, which cut to the bone and wrenched the actors' and audience members' hearts by reliving the abuses of the apartheid era, it was also seen as a therapeutic exercise for the community. After the one hour show, discussion time was allocated for questions and answers. The production is a prime example of how theatre can help with the reconciliation process, not only for the audience members, but also for the performers. An earlier example of this kind of production is *Ubu and the Truth Commission* by Jane Taylor, directed and designed by William Kentridge for the Handspring Puppet Company in association with Mannie Manim Productions at the 1997 Standard Bank National Arts Festival.

Another re-telling of South African history was to be found in Brett Bailey's *The Prophet*. The play was directed and designed by Bailey and deals with the history of Nongqawuse, a Xhosa girl in the nineteenth century who received a prophecy in a dream: utopia would start for the Xhosa nation if they kill all their cattle, destroy their food stocks and refrain from cultivating their fields. This utopia included immortal cattle herds, the rising of the dead Xhosa from their graves, and the eradication of the settlers. The result was a great famine for the Xhosa, many of whom died of hunger in pursuit of this dream. Bailey used the different accounts of the story, juxtaposing fable with historical writings in a performance filled with Xhosa traditions and rituals, to illuminate the rich cultural belief of the nation.

In *The Life and Times of Johnny Cockroach – a Morality play*, by Breyten Breytenbach, directed by Marthinus Basson, the idea of reviewing the past is found again. As the programme puts it, 'A tribunal of women – the wives, mothers, daughters, lovers and widows – meet to give a hearing to the protagonists of the major events of our last century. Those summoned play out one last time the convictions, passions and dreams that led to revolutions, wars and upheavals. They give us a review, as if in bird-flight, of the horrors and the beauty of our times.' This is a very simplistic description, but in this second collaboration between Breytenbach, a famous poet and painter, and multi-award winning director Basson, the complicated text (with music by Adriaan Brand, Tom van der Schueren and Ewald Cress) as well as the visual imagery became too much for the average festival patron. The play received critical acclaim in the press and played to full houses early in 2000 in Cape Town, but with notable alterations to the text, as well as some cast changes. The general lack of a strong narrative in the text is overshadowed by the poetic images and language, as well as the fine performances by the ensemble cast.

SOUTH AFRICA

This mentally challenging theatre piece was Breytenbach's second text for the theatre, and the strong appeal to the senses and feeling of the piece was largely misunderstood by its audiences.

In 2000, theatre practitioners revisited the history of the Anglo-Boer War (or the South African War as it has since been called) that began 100 years earlier. The production of *Skroot* (*Scrap*) by Nico Luwes, directed by Gerben Kamper, was a main festival attraction at the Klein Karoo National Arts Festival in Oudtshoorn. The play deals with aspects of a war that has long been considered a 'whites only' war, such as the concentration camps and Kitchener's 'scorched earth' policy. The well known history is retold, but through the eyes of the mute Sotho servant, Semumu, of the white Boer family in a concentration camp. The value of this production is that the untold part of the history of the war, the contribution to it of the black population, has been brought to the fore, correcting some of the misconceptions on this subject caused by the selective writing and censorship of the history books. Luwes also manages to paint the different sides of the coin, not pointing the finger, but showing the results of the war and the bigger captivities in which the characters found themselves. The central theme, that of reconciliation, is mixed with strong Christian morals and dogma, but is never pretentious. The simple staging, with a barbed wire fence between the audience and performers, not only emphasized the distance between them, but also showed how far we have come since the atrocities of the war.

The psyche of the Afrikaner male was examined in the production of Pieter Fourie's *Boetman is die Bliksem is* (*Boetman is Very Angry*), a documentary drama based on the open letter of Chris Louw to Willem de Klerk in the South African print media, which sparked a large scale debate on the issue of acceptance of guilt for the Apartheid government in connection with the war during the 80s in Angola. Staged and designed by Marthinus Basson, this piece dissected the past and the fight between two generations with a clinical scalpel and re-ignited the debate. The truth seemed to become too real and emotional reactions on the part of the audience could not be avoided. The significance of this play is that Fourie used letters printed in the columns of the different newspapers, transcriptions of interviews and other material gathered in connection to the issue, sculpting his work from material that came from the hearts of different South Africans. Apart from the performances at the Aardklop Festival in Potchefstroom, the production toured some of the major cities in South Africa, including Cape Town and Bloemfontein and was seen in 2001 at the Klein Karoo National Arts Festival and the Standard Bank National Arts Festival in Grahamstown.

Brett Bailey and Third World Bunfight's *Big Dada* depicted the rise and fall of Idi Amin Dada. With its psychotic paranoia and absurd action, the production was a satirical, harrowing look at the general who killed 350,000 people in his country before he was driven out to Saudi Arabia in 1978. Bailey again uses the past for contemporary political and social commentary, dedicating this production to 'His Excellency President Robert Mugabe of Zimbabwe' and drawing parallels between the leaders. Bailey's flair for design and different performance styles helps to hide the cutting edge of truth behind laughter and disbelief. The performance used different theatrical styles, incorporating song

(Dada's vicious and ironic rendition of 'My Way') and wild dances, framing the stage like a cartoon, especially in the depiction of Dada's rise, but the portrayal of the vicious acts committed by Dada is distorted with the character feasting on his enemies. Bailey gives the audience a very entertaining spectacle, but refrains from didacticism, opting instead for a distance from scrutinizing interrogation. He leaves the search for answers in the audience's hands.

In *On the Lake*, internationally renowned dramatist Reza de Wet once again revisits Chekov (this time *The Seagull*) in a dreamlike play. This tragicomic piece formed part of a dialogue with the physical theatre piece *lake... beneath the surface* conceived and choreographed by Gary Gordon and Juanita Finestone of the First Physical Theatre Company, with a text by Reza de Wet and Gary Gordon. Original music was commissioned from Leonhard Praeg, Francois le Roux and Rick van Heerden. The Chekhovian characters in this 'dance-play' are suffused with problems, all resonating and reflecting within the subconscious, like bodies beneath the surface of a lake. This meta-theatrical production speaks to audience members and artists, questioning the nature of their work. *lake...beneath the surface* will also have a run in 2002 at Cape Town's Artscape Theatre.

In the early years of the new democracy in South Africa, a debate raged over the subsidizing of eurocentric art forms such as opera and ballet by the apartheid government. It was felt that the promotion and development of indigenous art and performance forms had been neglected in favour of elitist, eurocentric forms. Performance forms like opera and ballet needed to be taken to the masses and popularized. The almost exclusive 'white' face of opera needed to become more representative of the people living in South Africa. The result of this debate was the staging of creative and relevant 'adaptations' of operas on the South African stage.

During the 2000/2001 season of the Spier Festival, held on the Spier Wine Estate near Stellenbosch in the West Cape Province, the Broomfield Opera Company, in collaboration with South African artists, produced *Carmen* by Bizet and *The Mysteries*, both productions combining Africa and Europe in a fresh style of musical theatre. These productions also played to critical acclaim in England and Australia and were restaged in Cape Town's Joseph Stone Auditorium. In *Carmen*, the libretto was sung not in the original French, but in English with some Afrikaans and Xhosa mixed in here and there. The setting was also typically South African, giving the production a more familiar look for the local audience. The same can be said of *The Mysteries – Yiimimamgaliso*, which used English, Latin, Afrikaans, Zulu and Xhosa to retell the stories of the Chester Mystery plays. The actors and singers are not only representative of the community, but the community can join in the pleasure of the productions. A result of these productions was the creation of the South African Academy of Performing Arts (SAAPA) by the artistic team of the Broomhill Opera from England. This provides a training ground and performance platform for previously disadvantaged communities.

Brett Bailey was responsible for the direction of Artscape's production of a revamped *Macbeth* by Verdi, also placing it in an African context. The opera was cut by Pieter van Dijk, a well-known composer, to run for one and a half hours. The important arias, duets and chorus were kept and sung in Italian (with English subtitles), thus emphasizing the story. Van Dijk composed extra choruses and added an extra layer of (African) instrumentation in the orchestration. His version is set in an African kraal, with the audience also seated on stage in a theatre-in-the-round production, drawing the audience deeper into the action. The (predominantly black) singers of this opera came from the Demidex Opera Studio and the University of Cape Town Opera School, showing the growing support for traditional 'Western' performance genres synthesized with indigenous energy and interpretations.

The 2001/2002 Opera season of the Spier festival yielded a varied and interesting crop of productions of high standard. The most impressive (and original) was certainly Paul Stern's adaptation of Henry Purcell's *Dido and Aeneas* with Dizu Plaatjies of Amapondo and the Free Flight Dance Company, funded by the National Arts Council and the Nederburg Foundation. Guy Willoughby noted in a review: 'Stern affects… dialogue by refashioning the prologue, epilogue and various climactic dances of Purcell's taut, concentrated drama as pre-Western African music, created by that wonderful percussive ensemble, Amapondo.' The exchange of dialogue between the distinctly different music styles (that formed a wonderful unity) was visually represented by the placing of the orchestras on different sides of the stage. The Free Flight Dance Company's dancers were used to underline the atmosphere and themes at different intervals of the opera, combining their unique dance and movement qualities to the exceptional (old and new) music.

It is not an easy task to summarize the highlights of the South African stage. The diverse nature of the people that are living in this country, their culture, their different languages and the art that they create can be described and praised in many books and articles, but the scene is not always a very romantic one. The social climate of the country means that poverty, AIDS and education are all matters that the government feels need to be addressed before the arts can be fully developed. This does not mean that the government does not support the arts, but more money and clearer structures of policies and programmes need to be formulated to stimulate development and overcome biased views of the nature of culture and performance in South Africa. Until then it is up to the artists themselves – and the private sector – to fill the financial gaps, because theatre is not only an art form, it is a business.

Petrus du Preez *is at the University of Stellenbosch Centre for Theatre and Performance Studies.*

SWEDEN

LARS RING

Swedish theatre is, of course, not uniform – quite the contrary. It offers a medley of semi-official theatrical institutions, differing artistic and social visions, attempts to play to the gallery, theatre for children that can be both pedagogical and ferocious, community theatres, amateur productions, regional theatres and young, angry groups in revolt. All of it is performed under particular circumstances, with various underlying premises and for specific audiences. Summarising Swedish theatre is all but impossible. The most effective and the simplest solution is to superimpose a screen of some kind over its entirety, as provided by the decennial or millennial changes, the *Annual Review of the Theatre* or the proceedings of a theatre biennale, so as to allow patterns to emerge.

The points of intersection between several of the topics for debate at the Swedish Theatre Biennale 2001 manage, in my view, to capture the current state of the Swedish stage: one of the discussions focused on how dramatists portray society, another on the documentary drive in Swedish theatre, while a third dealt with politically revolutionary theatre – in terms of both form and content. These boundaries encompass a number of interesting stage productions from the preceding theatre season: *Rannsakningen* (*The Investigation*) and *Om detta är en människa* (*If This Is a Man*) from the Riksteatern/ National Touring Theatre; *Bön för Tjernobyl* (*Prayer for Chernobyl*) from its young people's division, Unga Riks; *Ur funktion* (*Essex Girls*) from Uppsala Municipal Theatre; *Den europeiska kritcirkeln* (*The European Chalk Circle*) from the Gothenburg Municipal Theatre. Productions such as *Titta en älg* (*Look, an Elk*) from Brunnsgatan Fyra, *Don Juan* from the Royal Dramatic Theatre and *Erik XIV* from Teater Halland also coincide with these categories but are of interest primarily because they all make a powerful break for freedom from the accepted traditions of realism, using lyrically naïve Dreamplay-dramaturgy, dance, the influence of *commedia dell'arte* and improvisation.

Swedish theatre has never really been the same since the premiere of *Sju tre* (*Seven Three*) by Lars Norén and the ensuing debate – and the events that unfolded in its wake: once the production had finished its run, one of the performers (in real life a prison inmate) participated in the shooting of two policemen in the course of a robbery. There were those who suggested that all the attention he had had received during the production had served to accentuate his psychopathic tendencies, and that the whole thing was the fault of Norén. The effect of the text of this play and its underlying premises was to shift the consensus. Suddenly the theatrical community found itself adopting radically different positions and the issue of why and how theatre is performed became appallingly topical.

Taken unawares by a reality he had never dreamed of, Norén felt he had to tackle the situation and portray it in semi-documentary form for the general public: the growth of Nazism with the prisons as its hotbed, the source of a good deal of crime, and young men with a hazy not to say perverse image of masculinity. The outcome, without any lecturing or simplistic solutions, laid the burden fair and square on the shoulders of the audience. Theatre was once more taking on, quite mercilessly, the role of discussing society, our common responsibilities, the care of offenders and the wave of neo-Nazism enveloping the country. The events that followed the production helped intensify the discussion even more. Norén was held responsible because he was said to have increased the need for attention of the prison inmates. Instead of a debate about ideology, punishment and alienation, the subject became what can and should be shown on stage. And views on this were legion.

Lars Norén, however, refused to give up. As Head of Drama at the National Touring Theatre he stubbornly persisted in his efforts to stay on the track of contemporary xenophobia. Both *Rannsakningnen* and *Om detta är en människa* are the result. And both productions have split the theatrical community since the directors Etienne Glaser and Lars Norén have renounced aesthetic performance for the theatre as a sophisticated form of entertainment. *Rannsakningen* by Peter Weiss uses only documentary material from the Auschwitz trials held in Frankfurt after the Second World War. Etienne Glaser uses local amateurs in his stage version, which has toured throughout the country: the testimony is uttered in various dialects, fumbling its way through the horrors. This helps make the interpretation a requiem for untrained voices. The amateur actors lend the production a 'rasping' quality that helps to clarify the documentary material. The real becomes more real, the veil of fiction is torn away.

Om detta är en människa also makes use of artlessness as a technique. An actor reads aloud from Primo Levi's book about his own experience of the concentration camps, alone on stage with only the words.

In the view of some people, the documentary form is a cul-de-sac. I do not think so. On the contrary, nowadays we find ourselves being poisoned by fiction. We are inundated on a daily basis via books and film with drama after drama, one piece of production-line dramaturgy after another. Many people feel so exhausted by fiction that real life is able to cut like a blade through the shell of the predictable. *Bön för Tjernobyl* by the journalist Svetlana Alexeivich, which describes the inferno after the nuclear meltdown at Chernobyl, also belongs in this category – the director, Åsa Kalmér, has arranged to stage the production in various churches with a choir that changes with the venue. This unusual location for theatre means that customary expectations are negated. The production turns into a mass for the dead, with a liturgical dramaturgy which provides a wealth of different focal points: the events take place 'to one side' while the vaulted spaces of the church echo to the existential issues.

So are reality, society and political theatre about to re-conquer the stage after a period of post-1968 introspection? Perhaps. When it comes to the independent theatre groups, two stand out as clearly political: Teater Tribunalen in Stockholm and Teatermaskinen from Riddarhyttan in the province of Bergslagen. The director Richard Turpin states quite openly that he is a Marxist-Leninist, trained at the University of Moscow before 1989. The trio behind Teatermaskinen mix sophisticated ideas from Brecht and Heiner Müller with the kind of raw, brutal aesthetics to be found in Artaud. Both groups are clearly visually-oriented, and while abjuring the theatre of political placards, they use form and irony as the means to affect their audiences, not in direct fashion by focusing on the substantive issues but indirectly by being questioning and critical. *Den europeiska kritcirkeln*, an

ABOVE: scene from Rebecca Prichard's *Essex Girls*, directed by Birgitta Englin for Uppsala Municipal Theatre

(*photo:* Staffan Claesson)

BELOW: scene from Peter Weiss's *Rannsakningen* (*The Investigation*) by the Riksteatern (National Touring Theatre)

(*photo:* Urban Jören)

updated and theatrical version of Bertolt Brecht, at Gothenburg's Municipal Theatre, is another political piece in which the director Jasenko Selimovic, who is also artistic director of the theatre, shifts the play to the Europe of today – an open discussion about the information society and mankind in the light of the EU and the views of the sociologist Manuel Castells.

Yet another political play is *Ur funktion* (*Essex Girls*) from Uppsala Municipal Theatre, directed by Birgitta Englin – this time belonging to the neo-brutalist British school of in-yer-face theatre. Rebecca Prichard writes about four young girls headed unblinkingly toward a gender role defined by early pregnancies, bad jobs, the sexualisation of their bodies and mental degradation. Girls who call each other cunts. The staging is vital and frenetic – a mixture of anxiety on speed, expectation and panicked miscalculation. Quite superb.

A trio of Swedish playwrights were staged with unusual frequency during the previous season. Staffan Göthe's new play *Temperance* would appear to be his last play about the Cervieng family. Magnus Nilsson had his play *Pepparrotslandet* (*The Horseradish Patch*) performed by three theatres. The small stage Lilla scenen at the Royal Dramatic Theatre was re-opened with a play by Kristina Lugn, *Stulna juveler* (*Stolen Jewels*). This had been immediately preceded by her *Titta en älg* and *Eskil Johanssons flyttfirma* (*Eskil Johansson's Removal Firm*). *Nattorienterarna* (*The Night-Orienteers*) was performed on several stages, while *Rut och Ragnar* (*Ruth and Ragnar*) was staged by the National Touring Theatre.

Where Kristina Lugn is a confessional poet whose work often revolves around death and whose poetic and obstinate linguistic style succeeds in escaping theatrical routine, both Staffan Göthe's and Magnus Nilsson's work are concerned with equal intensity to depict a bygone paradise – an obviously Swedish, gauche, small-town or rural middle-class in which artists (musicians or cabaret artistes) wander aimlessly around the action. Göthe's dramatic work portrays the remnants of an unquestioning Swedish Welfare State and the unquestioned ideals that underpin it with a kind of hilarious sorrow. I once referred to him as a nostalgist, as distinct from a utopian. And I realise – having read *Nostalgia*, a book by the historian of ideas Karin Johannesson – that I was right. The word, which derives from *nostos*, homecoming and *algos*, pain, was originally, in 1678, a diagnosis of illness in young soldiers from the countryside who suffered from a severe form of homesickness: a condition of grief and longing. Nostalgia is thus not a method of looking backward in melancholy but an active pain spot that contrasts the past with the present – and in so doing criticises the latter: a period without ideology and to which there can be no homecoming.

While both Kristina Lugn – that peculiar mixture of Pippi Longstocking and the eighteenth-century Swedish poet Stagnelius – and the director Thorsten Flinck may be tearing a whole tradition of psychological realism to shreds, they are doing so in order to get closer to the bone. At the Plaza Theatre, Flinck rushes at Strindberg's *The Father* like a bull in order to discuss a father-son relationship, male sexuality, black pedagogy, masks and love. Flinck attacks the text with various stage techniques in order to create a multi-faceted artwork with emotional intelligence, showmanship and subtlety on the theme of being exposed in all one's vulnerability.

The opposition to custom and tradition is, as we have seen, becoming more clearly defined. The kind of theatre they are attacking – 'theatre the way it's supposed to be' – still remains the province of the vast majority of productions.

While Ingmar Bergman continues to create theatre within the Stanislavsky tradition of introverted realism, his work ranks among the very best and the tenor of his productions is always in keeping with the nature of the play. The method of reading a text through a different set of expectations, even though these may be found within the work of the same individual, recurs frequently in Bergman's work. Botho Strauss as Strindberg, Shakespeare's *A Winter's Tale* refracted through the Swedish 19th century writer Almqvist, by way of example. He has just finished looking at *Maria Stuart* by Schiller through the lens of the latter's *The Maid of Orleans*. He radically alters the fundamentals, making Elizabeth the lecherous one, playing on her sexuality, and turning Mary Stuart into a woman struggling fervently for her Catholic faith. Once again it is the extraordinary excellence of Bergman's craftsmanship that is most on display, in the way events and scenes are blended, in the ingenuity of the staging and in the exemplary quality of the rhythm and the delivery. If *The Ghost Sonata* at the Royal Dramatic Theatre was Bergman's take on feeling disgust with life, *Maria Stuart* offers room for faith.

And all the while the English have been invading Sweden's stages. First up was the autumn program of Stockholm's Municipal Theatre which was filled with guest performances by English companies – a marvellous opportunity for Swedish theatre to study cerebral, well-paced acting with a vocal emphasis that does not labour under the ballast of Stanislavskian seriousness and physicality. Then it was the turn of the Royal Dramatic Theatre and its spring season, although this was more problematic in that English work was being shown in Swedish versions. As a result what was light-hearted was made cheerless and what was furious was turned into dance. Several plays, such as David Hare's *The Blue Room*, based on Arthur Schnitzler, were turned into embarrassing efforts at ingratiation. And then there was *A Midsummer Night's Dream*, in a production by John Caird, which was a lavish and charming but thin attempt to seduce. It would appear that what our 'National Theatre' lacks is that very necessary sense of its own identity, particularly if its artistic direction believes that anything is to be gained by promoting easy-going Anglo-Saxon works.

Municipal theatres rise and fall with the careers of their artistic directors and at the whim of municipal politicians. Gothenburg has made a striking recovery with the help of the knowledgeable and socially involved Jasenko Selimovic as its driving force. Malmö Dramatic Theatre labours under a peculiar local government system of councils and administrative bodies and the outcome in artistic terms is what you would expect. Stockholm's City Theatre intersperses unjustifiably ordinary work with bold choices. There has been a new spring at the National Touring Theatre with Thomas Lyrevik's defence of artistic integrity in tandem with Lars Norén while simultaneously acquiring more easily-digested productions from independent groups and regional theatres.

Is this the direction we are heading in? A state of affairs in which a couple of daring productions have to provide an alibi for an increasingly superficial theatre of entertainment that fills in the spaces? Strip-shows at Östgötateatern are picked up by the National Touring Theatre and turned into commercial productions once they have finished touring. Västmanland offers one programme of musical theatre after another. Who knows. I hope not.

Lars Ring *is theatre critic for the leading Swedish newspaper* Svenska Dagbladet.

SWITZERLAND

KATHRIN STRAUB

On June 2, 2002 the people of the city of Zurich voted on payments to its main theatre, the Schauspielhaus (Playhouse). One bill concerned subsidies for the maintenance of the building, and a one-off contribution towards the cost overrun incurred by the Schauspielhaus during the building of the Schiffbau (Ship Building), its new cultural and creative centre, housing a large stage, a small stage, rehearsal rooms and workshops. The hall, formerly used for shipbuilding, is a huge space that makes the hearts of those who make theatre beat more quickly. The other bill contained a proposal for a subsidy increase, mainly to cover increased personnel costs due to new regulations in labour law. A total of nearly 10 million Swiss francs was at issue, not an outrageously high amount for Zurich, but the money was 'to be or not to be' for Christoph Marthaler as director of Zurich's Schauspielhaus; something akin to a vote of confidence in politics.

Since Marthaler's return to the city on the Limmat – he started out in the independent Zurich scene, going on to triumph on the best known stages in Germany – major papers, including the *New York Times*, report regularly on Schauspielhaus productions in their arts pages. One season in the hands of Marthaler was enough for people to start talking about it and, for the first time in its history, to make it Theatre of the Year, 2001. An illustrious group of critics from *Theater Heute* (Theatre Today), *the* theatre magazine for the German-speaking world, honoured the Schauspielhaus with the award. At the same time, in Ueli Jäggi, the group selected an Actor of the Year from the Schauspielhaus ensemble. The fact that several productions originating from Marthaler's house in 2001 and 2002 – the master's own interpretation of Shakespeare's *Twelfth Night* and Christoph Schlingensief's controversial Zurich *Hamlet* in 2001; Stefan Pucher's cleverly reduced and convincingly contemporary version of Chekhov's *Three Sisters*; *Alibi*, a work by dancer and choreographer Meg Stuart, and Christoph Marthaler's theatrical conversion of Franz Schubert's song cycle *Die Schöne Müllerin* in 2002 – were invited to the Berliner Theatertreffen surprised nobody in theatre circles; after all, the Swiss director ranks among the big names in German-speaking theatre. The local public took note of this, but that was all.

Schauspielhaus Zurich – like Swiss theatres in general – has an extremely high self-financing quota in comparison with theatres in other German-speaking areas. The subsidies do not even cover the fixed personnel costs, as they normally do in Germany. The Schauspielhaus must independently raise around 4.5 million Swiss francs through ticket sales and sponsors, while the opera house has to raise as much as 14 million. It was a close call, but success came with 53% of the citizens of Zurich voting 'yes' to the financial aid packages. This will ward off the Schauspielhaus' bankruptcy and Marthaler will stay, but the financial difficulties are far from over.

Patrizia Perlini (*Wendla*) and Andreas Bürgisser (*Melchior*) in a scene from Louis Naef's open-air, landscape production of Frank Wedekind's *Frühlings Erwachen (Spring Awakening)* in Lenzburg

SWITZERLAND

Zurich has a lot to offer culturally, especially in the area of theatre. In addition to the Schauspielhaus there is also Theaterhaus Gessnerallee, the house for independent theatre groups and international guest performances. Peter Brook, among others, is a regular guest here and, in 2000, the Gessnerallee was the venue for *Schlachten*, Luk Perceval's marathon production of Shakespeare's royal dramas – an unforgettable theatre experience. On top of that is a whole series of smaller and fringe theatres offering a wide range of theatre forms. The fear that these would remain empty after Marthaler and Co. moved in and after the opening of the Schiffbau is as yet unfounded. Indeed, last season, the Theater Neumarkt, one of the top league of Swiss theatres, both in terms of size and artistic merit, rose to become the most frequented theatre with around 85% capacity. It picked itself up after a change of management and a difficult first season. The manner in which the director pair Crescentia Dünsser and Otto Kukla consistently pursued a theatre language of their own has paid off. Following a successful season, artistically and financially, in 2000–01, 2001–02 was a also good year. A highlight in an attractive programme of original productions and guest performances was the atmospherically stylised and, in terms of stage setting, beautiful production of John Ford's *Tis Pity She's a Whore*, in the hands of the young director, Simone Blattner. The previous year she had staged a fascinating interpretation of Ben Jonson's *Volpone*, spiked with wonderful flashes of comic genius. With the live installation by the London artist Gary Stevens, *And*, Theater Neumarkt provided one of the rare co-productions – the partners being the Théâtre Arsenic in Lausanne and the Théâtre de l'Usine, Geneva – to transcend domestic Swiss language boundaries. This is something which people still have difficulty coming to terms with. Very rarely are there guest performances in the other language areas, let alone projects that bridge the gap between them. Wisely, this performance remains largely in the non-verbal or pre-verbal area. In the 2000/01 season, the Schauspielhaus worked together with the Théâtre Vidy of Lausanne in an effort to contribute to domestic cultural exchange with a stage adaptation of Gottfried Keller's *Romeo und Julia auf dem Dorfe* (*A Village Romeo and Juliet*).

There is no definitive Swiss theatre. Various models are practised depending on language and cultural area. The established German-Swiss theatre functions according to the city theatre model typical of German-speaking theatre operations, with subsidised permanent houses and ensembles attached to them, often organised into three-part operations (dance, opera and spoken theatre all under one roof). In the French-speaking western part of Switzerland, theatre is based on the French model with permanent establishments - usually, however, without their own ensembles. Instead, these are formed *ad hoc* for each production, and co-productions with other theatres are not uncommon. In the small area of Ticino, theatre is geared towards the Italian model, with predominantly touring companies and independent groups. The Teatro Sociale Bellinzona also operates on a guest performance basis. Another traditional body in Ticino is the Cooperativa Scuola e Teatro Dimitri in Verscio. If it is the Schauspielhaus Zurich and German-language spoken theatre in general, along with the two other exponents, namely the Theater Basel and Luzerner Theater, that are mainly covered here, this can be justified by considering the fact that theatre in the Basel-Lucerne-Zurich triangle has developed into a centre of committed and innovative theatre. It is symptomatic that, according to the criteria governing the Berliner

Theatertreffen, four out of ten of the outstanding productions of the 2001–2002 season originated in Switzerland. In addition to the three from Zurich already mentioned, Ibsen's *John Gabriel Borkmann*, directed by the Theater Basel's Sebastian Nübling, also made the trip to Berlin. On top of that, theatre in German Switzerland was – and is – exposed to stronger turbulence than in Western and Southern Switzerland where 'business as usual' – not meant negatively – largely prevails. However, the creativity so characteristic of the theatre scene in the Basel-Lucerne-Zurich triangle, and the international importance awarded it, does not please everyone. Condescendingly dismissed as 'underwear theatre' by certain, rather conservative circles of traditional theatre enthusiasts, these theatre aesthetics give rise to controversy – but then, what could be better for theatre than being talked about?

Theatre is turning into a political issue, as illustrated by the current example of the Schauspielhaus. The pattern is practically the same for all three: artistically interesting and inovative theatre is making its mark across borders and receiving good reviews, but the public is left out in the cold (in both senses of the expression). Many regular theatre-goers, who do not want to change their viewing habits, have no appreciation for what is offered on stage and as a result no longer attend the theatre, cancelling their season tickets. Before new audiences come to fill those empty seats, things will become financially precarious and this could be used by conservative circles in Switzerland to attack unpopular theatre on a political level. And, as it is the taxpayer who funds the theatre, this is entirely possible. But, without this support it is impossible to have artistic, formal theatre with a challenging content.

Of the three, the Theater Basel was the only one able to stop the exodus, thanks to an initiative headed by a few rich ladies from Basel who contributed 16 million to the 21 million Swiss franc cost of of a new theatre to replace the old comedy theatre at the beginning of 2002. Capacity has risen somewhat once again. Plenty of public discussion may well have had a confidence-building effect, and on top of that there were productions, such as one of the *Zauberflöte* (*The Magic Flute*), which proved to be real hits. And, of the three, Basel has been in the 'underwear' league the longest, perhaps allowing the effects of habit to contribute to the positive development.

Both ensembles put together for each production and permanent theatre companies are active on the lively independent scene. Included among these are the traditional troupe Klara from Basel, the group Mass&Fieber assembled by the director Niklaus Helbling and the young actress Fabienne Hadorn, whose first production – really low-budget – *Bambifikation* from 1999 has, in the meantime, achieved cult status, and whose latest production, *Krazy Kat,* is also well on its way to doing the same. Mass&Fieber's trademark is swift, imaginatively rich parodistic clashes between genres and modern myths in a pleasant combination of theatre and music.

Actress/director Meret Matter and her Berner Theater Club 111 have made a name for themselves with series theatre and were among the first to perform theatre soaps on stage. The group 400asa, directed by Samuel Schwarz, caused quite a stir with its interpretation of ancient plays; *Bakchen* for example, was played almost completely in the dark. Never before has there been so much theatre put on in Switzerland, both in established theatres and in the independent scene, in professional as well as amateur theatres and with the most varied of aesthetic means. Each year, institutions promoting culture receive more and more applications for funding.

Once again open-air amateur theatre groups also enjoyed great success. Up and down the country, districts, whole villages and small towns were transformed into theatres as the people caught the theatre bug. Two representative highlights include: Calderon de la Barca's *Welttheater* (*Great Theatre of the World*) and Frank Wedekind's *Frühlings Erwachen* (*Spring Awakening*). The *Welttheater* is performed regularly – and in 2000 it was time for it again – in the square with Einsiedeln's imposing baroque monastery church as backdrop. Thomas Hürlimann, next to Urs Widmer the most popular and productive contemporary playwright in the country, wrote a completely new version for this occasion, one that did not mince words. Volker Hesse, formerly in charge of the Theater Neumarkt in Zurich, directed. Thousands flocked to this historic place of pilgrimage in the interior of Switzerland for this theatrical experience. It was in the historic town of Lenzburg with its castle and accompanying hill that Louis Naef, a specialist in projects such as these, together with professional actors and actresses as well as many, for the most part young, amateurs and a feel for enchantingly beautiful (natural) images, produced Frank Wedekind's *Frühlings Erwachen* as landscape theatre.

Amateur theatre has a long and rich tradition in Switzerland. Gone are the days when only operettas and farces were performed; instead, there are serious and difficult contemporary plays as well. After months of rehearsal, the result is then performed for local audiences. All this work has an important communicative, social and also integrating function for the village or community in which it originates. All over the country, acting is a favourite leisure activity for the average Swiss. In the German-speaking part of Switzerland alone there are over 600 amateur dramatic clubs, organised into regional societies and all under the authority of the Zentralverband Schweizer Volkstheater (Central Society of Popular Swiss Theatre).

The most famous drama theatre in French-speaking Switzerland is still the Théâtre Vidy in Lausanne, under the direction of René Gonzales. The direction at the Comédie de Genève has changed hands from Claude Stratz to Anne Bisang. There has also been a change at the helm of the Théâtre Populaire Romand. After more than 30 years its founder and manager, moving spirit and long-time director Charles Joris had to give up the reins. His successor is Gino Zampieri. Like Christoph Marthaler and Stefan Bachmann, director of drama at the Theater Basel, the new Directrice of the Comédie comes from the independent scene. This is symptomatic for development in theatre: the merging of the borders between established and independent theatre. Some, among them also Swiss directors, continue to do the one – working with independent theatre groups – without giving up the other – producing at permanent houses. Barbara Frey, Samuel Schwarz, Meret Matter and Niklaus Helbling, among others, belong to this category. In the meantime, four women have joined the ranks of Swiss theatre management: along with Anne Bisang, Barbara Mundel in Lucerne and Crescentia Dünsser at the Zürcher Neumarkt, Franziska Severin is head of opera in the triumvirate of the Theater St.Gallen.

The most internationally well-known opera house in Switzerland, at which all the big international stars regularly appear, is the Opernhaus Zurich. For unconventional productions, the three-in-one houses in Basel and Lucerne are good addresses and the Theater St.Gallen often offers premieres. This theatre, the largest in Eastern Switzerland, celebrated its 200-year anniversary in 2001, making it the oldest permanent professional theatre in Switzerland. In honour of the anniversary, a special programme made up exclusively of first performances and produced especially for the occasion was shown for one straight week. Peter Schweiger, the play director in a team of three equals, is still *the* man for contemporary Swiss dramas. In 2001 he was the recipient of the Hans Reinhart Ring, the most prestigious award in Swiss theatre.

Dance has its audiences in Switzerland and there are some good companies, for example that of Phillipe Saire. Phillip Egli from the independent dance scene has been head of the Theater St. Gallen since last season and at the Stadttheater Bern, Felix Dumeril took over from Martin Schläpfer. But along with Heinz Spoerli in Zurich it is still the dance freak Maurice Béjart, in Lausanne, who causes sensations with his ballet, far beyond Swiss borders. Basel and Lucerne both make do without a permanent, traditional ballet, also due to financial reasons. Instead, Basel, with Joachim Schlömer, has opted for dance theatre and Lucerne has hosted guest performances put on by nationally and internationally acclaimed modern dance companies. The Schauspielhaus Zurich is cultivating a special kind of co-operation with the choreographer and dancer, Meg Stuart. She produces works on a regular basis with the actors and actresses of the ensemble. It is unusual, and a speciality of Marthaler's house, for a choreographer to work regularly on a stage which is purely for spoken theatre.

2002 is the year of the Swiss National Exhibition. In addition to a host of other attractions, the Swiss UNESCO commission is also presenting a theatre project: five stand-alone plays which examine signs of the times from an ethical point of view.

Good, new theatre texts are few and far between, although much is done to promote up-and-coming talent. Three mid-size theatres have joined forces in the 'drama processor', to give inexperienced authors a chance to develop their first tentative dramatic steps under the guidance of professionals. The 'women's drama lab' has the same goal. This is a project sponsored by Frauen im Theater (Women in Theatre), in a special effort to promote female playwrights, since plays by women for German-speaking stages are still under-represented. Masterclass MC 6 is a project in place to promote young goal-orientated playwrights, both male and female, who already have some experience and have published texts. In the first round, four participants were selected from 15 works received. Those plays completed by the end of 2002 in the MC 6 workshops, with the guidance of the renowned prose author and dramatist Marlene Streeruwitz, will be premiered at the Theater Neumarkt in Zurich and at the Bern and Lucerne theatres as well as at the 'ensemble' Theater Biel-Solothurn. MC 6 is a project of the Swiss Centre of the International Theatre Institute. Hope&Glory, a joint project of the Zurich theatres Gessnerallee and Neumarkt, is also meant to promote the next generation. The Festival of Young Theatre Talent gives these youngsters a platform on which to present their work and took place this year for the fifth time. There is to be a continuation next year in a slightly different form.

Kathrin Straub *studied at Zurich University. She is a lecturer, and a radio play editor at Swiss Radio DRS. Her journalistic work focuses on theatre and radio plays.*

TOGO

RAMSÈS ALFA

In these recent years Togo's theatrical activity has become more and more intense, showing a number of new thematic and scenic options which started to appear at the beginning of the 90s, due to the socio-political climate.

Many theatre groups are arriving on the scene, in response to young people's need to express themselves. As a result, the entertainment theatre has given way to another kind of theatrical expression, a much more committed one, which takes up themes like war, famine, democracy and AIDS with a deep desire to draw the audience's attention to these subjects. In spite of heavy financial problems Togo's theatre can expect good times ahead of it, and brave private initiatives are helping to make this hope concrete.

Let us note first the Festival de Théâtre de la Fraternité (FESTHEF) which has offered since 1992, at first every two years, then from 1999 every year, a promotional opportunity to the troupes and their new productions. Other theatrical events such as DJA'LELE and FITHAP (Festival International de Théâtre et des Arts Plastiques), although they no longer exist, have contributed to the blossoming of theatre until the year 2000. Nor should we overlook the school festivals such as DANA, which had its first edition last year in Tsevié, a city located 45km away from Lomé, Togo's capital, or FESTHA, held at Lomé's Technical College every year since 2000.

There is yet another event, called Les Karnak, a dramatic art training course with more than a hundred trainees every year.

Apart from festivals and training courses, new cultural spaces play a considerable role in the promotion of the stage crafts in Togo. For example, the AREMA space, the Degnigban centre or the Nathanael space in Lomé, and many others elsewhere in the country, have allowed the enlargement of performance possibilities. These were previously limited to Lomé's Centre Culturel Français, both for groups belonging to the capital and for groups in other parts of the country.

Let us also mention KEWEWA(Fédération Togolaise des Hommes de Théâtre) and the recently created Togolese ITI Centre, which are structures designed to encourage mutual support activities between companies and actors. But the biggest part of the credit for the growth in our theatre is due to the theatre workers themselves. Indeed, our directors, playwrights, actors and technicians, though they cannot hope for any State support, work very hard and without cease to give life to their profession.

It would be ungrateful not to mention institutions such as the Service de Co-opération et d'Action Culturelle (SCAC), the Centre Culturel Français (CCF), the Agence Intergouvernementale de la Francophonie (AIF) and the European Union's Programme de Soutien aux Initiatives Culturelles Décentralisées (PSICD) which are the only ones giving financial support to cultural activities, even if this support is very limited, compared to the scale of demand.

In short, in spite of the difficulties, theatre people are making theatre, against winds and tides, for a varied and very attentive public. More than a hundred theatre groups take part in theatre production in Togo. But we have to stress that this is not necessarily a professional activity: very few companies succeed in gaining real recognition on the African or world theatre market.

Let us mention companies such as Luxor, Tambours Théâtre de Lomé, the Atelier Théâtre de Lomé, l'Ensemble Artistique de Lomé and the troupe du Club Unesco Etudiant de l'Université de Lomé, which are known abroad. It is around those companies that we will concentrate this report of theatre activity during the three seasons 1999–2000, 2000–2001, 2001–2002.

The Atelier Théâtre de Lomé (ATL) is responsible for numerous activities.. In 1999, the company toured with *La Récupération (The Recovery)* by Josué Kossi Efoui, directed by Kangni Elem and Gaétan Noussoglo, with the support of Lomé and Cotonou's Centre Culturel Français. This production was also at the MASA 99, and in 2000 played first at the KIFT in Korea and later at the FESTHEF in Togo.

In 2001 ATL created *Tchakatchaka* from texts by the Togolese authors Kangni Alem, Gnoussira Analla, Hilla-Laobé Amele, Cossy Guenou and Jenuina Fiadjoe, directed by Gaétan Noussoglo. The same year saw the production of *Choboun* from O'Tae Sok, staged by Kangni Elem and Gaétan Noussoglo.

In 2002, ATL first revived *The Recovery* before going to Bordeaux in April with a new piece, *Atterrissage (Landing)* by Kangni Elem, a production which was also presented at the Francophonies théâtrales of Maintes-la-Jolie (France).

Although the UNESCO Students' Club of the Université de Lomé was less active, nevertheless in 1999 it was at the FESCUAO 99 in Yamoussoukro (Ivory Coast) with *L'Epopée de Djabatore (Djabatore's epic)* in Ramsès Alfa's production. This production was also seen in FESTHEF, where it was awarded first prize in the festival, as well as gaining the best actor prize for Dawa Litaaba-Kagnita and best actress for Eyno Tatrabor. In 2000, after taking part in the FITD in Burkina Faso, the company toured only in Togo.

As for CUE-UL, it was in Bamako (Mali) during 2001 for the Festival Culturel des Clubs UNESCO de l'Afrique de l'Ouest (FESCUAO), with *Bal masque (Masked Ball)* written and staged by the same Ramsès Alfa.

The Ensemble Artistique de Lomé (ENAL) is one of the companies that the Togolose audience appreciates particularly. In October 1999, it toured in French Guyana and after that went to Besançon (France) with *Les Veillées de Kadjika (Kadjika's Nights)* by Mèwe Banissa. After this production, ENAL created another Mèwe Banissa play, *Paroles de cauris en pile et face*, with which they took part in FESTHEF, Racines 2000 (Benin) and FIADFUP (Tchad). In 2000 the company produced Lamko Koulsy's *Paillon de Nuit (Moth)* staged by Mèwe Banissa, who in 2001 also staged Xavier Durringer's *Une envie de tuer sur le bout de la langue (Desire to Kill on the Tip of the Tongue)*.

Besides ENAL, Lomé's Tambours Théâtre is a company which, since 1997, has been trying out new ways of staging, working in experimental theatre with performances without scenery or props, making use of the actor's body as a table or a piece of office equipment. In 1999, Tambours toured the country with *La Répétition (The Rehearsal)* from Claude Kokou Amegan's *La sentence des derniers (The Sentence of the Last)* staged by Armand Brown. It was presented in Racines 99. After that Armand Brown created *Sans façons (No way)*.

TOGO

In 2000, Lomé's Tambours Théâtre produced a new piece, *Délire (Delirium)* by Alexandre Koffi Monde, staged by Richard Lakpassa; in 2001 came the new version of *Du lampion au théâtre*, written by Richard Lakpassa and staged by Julien Mensah. It should be said that Lomé's Tambours Théâtre has been the great revelation of Togolese theatre since 1995. Unfortunately, the company is presently facing extreme difficulties, because of the death of its actor Armand Brown during the festival Racines 99 in Benin and, after that, the death of the talented Marc Kodjo Ayivor in December 2001. The group is now trying to survive as best they can.

On the other hand, Luxor is going well, with many activities. In 2000, it took part in FESTHEF with *La Chute (The Fall)* by Ramsès Alfa and *Le Cid en rap*, a rap version of Pierre Corneille's *Le Cid*. This production toured in West Africa in March and April.

We cannot close this article without mentioning Abdou-Razac Bah-Traoré, Chairman of the Fédération Togolaise des Hommes de Théâtre, who has still not recovered from a traffic accident, on the occasion of the celebration of World Theatre Day on 27th March 2001. We wish him well.

After this panorama of theatre activity, we are in a position to say that the Togolese theatre is in good shape, in spite of the many problems it has to face. We deeply regret that Togolese actors do not take part in international training courses and we would like to launch a resounding call to any cultural institutions that can help us to overcome this deficiency. Finally, we want to thank all those people who continue to support Togolese theatre: we ask them to keep on backing us, so that our craft, the theatre, can live.

TURKEY

EMRE ERDEM

Turkey has been going through a difficult period in recent years. First, there was the devastating earthquake of 1999. Then, in early 2001, the woes of chronic inflation were greatly exacerbated by an economic crisis of equally seismic proportions. Shock waves of the September 11 incident added to the problems. Theatre was of course affected. Uncertainty dampened spirits. Caution replaced audacity. Infighting within companies grew. Lavish productions were out, as was experimentation.

There were nevertheless exceptions. In her own theatre The Kenter Players, Istanbul's Yildiz Kenter played herself, her mother, and her daughter in an auto-biographical presentation titled *Always There Was Love*. BKM Players, Istanbul, founded by playwright-director-actor Yilmaz Erdogan, have been making a significant contribution to Turkish black comedy. Their production of Erdogan's *Ever Seen a Firefly?* won several prizes. Another private company owned by its director, the Ali Poyrazoglu Theatre, also won accolades when it staged Poyrazoglu's adaptation of D. Keyes' *Guinea Pig*. The director-actor's characterisation of a man with Down's Syndrome fascinated audiences.

Dostlar Theatre celebrated its 30th anniversary. Since its foundation by the famous actor and director Genco Erkal, the company has performed plays by Bertolt Brecht, Tankred Dorst, Vaclav Havel, Vasif Ongeren and Nazim Hikmet. One man shows have taken a place in the Dostlar repertory, directed and acted by Genco Erkal. He has adopted the poems and stories of Nazim Hikmet and Aziz Nesin. He has toured all around Turkey and the world with the works of well known poets and writers. In commemoration of the contemporary poet Can Yücel, who passed away in 2000, Dostlar Theatre celebrated the anniversary with a memorial production, *Can*.

Martin McDonagh's slice of Irish life, *The Beauty Queen of Leenane*, was directed by Cuneyt Caliskur in the Istanbul State Theatre. Sumru Yavrucuk acted the main character Leanne, the single woman who lives under the pressure of her old fashioned mother, with great success. The director commented on the similarities between Irish and Turkish traditions.

The State Theatre of Turkey co-operated with the National State Theatre of Russia to give some reality to the conventional aspiration of developing international cultural relations. In December 2000, a Russian–Turkish Drama Festival was held in Moscow. Eleven Turkish plays were presented by prestigious companies of the Russian Federation. Most are still (June 2002) continuing successful runs in Moscow, Voronezh, Perm, Yaroslavl, Samara, and Ufa. Reciprocally, numerous Russian plays have been and will be presented during festivals in Turkey, under the auspices of the State Theatre and the Ministry of Culture.

One such institution is the International Drama Festival of Countries of the Black Sea Region, first held in May 2000. Repeated in 2001 and again in 2002, the festival has become an ongoing annual event with participating countries including Bulgaria, Romania, Belarus, Ukraine, Russia, Georgia, Azerbaijan and Turkey.

With the organisational support of the Ministries of Culture of Greece and Turkey, the Istanbul State Theatre hosted a Drama Encounter in May 2002. Greek companies staged three Turkish plays, while local groups presented two Greek plays. It was decided to repeat the event in Athens in 2003.

The Istanbul International Theatre Festival, organized by the Istanbul Art and Culture Foundation, is also continuing. Due to economic difficulties, however, this annual event will henceforth be held every other year. The 2002 festival included Heiner Goebbels' *Hashirigaki*, as well as *Rose Rage*, an adaptation of Shakespeare's *Henry VI* plays, directed by Edward Hall, son of the former director of Britain's National Theatre, Peter Hall, and a production of two Sarah Kane plays by a Turkish director, Emre Koyuncuoglu.

The Turkish Centre of the ITI has been actively encouraging the construction of new theatre buildings. In a widely publicized ceremony in July 2001, it awarded prizes to persons and institutions for their contributions to the infrastructure of theatre.

Turkish theatre lost two of its most prolific playwrights in 2001. Necati Cumali and Memet Baydur died, and were honoured by long runs of special productions of their works. Cumali's plays *Derya Gülü* (*The Rose of The Sea*), *Mine* (*Enamel*), *Susuz Yaz* (*Summer Without Water*) and *Nalinlar* (*The Clogs*), a classic of Turkish theatre, were performed in many other countries by Kenter Players. Baydur's plays *Yesil Papagan Limited* (*Green Parrot Ltd*), *Kamyon* (*Truck*) and *Tensing* visualized the society of Turkey. Another loss was the closure of the decades-old Dormen Theatre.

The current of fascism is rising all around the world day by day, trying to recruit more supporters. Theatre cries out against its darkness. Theatre Studio, Istanbul has been producing plays about fascism for the last two seasons. Esther Vilar's *Speer* was directed by the founder of the theatre, Ahmet Levendoglu. *Speer* was an ensemble work of the company that told about the Third Reich through the eyes of Hitler's architect, Albert Speer. Another accomplishment was *Breaking the Code* by Hugh Whitemore, also directed by Levendoglu, about the life of Alan Turing, who cracked the German Army's secret codes. Bertolt Brecht's *Schweyk*, with its panorama of World War II, was directed by Yücel Erten in Istanbul's Municipal Theatre, with the use of sound a notable feature.

Istanbul is Turkey's capital city for culture and art. It is possible to watch any type of artistic event, modern or postmodern. The city's fringe companies have existed from the beginning of the 90s. Some are still amateurs but others have gained professional recognition. For instance, Besinci Sokak Theatre, founded by director Mustafa Avkiran has been performing successful plays by young Turkish playwrights. The company had a co-operation with Hebbel Theatre, Germany and was invited to many international festivals abroad with Murathan Mungan's mysterious play *Dumrul ve Azrail* (*The Angel of Death*). Their last production *Ay Tedirginligi* (*Moon Perturbation*) by Ozen Yula criticised the life of a man and a woman in the period of the 50s in Turkey and was performed at the 2002 Bonn Biennale. Bilsak Atelier is another example of a

Othello, directed by Sükru Türen for the Istanbul Municipal Theatre in the 2002 Istanbul Theatre Festival
(*photo*: Orhan Burian)

TURKEY

group which has been searching for new styles of acting, dramaturgy and interdisiciplinary work. Atelier performed two experimental productions, *Birthday* by Ludmila Petrushevskaya and *Traveller* by Nazim Hikmet.

Kenter Players' production of David Auburn's *Proof* was directed by Yildiz Kenter with the new generation of Kenter players acting alongside the older generation. With the harmony of the old and the young ones, the life of the senile Maths professor came into sharper focus. The stage design, by Osman Sengezer, was compact and pure, in keeping with the text. Sengezer, a master stage and costume designer, also designed the set of Yildiz Kenter's *Always There Was Love*, leaving unforgettable pictures in the mind.

Other notable productions during the period in question include Büchner's *Woyzeck*, directed by Mehmet Ulusoy at the Istanbul Municipal Theatre, and a collage of Chekhov's plays, arranged and directed by Basar Sabuncu, also at the Istanbul Municipal Theatre. Tankred Dorst's *I, Feuerbach* was another remarkable production, directed by Genco Erkal at the Dostlar Theatre, Istanbul.

The opening, on World Theatre Day 2002, of a new theatre in its own building in Istanbul, Oyun Atölyesi (The Play Atelier), by a husband and wife acting team, Haluk Bilginer and Zuhal Olcay, was a welcome event. Their production of Anthony Horowitz's *Mindgame*, directed by Isil Kasapoglu, received critical acclaim and was invited to the Istanbul Festival.

With the world wide blessing of UNESCO, 2002 is being celebrated as the centenary of Nazim Hikmet's birth. In Russia, the United States, England, France, Germany, Australia and many other countries, admirers of the martyred poet-dramatist have staged celebratory performances to honour his memory. In London's Queen Elizabeth Hall, for instance, Turkish actors were joined by Julie Christie and Mark Rylance in a dramatic presentation of his poetry. All over Turkey, private and subsidized theatres are trying to outdo each other in staging his plays throughout the year, although Turkish citizenship has not been posthumously returned to him despite the best efforts of his supporters. Still, the officially sanctioned celebrations may be seen as a measure of how far artistic freedom has progressed since the days when hysterical repression made Nazim Hikmet's name unmentionable in his own country.

One hopes the trend will continue.

Emre Erdem *is a theatre critic, dramaturg, and researcher, writing for* Shalom *(the Turkish Jewish weekly), and* Cumhuriyet *(daily); he is a member of ITI and IATC and currently working for the Yehudi Menuhin Foundation.*

UNITED KINGDOM

England
PETER HEPPLE

If *Theatre Record* is to be believed, and this is a journal which reviews all the London and many regional openings, English theatre is in a state of numerical decline. In 1999 it carried reviews of 804 London shows, in 2000 708 and in 2001 674.

Is this a worrying trend? Well, in one respect it obviously is. Fewer productions mean less work for actors and reduced opportunities for writers. Or, and this is my personal contention, it more likely means less inclination to take a chance on the unknown, more care in choosing plays and productions, and possibly a reduction in the number of London's fringe theatres.

It does not necessarily mean a decline in interest on the part of the public. Despite the events of September 11, 2001 and an alarming increase in the cost of West End theatre seats over the past few years, there is some evidence that theatre attendance is going up. But bodies like the Society of London Theatre are past masters at massaging figures, whether it be box office receipts or the size of audiences, and it is a fact that a full theatre with tickets bought at half price yields the same return as a half-full one paying full price. An increase in receipts could even be explained by the hefty service charges most theatres now impose on seats booked by phone or through the net.

What is certain is that the theatre is no place for gamblers. One new management went into speedy liquidation simply because its transfer of a National Theatre production failed, and although some plays from subsidised and fringe theatres have been enormous successes when they moved to the West End, for example *Stones in His Pockets*, by and large the last two or three years seem to have proved what I have believed for two decades or more, that there are at least two kinds of audience – the dedicated followers of theatre, who go to the National, the RSC and the principal fringe theatres as a matter of course, and the mass audience, drawn to a show because of the skill of its marketing, unanimously good reviews or simply because it is the basis of a night out.

This is what exercises the minds of artistic directors, whether in the commercial or subsidised theatre, because the New Labour government, like most governments in fact, has not until very recently delivered the extra funding it promised. This is not to say that things are worse, but they are not much better, and despite some tinkering with funding bodies, the money has taken a long time to trickle down.

There have been new theatres, notably the Lowry at Salford, and major refurbishments to others, like the Birmingham Hippodrome and the long-delayed improvements to the Theatre Royal, Stratford East. But essentially the *status quo* of the previous review is still in place.

UNITED KINGDOM

The shifts are more subtle than tectonic, though they do proceed under the surface. Possibly this is because when something really far-reaching is proposed it will be almost universally condemned. One man in the firing line over the last year or two is Adrian Noble, director of the Royal Shakespeare Company. His scheme to demolish the much-loved but often criticised Royal Shakespeare Theatre at Stratford upon Avon and replace it with a smaller but better building, accompanied by a range of aids to the understanding of Shakespeare, with an educational bias, heaped coals of fire on his head, bringing accusations of his wanting to create a kind of theme park.

Add to this a perceived diminishing in the standard of RSC productions, a withdrawal from the Barbican, its London base since 1982, the disbanding of a large regular company, the booking of Stratford productions into West End theatres, and a temporary, and profitable, withdrawal from the arts scene altogether to direct *Chitty Chitty Bang Bang* at the London Palladium made Noble a man under siege, which was eventually brought to an end by his resignation, with effect from March 2003. Michael Boyd will replace him.

But there has been an upheaval in additional quarters as well, caused by the decision of other artistic directors to desert their posts. Trevor Nunn is leaving the National at the end of his contract, having weathered a few storms in his time, though there is approval for his alterations to the Lyttelton, its proscenium space. He is being replaced by Nicholas Hytner, highly regarded but somehow suspected of being cut from the same cloth as his predecessor, presumably because he has directed a successful musical or two, and some films.

Also departed are the directors of London's most fashionable fringe theatres, Sam Mendes from the Donmar Warehouse, and the Jonathan Kent–Ian McDiarmid team from the Almeida. They have both been exemplars of a certain style of theatre. To be sure, they have had a good record of artistic success, though not particularly with new plays, even if some of them were new to London. No one is doubting their skill as directors, but they have also tapped into the spirit of the times, in which venues, be they restaurants, clubs or theatres, can be made fashionable overnight.

In their favour, they have not jeopardised their integrity, but with few exceptions, and with a commendable eclecticism, they have consistently provided a good night out in less than comfortable conditions, thanks to some high-profile American actors and television personalities who were prevailed upon to appear for very modest fees. Kent and McDiarmid have managed to secure funds for the refurbishment of the Almeida's base in stylish Islington, no mean achievement, and spent the intervening period in a converted bus station in distinctly unstylish King's Cross, in addition to making an occasional foray into the West End and, in the case of an uneven Shakespeare season, to the former Gainsborough Film Studios before it was transformed into an expensive apartment block.

The new incumbent at the Donmar Warehouse is Michael Grandage, an actor turned director who has accomplished some good productions at the Donmar but made his reputation at the Crucible in Sheffield, to which he has brought London critics flocking as a matter of course. At the Almeida the new man is Michael Attenborough, son of Richard and regarded as a safe pair of hands.

ABOVE: Paul Rudd, Rachel Weisz, Gretchen Mol and Frederick Weller in Neil LaBute's *The Shape of Things*, premiered at the Almeida　　　　　　　　　　　　　　　　(*photo*: Ivan Kyncl)

BELOW: *The Ramayana*, adapted by Peter Oswald and performed both in Birmingham and at the National Theatre in London　　　　　　　　　　　　　　　(*photo*: Nobby Clark)

UNITED KINGDOM

Other changes in a busy 12 months are Jenny Topper, who left Hampstead Theatre after many years, and just before it moved into its newly-built premises 200 yards away, and Jude Kelly of the West Yorkshire Playhouse in Leeds, touted at one time as being a successor to Nunn at the National, who moved to London and will doubtless not lack for employment, as she is both competent and innovative, having cradled what must be regarded as the cult hit of the past few years, *Shockheaded Peter*, a bizarre horror pantomime which went on to three seasons at the Lyric, Hammersmith and another at the Albery.

But behind all these changes have been considerable upheavals in the bricks and mortar side of the London theatre. The majority of West End playhouses are now owned by two large companies, the Really Useful Group, headed by Andrew Lloyd Webber, which took over most of the Stoll Moss theatres, and the Ambassador Theatre Group, which acquired its theatres by a perhaps more stealthy approach.

What they have in common is a willingness, in fact a necessity, to create product for their theatres, which are of varying capacities. They are not necessarily producing it themselves, but they have smart young producers in house who comb fringe and regional theatres and develop productions of their own.

ATG, in particular, is in the business of making creative alliances. It has a large and growing number of big regional theatres and is anxious to develop one or two of them as production bases. But it keeps a businesslike eye on theatres like the Royal Court, which has actually increased the number of its productions under the directorship of Ian Rickson in its rebuilt Sloane Square theatre, and the always interesting Bush, which has an excellent track record of new writing. It also has alliances with the Young Vic and the young film stars of Working Title Pictures, plus Carlton Television, feeling that there might be some scope for the transfer of stage plays to television and vice versa. The company also entered into a partnership with the National to produce the highly successful revival of *Noises Off*, which began in the Lyttelton, moved into the West End and thence to Broadway.

The most striking above-the-ground feature of the West End has been the apparent demise of the blockbusting sung-through musicals pioneered by Andrew Lloyd Webber and carried on by the French team of Boublil and Schonberg. *Cats* has finished after over 20 years. So have *Starlight Express* and *Miss Saigon*, though *Les Miserables* and *Phantom of the Opera* carried on and Cameron Mackintosh and Lloyd Webber will be kept profitably engaged staging their past shows elsewhere.

Now the emphasis has switched to revivals, of *My Fair Lady* and *South Pacific*, both staged at the National, *Kiss Me Kate*, a Broadway revival, tribute shows like *Mamma Mia!* and *We Will Rock You* (featuring the music of Abba and Queen respectively) and film adaptations such as *Chitty Chitty Bang Bang*. The fact is that new large-scale musicals are either not being written, or not worth taking an expensive chance on: witness the disappointing reception for *The Witches of Eastwick* and Lloyd Webber's *The Beautiful Game*. New musicals have to be created by a team, it seems, as was the case with the Broadway import *The Full Monty* – originally a UK film, of course.

Revivals of plays are more likely to be successful than new ones. To *Noises Off* one can add Pinter's *No Man's Land* and *The Caretaker*, Peter Nichols' *Privates on Parade* and *A Day in the Death of Joe Egg*, Arthur Miller's *All My Sons*, Brian Friel's *Faith Healer*, Alan Ayckbourn's *Bedroom Farce* and pieces by Tennessee Williams and Eugene O'Neill; even these can only be guaranteed success if big British or American names are in them.

There have certainly been many visitors from the States since the start of the new Millennium – Kathleen Turner, the first of several who appeared in *The Graduate*, George Segal, in one of the ever-changing casts of *Art*, Jessica Lange, Gwyneth Paltrow, Matt Damon, Macaulay Culkin, Nicole Kidman ('pure theatrical Viagra' in the memorable phrase coined by critic Charles Spencer), and the ever in the news Madonna.

London has also seen a spate of 'in-yer-face' theatre, inspired, I suppose, by Irvine Welsh's *Trainspotting*: plays containing violence, graphic sex (hetero and homo) and heavy ingestion of drugs and alcohol, mainly restricted to smaller theatres but occasionally raising their heads in the West End. Most of these, I suspect, will end up as museum pieces like the angry young men of the 50s. Mark Ravenhill may be the most notable of the writers, his *Mother Clap's Molly House* being a major success at the National, though failing disastrously when it moved to the West End.

The young Irish writers, led by Martin McDonagh and Conor McPherson, continue to provide some of the most stimulating work of recent years, and Lee Hall, from North-East England, has had an extraordinarily productive two or three years.

But English theatre remains to my mind firmly insular. Whereas the work of English writers often continues to be produced in Europe, the States and even further afield, often long after they have fallen out of fashion in their native land, for example Edward Bond and Arnold Wesker, England seldom has the chance to see any recent plays from abroad, *Art* being the most notable exception.

When they do reach a London stage, it is almost inevitable that it will be in the small upstairs auditorium at the Royal Court or the National's Cottesloe, or in a festival like Edinburgh. LIFT (the London International Festival of Theatre) is now with us in name only, the original concept of its founders having now changed to staging occasional productions in smaller theatres. Something like *The Mysteries*, a black South African reworking of the medieval mystery cycle, which did reach the West End, is regarded as an exotic import, applauded because of its music, dance and visual appeal.

Yet despite everything English theatre remains almost uniquely vibrant. I would guess that there are still more theatres in this country than anywhere else in the world, even if many of them would not be recognised as such by many theatre practitioners because they are not in full-time use as theatres, being venues in which theatre can be presented alongside other forms of mainly light entertainment.

It is, I think, because the English have a deep suspicion of words like 'arts' and 'culture' and resent too much money being spent on it. But strangely enough there is a national instinct that the theatre is the best medium for conveying comedy, tragedy, spectacle and performance skills, and is still the goal to which performers in every field aspire.

UNITED KINGDOM

Scotland
MARK FISHER

Do you know when you're living through a time of transition? Is it only afterwards that you can tell? Maybe, but if I were to take a guess, I'd say transition is what Scottish theatre has been going through over the past three years.

Actually, make that six. In a newspaper article at the end of 1999, I commented that the theatre industry in Scotland was at last getting back up to speed. That was after the financial crisis sparked by local authority reorganisation three years earlier in 1996. Firm foundations had been laid down, I wrote, and if the theatre community held its nerve, I reckoned it would begin the new century in robust form.

Well, maybe 'robust' was too bold a hope. Writing in 2002, it feels as if the foundations are still being laid for something better to come. And there are signs that health will be restored. Such health will depend on three things: first, the injection of more money; second, the implementation of a visionary national theatre plan; and third, the emergence of a generation of directors worthy of the country's formidable acting and writing talent.

All are possible, though if the third happens, it will be by fluke and good fortune. As I write, the country's two major rep theatres are preparing for a change of artistic directors. In Edinburgh, the Royal Lyceum's Kenny Ireland will stand down in the spring of 2003, ending a ten-year rein. He will be remembered as a solid programmer of no great pretensions, who secured a steady middle-brow audience with the occasional hit, at the expense of anything too radical or risky.

At about the same time, Giles Havergal will retire from Glasgow's Citizens' Theatre: not only the longest stint of any director currently at work in Britain, but also one of the most artistically significant. Havergal has been there since 1969 and, together with fellow directors Philip Prowse and Robert David MacDonald, set about redefining the Citizens' as a kind of European outpost that bypassed the provincialism of London in favour of a continental panache that was as visual as it was literary. Remarkably, much of that spirit survives in the proscenium theatre and its two studios today. David Mark Thomson from the Brunton Theatre in Musselburgh will move in to the Ireland job, but there are no obvious contenders for the Citizens', whose formidable reputation will be hard to live up to.

Scotland is a country of powerful actors and strong writers, but rarely more than competent directors. There was a time when you would head to a play simply because it was directed by Gerry Mulgrew, whose Communicado company dominated the theatre scene for the best part of two decades before its untidy demise in 1998 and eventual rebirth. Even though Mulgrew is back from the artistic wilderness – attracting praise most recently for *Brave*, a show about native Americans, produced with Sounds of Progress in 2002 – there is no director with anything like the appeal he held in his creative prime. The death in January 2002 of John McGrath, writer, director and founder of 7:84 Theatre

Vicki Liddelle and Gavin Mitchell in David Greig's *Casanova*, for the Glasgow company Suspect Culture   (*photo*: Kevin Low)

UNITED KINGDOM

Company (Scotland), author of the seminal polemical essay collection *A Good Night Out* and the legendary drama *The Cheviot, the Stag and the Black, Black Oil*, only emphasised the lack of a creative successor.

To say more would be speculation. The field is open. Let's hope creative things happen as a result of the changes. But there is a reasonable chance of my first two ingredients for a healthy future – more money and a national theatre – coming about. And if they do, then this period – the late 90s and early noughties – will be remembered as the calm before the storm.

Or rather, the calm *between* the storms, because the years from 1990 until the middle of the decade are already looking like a lost golden age. This was when Glasgow was European City of Culture (1990), when Michael Boyd was artistic director of Glasgow's Tron Theatre (he's now to head the Royal Shakespeare Company in Stratford), when Mulgrew's Communicado was in full swing, and when Mayfest, the now defunct Glasgow arts festival, extended the theatrical calendar a month or two closer to the adrenalin surge of the August Edinburgh Festival and Fringe. Since that time, political and artistic changes have stunted the growth of a once flourishing theatre sector.

Amends have started to be made. In January 2002, the Scottish Arts Council (SAC) announced it would increase the funding of drama by £3.5m over the forthcoming three years. This is a welcome boost after a period of steady decline, but it's worth putting into perspective. It goes only part of the way to redress drama's historic funding deficit. And, contrary to the impression given, it does not bear comparison with the £25m cash injection into English theatre in 2001 prompted by the Boyden report, which has led to an upsurge in output and audiences.

Opinions are divided among the theatre community, but the general feeling is that the new money returns the industry to the position it was in roughly ten years ago. It is the bare minimum of structural support necessary if the radical plan for a Scottish national theatre is going to have any chance. This country of five million has many a national organisation – Scottish Ballet, Scottish Opera, the Scottish National Orchestra, the Scottish National Galleries – but it has never had a national theatre. It's not for want of trying. The stories are legion of the companies that aspired to national status, from the Scottish National Players, an amateur group inspired by the Abbey in the 1920s, to the Scottish Theatre Company, a professional touring group in the 1980s. But one way or another, it never worked out.

But in 2001, the SAC accepted the broad recommendations of an independent working group report on the feasibility of just such a body. The SAC then put a 'strong case' for extra funding to the Scottish Executive (the government in Scotland for all devolved matters) to ensure the project's success. The Executive, which in its cultural strategy had already expressed a desire for a national theatre, has delayed full commitment until it is convinced the broader theatre landscape is secure enough, but it is claiming still to be positive about the plan.

So why the change? Well, although the establishment of a Scottish parliament in 1999 helped get the idea moving, it was a change of tactics on behalf of the theatre lobby – in particular the Federation of Scottish Theatre – that made the real difference.

The idea is this. There will be no building. No monolith. No cash-guzzling mausoleum. No shrine to an earlier generation's vision of what theatre is. Instead, there will be an organisation. It will not be a performing company, but a small administration with an artistic director fulfilling a role similar to that of the director of a festival. Imagine the whole of Scottish theatre being the director's resource. The national theatre could team a playwright from Inverness with the production department of Glasgow's Tron Theatre and a director from Lithuania. It could take note when the tiny island Mull Theatre did a brilliant show and invest in it, so that it could be seen on bigger stages in different places. One week Dundee Rep would be the Scottish national theatre, the next it might be Edinburgh's Royal Lyceum.

The beauty of the scheme is in its recognition that Scotland already has a national theatre in the sum of its existing buildings and companies. The proposed national theatre wouldn't compete with the industry, draining it of money and resources, but would enhance it, celebrate it, be properly of it. It's significant that the SAC proposal insists not only on an annual £1.2m for the national theatre itself, but also an annual £1m to enhance the theatre at large. There's no point in having a company that celebrates the theatre of the nation if there is little theatre left to celebrate.

In May 2002 the Scottish Arts Council convened a national theatre steering group to advise on plans, time scale, budget and potential chair and board members.

So if Scotland already has a national theatre, in the sense of all the theatres in the nation, what exactly are its constituent parts and how well are they faring? Broadly, it's a varied landscape that ranges from the well-made summer rep playing to the tourists in Pitlochry Festival Theatre to the club-friendly young people's theatre pioneered by the touring company Boilerhouse. While Edinburgh's Theatre Workshop is turning disability into a political issue with a permanent company of actors in wheelchairs and on crutches, Cathie Boyd's Theatre Cryptic is developing lush music-theatre-installation crossovers that play on the senses.

Among this eclecticism, two names stand out. They are the playwrights Liz Lochhead and David Greig. Lochhead is of an older generation – she is still best known for *Mary Queen of Scots Got her Head Chopped Off*, first produced by Communicado in 1987 – but after a number of years in which she concentrated on poetry and other writing, she returned to the theatre with a vengeance in 1998 with the midlife crisis comedy *Perfect Days*; it seems like she has rarely been off the stage since. An indication of her reputation was the way *Miseryguts*, her adaptation of Molière's *Le Misanthrope*, was marketed by Edinburgh's Royal Lyceum on its debut in 2002. The name of Liz Lochhead dominated the adverts and posters in big letters, dwarfing all other information.

Other work by Lochhead seen in this period includes an intelligent translation of Chekhov's *Three Sisters,* adapted with a breezy wit to post-war rural Scotland, and performed at the Royal Lyceum in 2000 and, in the same year, an earthy, poetic, richly Scots version of *Medea* for the Glasgow touring company Theatre Babel. That production, given a gutsy lead performance by Maureen Beattie, was revived on the Edinburgh Festival Fringe for two successive years and toured internationally.

So to the younger generation, and a writer even more prolific than Lochhead. In 1999 alone, there were at least five David Greig productions. They included

UNITED KINGDOM

Suspect Culture's *Mainstream*, two stagings of *The Cosmonaut's Last Message to the Woman he Once Loved in the Former Soviet Union*, the Edinburgh International Festival production of *The Speculator,* and a Traverse Theatre production called *Danny 306 + Me (4 ever)*. Subjects covered included global alienation, the foundation of capitalism and how children can find confidence in a crazy adult world. Theatrical styles ranged from Brecht to Barker to puppet theatre.

The following year Greig produced adaptations and new plays including *The Golden Ass, Oedipus, Candide* and *Victoria* (this last for the Royal Shakespeare Company) and, more recently *Dr Korczak's Example* for Glasgow's young people's company TAG, *Casanova* and *Lament* for Suspect Culture. As I write, the Traverse Theatre is going into production with its Edinburgh Festival Fringe 2002 production of *Outlying Islands*, a play Greig first wrote for Radio 3. There are times, particularly with the devised work of his own company Suspect Culture, when Greig can get lost in the post-modern, but there is never anything predictable about his plays and they always have the ambition, scope and intellectual chutzpah of major drama.

To focus on these two playwrights is not to diminish the contribution of their peers, notable among them Iain Heggie, David Harrower, Nicola McCartney, John Clifford, Stuart Paterson, Gregory Burke, Douglas Maxwell and . . . well I could go on. But it's true to say that Lochhead and Greig have succeeded better than anyone in building an audience that is ready and eager for their work.

Three structural changes during this period to note. One is the needless demise of the Brunton Theatre Company in Musselburgh (just outside Edinburgh), caught in an obstinate funding trap between the SAC and its local authority; the former refused to start funding it, the latter refused to continue. This despite some fine, accessible work from artistic director David Mark Thomson, notably his own hostage drama, the brilliant *A Madman Sings to the Moon*, which was my personal find in the Edinburgh Festival Fringe of 1999. The end of the company in 2002 marks the loss of a very worthwhile local theatre (and I should mention also the demise in 2002 of two enterprising touring companies, lookOUT and Raindog).

Second, and much more positive, is the story of Dundee Rep. Backed by a £286,516 lottery grant in 1999, the Tayside theatre reinvented itself as a permanent ensemble in the Eastern European manner, giving 14 actors the chance of continued work, training, and development for three years. It's not that much of its work has been out of the ordinary, it's that the long-term benefits both artistic and commercial are too compelling to ignore. The actors are an ever tighter unit, comfortable with working with each other; productions can remain in the repertoire to be revived in the summer months or toured around the country; the relationship with the Dundee audience is ever more close; and when the company gets the chance to work with a visionary director, as it did with Lithuania's Rimas Tuminas on a radical version of Chekhov's *The Seagull* in 2001, it has proved itself capable of stunning originality.

Third, and most ambiguous, is the story of the Tron Theatre in Glasgow. When artistic director Irina Brown departed in the autumn of 1999, the theatre decided not to replace her. The reasoning was that the level of funding, which permits two, maybe three, productions in a year, wasn't sufficient to justify keeping someone in a full-time artistic post. Instead, the role of Neil Murray as administrative director has expanded so that as well as programming the venue's long list of touring companies, music acts and comedians, he's been commissioning outside directors to stage the Tron's own productions. Not to have a permanent director is to risk losing a sense of company identity, to miss out on a catalytic presence for other artists, and to deprive audiences of the chance to follow one person's creative development. Murray is aware of that risk and has so far managed to maintain the theatre's reputation for lively drama, having brought in guest directors for a number of fine productions including *Further Than the Furthest Thing* by Zinnie Harris, *The Beauty Queen of Leenane* directed by playwright Iain Heggie and Heggie's own *Love Freaks,* an obscene Marivaux adaptation, directed by Suspect Culture's Graham Eatough.

Finally, a few name checks. Some directors: Ben Harrison, for his imaginative site-specific work with Grid Iron; Angus Farquhar, whose work with NVA can rarely be called theatre, taking place up mountains or in graveyards, but frequently creating the rare sense of an event; John Tiffany, who directed many of the Traverse Theatre's most popular shows and has now moved to England's Paines Plough; and Cathie Boyd who, like Farquhar, can't easily be categorised but, with her Theatre Cryptic company, has built a reputation for bringing together her eclectic influences of music, literature and art.

One more theatre: the Arches in Glasgow was established in the aftermath of a subterranean exhibition in 1990, and somehow battled on with next to no resources, a dank and gloomy warren of bare-bricked performance spaces and a cacophonous rumble from the ceiling every time a train left the city's Central Station. Thanks to the energy and dedication of artistic director Andy Arnold, it has survived, raw and damp, yes, but all the more atmospheric for it. It was relaunched at the start of 2001 after a refurbishment and the resident company, a rough and ready outfit that makes up in spirit what it lacks in polish, looks ever more secure.

And finally some more productions: *A Solemn Mass For A Full Moon In Summer* (2000) was another fantastic translation into Scots by Martin Bowman and Bill Findlay of the French Canadian writer Michel Tremblay at the Traverse; and in the autumn of 1999, three marvellous shows from the Citizens' Theatre in its 30th anniversary year: Philip Prowse's *Pygmalion*, Giles Havergal's *Who's Afraid of Virginia Woolf?*, and Prowse's *Cavalcade*, all three consummate examples of stagecraft, ravishingly beautiful, powerfully acted and intelligently interpreted.

Wales - *Theatre in English*
DAVID ADAMS

Professional theatre provision is still relatively recent in Wales. It was introduced in the 60s and at the end of the twentieth century, less than half-a-century old, it underwent a major upheaval. As reported in the last *World of Theatre*, this overhaul of official support for drama came as part of a comprehensive review of arts funding from the Arts Council of Wales and within the context of Wales's new autonomy as a nation within the United Kingdom, with its own Assembly. As we predicted, the last three years have seen major changes in many aspects of theatre provision, with the net result of less work, more money and changed priorities.

UNITED KINGDOM

The National Assembly of Wales and its culture committee has emerged as the main force in policy-making (it was their support that brought about the establishment of the Wales ITI Centre), with the hitherto all-powerful Arts Council now little more than an agency to implement Assembly policy. The Assembly's priority is accessibility and participation rather than the art and this review of Welsh theatre must be seen within this context – and within the context of a changing theatre scene that has yet to come to terms with the new times.

The 1998 Arts Council drama strategy, the trigger for professional opposition, media criticism and Assembly intervention, as reported in *World of Theatre 2000*, was revised. The core issue, cutting several companies and budgets in order to find more funds for an English-language national theatre company, remained (though at the time of writing that company, based on Clwyd Theatr Cymru in North Wales, faces severe financial problems because of the withdrawal of support from its local authority). The objective of establishing a Welsh-language national theatre company has yet to be achieved. But the threat to community and young peoples' theatre provision, which many consider to be Welsh theatre's great strength, was removed. Indeed, Wales as a centre for young people's theatre has received a boost. One of the country's most committed and energetic directors, Arad Goch's Jeremy Turner, is now ASSITEJ chair and hopes to make Wales an important player in international young people's theatre over the next few years. Arad Goch themselves had a major success in 2001/2 with *The Stones*, a co-production with Australia's Zeal Theatre, directed by the writers Tom Lycos and Stefo Nantsou, and performed in English and Welsh.

The National Assembly for Wales's cultural strategy specifically targets young people and, indeed, many of the recent theatrical successes are productions from this sector. A highlight of the summer has become the productions from the theatre and dance companies of the National Youth Arts Wales organisation, both utilising top directors. Cardiff-based Italian Firenze Guidi has coaxed amazing performances from her young (mostly teenage) charges in her stunning and complex site-specific 'montage' productions of *Faust* (2000) and *Hamlet* (2001), with 2002's *Woyzeck* promising to complete a hat-trick of visually and conceptually exciting shows. Choreographer Wayne McGregor, founder of Sadlers Wells-based Random Dance, is the National Youth Dance Wales director and the new company's *Brew/Hive* (2001) was characteristically radical and innovative. It was staged in the grounds of the National Botanic Garden in West Wales and the ecological environment, with Norman Foster's breathtaking domed glasshouse at the centre, proved a great stimulus for the work.

With a dearth of new writing for the main stage, it is the small young people's theatre companies (that is, companies making theatre *for* young people rather than with them) who have commissioned new plays – for example Louise Osborn's first play, *Lizard's Tale*, for Gwent Theatre, and Mark Ryan's various pieces for Spectacle Theatre. Theatr Iolo, under Kevin Lewis, continue to make wonderful small-scale theatre, often with international partners or perspectives. One of the longer-lasting relationships has been that between Spectacle Theatre (based in the Rhondda Valleys, former mining communities where social problems are rife) and writer Dic Edwards. Director Steve Davis and a small but dedicated company have used Edwards's often difficult scripts to create highly theatrical short plays for young people.

Russell Gomer and Maria Pride in the Sherman Theatre, Cardiff production of *Everything Must Go*, by Patrick Jones   (*photo*: Dave Daggers)

Interestingly, one of Edwards's plays was also the most controversial theatrical event for many years – perhaps since a play called *Taffy* (derogatory slang for 'Welshman') by Caradoc Evans caused riots and police intervention when it opened in London in 1923. Edwards's comedy *Franco's Bastard*, staged by Sgript Cymru (Wales's bi-lingual new writing company) in Cardiff in Spring 2002, brought walk-outs, stink-bombs in the theatre and a long and bitter exchange in the media. The cause lay in Edwards's fictionalisation of the life and ideas of a Welsh nationalist of the 60s, Julian Cayo Evans, whose radical militancy still attracts supporters today: Edwards made his Carlo character, unmistakably based on Cayo, a figure of ridicule and so incurred the wrath of many nationalists. Others found the play's political satire unsatisfying but it was ceretainly a *succés de scandale*.

The only other controversial staging in the period under review was an earlier production by Sgript Cymru. *Crazy Gary's Mobile Disco*, the first play from writer Gary Owen, produced in Spring 2001 in collaboration with London-based Paines Plough, also caused audiences to walk out and became the subject of heated media debate, mainly because of its presumed sexism and, for some, its language and its portrayal of Welsh men. It was an impressive debut that explored familiar Welsh themes of identity, entrapment and machismo; but in its innovative form (the plot unfolds through three monologues), writing and performances it was a memorable production.

UNITED KINGDOM

It probably isn't surprising that a lot of Welsh theatre has been about identity and the monologue has been the dominant form. A continuing success is Mark Jenkins's *Playing Burton*, about the Welsh actor almost as well-known for his tempestuous relationship with Elizabeth Taylor, which is now about to play off-Broadway. Pirandellian in many ways, the play has the dead actor recalling his many roles and trying to separate his own life from the fictional characters he has portrayed.

Wales's most famous export, Volcano Theatre, maintained their reputation for unpredictability and immaculate performance work with two very different shows. *Private Lives*, hitherto regarded as an amusing period piece from a gentle satirist of the upper-classes, Noel Coward, was radically reinterpreted as a manic critique of bourgeois life, set in a residential home-cum-asylum. It was very, very funny, very physical, conceptually challenging and an intellectually stimulating questioning of normality – and not allowed to be performed in England, presumably because it wasn't quite the same Noel Coward that English theatres recognised.

Volcano's other major production was the first English-language staging of Thomas Bernhard's *Destination (Am Ziel),* also designated a comedy but so black an allegory of Austria's guilty past that the audience might feel as oppressed as the dominated daughter of the guilt-ridden mother trapped initially in a derelict foundry. Translated by Jan-Willem van den Bosch and directed by Kathryn Hunter, it was a powerful, uncomfortable experience with an outstanding central performance from Fern Smith.

But perhaps the best show to come out of Wales in the last few years has been a remarkable one-person piece from Eddie Ladd, *Scarface*. This graceful, diminutive performer has taken the Al Pacino film and transplanted the Miami tale of vice, violence, murder, gangsters, automobiles and urban living to the peaceful rolling hills of slow-moving rural West Wales, specifically the farmhouse of her uncle and aunt. She does it by relating and re-enacting the story, to thumping Welsh-language techno music and dressed in Pacino-style black suit on one half of the stage, to a camera that then superimposes her on to film of the farmstead projected on to a screen on the other half of the stage. The result is a funny, fascinating, inventive, thought-provoking piece of postmodern theatre. *Scarface* has, understandably (and despite being in both of Wales's languages), been a success all over Europe since its premiere at Chapter in Cardiff in Spring 2001.

Wales - *Theatre in Welsh*
HAZEL WALFORD DAVIES

Underfunding, and the chaos resulting from the misguided decision of the Arts Council of Wales to axe several of its funded Theatre for Young People companies, has meant that no major developments have been possible in Welsh-medium theatre since 1999. Although the Arts Council of Wales was forced to reconsider its decision, its inability to gauge the popularity of its funded companies meant that the Council rapidly lost the confidence of the theatre constituency. It also meant that some theatre companies looked for partnerships and outreach outside Wales, and much of the exciting new development within Welsh-language theatre since 1999 has resulted from the forging of international links.

The recent establishment of a Welsh Assembly level of government in Wales, with its strong European links, gave added impetus to this crucial aim of international outreach. Bara Caws (Bread and Cheese), based in North Wales, has forged valuable connections with Tryater Theatre Company in Friesland and with OFFSPRING, a body that facilitates multilingual productions in Europe. In 2000 Bara Caws took its production of *D.J. Faust* to Nîmes in France, and in 2002 the company participated in the highly acclaimed co-production, *Salted*, premiered in Friesland. Arad Goch (Red Plough), a mid-Wales Theatre for Young People company, is also noted for its world-wide theatre outreach. The company's director, Jeremy Turner, currently the British representative of ASSITEJ, masterminded the highly successful international theatre for young people festival, Agor Drysau (Opening Doors) which took place in Wales in 2000. Arad Goch has performed in America, Canada and Europe, and in 2002 the company facilitated a production in Korea by the theatre company Y Gymraes (The Welsh Woman) of S.M. Williams's play *Mab (Son)*.

Cwmni'r Fran Wen (the White Rook Company), based in Harlech in North Wales, has over the last two years widened its brief, and now has a community as well as a school audience. Two other companies, Na Nog and Iolo, based in West and South Wales, have continued to work in the field of Theatre in Education. Na Nog has also ventured into musicals with its production of *Nia Ben Aur (Nia of the Golden Hair)*.

The main energy, then, in Welsh-language theatre in the period 1999-2002 has been within community theatre, Theatre in Education, and Theatre for Young People. In contrast, the main stage company, Theatr Gwynedd in Bangor, North Wales, has not flourished. With a few exceptions (most notably Graham Laker's Welsh-medium production of *Amadeus*), it has not succeeded in attracting and keeping audiences.

In the area of new writing, it is the companies already mentioned that have succeeded in guaranteeing and encouraging new scripts and new writers. Sgript Cymru (Wales Script), a company with a specific brief for nurturing new writing, has suffered on the Welsh-language front from the departure for television of Bethan Jones, an experienced bilingual director. The company has, however, continued to work with the National Eisteddfod of Wales on the development and production of the annually commissioned play. In supporting younger dramatists, Urdd Gobaith Cymru (The Welsh League of Youth) has played a prominent part through its award of a Drama Medal at its annual Eisteddfod.

Recently, a newly constituted and restructured Arts Council of Wales has approved a strategy to establish a Welsh National Theatre Company working exclusively through the medium of Welsh. This is a significant development and the new Company should be in place by 2004.

About the contributors: **David Adams** *is a theatre critic of long experience, with newspapers such as the* Guardian. *He teaches theatre criticism at the University of Glamorgan;* **Mark Fisher** *is one of Scotland's leading critics, and editor of the events magazine for Glasgow and Edinburgh,* The List; **Peter Hepple** *is a former Secretary of the Critics' Circle, London, and editor of* The Stage *newspaper;* **Hazel Walford Davies** *teaches at the University of Glamorgan, Wales. A native Welsh speaker, she has published widely on both Welsh and English medium theatre in Wales, and has been Visiting Professor in drama at various American universities. She is a member of the Arts Council of Wales.*

UNITED STATES

JIM O'QUINN

Whither the American musical? No answer to that well-worn question was forthcoming in recent American theatrical seasons, but it was a topic on many minds. As the millennium approached, serious plays seemed to be in vogue, especially in the commercial theatre, where Arthur Miller's ever-dependable *Death of a Salesman* enjoyed a long and profitable Broadway run; August Wilson debuted *King Hedley II*, a powerful new entry in his decade-by-decade examination of the African American experience; and a talky drama about nuclear physics, Michael Frayn's *Copenhagen*, was not only a Tony winner for 2000's best play but a genuine hot ticket. Musicals, though – that signature commodity of the American theatre's golden age, the only theatrical form verifiably invented on US soil – were in alarmingly short supply.

Where was Stephen Sondheim? Tinkering with old shows, perfecting them for posterity, perhaps. What was Broadway offering? Disney's animation re-treads *Beauty and the Beast* and *The Lion King*, joined in March 2000 by the megamusical *Aida* (based on the operatic warhorse, with Elton John tunes, Tim Rice lyrics, and a cast of 25); the long-running pop concoctions of Frank Wildhorn, *Jekyll & Hyde* and *The Scarlet Pimpernel*; and lukewarm stage renditions of the movies *Footloose* and *Saturday Night Fever*. The golden age of musicals seemed far away indeed.

Against this backdrop, the arrival in November 1999 of Michael Blakemore's exuberant, cartoon-bright revival of Cole Porter's 1948 *Kiss Me, Kate* – if not a new musical, at least a top-flight old one – was seen as good news. At the same time, a surge of creativity from the non-commercial sector turned the conversation about American musicals in provocative new directions.

First, a high-profile pair of serious (and seriously flawed) new musicals emerged in New York from Playwrights Horizons and the Lincoln Center Theater Company. From the former came *James Joyce's The Dead*, an earnest, frequently effective musicalisation by Shaun Davey and Richard Nelson of Joyce's famous story of a Christmastime gathering in Dublin; and from the latter came the première of composer Michael John LaChiusa's *Marie Christine*, an ambitious, florid updating of *Medea* to the 19th-century US. *The Dead* went on in subsequent seasons to be widely produced as a chamber musical by regional theatres across the country. *Marie Christine* has not been so lucky thus far; with its sumptuous designs and overheated direction by Graciela Daniele, it was seen primarily as a dazzling showcase for the vocal and dramatic gifts of Broadway's current ingenue extraordinaire, Audra McDonald.

Other musicals were gestating and thriving far from the glare of East Coast scrutiny. At California's Pasadena Playhouse, artistic director Sheldon Epps mounted his already well-travelled *Play On!*, a musical jazzily based on *Twelfth Night*, set in 40s Harlem and scored with Duke Ellington songs. Avant-garde

ABOVE: The Wooster Group in *To You, the Birdie!*, a version of Racine's *Phèdre*
(*photo*: Mary Geart)

BELOW: Lindsay Duncan and Alan Rickman took Noel Coward's *Private Lives* to Broadway
(*photo*: Ivan Kyncl)

composer Philip Glass and director JoAnne Akalaitis, his collaborator and former wife, debuted *In the Penal Colony*, an experimental musical based on a brooding story by Franz Kafka, to general acclaim in Seattle, and brought it to New York. The tiny-but-spunky Signature Theatre of Arlington, Va., continued to solidify its reputation as an important developer and producer of musicals, despite the abrupt failure in early 2000 of its latest venture, an effort by the veteran team of John Kander and Fred Ebb to musicalize Thornton Wilder's *The Skin of Our Teeth*. (Eric Schaffer, the Signature's 36-year-old artistic director, would go on to supervise the grand-scale retrospective of Sondheim works at Washington, DC's Kennedy Center in 2002).

Were these varied attempts to revitalize the musical leading anywhere? The puzzlement escalated to the level of feverish debate in June 2000, when *Contact* – an episodic dance drama with no singing, little dialogue, and (in an alarming development for the Broadway musicians' union) a prerecorded score – won the top musical awards. The Lincoln Center Theater Company production was a vehicle for Susan Stroman's witty and emotion-drenched choreography but its success served to confirm traditionalist fears that the art form as they had known it was up for grabs.

More unconventional forays into the musical form quickly followed. The actor-centred Steppenwolf Theatre Company of Chicago tested the waters with composer Mike Reid's *The Ballad of Little Jo*, based on a 1993 film about the fate of a woman who makes her way in the American West of the late 1800s by disguising herself as a man. Directed by ensemble member Tina Landau, *Little Jo* was characterized by a quasi-operatic style and musical eclecticism.

Two musicals of identical title, *The Wild Party*, kicked up a storm of publicity in the spring of 2000 by facing off at major New York non-profit theatres. Composer Andrew Lippa's Manhattan Theatre Club version of the louche Jazz-Age poem by Joseph Moncure March fared somewhat better than LaChiusa and George C. Wolfe's adaptation at the Joseph Papp Public Theater, but neither was a critical or financial success. Those hoping to discover a well-defined route toward the musical's future were left at a crossroads with signs pointing in a dozen directions.

Musicals aside, recent seasons in the American theatre have offered food for thought on a surprisingly wide range of social issues. One of the most-produced works of 1999–2000 nationwide was *Gross Indecency: The Three Trials of Oscar Wilde*, a fascinating documentary-style examination of the infamous 1895 court proceedings that destroyed the life and career of the effete novelist and playwright and shaped public attitudes about homosexuality for decades to come. The show's creator and original director Moisés Kaufman, who developed *Gross Indecency* in tandem with his Tectonic Theater Project, had debuted it in New York in March 1996, at which point productions began to proliferate in cities across the US, Canada, and Europe (Corin Redgrave played Wilde in the London production). More recently, Kaufman and Tectonic's *The Laramie Project*, about the much-publicized murder of gay college student Matthew Shepard, has enjoyed similar international exposure.

In 2000–01, a number of established playwrights debuted important works. Edward Albee had a *succés d'estime* with his esoteric and literate theatrical fable *The Play About the Baby*, in an Off-Broadway production that made glorious use of the talents of veteran actors Marian Seldes and Brian Murray. Suzan-Lori Parks followed up her raw 1999 drama *In the Blood*, inspired by the themes of *The Scarlet Letter*, with an ostensibly realistic comedy-drama *Topdog/Underdog*, in which a pair of down-and-out brothers fret and feud. George C. Wolfe's taut Public Theater production moved to Broadway in 2001, and the play won Parks a Pulizer Prize. Historian-turned playwright Charles L. Mee made 'love' the operative word in a trilogy of dissimilar plays – *Big Love*, *First Love*, and *True Love* – that alternately engaged and puzzled audiences across the country with their collage-like texts and juggled time frames.

The 2001–02 season was indelibly marked, almost before it started, by September 11. As in other sectors of American life, the terrorist attacks reverberated through the nation's theatre community. Performances were postponed, cancelled, modified, and re-examined as theatres in New York and Washington DC struggled with logistical problems, and those in other parts of the country deferred to the mood of a shocked and mourning public. Some plays no longer seemed appropriate – a Broadway revival of Sondheim's dark musical *Assassins* was delayed, for example – and others took on surprising new resonances. It seemed certain that the economic consequences for theatre would be severe; with some governmental assistance, the commercial theatre (which suffered disastrously during the first weeks after the attack) quickly regained stability, but the not-for-profit theatre nationwide can expect to bear the brunt of a vastly diminished pool of resources available for the arts.

In the shadow of September 11, the premiere in mid-December 2001 at New York Theatre Workshop of Tony Kushner's new play *Homebody/Kabul* became the most talked-about event of the theatre year. In fact, it was more coincidence than calculation that Kushner's three-and-a-half-hour drama about the West's contemporary and historic relationship to Afghanistan arrived on stage a scant two months after the US had all but declared war on that country. A writer with an ongoing interest in international affairs, Kushner had long indulged a fascination with Afghanistan and its geopolitical plight, and he had finished the initial version of *Homebody/Kabul* the previous winter. Nevertheless, the play's events – it follows the journey of a British woman who disappears into the chaos of Afghan life – bore a remarkable parallel to news events. Director Declan Donnellan's Off-Broadway production, repeated in London, has been followed by other mountings at US theatres.

The sensation of the past two commercial theatre seasons – and the only show to take the September 11 slump in its box-office stride – has been comedian Mel Brooks's deliriously tasteless musicalization of his own 1967 cult film *The Producers*. No fodder here for whither-the-musical prophecies: an all-pro cast, led by Nathan Lane as the hard-luck showman Max Bialystock and Matthew Broderick as his nebbishy accountant Leo Bloom (roles played in the film by Zero Mostel and Gene Wilder), abetted by Brooks's own silly-sophisticated songs and lyrics, proved irresistible to ticket buyers. Among the records broken were the biggest advance sale ever ($33 million), the most Tony nominations (15), and the most Tonys won (12).

David Auburn's Pulitzer-confirmed drama *Proof*, about an unstable young woman's relationship with her late father, a mathematical prodigy, was the second most honoured Broadway show of 2000–01. The post-Tony arrival of an unlikely but high-spirited musical, Mark Hollmann and Greg Kotis's savvy Brecht-Weill parody *Urinetown*, enlivened the theatre year, as did a crowd-pleasing, all-star New York City staging in Central Park of Chekhov's *The Seagull*, directed by Mike Nichols and reuniting long-ago stage confederates Meryl Streep and Kevin Kline. On the West Coast, a revival of another golden-age musical, Rodgers and Hammerstein's 1958 *Flower Drum Song*, politically revamped via David Henry Hwang's rewritten book, earned high marks at the Mark Taper Forum and set its sights, not surprisingly, on Broadway.

Some formally adventurous new works took the spotlight in 2001–02, including Chicago-based *auteur* Mary Zimmerman's visual spectacle *Metamorphoses*, based on Ovid and performed mostly in an onstage pool. As sceptics shook their heads, a New York engagement of the piece was extended for a Broadway run, to surprising success – including a best-director Tony for Zimmerman. The always-innovative avant-garde troupe, the Wooster Group, created a dazzling variation on Racine's *Phaedra*, retitled *To You, The Birdie!*, a reference (at least in part) to the badminton games its classical characters incongruously play. Following its limited, Obie-winning run in New York, the piece has been seen at a number of international festivals. Two other regulars on the festival circuit – veteran director Richard Foreman and avant-garde newcomer Richard Maxwell – also offered provocative new works that have been seen abroad. Foreman's *Maria del Bosco* is a typically esoteric meditation on female beauty that incorporates hints of 9/11, with an extraordinary actress, Juliana Francis, in the title part. Maxwell, who carries deadpan to new heights in his performance style, has attracted a devoted cult following for such pieces as his soap-opera-with-songs *The House*.

As the 2001–02 season moved to its close, there was further evidence that Edward Albee is in a rich period of late-career productivity: On the heels of *The Play About the Baby*, he opted for a straight-to-Broadway production of another new play, *The Goat, or Who Is Sylvia?*, a dark comedy about a man's sexual obsession with the animal of the title. Challenging subject matter notwithstanding – and bolstered by a sterling production featuring Bill Pullman as the goat-lover and Mercedes Ruehl as his alternately sorrowful and furious wife – Albee won the Tony for best play. The best musical award went to the movie-derived pastiche *Thoroughly Modern Millie*, a slick and meticulous wind-up toy of a musical that will run for years to come but offers no point of view whatsoever on the troublesome question with which this article began.

Jim O'Quinn *is the founding editor of* American Theatre *magazine. Some of these comments have appeared previously in the 1999, 2000 and 2001 editions of the* Encyclopaedia Britannica Book of the Year.

URUGUAY

ROGER MIRZA

Within the contemporary cultural context, the new forms that can be seen emerging from Uruguayan theatre, embodying a stylised 'art of dissolution', can be seen as an attempt to create a subjective space that can withstand the transience of both individuals and communities. At the same time, we are undergoing one of the deepest social and economic crises ever seen in this country, that has also wreaked havoc in the entire surrounding region. With unemployment officially at 15% (35% if temporary jobs are included) and 45% of children born and bred below the poverty line, Uruguayan society has seen both its employment rate and quality of life (housing, health, education) go steadily and implacably down for the past few years. Immersed in a culture of instability and the ephemeral, the country suffers from a relentless decline in its living conditions, together with the destruction of its symbolic safety nets – now full of hypocrisy and distorted political, social and cultural interpretations.

If art in general can create areas where the prevailing culture can be resisted, theatre can create multiple spaces where the rigidities and imposture of the official discourse and the powers that be can be broken. It is the above-mentioned art of dissolution that enables each spectator to explore his/her own identity amidst uncertainty; a subjective, intuitive appropriation of today's maddeningly heterogeneous culture.

Within this context, Uruguayan theatre is struggling with its own contradictions, under the constant threat of disappearing because of dwindling audiences or an inability to cover production costs due to the almost total lack of government subsidies. The Board of Trustees of the National Theatre Fund (COFONTE, in Spanish), set up by law in the past decade, has the current equivalent of US$ 2,800 a month to allocate, barely aiding a handful of productions each year. The Comedia Nacional (National Theatre) is the only fully subsidised company – its entire budget is paid by the Government of the City of Montevideo.

However, despite this distressing situation, the number of new shows has increased over the past few years. 40 or 45 shows for grown-ups are performed every weekend, ranging from universal classics such as Aeschylus, Shakespeare or Molière to contemporary authors such as Heiner Müller or Bernard-Marie Koltès. This abundance reflects an insatiable need for expression that cannot find other outlets (cinema or TV) due to the high costs involved. Unfortunately, it is not usually accompanied by high standards; many companies fall back on old box-office hits with tried and proven formulas, or hasty improvisations. There is also the temptation to attract audiences with light, easily digestible shows that provide innocuous entertainment. Thus, a strictly commercial form of theatre is starting to develop whilst a few isolated efforts – full of imagination, talent and high standards – struggle on, under the indifferent gaze of the national cultural authorities.

URUGUAY

Atentados (Attempts on Her Life) by Martin Crimp, directed by Mariana Percovich for the Comedia Nacional

A few years ago, increasing alarm at dwindling audiences led to the creation of the Socio Espectacular (Show Partner) card that reached a peak of 15,000 members. It was a timely attempt to keep some of the most important independent theatres from closing, such as Teatro El Galpón and Teatro Circular, two strongholds of Uruguayan independent theatre since the 50s. However, the increasing financial difficulties, together with the lack of preparation shown by some companies, had a predictably bad influence on production quality.

The Socio Espectacular system, launched in 1998, renewed audiences and through special rates granted easy access for young people and students to films and football matches as well as theatres. Conversely, the increased attendances brought shorter runs for many of the shows. After four years and in deteriorating economic conditions, the quality of the productions has declined significantly.

Owing to these difficult circumstances, few stable groups remain active today that can plan a high quality, demanding repertoire and see it through. Amongst those, one may note the following, despite a certain unevenness in their productions: Teatro Circular, especially in a streamlined version of Brecht's *Terror y miserias del Tercer Reich (Fear and Miseries of the Third Reich)*, directed by Maria Varela (2000), Teatro El Galpón with *El hermano olvidado (The Forgotten Brother)* by Ariel Mastandrea and *El sueño y la vigilia(Sleep and Wakefulness)* by Juan Carlos Gené, both under the exquisite direction of Nelly Goitiño in 2001, Teatro de la Gaviota with *Copenhague (Copenhagen)* by Michael Frayn and *Nuestro pueblo (Our Town)* by Thornton Wilder, directed by Jorge Denevi in 2001, as well as the younger group Puerto Luna with a remarkable production of *Jubileo (Jubilee)* by Georg Tabori (2000), as well as *El Cerdo (The Pig)* by Antonio Andrés Lapeña (2001), both directed by Alberto Rivero. Along with these companies, the Comedia Nacional is playing an increasingly active and central role, with an average of six new productions per year, among which *Tres mujeres altas (Three Tall Women)* by Edward Albee (2001), *Atentados (Attempts on Her Life)* by Martin Crimp (2001) and *El labrador y la muerte* (*Death and the Ploughman*) by Johannes Von Saaz (2001).

Alongside these well established groups, there are a number of ground breaking productions that are remarkable for their talented directors or the exceptional quality of their actors, such as the non-repertory production *Cuarteto* (*Quartet*, 1997), directed by Eduardo Schinca with actors from the Comedia Nacional, which reached peaks of concentration and expressive range that enhanced Heiner Müller's sarcastic text, or *Ajax* (Goethe Institut, 2000), also by Müller and creatively directed by Mariana Percovich, or *Greek* (1999) by Steven Berkoff, directed with excellent teamwork by Alfredo Goldstein. This was also the case of *El retorno del desierto* (*Return from the Desert*) by Koltès (Teatro Victoria, 2000), directed by Fernando Beramendi, or *Historias ajenas* (*Collected Stories*) by Donald Margulies, directed by Mariana Wainstein (Teatro Alianza 2001), to name a few.

At the same time, a new trend has developed, which experiments with new spaces and with the actors' means of expression, or with transgressive texts, largely initiated by young directors such as Mariana Percovich, Alberto Rivero, Roberto Suárez, Sebstián Bedarnik, Ruben Coletto, Sergio Blanco, along with more senior ones such as Iván Solarich, María Dodera, Alvaro Ahuncháin, Ernesto Clavijo, Luis Vidal, Leonel Dárdano. They target young audiences with whom they share common values. However, it is a trend in which even established directors such as Nelly Goitiño are also active participants. These directors, most of whom are also playwrights, share an experimental approach to the use of space, a break with discursive speech, a rejection of realism and mimesis as well as linear timelines and traditional notions of character. They explore sensations, image distortion or subconscious impulses in an antirealist, sometimes hyper-realist quest. This can be seen in the excessive bloodshed of *Una cita con Caligula; crónica de una conspiración* (*An Appointment with Caligula: Chronicle of a Conspiracy*; Teatro Florencio Sánchez, 1999) by Roberto Suárez, directed by María Dodera, a remarkably expressive production featuring bodies that have been abused, spent or destroyed as a result of torturous power plays, in postures or gestures that reveal a violent and perverted sexuality, with constant changes and re-alignment of the performance space and the relationship between actors and audience.

Archaic imagery together with sonorous and visual impacts appear in Ionesco's *La improvisación del alma* (*Improvisation, or The Shepherd's Chameleon*, 1998) as directed by Ruben Coletto. In *¿Qué pasó con B.N?* (*What Happened to B.N?*, 1999), by Verónica Perrota (performer) and Sebastián Bednarick (director), speech distortions reveal that behind the apparent candour and helplessness of a little girl lies a disturbing experience. The use of marginality, crime, forms of rebellion and violence that break away from the soothing representations usually found in the collective imagination and challenge deeply embedded myths, are all main features of productions like *Extraviada* (*Deviated*, Teatro Circular 2, 1998) directed by Mariana Percovich.

The image of Carlos Gardel, famous local tango and folk singer, and some transgressive renditions of his identity as popular music icon appear in *Cenizas en el corazón* (*Ashes in the Heart*, 1999) written and staged by Mariana Percovich in the unconventional space of the renovated Cervantes Hotel restaurant.

URUGUAY

Tres mujeres altas (*Three Tall Women*) by Edward Albee, directed by Nelly Goitiño for the Comedia Nacional

Other important role models have been Eugenio Barba and his latest plays: *Evangelio de Oxyrhincus* (*Oxyrrhincus Gospel*) *Antigona* (*Antigone*), *Caosmos* and more recently *Mythos* (*Myths*). Also the Andalucian company La Zaranda, that has visited our country on several occasions both during and between the International Theatre Festivals organized by the local chapter of the International Association of Theatre Critics.

Thus we can say there is an emerging Uruguayan drama which includes playwrights such as Raquel Diana, Mariana Percovich, Roberto Suárez, Margarita Musto, Lupe Barone, Sergio Blanco, Sebastián Bedarnik and Verónica Perrota as well as, more recently, Marina Rodríguez (*Piedras y pájaros* – *Rocks and Birds*, El Galpón 2002). Their major theatre productions started to appear six or seven years ago, around 1995. Earlier writers include Alvaro Ahunchaín, Ricardo Grasso, Ariel Mastandrea or even Carlos Liscano, an acknowledged writer of fiction since the eighties. One must bear in mind, however, the continuance of works by those authors who connect with the new generation and incorporate some of their characteristics in the process. Such is the case of Ariel Mastandrea in his première of *El hermano olvidado* (*The Forgotten Brother*, El Galpón 2001), directed by Nelly Goitiño, a production that renounces discursive speech in order to address the plasticity of objects and bodies, emotional tension between actors, metaphors and deeply meaningful symbols, within a dreamlike universe. In a different and deliberately grotesque style, Mastandrea this year offered *La Monstrua* (*The She-Monster*, 2002), efficiently directed by Marianella Morena.

As everybody knows, these innovative forms co-exist with more conservative trends, contrasting and complementing each other at a crossroads where old meets new, and submission to convention and pre-existing models meets with the most radical transgressions. Thus, alongside the aforementioned new generation of authors, firmly established authors such as Carlos Manuel Varela, Ricardo Prieto, Victor Manuel Leites, Dino Armas and Mauricio Rosencof continue with sustained creativity. These, together with Milton Schinca, Carlos

Maggi and Andrés Castillo, are intellectual heavyweights; they constitute a group of established playwrights that have started to lose their dominant position.

The themes of the emerging theatre are violence, impunity, the need for remembrance, dreams as both an escape from and a means to accept a reality that cannot be assimilated, disenchantment and distrust in official initiatives, attempts to create nets of solidarity preserving individualities, re-creation of collective social and psychological spaces that have been fragmented or destroyed. On another level, there has been an effort to overcome the collective trauma caused by the political persecution and state terrorism rampant during the years of Uruguay's military dictatorship, which has resulted in various cross-generational plays that have received different scenic interpretations, ranging from a prisoner's monologue in *El Bataraz* (1996) by Mauricio Rosencof and *El informante* (*The Informer*, Teatro de la Alianza Francesa, 1998) by Carlos Liscano, based on a narrator/victim whose objective is to preserve both his life and dignity, to the masquerades, violence and scenic display of *¿Dónde estaba usted el 27 de junio de 1973?* (*Where Were You on June 27, 1973?* – the date of the military coup – Teatro de la Alianza Francesa, 1996), or the more objective viewpoint of *El estado del alma* (*The Status of the Soul*[1], 2002), both plays by Alvaro Ahunchaín.

In the same vein, *En voz alta* (*Out Loud*, Puerto Luna 1998), written by Lupe Barone and directed by Iván Solarich, is a monologue by a woman describing the violence she has suffered. The intimate contact with her personal memories and ghosts as well as the simplicity of her physical appearance and acting style are of much greater impact. Barefoot and wearing a light nightgown, in a small venue seating no more than forty people that allows close contact with the public, the actress does not hesitate to show her helplessness and directly addresses each spectator with her voice and her stare.

In *Por debajo de los muros* (*Beneath the Walls*, Puerto Luna 1999), also written by Lupe Barone and directed by Iván Solarich, the same themes of oppression and terror appear from a resistance viewpoint, albeit treated in a more traditional manner. It describes the relationship between two friends and a woman, individuals who are pursued by the relentless ghosts of betrayal and shame, against the coming apart of the social fabric. In *Para abrir la noche* (*To Start the Evening*, Teatro Circular, 2001), author and director Horacio Buscaglia focuses – in a discursive and realistic fashion – on the issue of memory and the ability to deal with trauma through personal encounters within a group.

A different approach can be seen in *En honor al mérito* (*In Honour of Merit*, El Galpón 2001) by Margarita Musto, directed by Hector Guido, which deals with the disappearance and assassination of the opposition leaders Gutiérrez Ruiz and Zelmar Michelini, one the Speaker of the House of Commons, the other a prominent left-wing Senator, in 1976 during the military dictatorship. The issue is tackled from the viewpoint of two women whose attitudes of complicity or rejection are progressively revealed during the play. The production, although basically realistic, is built around two scenic areas: an area in

---

[1] Current President Jorge Batlle made reference to this 'status of the soul' at the beginning of his term of office (March 2000), when launching his efforts to uncover the truth behind the disappearance of some of the victims of the military, still 'missing'.

the foreground, in the middle of the stage, like a sort of dais, where the action and dialogue take place; and another in the background, where a mysterious character moves amongst various instruments: ropes, pulleys and ramps.

Along the same lines, *Cuentos de hadas* (*Fairy Tales*, El Galpón 1998), written by Raquel Diana and directed by Juan Carlos Moretti, shows an affectionate encounter between three generations of women. In this warm and evocative production, a feminine world, characterised by the absence of men (fathers, husbands or lovers), seems to seal the fate of the house under the pressures of going undercover, prison, torture and death, all elliptically mentioned. However, they manage to pursue private goals and affections during times of oppression and fear. Yet at the same time, rooted in a few permanent realities beyond historical circumstances, we have elements such as the simplicity of everyday affection, the archaic magical connection with earth, nature and its primitive legends as irrational responses that ease incomprehensible pain, the poetry of fairy tale used to face reality. All these result in parables of an impossible existence which, nevertheless, through memory and imagination, bring forth a form of irrational hope.

In a style that can be more directly linked to the emergent theatre of dissolution or disintegration, *Episodos de la vida postmoderna* (*Episodes of Post-Modern Life*, Teatro Circular, 2000) by Raquel Diana offers a radically different approach underlined by director Juan Carlos Moretti. Here exasperation, fragmented situations, tensions, are represented through speech and interaction between characters, with distorted gestures as well as lighting and sound effects, very much like a video-clip or a cartoon. An excellent musical should also be noted, *El fantasma de Canterville* (*The Canterville Ghost*, El Galpón 1997) written by Diana in collaboration with Helen Velando, as well as her most recent production of *Banderas en tu corazón* (*Banners in Your Heart,* El Galpón 2001) which deals with marginality in a humorous and effective way.

As to the relationship between the shows described here and the rest of the theatrical establishment, these new performances are creating a new audience comprised mostly of young people faithful to their favourite directors and actors, with even a preference for certain venues, all of which tends to create a division within the system. On the other hand, other audiences continue to appreciate more traditional and conventional forms of theatre, such as the one derived from Creole grotesque theatre, or critical realism, or the historic avant-garde of Ionesco and Beckett, not to mention the emergence of a commercial theatre circuit, in this end of a century characterised by an increasing complexity of the system.

Translated by **Stephanie Regner** (ITI World Secretariat) and **Dr César Herrera** (Uruguay Centre of ITI).

YUGOSLAVIA

ALEKSANDAR MILOSAVLJEVIC

It would be nice if we could claim that the renaissance of theatre activity in this country occurred at the same time as the political changes in Serbia. Yet despite the dramatic collapse of the Milosevic regime and the subsequent favourable attitude of the international community toward our country following October 2, 2000, the changes have come neither automatically nor easily, since the years of isolation, lack of funds and ideational disorientation have left deep scars on the theatre in Serbia and Montenegro, as on every other social – that is to say economic – level. It is impossible to erase these scars immediately, let alone heal them.

Too often, theatre in Serbia has been accused of fostering the growing nationalism. It has been said that some of its productions have affected the profusion of populism, and what is more, its frivolous content has offered escapism instead of mobilising forces against evil. It is true that the theatre in this country engaged in politics, sometimes even in a banal, almost journalistic way, and most often in an ethnically irrelevant way, but it must also be admitted that during the reign of Milosevic there was a persistent expression of rebellion and resistance to repression. There was not a civil protest in which the most prominent theatremakers did not take part, nor form of civil disobedience that did not include actors, directors and playwrights.

Truth to tell, the theatre neither created Milosevic nor did it topple him, but it paid an enormous price during his reign. Along with the other fields of society, especially of culture, it became extremely impoverished, lost adequate material support and to a great extent was relegated to the will of ignorant people, the whims of the market, based on a populist taste and the world view of the newly created social elite. In such circumstances, the repertoire of Serbian theatres most often featured productions with two or three characters, without a change of decor and in modern dress. The theatre survived, with the enthusiasm of its makers as its only energy.

And then, in March 1999, came the NATO bombing of Yugoslavia. In such a context it is difficult to explain the position of the theatremakers or even intellectuals in this country. On the one hand, officially, NATO was intervening against something that the majority of intellectuals in the country were also against. On the other hand, our country was being bombed, our people were being killed ...

In a country in which everything had stopped, the theatres continued to give performances – true, only matinees, but even those under air attack. Entrance was free. At that time, the Belgrade theatres performed a so-called war repertory, productions which by the number of their cast or by their themes fitted into the atmosphere of grim reality. Some theatres were specific kinds of 'shelters of the soul', where it was possible to find refuge from the daily hysteria of war, to isolate oneself (among like-minded people) and give oneself up to the magic of the theatre, while others became symbols of patriotic resistance to the aggressor, part of the Milosevic propaganda machine. In the first days of the bombardment the theatres were packed, as people who had previously never even thought of the theatre entered one for the first time; but their interest in the theatre soon waned, and they manifested their patriotic feelings on the bridges which the then government defended from bombing with a 'living wall' of citizens, while the theatres continued to gather true theatre lovers.

To our general surprise, after the end of bombardment, confronting the effects of destruction, and in the midst of the hysterical rhetoric of victory in the war with NATO, the theatres continued to operate, and there were even theatre festivals. That year, in 1999, the Sterijino Pozorje festival was held, the most renowned Yugoslav festival for productions based on Yugoslav drama, as well as BITEF (the Belgrade International Theatre Festival) devoted to new theatre trends, and the Budva City Theatre, a Mediterranean summer festival in which theatre is only part of the programme. In this context, on a wave of unfounded enthusiasm, some exceptional productions were created, as attempts at establishing a seriously founded repertory.

The word *attempts* is apt, since in current theatre production in this country it is difficult to establish the existence of a precisely formulated, firmly executed repertory policy. In the present conditions, long term planning is impossible: funds for a production are raised haphazardly, despite the regular but insufficient amounts from the funders (city, municipality, republic), so that additional sums have to be raised from private connections with sponsors.

Among these exceptions are productions of Yugoslav plays, a segment indicating the vitality of any theatre environment. Following a lull in the 90s and sporadic heights (*The Belgrade Trilogy* and *Family Tales* by Biljana Srbljanovic, *Caroline Neuber* by Nebojša Romcevic, *The Tour* and *Speech Defect* by Goran Markovic), in the 1999–2000 theatre season there was the production of *Yegor's Journey* by Vida Ognjenovic, who also directed the production for the Budva City Theatre. Written in a classical realistic style, the action of the play takes place in Budva at the time of Napoleon's conquests and is a testimony to the eternal sad fate of the people of this region, doomed to be a pawn in the political games of great powers. The personal dramas of the people in turbulent times are skilfully combined with the great drama of Europe, while the destinies of ordinary people mingle in an exciting way with the story of the creation of a new world order.

Politics managed to sneak into Yugoslav theatre in several ways: through clearly defined plays and productions – the so-called political theatre – and in a roundabout way through commercial or politicking productions. It should be borne in mind that in this country it is politics, not the eternal triangle, which is the basis of boulevard theatre. The latest play by the well known film director Goran Markovic, *Pandora's Box*, deals with the secret police files which have been opened up to citizens after the fall of Milosevic. The author himself directed this play in the Belgrade Dramatic Theatre, revealing that after fifty years of repressive rule no one is innocent, and that the overturned system of values has compromised even those who fought against tyranny.

Politics is also the key point of the dramatic writing of Biljana Srbljanovic, whose plays are being performed all over Europe. Still, she approaches politics in a considered way, from the standpoint of a 'lost generation' which has done

Yegor's Journey by Vida Ognjenovic, who also directed the production for the Budva City Theatre

Scene from *Garbage* by Ljubomira Đurkovica, directed by Nick Upper (Niko Goršic, Montenegro)

away with illusions and which formulates its dramaturgy as 'blood and sperm'. By finely contrived metaphors and daring political allusions, in a play entitled *The Fall* (directed by Gorcin Stojanovic, Budva City Theatre and BITEF, 1999), Srbljanovic makes a radical re-evaluation of the roots of Serbian nationalism, raising the concept of the political theatre to a higher level than is usual, and in her latest piece *Supermarket* (directed by Alisa Stojanovic, Yugoslav Dramatic Theatre, 2002) she directs the edge of her satire at the new Europe through the prism and its refraction of a predominantly petit bourgeois view of the world.

In a similar key are the productions which have marked the latest season at the Yugoslav Dramatic Theatre – *The Pavilion* by Milena Markovic (directed by Alisa Stojanovic), one of the plays which received an award at the Viennese Teater mbH Competition for the best plays from the ex-Yugoslavia region, and *Shopping and Fucking* by Mark Ravenhill (directed by Iva Miloševic), both of which are focused on the fate of young people in their unresolved conflict with a reality defined by forces beyond their reach.

A specific feature within the context of the above mentioned repertory of the Yugoslav Dramatic Theatre, as well as of theatre events in Serbia, is a production of *The Miser* by the Renaissance playwright from Dubrovnik, Marin Drzic, directed by Jagoš Markovica. Forceful in its long pauses, markedly slow in tempo, with a Renaissance enthusiasm placed on its head, focused on the dark side of man's being and with fascinating acting, this production has been one of the heights of the season and the basis of a hope for the future.

In many ways also specific is *The Siege of St. Saviour's Church* (National Theatre, Sombor, 2002) which is based on a novel by Goran Petrovic and directed by Kokan Mladenovic, who also adapted it for the stage. The director is one of the key young artists who has dealt with his own times without compromise and with conviction, most often through the past, as is the case with *The Maligning of the People in Two Parts* by Slobodan Selenic (National Theatre, Sombor, 1999) which searches for the causes of the present in the events of the past.

The high standards of the Serbian theatre have been consistently preserved by Atelje 212, the Belgrade theatre founded in its time as a space for the performance of the contemporary dramatic and stage avant-garde, later known for its satirical productions, and in the past season one of the rare domestic theatres which have, at the expense of a clear repertory concept, also engaged in risky moves, and still managing to preserve some of the most important characteristics of theatre life in Belgrade in its heyday – virtuoso acting, precise directing and critically applauded productions. This year the Atelier has come into the limelight with a production of *Leda* by the Croatian writer Miroslav Krleza and *The Miracle in Sargan* by the Serbian poet and playwright Ljubomir Simovic. Both productions were directed by Dejan Mijac, a director of the older generation, in a well thought out, measured manner which combines a realistic procedure with a carefully applied stylisation.

Krleza has also been placed in the repertory by the Serbian National Theatre from Novi Sad. *The Noble Glembays* has been brilliantly directed by Egon Savin, who has pointed out the connections between the dark sides of the middle class who suddenly became rich at the beginning of the last century and the true face of those who make up the social elite in equally murky times today.

Politics as a force which determines man's fate is also one of the main topics that the director Nebojša Bradic deals with in a series of productions based on adaptations of the major works of Yugoslav literature. Following her adaptation and direction of Meša Selimovic's novel *The Dervish and Death*, Bradic has achieved success with productions of a reduced directing procedure, powerful acting expression and reduced stage design, one based on the novel *The Damned Yard* by the Nobel Prize winner Ivo Andric and the other a part of the saga *The Golden Fleece* by Borislav Pekic. It is interesting to point out that both productions have resulted in co-operation with the best actors of the younger generation in the Yugoslav capital and one of the most enterprising provincial theatres – the Kruševac theatre.

The destiny of man pressured by history, politics and his finer emotions is also the subject of *The Boka D-Minor* by Stevan Koprivica directed by Milan Karadzic (The Cultural Centre, Tivat, 1999). The melodramatic tone of this story about the tragic love of a rebellious pirate and an unusual young girl was enough to turn it into a commercial production, untypical for the Yugoslav theatre, mainly aimed at unrefined tastes.

There are several productions which form the cornerstones of theatre life in Montenegro. The productions of Ibsen's *Nora* directed by Branislav Micunovic (1999); *Garbage* by Ljubomira Đurkovica, directed by Nick Upper (Niko Goršic, 2002); and Gorky's *Smug Citizens*, directed by Paolo Magielli (2001) at the Montenegrin National Theatre in Podgorica form a framework for a new gathering of theatremakers from ex-Yugoslavia in projects which are firmly founded on modern stage expression, indicating the new sensibility of the theatre in Montenegro. The productions of The Budva City Theatre, relying on actors and directors from Belgrade, have made it possible for theatre to survive even in the darkest time, and this was the place where some of the most representative Yugoslav theatre projects were created. The Podgorica Children's Theatre, which has lately been transformed into The Municipal Theatre, is a perfect example of the vitality and expansion of theatre life in Montenegro and it brings together the youngest and very vital generation of the Faculty of Dramatic Arts of Cetinje.

In the past years there have been very few musical productions in Yugoslavia, perhaps due to the fact that few people felt like singing in this country, and also partly due to the exceptionally demanding production standards implied by this type of stage art. At the same time, the only Serbian theatre which specialises in musicals, the Belgrade Terazije Theatre, has been under reconstruction for more than a decade now. For this reason the only representative example of this genre is *The Anniversary*, a production which is a call for help, a homage to musical comedy and a reminder of the golden days of this theatre.

Things stand differently with dance theatre. An alternative theatre by its nature, this type of theatre has continued to deal with re-examination, deepening its critical stance toward its times. Among the artists who perform choreodrama and theatre of movement, Sonja Vukicevic stands out and she is regularly a consultant for theatre productions which require a specific choreography of movement. She is an imaginative and daring dancer who has devoted her major productions of the late 90s to an analysis of the Kafkaesque nature of reality in this country: in her choreography and dance performances we also recognise Shakespearean topics (*Macbeth Against Macbeth*).

YUGOSLAVIA

A specific kind of permanent theatre research and (self-)examination, influenced by Barba, is cultivated by the Dah Theatre from Belgrade, a group of devotees of the theatre led by Dijana Miloševic and Jadranka Anđelic. This is also confirmed by their latest productions, *Documents of the Times* (1999), *Dances with the Dark* (2002) and *The Maps of Forbidden Memories* (2002).

An important segment of theatre production in Yugoslavia. though not in the sense of quantity, is the children's theatre. The leaders are the Bosko Buha Theatre and The Snail Little Theatre, which are based on very different conceptions. The first is oriented toward the staging of the classics and company productions, while the other is based on the attempt to achieve the effect of a stage spectacle by the imaginative use of reduced means. What they have in common is that they treat children as a serious audience which should not be condescended to.

Both theatres are also the best schools for the education of future audiences, places which refine the tastes of those who will tomorrow become both spectators and creators. Still, in order for both of these to have a place to come together, it is necessary to invest money today, and above all the will, knowledge and enthusiasm without which theatre in Serbia and Montenegro will not overcome the time of crisis. In this regard it is no great comfort to learn that European theatre has been in permanent crisis for more than 2000 years already, and that such a crisis can only be overcome by good productions, backed always by new and daring efforts. At least this experience can be a basis to build on, and growth can be achieved by the quick inclusion of all segments of Yugoslav theatre and culture into international trends.

The question of the reintegration of our country into the world is no longer a matter of the fulfilling of political will, but the fundamental question of our survival. For this reason we find it important also to learn of experience in the field of theatre legislation. Serbia, namely, still has no law on theatre. Its formulation has been awaited for several decades now, and with it the establishing of optimal relations within theatre life, relations which would define the rights and obligations of all the factors of this reality.

I believe that the opening of the theatres of Serbia and Montenegro to experience from abroad, the establishing of healthy, competitive relations between the world and Yugoslav theatres, and the passage of effective theatre legislation are the basic preconditions for the healing of the wounds of Serbian and Montenegrin theatres and for their regaining of the position that they once used to have.

Aleksandar Milosavljevic *is editor in chief of the theatre newspaper* Ludus, *and an editorial board member of the periodical* Scena. *He has published theatre reviews and essays in the most prominent daily papers and periodicals of the former Yugoslavia, and is now writing for* Glas Javnosti *and Radio Belgrade Programme III. He has a regular column in the newspaper* Danas. *He has worked as artistic director at the National Theatre Nepszinhaz, Subotica, and at The Museum of Theatre Arts of Serbia, Belgrade. He has been president of the Serbian Association of Theatre Critics, and a member of the Sterijino Pozorje Arts Council. He has edited several books on theatre and theatre history. His article has been translated by Vladislava Felbabov.*

International Theatre Institute

INTERNATIONAL EVENTS AND ACTIVITIES

May 2000 - October 2002

11 - 15 May 2000
MARSEILLES (France)
**CIDC Audience Development/Funding
Seminar** organised for representatives of ITI
Centres by the ITI Committee for Cultural
Identity and Development in the framework of
the 28th ITI World Congress. Under the
direction of Gerald Lidstone, BA MA ATC
FRGS, and Gerri Morris of Morris &
Hargreaves Ltd, Consultants, by special
courtesy. With the support of the Swedish
International Development organisation, SIDA.
Participants: Ljubisha Nikodinowski-Bish
(F.Y.R. of Macedonia), Almuth Fricke
(Germany), Youssuf Nasiruddin (Bangladesh),
Stephane Etienne (Cameroun), Koulitsa
Demetriou, Michaelis Charalambides, Nicos
Shiafkalis, Nadia Stylianou (Cyprus), Jenena
Nicolic, Emina Visnic (Croatia), Pila Sinisalu
(Estonia), Abate Mekuria (Ethiopia), Tamar
Telai (Georgia), Ilse Rudzite (Latvia),
Gankhuyag Olkonuud (Mongolia), Sunil
Pokharel (Nepal), Tatjana Azman (Slovenia),
Boel Höjeberg (Sweden).

11 and 12 May 2000 and duration of Congress
MARSEILLES (France)
**110th Session of the ITI Executive
Council** (19 May, first Meeting of the new
Executive Council)
Following the 28th Congress, Mr Kim Jeong-
Ok (Rep. of Korea) was elected President of
ITI and Messrs Pierre Santini (France) and
Jean-Pierre Guingané (Burkina Faso), Vice-
Presidents. Other Board members elected:
Manfred Beilharz (Germany), Heino Byrgesen
(Denmark), Martha Coigney (U.S.A.), Neville
Shulman (U.K.).

May 2000
News from the Secretariat N° 73. International
theatre news edited and published three times a
year in French and English versions by the
General Secretariat of ITI with the support of
UNESCO.

14 - 21 May 2000
MARSEILLES (France)
28th ITI World Congress organised by
the French Centre of the ITI. Opening
ceremony on Sunday 14th May featuring a
new production of *Giselle* directed by
Eric Quilleré, presented by the National
Ballet of Marseilles under the direction of
Marie-Claude Pietragalla.
Main lines of the Congress: an opening up
to different cultures and to youth,
collaboration with artists in the region,
accent on the decentralisation of culture,
involvement of the host city and regional
audiences.
As well as the General Assembly and the
other statutory sessions (Executive
Council meetings and Committee
meetings), essential elements of the
Congress, the programme included two
international colloquia open to the general
public.
Themes:
1: Cultural Diversities and the role of live
theatre in the construction of a culture of
peace: *Theatre a Weapon for Life*.
2: The ITI/ UNESCO Chair of Theatre:
artistic education – training and teaching,
An intensive artistic programme, with the
involvement of artists from Marseilles,
(theatres, opera and dance companies,
schools) and in particular the National
Ballet of Marseilles, the Centre national
de création des arts de la rue (National
Centre for Street Arts) as well as national
activities with the participation of
ADAMI, the SACD, Syndeac, the Private
Theatre sector and the Fédération du
Spectacle.

Events were organised in collaboration
with the ITI Committees, the
International Association of Theatre
Critics and other international theatre
organisations in relation with ITI.

ITI Events and Activities 2000-2002

May 2000
Launching of **The World of Theatre**, 6th (2000) edition, in the framework of the 28th ITI World Congress. Edited for the ITI Communication Committee by Ian Herbert (President) and Nicole Leclercq in collaboration with the General Secretariat of the ITI. Published in paperback by the Bangladesh Centre of the ITI. A hardback edition was subsequently published by Routledge.

May 2000
Launching of the **World Theatre Directory**, 5th edition, in the framework of the 28th ITI World Congress. Edited by Nicole Leclercq for the ITI Communication Committee in collaboration with the ITI General Secretariat. Published by the General Secretariat.

May 2000
Launching of the **World Theatre Directory on Internet.** A project of the ITI Communication Committee and the ITI General Secretariat. Implemented by Nicole Leclercq, Communication Commitee, and Jennifer Walpole, ITI General Secretariat, in collaboration with Jakub Sosnowski, ITI Internet services administrator.

May 2000
'We, the People of Theatre' Publication of the collected International Messages for World Theatre Day (1962–2000). In English, French and Bangla. Published by the Bangladesh Centre of ITI.

May 2000
'International Messages for International Dance Day 1982 - 2000'.
All the IDD Messages published in English and French. Edited by the International Dance Committee of the International Theatre Institute with the support of the French Centre and the Belgian ITI Centre (Flemish Community).

May 2000
Creation of a website for the 28th ITI World Congress
Under the auspices of ITI, a website devoted to the Congress was created by Jakub Sosnowski (ITI Internet Services) who organised training in information and communication tools developed by ITI for its members.

May 2000
Creation of the Ivory Coast Centre of ITI

15 June - 2 July 2000
BONN, (Germany)
European Writers and Translators' Workshop organised by the German Centre of ITI in co-operation with the Bonner Biennale. Main themes: rapid translation of new works, in particular for those in less widely used languages.

23 June – 2 July 2000
BRATISLAVA (Slovakia)
Project Istropolitana 2000. 13th International Festival of Theatre schools. Festival and workshops under the auspices of the Theatre Education Committee of ITI. Participation of a dozen tertiary level schools.

June 2000
An honorary degree **Docteur honoris causa** was awarded to **André-Louis Périnetti**, Secretary General of ITI, by the Council of Arts and Sciences of the Academy of Music and Drama of Bratislava (VSMU) and presented during a ceremony held in the framework of Istropolitana.

30 June 2000
BRATISLAVA (Slovakia)
Meeting of the Theatre Education Committee Board in conjunction with Istropolitana. Presence of André-Louis Périnetti, Secretary General of ITI.

4 - 9 July 2000
HANNOVER/BRAUNSCHWEIG (Germany)
Who wants to be a woman tomorrow ? Female Configurations in the Performing Arts of Today. Organised by the German ITI Centre in collaboration with the ITI Dramatic Theatre Committee and the Cultural Identity and Development Committee in conjunction with the Theaterformen Festival's Summer Academy. International meeting of women artists from different cultures and disciplines: actresses, stage directors, choreographers, scenographers, playwrights, composers, dramaturgists, scholars etc...

4 - 9 July 2000
BRAUNSCHWEIG (Germany)
Board Meeting of the Dramatic Theatre Committee in the framework of the encounter 'Who wants to be a woman tomorrow? Female Configurations in the Performing Arts of Today'.

ITI Events and Activities 2000-2002

July 2000
Creation of the Togolese Centre of ITI

3 – 13 July 2000
SINAIA (Romania**)**
**2ⁿᵈ Run of the International Theatre
Schools' Workshops.** Theme: 'Methods and
innovations in Theatre Education'
Organised by the ITI/UNESCO Chair Objective:
Exchange of experience in the field of theatre
teaching, between schools and university theatre
departments from different countries. Recording
of workshops on video and CD-Rom for diffusion
to other schools in the network. Presentation of
different teaching methods in 5 programmes on
Internet. Under the auspices of the ITI Theatre
Education Committee.

7 – 13 July 2000
SINAIA (Romania)
**2ⁿᵈ World Conference of Directors of Higher
Education Theatre Institutions**, organised by
the ITI-UNESCO Chair of Theatre and Culture
of Civilisations, brought together 30 schools from
Europe, North America, Asia and Australia. The
main aim of this event, which received support
through the framework agreement between ITI
and UNESCO, was to discuss and further develop
the programme of mobility and international
exchange in the field of tertiary level theatre
education already being implemented by the ITI/
UNESCO Chair.
The Conference, acting as a general assembly of
the ITI/UNESCO Chair, adopted **3 resolutions**::
the setting up of an International documentation
centre on educational methods in Liège (Belgium);
the implementation of new aspects of PrumACT,
UNESCO programme of Mobility in tertiary level
theatre teaching (1999- 2003) of the ITI/
UNESCO Chair; the creation of a second
Regional Bureau of the ITI/UNESCO Chair
based at the GITIS Academy of Dramatic Art
(Moscow).

8 - 15 July 2000
MONTERREY - Nuevo Leon (Mexico).
**The 1st International Congress of Classical
and Contemporary Ballet,** under the auspices
of the ITI International Dance Committee,
organised by the National Council for Culture and
the Arts through the National Institute of Fine
Arts. Aim: to study and define the main lines of
dance development in the 21st century. An in
depth study of physical, psychological and
educational questions. Discussions, master classes,
demonstrations by guest schools from Argentina,
Australia, Canada, China, Denmark, England,
France, Germany, Italy, Japan, Russia, USA.

19 –30 July 2000
MOTUVUN (Croatia)
**Motovun Drama Colony 'From Text to
Performance'** organised by the Croatian
Centre of ITI in collaboration with the
International Youth Theatre Festival
(MKFM), the International Centre of
Motovun, and the Theatre Institute, Prague
(Czech Centre of ITI). Aim: to facilitate
participation in low-cost production of
contemporary plays and to establish links
between similar international centres.
Direction, Sanja Nikcevic.

30 July – 27 August 2000
WOLFSEGG (Austria)
**26th Wolfsegg International Ballet
Seminar.** Event under the auspices of the
ITI International Dance Committee.
University level courses for ballet teachers
in the tradition of the Lunacharsky Instiute
of Theatre Arts (GITIS). Classical training
for dancers and ballet students. Organised
by the Dance Committee and Music Theatre
Committee of the Austrian ITI Centre. The
organisers covered course fees for one
candidate from each ITI National Centre
wishing to send a student.

5 - 6 August 2000
MALMÖ, (Sweden)
**Meeting of the Dramatic Theatre
Committee Board**, in the framework of
the Nordic Theatre Meeting on the theme:
Music theatre. At the invitation of the
Swedish Centre of ITI.

10 - 19 August 2000
TOKYO (Japan).
**International Workshop - KYOGEN
2000** Under the direction of Master
Mannojo NOMURA of the Iizumi School.
Theoretical training: Professor Kazuo
TAGUCHI. Organised by the Japanese
Centre of ITI.

20 July – 5 September 2000
DROUSHIA & PAPHOS (Cyprus)
ANCIENT GREEK DRAMA 2000:
Organised by the Cyprus Centre of the ITI
in collaboration with the ITI Committee for
Cultural Identity and Development, the
Droushia Cultural Centre, the Cultural
Services of the Ministry of Education and
Culture, the Cyprus Tourism Organisation
and the Paphos Municipality, this major
event, taking place over 6 weeks, consisted
of a number of interrelated projects:

ITI Events and Activities 2000-2002

20 August – 5 September - **Seminar and Festival of Higher Education Theatre Institutes**
20 July – 5 September- **Summer Course in Ancient Greek Drama**
20 July – 5 September - **Workshop production of the *Trojan Women* by Euripides**
20th August – 5 September - **Festival of Ancient Greek Drama** (Paphos Ancient Odeon)
2-5 September **6th International Symposium on Ancient Greek Drama:** Theme: Hubris and Blindness: Contemporary Stage Approaches Papers by specialists in Ancient Greek Drama. The Cyprus Centre of ITI hosted a delegate from all ITI Centres that wished to send a specialist in the field.

22 - 24 September 2000
BUENOS AIRES (Argentina)
VIth International Congress on Theatre Research organised by the Institute of Theatre Arts for the University of Buenos Aires and under the auspices of the Argentinian Centre of ITI. Topic: The various stages of Grotowski's work. Seminar, 25-30 September, on Grotowski's vision of Creativity.

28 September – 10 October 2000
NAJING, YANGZHOU, SUZHOU, CHANGZHOU and WUXI (China).
6th National Festival of the Arts, China. Under the auspices of the Ministry of Culture and with the participation of the Chinese Centre of the ITI. 104 theatre performances in all genres presented by companies from China and other countries.

13 - 22 October 2000
SEOUL (Republic of Korea)
7th BeSeTo Festival. Major regional event founded in 1994 and organised in turn by the Chinese, Korean and Japanese Centres of ITI. Performances: *Buna, coming out of a tree* Japanese production by Seienen Gekijo; *Peach Blossom Water in March* Chinese production by the Dalian Dramatic Theatre. *Chunhyang-jun (The Story of Chunhyang)*, the third play, the highlight of this year's festival, was the first collaborative production between the 3 countries. The play was based on a traditional Korean tale. This unique intercultural production consisted of 3 organic parts. Enacted in 3 different languages and performance styles, the first part was in Chinese traditional Yueji by a company of women, the second in Japanese Kabuki style and the third in Korean Chang-geuk, a modernised theatrical conception of the epic-narrative solo performance Pansori, by the Korean National Theatre.

18 - 20 October 2000.
SEOUL (Korea)
The Korean Centre of ITI invited representatives of the ITI **Music Theatre Committee** to attend the International Symposium 'Traditional Theatre in Asia and the future of the live performing arts', in the framework of the BeSeTo Festival.

19 –22 October 2000
SEOUL (Rep. of Korea)
Creation of a Regional Bureau of ITI for Asia. As a follow-up to the resolution adopted by the 28th Congress of ITI, the founding meeting of the Regional Bureau took place under the presidency of Dr Hyesook Yang, President of the Korean Centre of ITI, in the framework of the BeSeTo Festival. The meeting was followed by an International Symposium on the theme: 'How to promote the development of the performing arts in Asia'. The aim of the bureau is to promote the development of the performing arts in Asia and intercultural exchange at regional and international levels. Participants invited from: Australia, Brunei, Bangladesh, China, Japan, Mongolia, Nepal, Philippines, Indonesia, Singapore, Vietnam and North Korea. Presence of Secretary General, André-Louis Périnetti and Kim Jeong-Ok, President of ITI worldwide.

25 – 29 October 2000
TAPLOW, Berkshire (England)
The Power of the Arts. Co-organised by the Dramatic Theatre Committee of ITI, and led by its co-president Faynia Williams, the Seminar was part of an ongoing research project on 'The growing role of the arts in personal and social development'. During the meeting, an international group of practitioners in the field of the arts and sciences met to discuss themes such as 'the relationship between the arts and the mind'. Patrick Guinand, co-president of the Committee, gave a paper.

28 October – 4 November 2000
OUAGADOUGOU (Burkina Faso).
FITMO 2000 - 7th Edition of the International Festival of Theatre and Puppets, Ouagadougou. Theme: 'Theatre, Human Rights and Peace in Africa' Presence of troupes from more than a dozen African and European countries. Event organised with the support of UNESCO through the framework agreement between ITI and UNESCO. Festival under the direction of Jean-Pierre Guingané, President of the ITI African Regional Bureau. The programme included theatre performances, daily discussions on the previous night's

performances, workshops; discussions on the theme: **Theatre, Human Rights and Peace in Africa**; homage to Sony Labou Tansi organised in collaboration with the University of Ouagadougou; special Day 'Culture de Quartier' UNESCO programme; theatre Bookshop.

The **3rd Meeting of REFATH** brought together representatives of African Theatre Festivals. Under the joint patronage of the the the Union of Dramatic Ensembles of Ouagadougou (UNEDO) and the Burkinabé Centre of the ITI, the FITMO aims to:
Provide a local framework for encounters between African artists; Facilitate the circulation of artistic productions; Provide an opportunity for artists to discover each other's work and stimulate joint projects (co-productions, training workshops etc);
Create a market for performing arts, not only among African promoters but also for those from other parts of the world; Contribute to raising the artistic quality of theatre performances by encouraging the pursuit of excellence among participants and by enabling them to share in the multiplicity of enriching experiences provided by the various events; Offer the audience a diversity of dramatic approaches; Obtain audience fidelity and attract new audiences; Create and nourish a taste for theatre among young audiences.

October 2000
News from the secretariat N° 74
International theatre news edited and published three times a year in French and English versions by the General Secretariat of ITI with the support of UNESCO, Division of Arts and Cultural Enterprise.

10-12 November 2000
IZAMAL (Mexico)
Board Meeting of the ITI International Dance Committee hosted by the Mexican ITI Centre and the Government of Izamal in the framework of a festival organised in honour of the Committee.

17 – 19 November 2000
PARIS (France).
The **111th Session of the Executive Council of ITI** held at UNESCO House, was preceded by a meeting of the Executive Board in the morning of 17 November.

November 2000
Uchimura Prize 2000. Awarded by the ITI Executive Council to **Abel Solares** (Austria/ Guatemala) for his work in the field of Japanese

theatre and his production *Kinuta*, a modern version of the Noh play by Zeami. The presentation took place in TOKYO (Japan), during a ceremony organised by the Japanese Centre.
The Uchimura Prize was inaugurated in 1992 on the initiative of the Japanese Centre of the International Theatre Institute in honour of its former president Naoya Uchimura, a playwright who devoted his life to promoting mutual knowledge and understanding of theatre throughout the world. This annual award aims to stimulate and encourage initiatives taken by groups or by individual artists outside Japan, leading to an action or project featuring relations with Japanese theatre. The Uchimura Prize was created in collaboration with the Uchimura family who have generously endowed it since its inception.

25 November - 11 December 2000
BUDAPEST (Hungary)
Meeting of the Theatre Education Committee in Budapest in the framework of the Union of European Theatres International Theatre Festival (25/11 - 1/12/2000), hosted by the University of Drama and Film of Budapest. A paper was given by Andrew McKinnon: 'The development of international structures designed to aid emerging directors – the "hothouses" in the Netherlands'.

December 2000
Creation of the ITI Centre of the Republic of Congo (Pointe Noire)

ITI Events and Activities 2000-2002

2001

15 - 19 February
TOKYO (Japan)
3rd Conference of Asian Women and Theatre Theme: Asian women yesterday and today in their social and family context. Co-organised by the organising Committee of the 3rd Conference for Asian Women and Theatre, the Asian Centre of the Japan Foundation with the support of the Japan Centre of ITI, the Association of Stage directors and the Japan Playwrights Association.

14 - 20 February 2001 DHAKA (Bangladesh)
'Roots and Blossoms' International Seminar, Workshops and Festival of Indigenous Theatre. Organised by the Bangladesh Centre under the presidency of Ramendu Majumdar. Guests came from Bangladesh, China, Cyprus, Denmark, France, Germany, Korea, India, Japan, Nepal, and Sweden. Seminar opened by Her Excellency Sheikh Hasina, Prime Minister of the People's Republic of Bangladesh. Presence of the co-ordinator of the Asia-Pacific Regional Bureau, Dr Hyesook Yang, President of the Korean Centre, Heino Byrgesen (Denmark). President of the Danish Centre and Member of the Executive Bureau. Event in the 2001 UNESCO ITI framework agreement. The ITI General Secretariat was represented by Jennifer Walpole. The Bangladesh Centre offered hospitality to nine theatre companies from other countries as well as to all the foreign delegates. Through the seminar and the festival, the biggest theatre event ever organised in Bangladesh, the Centre brought together artists and scholars to study the current situation of indigenous theatre and to try to determine ways of encouraging a positive evolution of theatre traditions in the future. Held in seven venues in Dhaka, the festival included performances by Bangladeshi and visiting troupes - traditional theatre, contemporary theatre, university productions and a substantial programme of theatre for children. Alexander Stillmark (German ITI and CIDC) directed a workshop for directors and actors in collaboration with the Goethe Institute.

18 - 20 February 2001 DHAKA (Bangladesh)
The 2nd Meeting of the Asia Pacific Regional Bureau was hosted by the Bangladesh Centre in the framework of the International Festival. Presence of delegates from the following countries: Bangladesh, China Korea, Japan, India, Nepal. The General Secretariat was represented by Jennifer Walpole.

17 February 2001
Board Meeting of the Communication Committee hosted by the Bangladesh Centre in the framework of the Festival and Seminar on Indigenous Theatre 'Roots and Blossoms'.

17 February 2001
Board Meeting of the Cultural Identity and Development Committee hosted by the Bangladesh Centre in the framework of the Festival and Seminar on Indigenous Theatre 'Roots and Blossoms'.

21 February 2001
Following a proposal made by Bangladesh, UNESCO created **International Mother Language Day** in 1999. The date chosen was February 21st, in commemoration of the five students who died on this date in 1952 defending recognition of Bangla as the state language of the then East Pakistan which became Bangladesh after the war of liberation.
In a resolution adopted at its 28th World Congress in Marseilles (France), May 2000, the International Theatre Institute officially joined with UNESCO in observing International Mother Language Day on 21st February each year.
International Mother Language Day provides an opportunity to theatre people all over the world to project the uniqueness and diversity of each culture, language being at the core of the national culture ... When many national languages face threat of extinction, national theatres are also endangered. We strongly believe theatre can play an inspiring role in protecting the rights of the mother language.

February 2001
News from the secretariat N° 75 International theatre news edited and published three times a year in French and English versions by the General Secretariat of ITI with the support of UNESCO, Division of Arts and Cultural Enterprise.

24 – 31 March 2001
MEXICO CITY & XALAPA State of Vera Cruz (Mexico)
Meeting of the ITI Centres of the Americas and the Caribbean hosted by the Mexican Centre of ITI, Event within the 2001 UNESCO/ITI framework agreement. Presence of the Secretary General of ITI, André-Louis Périnetti. The event included an exhibition on Mexican Scenography held by OISTAT.
World Theatre Day was celebrated in Xalapa by the presentation of the medal 'Mi vida en el teatro' to a number of prominent artists from the Americas. The Message was read by the great actress Ana Ofelia Murguia and by author Hugo

Rascon Banda during a ceremony at the University of Vera Cruz. Guest of honour was Alfonso Sastre, Spanish playwright who gave a conference on the 28th March. Theatre personalities present also participated in a round table discussion. Presence of ITI Centres from: Argentina, Uruguay, Peru, Colombia, Jamaica, Costa Rica, U.S.A., Mexico. Observers from Guatemala, Panama and Bolivia.

22-23 March 2001
CIUDAD VICTORIA (Tamaulipas - Mexico)
CICD International Symposium 'Theatre, Cultural Identity and Development' in the framework of the **1st Intercontinental Festival for the Cultures of the World**. The Mexican ITI-UNESCO Centre, The Government of the State of Tamaulipas, Mexico, the Tamaulipan Institute for Culture & the Arts, Mexico's Foreign Affairs Ministry, the Mexican Council for Culture & the Arts, and the Cultural Identity & Development Committee of the ITI invited participation of theatre directors, actors, drama professors, stage designers etc. Themes:
1)Theatre and cultural identity
2)The social risks of globalization, the need to reaffirm cultural diversity in a world in constant evolution.
3)Theatre: a tool for globalization
4) Society & the media, Theatre and new technologies.

27 March 2001
World Theatre Day, created in 1961 by the International Theatre Institute is celebrated annually on 27th March by the ITI National Centres and the world theatre community. Numerous theatre events and activities are held on this occasion, one of the most important being the diffusion of the traditional International Message written by a theatre figure of world stature at the invitation of the International Theatre Institute. The author of the 2001 Message was Iakovos Kampanellis (Greece). Mr Kampanellis has written more than 50 plays for theatre and cinema and his deep influence on Greek theatre is reflected in the fact that post war Greek authors are referred to as the 'Kampanellis generation'. His plays are performed thoughout Greece and his works have been translated into many languages. Reports on the celebration of the World Theatre Day were received from all continents. Traditionally the Message is read in theatres, published in the daily newspapers and reviews, diffused and commented on by radio and television in all countries. Extracts of reports from National Centres and other members of the theatre community follow:

BANGLADESH: The Centre and the Bangladesh Group Theatre Federation held a joint celebration of World Theatre Day. Members of the theatre community in theatre costumes took part in the traditional rally followed by a gathering. Aly Zaker, eminent actor and director gave the annual lecture and a modern dance performance was presented by the company Nrityanchal.
CONGO Rep: The newly formed Congo Pointe-Noire Centre of ITI celebrated World Theatre Day in the following manner:: publication of a page devoted to the WTD in the journal *Ou bien ou bien* of the French Cultural Centre in Pointe-Noire; production of a special radio programme; at the Pagode, largest theatre in the city, celebration of the WTD in presence of special guests Ms Mambou Aimée Gnali, Minister of Culture and Arts in charge of Tourism, Mr. Ernest Fassbender, Representative of UNESCO for Congo – Brazzaville; reading of the International Message; official presentation of the board of the Congo Centre of ITI; staged readings of extracts of plays by playwrights from different countries.
D.R. CONGO: The Congo Centre observed World Theatre Day in collaboration with the Corporation of Women Artists of the Congo (Corfac). The theatre community's celebration was hosted by the Halle de la Gombe, (French Cultural Centre) under the direction of Jean-Michel Champault. Programme: an address by the president of the Congolese Centre; a performance by the Corfac troupe of *Poor Fatuma*, the subject of which was appropriately related to the theme of International Women's Month: 'Women and rights of succession and reproduction'; a paper from Professor Ndundu Kivwila on 'Perspectives of the Congolese theatre in the 20th century'; and the screening of a film on theatre.
COSTA RICA: Celebrating World Theatre Day for the first time, the Costa Rica Centre held a screening of the film *The Two Voyages of Jacques Lecoq* at the Alliance Française in Costa Rica. The Centre circulated the International Message to all the country's theatres, asking them to read it before performances on the 27th or to post it up in the theatre. The Costa Rican press published a number of articles on the Day.
CROATIA: The Centre celebrated WTD by: organising a Welsh Drama Week, the writing of a Croatian message, sending out both Messages (dance and theatre) to the media and the theatres, a drive to mark World Theatre Day in schools, free performances or shows at very reasonable prices in Croatian National Theatres

ITI Events and Activities 2000-2002

- Zagreb, Rijeka, Osijek, and Split, appropriate programmes in theatres throughout Croatia and promotion of the Bulletin, *Croatian Drama*, Issues 6–7, at the premises of the Croatian Association of Dramatic Artists.

CUBA: Many activities were organised under the auspices of the Ministry of Culture, the Council of the Performing Arts and the Cuban Centre of the ITI. The Message was circulated to the 158 professional artistic groups in Cuba and also broadcast on radio and television. Reading of the Message by Hector Quintero, President of the ITI Cuban Centre. Presentation by Abel Prieto, Minister of Culture, of the National Culture Award and the Alejo Carpentier Medal to distinguished performing arts personalities. Performance and launching of the review *Conjunto*. The Casa de las Americas also celebrated WTD, the Message being read by Ignacio Guttierez, President of Honour of the Cuban Centre, at the Superior Institute of Arts. On 27 March the Omar Valdes Medal was presented to a group of theatre and dance artists at the headquarters of the National Union of Writers and Artists of Cuba. The theatre group 'El Publico' prepared a special parade including all the characters from works it had presented. In the 15 provinces of Cuba there was a special season of performances.

CZECH Republic: Thanks to the excellent partnership established this year with Radio Cesky rozhlas 3 vltava, a station devoted to culture, the Czech Centre was able to promote both the Day and also theatre in the country in an extremely effective manner. The programme began with a reading of the Message followed by interviews with famous artists: actors, directors, writers as well as commentaries by critics live from the Theatre on the Balustrade. The radio programme also included reports on the theatre by Czech correspondents abroad as well as plays and premières. All theatre genres were represented in the broadcasts which continued from morning until night. Listeners had an opportunity to express their views and took part in a competition to win free theatre tickets.

During a gala evening at the National Theatre attended by the wife of President Havel, the Actors Association made its annual **Thalia awards**. The ceremony was telecast live. Many newspapers published the International Message as well as articles on the celebration of WTD. **GERMANY:** In Berlin and Northrhine–Westphalia, the Theatergemeinde (Association of Theatre Subscribers), held a reception and organised visits to theatres.

On World Theatre Day 2001, during a ceremony presided by Manfred Beilharz, President of the German ITI Centre, the Centre awarded its annual prize distinguishing a personality on the German theatre scene whose work has had an outstanding, international impact to the Forum Junger Bühnen-angehöriger (Forum for Young Theatre Professionals) and its director Manfred Linke. Manfred Linke, who has been active for many years in international theatre exchange and who was from 1982-91 director of the German ITI Centre, has sought to promote the Forum's engagement in contemporary theatre issues. Under his leadership, the it has been a place of lively exchange, frequently intervening in political and aesthetic debates. The Forum for Young Theatre Professionals is recognised and highly valued all over the world as a place for exchange and practical training.

JAMAICA: The Annual Actor Boy Awards for Excellence in Jamaican Theatre were presented during a gala in Kingston. Nearly twenty awards were given in various categories. Charles Hyatt received the ITI Jamaica Centre Lifetime Achievement Award, while Walliston 'Donald' Howell was given a special award for his contribution to Jamaican theatre in the area of set construction. One of Jamaica's leading Actresses, Leonie Forbes, received the Mexico ITI's medal 'My Life In Theatre'.

KUWAIT: The Kuwait Centre of the ITI participated in the 5th Kuwait Theatre Festival organised from 16-26 April 2001 (in the framework of Kuwait 2001 Arab Cultural Capital) under the patronage of the Minister of Information. The World Theatre Day Message was read at the opening ceremony. Speeches were made by the Secretary General of the National Council for Culture, Arts and Letters, Dr M. Al-Rumaihi, and Mr Fuad Al-Shatti, Director of the Festival and Member of the ITI Executive Council. The 5th Theatre Festival included six Kuwaiti competing plays, two Arab guest presentations and an adapted production of *Hamlet* by Solaiman al Bassam, and another Kuwaiti play. Nine prizes were awarded by a jury of five outstanding Arab theatre figures.

LEBANON: The Lebanese Centre of ITI celebrated World Theatre Day 2001 in collaboration with the Ministry of Culture and the Lebanon-American University (L.A.U). The ceremony was held in the Gulbenkian hall at the L.A.U. in the presence of the Director General of the Ministry, Dr Omar Halablab, the Minister's advisor, Dr Alexandre Najjar, the ITI Committee, the Actors Union, directors, writers, scenographers, theatre directors, journalists, critics and students of theatre. The programme published by the Lebanese Centre included the International Message in three languages - Arabic, French and English - a word from the President, Chakib Khoury, information on ITI, the projects of the Lebanese Centre and a list of its Committee members. The Lebanese Centre awarded medals to 2 actors, Abdullah Homsy and Elias Elias, to the actress Takla Chamoun, to the author, Oussama el Aref, and to the critic, Abdo Wazen. The Director General made the presentations on behalf of the Ministry and the Lebanese Centre following an address by the Centre's Vice-president, Saadeddine el Mokhalalati, and the reading of several extracts from the Message by Secretary General Dr Elie Lahoud. The multilingual programme which followed included items from theatre, opera, dance, mime and pantomime. Participation of the following universities: Lebanese, Lebanese-American, USJ (St Joseph), USEK (St Esprit, Kasslik) together with the Actors Union, the Committee of Former Students of Fine Arts and the Lebanese School of Ballet.

F.Y.R of MACEDONIA: Performances in Macedonian theatres all over the country began with a reading of the International Message together with the National Message by playwright Jordan Plevnes, Macedonia's Ambassador to France and UNESCO. Macedonian television prepared a special news programme on the evening of the 27th March, focusing on the history of World Theatre Day and on Macedonian theatre today. The Messages were published in many newspapers and magazines, and read on radio and television. Actors communities, as is the tradition, celebrated this day with a musical evening.

MEXICO: World Theatre Day was celebrated in Xalapa (*see above*) and in Ciudad Victoria.. On 27 March 2001 at Cd. Victoria, the Day was marked by the closing of the Intercontinental Festival for the Cultures of the World and the work of the CIDC ITI Symposium 'Theatre, Identity and Cultural Development'. The Instituto Tamulipeco por la Cultura et las Artes (ITCA) presented the play that won the 'Tirso de Molina' Prize in Spain in 1998, *The Voyage of the Singers* by Hugo Salcedo. More than 40 actors from all corners of Tamaulipas participated in this production under the direction of Luis Martín Garza. Ms Sari Bermúdez, President of the Mexican Council for the Culture and the Arts (CONACULTA), the Governor of Tamaulipas, Mr Tomás Yarrington, and the Education

Minister of Tamaulipas, Baltazar Hinojosa Ochoa, were present and addressed the gathering in celebration of World Theatre Day. The Message of Iakovos Kampanellis was read by Fernando Mier y Terán, Secretary of ITI's Committee for Cultural Identity and Development (CIDC) and Director General of the ITCA. Participants were invited to a dance by the Governor and a souvenir video was screened at the end of the evening. Alexander Stillmark (Germany) member of the CIDC, who had conducted a workshop for young Mexican performing arts professionals in the framework of the festival, and Biruté Marcinkevicité (Lithuania), thanked the organisers of the festival on behalf of the participants.

NEPAL: Kathmandu: a rally in which eminent theatre personalities and theatre groups active in Kathmandu participated was held by the Nepal Centre of ITI. Chanting the slogan 'Let's develop the habit of going to the Theatre' the rally proceeded from Basatpur to the Open Theatre on the premises of the Royal Nepal Academy where it was transformed into a meeting. Addressing the gathering, the President of Nepal Centre of ITI, Professor Abhi Subedi, spoke of the importance of ITI membership for the Nepal Centre and of its projects and perspectives. Other speakers included senior Nepalese theatre critics Satya Mohan Joshi and Shyam Krishna Bainshanav, Dr. Carol Davis, an American theatre critic as well as Sunil Pokharel, Nisha Sharma Pokharel, Vijaya Bisfot, Puskar Gurung and Govinda Sing Rawat. The 'Gopi Nath Aryal T.N.N.' Award and the 'Tribeni T.N.N.' prize were presented to Sunil Pokharel and Bagina Theatre group respectively by Hari Har Sharma, Director of Nepal Culture Corporation. Puskar Gurung from Dabali Theatre, Kathmandu announced a future Dabali Award for Theatre Critics. The Nepal Culture Corporation organised a Theatre Festival, inaugurated by the Culture Minister of Nepal, from 24th March to 30th March. Pokhara: eight active theatre groups of Pokhara organised a discussion on theatre and Anup Baral, a regional member of Nepal Centre of ITI read the World Theatre Day Message. Dharan: Active theatre groups marked the Day with a performance and the reading of the International Message by regional members of the Nepal Centre of ITI.

PERU: On the occasion of WTD the Peruvian Centre inaugurated its homepage on Internet in order to make ITI and its activities in Peru better known. http://wwwgeocities.com/itiperu

ITI Events and Activities 2000-2002

POLAND: On World Theatre Day, the Message was read in all Polish theatres before the performances. The Board of the Polish Centre of ITI awarded its annual Stanislaw Ignacy Witkiewicz Award for promoting Polish theatre culture abroad to Andrei Bazilevski - Russian scholar, publisher and translator of, among others, the works of Stanislaw Ignacy Witkiewicz. The winner of the Theatre Critics' Section of the Polish Centre's annual prize for promoting Polish theatre culture abroad was Tadeusz Bradecki (playwright, actor and theatre director, former director of Stary Theatre in Cracow) and its 'Theatre Book of the Year' prize went to Jolanta Kowalska for her monograph on Kazimierz Junosza-Stepowski, one of the best known Polish actors of the early 20th century.

ROMANIA: On 27 March, the National Theatre 'I.L. Caragiale' of Bucharest organised a colloquium of playwrights. Other theatres also presented special performances, organised tours, 'open days', free tickets and galas. Participation of the following major theatres: Theatre Nottara of Bucharest, Atheneum People's Theatre 'M. Gh Pastia' in Focsani, Theatre Radu Stanca of Sibiu, Theatre André Muresanu of Sfantu Gheorghe, Municipal theatre of Ploiesti and the Studio Cassandra of the University of Theatre and Cinema of Bucharest which presented the première of Molière's *Tartuffe*, preceded by a reading of Iakovos Kampanellis's International Message. The Hungarian language Theatre Csiki Cergely of Timisoara, in collaboration with the National Theatre of the same city and the German State Theatre, highlighted the multicultural nature of the region by organising a week dedicated to Poetry, Music and Theatre which concluded on the 27 March with World Theatre Day and the reading of the International Message in the 3 languages - Romanian, Hungarian and German. The Romanian Section of the IACT organised a Caravan of Critics at the Municipal Theatre 'Maria Filotti' of Braila, which culminated in a meeting between the critics and the artists, dialogues on creation and finally the reading of the WTD International Message. The National Theatre of Targu-Mures awarded diplomas to members of the company who had worked for more than 25 years in this theatre, and dedicated the event to World Theatre Day.

SENEGAL: In Senegal on the morning of 27 March, the International Message was read by Mr Moustapha Mbaye, President of the Senegalese Centre of ITI. This was followed by a Message from the Minister of Culture. The artistic programme at the Sorano Theatre included the play *Ngiaga-Ndiay* by the Nzonzi Theatre Troupe and a play presented by young French secondary school students. The well-known Troupe des Gueules Tapées presented the evening performance, *La Terre Compromise (The Com-promised Land)*

SRI LANKA: To celebrate World Theatre Day, the Dept. of Fine Arts of the Eastern University of Batticaloa organised a five day theatre festival bringing academics and village people together for the first time. A number of cultural communities which live in Batticaloa and in the surrounding area, Tamils, Muslims and Burghers, as well as plantation workers originally from India, each presented a performance. The festival was reported as having great importance in bringing the diverse groups of the population closer together in a region that has suffered enormously from almost 20 years of ethnic conflict.

TOGO: A five day celebration of World Theatre Day 2001 was organised by the new Togo Centre of the ITI. The Minister of Culture and the Director of ITI Togo spoke at the opening ceremony. The programme included included performances by the companies 'Gerades', 'Les 3C', the Tambour Theatre of Lomé, Echos d'Afrique and Aktion Theatre. A carnival procession was held. The programme also included a lecture-discussion on professionalism and the profitability of theatre in Togo, performances in schools and a Poetry Café with the presentation of poems and reading of the International Message. A televised discussion took place on the theme, Artists , actors and their role in Togolese society.

TUNISIA: WTD was celebrated by the Tunisian Centre under the auspices of the Minister of Culture. The events took place over five days, beginning with the reading of the Message and an address by the Minister of Culture at the theatre Quatrième Art, followed by the performance *Une Heure d'amour*. On 28 March, a performance of the workshop 'Body in motion, dramatic movement' took place in collaboration with the association 'La Voix du Sourd Tunisien'. (The voice of the Tunisian deaf). On the 29, a performance of *M'harem* was presented at the Quatrième Art. The following day, at the Espace Entr'Act, there was an encounter: 'Body Language breaks the sound barrier' (Le Langage du Corps dépasse le mur du son) followed by a reception in honour of the participants and, in the evening, a performance *Voyage* at the Quatrième Art Theatre.

ITI Events and Activities 2000-2002

14 –18 April 2001
ISTANBUL, (Turkey)
Board Meeting of the International Playwrights Forum hosted by Turgut A. Akter and the Turkish ITI Centre. Preparation of the **International Playwriting Competition** organised by the Forum.

29 April 2001
International Dance Day – International Message from the celebrated choreographer **William Forsythe.** In 1982 the Dance Committee of the International Theatre Institute (ITI – UNESCO) founded International Dance Day. The intention of International Dance Day and the Message is to bring all dance together on this day, to celebrate this art form and revel in its universality, to cross all political, cultural and ethnic barriers and bring people together in peace and friendship with a common language - Dance. Every year a message from a well-known dance personality is circulated throughout the world. The Message is diffused jointly by the ITI International Dance Committee and the World Dance Alliance

Many countries on all continents organise events to celebrate International Dance Day – reading the message before evening performances, holding special performances or awarding annual prizes. A number of ITI Centres have formed national Dance Committees (e.g Austria, Bangladesh, Croatia, Cuba, Japan, Mexico, Romania, Slovenia) responsible for organising dance events. As an example, the Dance Committee of Bangladesh ITI held a colourful rally to mark International Dance Day on April 29. Eminent dancers and young dance students took part wearing traditional dance costumes. In the evening there was a dance recital in memory of Uday Shankar, celebrated choreographer of the subcontinent.

May 2001
News from the secretariat N° 76 International theatre news edited and published three times a year in French and English versions by the General Secretariat of ITI with the support of UNESCO, Division of Arts and Cultural Enterprise.

23 – 27 May 2001
VÄXJÖ (Sweden)
Board Meeting of the Dramatic Theatre Committee in conjunction with the DTC Seminar: 'Whose Theatre is it anyway? The author's, the director's or the actor's?' (26 May) in the framework of the Swedish Biennial organised by the Swedish ITI Centre.

24 May – 10 June 2001
MÜLHEIM (RFA)
The **9th International Translators' Meeting.** Organised by the German ITI Centre in cooperation with the Mülheimer Theatertage, the Strälen Translators' Colloquium and the Goethe Institute and held in the framework of the Festival 'Stücke'. Aim: to introduce translators of German theatre to contemporary German plays in their first production on the stage and to inspire their translation into other languages in order to promote production abroad. Discussions and workshop sessions. All ITI Centres were invited to send a qualified participant.
To further develop the translators meeting, a fully-fledged and integrated **International Platform for Contemporary Theatre** was also launched. Produced in co-operation with the British Centre for Literary Translation, Maison Antoine Vitez (France), the Finnish Theatre Information Centre and the biennial play market of the Theatre National de Luxembourg, the Platform aims to translate, promote, and exchange new plays from Finland, France, Germany, and Great Britain.

26 May – 5 June 2001
HELSINKI (Finland)
Helsinki International Dance Competition and Choreography Competition (3-4 June **Symposium Dance and Medicine**). The Competition belongs to the cycle of international ballet competitions organised in Jackson, New York, Moscow, Paris and Varna under the patronage of the ITI International Dance Committee. The Competitions are organised by the Finnish Theatre Information Centre (Finnish Centre of ITI) and the Finnish National Ballet. Artistic Director Mr Jorma Uotinen. General Administrator: Riitta Seppälä.

May-June 2001
MOSCOW (Russia)
International Theatre Workshops in the framework of the 3rd World Theatre Olympiad, organised by the Russian ITI Centre.
19 & 22 June 2001
PARIS (France) UNESCO Headquarters **112th Session of the ITI Executive Council**

20 - 23 June 2001
PHILADELPHIA (USA)
Board Meeting of the ITI Dramatic Theatre Committee in the framework of its Seminar 'Working in other languages' held in the framework and at the invitation of the **TCG 13th Biennial National Conference of American Theatres** (USA Centre of ITI)

ITI Events and Activities 2000-2002

22 - 23 June 2001
LONDON (UK)
Formation of the Artists' and Artistic Rights Network – AARN (formerly Artsnet). Based at the headquarters of PEN International and set up on the initiative of UNESCO, AARN is a network of international and regional organisations operating in the field of the arts. Aim: to monitor attacks on artists and their rights, to share information received and to facilitate co-operation between organisations working for the defence of artists and artistic rights. The International Theatre Institute is represented by Peter Bensted (board member of the Danish ITI Centre and Artistic Director of Teatergadesjakket in Odense).

10 – 17 July 2001
MOTUVUN (Croatia)
3rd Motovun International Drama Colony 'From Text to P erformance' organised by the Croatian Centre of ITI in co-operation with the Czech and Slovenian Centres.

19 - 20 July 2001
ZURICH (Switzerland)
Summer Academy in the framework of the **'Zürcher Festspiele' 2001.** Further training for performing arts professionals organised by the Swiss Centre of ITI.

9-12 July 2001
St PETERSBURG (Russia)
Summer Course of the ITI/UNESCO Chair in co-operation with the Academy of St Petersburg.

23-31 July 2001
SINAIA (Romania)
3rd International Theatre Schools Workshops Theme: 'The comic mechanism in Shakespeare' organised by the ITI/UNESCO Chair under the direction of Professor Corneliu Dumitriu. Diffusion on CD-Rom of the workshops illustrating different teaching methods and work presented by the schools. 10 countries participating and observers from 15. Doll puppets and marionettes. Post-graduate scenography workshops and post-graduate courses on the 'Training of teachers'. Presence of Jan Sadlak, Head of the CEPES, UNESCO European Bureau for Higher Education. Presence of Sonia Simkova, President of the Theatre Education Committee and Jean-Henri Drèze from the Conservatoire de Liège (Belgium), member of the Theatre Education Committee. Jennifer Walpole represented the ITI General Secretariat.

23 - 24 July 2001
GRIPSHOLM (Sweden)
Board Meeting of the Theatre Education Committee in the framework of Methodika, International Festival of Methods in Theatre Training, (artistic director, Juri Alschitz), organised by the European Association for Theatre Culture. Presence of André-Louis Périnetti, Secretary General of ITI. 'The training of directors', examples from the USA by Tom Cooke. 'The function of intellectual education in the framework of dramatic art studies; historical and theoretical subjects for future actors and directors', an open session chaired by Sona Simkova in the presence of participants of Methodika.

27 July – 5 August 2001
TOKYO (Japan)
International Workshop - Nihon Buyo. Course on Kabuki Dance for 20 performing arts professionals. Under the direction of great masters of the Hanayagi School. Organised by the Japanese Centre of ITI.

29 – 31 July 2001
MONTE CARLO (Monaco)
A **Meeting of the European ITI Centres & IATA/IIT Colloquium** organised by the Monaco ITI Centre was held in the framework of the 2nd 'Mondial du Théâtre,' (World Festival of Amateur Theatre). The Monaco Centre of ITI hosted representatives from 15 Centres in a meeting designed to promote greater co-ordination of activities and facilitate exchange among European ITI Centres.

29 July – 26 August 2001
WOLFSEGG (Austria)
27th Wolfsegg International Ballet Seminar. University level courses for ballet teachers in the tradition of the Lunacharsky Instiute of Theatre Arts (GITIS). Classical training for dancers and ballet students. Organised by the Dance Committee and Music Theatre Committee of the Austrian ITI Centre. The organisers covered course fees for one candidate from each ITI National Centre wishing to send a student. Event under the auspices of the International Dance Committee of ITI.
20 July – 31 August 2001.

DROUSHIA & PAPHOS (Cyprus)
'ANCIENT GREEK DRAMA 2001': Composed of a **Festival of Ancient Greek Drama** (August); a **Summer course** (20/07-31/8); a **Workshop/Performance**, a **Meeting and festival of Theatre schools** (27-31/8). Organised by the Cyprus Centre of ITI under the direction of Nicos Shiafkalis.

The Centre hosted teachers and students from theatre schools who presented work illustrating the diversity of approaches used in contemporary productions of ancient Greek drama. Like the workshops of the ITI/UNESCO Chair, the regular Cyprus encounter is an exemplary expression of ITI's commitment to artistic education.

15 August – 28 October 2001
TOKYO and province (Japan)
BeSeTo Festival, Annual theatre festival organised in turn by the Chinese, Japanese and Korean ITI Centres. Venues: Toyama (Village of Toga Aug..25 - Sep.8), Tokyo (August 29 – Sep. 15), Shizuoka. (Sep.29 - Oct.20) - and again in Tokyo (Oct. 21 – 28.). Performances and symposia organised in 2001 by the Japanese Centre of ITI in collaboration with the Japan Performing Arts Foundation. The latter was in charge of contemporary and experimental performing arts while the Japanese Centre organised the section devoted to traditional performing arts. Theme 'Seeking the origin of the performing arts in the folk tradition'. A main theme was 'The aesthetics of reincarnation in Asia'.

September 2001
ATHENS (Greece)
Board meeting of the International Playwrights Forum. Hosted by Lia Karavia and the Hellenic ITI Centre. Launching of the **International Playwriting Competition** organised by the Forum.

18 – 25 September 2001
ULAN BATOR (Mongolia)
1st International Festival of Theatre, Symposium, Workshop. Mongolian Centre of ITI. Independent Theatre calls for Mongolia including 'Shakespeare in the new Millennium'. Organised by the ITI Centre with support from the Soros Foundation. Major goals of this project were to extend the new general policy of encouraging international exchange to the field of the arts, by introducing Mongolian theatre to the world, bringing the latest achievements of world theatre into Mongolia, sharing experiences, promoting international co-operation. and contributing to the development of contemporary theatre. Performances, Conference and Workshops. Participants from Russia, Lithuania, Slovenia, Hungary, Yugoslavia, Bulgaria, England, Canada, Korea, Vietnam and Mongolia.

22 September 2001. **International conference on 'New Trends in World Theatre'** in conjunction with the festival; Aim: to examine the influence of contemporary world drama on Mongolian theatre development; to enable Mongolian theatre professionals to learn about new methods of theatre production and to establish co-operation with their international counterparts. Facilitator: Faynia Williams (UK), co-president of the International Theatre Institute's

Dramatic Theatre Committee. Event receiving support within the 2001 framework- agreement between UNESCO and ITI. Presence of the Secretary General of ITI, André-Louis Périnetti.

18 – 25 September 2001
ULAN BATOR (Mongolia)
Meeting of the ITI Dramatic Theatre Committee in the framework of the 1st International Festival of Theatre in Mongolia. Participation in the Symposium New Trends in Theatre). Faynia Williams ran a workshop on *Hamlet*, with British and Mongolian artists. Ann Mari Engel (Sweden) gave a paper on Theatre and Society. Presence of André-Louis Périnetti, Secretary General of ITI.

30 September – 7 October 2001
SANTA MARTA (Colombia)
International colloquium and workshop for young performing artists: 'Africa en la memoria de America' on the occasion of the 150th anniversary of the abolition of slavery. An event in the UNESCO/ITI 2001 framework agreement. Organised by the Colombian Centre. Presence of the Secretary General, André-Louis Périnetti.

October 2001
News from the secretariat N° 77 International theatre news edited and published three times a year in French and English versions by the General Secretariat of ITI with the support of UNESCO, Division of Arts and Cultural Enterprise.

October 2001
Theatre Studies First issue of the new journal of the **ITI/UNESCO Chair** devoted to the 3rd run of the international theatre schools' workshops organised by the Chair. Introduction by Jan Sadlak, Director of the UNESCO European Centre for Higher Education, UNESCO-CEPES. Preface by André-Louis Périnetti, Secretary General of ITI. Syntheses of the work presented by schools from Australia, China, Korea, Egypt, Portugal, Yugoslavia, Russia and Romania (2), written by Jean-Henri Drèze (Belgium) and Jennifer Walpole (Australia). Articles by Corneliu Dumitriu, director of the UNESCO Chair, Jeremy Stockwell from RADA (UK) and Calvin McClinton (USA).

October 2001
ATHENS (Greece)
Meeting of the Co-Presidents of the International Playwrights Forum, Lia Karavia and Tobias Biancone. Organisation of the presentation of prizes to winners of the International Playwrights Competition and the performance of their plays in the framework of the 29th ITI World Congress.

ITI Events and Activities 2000-2002

14-21 October. 2001.
ZAGREB (Croatia)
4th Theatre Forum: Theatre Publications Today.
Symposium, Workshop. Organised by the Croatian
Centre of ITI.

19 October 2001
ZAGREB (Croatia) **Meeting of the ITI
Communication Committee** hosted by the Croatian
Centre in the framework of the 4th Theatre Forum
'Theatre Publications Today'.

15 October - 3 November 2001
PARIS (France)
The 31st UNESCO General Conference was held
at UNESCO headquarters. The ITI, non-governmental
organisation in formal associate relations with
UNESCO, was invited to participate as observer in the
work of Commission IV (Culture), and in the
conference plenary sessions.
Jennifer Walpole spoke on behalf of ITI. ITI expressed
its support of the **Universal Declaration on
Cultural Diversity** adopted by UNESCO, first major
normative instrument conceived for promoting this
diversity, as well as for the action plan to aid its
implementation and the **Global Alliance for
Cultural Diversity,** a concrete project promoting
cultural diversity and designed to link the various
partners to work for more equality and justice in the
circulation of cultural goods.

27 October – 3 November 2001
OUAGADOUGOU (BURKINA FASO)
**8th Edition of the International Festival of
Theatre and Puppets of Ouagadougou (FITMO)**
Theme: Cultural Decentralization in Burkina Faso. Held
in collaboration with district authorities, with
performances also in Bobo-Dioulasso, Koudougou,
Kaya, Fada and Ouahigouya. Organised by the Burkina
Faso ITI Centre and the African Regional Bureau under
the Presidency of Jean-Pierre Guingané, Vice-President
of ITI.

5 – 11 November 2001
YAOUNDE (Cameroon)
**Festival of the Cameroon International Theatre
Meetings RETIC** (Rencontres Théâtrales
Internationales du Cameroun - RETIC). Under the
patronage of the Organisation of African Unity (OUA)
and the Cameroon Ministry of Culture. Organised by
the Cameroon Centre of the International Theatre
Institute under the direction of Ambroise M'bia. A
meeting point for artists and managers and the
development of co-operation between theatre and
dance professionals.

9-14 November 2001.
NANJING (China)
**Third Meeting of the ITI Asia Pacific Regional
Bureau AP-IIT** hosted by the Chinese ITI Centre in
the framework of the 7th China Theatre Festival.
Presence of A-L Périnetti, Secretary General.

11 and 12 November 2001.
MEXICO CITY (Mexico)
**Board Meeting of the International Dance
Committee** hosted by the Committee's Vice-President,
Anastacio A. Hernandez with the support of Hector
Garay, national co-ordinator for dance at the National
Institute of Fine Arts (INBA) of Mexico.

November 2001
BUDAPEST (Hungary).
**Board Meeting of the International Playwrights
Forum** hosted by Andras Nagy, President of the
Hungarian ITI Centre.

1 – 9 December 2001
TUNIS, (Tunisia)
**Workshop-Session of the University of the
Theatre of Nations: The Mediterranean region
through its tales –** For young performing arts
professionals. Narrative techniques and practices in the
region. An event included in the UNESCO/ITI 2001
framework agreement. Presence of the Secretary
General of ITI

15 - 20 December 2001
MUNICH (Germany)
**7th International Music Theatre Workshop –
New Works in Music Theatre** Video presentation
of new works in music theatre. Organised by the
German ITI Centre, the Music Theatre Committee of
ITI, and their partners. Artistic Director: Hellmuth
Matiasek. Consisting of the video presentation of the
first productions of recent music theatre works, the
workshop is intended to promote international
exchange of experience in the field of contemporary
music theatre and to identify new trends.

15 - 20 December 2001
MUNICH (Germany)
**Board meeting of the ITI Music Theatre
Committee** under the presidency of Hellmuth
Matiasek, in the framework of the 7th International
Music Theatre Workshop – New Works in Music
Theatre. Presence of the Secretary General, André-
Louis Périnetti.
On this occasion the Committee awarded the **Wolf
Ebermann Prize** to the Korean composer, Ji Hi Kim
for the work *Dong Dong Touching the Moons.*

2002

12 - 14 January 2002
PARIS (France) UNESCO Headquarters
113th Session of the ITI Executive Council

January 2002
The 2001 **Uchimura Prize** was awarded by the ITI Executive Council to Christina Nygren - scholar, lecturer and writer specialising in Asian theatre, for her studies on Japanese theatre and her work over more than 15 years making Japanese theatre known in Sweden.

January 2002
Membership of a new Co-operating Member, **Lalit Kala Kendra – Performing Arts Centre** of the University of Pune (India)

January 2002
TEHERAN (Iran)
20th International Fajr Festival Iranian Centre of ITI.

21 January 2002
PARIS (France)
Wallonie-Brussels Centre.
René Hainaux, 60 years in the service of theatre. Celebration of the work of René Hainaux, President of Honour of the Theatre Education Committee. Participation of representatives from UNESCO, Intergovernmental Agency for French Speakers, the French and Belgian ITI Centres, the ITI Theatre Education Committee, the René Hainaux Foundation, the Ministry of Culture and the Communauté Wallonie-Bruxelles, the National Library of France, AITU, FIRT-SIBMAS, etc., who met to discuss 3 major projects initiated by René Hainaux: A selective universal bibliography of the Performing Arts; an exhaustive bibliography of works published in French in the 2nd half of the 20th Century; a collection of video cassettes of masterpieces of French theatre. André-Louis Perinetti and Jennifer Walpole represented the ITI General Secretariat.

4 February 2002
PARIS (FRANCE)
The signature of the new Framework Agreement between UNESCO and ITI took place at UNESCO headquarters. UNESCO was represented by the Deputy Director General for Culture, Mounir Bouchenaki and ITI by its Secretary General, André-Louis Périnetti. The 31st UNESCO General Conference (15 October - 3 November 2001) renewed the International Theatre Institute's formal associate relations with UNESCO and approved the renewal of its Framework agreement with ITI for the six-year period 2002- 2007.

February 2002
News from the secretariat N° 78
International theatre news edited and published three times a year in French and English versions by the General Secretariat of ITI with the support of UNESCO, Division of Arts and Cultural Enterprise.

21 February 2002
Celebration of **International Mother Language Day** declared by UNESCO and observed by the International Theatre Institute. The event took place at UNESCO headquarters on Thursday 21 February under the chairmanship of Mr Mounir Bouchenaki, Deputy Director General for Culture. Part of the meeting was devoted to the presentation of the 2nd edition of the *Atlas of the World's Languages in Danger of Disappearing* published by UNESCO; homage was paid to the memory of Professor Stephen Wurm, chief editor of the *Atlas* and world renowned linguist. Speakers stressed the importance of the mother language in enabling the affirmation of a person's cultural identity and warned against policies and actions leading to the irreversible destruction of languages. Jennifer Walpole, Assistant Executive, represented ITI at this meeting.
The ITI Centre of the **Congo Republic** launched the **Tchicaya de Boa-Empire Prize** for the promotion of the Loango languages. The Prize, which is awarded for a work written in one of the Loango languages, was awarded for the first time in the framework of the International Mother Language Day. The Diploma for Excellence went to Joseph Tchiamas for his poem 'Luzala lu Mueka ku sukule ve Busu'.

March 2002
Creation of the **AZERBAIJAN** Centre of ITI

15 – 31 March 2002
BOGOTA (Colombia)
The **8th Festival Iberoamericano de Teatro 'Theatre of the Nations'** under the auspices of ITI.

ITI Events and Activities 2000-2002

16 – 27 March 2002
COTONOU (Benin).
6th International Theatre Festival of Benin (FITHEB). Created originally by a French-Benin trio, this festival was adopted by the State of Benin with the support of other national and foreign partners and the intellectual and organisational support of the Benin Centre of ITI. This edition brought together more than a dozen countries in Africa, Europe and America. All genres of the performing arts were represented: dance, theatre, circus, puppets, tales. Colloquium: 'What kind of theatre for Africa?'

25 – 28 March 2002
KINSHASA (RD Congo)
25th Anniversary and Hommage to Mobyem Mikanza: Colloquium on the Congolese theatre figure, Norbert Mikanza Mobyem, first Secretary General of the Congolese ITI Centre: performances, workshop, exhibition organised by the Centre. Theme: 'Theatre, a tool for dialogue'. Event included in the 2001 framework agreement between UNESCO and ITI.

25 – 28 March 2002
KINSHASA (RD Congo)
Regional Meeting of African ITI Centres. Hosted by the Congolese Centre of ITI. Presence of representatives of eight African ITI Centres: Pedro Noa Wete, Angola, Jean-Pierre Guingané, ITI Vice-President - Burkina Faso, Ambroise M'Bia – Cameroun, M.Y. Mitendo, President - R.D. Congo, Pierre Claver Mabial - Congo Rep, Evans Oma Hunter, Secretary general - Ghana, Elvira Bobson Kamara, President - Sierra Leone, Yao Julien Mensah, information officer – Togo. The meeting was chaired by Jean-Pierre Guingané, President of the African ITI Regional Bureau and Vice-president of the ITI Executive Council.

27 March 2002 **World Theatre Day International Message** by **Girish KARNAD**, playwright (India). Girish Karnad writes in Kannada, the language of the state of Karnataka where he lives, and has had his plays translated into English. His second play, *Tughlaq* (1966), established him as a playwright of all-India stature. In 1999 he was awarded the Bharatiya Jnanpith, India's highest literary prize. His play *Bali, The Sacrifice*, was commissioned by the Leicester (UK) Haymarket Theatre and opened in June 2002.
Thanks to the participation of ITI National Centres, Co-operating members (Centre for Performing Arts, Lalit Kala Kendra University of Pune) and other members of the theatre community the World Theatre Day Message may be found on the ITI website in 21 languages.: English (original), French,

Spanish, Arabic, Basque, Croatian, Czech, Danish, Estonian, Farsi, Filipino, Finnish, German, Greek, Nepali, Romanian, Slovak, Slovenian, Swedish, Marathi (Indian regional language) Fiote 'Vili ' (African language)
Reports of events celebrating World Theatre Day were received from all continents where the Message is diffused by ITI Centres, read in theatres, published in newspapers and journals and commented on by radio and television. Below are highlights from some of the reports received.
BANGLADESH: Bangladesh ITI and Bangladesh Group Theatre Federation jointly observed the Day on March 27. A colourful rally of theatre enthusiasts in the city streets was followed by a get-together. The World Theatre Day lecture was delivered by Prof. Abdus Selim, eminent translator and critic. Sara Zaker, Chairman of Bangladesh Group Theatre Federation welcomed the guests, Bangladesh ITI General Secretary Ataur Rahman read out the Bangla translation of Girish Karnad's World Theatre Day message. Two posthumous awards were made to eminent playwright-actor-director S.M. Solaiman and lighting designer Siraj Ahmed. Bangladesh ITI President, Ramendu Majumdar presided over the function which was rounded off by a dance recital by Nrityadhara.
CONGO Republic: Performing artists and media representatives met together in the Swedish Cultural Centre (SUECO). The Regional Director of the Arts in Kouilou congratulated the new Centre for what it had achieved in such a short time, referring particularly to the celebration of International Mother Language Day, the translation of the World Theatre Day messages into the Fiote (Vili) language and the adhesion of the Congolese National Ballet Centre and the Congolese National Theatre.
CUBA: The Cuban Centre's national Message was written by playwright Abelardo Estorino. National Theatre Prize 2002: the Centre organised a special programme in collaboration with the National Council of the Performing Arts in all the provinces. In collaboration with the Association of Performing Artists and the National Union of Writers and Artists (UNEAC) presentation of the 'Omar Valdés' Prize to Veronica Lynn, and special awards to the theatre company 'Rita Montaner' and the National Opera of Cuba.
CZECH Republic: During a gala evening at the National Theatre attended by Mrs Vaclav Havel, wife of the President of the Czech Republic, the annual Thalia Prizes were awarded by the Actors' Association. Of particular interest among the Czech events, was the project of <u>Vychodoceske Divadlo</u> (Theatre of East Bohemia), Pardubice, who invited its audience to an 'Open day' and held a special programme on the origins and history of theatre. Inspired by the impact of this event, the Czech ITI

Centre will encourage other theatres to organise similar programmes on World Theatre Day next year.

GERMANY: On World Theatre Day 2002, the German ITI Centre awarded its annual prize distinguishing a personality on the German theatre scene whose work has had an outstanding international impact to the Theater an der Ruhr. 'A creative force on the theatre scene for twenty years now, the Theater an der Ruhr represents a unique and innovative theatre model - aesthetically, organisationally and in terms of the cultural policy it pursues. Artistic Director Roberto Ciulli has succeeded in realising and sustaining a dialogue among cultures and The Theatre an der Ruhr remains an unflagging pioneer, forging contacts in zones of tension and transition'

INDIA: World Theatre Day was celebrated all over the country with the World Theatre Day message by Indian playwright Girish Karnad being broadcast on All India Radio in English, Hindi and 15 other regional languages, and read before the evening performances of drama all over the country. TV channels celebrated the day with chat shows and interviews with eminent theatre persons. Around 300 stage artists from the state of Punjab assembled at Chandigarh on 26th March, 2002 and launched the World Theatre Day celebration events with a torch-light march through Chandigarh from the residence of M. S. Randhawa, a renowned Arts Administrator responsible for promotion and preservation of performing and plastic arts, to the headquarters of the Academy of Dance, Drama and Music. Two full length plays were staged on the night of 26th March. On 27th March, 2002 there was a seminar and meeting with Punjabi playwright, Charan Das Sidhu.

Centre for Performing Arts, University of Pune, India (Lalit Kala Kendra), a new Co-operating Member of ITI, celebrated World Theatre Day, 27th March 2002, with a production of Molière's *Tartuffe* in Marathi with text & direction by Praveen Bhole, Lecturer (Drama), and a cast of: graduate and post-graduate theatre course students. Venue: Namdeo Auditorium, Arts Faculty, University of Pune. The World Theatre Day International message by Girish Karnad was read in Marathi before the show. Copies of Girish Karnad's message, translated into Marathi, were distributed to the audience

IRAN: A ceremony in honour of World Theatre Day was held in the main hall of City Theatre (Theatre Shahr) in the presence of the president of the UNESCO Bureau in Iran, the Minister of Culture, the Minister of Higher Education, the President of the Centre for Dialogue between Civilizations, cultural and artistic authorities and artists. The ceremony began with the reading of the

International Message after which Iran's message for World Theatre Day, written by the President of the Iranian ITI Centre (who is also the President of Dramatic Arts Centre), was read by the author. The annual report concerning Iran's current situation and past theatre activities followed, together with a presentation of future plans. Later in the evening, there was a social event to express appreciation to theatre artists and staff. A theatrical performance ended the celebration.

KUWAIT: The Kuwait Centre of the ITI (KCITI) celebrated World Theatre Day by reading Girish Karnad's International Message along with the author's biodata, translated into Arabic, and by sending the text to the local journals for publication and to concerned bodies and theatre groups in Kuwait and the Gulf Cooperation Council (GCC). Mr Fuad Al-Shatti, President of the KCITI, went to the Emirate of Sharja (United Arab Emirates) to give a lecture on the history of ITI, and its important international role in the world of contemporary theatre.

MONGOLIA: After the very successful First International Theatre Festival in Mongolia held in September 2001, the Mongolian Language Theatre Festival, in which the country's five provinces and Buriat, Inner Mongolian and other Mongolian Language theatres participated, took place in October 2001 in Ulanbaatar. In the period around World Theatre Day this intense activity continued with the organisation of training sessions focusing on contemporary dramaturgy.

NEPAL: The Centre organised a discussion on 'Theatre in Nepal in these times' at the Royal Nepal Academy, Kathmandu. Abhi Subedi, the President of Nepal ITI, read out the World Theatre Day message by Indian dramatist, Girish Karnad. The national message written by Abhi Subedi was read by director, Sunil Pokharel,

This year three awards were made. The annual 'Dabali Award' funded by Dabali Theatre Group went to Abhi Subedi, for his outstanding role in making Nepali theatre known to the international community through his articles and seminar papers. This year's 'Gopinath Aryal Award' went to Ashesh Malla, one of the founders of street theatre in Nepal for his role in giving Nepali theatre a new dimension. Mr. Nir Shah, a senior Nepali theatre artist, is the patron of this award. The 'Triveni Award' went to the Pratibimba Theatre Group of Pokhara for its efforts toward decentralising theatre performances. During the discussion, speakers Satyamohan Joshi and Tulasi Diwas, highly respected members of the theatre community, highlighted different movements and traditions in Nepali theatre. The discussion was followed by a performance which conveyed a profound message to the audience about Nepali theatre at this critical period in the country's history.

ITI Events and Activities 2000-2002

In Dharan, artists marked the Day by organising an interactive programme on Nepali theatre along with the reading of the international and national Messages.

POLAND: Outstanding Actor, Andrzej Seweryn of the Comédie Française addressed a message specifically to the Polish theatre community and to Polish audiences entitled 'We Are All Responsible for the Theatre'. The message was published by the press and read before performances in all the theatres on World Theatre Day.

The Stanisław Ignacy Witkiewicz Award for promoting Polish theatre culture abroad was given to the French theatre director, Jacques Rosner in appreciation of his productions of plays by Gombrowicz, especially *The Marriage* staged at the Comédie Francaise in April 2001. Two Polish theatre groups from Lublin - Provisorium and Kompania Teatr received the Polish Theatre Critics Award for promoting Polish theatre abroad. The book *Teatr bezpoœredni Petera Brooka* (Peter Brook's Immediate Theatre) by Grzegorz Ziółkowski was voted Theatre Book of the Year.

ROMANIA: A feature of this year's World Theatre Day celebration was the launching of a special project 'Artists for Artists' An initiative of UNITER and its President, the celebrated actor Ion Caramitru, the aim of this programme which is supported by the Ministry of Culture, is to raise funds to aid retired artists and those suffering from ill-health. All the theatres in the country paid the profits from ticket sales for performances presented in honour of World Theatre Day into this fund. This will henceforth become an annual event.

TOGO: The second celebration of World Theatre Day by the Togolese Centre took place over a ten day period with the involvement of numerous theatre and dance troupes. It was marked by a series of events, including radio and television programmes and a series of lecture-discussions. In collaboration with the Federation of Theatre artists of Togo (éwéwa) the Togolese ITI Centre focused on the theme: 'Theatre and Social Change: awareness for sustainable development' with a television programme on the theme 'The concrete contribution of theatre to Togolese society'. The Centre's programme also included a lecture-discussion at the technical lycée of Adidogome and a carnival procession. There were special thoughts for Traore-Ba Razak (Director of the Centre) still in hospital since his accident on 27th March 2001 when he was on his way to a television station to participate in a World Theatre Day programme.

UGANDA: The Centre organised a symposium on the theme 'Theatre: the way forward'. Three hundred performing artists attended this meeting held in the presence of guest of honour John Sebaana Kizito, Mayor of Kampala. Main themes and speakers included: 'Copyright law in Uganda', by James Wasula, 'Theatre for tomorrow with emphasis on standards and audience expectations', by Senkubuge Charles; 'Traditional Theatre and Dance', by Kizza Salongo; 'Music and Musicians', by Moses Matovu; 'Theatre and Politics', by the Hon. Sulaiman Madada; 'ITI present and future', by Jackson Ndawula, President of the ITI Centre.

UK: On World Theatre Day 2002, the British Centre of the ITI held its annual celebration at the Theatre Museum, London. At this reception, the British Centre made its annual Awards for Excellence in International Theatre and Dance. Angela Rippon and Maria Friedman presented the Award for Excellence in Theatre to David Lavender and Komedia (Brighton) for their 'Aurora Nova' season at St Stephen's Church during the Edinburgh Festival Fringe 2001 and the Excellence in Dance Award to Nikki Millican for the 'New Territories' season in Glasgow.

28 –31 March 2002
LAUSANNE (Switzerland) **Board Meeting of the International Playwrights Forum and Meeting of the Jury of the International Playwriting Competition** hosted by Tobias Biancone, the Swiss Centre of ITI and the Société Suisse des Auteurs.

27 March 2002
JAPAN **Theatre in Japan 2001.** International diffusion of the yearbook published by the Japanese ITI Centre.

10 April 2002
PARIS (France) UNESCO headquarters
Year of the United Nations for Cultural Heritage 2002. Mr Mounir Bouchnaki, Deputy-Director General for Culture, chaired an information session on the UN year for Cultural Heritage 2002. ITI was represented by the Secretary General, André-Louis Périnetti and Jennifer Walpole, Assistant executive. ITI supports the action undertaken by UNESCO, the objectives of which are the following: (Res. of the UN 56/8). Implement programmes, activities and projects aimed at the promotion and protection of the world cultural heritage; promote education and raise public awareness to foster respect for the national and world cultural heritage; encourage voluntary contributions to finance and support activities aimed at the promotion and protection of the national and world cultural heritage. ITI is contributing to UNESCO's action in its own area and in particular through 'Artistic education of young people encouraging exchange between cultures'.

ITI Events and Activities 2000-2002

29 April 2002
International Dance Day – International Message by Katherine Dunham. One of the first African Americans to enrol at the University of Chicago, Katherine Dunham obtained a PhD in anthropology. Through her innovative work on Brazilian and Caribbean dance she established dance anthropology as a new university discipline. The international message was distributed by the ITI International Dance Committee in collaboration with the General Secretariat and the World Dance Alliance.

April 2002
Creation of the Moroccan Centre of ITI

2 - 5 May 2002
LUXEMBURG
1st International Platform - Contemporary Theatre . A meeting of the partners was held in the framework of the Luxemburg Play Market. Project target: creation of a lasting support structure to promote and increase the flow of contemporary drama throughout Europe, independent of the short-term pressures and selectivity of the market place. Project duration: June 2001 to August 2003. Co-operation partners: German ITI Centre, Maison Antoine Vitez (France), British Centre for Literary Translation (UK), Finnish Theatre Information Centre (Finnish ITI Centre), Théâtre National du Luxembourg.

14 – 15 May 2002
SEOUL (Korea)
Extraordinary Meeting of the **Asia-Pacific Regional Bureau of ITI (AP-ITI)** Organised by the President Hyesook Yang in co-operation with a group of parliamentarians of the Korean National Assembly which is preparing the formation of an International Association of Parliamentarians for the Protection of Cultural Diversity. Among the themes discussed: setting up an Asia-Pacific Cultural Foundation and the organisation of an Asian Pacific Festival of Performing Arts. ITI delegates were invited to attend the meeting, accompanied by a member of parliament from their own country interested in these issues. Presence of delegates from: Bangladesh, China, Korea, Japan, India, Nepal, Philippines, Mongolia, Sri Lanka, Vietnam The Secretary General of ITI, André-Louis Périnetti took part in this meeting.

26 - 27 May 2002
KUWAIT
114th Session of the ITI Executive Council hosted by the Kuwait Centre of ITI and the Kuwait National Council for Culture, Arts and Letters from 23 to 30 May.

May 2002
News from the secretariat N° 79 International theatre news edited and published three times a year in French and English versions by the General Secretariat of ITI with the support of UNESCO, Division of Arts and Cultural Enterprise.

June 2002
Creation of the Welsh Centre of ITI

6 - 8 June 2002
SALZBURG (Austria)
'Art and Technology: a team'. A Meeting on Stage Technology including lectures, workshops, an exhibition and discussion organised by the Austrian Society for Theatre Technology (OETHG) - a member of the Austrian ITI Centre - the German Society for Theatre Technology (DTHG) and the Swiss Association of Theatre Technological Professions (svtb).

15 – 20 June 2002
BRATISLAVA (Slovakia)
Project Istropolitana 2002 – 14th Meeting and Festival of Theatre Academies. Organised by the Academy of Dramatic Art and Music in collaboration with the Slovak Centre of ITI and under the auspices of the ITI Theatre Education Committee. Presence of the Secretary General of ITI, André-Louis Périnetti. The event is included in the 2001 framework agreement between UNESCO and ITI This non-competitive, international biennial meeting of theatre schools is the culmination of an intensive two-year period devoted to the development of training in theatre arts. The Festival's aim is to create the conditions for a genuine encounter of young artists, involving a meeting between different cultures and ways of teaching and learning.
International Symposium 'The Perspectives of Theatre Education' in conjunction with the Istropolitana festival. Meeting of the Theatre Education Committee in the framework of this event.

21 –30 June 2002
BONN, DUSSELDORF, DUISBERG and COLOGNE (Germany)
Theater der Welt International festival of the German ITI Centre under the direction of Martin Roeder-Zerndt. Artistic Direction: Manfred Beilharz: 40 premières, 10 days, 4 cities. The 2002 festival focused on Dutch and Argentinian theatre. Other events in conjunction with the Festival: A weekend on **The power of negation** with journalists, critics: films, lecture discussions.

ITI Events and Activities 2000-2002

12 – 22 June 2002
BONN (Germany)
Workshop for Young European playwrights, writing workshops and discussion of new European plays in the framework of the Bonner Bienniale 2002. Organised by the German ITI Centre.

12-30 June 2002
BONN (Germany)
International Theatre Workshop 'Image Construction Site' (ITI Germany / Theatre der Welt). Meeting of German theatre professionals (actors, dancers, directors) with their colleagues from the Mashriq region. The project aims at a dialogue on theatre with the means of theatre, and at positioning contemporary theatre cultures in a radicalised social and political context.

7 – 14 July 2002
MOTUVUN (Croatia)
5th Motovun International Drama Colony: 'From Text to Performance' Co-Organisers: Croatian ITI Centre, MKFM and the Motovun International Centre, Mexican Centre of ITI. Objectives: to try out new international and Croatian drama texts in low-cost productions and to establish co-operation between Croatian artists and those from other countries.

12- 22 June 2002
BONN (Germany)
Workshop for Young European Playwrights: practical writing workshop and exchange on new European drama in the framework of the Bonner Bienniale 2002.

10 - 20 July 2002
SINAIA (Romania)
Summer Courses of the ITI/UNESCO Chair: Stanislavski, Chekhov, Doll puppets and Marionettes, Scenography.

20-28 July 2002
SINAIA (Romania)
4th run of the International Theatre schools Workshops organised by the ITI/UNESCO Chair under the direction of Corneliu Dumitriu. An occasion for encounters between young artists of different cultures. Theme: 'The tragic character: Sophocles' *Antigone*'. In 2002 the workshops explored the universal dimensions of an element of the European, and more specifically Greek, cultural heritage. Diffusion of the workshops on Internet illustrating different teaching methods and the schools' performances.
Meeting of an international jury chaired by the Secretary General of ITI and including

representatives of the Theatre Education Committee, the Director of the Chair and the President of the Hellenic Centre to select the 8 schools (3 from Europe, 2 from Asia and Australia, 1 from Latin America, 1 from North America, 1 from Africa and the Middle East) to participate in the World Festival of Theatre Schools to be held in Athens (Greece) in the framework of the 29th World Congress.

24 –28 July 2002
SINAIA (Romania)
3rd World Conference of Directors of Higher Education Theatre Institutions. Organised by the Chair UNESCO-ITI Theatre and culture of civilisations. Participation of 30 directors. Theme: **'The Concept of Mobility'** – Chair ITI/UNESCO Programme for the 2003-2007 period. Attending the workshop on Sophocles' *Antigone*; Attending the experimental Workshop on French drama, Launching the CD-Roms and the Bulletin of ITI/UNESCO Chair.

24 -28 July 2002
SINAIA (Romania)
Board Meeting of the ITI Theatre Education Committee in the framework of the World Conference of Directors of Higher Education Theatre Institutions. organised by the ITI/UNESCO Chair.

7 July – 2 September 2002.
DROUSHIA & PAPHOS (Cyprus)
Ancient Greek Drama 2002
Festival of Ancient Greek Drama (August) - Paphos Ancient Odeon;
Summer Course (7/07-6/08); **Workshop/ Performance (**7/7-6/08),
Encounter and Festival of Theatre Schools.

30 August – 2 September 2002
DROUSHIA (Cyprus)
7th international Symposium on Ancient Greek Drama Theme: 'The democratic ideal as portrayed in Ancient Greek Drama and its relevance to today's world'. Invited speakers: Oliver Taplin, Christopher Rocco, Michael Walton, James Diggle, Marianne McDonald, Freddy Decreus, Gregory McCart, Elie Lahoud, Nicos Hourmouziades and Martin West. All ITI Centres were invited to designate a representative specialising in Ancient Greek Drama to be hosted by the Cyprus Centre
(7/7-6/08) **Meeting and festival of Theatre Schools**. The Cyprus Centre invited ITI National Centres to select a theatre school to participate in this encounter. Hosted by the Cyprus Centre, the schools, represented by two or three students and their teacher, presented scenes from ancient Greek plays

illustrating the diversity of approaches in contemporary performance of ancient Greek drama. Facilitating encounters between artists, students and teachers from different countries, this annual event is an exemplary expression of the priority given by ITI to artistic education, also one of UNESCO's major concerns.

28 July - 25 August 2002
WOLFSEGG (Austria)
Wolfsegg, 28th International Ballet Seminar.
University level courses for ballet teachers in the tradition of the Lunacharsky Instiute of Theatre Arts (GITIS). Classical training for dancers and ballet students. Organised by the Dance Committee and the Music Theatre Committee of the Austrian ITI Centre of ITI. Under the auspices of the International Dance Committee of ITI. The organisers covered course fees for one candidate from each ITI National Centre wishing to send a student.

August 2002
KALAMATA (Greece)
Festival of Ancient Theatre Hellenic Centre of ITI

7-11 August, 2002
TORSHAVN (Faroe Isles)
Workshops for young performing arts practitioners in the framework of the Nordic Theatre Days. Organised by the Icelandic Centre and the Danish Centre of ITI.

11- 21 August 2002
TOKYO (Japan)
International Workshop GAGAKU under the direction of celebrated dancers and musicians of Ono gagaku-kai: Ono Takashi, Manabe Naoyuki, Nishihara Yuji, Nishiura Koichi. Organised by the Japanese Centre for 20 performing artists.

10 September – 31 October 2002
JERUSALEM
12th International Puppet Festival 2002.
Organised and hosted by the Palestinian National Theatre. The Palestinian ITI Centre invited ITI Centres to propose groups from their countries to participate in this important cultural event designed to be a tool for peace, where artists from the entire world meet and exchange ideas and experiences.

4 -11 October 2002
MOSCOW (Russia)
International Festival of one person shows, workshops for young actors and critics and a seminar on cultural management. Organised by the Russian Centre of the ITI and the National

House of Folklore and Popular Arts with the support of the Ministry of Culture of the Russian Federation. Main theme: 'Tolerance in our world'. The objective of this non-commercial festival is to promote artistic exchange among theatre professionals. Participation of young actors and critics from Germany, Poland, Lithuania, Ukraine, Latvia and Russia.

14 – 21 October 2002
ATHENS (Greece)
29th ITI WORLD CONGRESS. Organised by the Hellenic Centre of ITI.
Main projects of ITI Committees and other ITI bodies:
An International festival of theatre school workshops . Theme: 'Sophocles' *Antigone* '. Participation of schools selected during the ITI/UNESCO Chair's Workshop in July 2002. Presentation of a set of 6 CD-rom on the work of the schools. Under the direction of Corneliu Dumitriu, ITI/UNESCO Chairholder. A project of the ITI/UNESCO Chair with the support of the Theatre Education Committee.
A Dance-theatre production proposed by the NPG (New Project Group), under the responsibility of the German Centre. Entitled *Ariadne and Anger*, it focuses on the myths of Ariadne and Thymos and looks at violence as an aspect that establishes a strong connection between the two.
Events planned by the Communication Committee (including exhibition of publications on Greek theatre and the launching of new editions of *The World of Theatre*, the *World Theatre Directory* and other ITI publications.)
A Seminar organised by the Dramatic Theatre Committee, 'Working in a foreign language'.
A staged reading by Greek actors of the two winning plays of the International Playwriting Competition and the presentation of awards to the winners by the ITI International Playwrights Forum IPF
A Round Table Discussion, on the theme, 'How should we approach dance in the XXIst Century' and a Dance Photography Exhibition, 'Dance Positives', proposed by the International Dance Committee.
Access to email and Internet and training for delegates.

iTi

International Theatre Institute

UNESCO, 1 rue Miollis
75732 PARIS CEDEX 15   FRANCE
Tel: (33) 1 45 68 26 50   ***Fax***: (33) 1 45 66 50 40
e-mail: iti@unesco.org   *http*://www.iti-worldwide.org

ITI SECRETARIAT

Secretary General: André-Louis Perinetti
Assistant Executive: Jennifer M. Walpole

EXECUTIVE COUNCIL

May 2000 - June 2002

President:
KIM Jeong-Ok *(Korea)*

Vice-Presidents:
GUINGANE Jean-Pierre *(Burkina Faso)*
SANTINI Pierre *(France)*

Members:
BEILHARZ Manfred *(Germany)*
MAJUMDAR Ramendu *(Bangladesh)*
SHIAFKALIS Nicos *(Cyprus)*
NIKCEVIC Sanja *(Croatia)*
BYRGESEN Heino *(Denmark)*
PETERSON Lembit *(Estonia)*
COIGNEY Martha W. *(USA)*
ANDREADIS Yangos *(Greece)*
SHARMA Reoti Saran *(India)*
ODAGIRI Yoko *(Japan)*
AL-SHATTI Fuad *(Kuwait)*
MONTORO Manuel *(Mexico)*
SEMIL Malgorzata *(Poland)*
OULIANOV Mikhail/
KHASANOV Valery *(Russia)*
SHULMAN Neville *(UK)*
SIMKOVA Sonia *(Slovakia)*
GARZON Nelly *(Venezuela)*

Technical Advisers:
SEPPÄLÄ Riitta *(Finland)*
GEBARA Georgette *(Lebanon)*
MALEH Ghassan *(Syria)*

ITI REGIONAL OFFICES

African Regional Office
Jean-Pierre Guingané (*President*)
01 BP 3479, Ouagadougou
BURKINA FASO
Tel/Fax: 226/36 59 42
email: jp.guingane@liptinfor.bf

Regional Office for Latin America and the Caribbean
Ms Nelly Garzon (*Director*)
c/o Venezuelan Centre ITI,
Apartado 51-440, CARACAS 1050 -
VENEZUELA
Tel: 58/2/76 199 13 *Fax*: 761 99 13 ou 71 57 23 *email*: itiven@reacciun.ve

ITI Asia Pacific Regional Bureau
c/o Korean ITI Centre
#201 Samtoh BD 1-115, Dong Soong-dong,
Jongro-Ku Seoul 110-510, KOREA
President: Ms Hyesook YANG
Tel: 82/2/741-2971, *Fax*: 82/2/741-2972
email: itikor@orgio.net   iti@iti.or.kr

ITI Inter-Regional Liaison Bureau (Arab Countries, Subsaharan Africa, Mediterranean Basin)
Mohamed Driss (President)
Centre Tunisien de l'ITI
Théâtre National Tunisien
Palais du Théâtre
El Halfaouine, BP 183, 1006 Tunis
TUNISIA
Tel: 216/1/565-693 or 244 779
Fax: 565-640

Regional Bureau for Gulf Countries
Kuwaiti Centre of the ITI,
PO Box 5338, Safat, N 13054,
KUWAIT-KHAITAN
Tel: 965/47 42 574 *Fax*: 965/47 64 194
email: kciti@hotmail.com

Documentation & Archive Centre, Asia
c/o Bangladesh Centre of the ITI
144 New Bailey Road
Dacca 1000 - BANGLADESH
Tel:880/2/956 23 80 & 956 83 26
Fax: 956 08 82
email: iti@adexpressions.com

ITI/UNESCO Chair
'Theatre and Culture of Civilisations'
Director: Corneliu DUMITRIU
75-77 Matei Voievod, Bucharest 2,
ROMANIA
Tel/Fax: 40/1/252 7456
email: chair_iti@abritech.ro

ITI Centres

ITI NATIONAL CENTRES

Centres in **BOLD TYPE** have articles in this edition of *The World of Theatre*

ANGOLA
Angolan Centre of the ITI
B.P. 5520, Luanda , ANGOLA
President: Gabriel LEITAO
Director: Noa WETE
Tel: 244/2/334766
Fax: 244/2/397033 or 397 731

ARGENTINA
Argentine ITI Centre
c/o Argentores, Pacheco de Melo 1820
Buenos Aires 1126, ARGENTINA
President: Jorge RIVERA LOPEZ
Vice-President: Guillermo de la TORRE
Secretary General: Francisco JAVIER
Tel: 54/1/41 25 82 *Fax*: 54/1/343 27 33
(F.Javier) *email*: artespec@filo.uba.ar

AUSTRALIA
Australian Centre of the ITI (Associate)
Artslink PO Box 1480
Crows Nest 1585, AUSTRALIA
Director: Dirk PETTIGREW
Tel: 61/2/99668718 *Fax*: 61/2/99668719
mail@artslink.org.au

AUSTRIA
Austrian Centre of the ITI
Türkenstrasse 19, Mezzanine
A-1090 Vienna, AUSTRIA.
President: Helga DOSTAL
Representative: Franz Eugen DOSTAL
Tel: 43/1/317 06 99
Fax: 43/1/ 310 82 92
helga.dostal@iti-arte.at
http://www.iti-arte.at

AZERBAIJAN
Azerbaijan Centre of the ITI
c/o Mr H. Turabov
Khaqani Str. 10
Baku 370000, AZERBAIJAN
President: Hasan TURABOV
Secretary General: Vahid SHARIFOV
Vice-President: Azer NEJMATOV
Tel: 994/12/ 98 52 52
Fax: 994/12/98 52 52

BANGLADESH
Bangladesh Centre of the ITI
144 New Bailey Road,
Dacca 1000, BANGLADESH
President: Ramendu MAJUMDAR
Secretary General: Ataur RAHMAN
Tel: 880/2/956 23 80 & 880/2/956 83 26
Fax: 880/2/956 08 82
iti_exprns@yahoo.com
iti@adexpressions.com

BELARUS
Belarus Centre of the ITI
Volodarskogo Str. 5
220050 MINSK
BELARUS
Secretary General: Antonina MIKHALTSOVA
Tel/Fax: 375/172/ 20 32 80
　　　　375/172/20 83 45

BELGIUM (Flemish Community)
Belgian Centre of the ITI (Com.Fl.)
Minderbroedersstraat 24
2018 Antwerp, BELGIUM
President: Jaak VAN SCHOOR
Vice-President: Roger RENNENBERG
Secretary General: Mark HERMANS
Tel: 32/3/238 51 77
Fax: 32/3/2888402
iti.vlaams.centrum@pi.be
http://www.iti-sibmas.be

BELGIUM (Francophone Community)
Centre Belge de l'IIT (Com.Fr.)
Archives & Musée de la Littérature
Bd de l'Empéreur 4
Brussels 1000, BELGIUM
President: Jacques DE DECKER
Secretary General: Nicole LECLERCQ
Tel: 32/2/519 55 80
Fax: 32/2/519 55 83
nicole-iit@netcourrier.com
info.aml@yucom.be
http://www.iti-sibmas.be

BENIN
Centre Béninois de l'IIT
03 BP -4448
Jericho, Cotonou
BENIN
President: Pascal WANOU
Secretary General: Florent HESSOU
Tel: 229/98 3474
Fax: 229/32 5083 ?
email: wapas_bj@yahoo.fr
pascal_wanou@hotmail.com

BULGARIA
Bulgarian ITI Centre
12 Place "Narodno sabranie"
Sofia 1000, BULGARIA
President: Iskra RADEVA
Secretary.: N. KOLEWSKA-KOURTEVA
Tel: 359/2/738 288
Fax: 359/2/443 290
ikourtev@inet.bg

BURKINA FASO
Centre Burkinabè de l'IIT
01 BP 5743, OUAGADOUGOU 01
BURKINA FASO
President.: Etienne MINOUNGOU
Vice- Presidents: Amadou BOUROU
    Jean-Pierre GUINGANE
Secretary General: Ousmane BOUNDAONE
Tel/Fax: 226/36 59 42 & 36 56 35
Tel: 226/25 07 32 (*Mobile*)
Tel/Fax: 226/ 36 16 94 (J-PG)
jp.guingane@liptinfor.bf

CAMEROON
Centre Camerounais de l'IIT
BP 8163, Yaounde, CAMEROUN
President: Ambroise M'BIA
Vice-Presidents: Samuel N'FOR,
Elise MEKA MBALLA
Secretary General: Judith BISUH
Tel: 237/2 22 13 13 (M'Bia)
(*Telex* - MINFOC 8215KN - Att. M'Bia)
Fax: 237/2 23 30 22 *email*: retic@iccnet.cm

CANADA (Quebec)
Centre Québecois de l'IIT
c/o Conseil québecois du Théâtre
460 Sainte Catherine Ouest (Bur 808)
Montreal , Quebec
CANADA H2T 1S6
President: Pierre MacDUFF
Director: Raymonde GAZAILLE
Tel: 1/514/954 0270   *Fax*: 1/514/954 0165
cqt@cqt.qc.ca http://www.cqt.ca

CENTRAFRICA
Centre Centrafricain de l'IIT
BP 1520
Bangui, CENTRAFRICA
President: Faustin NIAMOLO
Secretary General: Rassidi ZACHARIA

CHAD
Centre Tchadien de l'IIT
B.P. 4330, Njamena, CHAD
President: Dorsouma VANGDAR
Secretary General: Christophe NGAROYAL

Tel: 235/5172 83 *Fax*: 235/51 77 05
email: themacult@yahoo.fr

CHINA
Chinese Centre of ITI,
(Chinese Theatre Association)
52 Dun Siba Tiao, Beijing
CHINA
President: LI Moran
Secretary General: WANG Yunming
Tel: 86/10/84043352
Fax: 86/10/84043352
email: ctawl@public.bta.net.cn

COLOMBIA
Centre colombien de l'IIT
c/o Festicaribe, Calle 16 N°5-10
Santa Marta, COLOMBIA
Secretary General:
Luz Patricia MORENO-LINERO
Fax: 57/543 11 281
email: fecaribe@tutopia.com
fecaribe@latinmail.com

ITI Centres

CONGO (DEMOCRATIC REPUBLIC)
Centre de la République Démocratique
du Congo de l'IIT
BP 6264, Kinshasa VI,
CONGO (Rép.démocratique.)
President: Mwadi Yinda MITENDO
Secretary General: Kosi-Basak NGAKI
Fax: 243/1246 593
iitrdcongo@yahoo.fr

CONGO (REPUBLIC)
Centre de la République
du Congo de l'IIT
Direction régionale de la Culture
et des Arts à Kouilou
BP 1225, Point Noire
Rép. du CONGO
President: Frédéric PAMBOU
Secretary General:: NGougel Jean Léopold
Tel: 242/94 15 79

COSTA RICA
Costa Rican Centre of the ITI
c/o Teatro Abya Yala
Apdo. 656 Moravia 2150
COSTA RICA
President: Daniel GALLEGOS
Secretary General: Roxana AVILA
Tel/Fax: 506/ 268 7629
email: dgallego@racsa.co.cr
email: dkorish@racsa.co.cr

CROATIA
Croatian Centre of the ITI
B. Magovca bb,pp 499
10010 Zagreb, CROATIA
President: Zeljka TURCINOVIC
Secretary.: Lidija ZOZOLI
Tel: 385/1/6670 137 *Tel/Fax*: 385/1/6670
143
email: hc-iti@zg.tel.hr
http://www.tel.hr/hc-iti-teatar

CUBA
Cuban Centre of the ITI
Cruz del Padre No.5 e/Calzada del
Cerro y Carballo. Cerro,
CP. 10600
Havana, CUBA.
President: Hector QUINTERO
Vice-President: A. SUAREZ DEL VILLAR
Secretary General: Miriam MORALES
Tel: 537/31 1357 *Fax*: 53-7-535773
escenart@cubarte.cult.cu

CYPRUS
Cyprus Centre of the ITI
38 Regaena Street
Nicosia 104 - CYPRUS
President: Christakis GEORGIOU
Director: Nicos SHIAFKALIS
Tel: 357/2/67 49 20
Fax: 357/2/68 08 22
email: ccoiti@cylink.com.cy
http://www.cyprus-theatre-iti.org

CZECH Republic
Czech Centre of the ITI
c/o Divadelni Ustav
Celetna 17, 110 00 Prague
CZECH REPUBLIC
President: Tana FISHEROVA
Director Exec.: Ondrej CZERNY
Tel: 420/2/2481 2754
Fax: 420/2/2481 0278
email: iti@theatre.cz
http://www.czech-theatre.cz

DENMARK
Danish Centre of the ITI
Vesterbrogade 26,3
1620 Copenhagen V
DENMARK
President: Heino BYRGESEN
Manager: Jan G. CHRISTIANSEN
Tel: 45/33/861210
Fax: 45/33/24 01 57
dititu@image.dk
http://www.image.dk/~dititu/

ECUADOR

Centre Equatorien de l'IIT
Los Rios 1074, La Tola
Quito, ECUADOR
President: Eduardo Almeida NAVEDA
Vice-President: Pilar OLMEDO
Secretary: José ALVEAR
Tel: 593/2/ 228 9567
Fax: 1/775/2579537

EGYPT

Egyptian Centre of the ITI
36 Abubakelsedik, Dokki
Cairo, EGYPT
President: Ahmed ZAKI
Tel 20/2/3600063 or 3357333
Fax: 20/2/335 7333 (A. Zaki)

ESTONIA

Estonian Centre of the ITI
Uus 5, Tallinn 200 001
ESTONIA
President: Lembit PETERSON
Vice-President: Jaak ALLIK
Sec.: Riina VIIDING
Tel: 372/2/6464 512 *Fax:* 372/2/6464 516
teater@estpak.ee http://www.teatriliit.ee

FINLAND

Finnish Centre of the ITI
Teatterikulma, Meritullinkatu 33
00170 Helsinki 17, FINLAND
President: Raija Sinikka RANTALA
Director: Riitta SEPPÄLÄ
Assistant Director: Anneli KURKI
Tel: 358/9/135 7861 (RS)
Tel: 358/9/135 7887 (AK)
Fax: 358/9/135 55 22
email: tinfo@teatteri.org
http://www.teatteri.org

FRANCE

Centre Français de l'IIT
10 rue de la Chaussée d'Antin
75009 Paris, FRANCE
President: Jacques TEPHANY
Tel: 33/1/46035833
Fax: 33/1/46035833
c_f_t@club-internet.fr

GEORGIA

Centre Géorgien de l'IIT
45 Chavchavadze av
380062 Tbilisi, GEORGIA
President: Atvandil VARSIMASHVLI
Secretary General: Levan KHETAGURI
Tel: 99532/ 250089 *Fax:* 99532/29 43 06
email: scf@lingua.edu.ge

GERMANY

German Centre of the ITI
PF 41 11 28, D-12121 Berlin
GERMANY
President: Manfred BEILHARZ
Vice-President: Jürgen SCHITTHELM
       Volker LUDWIG
Director: Martin ROEDER-ZERNDT
Assistant Director: Thomas ENGEL
Tel: 49/30/791 17 77
Fax: 49/30/791 18 74
info@iti-germany.de
http://www.iti-germany.de

GHANA

Ghana Centre of the ITI
c/o National Commission on Culture
Private Mail Bag
Ministries' Post Office
Accra
GHANA
President: George HAGAN
Secretary General: Evans Oma HUNTER
Nat.Organizer: Togbi EHLAH
Tel: 233/21 66 49 98
Fax: 233/21/66 20 47
omahunter75@hotmail.com

GREECE

Hellenic Centre of the ITI
19 Soultani Str.
Athens 106 82
GREECE
President: Christina BABOU-PAGOURELI
Vice-President: Apostolos VETTAS
Secretary General: N. ARMAOS,
K. ARSENI-ALTERN
Tel/fax: +30/ 10 /33 06 115
email: itigrece@otenet.gr

ITI Centres

HUNGARY
Hungarian Centre of the ITI
Krisztina Krt.57
Budapest 1016, HUNGARY
President: Peter FABRI
Vice-President: Janos NOVAK
Tel: 36/1/212 5247 or 375 23 72
Fax: 36/1/212 5247 or 375 11 84
itihun@freemail.c3.hu
http://www.itihun.hu

ICELAND
Icelandic Centre of the ITI
Thingholts str. 24,
101 Reykjavik,
ICELAND
President: Gudjon PEDERSEN
Sec: Viðar Eggertsson
Tel: 354/562 2762 (Pres)
Tel: 354/ 568 5500
Fax: 354/568 03 83
vidaregg@islandia.is

INDIA
Indian Centre of the ITI
Bharatiya Natya Sangh, F-34 Shanker Market,
Connaught Place
New Delhi 110 001
INDIA
President: Shymanand JALAN
Secretary General: Reoti Saran SHARMA
Tel: 91/11/4670 135 (Mr Sharma)
Fax: 91/11/68 72 515 c/o P.O. + address
Centre

IRAN
Iranian Centre of ITI
(Centre of Dramatic Arts)
Vahdat Hall,
Ostad Shahryar, Hafez Av
Teheran, IRAN
President: Majid SHARIFKHODAEI
Secretary: Farah YEGANEH
Tel: 98/21/670 8861 or 672 6478
Fax: 98/21/6725316
dac@neda.net

IRAQ
Iraqi Centre of the ITI
I.T.C.,
PO Box 8072 - Salhia
Baghdad
IRAQ
President: Yousif AL- ANI
Secretary General: Adel KHADIM

IRELAND
Irish Centre of the ITI (Associate)
(*att* S.Wilmer)
Samuel Beckett Centre
for Drama & Theatre Studies
Trinity College, Dublin University
Dublin 2
IRELAND
Steve WILMER (Representative)
Tel: 353/1/702 1239
Fax: 353/1/679 34 88

ISRAEL
Israeli Centre of the ITI
Habimah National Theatre of Israel
Habimah Plaza, POB 222
Tel Aviv
ISRAEL
Representative: Ruth TONN-MENDELSON
Tel: 972/3/52 66 666
Fax: 972/3/52 66 677

IVORY COAST
Centre Ivoirien de l'IIT
BP 527 Adzope, COTE D'IVOIRE
Vice-President: Abel BOTCHI
Tel: 00 225 /05 68 74 56
Fax: 225/20 22 58 98 (Personnel)
email: abel.botchi@caramail.com

JAMAICA
Jamaica Centre of the ITI
The Barn Theatre
5 Ripon Road
Kingston 5, JAMAICA
President: David HERON
d.heron@cwjamaica.com

JAPAN

Japanese Centre of the ITI
c/o National Noh Theatre,
Sendagaya 4-18-1, Shibuya-Ku
Tokyo 151, JAPON
President.: NAGAYAMA Takeomi
Vice-President: SAÏMYOJI Ikuko
Directors: Tatsuji IWABUCHI, Shuji
ISHIZAWA
Tadeo NAKANE, Hideki HAYASHI
Secretary General: Yoko ODAGIRI
Tel&Fax: 81/3/3478-2189
Fax: 81/3/3478 7218
iti@ceres.dti.ne.jp

JORDAN

Jordanian Centre of the ITI
c/o Sawsan Darwarza
P.O.Box 5701 Zahran
Amman, JORDAN
President: Sawsan Darwaza
Secretary General: Zein Ghanma
Tel: (9626)-5518781
Fax: (9626)-5537855
email: datco@go.com.jo

KENYA

Kenya Centre of the ITI
PO Box 13015
Nairobi, KENYA
Secretary General: Fred ODUOR
Tel: 254/2/334244 *ext* 28081
Tel: 254/2/562 170
Fax: 254/2/33 6885

KOREA (Republic of)

Korean Centre of the ITI
#201 Samtoh BD 1-115, Dong Soong-dong,
Jongro-Ku
Seoul 110-510, KOREA
President: Hye Suck YANG
Vice President: Il Soo SHIN, Soo Ho KUK,
Seung Hoon CHAE,
Secretary General: Woo Young YOON
Tel: 82/2/741-2971
Fax: 82/2/741-2972
email:: itikor@orgio.net *email*: iti@iti.or.kr

KUWAIT

Kuwaiti Centre of the ITI
PO Box 5338, Safat, N 13054
KUWAIT-KHAITAN
President: Fuad AL-SHATTI
Vice-President: Suad ABDULLAH
Secretary General:
 Hussein A. AL-MUSSALEM
Tel: 965/47 42 574
Fax: 965/47 64 194
kciti@hotmail.com

LATVIA

Latvian Centre of the ITI
c/o Riga Latvian Society
Merkela 13-426
LV 1050 Riga
LATVIA
President: Arnis OZOLS
Vice-President: Brigita SILINA
Secretary General: Guna ZELTINA
Tel: 371/9470990 (*mobile*)
Fax: 371/7/270424
email: brig15@hotmail.com

LEBANON

Centre Libanais de l'IIT
c/o Dr Shakib Khoury
B.P.293, Ain Arr 1207
LEBANON
President: Shakib KHOURY
Vice-President: Saadeddine
 MOKHALALATY
Secretary General: Elie LAHOUD
Tel: 961/9/218 577
Fax: 961/9/218 477
nss@cyberia.net.lb

LITHUANIA

Lithuanian Centre of the ITI
Gedimino pr. 1
202 Vilnius,
LITHUANIA
President: Juozas BUDRAITIS
Tel: 370/262 35 86
Fax: 370/261 08 14

ITI Centres

MACEDONIA F.Y.R
Macedonian Centre of the ITI
c/o Ljubisha NIKODINOVSKI-BISH
Kej. Dimitar Vlahov b.b.,
P.O. Box 690, 9100 Skopje
Republic of MACEDONIA
President: Goran STEFANOVSKI
Secretary General: L. NIKODINOVSKI-BISH
Tel: 389/**2**/114 641 *Fax*: 389/**2**/114 641
email: iti-mac@unet.com.mk
http://www.unet.com.mk/iti-macedonia

MALI
Centre Malien de l'IIT
BP 91, Bamako, MALI
President: Gaoussou DIAWARA
Secretary General: Younoussa TOURE

MEXICO
Mexican Centre of the ITI
Miguel Angel de Quevedo # 687
Cuadrante de San Francisco/ Coyoacán
04320 México D.F., MEXICO
President: José SOLE
Vice-President: Hector GOMEZ
Secretary General: Isabel QUINTANAR
Tel: 52/5/6 59 10 94*Tel*/*Fax*:52/5/658 21 39
email: cemex_iti.unesco@starmedia.com

MOLDOVA
Moldova Centre of the ITI (Associate)
c/o Valeriu Turcanu, Dean, Theatre Faculty
State University of Arts, Chisinau
Str. A. Mateevici 111
Chisinau 2014 MOLDOVA
Representative: Valeriu TURCANU
Tel: 373/22/:23 82 10 or 373/2/23 87 74
Tel/*Fax* 373/2/ 227953
turcanu@moldovacc.md
ctheatre@moldtelecom.md

MONACO
Centre Monégasque de l'IIT
c/o M. Rocchi, Director des Affaires cult.
8 rue Louis Notari
MC 98000 MONACO
Representative: Rainier ROCCHI
Tel:377/93 15 83 03 *Fax* 377/93 50 66 94

MONGOLIA
Mongolian Centre of the ITI
Dramatic Centr Teatre
Centre Posta 346, Ulan Bator
MONGOLIA
President: Namsrai SUVD
Secretary: Choisuren ODONCHIMEC
Tel: 976/1/325756 *Fax*: 976/11/312 841
email: suvd_iti@hotmail.com

MOROCCO
Centre Marocain de l'IIT
c/o M. Hassan NEFFALI
Secretary General du SNPT
BP 15604, 20001 Casablanca
MOROCCO
President: Jamal Eddine DKHISSI
Representative: Hassan NEFFALI
Fax: 212/37 702100
email: smpt@menara.co.ma

NEPAL
Nepal Centre of the ITI
G.P.O. Box 7736, Kathmandu, NEPAL
President: Abhi SUBEDI
Secretary: Sunil POKHAREL
Tel: 977/1/221391 *Fax*: 977/1/434407
email: sunil@ccsl.com.np
girish@unlimit.com

NETHERLANDS
Netherlands Centre of the ITI
Theater Instituut Nederland
P.O.Box 19304, 1000 GH Amsterdam
NETHERLANDS
Representative: Titia VUYK
Tel: 31/20/551 33 00
Fax: 31/20/551 33 03
email: titiav@tin.nl

NIGERIA
Nigerian Centre of the ITI
University of Ibadan
Dept. of Theatre Arts
Ibadan, NIGERIA
President: Wole SOYINKA
Secretary General: Dapo ADELUGBA
Tel: 234/2/62550
Cable UNIBADAN

NORWAY
Norwegian Centre of the ITI
Welhavens gate 1, N-0166 Oslo
NORWAY
President: Bernhard RAMSTAD
Secretary: Ellen von SCHANTZ
Tel: 47/23 29 29 30
Fax: 47/23 29 29 31
iti.norway@nto.no

PALESTINE (Associate)
Palestinian Centre of the ITI
Centre Arabe d'Arts et de Culture
rue Abou Oubaida, BP 20462
East Jerusalem 97200
President: Jamal GHOSHEH
Tel: 972/2/6280 957 *Fax*: 972/2/6276293
pnt@palnet.com

PAPUA NEW GUINEA (Associate)
Papua-New Guinea Centre of the ITI
c/o National Cultural Commission
PO Box 7144, Boroko N.C.D.
PAPUA NEW GUINEA
Director: Jacob L. SIMET
Tel: 675/27 25 21 *Fax*: 675/25 91 19

PERU
Centre Péruvien de l'IIT
Avda. Benavides 1294, Lima 18
PERU
President: Violeta CACERES
Secretary General: Fernando TORRES
Tel: 51/1/460 27 67 *Fax*: 51/1/460 27 55
vcacere@pucp.edu.pe
http://www.geocities.com/itiperu

PHILIPPINES
Philippines Centre of the ITI
World Theatre Dance Secretariat Unit
1203 Gotesco Twin Towers B
Concepcion Street, Ermita,
Manila, PHILIPPINES
President: Alejandro ROCES
Secretary General: Cécile GUIDOTE-ALVAREZ
Tel: 63/2/527 77 71 & 931 5369
Fax: 632/527 8713 & 63/2/931 5369
cecilealvarez@yahoo.com
itiphilippines@yahoo.com

POLAND
Polish Centre of the ITI
Pl. Pilsudskiego 9
00 078 Warsaw, POLAND
President: Bogdan HUSSAKOWSKI
Secretary General: Malgorzata SEMIL
Director: Malgorzata MAJEWSKA
Tel: 48/22/826 17 71 & 826 30 27
Fax: 48/22/826 30 27
msemil@tenbit.pl

ROMANIA
Romanian ITI Centre
c/o UNITER
Str.George Enescu 2-4
70141 Bucarest , ROMANIA
President: Ion CARAMITRU
Secretary General: Margareta BARBUTZA
Tel: 40/1/315 36 36 or 311 32 14
Fax: 40/1/312 09 13
email: uniter@fx.ro

RUSSIA
Russian ITI Centre
c/o Valery Khasanov, GRDNT
Sverchkov 8 per Bldg 3
Moscow 101000
RUSSIA
President: Mikhail OULIANOV
Secretary General: Valery KHASANOV
Tel: 7/095/921 9284
Fax: 7/095/921 7917
rusiti@com2com.ru
grdnt@mail.cnt.ru

SENEGAL
Centre sénégalais de l'IIT
BP 5500
Dakar
SENEGAL
President: Moustapha M'BAYE
Secretary General: Ousmane DIAKHATE
Tel: 221/822 1715 *Tel/Fax*: 221/822 3879
Tel/ Fax: 221/823 93 36 (O. Diakhate)
sorano@metissacana.sn

ITI Centres

SIERRA LEONE
Sierra Leone Centre of the ITI
Room 803W, 8th Floor, Youyi Building
Brookfields, Freetown
SIERRA LEONE
President: Elvira M.J.
 BOBSON-KAMARA
Secretary General(*Acting*): Foday JALLOH
Tel: 232/22/240 911 or 240670
Fax: 232/22/241 757 (Mohamed Sheriff)

SLOVAKIA
Slovak Centre of the ITI
Theatre Institute (Divadelny ustav)
Jakubovo nam. 12, 81357 Bratislava
SLOVAKIA
President: Martin PORUBJAK
Vice-President: Darina KAROVA
Secretary General: Zuzana ULICIANSKA
Tel:421/7/529 31535 *Fax*:421/7/529 31571
email: zuzana@du.savba.sk

SLOVENIA
Slovenian Centre of the ITI
c/o SNG Opera in balet
Cankarjeva 11, 1000 Ljubljana, SLOVENIA
President: Ira RATEJ
Secretary General: Tatjana AZMAN
Tel: 386/61/24 11 700 or 24 11 715
Fax: 386/61/126 22 49
tatjana.azman1@guest.arnes.si

SPAIN
Centre Espagnol de l'IIT
Maria PAZ BALLESTEROS
Alberto Aguilera 11C- 3C
28015 Madrid
SPAIN
Tel/ Fax: 34/91 44 50 345

SRI LANKA
Sri Lanka Centre of the ITI
Mr Dharmakirti
Tower Hall Theatre Foundation
Sausiripaya, 123 Wiyrama Mawatha
Colombo 7, SRI LANKA
Representative: Ranjit DHARMAKIRTI
Tel: 94/1/68 60 80 *Fax*: 94/1/69 97 38
towersl@sltnet.lk

SUDAN
Sudanese Centre of ITI
c/o Ali MAHDI
P.O. Box 1988
Dairat el-Mahdi Gamhoria St
Khartoum, SUDAN
Secretary General: Ali MAHDI
Tel: 249/11/ 782072 & 781419
Fax: 249/11 /771621
email: alimahdi@sudanmail.net

SWEDEN
Swedish Centre of the ITI
(Kvarnholmsvägen 56, Gäddviken)
Box 15035
Stockholm 10465, SWEDEN
President: Lars EDSTRÖM
Director: Ann Mari ENGEL
Tel: 46/8/462 25 30
Fax: 46/8/462 25 35
swedish@iti.a.se

SWITZERLAND
Swiss ITI Centre
Gessnerallee 13
8001 Zurich
SWITZERLAND
President: Beat SCHLÄPFER
Secretary: Annelis KÖNG
Tel: 41/1/226 19 10
Fax: 41/1/226 19 11
iti-swiss@swissonline.ch
http://www.iti-swiss.ch

SYRIA
Centre Syrien de l'IIT
Ministère de la Culture
Damascus, SYRIA
President: Assad FEDDA
Fax: 963/11/224 94 02

TOGO
Centre Togolais de l'IIT
BP 81090, Lomé, TOGO
Tel/Fax: 228/222 44 00
email: ititogo@yahoo.fr
President: Abdou Razak BAH-TRAORE
Secretary General: Kinvi Mihom T. GBADOE

TUNISIA
Centre Tunisien de l'IIT
Théâtre National Tunisien
El Halfaouine BP 183
106 Tunis, TUNISIA
President: Mohamed DRISS
Secretary General: Hamdi HEMAÏDI
Tel: 216/71/565 693 *Tel*: 216/1/351783
Fax: 216/71/565 640 *Fax* 216/1/333871

TURKEY
Turkish Centre of the ITI
c/o R. Erduran
Kasaneler Sok 11
Erenkoy, Istanbul
TURKEY
President: Refik ERDURAN
Vice-President: Recep BILGINER
Fax:90/216/ 363 4556
r.erduran@veezy.com

UGANDA
Uganda Centre of the ITI
PO Box 930, Kampala
UGANDA
President: Jackson NDAWULA
V-President: Christopher KIZZA
SSALONGO, Moses MATOVU
Secretary General: Augustine BAZAALE
Tel: 256/41/251 229 & 232350
Fax: 256/41/345598

UK
British Centre of the ITI
ITI at Goldsmiths College,
University of London
Lewisham Way, New Cross
London SE14 6NW
UNITED KINGDOM
Director: Neville SHULMAN
Secretary: Glyn CANNON
Tel: 44/20/7919 7276
Tel: 44/20/7486 6363 (N. Shulman)
Fax: 44/20/7919 72 77
email: iti@gold.ac.uk
http://iti.gold.ac.uk

UKRAINE (Associate)
Ukrainian Centre of the ITI
c/o Union of Theatre Artists of Ukraine,
P.O. Box 329 (Skovoroda St 2), Kiev 34
UKRAINE 04070,
President: Larysa KADYROVA
Sec.: Vera BILYK
Tel/Fax: 380/44/241 0423
email: iti-ukraine@svitonline.com

USA
U.S. Centre of the ITI
Theatre Communications Group
355 Lexington Avenue,
New York, NY10017-6603, USA
President: Kent THOMPSON
Director: Martha COIGNEY
Tel: 1/212/697 5230
Fax: 1/212/983 4847
mcoigney@tcg.org
http://www.tcg.org

URUGUAY
Centre Uruguayen de l'IIT
Mercedes 933, 11100 Montevideo
URUGUAY
President: Andrés CASTILLO
Vice-President: Irma ABIRAD
Secretary General: César CAMPODONICO
Tel: 598/2/900 48 69 *Tel*: 598/2/901 94 12
Fax: 598/2/902 40 54
email: ccampodo@adinet.com.uy

VENEZUELA
Centre vénézuélien de l'IIT
Apartado 51-440, Caracas 1050
VENEZUELA
President: Maria T. CASTILLO
Director: Nelly GARZON
Tel: 58/2/76 199 13
Fax: 58/2/761 99 13 or 763 57 23
itiven@reacciun.ve

ZIMBABWE (restructuring)
Zimbabwe Centre of the ITI
PO Box CY 2651, Causeway
Harare, ZIMBABWE
Stephen CHIFUNYISE(Coordinator)

International Theatre Institute
Co-operating Members

International Organisation

European Festivals Association
Château de Coppet
Case Postale 26
1296 Coppet, SWITZERLAND
Tel: + 41-22-776 86 73
Fax: + 41-22-776 42 75
email: geneva@euro-festival.net
http://www.euro-festival.net
President: Frans de RUITER
General Secretary: Tamás KLENJANSKY

National Organisations

Professor Devendra Raj Ankur
Director,
National School of Drama
Bahawalpur House
Bhagwandas Road
NEW DELHI 110001
INDIA
*Tel:*91/11/3387137
Fax: 91/11/338 4288
nsdr@bol.net.in
drama_school_in@yahoo.com

Satish Alekar, Professor & Head,
Centre for Performing Arts
(Lalit Kala Kendra),
University of Pune
Pune - 411 007
Maharashtra
INDIA
Tel: 91-20-569 2182
Fax: 91-20-569 3899
email: alekar@unipune.ernet.in

Dr Madhuchhanda Chatterjee
Executive Director
Anamika Kala Sangam
4 Bishop Lefroy Road
Calcutta 700 020
INDIA
Tel: 91/247/4129

Mr Ranbir SINH, Vice Chairman
Indian People's Theatre Association
Dundlod House, Hawa Sarak
Jaipur (Rajasthan)
INDIA
Fax: 91/141/211 276
Fax: 91/1594/52519